THE SCOPE OF THE MODERN THEATER

It can convey the rare spirit of nobility and beauty of Cyrano de Bergerac. Or be alive with the dancing wit and cunningly barbed social satire of Pygmalion. Or expand the accepted boundaries of the stage with the rich humanity of Our Town. Or be charged with the burning relevance of The Crucible. Or attain the point where realism takes on the hauntingly symbolic quality of An Enemy of the People.

But whatever its methods and point of view, the goal of the modern theater—as these five plays magnificently demonstrate—is to illumine our hopes, our fears, our dreams, our world, and the lives we lead.

ABOUT THE EDITOR: RICHARD H. GOLDSTONE is a member of the English faculty of City College, New York, where he teaches modern drama. A graduate of the University of Wisconsin with a Ph.D. from Columbia, Professor Goldstone has been published in many major magazines, including THE NEW YORK TIMES BOOK REVIEW, THE PARIS REVIEW, THE SATURDAY REVIEW and others. He is the author of several works on drama and is currently preparing a biographical study of Thornton Wilder.

Modern Plays in SIGNET Editions

☐ **BECKET by Jean Anouilh.** The compelling historical play about the relationship between Becket, Archbishop of Canterbury, and his friend-turned-enemy, Henry II of England. A great motion picture starring Richard Burton and Peter O'Toole. (#P2453—60¢)

☐ **A RAISIN IN THE SUN and THE SIGN IN SIDNEY BRUSTEIN'S WINDOW by Lorraine Hansberry.** Two outstanding plays: one, winner of the New York Drama Critics Award, about a young Negro father's struggle to break free from the barriers of prejudice, the other, portraying a modern-day intellectual's challenge of the negation and detachment of his fellow intellectuals. With a foreword by John Braine and an introduction by Robert Nemiroff. (#T2926—75¢)

☐ **MY FAIR LADY by Alan Jay Lerner.** The complete play and lyrics of the famous musical based on the Pygmalion story. (#P2536—60¢)

☐ **LUTHER by John Osborne.** A brilliant play about the rebellious priest who challenged, and changed, the spiritual world of his time. By the author of **Look Back in Anger.** (#Q3677—95¢)

☐ **SUNRISE AT CAMPOBELLO by Dore Schary.** The superb drama about Franklin D. Roosevelt's bout with polio and his triumphant emergence from his ordeal. (#T3515—75¢)

THE NEW AMERICAN LIBRARY, INC., P.O. Box 2310, Grand Central Station, New York, New York 10017

Please send me the SIGNET BOOKS I have checked above. I am enclosing $_____ (check or money order—no currency or C.O.D.'s). Please include the list price plus 10¢ a copy to cover mailing costs. (New York City residents add 5% Sales Tax. Other New York State residents add 2% plus any local sales or use taxes.)

Name_____

Address_____

City_____State_____Zip Code_____
Allow at least 3 weeks for delivery

Mentor Masterworks of Modern Drama: Five Plays

Edited and with an Introduction by

RICHARD H. GOLDSTONE, comp.

A MENTOR BOOK

Published by The New American Library,
New York and Toronto

PN
6112
.G 635

MENTOR TRADEMARK REG. U.S. PAT. OFF. AND FOREIGN COUNTRIES
REGISTERED TRADEMARK—MARCA REGISTRADA
HECHO EN CHICAGO, U.S.A.

MENTOR BOOKS are published *in the United States* by
The New American Library, Inc.,
1301 Avenue of the Americas, New York, New York 10019,
in Canada by The New American Library of Canada Limited,
295 King Street East, Toronto 2, Ontario

FIRST PRINTING, MARCH, 1969

PRINTED IN THE UNITED STATES OF AMERICA

Contents

MENTOR MASTERWORKS OF MODERN DRAMA

General Introduction

The five plays in this volume—each of them a masterwork by a master playwright—have in common one supreme element: their universal and durable appeal. Though each of the plays is clearly the product of the country that produced it, all of them have long since become fixed in the matrix of the culture of the entire Western world. *An Enemy of the People,* for example, quickly entered the repertory of the English and German stage; *Cyrano de Bergerac,* as performed by Richard Mansfield and later by Walter Hampden, was played throughout the United States for thirty years. *Pygmalion,* after its transformation into a classic film and then into a musical comedy (from which another film emerged), is probably unrivaled in worldwide popularity; *Our Town,* as *Piccola Città,* provoked riots at its Italian premiere and then went on to become one of Italy's most cherished plays; *The Crucible,* transformed by the French into an existentialist movie, had as the author of the screen play Nobel Laureate Jean-Paul Sartre.

Their Modernity

But the plays, produced over a period of seventy years (1882–1952), have another element in common: their modernity. When we use the term *modern* in relation to a literary work, we are speaking of literature that derives its impulse from the values of a democratic society, literature that concerns itself with the problems inherent in democratically structured communities.

This is not to say that any of the plays in this volume are topical. On the contrary, it is precisely because they are not topical that they are not dated. These are not topical plays, but they are plays for today—and for tomorrow. Two of the plays, *An Enemy of the People* and *Cyrano de*

11

Bergerac, are from the nineteenth century, but they are modern enough to touch our sensibilities and to disturb our complacencies. *Pygmalion* is essentially about education, a subject that is even more deeply considered and more widely discussed than it was in 1912 when Shaw began writing the play. *Our Town* (1938) and *The Crucible* (1952) are contemporary works set in the past; but their idiom is unmistakably that of today.

Cyrano de Bergerac

Edmond Rostand wrote *Cyrano* in a reaction against the realism and naturalism which had become ascendant in the plays and the fiction of the late nineteenth century. Then, as now, there came a moment when people no longer wanted to see their own reflection on the stage (or in the movies, or in the books they read). Audiences traditionally want to turn to an idealized, romanticized past. Americans look back to the old West; the English to the chivalric middle ages; the French to their days of glory in the seventeenth century. *Cyrano* reveals what Rostand and the millions among his audiences miss in today's world: selflessness and sacrifice; integrity and courage; elegance and honor. These aristocratic virtues revealing themselves in so earthy a man as Cyrano— the witty guardsman from the provinces, without wealth, without influence, without rank—make him the only romantic hero of modern drama, a hero who never seems absurd, strained, or pretentious. He is as real as Norman Mailer, and as irrepressibly articulate. Cyrano can call attention to his nose as unselfconsciously as Dick Gregory has used the fact of his race in his ironic monologues. But Cyrano has seen his reflection in the eyes of shallow and ignorant people; and though what he has seen has broken his heart, it has enlarged his humanity.

We, today, find in a play like *Cyrano de Bergerac* a reassurance that princely character and behavior are not beyond the range of possibility for men who are of less than noble birth. We are told by the widow of John F. Kennedy that the late president was both moved and inspired by *Camelot,* the musical play based on Arthurian legend. John F. Kennedy was the kind of American who could appreciate the possibilities inherent in the fusion of the democratic impulse and nobility of style, a fusion which characterizes Rostand's tragicomic hero.

Our Town

In *Our Town* we find another play which takes us back in time. But where Rostand carries us back two and a half centuries, Thornton Wilder, in 1938, was writing of a genera- tion barely once removed from his own. That is to say, for the majority of *Our Town's* first audiences, the action of the play almost coincided with their own time of growing up. Even today, particularly for those who have grown up in small towns, or even in the suburbs of larger cities, *Our Town* is both an exercise in nostalgia and a reminder of our failure to realize life while we're living it.

A play in the form of a landscape, *Our Town* introduces us to the town of Grover's Corners much as though we were seeing it on a huge animated relief map. Grover's Corners looks like the New England village of our dreams; it has clean air, fresh-faced children, no violence nor crime nor slums; there is neither excessive wealth nor hopeless poverty. (Those who are helpless are taken care of by the com- munity.) In choosing the years before the two great wars, the author can ignore the depression that plagued the nine- teen thirties; and in setting his play in New England, Mr. Wilder can ignore the racial tensions that beset the South and the problems of industrial complexes and mining areas. Grover's Corners appears to be without any disease worse than whooping cough; without divorces or domestic strife; without sexual irregularities or juvenile delinquencies. The only addiction seems to be to coffee.

Grover's Corners, in fact, would seem to be the fulfillment of the American Dream, the apogee of Puritan aspiration, the utmost achievement of a democratic society. To some degree it was what it seems; millions of white, native-born Ameri- cans born in the decades between the Civil War and the turn of the century could, if they were not greatly ambitious, ignore the squalor, the strain, and the ugliness of city life in America. The small towns of New England, New York, and Ohio, supported by the farming communities around them and by small industries "across the tracks," were gen- erally free and even unaware of the malignancies that beset the tenement dwellers of the great cities of the North and the tenant farmers of the South. Of the inhabitants of Grover's Corners one might observe that "where ignorance is bliss, 'tis folly to be wise."

But *Our Town* is interesting to us, not for what it leaves

out, but for its extraordinary rich comprehensiveness and inclusiveness. There is life enough, as much as we can absorb in two hours' time. We come to realize, moreover, that even in so idyllic a setting, existence leaves a great deal to be desired. Emily makes clear that though she and her community of relatives and friends are an accepting lot, they rarely achieve real happiness and never experience aesthetic or spiritual ecstasy. The only person in the play who seems to have intimations of life's glorious intensity is a drunkard and a suicide.

Thus part of *Our Town's* impact lies in its capacity to remind us of a lost innocence, of those best moments in our growing up in the warm center of our family. The play gives us a second chance—not only to relive what was good and satisfying in that part of our life now behind us, but to become more aware of the poignancy and the excitement of sheer existence. For we see that the inhabitants of Grover's Corners who had so much going for them were blind to the possibilities, the variations, the adventures that life can offer. Mrs. Gibbs would somehow like to see Paris, but she doesn't go; George Gibbs rejects college in favor of the safe and the familiar; Dr. Gibbs returns each year to the battlefields of Gettysburg; and Editor Webb's intellectual interests don't seem to go beyond the life of Napoleon.

Thornton Wilder is not implying that travel or wide reading or application to intellectual problems are the keys to happiness or to fulfillment. But he does suggest that the timidity, the complacency, the limited range of Grover's Corners' inhabitants have deprived them of a good deal of the excitement of a complete life. In a democratic society, all that is good and beautiful and wholesome in the daily lives of Grover's Corners should be assured to everyman: a clean, decent home, nourishing food, good schools, the respect of his neighbors, the opportunity to practice a livelihood commensurate with his abilities. Such an assumption is implicit in the play. But Wilder reminds us also that the satisfaction of our basic needs brings us to the point where— with our first intimations of death—we ask ourselves: Is that all there is? Could there perhaps have been something more?

Our Town in the short space of little more than three decades has become the most widely read and performed play by an American. While success is not necessarily a guarantee of literary distinction, *Our Town* is as representative of the American genius as any dramatic work that we can identify. For not only does it depict the commendable modesty of our collective aspirations, it lays bare forth-rightly and mercilessly the aesthetic-spiritual-passional torpor that afflicts the great majority of Americans. *Our Town* has been called an optimistic play, and to the extent that it is a celebration of life it is an affirmative work of art. But even though it is written in the form of a New England landscape, it is by no means a naive Grandma Moses period piece. There are shadows in the very first scene, shadows that lengthen until, in the last act, the play and all its *dramatis personae* are overcast, until close to the very end, the audience itself receives the full force of Simon Stimson's final outburst. Suddenly then the shadows are lifted, the stars are shining, and our town resumes "the noiseless tenor of its way."

Today's audiences know that the Grover's Corners of the turn of the century no longer exists; but part of it—the best part, perhaps—may yet survive so long as we keep straining, in Mr. Wilder's words, to make something better of what we already have.

Pygmalion

Pygmalion, possibly because it is Bernard Shaw's most overwhelmingly popular success, is the most underrated of his plays. In its first English production, it triumphantly starred the celebrated actress, Mrs. Patrick Campbell. A generation later it was transformed, with additional material by Shaw, into a classic film with Wendy Hiller and the late Leslie Howard. Finally came its most extraordinary incarnation as *My Fair Lady,* originally produced with Rex Harrison and Julie Andrews. *My Fair Lady,* both as a staged musical comedy and subsequently as a film, has had the effect of eclipsing Shaw's play. The musical version of *Pygmalion,* with its appealing score and its colorful evocation of the period, is not the play that Shaw wrote; *My Fair Lady* simplifies and diminishes one of Shaw's most fully and suc-cessfully realized stage works.

George Bernard Shaw composed his plays, usually, in the framework of one or another of his intellectual-political-economic-philosophical ideas; e.g., the technique of success-ful government (*Caesar and Cleopatra*); the evolutionary development of man's intellectual and physical capacities (*Man and Superman*); munitions making and the capitalist system (*Major Barbara*); the artist's role in society (*The Doctor's Dilemma*); world war and the problem of nationalism (*Heartbreak House*); tradition and change in collision (*Saint Joan*).

Pygmalion, by contrast, seems to be merely the portrayal of the involvement of three men with a girl (though Shaw wrote a long preface explaining that his play is really about phonetics. Later he wrote an afterword asserting that Eliza ultimately married Freddy; and, reverting to his early career as a novelist, Shaw constructs an elaborate summary of Eliza and Freddy's life together as man and wife.) Shaw's disclaimers to the contrary, we are confronted by the fascinating dramatic situation that arises when a Pygmalion creates a Galatea; it is precisely the element that Shaw in his afterword attempts to deflect our attention from, which makes the play one of his artistically most satisfying: those emotional currents generated in a student-teacher relationship when the teacher is suffering from emotional malnutrition and the student is an attractive young woman.

Shaw regarded himself as a teacher and he regarded his plays as a means by which he might educate his generation. He despised most of the dramatic work of his time because the bulk of it was either melodrama or drawing room comedy. He even deplored what he regarded as the moral purposelessness of Shakespeare; plays about love affairs, Shaw contended in his preface to *Caesar and Cleopatra,* were not worthy of the attention of serious, mature people. But *Pygmalion* is a play about people in love, and what is more, it is one of the few plays of Shaw that reveal something of his deeply personal feelings. In his late fifties when he wrote *Pygmalion,* Shaw had become infatuated with the beautiful and fascinating Mrs. Campbell. Mrs. Campbell, though she welcomed the attentions of a distinguished and brilliant playwright and critic, allowing herself to become intimately involved with Shaw, was not in love with him and ultimately rejected his ardent advances to marry a younger man. Shaw's passion, his frustration and the wound to his amour propre all spill over into the play, which appropriately opened in London (1914)—as Shaw had envisaged it in his writing of the play—with Mrs. Campbell in the role of Eliza. A record of the stormy correspondence between the playwright and the actress remains; as we read the letters we hear echoes of the play—with an important exception. In the play, the man retains his mastery of the situation.

My Fair Lady simplifies and conventionalizes the tortured relationship between the two principals. The requirements of a musical comedy result in the music and lyrics displacing half the dialogue of the play. Liza and Henry Higgins of the musical, consequently, lose some of their individuality, some of their humanity. Liza becomes Cinderella and Higgins is transformed into a slightly crusty prince. Shaw had maintained in his afterword that Higgins and Liza never marry one another because they both realize that they would make each other miserable. No reservation of that kind would occur to the audiences of the musical version. In *My Fair Lady* there is an unambiguously happy ending: Shaw's ending is deliberately inconclusive. What we know when the curtain comes down is that Liza and Higgins have finally come to terms with their mutual need. And that is resolution enough . . . enough for Shaw, and enough for us, once we have become reconciled to the idea that in art, just as in life, we cannot expect unqualifiedly happy endings.

Pygmalion is one of Shaw's least didactic plays; but that is not to say that Shaw had eliminated his characteristically incisive social analysis. England in the early decades of the twentieth century was obsessed by the matter of class status, by the gradations of the rigid social structure. The upper middle class—that is to say, Britain's *ladies* and *gentlemen*— achieved their precious status through the fortuitous combination of birth, education, profession (if any), and manner of dress. Money was normally a prerequisite to status, but one could struggle along without very much of it if one belonged to the right family.

Shaw observes in *Pygmalion* that the right accent (together with the right clothes) could carry the day. His position in relation to class was not that society should eliminate the concept of *ladies* and *gentlemen* but that the status of lady or gentleman might be attained by anyone with intelligence and character who aspired to the part. Shaw makes clear that class distinctions lose their force when a decent education can transform a street vendor into a "duchess"; that education made available to all those with the intellectual means of profiting from it would eliminate the outworn concepts of caste and class.

The Crucible

Miller's *The Crucible* documents two shameful and not unrelated interludes in American history. The first, of course, was the Salem witch trials, those outrages that made Hathorne, their presiding judge, eternally infamous and left an indelible stain on the pages of American history. If *The Cru-*

cible had done no more than recreate for us those incredible horrors of 1692, it would have been well worth our attention. But Arthur Miller wrote his play during another shameful episode in our national history, an episode, national in scope, enacted in the nation's capital. Just as we now ask ourselves how could the decent colonists of Massachusetts have countenanced the witch trials that resulted in the deaths of innocent people, so today we ask how a United States senator, sponsored and financed by the federal government (and aided by a network of anonymous informers in dozens of major government departments and bureaus, including the FBI) could have destroyed the careers of innumerable innocent public servants, threatened and intimidated high officials and officers of the Department of the Army and of State, compelled dozens of prominent and respected Americans to reveal the names of associates whose sympathies were, at one time or another, enlisted in leftist causes and organizations.

Arthur Miller himself, unlike a number of his prominent associates in the theater, refused to name leftist sympathizers who were known to him. Both he and playwright Lillian Hellman were threatened with jail for refusing to name names, but their prosecution for "contempt of Congress" was never carried out. Instead, it was ultimately Senator Joseph McCarthy who was stripped of his powers and reprimanded by the Senate; the detection of subversives and saboteurs was entrusted to more appropriate and qualified government agencies. McCarthyism has become a horrid memory and an ugly paragraph in American history.

The Crucible is a reminder to us of those bewildering months when so great an American as General George Marshall could be denounced as a traitor. Arthur Miller, however, was not intent, when he wrote *The Crucible*, on producing a play that would vindicate himself or lash out at his tormentors. Rather, Miller wrote his play as nothing less than an indictment of an American collective impulse which rises to the surface from time to time, the impulse which denies life or the means of livelihood to those who remain faithful either to their deeply felt personal beliefs, or to their political or religious attitudes. In connection with this we should recall that the McCarthy committee did not prosecute government and nongovernment employees for what they *did*, but for what they *were* (or seemed to be) or for what they privately *believed*.

The tragedy of *The Crucible*—and it is an example of modern tragedy—does not lie in the acts of John Proctor (whose expiation through anguish and repentance has begun before the action of the play); the tragedy that Miller is pointing to is an American tragedy. Here is a country that even in its beginnings had a tragic flaw. The Puritans who initially provided the predominant temper of America, a temper that survives to this day, established the principle of economic and religious democracy. But the proper atmosphere for political dissent (so striking in England) and for moral freedom (for which America has alternately envied and condemned France) was missing at the outset. Miller's text implies that this atmosphere is missing still. We are not content with prosecuting lawbreakers or scotching the acts of subversives; we must, at various intervals, search out and persecute citizens for their beliefs, even for their psychological divergencies.

This flaw in the American psyche is hinted at but not developed in *Our Town*. *Our Town* and *The Crucible* are the reverse faces of the American democratic impulse. That part that is affirmative rings out clear in Wilder's celebration of the egalitarian spirit. The potential for evil in a democratic society—i.e., the tyranny by the majority over the minority, particularly of those minorities who most jealously guard their particular individuality—is the subject of Miller's tragic play.

The Crucible was not so well received in its initial production in New York as was *Our Town*. Its first great success was in France. And five years after its New York premiere —after the disappearance of Joseph McCarthy from the American political scene—its 1957 revival in New York was a triumphant vindication of the play. The durability of *The Crucible* is, in itself, a hopeful sign of change. But before we become too hopeful, we should remember the pendulum swing of our history. Not inconceivably in some future decade, we may be denied the right to read *The Crucible*, unless the implications of the play sink deeply enough into the consciences and minds of the American people as to make impossible another witch-hunt—another period of terror for those whose ideas or mores are in violent conflict with those of the radical right.

An Enemy of the People

Of the five plays in this volume, *An Enemy of the People* is the most perplexing, the most difficult to come to terms with. Dr. Stockmann, its protagonist, is an honest man who would zealously cleanse his community of corruption. But ultimately he finds that for his pains every force in the community turns against him so that he stands, at the end—together with his bewildered wife and children—stripped of his position and painfully alone.

A careless reading of the play has often encouraged one writer or another to label *An Enemy of the People* as anti-democratic in spirit, as evidence of Ibsen's contempt for the democratic process, even of his bitter arrogance and monumental self-regard.

There is good reason for viewing the play as an expression of Ibsen's personal feelings toward popular institutions. *Ghosts,* the play of Ibsen which preceded *An Enemy of the People,* shocked Europe, England, and America in its unmistakable reference to what was then a taboo subject, sexual disease. Ibsen was denounced in terms which even now seem both incredibly harsh and patently absurd. *An Enemy of the People* was Ibsen's response to the press and to the public; the play conveys Ibsen's contempt not only for community indifference to the filth and disease lying under the veneer of middle class respectability, but also for the moral cowardice and stupidity—even in the liberal press—that formulated the unconscionable attacks upon Ibsen's integrity and upon his honor.

But we misread the play if we assume that Dr. Stockmann is intended as a self-portrait or a paradigm of the selfless man of truth crucified by self-seekers and fools. Stockmann is bewildered when the town which he thought would honor him isolates him. Stockmann saw himself as a public hero and he gloried in the thought of the homage he expected to be paid him. At the end of the first act, for example, he is crowing like a cock and publicly refusing a rise in salary that no one has even thought of offering him. Ibsen is portraying a man who is incredibly naive about community affairs and childishly eager for recognition and appreciation. The same man who can proclaim that "the strongest man in the world is he who stands most alone," is also capable of exasperating folly.

Nevertheless, the inescapable fact is that Stockmann is right. The central symbolic fact of the play is the contaminated water which the town expects will sustain it and make it prosper. Is the implication that the playwright believes that a democratic society necessarily flourishes only amidst corruption, that the majority *must* always be wrong?

Ibsen the idealist and the individualist, of course, had no

Whitman-like love of the masses. (And the masses have returned the compliment by their indifference to or their dislike for his plays.) But neither was Ibsen an advocate of totalitarianism, a system that would have been abhorrent to him. Ibsen, in fact, never formulated any political philosophy; he accepted government as a necessary evil whose financial support he welcomed for the better part of his life. Ibsen, in short, accepted the idea of representative government in the same spirit with which he accepted the weather: something you either live with or move away from.

And he viewed society in general as corrupt, misgoverned, and hostile to change. He saw people as badly educated, poorly fed, susceptible to the blandishments of fools and knaves. To Ibsen, public morality was a farce. *An Enemy of the People* represents another twist of the knife in that Ibsen depicts a corrupt society in dramatic conflict with a Stockmann—high-minded, pure of heart, but a bungling incompetent, a seeker after glory or, if that be denied him, martyrdom. What can one expect of ordinary people, Ibsen implies, if its leaders are either venal, cowardly, or self-seeking?

Unlike Shaw, Ibsen proposes no solutions, provides no answers to the questions he raises. But those questions haunt us to this very hour. Ibsen died thirty years before Hitler came to power, but the rise of Hitler would have been no surprise to Ibsen. Nazi Germany was precisely what Ibsen would have expected. Corruption kept under cover ultimately rises to the surface, and no member of the community is immune to its effects. Such a conclusion is perhaps the most important lesson a democratic society can learn from the greatest dramatist of its age. But that lesson must be taught with patience, with humility, with understanding and detachment, qualities that Dr. Stockmann—unfortunately for the community he wished to serve, unfortunately for himself—did not possess. There is a lesson in that, too.

Edmond Rostand:

Cyrano de Bergerac

Edmond Rostand (1868–1918), the French poet-playwright, is known in the United States chiefly for *Cyrano de Bergerac*. But the first act of his early play *Les Romanesques* was converted into a musical comedy and achieved the longest run of any work in the history of the New York stage. The musical, titled *The Fantasticks*, adheres closely to the spirit of Rostand's stage work. Rostand's other well-known plays are *L'Aiglon*, which starred Sarah Bernhardt, and *Chantecler*, which was performed in America with Maude Adams.

A young man offered a choice between being brave and true, articulate and imaginative on the one hand, or being strikingly handsome on the other, would have no difficulty in making a decision. For he knows what choice between two such men women (and, alas, too often, men) make. The world, he knows, instinctively favors the well-favored man, though given enough time the world reverses itself. The plain man, if he is good, becomes beautiful; the handsome man, if his looks are a mere facade, becomes plain.

Upon this premise Edmond Rostand structured *Cyrano de Bergerac*. His brave and true hero, a poet-soldier supreme, has the visage of a clown. The Adonis of the play is an inarticulate, unimaginative, entirely uninteresting young man. And Roxane, the woman beloved by both men, demands the very best that the two men possess between them: beauty, intelligence, poetic ardor, fidelity, courage, and integrity.

Rostand's play, though it is essentially a love story, is something more. A great deal more. It recreates an epoch, it reveals to us a colorful and fascinating past. In choosing as his setting the years when France's glory was at its apogee, Rostand reminds us of values held to in the past that we are now apparently disregarding or abandoning. The central symbol of the play—Cyrano's white plume—underscores the im-

23

portance that Rostand attaches to the ideal of honor which contemporary civilization is rendering obsolete.

The question Rostand raises—apart from the matter of Roxane's curious ambivalence—has to do with whether there is room in the twentieth century world for men such as Cyrano de Bergerac. His principles, his integrity, his valor made existence for him, even in his own time, hazardous; how long could he, or would he wish to survive in ours?

Rostand wrote *Cyrano* in rhymed alexandrines, a verse form that contains twelve beats to the line. The celebrated Brian Hooker translation uses the traditional blank verse of English dramatic poetry.

Cyrano de Bergerac

A NEW VERSION IN ENGLISH VERSE
BY BRIAN HOOKER

It was to the soul of CYRANO *that I intended to
    dedicate this poem.
But since that soul has been reborn in you,
    COQUELIN, it is to you that I dedicate it.*

E. R.

Characters

CYRANO DE BERGERAC.	THE PORTER.
CHRISTIAN DE NEUVILLETTE.	A CITIZEN.
COMTE DE GUICHE.	HIS SON.
RAGUENEAU.	A CUTPURSE.
LE BRET.	A SPECTATOR.
CARBON DE CASTEL-JALOUX.	A SENTRY.
THE CADETS.	BERTRANDOU THE FIFER.
LIGNIÈRE.	A CAPUCHIN.
VICOMTE DE VALVERT.	TWO MUSICIANS.
A MARQUIS.	THE POETS.
SECOND MARQUIS.	THE PASTRYCOOKS.
THIRD MARQUIS.	THE PAGES.
MONTFLEURY.	ROXANE.
BELLEROSE.	HER DUENNA.
JODELET.	LISE.
CUIGY.	THE ORANGE GIRL.
BRISSAILLE.	MOTHER MARGUÉRITE DE JESUS.
A MEDDLER.	SISTER MARTHE.
A MUSKETEER.	SISTER CLAIRE.
ANOTHER MUSKETEER.	AN ACTRESS.
A SPANISH OFFICER.	A SOUBRETTE.
A CAVALIER.	THE FLOWER GIRL.

THE CROWD, CITIZENS, MARQUIS, MUSKETEERS, THIEVES,
PASTRYCOOKS, POETS, CADETS OF GASCOYNE, ACTORS, VIO-
LINS, PAGES, CHILDREN, SPANISH SOLDIERS, SPECTATORS, IN-
TELLECTUALS, ACADEMICIANS, NUNS, ETC.

25

ACT I

(A PERFORMANCE AT THE HÔTEL DE BOURGOGNE)

(The Hall of the Hôtel de Bourgogne in 1640. A sort of tennis court, arranged and decorated for theatrical productions.

The hall is a long rectangle; we see it diagonally, in such a way that one side of it forms the back scene, which begins at the first entrance on the right and runs up to the last entrance on the left, where it makes a right angle with the stage which is seen obliquely.

This stage is provided on either hand with benches placed along the wings. The curtain is formed by two lengths of tapestry which can be drawn apart. Above a harlequin cloak, the royal arms. Broad steps lead from the stage down to the floor of the hall. On either side of these steps, a place for the musicians. A row of candles serving as footlights. Two tiers of galleries along the side of the hall; the upper one divided into boxes.

There are no seats upon the floor, which is the actual stage

*of our theater; but toward the back of the hall, on the right,
a few benches are arranged; and underneath a stairway on the
extreme right, which leads up to the galleries, and of which
only the lower portion is visible, there is a sort of sideboard,
decorated with little tapers, vases of flowers, bottles and
glasses, plates of cake, et cetera.*

*Farther along, toward the center of our stage is the entrance
to the hall; a great double door which opens only slightly to
admit the audience. On one of the panels of this door, as also
in other places about the hall, and in particular just over the
sideboard, are playbills in red, upon which we may read the
title La Clorise.*

*As the curtain rises, the hall is dimly lighted and still
empty. The chandeliers are lowered to the floor, in the middle
of the hall, ready for lighting.*

Sound of voices outside the door. Then a CAVALIER *enters
abruptly.*)

THE PORTER (*follows him*): Halloa there!—Fifteen sols!

THE CAVALIER: I enter free.

THE PORTER: Why?

THE CAVALIER: Soldier of the Household of the King!

THE PORTER (*turns to another* CAVALIER *who has just entered*): You?

SECOND CAVALIER: I pay nothing.

THE PORTER: Why not?

SECOND CAVALIER: Musketeer!

FIRST CAVALIER (*to the second*): The play begins at two.
Plenty of time—
And here's the whole floor empty. Shall we try
Our exercise?

(*They fence with the foils which they have brought.*)

A LACKEY (*enters*): —Pst! . . . Flanquin! . . .

ANOTHER (*already on stage*): What, Champagne?

FIRST LACKEY (*showing games which he takes out of his
doublet*): Cards. Dice. Come on (*sits on the floor*).

SECOND LACKEY (*same action*): Come on, old cock!

FIRST LACKEY (*takes from his pocket a bit of candle, lights
it, sets it on the floor*): I have stolen
A little of my master's fire.

A GUARDSMAN (*to a* FLOWER GIRL *who comes forward*):
How sweet
Of you, to come before they light the hall! (*puts his arm
around her*).

FIRST CAVALIER (*receives a thrust of the foil*): A hit!
SECOND LACKEY: A club!
THE GUARDSMAN (*pursuing the girl*): A kiss!
THE FLOWER GIRL (*pushing away from him*): They'll see
us!—
THE GUARDSMAN (*draws her into a dark corner*):
                                        No danger!
A MAN (*sits on the floor, together with several others who
have brought packages of food*): When we come early, we
have time to eat.
A CITIZEN (*escorting his son, a boy of sixteen*): Sit here,
my son.
FIRST LACKEY: Mark the Ace!
ANOTHER MAN (*draws a bottle from under his cloak and
sits down with the others*):   Here's the spot
For a jolly old sot to suck his Burgundy—(*drinks*)
Here—in the house of the Burgundians!
THE CITIZEN (*to his son*): Would you not think you were
in some den of vice? (*points with his cane at the drunkard*)
Drunkards—(*in stepping back, one of the cavaliers trips him
up*) Bullies!—
(*He falls between the lackeys.*) Gamblers!—
THE GUARDSMAN (*behind him as he rises, still struggling
with the* FLOWER GIRL): One kiss—
THE CITIZEN: Good God!—
(*draws his son quickly away*) Here!—And to think, my son,
that in this hall
They play Rotrou!
THE BOY: Yes father—and Corneille!
THE PAGES (*dance in, holding hands and singing*):
Tra-la-la-la-la-la-la-la-la-lère . . .
THE PORTER: You pages there—no nonsense!
FIRST PAGE (*with wounded dignity*): Oh, monsieur!
Really! How could you? (*to the second, the moment the*
PORTER *turns his back*) Pst!—a bit of string?
SECOND PAGE (*shows fishline with hook*): Yes—and a hook.
FIRST PAGE: Up in the gallery,
And fish for wigs!
A CUTPURSE (*gathers around him several evil-looking young
fellows*): Now then, you picaroons,
Perk up, and hear me mutter. Here's your bout—
Bustle around some cull, and bite his bung . . .
SECOND PAGE (*calls to other pages already in the gallery*):
Hey! Brought your pea-shooters?
THIRD PAGE (*from above*):   And our peas, too!

(*blows, and showers them with peas*)

THE BOY: What is the play this afternoon?

THE CITIZEN: Clorise.

THE BOY: Who wrote that?

THE CITIZEN: Balthasar Baro. What a play! . . . (*He takes the* BOY's *arm and leads him upstage.*)

THE CUTPURSE (*to his pupils*): Lace now, on those long sleeves, you cut it off—(*gesture with thumb and finger, as if using scissors*.)

A SPECTATOR (*to another, pointing upward toward the gallery*): Ah, *Le Cid!*—Yes, the first night, I sat there—

THE CUTPURSE: Watches—(*gesture as of picking a pocket*).

THE CITIZEN (*coming down with his son*): Great actors we shall see today—

THE CUTPURSE: Handkerchiefs—(*gesture of holding the pocket with left hand, and drawing out handkerchief with right*).

THE CITIZEN: Montfleury—

A VOICE (*in the gallery*):   Lights! Light the lights!

THE CITIZEN: Bellerose, l'Épy, Beaupré, Jodelet—

A PAGE (*on the floor*): Here comes the orange girl.

THE ORANGE GIRL: Oranges, milk, Raspberry syrup, lemonade—(*noise at the door*).

A FALSETTO VOICE (*outside*):   Make way, Brutes!

FIRST LACKEY: What, the Marquis—on the floor?

(*The* MARQUIS *enters in a little group.*)

SECOND LACKEY: Not long— Only a few moments: they'll go and sit On the stage presently.

FIRST MARQUIS (*seeing the hall half empty*): How now! We enter Like tradespeople—no crowding, no disturbance!— No treading on the toes of citizens? Oh fie! Oh fie! (*He encounters two gentlemen who have already arrived.*) Cuigy! Brissaille! (*great embracings*)

CUIGY: The faithful! (*looks around him*) We are here before the candles.

FIRST MARQUIS: Ah, be still! You put me in a temper.

SECOND MARQUIS: Console yourself, Marquis—The lamplighter!

THE CROWD (*applauding the appearance of the* LAMP-LIGHTER): Ah! . . .

(*A group gathers around the chandelier while he lights it.
A few people have already taken their place in the gallery.*
LIGNIÈRE *enters the hall, arm in arm with* CHRISTIAN DE NEU-
VILLETTE. LIGNIÈRE *is a slightly disheveled figure, dissipated
and yet distinguished-looking.* CHRISTIAN, *elegantly but rather
unfashionably dressed, appears preoccupied and keeps looking up at the boxes.*)

CUIGY: Lignière!—

BRISSAILLE (*laughing*): Still sober—at this hour?

LIGNIÈRE (*to* CHRISTIAN): May I present you?
(CHRISTIAN *assents.*) Baron Christian de Neuvillette. (*They
salute.*)

THE CROWD (*applauding as the lighted chandelier is hoisted
into place*):   Ah!—

CUIGY (*aside to* BRISSAILLE, *looking at* CHRISTIAN): Rather
A fine head, is it not? The profile . . .

FIRST MARQUIS (*who has overheard*):   Peuh!

LIGNIÈRE (*presenting them to* CHRISTIAN): Messieurs de
Cuigy . . . de Brissaille . . .

CHRISTIAN (*bows*):   Enchanted!

FIRST MARQUIS (*to the second*): He is not ill-looking; pos-
    sibly a shade
Behind the fashion.

LIGNIÈRE (*to* CUIGY):   Monsieur is recently
From the Touraine.

CHRISTIAN: Yes, I have been in Paris
Two or three weeks only. I join the Guards
Tomorrow.

FIRST MARQUIS (*watching the people who come into the
boxes*): Look—Madame la Présidente
Aubry!

THE ORANGE GIRL: Oranges, milk—

THE VIOLINS (*tuning up*): La . . . la . . .

CUIGY (*to* CHRISTIAN, *calling his attention to the increasing
crowd*):   We have
An audience today!

CHRISTIAN: A brilliant one.

FIRST MARQUIS: Oh yes, all our own people—the gay
world! (*They name the ladies who enter the boxes elaborately
dressed. Bows and smiles are exchanged.*)

SECOND MARQUIS: Madame de Guéméné . . .

CUIGY: De Bois-Dauphin . . .

FIRST MARQUIS: Whom we adore—

BRISSAILLE: Madame de Chavigny . . .

SECOND MARQUIS: Who plays with all our hearts—

LIGNIÈRE: Why, there's Corneille
Returned from Rouen!
THE BOY (*to his* FATHER):   Are the Academy
All here?
THE CITIZEN: I see some of them . . . there's Boudu—
Boissat—Cureau—Porchères—Colomby—
Bourzeys—Bourdon—Arbaut—
                                    Ah, those great names,
Never to be forgotten!
FIRST MARQUIS: Look—at last!
Our Intellectuals! Barthénoide,
Urimédonte, Félixérie . . .
SECOND MARQUIS (*languishing*):   Sweet heaven!
How exquisite their surnames are! Marquis,
You know them all?
FIRST MARQUIS: I know them all, Marquis!
LIGNIÈRE (*draws* CHRISTIAN *aside*):
My dear boy, I came here to serve you—Well,
But where's the lady? I'll be going.
CHRISTIAN: Not yet—
A little longer! She is always here.
Please! I must find some way of meeting her.
I am dying of love! And you—you know
Everyone, the whole court and the whole town,
And put them all into your songs—at least
You can tell me her name!
THE FIRST VIOLIN (*raps on his desk with his bow*): Pst—
Gentlemen! (*raises his bow*)
THE ORANGE GIRL: Macaroons, lemonade—
CHRISTIAN: Then she may be
One of those aesthetes . . . Intellectuals,
You call them— How can I talk to a woman
In that style? I have no wit. This fine manner
Of speaking and of writing nowadays—
Not for me! I am a soldier—and afraid.
That's her box, on the right—the empty one.
LIGNIÈRE (*starts for the door*): I am going.
CHRISTIAN (*restrains him*): No—wait!
LIGNIÈRE: Not I. There's a tavern
Not far away—and I am dying of thirst.
THE ORANGE GIRL (*passes with her tray*): Orange juice?
LIGNIÈRE: No!
THE ORANGE GIRL: Milk?
LIGNIÈRE: Pouah!
THE ORANGE GIRL: Muscatel?

LIGNIÈRE: Here! Stop! (*to* CHRISTIAN) I'll stay a little. (*to the* GIRL)   Let me see
Your Muscatel.

(*He sits down by the sideboard. The* GIRL *pours out wine for him.*)

VOICES (*in the crowd about the door, upon the entrance of a spruce little man, rather fat, with a beaming smile*): Ragueneau!

LIGNIÈRE (*to* CHRISTIAN):   Ragueneau,
Poet and pastry-cook—a character!

RAGUENEAU (*dressed like a confectioner in his Sunday clothes, advances quickly to* LIGNIÈRE): Sir, have you seen Monsieur de Cyrano?

LIGNIÈRE (*presents him to* CHRISTIAN): Permit me . . .
    Ragueneau, confectioner,
The chief support of modern poetry.

RAGUENEAU (*bridling*): Oh—too much honor!

LIGNIÈRE: Patron of the Arts—
Maecenas! Yes, you are—

RAGUENEAU: Undoubtedly,
The poets gather round my hearth,

LIGNIÈRE: On credit—
Himself a poet—

RAGUENEAU: So they say—

LIGNIÈRE: Maintains
The Muses.

RAGUENEAU: It is true that for an ode—

LIGNIÈRE: You give a tart—

RAGUENEAU: A tartlet—

LIGNIÈRE: Modesty!
And for a triolet you give—

RAGUENEAU: Plain bread.

LIGNIÈRE (*severely*): Bread and milk! And you love the theater?

RAGUENEAU: I adore it!

LIGNIÈRE: Well, pastry pays for all.
Your place today now— Come, between ourselves,
What did it cost you?

RAGUENEAU: Four pies; fourteen cakes.
(*looking about*) But—Cyrano not here? Astonishing!

LIGNIÈRE: Why so?

RAGUENEAU: Why— Montfleury plays!

LIGNIÈRE: Yes, I hear
That hippopotamus assumes the role
Of Phédon. What is that to Cyrano?

RAGUENEAU: Have you not heard? Monsieur de Bergerac
So hates Montfleury, he has forbidden him
For three weeks to appear upon the stage.

LIGNIÈRE (*who is, by this time, at his fourth glass*): Well?

RAGUENEAU: Montfleury plays—

CUIGY (*strolls over to them*):   Yes—what then?

RAGUENEAU: Ah! That
Is what I came to see.

FIRST MARQUIS: This Cyrano—
Who is he?

CUIGY: Oh, he is the lad with the long sword.

SECOND MARQUIS: Noble?

CUIGY: Sufficiently; he is in the Guards. (*points to a gentle-
man who comes and goes about the hall as though seeking
for someone*)
His friend Le Bret can tell you more. (*calls to him*)
Le Bret! (LE BRET *comes down to them.*)
Looking for Bergerac?

LE BRET: Yes. And for trouble.

CUIGY: Is he not an extraordinary man?

LE BRET: The best friend and the bravest soul alive!

RAGUENEAU: Poet—

CUIGY: Swordsman—

LE BRET: Musician—

BRISSAILLE: Philosopher—

LIGNIÈRE: Such a remarkable appearance, too!

RAGUENEAU: Truly, I should not look to find his portrait
By the grave hand of Philippe de Champagne.
He might have been a model for Callot—
One of those wild swashbucklers in a masque—
Hat with three plumes, and doublet with six points—
His cloak behind him over his long sword
Cocked, like the tail of strutting Chanticleer—
Prouder than all the swaggering Tamburlaines
Hatched out of Gascony. And to complete
This Punchinello figure—such a nose!—
My lords, there is no such nose as that nose—
You cannot look upon it without crying: "Oh, no,
Impossible! Exaggerated!" Then
You smile, and say: "Of course— I might have known;
Presently he will take it off." But that
Monsieur de Bergerac will never do.

LIGNIÈRE (*grimly*): He keeps it—and God help the man
who smiles!

RAGUENEAU: His sword is one half of the shears of Fate!

FIRST MARQUIS (*shrugs*): He will not come.

RAGUENEAU: Will he not? Sir, I'll lay you
A pullet à la Ragueneau!

FIRST MARQUIS (*laughing*): Done!

(*Murmurs of admiration;* ROXANE *has just appeared in her box. She sits at the front of the box, and her* DUENNA *takes a seat toward the rear.* CHRISTIAN, *busy paying the* ORANGE GIRL, *does not see her at first.*)

SECOND MARQUIS (*with little excited cries*): Ah!
Oh! Oh! Sweet sirs, look yonder! Is she not
Frightfully ravishing?

FIRST MARQUIS: Bloom of the peach—
Blush of the strawberry—

SECOND MARQUIS: So fresh—so cool,
That our hearts, grown all warm with loving her,
May catch their death of cold!

CHRISTIAN (*looks up, sees* ROXANE, *and seizes* LIGNIÈRE *by the arm*): There! Quick—up there—
In the box! Look—

LIGNIÈRE (*coolly*):   Herself?

CHRISTIAN: Quickly— Her name?

LIGNIÈRE (*sipping his wine, and speaking between sips*):
Madeleine Robin, called Roxane . . . refined . . .
Intellectual . . .

CHRISTIAN: Ah!—

LIGNIÈRE: Unmarried . . .

CHRISTIAN: Oh!—

LIGNIÈRE: No title . . . rich enough . . . an orphan . . .
cousin
To Cyrano . . . of whom we spoke just now . . .

(*At this point, a very distinguished-looking gentleman, the Cordon Bleu around his neck, enters the box, and stands a moment talking with* ROXANE.)

CHRISTIAN (*starts*): And the man? . . .

LIGNIÈRE (*beginning to feel his wine a little; cocks his eye at them*): Oho! That man? . . . Comte de Guiche . . .
In love with her . . . married himself, however,
To the niece of the Cardinal—Richelieu . . .
Wishes Roxane, therefore, to marry one
Monsieur de Valvert . . . Vicomte . . . friend of his . . .
A somewhat melancholy gentleman . . .
But . . . well, accommodating! . . . She says No . . .
Nevertheless, de Guiche is powerful . . .
Not above persecuting . . . (*he rises, swaying a little, and very happy*)   I have written

A little song about his little game . . .
Good little song, too . . . Here, I'll sing it for you . . .
Make de Guiche furious . . . naughty little song . . .
Not so bad, either— Listen! . . . (*He stands with his glass
held aloft, ready to sing.*)

CHRISTIAN: No. Adieu.

LIGNIÈRE: Whither away?

CHRISTIAN: To Monsieur de Valvert!

LIGNIÈRE: Careful! The man's a swordsman . . . (*nods
toward* ROXANE, *who is watching* CHRISTIAN) Wait! Someone
Looking at you—

CHRISTIAN: Roxane! . . .

(*He forgets everything, and stands spellbound, gazing
toward* ROXANE. *The* CUTPURSE *and his crew, observing him
transfixed, his eyes raised and his mouth half open, begin
edging in his direction.*)

LIGNIÈRE: Oh! Very well,
Then I'll be leaving you . . . Good day . . . Good day! . . .
(CHRISTIAN *remains motionless.*)
Everywhere else, they like to hear me sing!—
Also, I am thirsty.

(*He goes out, navigating carefully.* LE BRET, *having made
the circuit of the hall, returns to* RAGUENEAU, *somewhat reassured.*)

LE BRET: No sign anywhere
Of Cyrano!

RAGUENEAU (*incredulous*): Wait and see!

LE BRET: Humph! I hope
He has not seen the bill.

THE CROWD: The play— The play!—

FIRST MARQUIS (*observing* DE GUICHE, *as he descends from*
ROXANE'S *box and crosses the floor, followed by a knot of
obsequious gentlemen, the* VICOMTE DE VALVERT *among them*):
This man de Guiche—what ostentation!

SECOND MARQUIS: Bah!—
Another Gascon!

FIRST MARQUIS: Gascon, yes—but cold
And calculating—certain to succeed—
My word for it. Come, shall we make our bow?
We shall be none the worse, I promise you . . .
(*They go toward* DE GUICHE.)

SECOND MARQUIS: Beautiful ribbons, Count! That color,
    now,
What is it—"Kiss-me-Dear" or "Startled-Fawn"?

DE GUICHE: I call that shade "The Dying Spaniard."

FIRST MARQUIS: Ha!
And no false colors either—thanks to you
And your brave troops, in Flanders before long
The Spaniard will die daily.
   DE GUICHE: Shall we go
And sit upon the stage? Come, Valvert.
   CHRISTIAN (*starts at the name*):   Valvert!—
The Vicomte— Ah, that scoundrel! Quick—my glove—
I'll throw it in his face—(*Reaching into his pocket for his
glove, he catches the hand of the* CUTPURSE.)
   THE CUTPURSE: Oh!—
   CHRISTIAN (*holding fast to the man's wrist*): Who are you?
I was looking for a glove—
   THE CUTPURSE (*cringing*):   You found a hand.
(*hurriedly*) Let me go— I can tell you something—
   CHRISTIAN (*still holding him*):   Well?
   THE CUTPURSE: Lignière—that friend of yours—
   CHRISTIAN (*same business*):   Well?
   THE CUTPURSE: Good as dead—
Understand? Ambuscaded. Wrote a song
About—no matter. There's a hundred men
Waiting for him tonight—I'm one of them.
   CHRISTIAN: A hundred? Who arranged this?
   THE CUTPURSE: Secret.
   CHRISTIAN: Oh!
   THE CUTPURSE (*with dignity*): Professional secret.
   CHRISTIAN: Where are they to be?
   THE CUTPURSE: Porte de Nesle. On his way home. Tell
him so. Save his life.
   CHRISTIAN (*releases the man*): Yes, but where am I to find
him?
   THE CUTPURSE: Go round the taverns. There's the Golden
      Grape,
The Pineapple, the Bursting Belt, the Two
Torches, the Three Funnels—in every one
You leave a line of writing—understand?
To warn him.
   CHRISTIAN (*starts for the door*):
                        I'll go! God, what swine—a hundred
Against one man! . . . (*stops and looks longingly at* ROXANE)
Leave *her* here—(*savagely, turning toward* VALVERT) And
leave *him*—(*decidedly*) I must save Lignière!
(*Exit.* DE GUICHE, VALVERT, *and all the* MARQUIS *have dis-
appeared through the curtains, to take their seats upon the*

*stage. The floor is entirely filled; not a vacant seat remains
in the gallery or in the boxes.*)

THE CROWD: The play! The play!
Begin the play!

A CITIZEN (*as his wig is hoisted into the air on the end of
a fishline, in the hands of a page in the gallery*):   My wig! !

CRIES OF JOY: He's bald! Bravo,
You pages! Ha ha ha!

THE CITIZEN (*furious, shakes his fist at the boy*):
                                  Here, you young villain!

CRIES OF LAUGHTER (*beginning very loud, then suddenly
repressed*): HA HA! Ha Ha! ha ha . . . (*complete silence*)

LE BRET (*surprised*):   That sudden hush? . . .
(*A* SPECTATOR *whispers in his ear.*) Yes?

THE SPECTATOR: I was told on good authority . . .

MURMURS (*here and there*): What? . . . Here? . . . No . . .
        Yes . . . Look—in the latticed box—
The Cardinal! . . . The Cardinal! . . .

A PAGE: The Devil!—
Now we shall all have to behave ourselves!

(*Three raps on the stage. The audience becomes motionless. Silence*)

THE VOICE OF A MARQUIS (*from the stage, behind the curtains*): Snuff that candle!

ANOTHER MARQUIS (*puts his head out through the curtains*):
A chair! . . .

(*A chair is passed from hand to hand over the heads of the
crowd. He takes it, and disappears behind the curtains, not
without having blown a few kisses to the occupants of the
boxes.*)

A SPECTATOR: Silence!

VOICES: Hssh! . . . Hssh! . . .

(*Again the three raps on the stage. The curtains part.
TABLEAU. The* MARQUIS *seated on their chairs to right and
left of the stage, insolently posed. Back drop representing a
pastoral scene, bluish in tone. Four little crystal chandeliers
light up the stage. The violins play softly.*)

LE BRET (*in a low tone, to* RAGUENEAU): Montfleury enters
now?

RAGUENEAU (*nods*):   Opens the play.

LE BRET (*much relieved*): Then Cyrano is not here!

RAGUENEAU: I lose . . .

LE BRET: Humph!—
So much the better!

(*The melody of a musette is heard.* MONTFLEURY *appears*

*upon the scene, a ponderous figure in the costume of a rustic
shepherd, a hat garlanded with roses tilted over one ear,
playing upon a beribboned pastoral pipe.*)

THE CROWD (*applauds*):   Montfleury! . . . Bravo! . . .

MONTFLEURY (*after bowing to the applause, begins the
role of Phédon*):

"Thrice happy he who hides from pomp and power
In sylvan shade or solitary bower;
Where balmy zephyrs fan his burning cheeks——"

A VOICE (*from the midst of the hall*): Wretch. Have I not
forbade you these three weeks?

(*Sensation. Everyone turns to look. Murmurs.*)

SEVERAL VOICES: What? . . . Where? . . . Who is it? . . .

CUIGY: Cyrano!

LE BRET (*in alarm*):   Himself!

THE VOICE: King of clowns! Leave the stage—*at once!*

THE CROWD: Oh!—

MONTFLEURY: Now,
Now, now—

THE VOICE: You disobey me?

SEVERAL VOICES (*from the floor, from the boxes*): Hsh!
Go on—

Quiet!—Go on, Montfleury!—Who's afraid?—

MONTFLEURY (*in a voice of no great assurance*):
"Thrice happy he who hides from . . ."

THE VOICE (*more menacingly*): Well? Well? Well? . . .
Monarch of mountebanks! Must I come and plant
A forest on your shoulders?

(*A cane at the end of a long arm shakes above the heads
of the crowd.*)

MONTFLEURY (*in a voice increasingly feeble*):
                                          "Thrice hap—"

(*The cane is violently agitated.*)

THE VOICE: GO! ! !

THE CROWD: Ah . . .

CYRANO (*arises in the center of the floor, erect upon a
chair, his arms folded, his hat cocked ferociously, his moustache bristling, his nose terrible*): Presently I shall grow
angry! (*sensation at his appearance*)

MONTFLEURY (*to the* MARQUIS):   Messieurs,
If you protect me—

A MARQUIS (*nonchalantly*):   Well—proceed!

CYRANO: Fat swine!
If you dare breathe one balmy zephyr more,
I'll fan your cheeks for you!

THE MARQUIS: Quiet down there!
CYRANO: Unless these gentlemen retain their seats,
My cane may bite their ribbons!
ALL THE MARQUIS (*on their feet*):   That will do!—
Montfleury—
CYRANO: Fly, goose! Shoo! Take to your wings,
Before I pluck your plumes, and draw your gorge!
A VOICE: See here—
CYRANO: Off stage! I
ANOTHER VOICE: One moment—
CYRANO: What—still there?
(*turns back his cuffs deliberately*) Very good—then I enter—
    Left—with knife—
To carve this large Italian sausage.
MONTFLEURY (*desperately attempting dignity*):   Sir,
When you insult me, you insult the Muse!
CYRANO (*with great politeness*): Sir, if the Muse, who never
    knew your name,
Had the honor to meet you—then be sure
That after one glance at that face of yours,
That figure of a mortuary urn—
She would apply her buskin—toward the rear!
THE CROWD: Montfleury! . . . Montfleury! . . . The play!
The play!
CYRANO (*to those who are shouting and crowding about
him*): Pray you, be gentle with my scabbard here—
She'll put her tongue out at you presently!—
    (*The circle enlarges.*)
THE CROWD (*recoiling*): Keep back—
CYRANO (*To* MONTFLEURY):   Begone!
THE CROWD (*pushing in closer and growling*):
                                Ahr! . . . ahr! . . .
CYRANO (*turns upon them*):   Did someone speak?
(*They recoil again.*)
A VOICE (*in the back of the hall, sings*):
                Monsieur de Cyrano
                    Must be another Caesar—
                Let Brutus lay him low,
                    And play us *La Clorise!*
ALL THE CROWD (*singing*):
                    La Clorise! La Clorise!
CYRANO: Let me hear one more word of that same song,
And I destroy you all!
A CITIZEN: Who might you be?
Samson?—

CYRANO: Precisely. Would you kindly lend me
Your jawbone?

A LADY (*in one of the boxes*): What an outrage!

A NOBLE: Scandalous!

A CITIZEN: Annoying!

A PAGE: What a game!

THE CROWD: Kss! Montfleury!
Cyrano!

CYRANO: Silence!

THE CROWD (*delirious*):   Woof! Woof! Baaa! Cockadoo!

CYRANO: I—

A PAGE: Meow!

CYRANO: I say be silent!—

(*His voice dominates the uproar. Momentary hush.*)

                                                And I offer
One universal challenge to you all!
Approach, young heroes—I will take your names.
Each in his turn—no crowding! One, two, three—
Come, get your numbers—who will head the list—
You sir? No— You? Ah, no. To the first man
Who falls I'll build a monument! . . . Not one?
Will all who wish to die, please raise their hands? . . .
I see. You are so modest, you might blush
Before a sword naked. Sweet innocence! . . .
Not one name? Not one finger? . . . Very well,
Then I go on (*turning back toward the stage, where* MONT-
FLEURY *waits in despair*) I'd have our theater cured
Of this carbuncle. Or if not, why then—(*his hand on his sword
hilt*)
The lancet!

MONTFLEURY: I—

CYRANO (*descends from his chair, seats himself comfortably
in the center of the circle which has formed around him,
and makes himself quite at home*): Attend to me—full moon!
I clap my hands, three times—thus. At the third
You will eclipse yourself.

THE CROWD (*amused*):   Ah!

CYRANO: Ready? One!

MONTFLEURY: I—

A VOICE (*from the boxes*): No!

THE CROWD: He'll go— He'll stay—

MONTFLEURY: I really think,
Gentlemen—

CYRANO: Two!

MONTFLEURY: Perhaps I had better—

CYRANO: Three!
(MONTFLEURY *disappears, as if through a trapdoor. Tempest of laughter, hoots and hisses.*)
THE CROWD: Yah!—Coward— Come back—
CYRANO (*beaming, drops back in his chair and crosses his legs*): Let him—if he dare!
A CITIZEN: The Manager! Speech! Speech!
(BELLEROSE *advances and bows.*)
THE BOXES: Ah! Bellerose!
BELLEROSE (*with elegance*): Most noble—most fair—
THE CROWD: No! The Comedian— Jodelet!—
JODELET (*advances, and speaks through his nose*): Lewd fellows of the baser sort—
THE CROWD: Ha! Ha! Not bad! Bravo!
JODELET: No Bravos here!
Our heavy tragedian with the voluptuous bust
Was taken suddenly—
THE CROWD: Yah! Coward!
JODELET: I mean . . .
He had to be excused—
THE CROWD: Call him back— No!— Yes!—
THE BOY (*to* CYRANO): After all, Monsieur, what reason have you
To hate this Montfleury?
CYRANO (*graciously, still seated*): My dear young man,
I have two reasons, either one alone
Conclusive. *Primo:* A lamentable actor,
Who mouths his verse and moans his tragedy,
And heaves up— Ugh!—like a hod-carrier, lines
That ought to soar on their own wings. *Secundo:*—
Well—that's my secret.
THE OLD CITIZEN (*behind him*): But you close the play—
La Clorise—by Baro! Are we to miss
Our entertainment, merely—
CYRANO (*respectfully, turns his chair toward the old man*):
My dear old boy,
The poetry of Baro being worth
Zero, or less, I feel that I have done
Poetic justice!
THE INTELLECTUALS (*in the boxes*): Really!—our Baro!—
My dear!—Who ever?—Ah, dieu! The idea!—
CYRANO (*gallantly, turns his chair toward the boxes*):
Fair ladies—shine upon us like the sun,

Blossom like the flowers around us—be our songs,
Heard in a dream— Make sweet the hour of death,
Smiling upon us as you close our eyes—
Inspire, but do not try to criticize!
   BELLEROSE: Quite so!—and the mere money—possibly
You would like that returned— Yes?
   CYRANO: Bellerose,
You speak the first word of intelligence!
I will not wound the mantle of the Muse—
Here, catch!—(*throws him a purse*)
              And hold your tongue.
   THE CROWD (*astonished*):   Ah! Ah!
   JODELET (*deftly catches the purse, weighs it in his hand*):
                       Monsieur,
You are hereby authorized to close our play
Every night, on the same terms.
   THE CROWD: Boo!
   JODELET: And welcome!
Let us be booed together, you and I!
   BELLEROSE: Kindly pass out quietly . . .
   JODELET (*burlesquing* BELLEROSE): Quietly . . .
   (*They begin to go out, while* CYRANO *looks about him with
satisfaction. But the exodus ceases presently during the en-
suing scene. The ladies in the boxes who have already risen
and put on their wraps, stop to listen, and finally sit down
again.*)
   LE BRET (*to* CYRANO): Idiot!
   A MEDDLER (*hurries up to* CYRANO):
                 But what a scandal! Montfleury—
The great Montfleury! Did you know the Duc de Candale
was his patron? Who is yours?
   CYRANO: No one.
   THE MEDDLER: No one—no patron?
   CYRANO: I said no.
   THE MEDDLER: What, no great lord, to cover with his
name—
   CYRANO (*with visible annoyance*): No, I have told you
    twice. Must I repeat?
No sir, no patron—(*his hand on his sword*)
                  But a patroness!
   THE MEDDLER: And when do you leave Paris?
   CYRANO: That's as may be.
   THE MEDDLER: The Duc de Candale has a long arm.
   CYRANO: Mine
Is longer (*drawing his sword*)

by three feet of steel.

THE MEDDLER: Yes, yes,
But do you dream of daring—

CYRANO: I do dream
Of daring . . .

THE MEDDLER: But—

CYRANO: You may go now.

THE MEDDLER: But—

CYRANO: You may go—
Or tell me why are you staring at my nose!

THE MEDDLER (*in confusion*): No—I—

CYRANO (*stepping up to him*): Does it astonish you?

THE MEDDLER (*drawing back*): Your grace
Misunderstands my—

CYRANO: Is it long and soft
And dangling, like a trunk?

THE MEDDLER (*same business*): I never said—

CYRANO: Or crooked, like an owl's beak?

THE MEDDLER: I—

CYRANO: Perhaps
A pimple ornaments the end of it?

THE MEDDLER: No—

CYRANO: Or a fly parading up and down?
What is this portent?

THE MEDDLER: Oh—

CYRANO: This phenomenon?

THE MEDDLER: But I have been careful not to look—

CYRANO: And why
Not, if you please?

THE MEDDLER: Why—

CYRANO: It disgusts you, then?

THE MEDDLER: My dear sir—

CYRANO: Does its color appear to you
Unwholesome?

THE MEDDLER: Oh, by no means!

CYRANO: Or its form
Obscene?

THE MEDDLER: Not in the least—

CYRANO: Then why assume
This deprecating manner? Possibly
You find it just a trifle large?

THE MEDDLER (*babbling*): Oh no!—
Small, very small, infinitesimal—

CYRANO (*roars*): What?
How? You accuse me of absurdity?

Small—*my nose?* Why—
  THE MEDDLER (*breathless*): My God!—
  CYRANO: Magnificent,
My nose! . . . You pug, you knob, you button-head,
Know that I glory in this nose of mine,
For a great nose indicates a great man—
Genial, courteous, intellectual,
Virile, courageous—as I am—and such
As you—poor wretch—will never dare to be
Even in imagination. For that face—
That blank, inglorious concavity
Which my right hand finds—
  (*He strikes him.*)
  THE MEDDLER: Ow!
  CYRANO: —on top of you,
Is as devoid of pride, of poetry,
Of soul, of picturesqueness, of contour,
Of character, of NOSE in short—as that (*takes him by the
shoulders and turns him around, suiting the action to the
word*)
Which at the end of that limp spine of yours
My left foot—
  THE MEDDLER (*escaping*): Help! The Guard!
  CYRANO: Take notice, all
Who find this feature of my countenance
A theme for comedy! When the humorist
Is noble, then custom is to show
Appreciation proper to his rank—
More heartfelt . . . and more pointed. . . .
  DE GUICHE (*who has come down from the stage, surrounded
by the* MARQUIS):   Presently
This fellow will grow tiresome.
  VALVERT (*shrugs*): Oh, he blows
His trumpet!
  DE GUICHE: Well—will no one interfere?
  VALVERT: No one? (*looks around*) Observe. I myself will
    proceed
To put him in his place.
  (*He walks up to* CYRANO, *who has been watching him, and
stands there, looking him over with an affected air.*)
                     Ah . . . your nose . . . hem! . . .
Your nose is . . . rather large!
  CYRANO (*gravely*): Rather.
  VALVERT (*simpering*):   Oh well—
  CYRANO (*coolly*): Is that all?

VALVERT (*turns away with a shrug*): Well, of course—
CYRANO: Ah, no, young sir!
You are too simple. Why, you might have said—
Oh, a great many things! Mon dieu, why waste
Your opportunity? For example, thus:—
AGGRESSIVE: I, sir, if that nose were mine,
I'd have it amputated—on the spot!
FRIENDLY: How do you drink with such a nose?
You ought to have a cup made specially.
DESCRIPTIVE: 'Tis a rock—a crag—a cape—
A cape? say rather, a peninsula!
INQUISITIVE: What is that receptacle—
A razor-case or a portfolio?
KINDLY: Ah, do you love the little birds
So much that when they come and sing to you,
You give them this to perch on? INSOLENT:
Sir, when you smoke, the neighbors must suppose
Your chimney is on fire. CAUTIOUS: Take care—
A weight like that might make you topheavy.
THOUGHTFUL: Somebody fetch my parasol—
Those delicate colors fade so in the sun!
PEDANTIC: Does not Aristophanes
Mention a mythologic monster called
Hippocampelephantocamelos?
Surely we have here the original!
FAMILIAR: Well, old torchlight! Hang your hat
Over that chandelier—it hurts my eyes.
ELOQUENT: When it blows, the typhoon howls,
And the clouds darken. DRAMATIC: When it bleeds—
The Red Sea! ENTERPRISING: What a sign
For some perfumer! LYRIC: Hark—the horn
Of Roland calls to summon Charlemagne!—
SIMPLE: When do they unveil the monument?
RESPECTFUL: Sir, I recognize in you
A man of parts, a man of prominence—
RUSTIC: Hey? What? Call that a nose? Na na—
I be no fool like what you think I be—
That there's a blue cucumber! MILITARY:
Point against cavalry! PRACTICAL: Why not
A lottery with this for the grand prize?
Or—parodying Faustus in the play—
"Was this the nose that launched a thousand ships
And burned the topless towers of Ilium?"
These, my dear sir, are things you might have said
Had you some tinge of letters, or of wit

To color your discourse. But wit,—not so,
You never had an atom—and of letters,
You need but three to write you down—an Ass.
Moreover,—if you had the invention, here
Before these folks to make a jest of me—
Be sure you would not then articulate
The twentieth part of half a syllable
Of the beginning! For I say these things
Lightly enough myself, about myself,
But I allow none else to utter them.

DE GUICHE (*tries to lead away the amazed* VALVERT):
Vicomte—come.

VALVERT (*choking*): Oh— These arrogant grand airs!—
A clown who—look at him—not even gloves!
No ribbons—no lace—no buckles on his shoes—

CYRANO: I carry my adornments on my soul.
I do not dress up like a popinjay;
But inwardly, I keep my daintiness.
I do not bear with me, by any chance,
An insult not yet washed away—a conscience
Yellow with unpurged bile—an honor frayed
To rags, a set of scruples badly worn.
I go caparisoned in gems unseen,
Trailing white plumes of freedom, garlanded
With my good name—no figure of a man,
But a soul clothed in shining armor, hung
With deeds of decorations, twirling—thus—
A bristling wit, and swinging at my side
Courage, and on the stones of this old town
Making the sharp truth ring, like golden spurs!

VALVERT: But—

CYRANO: But I have no gloves! A pity too!
I had one—the last one of an old pair—
And lost that. Very careless of me. Some
Gentleman offered me an impertinence.
I left it—in his face.

VALVERT: Dolt, bumpkin, fool,
Insolent puppy, jobbernowl!

CYRANO (*removes his hat and bows*): Ah, yes?
And I—Cyrano-Savinien-Hercule De Bergerac!

VALVERT (*turns away*): Buffoon!

CYRANO (*cries out as if suddenly taken with a cramp*):
                                                    Oh!

VALVERT (*turns back*): Well, what now?

CYRANO (*with grimaces of anguish*):

I must do something to relieve these cramps—
This is what comes of lack of exercise—
Ah!—
   VALVERT: What is all this?
   CYRANO: My sword has gone to sleep!
   VALVERT (*draws*): So be it!
   CYRANO: You shall die exquisitely.
   VALVERT (*contemptuously*): Poet!
   CYRANO: Why yes, a poet, if you will;
So while we fence, I'll make you a Ballade
Extempore.
   VALVERT: A Ballade?
   CYRANO: Yes. You know
What that is?
   VALVERT: I—
   CYRANO: The Ballade, sir, is formed
Of three stanzas of eight lines each—
   VALVERT: Oh, come!
   CYRANO: And a refrain of four.
   VALVERT: You—
   CYRANO: I'll compose
One, while I fight with you; and at the end
Of the last line—thrust home!
   VALVERT: Will you?
   CYRANO: I will.
(*declaims*) "Ballade of the duel at the Hôtel de Bourgogne
Between de Bergerac and a Boeotian."
   VALVERT (*sneering*): What do you mean by that?
   CYRANO: Oh, that? The title.
   THE CROWD (*excited*): Come on—
                           A circle—
                               Quiet—
                          Down in front!
   (TABLEAU. *A ring of interested spectators in the center of
the floor, the* MARQUIS *and the* OFFICERS *mingling with the
citizens and common folk. Pages swarming up on men's
shoulders to see better; the Ladies in the boxes standing and
leaning over. To the right,* DE GUICHE *and his following; to
the left,* LE BRET, CUIGY, RAGUENEAU, *and others of* CYRANO'S
friends.)
   CYRANO (*closes his eyes for an instant*): Stop . . . Let me
choose my rimes. . . . Now!
                        Here we go—
   (*He suits the action to the word, throughout the following.*)
Lightly I toss my hat away,

Languidly over my arm let fall
The cloak that covers my bright array—
    Then out swords, and to work withal!
    A Launcelot, in his Lady's hall . . .
A Spartacus, at the Hippodrome! . . .
    I dally awhile with you, dear jackal,
Then, as I end the refrain, thrust home!
    (*The swords cross—the fight is on.*)
Where shall I skewer my peacock? . . . Nay,
    Better for you to have shunned this brawl!—
Here, in the heart, thro' your ribbons gay?
    —In the belly, under your silken shawl?
    Hark, how the steel rings musical!
Mark how my point floats, light as the foam,
    Ready to drive you back to the wall,
Then, as I end the refrain, thrust home!

Ho, for a rime! . . . You are white as whey—
    You break, you cower, you cringe, you . . . crawl!
Tac!—and I parry your last essay:
    So may the turn of a hand forestall
Life with its honey, death with its gall;
    So may the turn of my fancy roam
Free, for a time, till the rimes recall,
Then, as I end the refrain, thrust home!
    (*He announces solemnly.*)
Refrain:
    Prince! Pray God, that is Lord of all,
Pardon your soul, for your time has come!
    Beat—pass—fling you aslant, asprawl—
Then, as I end the refrain . . .
    (*He lunges;* VALVERT *staggers back and falls into the arms of his friends.* CYRANO *recovers, and salutes.*)
                                        —Thrust home!
    (*Shouts. Applause from the boxes. Flowers and handkerchiefs come fluttering down. The Officers surround* CYRANO *and congratulate him.* RAGUENEAU *dances for joy.* LE BRET *is unable to conceal his enthusiasm. The friends of* VALVERT *hold him up and help him away.*)
    THE CROWD (*in one long cry*): Ah-h!
    A CAVALIER: Superb!
    A WOMAN: Simply sweet!
    RAGUENEAU: Magnelephant!
    A MARQUIS: A novelty!
    LE BRET: Bah!

THE CROWD (*thronging around* CYRANO): Compliments—
    regards—
Bravo!—
    A WOMAN'S VOICE: Why, he's a hero!
    A MUSKETEER (*advances quickly to* CYRANO, *with out-
stretched hands*):   Monsieur, will you
Permit me?—It was altogether fine!
I think I may appreciate these things—
Moreover, I have been stamping for pure joy!
    (*He retires quickly.*)
    CYRANO (*to* CUIGY): What was that gentleman's name?
    CUIGY: Oh . . . D'Artagnan.
    LE BRET (*takes* CYRANO'S *arm*): Come here and tell me—
    CYRANO: Let this crowd go first—
    (*to* BELLEROSE): May we stay?
    BELLEROSE (*with great respect*): Certainly! (*cries and cat-
calls off stage*)
    JODELET (*comes down from the door where he has been
looking out*):   Hark!— Montfleury—
They are hooting him.
    BELLEROSE (*solemnly*): "Sic transit gloria!" (*changes his
tone and shouts to the* PORTER *and the* LAMPLIGHTER)—
Strike! . . . Close the house! . . . Leave the lights—
                                We rehearse
The new farce after dinner.
    (JODELET *and* BELLEROSE *go out after elaborately saluting*
CYRANO.)
    THE PORTER (*to* CYRANO): You do not dine?
    CYRANO: I?— No!
    (*The* PORTER *turns away.*)
    LE BRET: Why not?
    CYRANO (*haughtily*): Because— (*changing his tone when
he sees the* PORTER *has gone*) Because I have
No money.
    LE BRET (*gesture of tossing*): But—the purse of gold?
    CYRANO: Farewell,
Paternal pension!
    LE BRET: So you have, until
The first of next month—?
    CYRANO: Nothing.
    LE BRET: What a fool!—
    CYRANO: But—what a gesture!
    THE ORANGE GIRL (*behind her little counter; coughs*): Hem!
    (CYRANO *and* LE BRET *look around; she advances timidly.*)
                                Pardon, monsieur . . .

A man ought never to go hungry . . . (*indicating the side-board*)

   See,
I have everything here . . . (*eagerly*)
        Please!—
 CYRANO (*uncovers*):   My dear child,
I cannot bend this Gascon pride of mine
To accept such a kindness— Yet, for fear
That I may give you pain if I refuse,
I will take . . .
  (*He goes to the sideboard and makes his selection.*)
        Oh, not very much! A grape . . .
  (*She gives him the bunch; he removes a single grape.*)
One only! And a glass of water . . .
  (*She starts to pour wine into it; he stops her.*)
          Clear!
And . . . half a macaroon!
  (*He gravely returns the other half.*)
 LE BRET: Old idiot!
 THE ORANGE GIRL: Please!— Nothing more?
 CYRANO: Why yes— Your hand to kiss.
  (*He kisses the hand which she holds out, as he would the hand of a princess.*)
 THE ORANGE GIRL: Thank you, sir. (*She curtseys.*) Good-night. (*She goes out.*)
 CYRANO: Now, I am listening. (*plants himself before the sideboard and arranges thereon—*)
Dinner!—(*—the macaroon*)
      Drink!—(*—the glass of water*)
      Dessert!—(*—the grape*)
      There—now I'll sit down.
 (*seats himself*) Lord, I was hungry! Abominably! (*eating*)
            Well?

 LE BRET: These fatheads with the bellicose grand airs
Will have you ruined if you listen to them;
Talk to a man of sense and hear how all
Your swagger impresses him.
 CYRANO (*finishes his macaroon*): Enormously.
 LE BRET: The Cardinal—
 CYRANO (*beaming*): Was he there?
 LE BRET: He must have thought you—
 CYRANO: Original.
 LE BRET: Well, but—
 CYRANO: He is himself
A playwright. He will not be too displeased

That I have closed another author's play.
   LE BRET: But look at the enemies you have made!
   CYRANO (*begins on the grape*):
How many—do you think?
   LE BRET: Just forty-eight
Without the women.
   CYRANO: Count them.
   LE BRET: Montfleury,
Baro, de Guiche, the Vicomte, the Old Man,
All the Academy—
   CYRANO: Enough! You make me
Happy!
   LE BRET: But where is all this leading you?
What is your plan?
   CYRANO: I have been wandering—
Wasting my force upon too many plans.
Now I have chosen one.
   LE BRET: What one?
   CYRANO: The simplest—
To make myself in all things admirable!
   LE BRET: Hmph!— Well, then, the real reason why you hate
Montfleury— Come, the truth, now!
   CYRANO (*rises*):   That Silenus,
Who cannot hold his belly in his arms,
Still dreams of being sweetly dangerous
Among the women—sighs and languishes,
Making sheeps' eyes out of his great frog's face—
I hate him ever since one day he dared
Smile upon—
         Oh, my friend, I seemed to see
Over some flower a great snail crawling!
   LE BRET (*amazed*):   How,
What? Is it possible?—
   CYRANO (*with a bitter smile*): For me to love? . . .
(*changing his tone; seriously*) I love.
   LE BRET: May I know? You have never said—
   CYRANO: Whom I love? Think a moment. Think of me—
Me, whom the plainest woman would despise—
Me, with this nose of mine that marches on
Before me by a quarter of an hour!
Whom should I love? Why—of course—it must be
The woman in the world most beautiful.
   LE BRET: Most beautiful?
   CYRANO: In all this world—most sweet:
Also most wise; most witty; and most fair!

LE BRET: Who and what is this woman?

CYRANO: Dangerous

Mortally, without meaning; exquisite
Without imagining. Nature's own snare
To allure manhood. A white rose wherein
Love lies in ambush for his natural prey.
Who knows her smile has known a perfect thing.
She creates grace in her own image, brings
Heaven to earth in one movement of her hand—
Nor thou, O Venus! balancing thy shell
Over the Mediterranean blue, nor thou,
Diana! marching through broad, blossoming woods,
Art so divine as when she mounts her chair,
And goes abroad through Paris!

LE BRET: Oh, well—of course,

That makes everything clear!

CYRANO: Transparently.

LE BRET: Madeleine Robin—your cousin?

CYRANO: Yes; Roxane.

LE BRET: And why not? If you love her, tell her so!
You have covered yourself with glory in her eyes
This very day.

CYRANO: My old friend—look at me,
And tell me how much hope remains for me
With this protuberance! Oh I have no more
Illusions! Now and then—bah! I may grow
Tender, walking alone in the blue cool
Of evening, through some garden fresh with flowers
After the benediction of the rain;
My poor big devil of a nose inhales
April . . . and so I follow with my eyes
Where some boy, with a girl upon his arm,
Passes a patch of silver . . . and I feel
Somehow, I wish I had a woman too,
Walking with little steps under the moon,
And holding my arm so, and smiling. Then
I dream—and I forget. . . .

                                          And then I see

The shadow of my profile on the wall!

LE BRET: My friend! . . .

CYRANO: My friend, I have my bitter days,
Knowing myself so ugly, so alone.
Sometimes—

LE BRET: You weep?

CYRANO (*quickly*):   Oh, not that ever! No,

That would be too grotesque—tears trickling down
All the long way along this nose of mine?
I will not so profane the dignity
Of sorrow. Never any tears for me!
Why, there is nothing more sublime than tears,
Nothing!— Shall I make them ridiculous
In my poor person?
    LE BRET: Love's no more than chance!
    CYRANO (*shakes his head*):
No. I love Cleopatra: do I appear
Cæsar? I adore Beatrice; have I
The look of Dante?
    LE BRET: But your wit—your courage—
Why, that poor child who offered you just now
Your dinner! She—you saw with your own eyes,
Her eyes did not avoid you.
    CYRANO (*thoughtful*): That is true . . .
    LE BRET: Well then! Roxane herself, watching your duel,
Paler than—
    CYRANO: Pale?—
    LE BRET: Her lips parted, her hand
Thus, at her breast— I saw it! Speak to her
Speak, man!
    CYRANO: Through my nose? She might laugh at me;
That is the one thing in this world I fear!
    THE PORTER (*followed by the* DUENNA, *approaches* CYRANO
respectfully): A lady asking for Monsieur.
    CYRANO: Mon dieu . . .
Her Duenna!—
    THE DUENNA (*a sweeping curtsey*): Monsieur . . .
                      A message for you:
From our good cousin we desire to know
When and where we may see him privately.
    CYRANO (*amazed*): To see me?
    THE DUENNA (*an elaborate reverence*):
                    To see you. We have certain things
To tell you.
    CYRANO: Certain—
    THE DUENNA: Things.
    CYRANO (*trembling*): Mon dieu! . . .
    THE DUENNA: We go
Tomorrow, at the first flush of the dawn,
To hear Mass at St. Roch. Then afterward,
Where can we meet and talk a little?
    CYRANO (*catching* LE BRET'S *arm*):   Where?—

I—Ah, mon dieu! . . . mon dieu! . . .

THE DUENNA: Well?

CYRANO: I am thinking . . .

THE DUENNA: And you think?

CYRANO: I . . . The shop of Ragueneau . . .
Ragueneau—pastrycook . . .

THE DUENNA: Who dwells?—

CYRANO: Mon dieu! . . .
Oh, yes . . . Ah, mon dieu! . . . Rue St.-Honoré.

THE DUENNA: We are agreed. Remember—seven o'clock.
(*reverence*) Until then—

CYRANO: I'll be there.

  (*The* DUENNA *goes out.*)

CYRANO (*falls into the arms of* LE BRET): Me . . . to see
me . . .

LE BRET: You are not quite so gloomy.

CYRANO: After all,
She knows that I exist—no matter why!

LE BRET: So now, you are going to be happy.

CYRANO: Now! . . .
(*beside himself*) I—I am going to be a storm—a flame—
I need to fight whole armies all alone;
I have ten hearts; I have a hundred arms; I feel
Too strong to war with mortals—
(*He shouts at the top of his voice.*)   BRING ME GIANTS!
  (*A moment since, the shadows of the* COMEDIANS *have been
visible moving and posturing upon the stage. The* VIOLINS *have
taken their places.*)

A VOICE (*from the stage*): Hey—pst—less noise! We are
rehearsing here!

CYRANO (*laughs*): We are going.
  (*He turns up stage. Through the street door enter* CUIGY,
BRISSAILLE, *and a number of officers, supporting* LIGNIÈRE,
who is now thoroughly drunk.)

CUIGY: Cyrano!

CYRANO: What is it?

CUIGY: Here—
Here's your stray lamb!

CYRANO (*recognizes* LIGNIÈRE): Lignière—What's wrong
with him?

CUIGY: He wants you.

BRISSAILLE: He's afraid to go home.

CYRANO: Why?

LIGNIÈRE (*showing a crumpled scrap of paper and speaking with the elaborate logic of profound intoxication*):

This letter—hundred against one—that's me—
I'm the one—all because of little song—
Good song— Hundred men, waiting, understand?
Porte de Nesle—way home— Might be dangerous—
Would you permit me spend the night with you?
    CYRANO: A hundred—is that all? You are going home!
    LIGNIÈRE (*astonished*): Why—
    CYRANO (*in a voice of thunder, indicating the lighted lantern which the* PORTER *holds up curiously as he regards the scene*): Take that lantern!
    (LIGNIÈRE *precipitately seizes the lantern.*)
                             Forward march! I say
I'll be the man tonight that sees you home.
(*to the officers*) You others follow—I want an audience!
    CUIGY: A hundred against one—
    CYRANO: Those are the odds
Tonight!
    (*The* COMEDIANS *in their costumes are descending from the stage and joining the group.*)
    LE BRET: But why help this—
    CYRANO: There goes Le Bret
Growling!
    LE BRET: —This drunkard here?
    CYRANO (*his hand on* LE BRET'S *shoulder*): Because this
    drunkard—
This tun of sack, this butt of Burgundy—
Once in his life has done one lovely thing:
After the Mass, according to the form,
He saw, one day, the lady of his heart
Take holy water for a blessing. So
This one, who shudders at a drop of rain,
This fellow here—runs headlong to the font
Bends down and drinks it dry!
    A SOUBRETTE: I say that was
A pretty thought!
    CYRANO: Ah, was it not?
    THE SOUBRETTE (*to the others*): But why
Against one poor poet, a hundred men?
    CYRANO: March!
(*to the officers*) And you gentlemen, remember now,
No rescue— Let me fight alone.
    A COMEDIENNE (*jumps down from the stage*): Come on!
I'm going to watch—
    CYRANO: Come along!
    ANOTHER COMEDIENNE (*jumps down, speaks to a* COMEDIAN

costumed as an old man):   You, Cassandre?

CYRANO: Come all of you—the Doctor, Isabelle,
Léandre—the whole company—a swarm
Of murmuring, golden bees—we'll parody
Italian farce and Tragedy-of-Blood;
Ribbons for banners, masks for blazonry,
And tambourines to be our rolling drums!

ALL THE WOMEN (*jumping for joy*): Bravo!— My hood—
My cloak— Hurry!

JODELET (*mock heroic*):   Lead on!—

CYRANO (*to the* VIOLINS): You violins—play us an over-
        ture—

(*The violins join the procession which is forming. The
lighted candles are snatched from the stage and distributed;
it becomes a torchlight procession.*)

Bravo!—Officers— Ladies in costume—
And twenty paces in advance . . .
(*He takes his station as he speaks.*) Myself,
Alone, with glory fluttering over me,
Alone as Lucifer at war with heaven!
Remember—no one lifts a hand to help—
Ready there? One . . . two . . . three! Porter, the doors! . . .

(*The* PORTER *flings wide the great doors. We see in the
dim moonlight a corner of old Paris, purple and picturesque.*)

Look—Paris dreams—nocturnal, nebulous,
Under blue moonbeams hung from wall to wall—
Nature's own setting for the scene we play!—
Yonder, behind her veil of mist, the Seine,
Like a mysterious and magic mirror
Trembles—
              And you shall see what you shall see!

ALL: To the Porte de Nesle!

CYRANO (*erect upon the threshold*): To the Porte de Nesle!
(*He turns back for a moment to the* SOUBRETTE.) Did you
        not ask, my dear, why against one
Singer they send a hundred swords?
(*quietly, drawing his own sword*) Because
They know this one man for a friend of mine!

(*He goes out. The procession follows:* LIGNIÈRE *zigzagging
at its head, then the* COMEDIENNES *on the arms of the* OF-
FICERS, *then the* COMEDIANS, *leaping and dancing as they
go. It vanishes into the night to the music of* VIOLINS, *il-
luminated by the flickering glimmer of the candles.*)

ACT II

(THE BAKERY OF THE POETS)

(The shop of Ragueneau, baker and pastrycook: a spacious affair at the corner of the Rue St.-Honoré and the Rue de l'Arbre Sec. The street, seen vaguely through the glass panes in the door at the back, is gray in the first light of dawn.

In the foreground, at the left, a counter is surmounted by a canopy of wrought iron from which are hanging ducks, geese, and white peacocks. Great crockery jars hold bouquets of common flowers, yellow sunflowers in particular. On the same side farther back, a huge fireplace; in front of it, between great andirons, of which each one supports a little saucepan, roast fowls revolve and weep into their dripping-pans. To the right at the first entrance, a door. Beyond it, second entrance, a staircase leads up to a little dining room under the eaves, its interior visible through open shutters. A table is set there and a tiny Flemish candlestick is lighted; there one may retire to eat and drink in private. A wooden gallery, extending from the head of the stairway, seems to lead to other little dining rooms.

In the center of the shop, an iron ring hangs by a rope over a pulley so that it can be raised or lowered; adorned with game of various kinds hung from it by hooks, it has the appearance of a sort of gastronomic chandelier.

In the shadow under the staircase, ovens are glowing. The spits revolve; the copper pots and pans gleam ruddily. Pastries in pyramids. Hams hanging from the rafters. The morning baking is in progress: a bustle of tall cooks and timid scullions and scurrying apprentices; a blossoming of white caps adorned with cock's feathers or the wings of guinea fowl. On wicker trays or on great metal platters they bring in rows of pastries and fancy dishes of various kinds.

Tables are covered with trays of cakes and rolls; others with chairs placed about them are set for guests.

One little table in a corner disappears under a heap of

papers. At the curtain rise RAGUENEAU *is seated there. He is writing poetry.)*

A PASTRYCOOK (*brings in a dish*): *Fruits en gelée!*

SECOND PASTRYCOOK (*brings dish*): Custard!

THIRD PASTRYCOOK (*brings roast peacock ornamented with feathers*):   Peacock *rôti!*

FOURTH PASTRYCOOK (*brings tray of cakes*): Cakes and confections!

FIFTH PASTRYCOOK (*brings earthen dish*): Beef *en casserole!*

RAGUENEAU (*raises his head; returns to mere earth*):
Over the coppers of my kitchen flows
The frosted-silver dawn. Silence awhile
The god who sings within thee, Ragueneau!
Lay down the lute—the oven calls for thee!
(*rises; goes to one of the cooks*)
Here's a hiatus in your sauce; fill up
The measure.

THE COOK: How much?

RAGUENEAU (*measures on his finger*): One more dactyl.

THE COOK: Huh? . . .

FIRST PASTRYCOOK: Rolls!

SECOND PASTRYCOOK: Roulades!

RAGUENEAU (*before the fireplace*): Veil, O Muse, thy virgin eyes
From the lewd gleam of these terrestrial fires!
(*to* FIRST PASTRYCOOK) Your rolls lack balance. Here's the proper form—
An equal hemistich on either side,
And the caesura in between.
(*to another, pointing out an unfinished pie*) Your house
Of crust should have a roof upon it.
(*to another, who is seated on the hearth, placing poultry on a spit*)   And you—
Along the interminable spit, arrange
The modest pullet and the lordly Turk
Alternately, my son—as great Malherbe
Alternates male and female rimes. Remember,
A couplet, or a roast, should be well turned.

AN APPRENTICE (*advances with a dish covered by a napkin*): Master, I thought of you when I designed
This, hoping it might please you.

RAGUENEAU: Ah! A lyre—

THE APPRENTICE: In puff-paste—

RAGUENEAU: And the jewels—candied fruit!

THE APPRENTICE: And the strings, barley-sugar!

RAGUENEAU (*gives him money*): Go and drink
My health. (LISE *enters.*) St!—My wife— Circulate, and hide
That money! (*shows the lyre to* LISE, *with a languid air*)
                                        Graceful—yes?

LISE: Ridiculous! (*She places on the counter a pile of paper bags.*)

RAGUENEAU: Paper bags? Thank you . . .
(*He looks at them.*)   Ciel! My manuscripts!
The sacred verses of my poets—rent
Asunder, limb from limb—butchered to make
Base packages of pastry! Ah, you are one
Of those insane Bacchantes who destroyed
Orpheus!

LISE: Your dirty poets left them here
To pay for eating half our stock-in-trade:
We ought to make some profit out of them!

RAGUENEAU: Ant! Would you blame the locust for his song?

LISE: I blame the locust for his appetite!
There used to be a time—before you had
Your hungry friends—you never called me Ants—
No, nor Bacchantes!

RAGUENEAU: What a way to use
Poetry!

LISE: Well, what is the use of it?

RAGUENEAU: But, my dear girl, what would you do with prose?
(*Two children enter.*) Well, dears?

A CHILD: Three little patties.

RAGUENEAU (*serves them*): There we are!
All hot and brown.

THE CHILD: Would you mind wrapping them?

RAGUENEAU: One of my paper bags! . . .
                                        Oh, certainly.
(*reads from the bag, as he is about to wrap the patties in it*)
"Ulysses, when he left Penelope"—
Not that one! (*takes another bag; reads*)
                        "Phoebus, golden-crowned"—
                                        Not that one.

LISE: Well? They are waiting!

RAGUENEAU: Very well, very well!—
The Sonnet to Phyllis . . .
                            Yet—it does seem hard . . .

LISE: Made up your mind—at last! Mph!—Jack-o'-Dreams!

RAGUENEAU (*as her back is turned, calls the children, who are already at the door*): Pst!—Children—Give me back the bag. Instead

Of three patties, you shall have six of them!

(*Makes the exchange. The children go out. He reads from the bag, as he smooths it out tenderly.*)

"Phyllis"—

A spot of butter on her name!—

"Phyllis"—

CYRANO (*enters hurriedly*): What is the time?

RAGUENEAU: Six o'clock.

CYRANO: One

Hour more . . .

RAGUENEAU: Felicitations!

CYRANO: And for what?

RAGUENEAU: Your victory! I saw it all—

CYRANO: Which one?

RAGUENEAU: At the Hôtel de Bourgogne.

CYRANO: Oh—the duel!

RAGUENEAU: The duel in Rime!

LISE: He talks of nothing else.

CYRANO: Nonsense!

RAGUENEAU (*fencing and foining with a spit, which he snatches up from the hearth*): "Then, as I end the refrain, thrust home!"

"Then as I end the refrain"—

Gods! What a line!

"Then, as I end"—

CYRANO: What time now, Ragueneau?

RAGUENEAU (*petrified at the full extent of a lunge, while he looks at the clock*):

Five after six—(*recovers*) "—thrust home!"

A Ballade, too!

LISE (*to* CYRANO, *who in passing has mechanically shaken hands with her*): Your hand—what have you done?

CYRANO: Oh, my hand?—Nothing.

RAGUENEAU: What danger now—

CYRANO: No danger.

LISE: I believe

He is lying.

CYRANO: Why? Was I looking down my nose?

That must have been a devil of a lie!

(*changing his tone; to* RAGUENEAU) I expect someone. Leave us here alone,

When the time comes.

RAGUENEAU: How can I? In a moment,
My poets will be here.

LISE: To break their . . . fast!

CYRANO: Take them away, then, when I give the sign.
—What time?

RAGUENEAU: Ten minutes after.

CYRANO: Have you a pen?

RAGUENEAU (*offers him a pen*): An eagle's feather!

A MUSKETEER (*enters, and speaks to* LISE *in a stentorian voice*): Greeting!

CYRANO (*to* RAGUENEAU): Who is this?

RAGUENEAU: My wife's friend. A terrific warrior,
So he says.

CYRANO: Ah— I see. (*takes up the pen; waves* RAGUENEAU *away*) Only to write—
To fold— To give it to her—and to go . . . (*throws down the pen*) Coward! And yet—the Devil take my soul
If I dare speak one word to her . . .
(*to* RAGUENEAU) What time now?

RAGUENEAU: A quarter after six.

CYRANO (*striking his breast*): —One little word
Of all the many thousand I have here!
Whereas in writing . . . (*takes up the pen*) Come, I'll write
    to her
That letter I have written on my heart,
Torn up, and written over many times—
So many times . . . that all I have to do
Is to remember, and to write it down.

(*He writes. Through the glass of the door appear vague and hesitating shadows. The* POETS *enter, clothed in rusty black and spotted with mud.*)

LISE (*to* RAGUENEAU): Here come your scarecrows!

FIRST POET: Comrade!

SECOND POET (*takes both* RAGUENEAU'S *hands*):
My dear brother!

THIRD POET (*sniffing*): O Lord of Roasts, how sweet thy
dwellings are!

FOURTH POET: Phoebus Apollo of the Silver Spoon!

FIFTH POET: Cupid of Cookery!

RAGUENEAU (*surrounded, embraced, beaten on the back*):
These geniuses,
They put one at one's ease!

FIRST POET: We were delayed
By the crowd at the Porte de Nesle.

SECOND POET: Dead men

All scarred and gory, scattered on the stones,
Villainous-looking scoundrels—eight of them.
    CYRANO (*looks up an instant*):
Eight? I thought only seven—
    RAGUENEAU: Do you know
The hero of this hecatomb?
    CYRANO: I? . . . No.
    LISE (*to the* MUSKETEER): Do you?
    THE MUSKETEER: Hmm—perhaps!
    FIRST POET: They say one man alone
Put to flight all this crowd.
    SECOND POET: Everywhere lay
Swords, daggers, pikes, bludgeons—
    CYRANO (*writing*): "Your eyes . . ."
    THIRD POET: As far
As the Quai des Orfevres, hats and cloaks—
    FIRST POET: Why, that man must have been the devil!
    CYRANO: "Your lips . . ."
    FIRST POET: Some savage monster might have done this
thing!
    CYRANO: "Looking upon you, I grow faint with fear . . ."
    SECOND POET: What have you written lately, Ragueneau?
    CYRANO: "Your Friend— Who loves you . . ."
                         So. No signature;
I'll give it to her myself.
    RAGUENEAU: A Recipe
In Rime.
    THIRD POET: Read us your rimes!
    FOURTH POET: Here's a brioche
Cocking its hat at me. (*He bites off the top of it.*)
    FIRST POET: Look how those buns
Follow the hungry poet with their eyes—
Those almond eyes!
    SECOND POET: We are listening—
    THIRD POET: See this cream-puff—
Fat little baby, drooling while it smiles!
    SECOND POET (*nibbling at the pastry lyre*): For the first
time, the lyre is my support.
    RAGUENEAU (*coughs, adjusts his cap, strikes an attitude*):
"A Recipe in Rime"—
    SECOND POET (*gives* FIRST POET *a dig with his elbow*):
Your breakfast?
    FIRST POET: Dinner!
    RAGUENEAU (*declaims*):
        "A Recipe for Making Almond Tarts"

Beat your eggs, the yolk and white,
  Very light;
Mingle with their creamy fluff
  Drops of lime-juice, cool and green;
   Then pour in
Milk of Almonds, just enough.

Dainty patty-pans, embraced
  In puff-paste—
Have these ready within reach;
  With your thumb and finger, pinch
   Half an inch
Up around the edge of each—

Into these, a score or more,
  Slowly pour
All your store of custard; so
  Take them, bake them golden-brown—
   Now sit down! . . .
  Almond tartlets, Ragueneau!
 THE POETS: Delicious! Melting!
 A POET (*chokes*): Humph!
 CYRANO (*to* RAGUENEAU): Do you not see
Those fellows fattening themselves?—
 RAGUENEAU: I know.
I would not look—it might embarrass them—
You see, I love a friendly audience.
Besides—another vanity—I am pleased
When they enjoy my cooking.
 CYRANO (*slaps him on the back*): Be off with you!—
 (RAGUENEAU *goes upstage.*)
Good little soul! (*calls to* LISE) Madam!—(*She leaves the*
MUSKETEER *and comes down to him.*) This musketeer—
He is making love to you?
 LISE (*haughtily*): If any man
Offends my virtue—all I have to do
Is look at him—once!
 CYRANO (*looks at her gravely; she drops her eyes*):
           I do not find
Those eyes of yours unconquerable.
 LISE (*panting*):   —Ah!
 CYRANO (*raising his voice a little*): Now listen— I am fond
  of Ragueneau;
I allow no one—do you understand?—
To . . . take his name in vain!

LISE: You think—

CYRANO (*ironic emphasis*):   I think
I interrupt you.

(*He salutes the* MUSKETEER, *who has heard without daring
to resent the warning.* LISE *goes to the* MUSKETEER *as he returns* CYRANO'S *salute.*)

LISE: You—you swallow that?—
You ought to have pulled his nose!

THE MUSKETEER: His nose?—His nose! . . .

(*He goes out hurriedly.* ROXANE *and the* DUENNA *appear
outside the door.*)

CYRANO (*nods to* RAGUENEAU): Pst!—

RAGUENEAU (*to the* POETS): Come inside—

CYRANO (*impatient*): Pst! . . . Pst! . . .

RAGUENEAU: We shall be more
Comfortable . . .

(*He leads the* POETS *into inner room.*)

FIRST POET: The cakes!

SECOND POET: Bring them along!

(*They go out.*)

CYRANO: If I can see the faintest spark of hope,
Then—(*throws door open—bows*)
Welcome!

(ROXANE *enters, followed by the* DUENNA, *whom* CYRANO
detains.)

                   Pardon me—one word—

THE DUENNA: Take two.

CYRANO: Have you a good digestion?

THE DUENNA: Wonderful!

CYRANO: Good. Here are two sonnets, by Benserade—

THE DUENNA: Euh?

CYRANO: Which I fill for you with éclairs.

THE DUENNA: Ooo!

CYRANO: Do you like cream-puffs?

THE DUENNA: Only with whipped cream.

CYRANO: Here are three . . . six—embosomed in a poem
By Saint-Amant. This ode of Chapelin
Looks deep enough to hold—a jelly roll.
—Do you love Nature?

THE DUENNA: Mad about it.

CYRANO: Then
Go out and eat these in the street. Do not
Return—

THE DUENNA: Oh, but—

CYRANO: Until you finish them.

(*down to* ROXANE) Blessed above all others be the hour
When you remembered to remember me,
And came to tell me . . . what?

ROXANE (*takes off her mask*):   First let me thank you
Because . . . That man . . . that creature, whom your sword
Made sport of yesterday— His patron, one—

CYRANO: De Guiche?—

ROXANE: —who thinks himself in love with me
Would have forced that man upon me for—
                                        a husband—

CYRANO: I understand—so much the better then!
I fought, not for my nose, but your bright eyes.

ROXANE: And then, to tell you—but before I can
Tell you— Are you, I wonder, still the same
Big brother—almost—that you used to be
When we were children, playing by the pond
In the old garden down there—

CYRANO: I remember—
Every summer you came to Bergerac! . . .

ROXANE: You used to make swords out of bulrushes—

CYRANO: Your dandelion-dolls with golden hair—

ROXANE: And those green plums—

CYRANO: And those black mulberries—

ROXANE: In those days, you did everything I wished!

CYRANO: Roxane, in short skirts, was called Madeleine.

ROXANE: Was I pretty?

CYRANO: Oh—not too plain!

ROXANE: Sometimes
When you had hurt your hand you used to come
Running to me—and I would be your mother,
And say— Oh, in a very grown-up voice (*She takes his hand.*):
"Now, what have you been doing to yourself?
Let me see—"
(*She sees the hand—starts.*) Oh!—
                    Wait— I said, "Let me see!"
Still—at your age! How did you do that?

CYRANO: Playing
With the big boys, down by the Porte de Nesle.

ROXANE (*sits at a table and wets her handkerchief in a glass
of water*): Come here to me.

CYRANO: —Such a wise little mother!

ROXANE: And tell me, while I wash this blood away,
How many you—played with?

CYRANO: Oh, about a hundred.

ROXANE: Tell me.

CYRANO: No. Let me go. Tell me what you
Were going to tell me—if you dared?
ROXANE (*still holding his hand*): I think
I do dare—now. It seems like long ago
When I could tell you things. Yes—I dare . . .
                                    Listen:

I . . . love someone.
  CYRANO: Ah! . . .
  ROXANE: Someone who does not know.
  CYRANO: Ah! . . .
  ROXANE: At least—not yet.
  CYRANO: Ah! . . .
  ROXANE: But he will know
Some day.
  CYRANO: Ah! . . .
  ROXANE: A big boy who loves me too,
And is afraid of me, and keeps away,
And never says one word.
  CYRANO: Ah! . . .
  ROXANE: Let me have
Your hand a moment—why how hot it is!—
I know. I see him trying . . .
  CYRANO: Ah! . . .
  ROXANE: There now!
Is that better?—(*She finishes bandaging the hand with her
handkerchief.*) Besides—only to think—
(This is a secret.) He is a soldier too,
In your own regiment—
  CYRANO: Ah! . . .
  ROXANE: Yes, in the Guards,
Your company too.
  CYRANO: Ah! . . .
  ROXANE: And such a man!—
He is proud—noble—young—brave—beautiful—
  CYRANO (*turns pale; rises*): Beautiful!—
  ROXANE: What's the matter?
  CYRANO (*smiling*):   Nothing—this—
My sore hand!
  ROXANE: Well, I love him. That is all.
Oh—and I never saw him anywhere
Except the *Comédie*.
  CYRANO: You have never spoken?—
  ROXANE: Only our eyes . . .
  CYRANO: Why, then— How do you know?—
  ROXANE: People talk about people; and I hear

Things . . . and I know.

CYRANO: You say he is in the Guards:
His name?

ROXANE: Baron Christian de Neuvillette.

CYRANO: He is not in the Guards.

ROXANE: Yes. Since this morning.
Captain Carbon de Castel-Jaloux.

CYRANO: So soon! . . .
So soon we lose our hearts!—

                                      But, my dear child,—

THE DUENNA (*opens the door*):
I have eaten the cakes, Monsieur de Bergerac!

CYRANO: Good! Now go out and read the poetry!
(*The* DUENNA *disappears*.)

—But, my dear child! You, who love only words,
Wit, the grand manner— Why, for all you know,
The man may be a savage, or a fool.

ROXANE: His curls are like a hero from D'Urfé.

CYRANO: His mind may be as curly as his hair.

ROXANE: Not with such eyes. I read his soul in them.

CYRANO: Yes, all our souls are written in our eyes!
But—if he be a bungler?

ROXANE: Then I shall die—
There!

CYRANO (*after a pause*): And you brought me here to tell
me this?
I do not yet quite understand, Madame,
The reason for your confidence.

ROXANE: They say
That in your company— It frightens me—
You are all Gascons . . .

CYRANO: And we pick a quarrel
With any flat-foot who intrudes himself.
Whose blood is not pure Gascon like our own?
Is that what you have heard?

ROXANE: I am so afraid
For him!

CYRANO (*between his teeth*): Not without reason!—

ROXANE: And I thought
You . . . You were so brave, so invincible
Yesterday, against all those brutes!—If you,
Whom they all fear—

CYRANO: Oh well— I will defend
Your little Baron.

ROXANE: Will you? Just for me?

Because I have always been—your friend!

CYRANO: Of course . . .

ROXANE: Will you be *his* friend?

CYRANO: I will be his friend.

ROXANE: And never let him fight a duel?

CYRANO: No—never.

ROXANE: Oh, but you are a darling!—I must go—
You never told me about last night— Why,
You must have been a hero! Have him write
And tell me all about it—will you?

CYRANO: Of course . . .

ROXANE (*kisses her hand*): I always did love you—A
hundred men
Against one— Well . . . Adieu. We are great friends,
Are we not?

CYRANO: Of course . . .

ROXANE: He *must* write to me—
A hundred— You shall tell me the whole story
Some day, when I have time. A hundred men—
What courage—

CYRANO (*salutes as she goes out*): Oh . . . I have done
better since!

(*The door closes after her.* CYRANO *remains motionless,
his eyes on the ground. Pause. The other door opens;* RAGUE-
NEAU *puts in his head.*)

RAGUENEAU: May I come in?

CYRANO (*without moving*): Yes . . .

(RAGUENEAU *and his friends re-enter. At the same time,*
CARBON DE CASTEL-JALOUX *appears at the street door in uniform as Captain of the Guards; recognizes* CYRANO *with a
sweeping gesture.*)

CARBON: Here he is!—Our hero!

CYRANO (*raises his head and salutes*): Our Captain!

CARBON: We know! All our company
Are here—

CYRANO (*recoils*): No—

CARBON: Come! They are waiting for you.

CYRANO: No!

CARBON (*tries to lead him out*): Only across the street—
Come!

CYRANO: Please—

CARBON (*goes to the door and shouts in a voice of thunder*):   Our champion
Refuses! He is not feeling well today!

A VOICE OUTSIDE: Ah! Sandious! (*noise outside of swords and trampling feet approaching*)

CARBON: Here they come now!

THE CADETS (*entering the shop*):   Mille dious!—
Mordious!—Capdedious!—Pocapdedious!

RAGUENEAU (*in astonishment*):   Gentlemen—
You are all Gascons?

THE CADETS: All!

FIRST CADET (*to* CYRANO):   Bravo!

CYRANO: Baron!

ANOTHER CADET (*takes both his hands*): Vivat!

CYRANO: Baron!

THIRD CADET: Come to my arms!

CYRANO: Baron!

OTHERS: To mine!—To mine!—

CYRANO: Baron . . . Baron . . . Have mercy—

RAGUENEAU: You are all Barons too?

THE CADETS: *Are* we?

RAGUENEAU: Are they? . . .

FIRST CADET: Our coronets would star the midnight sky!

LE BRET (*enters; hurries to* CYRANO): The whole town's
    looking for you! Raving mad—
A triumph! Those who saw the fight—

CYRANO: I hope
You have not told them where I—

LE BRET (*rubbing his hands*):   Certainly
I told them!

CITIZEN (*enters, followed by a group*):
                        Listen! Shut the door—Here comes
All Paris!

(*The street outside fills with a shouting crowd. Chairs and carriages stop at the door.*)

LE BRET (*aside to* CYRANO, *smiling*): And Roxane?

CYRANO (*quickly*):   Hush!

THE CROWD OUTSIDE: Cyrano!

(*A mob bursts into the shop. Shouts, acclamations, general disturbance.*)

RAGUENEAU (*standing on a table*):
My shop invaded— They'll break everything—
Glorious!

SEVERAL MEN (*crowding about* CYRANO): My friend! . . .
My friend! . . .

CYRANO: Why, yesterday
I did not have so many friends!

LE BRET: Success
At last!

A MARQUIS (*runs to* CYRANO, *with outstretched hands*):
My dear—really!—

CYRANO (*coldly*):   So? And how long
Have I been dear to you?

ANOTHER MARQUIS: One moment—pray!
I have two ladies in my carriage here;
Let me present you—

CYRANO: Certainly! And first,
Who will present you, sir,—to me?

LE BRET (*astounded*):   Why, what
The devil?—

CYRANO: Hush!

A MAN OF LETTERS (*with a portfolio*):
                                    May I have the details? . . .

CYRANO: You may not.

LE BRET (*plucking* CYRANO'S *sleeve*):
                             Theophraste Renaudot!—Editor
Of the *Gazette*—your reputation! . . .

CYRANO: No!

A POET (*advances*): Monsieur—

CYRANO: Well?

THE POET: Your full name? I will compose
A pentacrostic—

ANOTHER: Monsieur—

CYRANO: That will do!

(*Movement. The crowd arranges itself.* DE GUICHE *appears,
escorted by* CUIGY, BRISSAILLE, *and the other officers who
were with* CYRANO *at the close of Act I.*)

CUIGY (*goes to* CYRANO): Monsieur de Guiche!—(*murmur; everyone moves.*)   A message from the Marshal
De Gassion—

DE GUICHE (*saluting* CYRANO): Who wishes to express
Through me his admiration. He has heard
Of your affair—

THE CROWD: Bravo!

CYRANO (*bowing*):   The Marshal speaks
As an authority.

DE GUICHE: He said just now
The story would have been incredible
Were it not for the witness—

CUIGY: Of our eyes!

LE BRET (*aside to* CYRANO): What is it?

CYRANO: Hush!—

LE BRET: Something is wrong with you;
Are you in pain?

CYRANO (*recovering himself*): In pain? Before this crowd?
(*His moustache bristles; he throws out his chest.*) I? In pain?
You shall see!

DE GUICHE (*to whom* CUIGY *has been whispering*):
Your name is known
Already as a soldier. You are one
Of those wild Gascons, are you not?

CYRANO: The Guards,
Yes. A Cadet.

A CADET (*in a voice of thunder*): One of ourselves!

DE GUICHE: Ah! So—
Then all these gentlemen with the haughty air,
These are the famous—

CARBON: Cyrano!

CYRANO: Captain?

CARBON: Our troop being all present, be so kind
As to present them to the Comte de Guiche!

CYRANO (*with a gesture presenting the* CADETS *to* DE
GUICHE, *declaims*):
The Cadets of Gascoyne—the defenders
    of Carbon de Castel-Jaloux:
Free fighters, free lovers, free spenders—
The Cadets of Gascoyne—the defenders
Of old homes, old names, and old splendors—
    A proud and a pestilent crew!
The Cadets of Gascoyne, the defenders
    Of Carbon de Castel-Jaloux.

Hawk-eyed, they stare down all contenders—
    The wolf bares his fangs as they do—
Make way there, you fat moneylenders!
(Hawk-eyed, they stare down all contenders)
Old boots that have been to the menders,
    Old cloaks that are worn through and through—
Hawk-eyed, they stare down all contenders—
    The wolf bares his fangs as they do!

Skull-breakers they are, and sword-benders;
    Red blood is their favorite brew;
Hot haters and loyal befrienders,
Skull-breakers they are, and sword-benders.
Wherever a quarrel engenders,
    They're ready and waiting for you!

Skull-breakers they are, and sword-benders;
    Red blood is their favorite brew!

Behold them, our Gascon defenders
    Who win every woman they woo!
There's never a dame but surrenders—
Behold them, our Gascon defenders!
Young wives who are clever pretenders—
    Old husbands who house the cuckoo—
Behold them—our Gascon defenders
    Who win every woman they woo!

DE GUICHE (*languidly, sitting in a chair*): Poets are fashion-
    able nowadays
To have about one. Would you care to join
My following?

CYRANO: No, sir. I do not follow.

DE GUICHE: Your duel yesterday amused my uncle
The Cardinal. I might help you there.

LE BRET: Grand Dieu!

DE GUICHE: I suppose you have written a tragedy—
They all have.

LE BRET (*aside to* CYRANO):
                             Now at last you'll have it played—
Your *Agrippine!*

DE GUICHE: Why not? Take it to him.

CYRANO (*tempted*): Really—

DE GUICHE: He is himself a dramatist;
Let him rewrite a few lines here and there,
And he'll approve the rest.

CYRANO (*his face falls again*):   Impossible.
My blood curdles to think of altering
One comma.

DE GUICHE: Ah, but when he likes a thing
He pays well.

CYRANO: Yes—but not so well as I—
When I have made a line that sings itself
So that I love the sound of it—I pay
Myself a hundred times.

DE GUICHE: You are proud, my friend.

CYRANO: You have observed that?

A CADET (*enters with a drawn sword, along the whole blade
of which is transfixed a collection of disreputable hats, their
plumes draggled, their crowns cut and torn*):
                             Cyrano! See here—
Look what we found this morning in the street—

The plumes dropped in their flight by those fine birds
Who showed the white feather!

CARBON: Spoils of the hunt—
Well mounted!

THE CROWD: Ha-ha-ha!

CUIGY: Whoever hired
Those rascals, he must be an angry man
Today!

BRISSAILLE: Who was it? Do you know?

DE GUICHE: Myself!—
(*The laughter ceases.*)
I hired them to do the sort of work
We do not soil our hands with—punishing
A drunken poet . . .
(*Uncomfortable silence.*)

THE CADET (*to* CYRANO): What shall we do with them?
They ought to be preserved before they spoil—

CYRANO (*takes the sword, and in the gesture of saluting*
DE GUICHE *with it, makes all the hats slide off at his feet*):
Sir, will you not return these to your friends?

DE GUICHE: My chair—my porters here—immediately!
(*to* CYRANO *violently*)—As for you, sir!—

A VOICE (*in the street*): The chair of Monseigneur
Le Comte de Guiche!—

DE GUICHE (*who has recovered his self-control; smiling*):
                         Have you read *Don Quixote?*

CYRANO: I have—and found myself the hero.

A PORTER (*appears at the door*):   Chair
Ready!

DE GUICHE: Be so good as to read once more
The chapter of the windmills.

CYRANO (*gravely*):   Chapter Thirteen.

DE GUICHE: Windmills, remember, if you fight with them—

CYRANO: My enemies change, then, with every wind?

DE GUICHE:—May swing round their huge arms and cast
    you down
Into the mire.

CYRANO: Or up—among the stars!

(DE GUICHE *goes out. We see him get into the chair. The*
OFFICERS *follow murmuring among themselves.* LE BRET *goes*
up with them. The crowd goes out.)

CYRANO (*saluting with burlesque politeness those who go*
out without daring to take leave of him): Gentlemen. . . .
Gentlemen. . . .

LE BRET (*as the door closes, comes down, shaking his*

clenched hands to heaven):   You have done it now—
You have made your fortune!
 CYRANO: There you go again,
Growling!—
 LE BRET: At least this latest pose of yours—
Ruining every chance that comes your way—
Becomes exaggerated—
 CYRANO: Very well,
Then I exaggerate!
 LE BRET (*triumphantly*): Oh, you do!
 CYRANO: Yes;
On principle. There are things in this world
A man does well to carry to extremes.
 LE BRET: Stop trying to be Three Musketeers in one!
Fortune and glory—
 CYRANO: What would you have me do?
Seek for the patronage of some great man,
And like a creeping vine on a tall tree
Crawl upward, where I cannot stand alone?
No thank you! Dedicate, as others do,
Poems to pawnbrokers? Be a buffoon
In the vile hope of teasing out a smile
On some cold face? No thank you! Eat a toad
For breakfast every morning? Make my knees
Callous, and cultivate a supple spine,—
Wear out my belly groveling in the dust?
No thank you! Scratch the back of any swine
That roots up gold for me? Tickle the horns
Of Mammon with my left hand, while my right
Too proud to know his partner's business,
Takes in the fee? No thank you! Use the fire
God gave me to burn incense all day long
Under the nose of wood and stone? No thank you!
Shall I go leaping into ladies' laps
And licking fingers?—or—to change the form—
Navigating with madrigals for oars,
My sails full of the sighs of dowagers?
No thank you! Publish verses at my own
Expense? No thank you! Be the patron saint
Of a small group of literary souls
Who dine together every Tuesday? No
I thank you! Shall I labor night and day
To build a reputation on one song,
And never write another? Shall I find
True genius only among Geniuses,

Palpitate over little paragraphs,
And struggle to insinuate my name
In the columns of the *Mercury?*
No thank you! Calculate, scheme, be afraid,
Love more to make a visit than a poem,
Seek introductions, favors, influences?—
No thank you! No, I thank you! And again
I thank you!—But . . .

                      To sing, to laugh, to dream,
To walk in my own way and be alone,
Free, with an eye to see things as they are,
A voice that means manhood—to cock my hat
Where I choose— At a word, a *Yes*, a *No*,
To fight—or write. To travel any road
Under the sun, under the stars, nor doubt
If fame or fortune lie beyond the bourne—
Never to make a line I have not heard
In my own heart; yet, with all modesty
To say: "My soul, be satisfied with flowers,
With fruit, with weeds even; but gather them
In the one garden you may call your own."
So, when I win some triumph, by some chance,
Render no share to Caesar—in a word,
I am too proud to be a parasite,
And if my nature wants the germ that grows
Towering to heaven like the mountain pine,
Or like the oak, sheltering multitudes—
I stand, not high it may be—but alone!

    LE BRET: Alone, yes!—But why stand against the world?
What devil has possessed you now, to go
Everywhere making yourself enemies?

    CYRANO: Watching you other people making friends
Everywhere—as a dog makes friends! I mark
The manner of these canine courtesies
And think: "My friends are of a cleaner breed;
Here comes—thank God!—another enemy!"

    LE BRET: But this is madness!

    CYRANO: Method, let us say.
It is my pleasure to displease. I love
Hatred. Imagine how it feels to face
The volley of a thousand angry eyes—
The bile of envy and the froth of fear
Spattering little drops about me— You—
Good nature all around you, soft and warm—
You are like those Italians, in great cowls

Comfortable and loose— Your chin sinks down
Into the folds, your shoulders droop. But I—
The Spanish ruff I wear around my throat
Is like a ring of enemies; hard, proud,
Each point another pride, another thorn—
So that I hold myself erect perforce
Wearing the hatred of the common herd
Haughtily, the harsh collar of Old Spain,
At once a fetter and—a halo!

LE BRET: Yes . . .
(*after a silence, draws* CYRANO'S *arm through his own*)
Tell this to all the world— And then to me
Say very softly that . . . She loves you not.

CYRANO (*quickly*): Hush!

(*A moment since,* CHRISTIAN *has entered and mingled with
the* CADETS, *who do not offer to speak to him. Finally, he sits
down alone at a small table, where he is served by* LISE.)

A CADET (*rises from a table up stage, his glass in his hand*):
                                    Cyrano—Your story!

CYRANO: Presently . . . (*He goes up, on the arm of* LE
RBET, *talking to him. The* CADET *comes down stage.*)

THE CADET: The story of the combat! An example
For—(*He stops by the table where* CHRISTIAN *is sitting.*)
                              —this young tadpole here.

CHRISTIAN (*looks up*):   Tadpole?

ANOTHER CADET: Yes, you!—
You narrow-gutted Northerner!

CHRISTIAN: Sir?

FIRST CADET: Hark ye,
Monsieur de Neuvillette: You are to know
There is a certain subject—I would say,
A certain object—never to be named
Among us: utterly unmentionable!

CHRISTIAN: And that is?

THIRD CADET (*in an awful voice*): Look at me! . . . (*He
strikes his nose three times with his finger, mysteriously.*)
                              You understand?

CHRISTIAN: Why, yes; the—

FOURTH CADET: Sh! . . . We never speak that word—
(*indicating* CYRANO *by a gesture*) To breathe it is to have to
do with HIM!

FIFTH CADET (*speaks through his nose*): He has extermi-
    nated several
Whose tone of voice suggested . . .

SIXTH CADET (*in a hollow tone; rising from under the table on all fours*):   Would you die
Before your time? Just mention anything
Convex . . . or cartilaginous . . .
    SEVENTH CADET (*his hand on* CHRISTIAN'S *shoulder*):
                              One word—
One syllable—one gesture—nay, one sneeze—
Your handkerchief becomes your winding-sheet! (*Silence. In a circle around* CHRISTIAN, *arms crossed, they regard him expectantly.*)
    CHRISTIAN (*rises and goes to* CARBON, *who is conversing with an officer, and pretending not to see what is taking place*): Captain!
    CARBON (*turns, and looks him over*): Sir?
    CHRISTIAN: What is the proper thing to do
When Gascons grow too boastful?
    CARBON: Prove to them
That one may be a Norman, and have courage (*turns his back*).
    CHRISTIAN: I thank you.
    FIRST CADET (*to* CYRANO): Come—the story!
    ALL: The story!
    CYRANO (*come down*):   Oh,
My story? Well . . .
    (*They all draw up their stools and group themselves around him, eagerly.* CHRISTIAN *places himself astride of a chair, his arms on the back of it.*)
                              I marched on, all alone
To meet those devils. Overhead, the moon
Hung like a gold watch at the fob of heaven,
Till suddenly some Angel rubbed a cloud,
As it might be his handkerchief, across
The shining crystal, and—the night came down.
No lamps in those back streets— It was so dark—
Mordious! You could not see beyond—
    CHRISTIAN: Your nose.
    (*Silence. Every man slowly rises to his feet. They look at* CYRANO *almost with terror. He has stopped short, utterly astonished. Pause.*)
    CYRANO: Who is that man there?
    A CADET (*in a low voice*):   A recruit—arrived
This morning.
    CYRANO (*takes a step toward* CHRISTIAN):   A recruit—
    CARBON (*in a low voice*):   His name is Christian
De Neuvil—

CYRANO (*suddenly motionless*): Oh . . . (*He turns pale,
flushes, makes a movement as if to throw himself upon*
CHRISTIAN.) I—(*controls himself, and goes on in a choking
voice*)   I see. Very well,
As I was saying—(*with a sudden burst of rage*) Mordious! . . .
(*He goes on in a natural tone.*)   It grew dark,
You could not see your hand before your eyes.
I marched on, thinking how, all for the sake
Of one old souse (*They slowly sit down, watching him.*)
                                   who wrote a bawdy song
Whenever he took—
     CHRISTIAN: A noseful—
     (*Everyone rises.* CHRISTIAN *balances himself on two legs
of his chair.*)
     CYRANO (*half strangled*):   —Took a notion.
Whenever he took a notion— For his sake,
I might antagonize some dangerous man,
One powerful enough to make me pay—
     CHRISTIAN: Through the nose—
     CYRANO (*wipes the sweat from his forehead*):
                                   —Pay the Piper. After all,
I thought, why am I putting in my—
     CHRISTIAN: Nose—
     CYRANO:—My oar . . . Why am I putting in my oar?
The quarrel's none of mine. However—now
I am here, I may as well go through with it.
Come Gascon—do your duty!—Suddenly
A sword flashed in the dark. I caught it fair—
     CHRISTIAN: On the nose—
     CYRANO: On my blade. Before I knew it,
There I was—
     CHRISTIAN: Rubbing noses—
     CYRANO (*pale and smiling*):   Crossing swords
With half a score at once. I handed one—
     CHRISTIAN: A nosegay—
     CYRANO (*leaping at him*): Ventre-Saint-Gris! . . .
     (*The* GASCONS *tumble over each other to get a good view.
Arrived in front of* CHRISTIAN, *who has not moved an inch,*
CYRANO *masters himself again, and continues.*)
                                   He went down;
The rest gave way; I charged—
     CHRISTIAN: Nose in the air—
     CYRANO: I skewered two of them—disarmed a third—
Another lunged— Paf! And I countered—
     CHRISTIAN: Pif!

CYRANO (*bellowing*): TONNERRE! Out of here!—All of you!

(*All the* CADETS *rush for the door.*)

FIRST CADET: At last—
The old lion wakes!

CYRANO: All of you! Leave me here
Alone with that man!

(*The lines following are heard brokenly in the confusion of getting through the door.*)

SECOND CADET: Bigre! He'll have the fellow
Chopped into sausage—

RAGUENEAU: Sausage?—

THIRD CADET: Mince-meat, then—
One of your pies!—

RAGUENEAU: Am I pale? You look white
As a fresh napkin—

CARBON (*at the door*): Come!

FOURTH CADET: He'll never leave
Enough of him to—

FIFTH CADET: Why, it frightens ME
To think of what will—

SIXTH CADET (*closing the door*): Something horrible
Beyond imagination . . .

(*They are all gone: some through the street door, some by the inner doors to right and left. A few disappear up the staircase.* CYRANO *and* CHRISTIAN *stand face to face a moment, and look at each other.*)

CYRANO: To my arms!

CHRISTIAN: Sir? . . .

CYRANO: You have courage!

CHRISTIAN: Oh, that! . . .

CYRANO: You are brave—
That pleases me.

CHRISTIAN: You mean? . . .

CYRANO: Do you not know
I am her brother? Come!

CHRISTIAN: Whose?—

CYRANO: Hers—Roxane!

CHRISTIAN: Her . . . brother? You? (*hurries to him*)

CYRANO: Her cousin. Much the same.

CHRISTIAN: And she has told you? . . .

CYRANO: Everything.

CHRISTIAN: She loves me?

CYRANO: Perhaps.

CHRISTIAN (*takes both his hands*):

                        My dear sir—more than I can say,

I am honored—
  CYRANO: This is rather sudden.
  CHRISTIAN: Please

Forgive me—
  CYRANO (*holds him at arm's length, looking at him*):
                    Why, he is a handsome devil.

This fellow!
  CHRISTIAN: On my honor—if you knew

How much I have admired—
  CYRANO: Yes, yes—and all

Those Noses which—
  CHRISTIAN: Please! I apologize.
  CYRANO (*change of tone*): Roxane expects a letter—
  CHRISTIAN: Not from me?—
  CYRANO: Yes. Why not?
  CHRISTIAN: Once I write, that ruins all!
  CYRANO: And why?
  CHRISTIAN: Because . . . because I am a fool!

Stupid enough to hang myself!
  CYRANO: But no—

You are no fool; you call yourself a fool,
There's proof enough in that. Besides, you did not
Attack me like a fool.
  CHRISTIAN: Bah! Anyone

Can pick a quarrel. Yes, I have a sort
Of rough and ready soldier's tongue. I know
That. But with any woman—paralyzed,
Speechless, dumb. I can only look at them.
Yet sometimes, when I go away, their eyes . . .
  CYRANO: Why not their hearts, if you should wait and see?
  CHRISTIAN: No. I am one of those— I know—those men
Who never can make love.
  CYRANO: Strange . . . . Now it seems

I, if I gave my mind to it, I might
Perhaps make love well.
  CHRISTIAN: Oh, if I had words

To say what I have here!
  CYRANO: If I could be

A handsome little Musketeer with eyes!
  CHRISTIAN: Besides—you know Roxane—how sensitive—
One rough word, and the sweet illusion—gone!
  CYRANO: I wish you might be my interpreter.
  CHRISTIAN: I wish I had your wit—
  CYRANO: Borrow it, then!—

Your beautiful young manhood—lend me that,
And we two make one hero of romance!

   CHRISTIAN: What?

   CYRANO: Would you dare repeat to her the words
I gave you, day by day?

   CHRISTIAN: You mean?

   CYRANO: I mean

Roxane shall have no disillusionment!
Come, shall we win both together? Take
The soul within this leathern jack of mine,
And breathe it into you? (*touches him on the breast*)

                         So—there's my heart

Under your velvet, now!

   CHRISTIAN: But— Cyrano!—

   CYRANO: But— Christian, why not?

   CHRISTIAN: I am afraid—

   CYRANO: I know—

Afraid that when you have her all alone,
You lose all. Have no fear. It is yourself
She loves—give her yourself put into words—
My words, upon your lips!

   CHRISTIAN: But . . . but your eyes!
They burn like—

   CYRANO: Will you? . . . Will you?

   CHRISTIAN: Does it mean
So much to you?

   CYRANO (*beside himself*): It means—(*recovers, changes tone*)

                          A Comedy,
A situation for a poet! Come.
Shall we collaborate? I'll be your cloak
Of darkness, your enchanted sword, your ring
To charm the fairy Princess!

   CHRISTIAN: But the letter—
I cannot write—

   CYRANO: Oh yes, the letter. (*He takes from his pocket the letter which he has written.*)   Here.

   CHRISTIAN: What is this?

   CYRANO: All there; all but the address.

   CHRISTIAN: I—

   CYRANO: Oh, you may send it. It will serve.

   CHRISTIAN: But why
Have you done this?

   CYRANO: I have amused myself
As we all do, we poets—writing vows

To Chloris, Phyllis—any pretty name—
You might have had a pocketful of them!
Take it, and turn to facts my fantasies—
I loosed those loves like doves into the air;
Give them a habitation and a home.
Here, take it— You will find me all the more
Eloquent, being insincere! Come!

CHRISTIAN: First,
There must be a few changes here and there—
Written at random, can it fit Roxane?

CYRANO: Like her own glove.

CHRISTIAN: No, but—

CYRANO: My son, have faith—
Faith in the love of women for themselves—
Roxane will know this letter for her own!

CHRISTIAN (*throws himself into the arms of* CYRANO, *they
stand embraced*): My friend!

(*The door up stage opens a little. A* CADET *steals in.*)

THE CADET: Nothing. A silence like the tomb . . .
I hardly dare look—(*He sees the two.*) Wha-at?

(*The other* CADETS *crowd in behind him and see.*)

THE CADETS: No!—No!

SECOND CADET: Mon dieu!

THE MUSKETEER (*slaps his knee*): Well, well, well!

CARBON: Here's our devil . . . Christianized!
Offend one nostril, and he turns the other.

THE MUSKETEER: Now we are allowed to talk about his
nose! (*calls*) Hey, Lise! Come here—(*affectedly*)
                                        Snf! What a horrid smell!
What is it? . . . (*plants himself in front of* CYRANO, *and looks
at his nose in an impolite manner*) You ought to know about
such things;
What seems to have died around here?

CYRANO (*knocks him backward over a bench*): Cabbage-
heads!

(*Joy. The* CADETS *have found their old* CYRANO *again.
General disturbance.*)

ACT III

(ROXANE'S KISS)

(*A little square in the old Marais: old houses, and a glimpse of narrow streets. On the right, the house of* ROXANE *and her garden wall, overhung with tall shrubbery. Over the door of the house a balcony and a tall window; to one side of the door, a bench.*

Ivy clings to the wall; jasmine embraces the balcony, trembles, and falls away.

By the bench and the jutting stonework of the wall one might easily climb up to the balcony.

Opposite, an ancient house of the like character, brick and stone, whose front door forms an entrance. The knocker on this door is tied up in linen like an injured thumb.

At the curtain rise the DUENNA *is seated on the bench beside the door. The window is wide open on* ROXANE'S *balcony; a light within suggests that it is early evening. By the* DUENNA *stands* RAGUENEAU *dressed in what might be the livery of one attached to the household. He is by way of telling her something, and wiping his eyes meanwhile.*)

RAGUENEAU:—And so she ran off with a Musketeer!
I was ruined—I was alone— Remained
Nothing for me to do but hang myself,
So I did that. Presently along comes
Monsieur de Bergerac, and cuts me down,
And makes me steward to his cousin.

THE DUENNA: Ruined?—
I thought your pastry was a great success!

RAGUENEAU (*shakes his head*): Lise loved the soldiers, and
I loved the poets—
Mars ate up all the cakes Apollo left;
It did not take long. . . .

THE DUENNA (*calls up to window*): Roxane! Are you ready?
We are late!

VOICE OF ROXANE (*within*): Putting on my cape—

THE DUENNA (*to* RAGUENEAU, *indicating the house op-*
posite):   Clomire
Across the way receives on Thursday nights—
We are to have a psycho-colloquy
Upon the Tender Passion.
    RAGUENEAU: Ah—the Tender . . .
    THE DUENNA (*sighs*):—Passion! . . . (*calls up to window*)
                Roxane!—Hurry, dear—we shall miss
The Tender Passion!
    ROXANE: Coming!—(*music of stringed instruments off*
stage approaching)
    THE VOICE OF CYRANO (*singing*): La, la, la!—
    THE DUENNA: A serenade?—How pleasant—
    CYRANO: No, no, no!—
F natural, you natural born fool! (*enters, followed by two*
pages, carrying theorbos)
    FIRST PAGE (*ironically*): No doubt your honor knows F
    natural
When he hears—
    CYRANO: I am a musician, infant!—
A pupil of Gassendi.
    THE PAGE (*plays and sings*): La, la,—
    CYRANO: Here—
Give me that—(*He snatches the instrument from the* PAGE
and continues the tune.) La, la, la, la—
    ROXANE (*appears on the balcony*): Is that you, Cyrano?
    CYRANO (*singing*): I, who praise your lilies fair,
But long to love your ro . . . ses!
    ROXANE: I'll be down—
Wait—(*goes in through window*)
    THE DUENNA: Did you train these virtuosi?
    CYRANO: No—
I won them on a bet from D'Assoucy.
We were debating a fine point of grammar
When, pointing out these two young nightingales
Dressed up like peacocks, with their instruments,
He cries: "No, but I KNOW! I'll wager you
A day of music." Well, of course he lost;
And so until tomorrow they are mine,
My private orchestra. Pleasant at first,
But they become a trifle—(*to the* PAGES)   Here! Go play
A minuet to Montfleury—and tell him
I sent you! (*The* PAGES *go up to the exit;* CYRANO *turns to the*
DUENNA.) I came here as usual
To inquire after our friend—(*to* PAGES) Play out of tune.

And keep on playing! (*The* PAGES *go out; he turns to the*
DUENNA.)   Our friend with the great soul.
  ROXANE (*enters in time to hear the last words*): He is beau-
tiful and brilliant—and I love him!
  CYRANO: Do you find Christian . . . intellectual?
  ROXANE: More so than you, even.
  CYRANO: I am glad.
  ROXANE: No man
Ever so beautifully said those things—
Those pretty nothings that are everything.
Sometimes he falls into a reverie;
His inspiration fails—then all at once,
He will say something absolutely . . . Oh! . . .
  CYRANO: Really!
  ROXANE: How like a man! You think a man
Who has a handsome face must be a fool.
  CYRANO: He talks well about . . . matters of the heart?
  ROXANE: He does not *talk;* he rhapsodizes . . . dreams . . .
  CYRANO (*twisting his moustache*): He . . . writes well?
  ROXANE: Wonderfully. Listen now:
(*reciting as from memory*) "Take my heart; I shall have it
    all the more;
Plucking the flowers, we keep the plant in bloom—"
Well?
  CYRANO: Pooh!
  ROXANE: And this:

                      "Knowing you have in store
More heart to give than I to find heart-room—"
  CYRANO: First he has too much, then too little; just
How much heart does he need?
  ROXANE (*tapping her foot*):   You are teasing me!
You are jealous!
  CYRANO (*startled*): Jealous?
  ROXANE: Of his poetry—
You poets are like that . . .

                      And these last lines
Are they not the last word in tenderness?—
"There is no more to say: only believe
That unto you my whole heart gives one cry,
And writing, writes down more than you receive;
Sending you kisses through my fingertips—
Lady, O read my letter with your lips!"
  CYRANO: H'm, yes—those last lines . . . but he overwrites!
  ROXANE: Listen to this—
  CYRANO: You know them all by heart?

ROXANE: Every one!

CYRANO (*twisting his moustache*): I may call that flattering . . .

ROXANE: He is a master!

CYRANO: Oh—come!

ROXANE: Yes—a master!

CYRANO (*bowing*): A master—if you will!

THE DUENNA (*comes down stage quickly*):

                 Monsieur de Guiche!—

(*to* CYRANO, *pushing him toward the house*) Go inside—
If he does not find you here,
It may be just as well. He may suspect—

ROXANE:—My secret! Yes; he is in love with me
And he is powerful. Let him not know—
One look would frost my roses before bloom.

CYRANO (*going into house*): Very well, very well!

ROXANE (*to* DE GUICHE, *as he enters*): We were just going—

DE GUICHE: I came only to say farewell.

ROXANE: You leave
Paris?

DE GUICHE: Yes—for the front.

ROXANE: Ah!

DE GUICHE: And tonight!

ROXANE: Ah!

DE GUICHE: We have orders to besiege Arras.

ROXANE: Arras?

DE GUICHE: Yes. My departure leaves you . . . cold?

ROXANE (*politely*): Oh! Not that.

DE GUICHE: It has left me desolate—
When shall I see you? Ever? Did you know
I was made Colonel?

ROXANE (*indifferent*): Bravo.

DE GUICHE: Regiment
Of the Guards.

ROXANE (*catching her breath*): Of the Guards?—

DE GUICHE: *His* regiment
Your cousin, the mighty man of words!—(*grimly*)

                 Down there
We may have an accounting!

ROXANE (*suffocating*):   Are you sure
The Guards are ordered?

DE GUICHE: Under my command!

ROXANE (*sinks down, breathless, on the bench; aside*):
Christian!—

DE GUICHE: What is it?

ROXANE (*losing control of herself*): To the war—perhaps
Never again to— When a woman cares,
Is that nothing?

DE GUICHE (*surprised and delighted*):

You say this now—to me—
Now, at the very moment?—

ROXANE (*recovers—changes her tone*): Tell me something:
My cousin— You say you mean to be revenged
On him. Do you mean that?

DE GUICHE (*smiles*): Why? Would you care?

ROXANE: Not for him.

DE GUICHE: Do you see him?

ROXANE: Now and then.

DE GUICHE: He goes about everywhere nowadays
With one of the Cadets—de Neuve—Neuville—
Neuvillers—

ROXANE (*coolly*): A tall man?—

DE GUICHE: Blond—

ROXANE: Rosy cheeks?—

DE GUICHE: Handsome!—

ROXANE: Pooh!—

DE GUICHE: And a fool.

ROXANE (*languidly*):   So he appears . . .
(*animated*) But Cyrano? What will you do to him?
Order him into danger? He loves that!
I know what *I* should do.

DE GUICHE: What?

ROXANE: Leave him here
With his Cadets, while all the regiment
Goes on to glory! That would torture him—
To sit all through the war with folded arms—
I know his nature. If you hate that man,
Strike at his self-esteem.

DE GUICHE: Oh woman—woman!
Who but a woman would have thought of this?

ROXANE: He'll eat his heart out, while his Gascon friends
Bite their nails all day long in Paris here.
And you will be avenged!

DE GUICHE: You love me then,
A little? . . . (*She smiles.*)   Making my enemies your own,
Hating them—I should like to see in that
A sign of love, Roxane.

ROXANE: Perhaps it is one . . .

DE GUICHE (*shows a number of folded dispatches*): Here
   are the orders—for each company—

Ready to send . . . (*selects one*) So— This is for the
Guards—
I'll keep that. Aha, Cyrano! (*to* ROXANE)   You too,
You play your little games, do you?
  ROXANE (*watching him*):   Sometimes . . .
  DE GUICHE (*close to her, speaking hurriedly*): And you!—
Oh, I am mad over you!—

                               Listen—

I leave tonight—but—let you through my hands
Now, when I feel you trembling?—Listen— Close by,
In the Rue d'Orléans, the Capuchins
Have their new convent. By their law, no layman
May pass inside those walls. I'll see to that—
Their sleeves are wide enough to cover me—
The servants of my Uncle-Cardinal
Will fear his nephew. So—I'll come to you
Masked, after everyone knows I have gone—
Oh, let me wait one day!—
  ROXANE: If this be known,
Your honor—
  DE GUICHE: Bah!
  ROXANE: The war—your duty—
  DE GUICHE (*blows away an imaginary feather*):   Phoo!—
Only say yes!
  ROXANE: No!
  DE GUICHE: Whisper . . .
  ROXANE (*tenderly*):   I ought not
To let you . . .
  DE GUICHE: Ah! . . .
  ROXANE (*pretends to break down*): Ah, go!
                (*aside*)—Christian remains—
(*aloud—heroically*) I must have you a hero—Antoine . . .
  DE GUICHE: Heaven! . . .
So you can love—
  ROXANE: One for whose sake I fear.
  DE GUICHE (*triumphant*): I go!
             Will that content you? (*kisses her hand*)
  ROXANE: Yes—my friend!
  (*He goes out.*)
  THE DUENNA (*as* DE GUICHE *disappears, making a deep
curtsey behind his back, and imitating* ROXANE's *intense tone*):
Yes—my friend!
  ROXANE (*quickly, close to her*): Not a word to Cyrano—
He would never forgive me if he knew
I stole his war!

(*She calls toward the house.*) Cousin!

(CYRANO *comes out of the house; she turns to him, indicating the house opposite.*)

We are going over—
Alcandre speaks tonight—and Lysimon.

THE DUENNA (*puts finger in her ear*): My little finger says
    we shall not hear
Everything.

CYRANO: Never mind me—

THE DUENNA (*across the street*):   Look— Oh, look!
The knocker tied up in a napkin— Yes,
They muzzled you because you bark too loud
And interrupt the lecture—little beast!

ROXANE (*as the door opens*): Enter . . .

(*to* CYRANO)   If Christian comes, tell him to wait.

CYRANO: Oh—(ROXANE *returns.*)

            When he comes, what will you talk about?
You always know beforehand.

ROXANE: About . . .

CYRANO: Well?

ROXANE: You will not tell him, will you?

CYRANO: I am dumb.

ROXANE: About nothing! Or about everything—
I shall say: "Speak of love in your own words—
Improvise! Rhapsodize! Be eloquent!"

CYRANO (*smiling*): Good!

ROXANE: Sh!—

CYRANO: Sh!—

ROXANE: Not a word!

(*She goes in; the door closes.*)

CYRANO (*bowing*):   Thank you so much—

ROXANE (*opens door and puts out her head*): He must be
unprepared—

CYRANO: Of course!

ROXANE: Sh!—

(*goes in again*)

CYRANO (*calls*):   Christian!

(CHRISTIAN *enters.*) I have your theme—bring on your memory!—
Here is your chance now to surpass yourself,
No time to lose— Come! Look intelligent—
Come home and learn your lines.

CHRISTIAN: No.

CYRANO: What?

CHRISTIAN: I'll wait

Here for Roxane.
    CYRANO: What lunacy is this?
Come quickly!
    CHRISTIAN: No, I say! I have had enough—
Taking my words, my letters, all from you—
Making our love a little comedy!
It was a game at first; but now—she cares . . .
Thanks to you. I am not afraid. I'll speak
For myself now.
    CYRANO: Undoubtedly!
    CHRISTIAN: I will!
Why not? I am no such fool—you shall see!
Besides—my dear friend—you have taught me much.
I ought to know something . . . By God, I know
Enough to take a woman in my arms!
    (ROXANE *appears in the doorway, opposite.*)
There she is now . . . Cyrano, wait! Stay here!
    CYRANO (*bows*): Speak for yourself, my friend! (*He goes out.*)
    ROXANE (*taking leave of the company*): —Barthénoide!
Alcandre! . . . Grémione! . . .
    THE DUENNA: I told you so—
We missed the Tender Passion!
    (*She goes into* ROXANE'S *house.*)
    ROXANE: Urimédonte!—
Adieu! (*As the guests disappear down the street, she turns to* CHRISTIAN.) Is that you, Christian? Let us stay
Here, in the twilight. They are gone. The air
Is fragrant. We shall be alone. Sit down
There—so . . . (*They sit on the bench.*) Now tell me things.
    CHRISTIAN (*after a silence*):   I love you.
    ROXANE (*closes her eyes*):   Yes,
Speak to me about love . . .
    CHRISTIAN: I love you.
    ROXANE: Now
Be eloquent! . . .
    CHRISTIAN: I love—
    ROXANE (*opens her eyes*):   You have your theme—
Improvise! Rhapsodize!
    CHRISTIAN: I love you so!
    ROXANE: Of course. And then? . . .
    CHRISTIAN: And then . . . Oh, I should be
So happy if you loved me too! Roxane,
Say that you love me too!
    ROXANE (*making a face*): I ask for cream

You give me milk and water. Tell me first
A little, how you love me.
CHRISTIAN: Very much.
ROXANE: Oh—tell me how you *feel!*
CHRISTIAN (*coming nearer, and devouring her with his eyes*): Your throat . . . If only
I might . . . kiss it—
ROXANE: Christian!
CHRISTIAN: I love you so!
ROXANE (*makes as if to rise*): Again?
CHRISTIAN (*desperately, restraining her*): No, not again—
I do not love you—
ROXANE (*settles back*): That is better . . .
CHRISTIAN: I adore you!
ROXANE: Oh!—(*rises and moves away*)
CHRISTIAN: I know;
I grow absurd.
ROXANE (*coldly*): And that displeases me
As much as if you had grown ugly.
CHRISTIAN: I—
ROXANE: Gather your dreams together into words!
CHRISTIAN: I love—
ROXANE: I know; you love me. Adieu.
(*She goes to the house.*)
CHRISTIAN: No,
But wait—please—let me— I was going to say—
ROXANE (*pushes the door open*): That you adore me. Yes;
   I know that too.
No! . . . Go away! . . .
(*She goes in and shuts the door in his face.*)
CHRISTIAN: I . . . I . . .
CYRANO (*enters*): A great success!
CHRISTIAN: Help me!
CYRANO: Not I.
CHRISTIAN: I cannot live unless
She loves me—now, this moment!
CYRANO: How the devil
Am I to teach you now—this moment?
CHRISTIAN (*catches him by the arm*): —Wait!—
Look! Up there!—Quick—(*The light shows in* ROXANE'S *window.*)
CYRANO: Her window—
CHRISTIAN (*wailing*): I shall die!—
CYRANO: Less noise!
CHRISTIAN: Oh, I—

CYRANO: It does seem fairly dark—

CHRISTIAN (*excitedly*): Well?—Well?—Well?—

CYRANO: Let us try what can be done;
It is more than you deserve—stand over there,
Idiot—there!—before the balcony—
Let me stand underneath. I'll whisper you
What to say.

CHRISTIAN: She may hear—she may—

CYRANO: Less noise!
(*The* PAGES *appear up stage.*)

FIRST PAGE: Hep!—

CYRANO (*finger to lips*): Sh!—

FIRST PAGE (*low voice*): We serenaded Montfleury!—
What next?

CYRANO: Down to the corner of the street—
One this way—and the other over there—
If anybody passes, play a tune!

PAGE: What tune, O musical Philosopher?

CYRANO: Sad for a man, or merry for a woman—
Now go!
(*The* PAGES *disappear, one toward each corner of the street.*)

CYRANO (*to* CHRISTIAN): Call her!

CHRISTIAN: Roxane!

CYRANO: Wait . . . (*gathers up a handful of pebbles*)
Gravel . . .
(*throws it at the window*) There!—

ROXANE (*opens the window*): Who is calling?

CHRISTIAN: I—

ROXANE: Who?

CHRISTIAN: Christian.

ROXANE: You again?

CHRISTIAN: I had to tell you—

CYRANO (*under the balcony*): Good— Keep your voice down.

ROXANE: No. Go away. You tell me nothing.

CHRISTIAN: Please!—

ROXANE: You do not love me any more—

CHRISTIAN (*to whom* CYRANO *whispers his words*): No— no—
Not any more—I love you . . . evermore . . .
And ever . . . more and more!

ROXANE (*about to close the window—pauses*): A little better . . .

CHRISTIAN (*same business*): Love grows and struggles like
    . . . an angry child . . .
Breaking my heart . . . his cradle . . .
    ROXANE (*coming out on the balcony*): Better still—
But . . . such a babe is dangerous; why not
Have smothered it new-born?
    CHRISTIAN (*same business*):   And so I do . . .
And yet he lives . . . I found . . . as you shall find . . .
This new-born babe . . . an infant . . . Hercules!
    ROXANE (*further forward*): Good!—
    CHRISTIAN (*same business*): Strong enough . . . at birth
    . . . to strangle those
Two serpents—Doubt and . . . Pride.
    ROXANE (*leans over balcony*):   Why, very well!
Tell me now why you speak so haltingly—
Has your imagination gone lame?
    CYRANO (*thrusts* CHRISTIAN *under the balcony, and stands
in his place*): Here—
This grows too difficult!
    ROXANE: Your words tonight
Hesitate. Why?
    CYRANO (*in a low tone, imitating* CHRISTIAN): Through the
        warm summer gloom
They grope in darkness toward the light of you.
    ROXANE: My words, well aimed, find you more readily.
    CYRANO: My heart is open wide and waits for them—
Too large a mark to miss! My words fly home,
Heavy with honey like returning bees,
To your small secret ear. Moreover—yours
Fall to me swiftly. Mine more slowly rise.
    ROXANE: Yet not so slowly as they did at first.
    CYRANO: They have learned the way, and you have wel-
comed them.
    ROXANE (*softly*): Am I so far above you now?
    CYRANO: So far—
If you let fall upon me one hard word,
Out of that height—you crush me!
    ROXANE (*turns*):   I'll come down—
    CYRANO (*quickly*): No!
    ROXANE (*points out the bench under the balcony*): Stand
you on the bench. Come nearer!
    CYRANO (*recoils into the shadow*):   No!—
    ROXANE: And why—so great a *No*?
    CYRANO (*more and more overcome by emotion*):
                    Let me enjoy

The one moment I ever—my one chance
To speak to you . . . unseen!
   ROXANE: Unseen?—
   CYRANO: Yes!—yes . . .
Night, making all things dimly beautiful,
One veil over us both— You only see
The darkness of a long cloak in the gloom,
And I the whiteness of a summer gown—
You are all light— I am all shadow! . . . How
Can you know what this moment means to me?
If I was ever eloquent—
   ROXANE: You were
Eloquent—
   CYRANO: —You have never heard till now
My own heart speaking!
   ROXANE: Why not?
   CYRANO: Until now,
I spoke through . . .
   ROXANE: Yes?—
   CYRANO: —through that sweet drunkenness
You pour into the world out of your eyes!
But tonight . . . but tonight, I indeed speak
For the first time!
   ROXANE: For the first time— Your voice,
Even, is not the same.
   CYRANO (*passionately; moves nearer*): How should it be?
I have another voice—my own,
Myself, daring—(*He stops, confused; then tries to recover
himself.*) Where was I? . . . I forget! . . .
Forgive me. This is all sweet like a dream . . .
Strange—like a dream . . .
   ROXANE: How, strange?
   CYRANO: Is it not so
To be myself to you, and have no fear
Of moving you to laughter?
   ROXANE: Laughter—why?
   CYRANO (*struggling for an explanation*): Because . . . What
am I . . . What is any man,
That he dare ask for you? Therefore my heart
Hides behind phrases. There's a modesty
In these things too— I come here to pluck down
Out of the sky the evening star—then smile,
And stoop to gather little flowers.
   ROXANE: Are they
Not sweet, those little flowers?

CYRANO: Not enough sweet
For you and me, tonight!
ROXANE (*breathless*): You never spoke
To me like this . . .
CYRANO: Little things, pretty things—
Arrows and hearts and torches—roses red,
And violets blue—are these all? Come away,
And breathe fresh air! Must we keep on and on
Sipping stale honey out of tiny cups
Decorated with golden tracery,
Drop by drop, all day long? We are alive;
We thirst— Come away, plunge, and drink, and drown
In the great river flowing to the sea!
ROXANE: But . . . Poetry?
CYRANO: I have made rimes for you—
Not now— Shall we insult Nature, this night,
These flowers, this moment—shall we set all these
To phrases from a letter by Voiture?
Look once at the high stars that shine in heaven,
And put off artificiality!
Have you not seen great gaudy hothouse flowers,
Barren, without fragrance?—Souls are like that:
Forced to show all, they soon become all show—
The means to Nature's end ends meaningless!
ROXANE: But . . . Poetry?
CYRANO: Love hates that game of words!
It is a crime to fence with life— I tell you,
There comes one moment, once—and God help those
Who pass that moment by!—when Beauty stands
Looking into the soul with grave, sweet eyes
That sicken at pretty words!
ROXANE: If that be true—
And when that moment comes to you and me—
What words will you? . . .
CYRANO: All those, all those, all those
That blossom in my heart, I'll fling to you—
Armfuls of loose bloom! Love, I love beyond
Breath, beyond reason, beyond love's own power
Of loving! Your name is like a golden bell
Hung in my heart; and when I think of you,
I tremble, and the bell swings and rings—
                                        "Roxane!" . . .
"Roxane!" . . . along my veins, "Roxane!" . . .
                                        I know
All small forgotten things that once meant You—

I remember last year, the First of May,
A little before noon, you had your hair
Drawn low, that one time only. Is that strange?
You know how, after looking at the sun,
One sees red suns everywhere—so, for hours
After the flood of sunshine that you are,
My eyes are blinded by your burning hair!
   ROXANE (*very low*): Yes . . . that is . . . Love—
   CYRANO: Yes, that is Love—that wind
Of terrible and jealous beauty, blowing
Over me—that dark fire, that music . . .

                                         Yet

Love seeketh not his own! Dear, you may take
My happiness to make you happier,
Even though you never know I gave it you—
Only let me hear sometimes, all alone,
The distant laughter of your joy! . . .

                                  I never

Look at you, but there's some new virtue born
In me, some new courage. Do you begin
To understand, a little? Can you feel
My soul, there in the darkness, breathe on you?
—Oh, but tonight, now, I dare say these things—
I . . . to you . . . and you hear them! . . . It is too much!
In my most sweet unreasonable dreams,
I have not hoped for this! Now let me die,
Having lived. It is my voice, mine, my own,
That makes you tremble there in the green gloom
Above me—for you do tremble, as a blossom
Among the leaves— You tremble, and I can feel,
All the way down along these jasmine branches,
Whether you will or no, the passion of you
Trembling . . . (*He kisses wildly the end of a drooping spray of jasmine.*)
   ROXANE: Yes, I do tremble . . . and I weep . . .
And I love you . . . and I am yours . . . and you
Have made me thus!
   CYRANO (*after a pause; quietly*):
                       What is death like, I wonder?
I know everything else now . . .

                              I have done

This, to you—I, myself . . .
                       Only let me
Ask one thing more—
   CHRISTIAN (*under the balcony*): One kiss!

ROXANE (*startled*): One?—

CYRANO (*to* CHRISTIAN): You! ...

ROXANE: You ask me
For—

CYRANO: I ... Yes, but—I mean—(*to* CHRISTIAN)
You go too far!

CHRISTIAN: She is willing!— Why not make the most of it?

CYRANO (*to* ROXANE): I did ask ... but I know I ask too
much ...

ROXANE: Only one— Is that all?

CYRANO: All!—How much more
Than all!—I know—I frighten you—I ask ...
I ask you to refuse—

CHRISTIAN (*to* CYRANO): But why? Why? Why?

CYRANO: Christian, be quiet!

ROXANE (*leaning over*): What is that you say
To yourself?

CYRANO: I am angry with myself
Because I go too far, and so I say
To myself: "Christian, be quiet!"—(*The theorbos begin to
play.*) Hark—someone
Is coming—(ROXANE *closes her window;* CYRANO *listens to
the theorbos, one of which plays a gay melody, the other a
mournful one.*) A sad tune, a merry tune—
Man, woman—what do they mean?—

(*A* CAPUCHIN *enters; he carries a lantern, and goes from
house to house, looking at the doors.*)

Aha!—a priest!
(*to the* CAPUCHIN) What is this new game of Diogenes?

THE CAPUCHIN: I am looking for the house of Madame—

CHRISTIAN (*impatient*): Bah!—

THE CAPUCHIN: Madeleine Robin—

CHRISTIAN: What does he want?

CYRANO (*to the* CAPUCHIN; *points out a street*): This way—
To the right—keep to the right—

THE CAPUCHIN: I thank you, sir!—
I'll say my beads for you to the last grain.

CYRANO: Good fortune, father, and my service to you!
(*The* CAPUCHIN *goes out.*)

CHRISTIAN: Win me that kiss!

CYRANO: No.

CHRISTIAN: Sooner or later—

CYRANO: True ...
That is true ... Soon or late, it will be so
Because you are young and she is beautiful—

(*to himself*) Since it must be, I had rather be myself (*The window reopens;* CHRISTIAN *hides under the balcony.*) The cause of . . . what must be.

ROXANE (*out on the balcony*):   Are you still there? We were speaking of—

CYRANO: A kiss. The word is sweet—
What will the deed be? Are your lips afraid
Even of its burning name? Not much afraid—
Not too much! Have you not unwittingly
Laid aside laughter, slipping beyond speech
Insensibly, already, without fear,
From words to smiles . . . from smiles to sighs . . . from
    sighing,
Even to tears? One step more—only one—
From a tear to a kiss—one step, one thrill!

ROXANE: Hush—

CYRANO: And what is a kiss, when all is done?
A promise given under seal—a vow
Taken before the shrine of memory—
A signature acknowledged—a rosy dot
Over the i of Loving—a secret whispered
To listening lips apart—a moment made
Immortal, with a rush of wings unseen—
A sacrament of blossoms, a new song
Sung by two hearts to an old simple tune—
The ring of one horizon around two souls
Together, all alone!

ROXANE: Hush! . . .

CYRANO: Why, what shame?—
There was a Queen of France, not long ago,
And a great lord of England—a queen's gift,
A crown jewel!

ROXANE: Indeed!

CYRANO: Indeed, like him,
I have my sorrows and my silences;
Like her, you are the queen I dare adore;
Like him I am faithful and forlorn—

ROXANE: Like him,
Beautiful—

CYRANO (*aside*): So I am—I forgot that!

ROXANE: Then— Come; . . . Gather your sacred blossom . . .

CYRANO (*to* CHRISTIAN):   Go!—

ROXANE: Your crown jewel . . .

CYRANO: Go on!—

ROXANE: Your old new song . . .

CYRANO: Climb!—

CHRISTIAN (*hesitates*): No— Would you?—not yet—

ROXANE: Your moment made
Immortal . . .

CYRANO (*pushing him*): Climb up, animal!

(CHRISTIAN *springs on the bench, and climbs by the pillars,
the branches, the vines, until he bestrides the balcony railing.*)

CHRISTIAN: Roxane! . . . (*He takes her in his arms and
bends over her.*)

CYRANO (*very low*): Ah! . . . Roxane! . . .
                              I have won what I have won—
The feast of love—and I am Lazarus!
Yet . . . I have something here that is mine now
And was not mine before I spoke the words
That won her—not for me! . . . Kissing my words
My words, upon your lips! (*The theorbos begin to play.*)
                              A merry tune—
A sad tune— So! The Capuchin! (*He pretends to be running,
as if he had arrived from a distance; then calls up to the
balcony.*) Hola!

ROXANE: Who is it?

CYRANO: I. Is Christian there with you?

CHRISTIAN (*astonished*): Cyrano!

ROXANE: Good morrow, Cousin!

CYRANO: Cousin, . . . good morrow!

ROXANE: I am coming down. (*She disappears into the
house; the* CAPUCHIN *enters up stage.*)

CHRISTIAN (*sees him*): Oh—again!

THE CAPUCHIN (*to* CYRANO):   She lives *here*,
Madeleine Robin!

CYRANO: You said RO-LIN.

THE CAPUCHIN: No—
R-O-B-I-N.

ROXANE (*appears on the threshold of the house, followed
by* RAGUENEAU *with a lantern, and by* CHRISTIAN): What is it?

THE CAPUCHIN: A letter.

CHRISTIAN: Oh! . . .

THE CAPUCHIN (*to* ROXANE): Some matter profitable to the
        soul—
A very noble lord gave it to me!

ROXANE (*to* CHRISTIAN): De Guiche!

CHRISTIAN: He dares?—

ROXANE: It will not be for long;
When he learns that I love you . . . (*By the light of the*

lantern which RAGUENEAU *holds, she reads the letter in a low
tone, as if to herself.)*   "Mademoiselle
The drums are beating, and the regiment
Arms for the march. Secretly I remain
Here, in the Convent. I have disobeyed;
I shall be with you soon. I send this first
By an old monk, as simple as a sheep,
Who understands nothing of this. Your smile
Is more than I can bear, and seek no more.
Be alone tonight, waiting for one who dares
To hope you will forgive . . . —" etcetera—
(*to the* CAPUCHIN) Father, this letter concerns you . . .
(*to* CHRISTIAN)   —and you.
Listen (*The others gather around her; she pretends to read
from the letter, aloud.*) "Mademoiselle:
                                        The Cardinal
Will have his way, although against your will;
That is why I am sending this to you
By a most holy man, intelligent,
Discreet. You will communicate to him
Our order to perform, here and at once
The rite of . . . (*turns the page*)—Holy Matrimony. You
And Christian will be married privately
In your house. I have sent him to you. I know
You hesitate. Be resigned, nevertheless,
To the Cardinal's command, who sends herewith
His blessing. Be assured also of my own
Respect and high consideration—*signed,*
Your very humble and—etcetera—"
    THE CAPUCHIN: A noble lord! I said so—never fear—
A worthy lord!—a very worthy lord!—
    ROXANE (*to* CHRISTIAN): Am I a good reader of letters?
    CHRISTIAN (*motions toward the* CAPUCHIN):   Careful!—
    ROXANE (*in a tragic tone*): Oh, this is terrible!
    THE CAPUCHIN (*turns the light of his lantern on* CYRANO):
You are to be—
    CHRISTIAN: *I* am the bridegroom!
    THE CAPUCHIN (*turns his lantern upon* CHRISTIAN; *then, as
if some suspicion crossed his mind, upon seeing the young
man so handsome*): Oh—why, *you* . . .
    ROXANE (*quickly*): Look here—
"Postscript: Give to the Convent in my name
One hundred and twenty pistoles"—
    THE CAPUCHIN: Think of it!
A worthy lord—a worthy lord! . . .

(*to* ROXANE, *solemnly*) Daughter, resign yourself!

ROXANE (*with an air of martyrdom*): I am resigned . . .
(*While* RAGUENEAU *opens the door for the* CAPUCHIN *and*
CHRISTIAN *invites him to enter, she turns to* CYRANO.) De
Guiche may come. Keep him out here with you
Do not let him—

CYRANO: I understand!

(*to the* CAPUCHIN) How long
Will you be?—

THE CAPUCHIN: Oh, a quarter of an hour.

CYRANO (*hurrying them into the house*): Hurry—I'll wait
here—

ROXANE (*to* CHRISTIAN): Come!

(*They go into the house.*)

CYRANO: Now then, to make
His Grace delay that quarter of an hour . . .
I have it!—up here—(*He steps on the bench, and climbs up
the wall toward the balcony; the theorbos begin to play a
mournful melody.*)   Sad music— Ah, a man! . . .
(*The music pauses on a sinister tremolo.*) Oh—very much a
man! (*He sits astride of the railing and, drawing toward him
a long branch of one of the trees which border the garden
wall, he grasps it with both hands, ready to swing himself
down.*) So—not too high—(*He peers down at the ground.*) I
must float gently through the atmosphere—

DE GUICHE (*enters, masked, groping in the dark toward the
house*): Where is that cursed, bleating Capuchin?

CYRANO: What if he knows my voice?—the devil!—Tic-tac,
Bergerac—we unlock our Gascon tongue;
A good strong accent—

DE GUICHE: Here is the house—all dark—
Damn this mask!—

(*As he is about to enter the house,* CYRANO *leaps from the
balcony, still holding fast to the branch, which bends and
swings him between* DE GUICHE *and the door; then he releases the branch and pretends to fall heavily as though from
a height. He lands flatly on the ground, where he lies motionless, as if stunned.* DE GUICHE *leaps back.*)
What is that? (*When he lifts his eyes, the branch has sprung
back into place; he can see nothing but the sky; he does not
understand.*)   Why . . . where did this man
Fall from?

CYRANO (*sits up, and speaks with a strong accent*): —The
moon!

DE GUICHE: You—

CYRANO: From the moon, the moon!
I fell out of the moon!

DE GUICHE: The fellow is mad—

CYRANO (*dreamily*): Where am I?

DE GUICHE: Why—

CYRANO: What time is it? What place
Is this? What day? What season?

DE GUICHE: You—

CYRANO: I am stunned!

DE GUICHE: My dear sir—

CYRANO: Like a bomb—a bomb—I fell
From the moon!

DE GUICHE: Now, see here—

CYRANO (*rising to his feet, and speaking in a terrible
voice*):   I say, the moon!

DE GUICHE (*recoils*): Very well—if you say so—(*aside*)
                                   Raving mad!—

CYRANO (*advancing upon him*): I am not speaking meta-
phorically!

DE GUICHE: Pardon.

CYRANO: A hundred years—an hour ago—
I really cannot say how long I fell—
I was in yonder shining sphere—

DE GUICHE (*shrugs*): Quite so.
Please let me pass.

CYRANO (*interposes himself*): Where am I? Tell the truth—
I can bear it. In what quarter of the globe
Have I descended like a meteorite?

DE GUICHE: Morbleu!

CYRANO: I could not choose my place to fall—
The earth spun round so fast— Was it the Earth,
I wonder?—Or is this another world?
Another moon? Whither have I been drawn
By the dead weight of my posterior?

DE GUICHE: Sir, I repeat—

CYRANO (*with a sudden cry, which causes* DE GUICHE *to
recoil again*): His face! My God—black!

DE GUICHE (*carries his hand to his mask*):   Oh!—

CYRANO (*terrified*): Are you a native? Is this Africa?

DE GUICHE: —This mask!

CYRANO (*somewhat reassured*): Are we in Venice? Genoa?

DE GUICHE (*tries to pass him*): A lady is waiting for me.

CYRANO (*quite happy again*):   So this is Paris!

DE GUICHE (*smiling in spite of himself*): This fool becomes
amusing.

CYRANO: Ah! You smile?

DE GUICHE: I do. Kindly permit me—

CYRANO (*delighted*): Dear old Paris—
Well, well!—(*wholly at his ease, smiles, bows, arranges his
dress*) Excuse my appearance. I arrive
By the last thunderbolt—a trifle singed
As I came through the ether. These long journeys—
You know! There are so few conveniences!
My eyes are full of stardust. On my spurs,
Some sort of fur . . . Planet's apparently . . .
(*plucks something from his sleeve*) Look—on my doublet—
That's a Comet's hair!
(*He blows something from the back of his hand.*) Phoo!

DE GUICHE (*grows angry*): Monsieur—

CYRANO (*as* DE GUICHE *is about to push past, thrusts his leg
in the way*): Here's a tooth, stuck in my boot,
From the Great Bear. Trying to get away,
I tripped over the Scorpion and came down
Slap, into one scale of the Balances—
The pointer marks my weight this moment . . .
(*pointing upward*) See?
(DE GUICHE *makes a sudden movement;* CYRANO *catches his
arm.*) Be careful! If you struck me on the nose,
It would drip milk!

DE GUICHE: Milk!

CYRANO: From the Milky Way!

DE GUICHE: Hell!

CYRANO: No, no—Heaven. (*crossing his arms*)
Curious place up there—
Did you know Sirius wore a nightcap? True!
(*confidentially*) The Little Bear is still too young to bite.
(*laughing*) My foot caught in the Lyre, and broke a string.
(*proudly*) Well—when I write my book, and tell the tale
Of my adventures—all these little stars
That shake out of my cloak—I must save those
To use for asterisks!

DE GUICHE: That will do now—
I wish—

CYRANO: Yes, yes—I know—

DE GUICHE: Sir—

CYRANO: You desire
To learn from my own lips the character
Of the moon's surface—its inhabitants
If any—

DE GUICHE (*loses patience and shouts*): I desire no such
thing! I—

CYRANO (*rapidly*): You wish to know by what mysterious
    means
I reached the moon?—well—confidentially—
It was a new invention of my own.

DE GUICHE (*discouraged*): Drunk too—as well as mad!

CYRANO: I scorned the eagle
Of Regiomontanus, and the dove
Of Archytas!

DE GUICHE: A learned lunatic!—

CYRANO: I imitated no one. I myself
Discovered not one scheme merely, but six—
Six ways to violate the virgin sky!

   (DE GUICHE *has succeeded in passing him, and moves toward the door of* ROXANE'S *house.* CYRANO *follows, ready to
use violence if necessary.*)

DE GUICHE (*looks around*): Six?

CYRANO (*with increasing volubility*): As for instance—
Having stripped myself
Bare as a wax candle, adorn my form
With crystal vials filled with morning dew,
And so be drawn aloft, as the sun rises
Drinking the mist of dawn!

DE GUICHE (*takes a step toward* CYRANO):
                              Yes—that makes one.

CYRANO (*draws back to lead him away from the door;
speaks faster and faster*): Or, sealing up the air in a cedar
    chest,
Rarefy it by means of mirrors, placed
In an icosahedron.

DE GUICHE (*takes another step*): Two.

CYRANO (*still retreating*): Again,
I might construct a rocket, in the form
Of a huge locust, driven by impulses
Of villainous saltpeter from the rear,
Upward, by leaps and bounds.

DE GUICHE (*interested in spite of himself, and counting on
his fingers*): Three.

CYRANO (*same business*):   Or again,
Smoke having a natural tendency to rise,
Blow in a globe enough to raise me.

DE GUICHE (*same business, more and more astonished*):
                              Four!

CYRANO: Or since Diana, as old fables tell,

Draws forth to fill her crescent horn, the marrow
Of bulls and goats—to anoint myself therewith.
    DE GUICHE (*hypnotized*): Five!—
    CYRANO (*has by this time led him all the way across the
street, close to a bench*): Finally—seated on an iron plate,
To hurl a magnet in the air—the iron
Follows—I catch the magnet—throw again—
And so proceed indefinitely.
    DE GUICHE: Six!—
All excellent,—and which did you adopt?
    CYRANO (*coolly*): Why, none of them. . . . A seventh.
    DE GUICHE: Which was?—
    CYRANO: Guess!—
    DE GUICHE: An interesting idiot, this!
    CYRANO (*imitates the sound of waves with his voice, and
their movement by large, vague gestures*): Hoo! . . . Hoo! . . .
    DE GUICHE: Well?
    CYRANO: Have you guessed it yet?
    DE GUICHE: Why, no.
    CYRANO (*grandiloquent*):   The ocean! . . .
What hour its rising tide seeks the full moon,
I laid me on the strand, fresh from the spray,
My head fronting the moonbeams, since the hair
Retains moisture—and so I slowly rose
As upon angels' wings, effortlessly,
Upward—then suddenly I felt a shock!—
And then . . .
    DE GUICHE (*overcome by curiosity, sits down on the bench*):
                                      And then?
    CYRANO: And then—(*changes abruptly to his natural voice*)
                            The time is up!—
Fifteen minutes, your Grace!—You are now free;
And—they are bound—in wedlock.
    DE GUICHE (*leaping up*):   Am *I* drunk?
That voice . . . (*The door of* ROXANE'S *house opens; lackeys
appear, bearing lighted candles; lights up;* CYRANO *removes
his hat.*) And that nose!—Cyrano!
    CYRANO (*saluting*):   Cyrano! . . .
This very moment, they have exchanged rings.
    DE GUICHE: Who?
    (*He turns up stage.* TABLEAU: *between the lackeys,* ROXANE
and CHRISTIAN *appear, hand in hand. The* CAPUCHIN *follows
them, smiling.* RAGUENEAU *holds aloft a torch. The* DUENNA
*brings up the rear, in a negligée, and a pleasant flutter of
emotion.*)

Zounds!
(*to* ROXANE): You?—
(*recognizes* CHRISTIAN) He?—
(*saluting* ROXANE)   My sincere compliments!
(*to* CYRANO) You also, my inventor of machines!
Your rigmarole would have detained a saint
Entering Paradise—decidedly
You must not fail to write that book some day!

    CYRANO (*bowing*): Sir, I engage myself to do so. (*leads the bridal pair down to* DE GUICHE *and strokes with great satisfaction his long white beard*) My lord,
The handsome couple you—and God—have joined
Together!

    DE GUICHE (*regarding him with a frosty eye*): Quite so.
(*turns to* ROXANE) Madame, kindly bid
Your . . . husband farewell.

    ROXANE: Oh!—

    DE GUICHE (*to* CHRISTIAN):   Your regiment
Leaves tonight, sir. Report at once!

    ROXANE: You mean
For the front? The war?

    DE GUICHE: Certainly!

    ROXANE: I thought
The Cadets were not going—

    DE GUICHE: Oh yes, they are! (*taking out the dispatch from his pocket*) Here is the order—(*to* CHRISTIAN) Baron!
Deliver this.

    ROXANE (*throws herself into* CHRISTIAN'S *arms*): Christian!

    DE GUICHE (*to* CYRANO, *sneering*): The bridal night is not so near!

    CYRANO (*aside*): Somehow that news fails to disquiet me.

    CHRISTIAN (*to* ROXANE): Your lips again . . .

    CYRANO: There . . . That will do now— Come!

    CHRISTIAN (*still holding* ROXANE): You do not know how hard it is—

    CYRANO (*tries to drag him away*): I know!
(*The beating of drums is heard in the distance.*)

    DE GUICHE (*up stage*): The regiment—on the march!

    ROXANE (*as* CYRANO *tries to lead* CHRISTIAN *away, follows, and detains them*):   Take care of him
For me—(*appealingly*)
Promise me never to let him do
Anything dangerous!

    CYRANO: I'll do my best—
I cannot promise—

ROXANE (*same business*):   Make him be careful!
CYRANO: Yes—
I'll try—
ROXANE (*same business*): Be sure to keep him dry and
warm!
CYRANO: Yes, yes—if possible—
ROXANE (*same business; confidentially, in his ear*): See
     that he remains
Faithful!—
CYRANO: Of course! If—
ROXANE (*same business*): And have him write to me
Every single day!
CYRANO (*stops*): That, I promise you!

ACT IV

(THE CADETS OF GASCOYNE)

(*The post occupied by the company of* CARBON DE CASTEL-
JALOUX *at the siege of Arras.*
*In the background, a rampart traversing the entire scene;
beyond this, and apparently below, a plain stretches away to
the horizon. The country is cut up with earthworks and other
suggestions of the siege. In the distance, against the skyline,
the houses and the walls of Arras.*
*Tents; scattered weapons; drums, et cetera. It is near day-
break, and the east is yellow with approaching dawn. Sentries
at intervals. Campfires.*
Curtain rise discovers the CADETS *asleep, rolled in their
cloaks.* CARBON DE CASTEL-JALOUX *and* LE BRET *keep watch.
They are both very thin and pale.* CHRISTIAN *is asleep among
the others, wrapped in his cloak, in the foreground, his face
lighted by the flickering fire. Silence.*)

LE BRET: Horrible!
CARBON: Why, yes. All of that.
LE BRET: Mordious!
CARBON (*gesture toward the sleeping* CADETS): Swear gent-
ly— You might wake them.

(*to* CADETS)   Go to sleep—
Hush! (*to* LE BRET) Who sleeps dines.
   LE BRET: I have insomnia.
God! What a famine.
   (*Firing off stage.*)
   CARBON: Curse that musketry!
They'll wake my babies.
(*to the men*) Go to sleep!—
   A CADET (*rouses*):   Diantre!
Again?
   CARBON: No—only Cyrano coming home.
   (*The heads which have been raised sink back again.*)
   A SENTRY (*off stage*): Halt! Who goes there?
   VOICE OF CYRANO: Bergerac!
   THE SENTRY ON THE PARAPET: Halt! Who goes?—
   CYRANO (*appears on the parapet*): Bergerac, idiot!
   LE BRET (*goes to meet him*): Thank God again!
   CYRANO (*signs to him not to wake anyone*): Hush!
   LE BRET: Wounded?—
   CYRANO: No— They always miss me—quite
A habit by this time!
   LE BRET: Yes— Go right on—
Risk your life every morning before breakfast
To send a letter!
   CYRANO (*stops near* CHRISTIAN): I promised he should write
Every single day . . . (*looks down at him*) Hm— The boy
    looks pale
When he is asleep—thin too—starving to death—
If that poor child knew! Handsome, none the less . . .
   LE BRET: Go and get some sleep!
   CYRANO (*affectionately*): Now, now—you old bear,
No growling!—I am careful—you know I am—
Every night, when I cross the Spanish lines
I wait till they are all drunk.
   LE BRET: You might bring
Something with you.
   CYRANO: I have to travel light
To pass through— By the way, there will be news
For you today: the French will eat or die,
If what I saw means anything.
   LE BRET: Tell us!
   CYRANO: No—
I am not sure—we shall see!
   CARBON: What a war,
When the besieger starves to death!

LE BRET: Fine war—
Fine situation! We besiege Arras—
The Cardinal Prince of Spain besieges us—
And—here we are!

CYRANO: Someone might besiege *him*.

CARBON: A hungry joke!

CYRANO: Ho, ho!

LE BRET: Yes, you can laugh—
Risking a life like yours to carry letters—
Where are you going now?

CYRANO (*at the tent door*): To write another
(*goes into tent*).

(*A little more daylight. The clouds redden. The town of Arras shows on the horizon. A cannon shot is heard, followed immediately by a roll of drums, far away to the left. Other drums beat a little nearer. The drums go on answering each other here and there, approach, beat loudly almost on the stage, and die away toward the right, across the camp. The camp awakes. Voices of officers in the distance.*)

CARBON (*sighs*): Those drums!—another good nourishing sleep
Gone to the devil. (*The* CADETS *rouse themselves.*)
Now then!—

FIRST CADET (*sits up, yawns*): God! I'm hungry!

SECOND CADET: Starving!

ALL (*groan*): Aoh!

CARBON: Up with you!

THIRD CADET: Not another step!

FOURTH CADET: Not another movement!

FIRST CADET: Look at my tongue—
I said this air was indigestible!

FIFTH CADET: My coronet for half a pound of cheese!

SIXTH CADET: I have no stomach for this war—I'll stay
In my tent—like Achilles.

ANOTHER: Yes—no bread,
No fighting—

CARBON: Cyrano!

OTHERS: May as well die—

CARBON: Come out here!—You know how to talk to them.
Get them laughing—

SECOND CADET (*rushes up to* FIRST CADET *who is eating something*): What are you gnawing there?

FIRST CADET: Gun wads and axle-grease. Fat country this
Around Arras.

ANOTHER (*enters*): I have been out hunting!

ANOTHER (*enters*): Went fishing, in the Scarpe!

ALL (*leaping up and surrounding the newcomers*): Find anything?
Any fish? Any game? Perch? Partridges?
Let me look!

THE FISHERMAN: Yes—one gudgeon (*shows it*).

THE HUNTER: One fat . . . sparrow
(*shows it*).

ALL: Ah!—See here, this—mutiny!—

CARBON: Cyrano!
Come and help!

CYRANO (*enters from tent*): Well? (*silence; to the* FIRST
CADET *who is walking away, with his chin on his chest*)
                                   You there, with the long face?

FIRST CADET: I have something on my mind that troubles
me.

CYRANO: What is that?

FIRST CADET: My stomach.

CYRANO: So have I.

FIRST CADET: No doubt
You enjoy this!

CYRANO (*tightens his belt*): It keeps me looking young.

SECOND CADET: My teeth are growing rusty.

CYRANO: Sharpen them!

THIRD CADET: My belly sounds as hollow as a drum.

CYRANO: Beat the long roll on it!

FOURTH CADET: My ears are ringing.

CYRANO: Liar! A hungry belly has no ears.

FIFTH CADET: Oh for a barrel of good wine!

CYRANO (*offers him his own helmet*): Your casque.

SIXTH CADET: I'll swallow anything!

CYRANO (*throws him the book which he has in his hand*):
Try the "Iliad."

SEVENTH CADET: The Cardinal, he has four meals a day—
What does he care!

CYRANO: Ask him; he really ought
To send you . . . a spring lamb out of his flock,
Roasted whole—

THE CADET: Yes, and a bottle—

CYRANO (*exaggerates the manner of one speaking to a
servant*):   If you please,
Richelieu—a little more of the Red Seal . . .
Ah, thank you!

THE CADET: And the salad—

CYRANO: Of course—Romaine!

ANOTHER CADET (*shivering*): I am as hungry as a wolf.

CYRANO (*tosses him a cloak*): Put on
Your sheep's clothing.

FIRST CADET (*with a shrug*):   Always the clever answer!

CYRANO: Always the answer—yes! Let me die so—
Under some rosy-golden sunset, saying
A good thing, for a good cause! By the sword,
The point of honor—by the hand of one
Worthy to be my foeman, let me fall—
Steel in my heart, and laughter on my lips!

VOICES HERE AND THERE: All very well— We are hungry!

CYRANO: Bah! You think
Of nothing but yourselves. (*His eye singles out the old fifer
in the background.*) Here, Bertrandou,
You were a shepherd once— Your pipe now! Come,
Breathe, blow,— Play to these belly-worshippers
The old airs of the South—

                              "Airs with a smile in them,
Airs with a sigh in them, airs with the breeze
And the blue of the sky in them—"

                              Small, demure tunes
Whose every note is like a little sister—
Songs heard only in some long silent voice
Not quite forgotten— Mountain melodies
Like thin smoke rising from brown cottages
In the still noon, slowly— Quaint lullabies,
Whose very music has a Southern tongue—
(*The old man sits down and prepares his fife.*)
Now let the fife, that dry old warrior,
Dream, while over the stops your fingers dance
A minuet of little birds—let him
Dream beyond ebony and ivory;
Let him remember he was once a reed
Out of the river, and recall the spirit
Of innocent, untroubled country days . . .
(*The fifer begins to play a Provençal melody.*)
Listen, you Gascons! Now it is no more
The shrill fife— It is the flute, through woodlands
        far
Away, calling—no longer the hot battle-cry,
But the cool, quiet pipe our goatherds play!
Listen—the forest glens . . . the hills . . . the downs . . .
The green sweetness of night on the Dordogne . . .
Listen, you Gascons! It is all Gascoyne! . . .
    (*Every head is bowed; every eye cast down. Here and*

*there a tear is furtively brushed away with the back of a hand,
the corner of a cloak.*)

CARBON (*softly to* CYRANO): You make them weep—
CYRANO: For homesickness—a hunger
More noble than that hunger of the flesh;
It is their hearts now that are starving.
CARBON: Yes,
But you melt down their manhood.
CYRANO (*motions the drummer to approach*):

                                        You think so?

Let them be. There is iron in their blood
Not easily dissolved in tears. You need
Only—(*He makes a gesture; the drum beats.*)
ALL (*spring up and rush toward their weapons*):
What's that? Where is it?—What?—
CYRANO (*smiles*):   You see—
Let Mars snore in his sleep once—and farewell
Venus—sweet dreams—regrets—dear thoughts of home—
All the fife lulls to rest wakes at the drums!
A CADET (*looks up stage*): Aha— Monsieur de Guiche!
THE CADETS (*mutter among themselves*): Ugh! . . .
CYRANO (*smiles*):   Flattering
Murmur!
A CADET: He makes me weary!
ANOTHER: With his collar
Of lace over his corselet—
ANOTHER: Like a ribbon
Tied round a sword!
ANOTHER: Bandages for a boil
On the back of his neck—
SECOND CADET: A courtier always!
ANOTHER: The Cardinal's nephew!
CARBON: None the less—a Gascon.
FIRST CADET: A counterfeit! Never you trust that man—
Because we Gascons, look you, are all mad—
This fellow is reasonable—nothing more
Dangerous than a reasonable Gascon!
LE BRET: He looks pale.
ANOTHER: Oh, he can be hungry too,
Like any other poor devil—but he wears
So many jewels on that belt of his
That his cramps glitter in the sun!
CYRANO (*quickly*): Is he
To see us looking miserable? Quick—
Pipes!—Cards!—Dice!—(*They all hurriedly begin to play, on*

*their stools, on the drums, or on their cloaks spread on the
ground, lighting their long pipes meanwhile.)*

                                      As for me, I read Descartes.
*(He walks up and down, reading a small book which he
takes from his pocket.* TABLEAU: DE GUICHE *enters, looking
pale and haggard. All are absorbed in their games. General
air of contentment.* DE GUICHE *goes to* CARBON. *They look at
each other askance, each observing with satisfaction the condition of the other.)*

   DE GUICHE: Good morning! *(aside)* He looks yellow.
   CARBON *(same business)*:   He is all eyes.
   DE GUICHE *(looks at the* CADETS*)*: What have we here?
Black looks? Yes, gentlemen—
I am informed I am not popular;
The hill-nobility, barons of Béarn,
The pomp and pride of Périgord—I learn
They disapprove their colonel; call him courtier,
Politician—they take it ill that I
Cover my steel with lace of Genoa.
It is a great offense to be a Gascon
And not to be a beggar!
(Silence; they smoke; they play.) Well—Shall I have
Your captain punish you? . . . No.
   CARBON: As to that,
It would be impossible.
   DE GUICHE: Oh?
   CARBON: I am free;
I pay my company; it is my own;
I obey military orders.
   DE GUICHE: Oh!
That will be quite enough.
(to the CADETS*)* I can afford
Your little hates. My conduct under fire
Is well known. It was only yesterday
I drove the Count de Bucquoi from Bapaume,
Pouring my men down like an avalanche,
I myself led the charge—
   CYRANO *(without looking up from his book)*:
                                      And your white scarf?
   DE GUICHE *(surprised and gratified)*: You heard that
     episode? Yes—rallying
My men for the third time, I found myself
Carried among a crowd of fugitives
Into the enemy's lines. I was in danger
Of being shot or captured; but I thought

Quickly—took off and flung away the scarf
That marked my military rank—and so
Being inconspicuous, escaped among
My own force, rallied them, returned again
And won the day! . . . (*The* CADETS *do not appear to be lis-
tening, but here and there the cards and dice boxes remain
motionless, the smoke is retained in their cheeks.*) What do
        you say to that?
Presence of mind—yes?
    CYRANO: Henry of Navarre
Being outnumbered, never flung away
His white plume (*silent enjoyment; the cards flutter, the dice
roll, the smoke puffs out*).
    DE GUICHE: My device was a success,
However! (*same attentive pause, interrupting the games and
the smoking*)
    CYRANO: Possibly . . . An officer
Does not lightly resign the privilege
Of being a target. (*Cards, dice, and smoke fall, roll and float
away with increasing satisfaction.*) Now, if I had been there—
Your courage and my own differ in this—
When your scarf fell, I should have put it on.
    DE GUICHE: Boasting again!
    CYRANO: Boasting? Lend it to me
Tonight; I'll lead the first charge, with your scarf
Over my shoulder!
    DE GUICHE: Gasconnade once more!
You are safe making that offer, and you know it—
My scarf lies on the river bank between
The lines, a spot swept by artillery
Impossible to reach alive!
    CYRANO (*produces the scarf from his pocket*):
                                    Yes. Here . . .
    (*Silence. The* CADETS *stifle their laughter behind their cards
and their dice boxes.* DE GUICHE *turns to look at them. Im-
mediately they resume their gravity and their game. One of
them whistles carelessly the mountain air which the fifer was
playing.*)
    DE GUICHE (*takes the scarf*): Thank you! That bit of white
        is what I need
To make a signal. I was hesitating—
You have decided me. (*He goes up to the parapet, climbs
upon it, and waves the scarf at arm's length several times.*)
    ALL: What is he doing?—
What?—

THE SENTRY ON THE PARAPET: There's a man down there
running away!

DE GUICHE (*descending*): A Spaniard. Very useful as a spy
To both sides. He informs the enemy
As I instruct him. By his influence
I can arrange their dispositions.

CYRANO: Traitor!

DE GUICHE (*folding the scarf*): A traitor, yes; but useful ...
We were saying? ...

Oh, yes— Here is a bit of news for you:
Last night we had hopes of reprovisioning
The army. Under cover of dark,
The Marshal moved to Dourlens. Our supplies
Are there. He may reach them. But to return
Safely, he needs a large force—at least half
Our entire strength. At present, we have here
Merely a skeleton.

CARBON: Fortunately,
The Spaniards do not know that.

DE GUICHE: Oh, yes; they know.
They will attack.

CARBON: Ah!

DE GUICHE: From that spy of mine
I learned of their intention. His report
Will determine the point of their advance.
The fellow asked me what to say! I told him:
"Go out between the lines; watch for my signal;
When you see that, let them attack there."

CARBON (*to the* CADETS): Well,
Gentlemen!

(*All rise; noise of sword belts and breastplates being
buckled on.*)

DE GUICHE: You may have perhaps an hour.

FIRST CADET: Oh— An hour!

(*They all sit down and resume their games once more.*)

DE GUICHE (*to* CARBON): The great thing is to gain time.
Any moment the Marshal may return.

CARBON: And to gain time?

DE GUICHE: You will all be so kind
As to lay down your lives!

CYRANO: Ah! Your revenge?

DE GUICHE: I make no great pretense of loving you!
But—since you gentlemen esteem yourselves
Invincible, the bravest of the brave,
And all that—why need we be personal?

I serve the king in choosing . . . as I choose!

    CYRANO (*salutes*): Sir, permit me to offer—all our thanks.

    DE GUICHE (*returns the salute*): You love to fight a hundred against one;

Here is your opportunity! (*He goes up stage with* CARBON.)

    CYRANO (*to the* CADETS): My friends,

We shall add now to our old Gascon arms

With their six chevrons, blue and gold, a seventh—

Blood-red!

    (DE GUICHE *talks in a low tone to* CARBON *up stage. Orders are given. The defense is arranged.* CYRANO *goes to* CHRISTIAN *who has remained motionless with folded arms.*)

Christian? (*lays a hand on his shoulder*)

    CHRISTIAN (*shakes his head*): Roxane . . .

    CYRANO: Yes.

    CHRISTIAN: I should like

To say farewell to her, with my whole heart

Written for her to keep.

    CYRANO: I thought of that—

(*takes a letter from his doublet*) I have written your farewell.

    CHRISTIAN: Show me!

    CYRANO: You wish

To read it?

    CHRISTIAN: Of course! (*He takes the letter; begins to read, looks up suddenly.*) What?

    CYRANO: What is it?

    CHRISTIAN: Look—

This little circle—

    CYRANO (*takes back the letter quickly, and looks innocent*): Circle?—

    CHRISTIAN: Yes—a tear!

    CYRANO: So it is! . . . Well—a poet while he writes

Is like a lover in his lady's arms,

Believing his imagination—all

Seems true—you understand? There's half the charm

Of writing— Now, this letter as you see

I have made so pathetic that I wept

While I was writing it!

    CHRISTIAN: You—wept?

    CYRANO: Why, yes—

Because . . . it is a little thing to die,

But—not to see her . . . that is terrible!

And I shall never—

(CHRISTIAN *looks at him.*) We shall never—

(*quickly*) You

Will never—

CHRISTIAN (*snatches the letter*): Give me that!

(*noise in the distance on the outskirts of the camp*)

VOICE OF A SENTRY: Halt—who goes there?

(*shots, shouting, jingle of harness*)

CARBON: What is it?—

THE SENTRY ON THE PARAPET: Why, a coach.

(*They rush to look.*)

CONFUSED VOICES: What? In the Camp?
A coach? Coming this way— It must have driven
Through the Spanish lines—what the devil— Fire!—
No— Hark! The driver shouting—what does he say?
Wait— He said: "On the service of the King!"

(*They are all on the parapet looking over. The jingling
comes nearer.*)

DE GUICHE: Of the King?

(*They come down and fall into line.*)

CARBON: Hats off, all!

DE GUICHE (*speaks off stage*):   The King! Fall in,
Rascals!—

(*The coach enters at full trot. It is covered with mud and
dust. The curtains are drawn. Two footmen are seated behind. It stops suddenly.*)

CARBON (*shouts*): Beat the assembly—

(*Roll of drums. All the CADETS uncover.*)

DE GUICHE: Two of you,
Lower the steps—open the door—

(*Two men rush to the coach. The door opens.*)

ROXANE (*comes out of the coach*):   Good morning!

(*At the sound of a woman's voice, every head is raised.
Sensation.*)

DE GUICHE: On the King's service— You?

ROXANE: Yes—my own king—
Love!

CYRANO (*aside*): God is merciful . . .

CHRISTIAN (*hastens to her*):   You! Why have you—

ROXANE: Your war lasted so long!

CHRISTIAN: But why?—

ROXANE: Not now—

CYRANO (*aside*): I wonder if I dare to look at her . . .

DE GUICHE: You cannot remain here!

ROXANE: Why, certainly!
Roll that drum here, somebody . . . (*She sits on the drum,
which is brought to her.*)   Thank you—There!

(*She laughs.*) Would you believe—they fired upon us?
                                                    —My coach
Looks like the pumpkin in the fairy tale,
Does it not? And my footmen—(*She throws a kiss to* CHRIS-
TIAN.)   How do you do?
(*She looks about.*) How serious you all are! Do you know,
It is a long drive here—from Arras? (*sees* CYRANO) Cousin,
I am glad to see you!
     CYRANO (*advances*):   Oh— How did you come?
     ROXANE: How did I find you? Very easily—
I followed where the country was laid waste
—Oh, but I saw such things! I had to see
To believe. Gentlemen, is that the service
Of your King? I prefer my own!
     CYRANO: But how
Did you come through?
     ROXANE: Why, through the Spanish lines
Of course! ·
     FIRST CADET: They let you pass?—
     DE GUICHE: What did you say?
How did you manage?
     LE BRET: Yes, that must have been
Difficult!
     ROXANE: No— I simply drove along.
Now and then some hidalgo scowled at me
And I smiled back—my best smile; whereupon,
The Spaniards being (without prejudice
To the French) the most polished gentlemen
In the world—I passed!
     CARBON: Certainly that smile
Should be a passport! Did they never ask
Your errand or your destination?
     ROXANE: Oh,
Frequently! Then I dropped my eyes and said:
"I have a lover . . ." Whereupon, the Spaniard
With an air of ferocious dignity
Would close the carriage door—with such a gesture
As any king might envy, wave aside
The muskets that were leveled at my breast,
Fall back three paces, equally superb
In grace and gloom, draw himself up, thrust forth
A spur under his cloak, sweeping the air
With his long plumes, bow very low, and say:
"Pass, Señorita!"
     CHRISTIAN: But Roxane—

ROXANE: I know—
I said "a lover"—but you understand—
Forgive me!—If I said "I am going to meet
My husband," no one would believe me!
    CHRISTIAN: Yes,
But—
    ROXANE: What then?
    DE GUICHE: You must leave this place.
    CYRANO: At once.
    ROXANE: I?
    LE BRET: Yes—immediately.
    ROXANE: And why?
    CHRISTIAN (*embarrassed*):   Because . . .
    CYRANO (*same*): In half an hour . . .
    DE GUICHE (*same*): Or these quarters . . .
    CARBON (*same*): Perhaps
It might be better . . .
    LE BRET: If you . . .
    ROXANE: Oh— I see!
You are going to fight. I remain here.
    ALL: No—no!
    ROXANE: He is my husband—(*throws herself in* CHRISTIAN'S
arms) I will die with you!
    CHRISTIAN: Your eyes! . . . Why do you?—
    ROXANE: You know why . . .
    DE GUICHE (*desperate*):   This post
Is dangerous—
    ROXANE (*turns*): How—dangerous?
    CYRANO: The proof
Is, we are ordered—
    ROXANE (*to* DE GUICHE): Oh—you wish to make
A widow of me?
    DE GUICHE: On my word of honor—
    ROXANE: No matter. I am just a little mad—
I will stay. It may be amusing.
    CYRANO: What,
A heroine—our intellectual?
    ROXANE: Monsieur de Bergerac, I am your cousin!
    A CADET: We'll fight now! Hurrah!
    ROXANE (*more and more excited*): I am safe with you—
my friends!
    ANOTHER (*carried away*): The whole camp breathes of
lilies!—
    ROXANE: And I think,
This hat would look well on the battlefield! . . .

But perhaps—
(*looks at* DE GUICHE)
　　　　　　　　　　The Count ought to leave us. Any moment
Now, there may be danger.
　　DE GUICHE: This is too much!
I must inspect my guns. I shall return—
You may change your mind— There will yet be
　　　time—
　　ROXANE: Never! (DE GUICHE *goes out*).
　　CHRISTIAN (*imploring*): Roxane! . . .
　　ROXANE:　　　　　　　　　　　　　　　　No!
　　FIRST CADET (*to the rest*): She stays here!
　　ALL (*rushing about, elbowing each other, brushing off their
clothes*):　　　　　　　　　　　　　　　　A comb!—
Soap!—Here's a hole in my— A needle!—Who
Has a ribbon?—Your mirror, quick!—My cuffs—
A razor—
　　ROXANE (*to* CYRANO, *who is still urging her*): No! I shall
not stir one step!
　　CARBON (*having, like the others, tightened his belt, dusted
himself, brushed off his hat, smoothed out his plume and put
on his lace cuffs, advances to* ROXANE *ceremoniously*): In that
case, may I not present to you
Some of these gentlemen who are to have
The honor of dying in your presence?
　　ROXANE (*bows*): Please!—
　　(*She waits, standing, on the arm of* CHRISTIAN, *while*
CARBON—*presents*): Baron de Peyrescous de Colignac!
　　THE CADET (*salutes*): Madame . . .
　　ROXANE: Monsieur . . .
　　CARBON (*continues*): Baron de Casterac
De Cahuzac—Vidame de Malgouyre
Estressac Lésbas d'Escarabiot—
　　THE VIDAME: Madame . . .
　　CARBON: Chevalier d'Antignac-Juzet—
Baron Hillot de Blagnac-Saléchan
De Castel-Crabioules—
　　THE BARON:　　　　　　　　　　　　　Madame . . .
　　ROXANE: How many
Names you all have!
　　THE BARON:　　　　　　　　　　　　　Hundreds!
　　CARBON (*to* ROXANE):　　　　　Open the hand
That holds your handkerchief.
　　ROXANE (*opens her hand; the handkerchief falls*):
　　　　　　　　　　　　　　　　　　　Why?

(*The whole company makes a movement toward it.*)
    CARBON (*picks it up quickly*):   My company
Was in want of a banner. We have now
The fairest in the army!
    ROXANE (*smiling*): Rather small—
    CARBON (*fastens the handkerchief to his lance*): Lace—
and embroidered!
    A CADET (*to the others*):   With her smiling on me,
I could die happy, if I only had
Something in my—
    CARBON (*turns upon him*): Shame on you! Feast your eyes
And forget your—
    ROXANE (*quickly*): It must be this fresh air—
I am starving! Let me see . . .
                            Cold partridges,
Pastry, a little white wine—that would do.
Will someone bring that to me?
    A CADET (*aside*):   Will someone!—
    ANOTHER: Where the devil are we to find—
    ROXANE (*overhears; sweetly*):   Why, there—
In my carriage.
    ALL: Wha-at?
    ROXANE: All you have to do
Is to unpack, and carve, and serve things.
                                   Oh,
Notice my coachman; you may recognize
An old friend.
    THE CADETS (*rush to the coach*): Ragueneau!
    ROXANE (*follows them with her eyes*): Poor fellows . . .
Ah!
    THE CADETS (*acclamations*):   Ah!
Ah!
    CYRANO (*kisses her hand*): Our good fairy!
    RAGUENEAU (*standing on his box, like a mountebank before
a crowd*):   Gentlemen!—
(*enthusiasm*)
    THE CADETS: Bravo!
Bravo!
    RAGUENEAU: The Spaniards, basking in our smiles,
Smiled on our baskets! (*applause*)
    CYRANO (*aside, to* CHRISTIAN):   Christian!—
    RAGUENEAU: They adored
The Fair, and missed—(*He takes from under the seat a dish,
which he holds aloft.*) the Fowl!
    (*Applause. The dish is passed from hand to hand.*)

CYRANO (*as before, to* CHRISTIAN):   One moment—
RAGUENEAU: Venus
Charmed their eyes, while Adonis quietly
(*brandishing a ham*) Brought home the Boar!

(*Applause; the ham is seized by a score of hands outstretched.*)

CYRANO (*as before*): Pst— Let me speak to you—
ROXANE (*as the* CADETS *return, their arms full of provisions*):
Spread them out on the ground. (*calls*) Christian! Come here;
Make yourself useful.

(CHRISTIAN *turns to her, at the moment when* CYRANO *was leading him aside. She arranges the food, with his aid and that of the two imperturbable footmen.*)

RAGUENEAU: Peacock, *aux truffes!*
FIRST CADET (*comes down, cutting a huge slice of the ham.*):
                                                    Tonnerre!
We are not going to die without a gorge—(*sees* ROXANE; *corrects himself hastily*) Pardon—a banquet!
RAGUENEAU (*tossing out the cushions of the carriage*):
Open these—they are full
Of ortolans!

(*Tumult; laughter; the cushions are eviscerated.*)

THIRD CADET: Lucullus!
RAGUENEAU (*throws out bottles of red wine*):
                                        Flasks of ruby—
(*and of white*) Flasks of topaz—
ROXANE (*throws a tablecloth at the head of* CYRANO):
                        Come back out of your dreams!
Unfold this cloth—
RAGUENEAU (*takes off one of the lanterns of the carriage, and flourishes it*): Our lamps are bonbonnières!
CYRANO (*to* CHRISTIAN): I must see you before you speak
with her—
RAGUENEAU (*more and more lyrical*): My whip-handle is
one long sausage!
ROXANE (*pouring wine; passing the food*):   We
Being about to die, first let us dine!
Never mind the others—all for Gascoyne!
And if De Guiche comes, he is not invited!
(*going from one to another*) Plenty of time—you need not
        eat so fast—
Hold your cup—
(*to another*)   What's the matter?
                                            You are so good
THE CADET (*sobbing*):
To us . . .

ROXANE: There, there! Red or white wine?

           —Some bread
For Monsieur de Carbon!—Napkins— A knife—
Pass your plate— Some of the crust? A little more—
Light or dark?—Burgundy?—

 CYRANO (*follows her with an armful of dishes, helping to serve*):
               Adorable!

 ROXANE (*goes to* CHRISTIAN): What would you like?

 CHRISTIAN: Nothing.

 ROXANE: Oh, but you must!—
A little wine? A biscuit?

 CHRISTIAN: Tell me first
Why you came—

 ROXANE: By and by. I must take care
Of these poor boys—

 LE BRET (*who has gone up stage to pass up food to the sentry on the parapet, on the end of a lance*): De Guiche!—

 CYRANO: Hide everything
Quick!—Dishes, bottles, tablecloth—

              Now look
Hungry again—(*to* RAGUENEAU) You there! Up on your box—
—Everything out of sight?—

 (*In a twinkling, everything has been pushed inside the tents, hidden in their hats or under their cloaks.* DE GUICHE *enters quickly, then stops, sniffing the air. Silence.*)

 DE GUICHE: It smells good here.

 A CADET (*humming with an air of great unconcern*): Sing ha-ha-ha and ho-ho-ho—

 DE GUICHE (*stares at him; he grows embarrassed*): You there—
What are you blushing for?

 THE CADET: Nothing—my blood
Stirs at the thought of battle.

 ANOTHER: Pom . . . pom . . . pom! . . .

 DE GUICHE (*turns upon him*): What is that?

 THE CADET (*slightly stimulated*): Only song—only little song—

 DE GUICHE: You appear happy!

 THE CADET: Oh yes—always happy
Before a fight—

 DE GUICHE (*calls to* CARBON, *for the purpose of giving him an order*): Captain! I—(*stops and looks at him*)

            What the devil—
You are looking happy too!—

CARBON (*pulls a long face and hides a bottle behind his back*): No!

DE GUICHE: Here—I had
One gun remaining. I have had it placed (*He points off stage.*)
There—in that corner—for your men.

A CADET (*simpering*): So kind!—
Charming attention!

ANOTHER (*same business; burlesque*): Sweet solicitude!—

DE GUICHE (*contemptuous*): I believe you are both drunk— (*coldly*) Being accustomed
To guns—take care of the recoil!

FIRST CADET (*gesture*): Ah-h . . . Pfft!

DE GUICHE (*goes up to him, furious*): How dare you?

FIRST CADET: A Gascon's gun never recoils!

DE GUICHE (*shakes him by the arm*): You *are* drunk—

FIRST CADET (*superbly*): With the smell of powder!

DE GUICHE (*turns away with a shrug*): Bah!
(*to* ROXANE) Madame, have you decided?

ROXANE: I stay here.

DE GUICHE: You have time to escape—

ROXANE: No!

DE GUICHE: Very well—
Someone give me a musket!

CARBON: What!

DE GUICHE: *I* stay
Here also.

CYRANO (*formally*): Sir, you show courage!

FIRST CADET: A Gascon
In spite of all that lace!

ROXANE: Why—

DE GUICHE: Must I run
Away, and leave a woman?

SECOND CADET (*to* FIRST CADET): We might give him
Something to eat—what do you say?
(*All the food reappears, as if by magic.*)

DE GUICHE (*his face lights up*): A feast!

THIRD CADET: Here a little, there a little—

DE GUICHE (*recovers his self-control; haughtily*): Do you think
I want your leavings?

CYRANO (*saluting*): Colonel—you improve!

DE GUICHE: I can fight as I am!

FIRST CADET (*delighted*): Listen to him—
He has an accent!

DE GUICHE (*laughs*): Have I so?

FIRST CADET: A Gascon!—
A Gascon, after all!

(*They all begin to dance.*)

CARBON (*who has disappeared for a moment behind the parapet, reappears on top of it*): I have placed my pikemen
Here (*indicates a row of pikes showing above the parapet*).

DE GUICHE (*bows to* ROXANE): We'll review them; will you take my arm?

(*She takes his arm; they go up on the parapet. The rest uncover, and follow them up stage.*)

CHRISTIAN (*goes hurriedly to* CYRANO): Speak quickly!

(*At the moment when* ROXANE *appears on the parapet the pikes are lowered in salute, and a cheer is heard. She bows.*)

THE PIKEMEN (*off stage*): Hurrah!

CHRISTIAN: What is it?

CYRANO: If Roxane . . .

CHRISTIAN: Well?

CYRANO: Speaks about your letters . . .

CHRISTIAN: Yes—I know!

CYRANO: Do not make the mistake of showing . . .

CHRISTIAN: What?

CYRANO: Showing surprise.

CHRISTIAN: Surprise—why?

CYRANO: I must tell you! . . .
It is quite simple—I had forgotten it
Until just now. You have . . .

CHRISTIAN: Speak quickly!—

CYRANO: You
Have written oftener than you think.

CHRISTIAN: Oh—have I!

CYRANO: I took upon me to interpret you;
And wrote—sometimes . . . without . . .

CHRISTIAN: My knowing. Well?

CYRANO: Perfectly simple!

CHRISTIAN: Oh yes, perfectly!—
For a month, we have been blockaded here!—
How did you send all these letters?

CYRANO: Before
Daylight, I managed—

CHRISTIAN: I see. That was also
Perfectly simple!

                                    —So I wrote to her,
          How many times a week? Twice? Three times?
Four?

CYRANO: Oftener.

CHRISTIAN: Every day?

CYRANO: Yes—every day . . .
Every single day . . .

CHRISTIAN (*violently*): And that wrought you up
Into such a flame that you faced death—

CYRANO (*sees* ROXANE *returning*): Hush—
Not before her!

(*He goes quickly into the tent.* ROXANE *comes up to* CHRISTIAN.)

ROXANE: Now—Christian!

CHRISTIAN (*takes her hands*): Tell me now
Why you came here—over these ruined roads—
Why you made your way among mosstroopers
And ruffians—you—to join me here?

ROXANE: Because—
Your letters . . .

CHRISTIAN: Meaning?

ROXANE: It was your own fault
If I ran into danger! I went mad—
Mad with you! Think what you have written me,
How many times, each one more wonderful
Than the last!

CHRISTIAN: All this for a few absurd
Love letters—

ROXANE: Hush—absurd! How can you know?
I thought I loved you, ever since one night
When a voice that I never would have known
Under my window breathed your soul to me . . .
But—all this time—every one
Was like hearing your voice there in the dark,
All around me, like your arms around me . . . (*more lightly*)
At last,
I came. Anyone would! Do you suppose
The prim Penelope had stayed at home
Embroidering,—if Ulysses wrote like you?
She would have fallen like another Helen—
Tucked up those linen petticoats of hers
And followed him to Troy!

CHRISTIAN: But you—

ROXANE: I read them
Over and over. I grew faint reading them.
I belonged to you. Every page of them
Was like a petal fallen from your soul—
Like the light and the fire of a great love,

Sweet and strong and true—
    CHRISTIAN: Sweet . . . and strong . . . and true . . .
You felt that, Roxane?—
    ROXANE: You know how I feel! . . .
    CHRISTIAN: So—you came . . .
    ROXANE: Oh, my Christian, oh my king,—
Lift me up if I fall upon my knees—
It is the heart of me that kneels to you,
And will remain forever at your feet—
You cannot lift that!—
                            I came here to say
'Forgive me'—(It is time to be forgiven
Now, when we may die presently)—forgive me
For being light and vain and loving you
Only because you were beautiful.
    CHRISTIAN (*astonished*):   Roxane! . . .
    ROXANE: Afterwards I knew better. Afterwards
(I had to learn to use my wings) I loved you
For yourself too—knowing you more, and loving
More of you. And now—
    CHRISTIAN: Now? . . .
    ROXANE: It is yourself
I love now: your own self.
    CHRISTIAN (*taken aback*): Roxane!
    ROXANE (*gravely*):   Be happy!—
You must have suffered; for you must have seen
How frivolous I was; and to be loved
For the mere costume, the poor casual body
You went about in—to a soul like yours,
That must have been torture! Therefore with words
You revealed your heart. Now that image of you
Which filled my eyes first—I see better now,
And I see it no more!
    CHRISTIAN: Oh!—
    ROXANE: You still doubt
Your victory?
    CHRISTIAN (*miserably*): Roxane!—
    ROXANE: I understand:
You cannot perfectly believe in me—
A love like this—
    CHRISTIAN: I want no love like this!
I want love only for—
    ROXANE: Only for what
Every woman sees in you? I can do
Better than that!

CHRISTIAN: No—it was best before!

ROXANE: You do not altogether know me . . . Dear,
There is more of me than there was—with this,
I can love more of you—more of what makes
You your own self—Truly! . . . If you were less
Lovable—

CHRISTIAN: No!

ROXANE: —Less charming—ugly even—
I should love you still.

CHRISTIAN: You mean that?

ROXANE: I do
Mean that!

CHRISTIAN: Ugly? . . .

ROXANE: Yes. Even then!

CHRISTIAN (*agonized*):   Oh . . . God! . . .

ROXANE: Now are you happy?

CHRISTIAN (*choking*): Yes . . .

ROXANE: What is it?

CHRISTIAN (*pushes her away gently*):   Only . . .
Nothing . . . one moment . . .

ROXANE: But—

CHRISTIAN (*gestures toward the* CADETS): I am keeping you
From those poor fellows— Go and smile at them;
They are going to die!

ROXANE (*softly*): Dear Christian!

CHRISTIAN: Go—
(*She goes up among the* GASCONS *who gather round her
respectfully*.)
Cyrano!

CYRANO (*comes out of the tent, armed for the battle*):
What is wrong? You look—

CHRISTIAN: She does not
Love me any more.

CYRANO (*smiles*): You think not?

CHRISTIAN: She loves
You.

CYRANO: No!—

CHRISTIAN (*bitterly*): She loves only my soul.

CYRANO: No!

CHRISTIAN: Yes—
That means you. And you love her.

CYRANO: I?

CHRISTIAN: I see—
I know!

CYRANO: That is true . . .

CHRISTIAN: More than—
CYRANO (*quietly*):   More than that.
CHRISTIAN: Tell her so!
CYRANO: No.
CHRISTIAN: Why not?
CYRANO: Why—look at me!
CHRISTIAN: She would love me if I were ugly.
CYRANO (*startled*): She—
Said that?
CHRISTIAN: Yes. Now then!
CYRANO (*half to himself*):   It was good of her
To tell you that . . .
(*change of tone*) Nonsense! Do you believe
Any such madness—

                         It was good of her
To tell you. . . .
               Do not take her at her word!
Go on—you never will be ugly— Go!
She would never forgive me.
CHRISTIAN: That is what
We shall see.
CYRANO: No, no—
CHRISTIAN: Let her choose between us!—
Tell her everything!
CYRANO: No—you torture me—
CHRISTIAN: Shall I ruin your happiness, because
I have a cursed pretty face? That seems
Too unfair!
CYRANO: And am I to ruin yours
Because I happen to be born with power
To say what you—perhaps—feel?
CHRISTIAN: Tell her!
CYRANO: Man—
Do not try me too far!
CHRISTIAN: I am tired of being
My own rival!
CYRANO: Christian!—
CHRISTIAN: Our secret marriage—
No witnesses—fraudulent—that can be
Annulled—
CYRANO: Do not try me—
CHRISTIAN: I want her love
For the poor fool I am—or not at all!
Oh, I am going through with this! I'll know,
One way or the other. Now I shall walk down

To the end of the post. Go tell her. Let her choose
One of us.
  CYRANO: It will be you.
  CHRISTIAN: God—I hope so! (*He turns and calls.*) Roxane!
  CYRANO: No—no—
  ROXANE (*hurries down to him*): Yes, Christian?
  CHRISTIAN: Cyrano
Has news for you—important.
  (*She turns to* CYRANO. CHRISTIAN *goes out.*)
  ROXANE (*lightly*):   Oh—important?
  CYRANO: He is gone . . . (*to* ROXANE) Nothing—only
Christian thinks
You ought to know—
  ROXANE: I do know. He still doubts
What I told him just now. I saw that.
  CYRANO (*takes her hand*):   Was it
True—what you told him just now?
  ROXANE: It was true!
I said that I should love him even . . .
  CYRANO (*smiling sadly*):   The word
Comes hard—before me?
  ROXANE: Even if he were . . .
  CYRANO: Say it—
I shall not be hurt!—Ugly?
  ROXANE: Even then
I should love him. (*a few shots, off stage, in the direction in
which* CHRISTIAN *disappeared*) Hark! The guns—
  CYRANO: Hideous?
  ROXANE: Hideous.
  CYRANO: Disfigured?
  ROXANE: Or disfigured.
  CYRANO: Even
Grotesque?
  ROXANE: How could he ever be grotesque—
Ever—to me!
  CYRANO: But you could love him so,
As much as?—
  ROXANE: Yes—and more!
  CYRANO (*aside, excitedly*):   It is true!—true!—
Perhaps—God! This is too much happiness . . .
(*to* ROXANE) I—Roxane—listen—
  LE BRET (*enters quickly; calls to* CYRANO *in a low tone*):
Cyrano—
  CYRANO (*turns*): Yes?
  LE BRET: Hush! . . . (*whispers a few words to him*)

CYRANO (*lets fall* ROXANE's *hand*): Ah!

ROXANE: What is it?

CYRANO (*half stunned, and aside*): All gone . . .

ROXANE (*more shots*): What is it? Oh,
They are fighting!—(*She goes up to look off stage.*)

CYRANO: All gone. I cannot ever
Tell her, now . . . ever . . .

ROXANE (*starts to rush away*): What has happened?

CYRANO (*restrains her*): Nothing.
(*Several* CADETS *enter. They conceal something which they
are carrying, and form a group so as to prevent* ROXANE *from
seeing their burden.*)

ROXANE: These men—

CYRANO: Come away . . . (*He leads her away from the
group.*)

ROXANE: You were telling me
Something—

CYRANO: Oh, that? Nothing. . . . (*gravely*) I swear to you
That the spirit of Christian—that his soul
Was—(*corrects himself quickly*)
That his soul is no less great—

ROXANE (*catches at the word*): Was?
(*crying out*) Oh!—
(*She rushes among the men, and scatters them.*)

CYRANO: All gone . . .

ROXANE (*sees* CHRISTIAN *lying upon his cloak*): Christian!

LE BRET (*to* CYRANO): At the first volley.
(ROXANE *throws herself upon the body of* CHRISTIAN. *Shots;
at first scattered, then increasing. Drums. Voices shouting.*)

CARBON (*sword in hand*): Here
They come!—Ready—(*Followed by the* CADETS, *he climbs
over the parapet and disappears.*)

ROXANE: Christian!

CARBON (*off stage*): Come on, there. You!

ROXANE: Christian!

CARBON: Fall in!

ROXANE: Christian!

CARBON: Measure your fuse!
(RAGUENEAU *hurries up, carrying a helmet full of water.*)

CHRISTIAN (*faintly*): Roxane! . . .

CYRANO (*low and quick, in* CHRISTIAN's *ear, while* ROXANE
is dipping into the water a strip of linen torn from her dress):
I have told her; she loves you (CHRISTIAN *closes his eyes*).

ROXANE (*turns to* CHRISTIAN): Yes,
My darling?

CARBON: Draw your ramrods!

ROXANE (*to* CYRANO): He is not dead? . . .

CARBON: Open your charges!

ROXANE: I can feel his cheek
Growing cold against mine—

CARBON: Take aim!

ROXANE: A letter—
Over his heart—(*She opens it.*) For me.

CYRANO (*aside*): My letter . . .

CARBON: Fire! (*musketry, cries and groans; din of battle*)

CYRANO (*trying to withdraw his hand, which* ROXANE, *still upon her knees, is holding*):
But Roxane—they are fighting—

ROXANE: Wait a little . . .
He is dead. No one else knew him but you . . . (*She weeps quietly.*) Was he not a great lover, a great man,
A hero?

CYRANO (*standing, bareheaded*): Yes, Roxane.

ROXANE: A poet, unknown,
Adorable?

CYRANO: Yes, Roxane.

ROXANE: A fine mind?

CYRANO: Yes, Roxane.

ROXANE: A heart deeper than we knew—
A soul magnificently tender?

CYRANO (*firmly*): Yes,
Roxane!

ROXANE (*sinks down upon the breast of* CHRISTIAN): He is dead now . . .

CYRANO (*aside; draws his sword*):   Why, so am I—
For I am dead, and my love mourns for me
And does not know . . . (*trumpets in distance*).

DE GUICHE (*appears on the parapet, disheveled, wounded on the forehead, shouting*): The signal—hark—the trumpets! The army has returned— Hold them now!—Hold them! The army!—

ROXANE: On his letter—blood . . . and tears.

A VOICE (*off stage*): Surrender!

THE CADETS: No!

RAGUENEAU: This place is dangerous!—

CYRANO (*to* DE GUICHE): Take her away—I am going—

ROXANE (*kisses the letter; faintly*): His blood . . . his tears . . .

RAGUENEAU (*leaps down from the coach and runs to her*): She has fainted—

DE GUICHE (*on the parapet; savagely, to the* CADETS): Hold them!

VOICE OFF STAGE: Lay down your arms!

VOICES: No! No!

CYRANO (*to* DE GUICHE): Sir, you have proved yourself— Take care of her.

DE GUICHE (*hurries to* ROXANE *and takes her up in his arms*): As you will—we can win, if you hold on
A little longer—

CYRANO: Good! (*calls out to* ROXANE, *as she is carried away, fainting, by* DE GUICHE *and* RAGUENEAU) Adieu, Roxane!

(*Tumult, outcries. Several* CADETS *come back wounded and fall on the stage.* CYRANO, *rushing to the fight, is stopped on the crest of the parapet by* CARBON, *covered with blood.*)

CARBON: We are breaking—I am twice wounded—

CYRANO (*shouts to the* GASCONS):   Hardi!
Reculez pas, Drollos!
(*to* CARBON, *holding him up*) So—never fear!
I have two deaths to avenge now—Christian's
And my own! (*They come down;* CYRANO *takes from him the lance with* ROXANE'S *handkerchief still fastened to it.*)
Float, little banner, with her name!
(*He plants it on the parapet; then shouts to the* CADETS.)
Toumbé dessus! Escrasas lous!
(*to the fifer*) Your fife!
Music!

(*Fife plays. The wounded drag themselves to their feet. Other* CADETS *scramble over the parapet and group themselves around* CYRANO *and his tiny flag. The coach is filled and covered with men, bristling with muskets, transformed into a redoubt.*)

A CADET (*reels backward over the wall, still fighting; shouts*): They are climbing over!—(*and falls dead*)

CYRANO: Very good—
Let them come!— A salute now—
(*The parapet is crowned for an instant with a rank of enemies. The imperial banner of Spain is raised aloft.*)
Fire! (*general volley*)

VOICE (*among the ranks of the enemy*): Fire! (*Murderous counterfire; the* CADETS *fall on every side.*)

A SPANISH OFFICER (*uncovers*): Who are these men who are so fond of death?

CYRANO (*erect amid the hail of bullets, declaims*): The Cadets of Gascoyne, the defenders

Of Carbon de Castel-Jaloux—
Free fighters, free lovers, free spenders— (*He rushes forward, followed by a few survivors.*)
The Cadets of Gascoyne . . . (*The rest is lost in the din
of battle.*)

ACT V

(CYRANO'S GAZETTE)

(*Fifteen years later, in 1655: the park of the convent occupied by the Ladies of the Cross, at Paris.*

*Magnificent foliage. To the left, the house upon a broad
terrace at the head of a flight of steps, with several doors
opening upon the terrace. In the center of the scene an enormous tree alone in the center of a little open space. Toward
the right, in the foreground, among boxwood bushes, a semi-
circular bench of stone.*

*All the way across the background of the scene, an avenue
overarched by the chestnut trees, leading to the door of a
chapel on the right, just visible among the branches of the
trees. Beyond the double curtain of the trees, we catch a
glimpse of bright lawns and shaded walks, masses of shrubbery; the perspective of the park; the sky.*

*A little side door of the chapel opens upon a colonnade,
garlanded with autumnal vines, and disappearing on the right
behind the box-trees.*

*It is late October. Above the still living green of the turf
all the foliage is red and yellow and brown. The evergreen
masses of box and yew stand out darkly against this autumnal coloring. A heap of dead leaves under every tree. The
leaves are falling everywhere. They rustle underfoot along the
walks; the terrace and the bench are half covered with them.*

*Before the bench on the right, on the side toward the tree,
is placed a tall embroidery frame and beside it a little chair.
Baskets filled with skeins of many-colored silks and balls of
wool. Tapestry unfinished on the frame.*

*At the curtain rise the nuns are coming and going across
the park; several of them are seated on the bench around
MOTHER MARGUÉRITE DE JÉSUS. The leaves are falling.*)

SISTER MARTHE (*to* MOTHER MARGUÉRITE):
Sister Claire has been looking in the glass
At her new cap; twice!

    MOTHER MARGUÉRITE (*to* SISTER CLAIRE): It is very plain;
Very.

    SISTER CLAIRE: And Sister Marthe stole a plum
Out of the tart this morning!

    MOTHER MARGUÉRITE (*to* SISTER MARTHE): That was
      wrong;
Very wrong.

    SISTER CLAIRE: Oh, but such a little look!

    SISTER MARTHE: Such a little plum!

    MOTHER MARGUÉRITE (*severely*): I shall tell Monsieur
De Cyrano, this evening.

    SISTER CLAIRE: No! Oh, no!—
He will make fun of us.

    SISTER MARTHE: He will say nuns
Are so gay!

    SISTER CLAIRE: And so greedy!

    MOTHER MARGUÉRITE (*smiling*):   And so good . . .

    SISTER CLAIRE: It must be ten years, Mother Marguérite,
That he has come here every Saturday,
Is it not?

    MOTHER MARGUÉRITE: More than ten years; ever since
His cousin came to live among us here—
Her worldly weeds among our linen veils,
Her widowhood and our virginity—
Like a black dove among white doves.

    SISTER MARTHE: No one
Else ever turns that happy sorrow of hers
Into a smile.

    ALL THE NUNS: He is such fun!—He makes us
Almost laugh!—And he teases everyone—
And pleases everyone— And we all love him—
And he likes our cake, too—

    SISTER MARTHE: I am afraid
He is not a good Catholic.

    SISTER CLAIRE: Some day
We shall convert him.

    THE NUNS: Yes—yes!

    MOTHER MARGUÉRITE: Let him be;
I forbid you to worry him. Perhaps
He might stop coming here.

    SISTER MARTHE: But . . . God?

    MOTHER MARGUÉRITE: You need not

Be afraid. God knows all about him.

SISTER MARTHE: Yes . . .

But every Saturday he says to me,
Just as if he were proud of it: "Well, Sister,
I ate meat yesterday!"

MOTHER MARGUÉRITE: He tells you so?

The last time he said that, he had not eaten
Anything, for two days.

SISTER MARTHE: Mother!—

MOTHER MARGUÉRITE: He is poor;
Very poor.

SISTER MARTHE: Who said so?

MOTHER MARGUÉRITE: Monsieur Le Bret.

SISTER MARTHE: Why does not someone help him?

MOTHER MARGUÉRITE: He would be
Angry; very angry . . .

(*Between the trees up stage,* ROXANE *appears, all in black,
with a widow's cap and long veils.* DE GUICHE, *magnificently
grown old, walks beside her. They move slowly.* MOTHER
MARGUÉRITE *rises.*)

Let us go in—

Madame Madeleine has a visitor.

SISTER MARTHE (*to* SISTER CLAIRE): The Duc de Gram-
mont, is it not? The Marshal?

SISTER CLAIRE (*looks toward* DE GUICHE): I think so—yes.

SISTER MARTHE: He has not been to see her

For months—

THE NUNS: He is busy—the Court!—the Camp!—

SISTER CLAIRE: The world! . . .

(*They go out.* DE GUICHE *and* ROXANE *come down in silence, and stop near the embroidery frame. Pause.*)

DE GUICHE: And you remain here, wasting all that gold—
Forever in mourning?

ROXANE: Forever.

DE GUICHE: And still faithful?

ROXANE: And still faithful . . .

DE GUICHE (*after a pause*): Have you forgiven me?

ROXANE (*simply, looking up at the cross of the convent*):
I am here (*another pause*).

DE GUICHE: Was Christian . . . all that?

ROXANE: If you knew him.

DE GUICHE: Ah? We were not precisely . . . intimate . . .
And his last letter—always at your heart?

ROXANE: It hangs here, like a holy reliquary.

DE GUICHE: Dead—and you love him still!

ROXANE: Sometimes I think
He has not altogether died; our hearts
Meet, and his love flows all around me, living.
DE GUICHE (*after another pause*): You see Cyrano often?
ROXANE: Every week.
My old friend takes the place of my Gazette,
Brings me all the news. Every Saturday,
Under that tree where you are now, his chair
Stands, if the day be fine. I wait for him,
Embroidering; the hour strikes; then I hear,
(I need not turn to look!) at the last stroke,
His cane tapping the steps. He laughs at me
For my eternal needlework. He tells
The story of the past week—(LE BRET *appears on the steps.*)
There's Le Bret!—
(LE BRET *approaches.*) How is it with our friend?
    LE BRET: Badly.
    DE GUICHE: Indeed?
    ROXANE (*to* DE GUICHE): Oh, he exaggerates!
    LE BRET: Just as I said—
Loneliness, misery—I told him so!—
His satires make a host of enemies—
He attacks the false nobles, the false saints,
The false heroes, the false artists—in short,
Everyone!
    ROXANE: But they fear that sword of his—
No one dare touch him!
    DE GUICHE (*with a shrug*):   H'm—that may be so.
    LE BRET: It is not violence I fear for him,
But solitude—poverty—old gray December,
Stealing on wolf's feet, with a wolf's green eyes,
Into his darkening room. Those bravoes yet
May strike our Swordsman down! Every day now,
He draws his belt up one hole; his poor nose
Looks like old ivory; he has one coat
Left—his old black serge.
    DE GUICHE: That is nothing strange
In this world! No, you need not pity him
Overmuch.
    LE BRET (*with a bitter smile*): My lord Marshal! . . .
    DE GUICHE: I say, do not
Pity him overmuch. He lives his life,
His own life, his own way—thought, word, and deed
Free!
    LE BRET (*as before*): My lord Duke! . . .

DE GUICHE (*haughtily*):   Yes, I know—I have all;
He has nothing. Nevertheless, today
I should be proud to shake his hand . . . (*saluting* ROXANE)
                                                            Adieu.

ROXANE: I will go with you.

(DE GUICHE *salutes* LE BRET, *and turns with* ROXANE *toward
the steps.*)

DE GUICHE (*pauses on the steps, as she climbs*): Yes—I
     envy him
Now and then . . .
                              Do you know, when a man wins
Everything in this world, when he succeeds
Too much—he feels, having done nothing wrong
Especially, Heaven knows!—he feels somehow
A thousand small displeasures with himself,
Whose whole sum is not quite Remorse, but rather
A sort of vague disgust . . . The ducal robes
Mounting up, step by step, to pride and power,
Somewhere among their folds draw after them
A rustle of dry illusions, vain regrets,
As your veil, up the stairs here, draws along
The whisper of dead leaves.

ROXANE (*ironical*): The sentiment
Does you honor.

DE GUICHE: Oh, yes . . . (*pausing suddenly*)
                              Monsieur Le Bret!—
(*to* ROXANE) You pardon us?—(*He goes to* LE BRET, *and
speaks in a low tone.*) One moment— It is true
That no one dares attack your friend. Some people
Dislike him, none the less. The other day
At Court, such a one said to me: "This man
Cyrano may die—accidentally."

LE BRET (*coldly*): Thank you.

DE GUICHE: You may thank me. Keep him at home
All you can. Tell him to be careful.

LE BRET (*shaking his hands to heaven*):   Careful!—
He is coming here. I'll warn him—yes, but! . . .

ROXANE (*still on the steps, to a* NUN *who approaches her*):
                                                            Here
I am—what is it?

THE NUN: Madame, Ragueneau
Wishes to see you.

ROXANE: Bring him here.

(*to* LE BRET *and* DE GUICHE)   He comes
For sympathy—having been first of all

A Poet, he became since then, in turn,
A Singer—
  LE BRET: Bathhouse keeper—
  ROXANE: Sacristan—
  LE BRET: Actor—
  ROXANE: Hairdresser—
  LE BRET: Music master—
  ROXANE: Now,
Today—
  RAGUENEAU (*enters hurriedly*): Madame!—
(*He sees* LE BRET.) Monsieur!—
  ROXANE (*smiling*):   First tell your troubles
To Le Bret for a moment.
  RAGUENEAU: But Madame—
  (*She goes out, with* DE GUICHE, *not hearing him.* RAGUE-
NEAU *comes to* LE BRET.)
After all, I had rather— You are here—
She need not know so soon— I went to see him
Just now— Our friend— As I came near his door,
I saw him coming out. I hurried on
To join him. At the corner of the street,
As he passed— Could it be an accident?—
I wonder!—At the window overhead,
A lackey with a heavy log of wood
Let it fall—
  LE BRET: Cyrano!
  RAGUENEAU: I ran to him—
  LE BRET: God! The cowards!
  RAGUENEAU: I found him lying there—
A great hole in his head—
  LE BRET: Is he alive?
  RAGUENEAU: Alive—yes. But . . . I had to carry him
Up to his room—Dieu! Have you seen his room?—
  LE BRET: Is he suffering?
  RAGUENEAU: No; unconscious.
  LE BRET: Did you
Call a doctor?
  RAGUENEAU: One came—for charity.
  LE BRET: Poor Cyrano!—We must not tell Roxane
All at once . . . Did the doctor say?—
  RAGUENEAU: He said
Fever, and lesions of the— I forget
Those long names— Ah, if you had seen him there,
His head all white bandages!—Let us go
Quickly—there is no one to care for him—

All alone— If he tries to raise his head,
He may die!

LE BRET (*draws him away to the right*):
                              This way— It is shorter—through
The chapel—

ROXANE (*appears on the stairway, and calls to* LE BRET *as
he is going out by the colonnade which leads to the small
door of the chapel*): Monsieur Le Bret!—(LE BRET *and*
RAGUENEAU *rush off without hearing.*)   Running away
When I call to him? Poor dear Ragueneau
Must have been very tragic!
(*She comes slowly down the stair, toward the tree.*)
                                        What a day! . . .

Something in these bright Autumn afternoons
Happy and yet regretful—an old sorrow
Smiling . . . as though poor little April dried
Her tears long ago—and remembered . . . (*She sits down at
her work; two* NUNS *come out of the house carrying a great
chair and set it under the tree.*)   Ah—
The old chair, for my old friend!—

SISTER MARTHE: The best one
In our best parlor!—

ROXANE: Thank you, Sister—(*The* NUNS *withdraw.*)
                                                    There—

(*She begins embroidering; the clock strikes.*)
The hour!—He will be coming now—my silks—
All done striking? He never was so late
Before! The sister at the door—my thimble . . .
Here it is—she must be exhorting him
To repent all his sins . . . (*a pause*) He ought to be
Converted, by this time— Another leaf—(*A dead leaf falls
on her work; she brushes it away.*)
Certainly nothing could—my scissors—ever
Keep him away—

A NUN (*appears on the steps*): Monsieur de Bergerac.

ROXANE (*without turning*): What was I saying? . . . Hard,
    sometimes, to match
These faded colors! . . .

(*While she goes on working,* CYRANO *appears at the top of
the steps, very pale, his hat drawn over his eyes. The* NUN
*who has brought him in goes away. He begins to descend the
steps leaning on his cane, and holding himself on his feet
only by an evident effort.* ROXANE *turns to him, with a tone
of friendly banter.*)

                              After fourteen years,

Late—for the first time!

CYRANO (*reaches the chair, and sinks into it; his gay tone contrasting with his tortured face*): Yes, yes—maddening! I was detained by—

ROXANE: Well?

CYRANO: A visitor.
Most unexpected.

ROXANE (*carelessly, still sewing*): Was your visitor Tiresome?

CYRANO: Why, hardly that—inopportune, Let us say—an old friend of mine—at least A very old acquaintance.

ROXANE: Did you tell him To go away?

CYRANO: For the time being, yes.
I said: "Excuse me—this is Saturday—
I have a previous engagement, one
I cannot miss, even for you— Come back
An hour from now."

ROXANE: Your friend will have to wait;
I shall not let you go till dark.

CYRANO (*very gently*): Perhaps
A little before dark, I must go . . .
(*He leans back in the chair, and closes his eyes.* SISTER MARTHE *crosses above the stairway.* ROXANE *sees her, motions her to wait, then turns to* CYRANO.)

ROXANE: Look—
Somebody waiting to be teased.

CYRANO (*quickly, opens his eyes*): Of course!
(*in a big, comic voice*) Sister, approach!
(SISTER MARTHE *glides toward him.*) Beautiful downcast
        eyes!—
So shy—

SISTER MARTHE (*looks up, smiling*): You—(*She sees his face.*) Oh!—

CYRANO (*indicates* ROXANE): Sh!—Careful!
(*resumes his burlesque tone*)   Yesterday,
I ate meat again!

SISTER MARTHE: Yes, I know. (*aside*) That is why
He looks so pale . . .
(*to him: low and quickly*) In the refectory,
Before you go—come to me there—

                                        I'll make you
A great bowl of hot soup—will you come?

CYRANO (*boisterously*): Ah—

Will I come!

SISTER MARTHE: You are quite reasonable
Today!

ROXANE: Has she converted you?

SISTER MARTHE: Oh, no—
Not for the world!—

CYRANO: Why, now I think of it,
That is so— You, bursting with holiness,
And yet you never preach! Astonishing
I call it . . . (*with burlesque ferocity*) Ah—now I'll as-
      tonish you—
I am going to—(*with the air of seeking for a good joke and
finding it*)—let you pray for me
Tonight, at vespers!

ROXANE: Aha!

CYRANO: Look at her—
Absolutely struck dumb!

SISTER MARTHE (*gently*): I did not wait
For you to say I might. (*She goes out.*)

CYRANO (*returns to* ROXANE, *who is bending over her
work*): Now, may the devil
Admire me, if I ever hope to see
The end of that embroidery!

ROXANE (*smiling*): I thought
It was time you said that.
      (*A breath of wind causes a few leaves to fall.*)

CYRANO: The leaves—

ROXANE (*raises her head and looks away through the
trees*): What color—
Perfect Venetian red! Look at them fall.

CYRANO: Yes—they know how to die. A little way
From the branch to the earth, a little fear
Of mingling with the common dust—and yet
They go down gracefully—a fall that seems
Like flying!

ROXANE: Melancholy—you?

CYRANO: Why, no,
Roxane!

ROXANE: Then let the leaves fall. Tell me now
The Court news—my gazette!

CYRANO: Let me see—

ROXANE: Ah!

CYRANO (*more and more pale, struggling against pain*):
Saturday, the nineteenth; the King fell ill,
After eight helpings of grape marmalade.

His malady was brought before the court,
Found guilty of high treason; whereupon
His Majesty revived. The royal pulse
Is now normal. Sunday, the twentieth:
The Queen gave a grand ball, at which they burned
Seven hundred and sixty-three wax candles. Note:
They say our troops have been victorious
In Austria. Later: Three sorcerers
Have been hung. Special post: The little dog
Of Madame d'Athis was obliged to take
Four pills before—

ROXANE: Monsieur de Bergerac,
Will you kindly be quiet!

CYRANO: Monday . . . nothing.
Lygdamire has a new lover.

ROXANE: Oh!

CYRANO (*his face more and more altered*): Tuesday,
The twenty-second: All the Court has gone
To Fontainebleau. Wednesday: The Comte de Fiesque
Spoke to Madame de Montglat; she said No.
Thursday: Mancini was the Queen of France
Or—very nearly! Friday: La Montglat
Said Yes. Saturday, twenty-sixth. . . . (*His eyes close; his
head sinks back; silence.*)

ROXANE (*surprised at not hearing any more, turns, looks
at him, and rises, frightened*): He has fainted—
(*She runs to him, crying out.*) Cyrano!

CYRANO (*opens his eyes*): What . . . What is it? . . . (*He
sees* ROXANE *leaning over him, and quickly pulls his hat down
over his head and leans back away from her in the chair.*)
No—oh no—
It is nothing—truly!

ROXANE: But—

CYRANO: My old wound—
At Arras—sometimes—you know. . . .

ROXANE: My poor friend!

CYRANO: Oh it is nothing; it will soon be gone. . . . (*forcing a smile*) There! It is gone!

ROXANE (*standing close to him*):
We all have our old wounds—
I have mine—here . . .
(*her hand at her breast*) under this faded scrap
Of writing. . . . It is hard to read now—all
But the blood—and the tears. . . .
(*Twilight begins to fall.*)

CYRANO: His letter! . . . Did you
Not promise me that some day . . . that some day . . .
You would let me read it?
ROXANE: His letter?—You . . .
You wish—
CYRANO: I do wish it—today.
ROXANE (*gives him the little silken bag from around her
neck*) Here. . . .
CYRANO: May I . . . open it?
ROXANE: Open it, and read. (*She goes back to her work,
folds it again, rearranges her silks.*)
CYRANO (*unfolds the letter; reads*): "Farewell Roxane, be-
cause today I die—"
ROXANE (*looks up, surprised*): Aloud?
CYRANO (*reads*): "I know that it will be today,
My own dearly beloved—and my heart
Still so heavy with love I have not told,
And I die without telling you! No more
Shall my eyes drink the sight of you like wine,
Never more, with a look that is a kiss,
Follow the sweet grace of you—"
ROXANE: How you read it—
His letter!
CYRANO (*continues*): "I remember now the way
You have, of pushing back a lock of hair
With one hand, from your forehead—and my heart
Cries out—"
ROXANE: His letter . . . and you read it so . . .
(*The darkness increases imperceptibly.*)
CYRANO: "Cries out and keeps crying: 'Farewell, my dear,
My dearest—' "
ROXANE: In a voice. . . .
CYRANO: "—My own heart's own,
My own treasure—"
ROXANE (*dreamily*): In such a voice. . . .
CYRANO: —"My love—"
ROXANE: —As I remember hearing . . . (*She trembles.*)
                              —long ago. . . .
(*She comes near him, softly, without his seeing her; passes
the chair, leans over silently, looking at the letter. The dark-
ness increases.*)
CYRANO: "—I am never away from you. Even now,
I shall not leave you. In another world,
I shall be still that one who loves you, loves you
Beyond measure, beyond—"

ROXANE (*lays her hand on his shoulder*):

How can you read
Now? It is dark. . . . (*He starts, turns, and sees her there
close to him—a little movement of surprise, almost of fear;
then he bows his head; a long pause; then in the twilight now
completely fallen, she says very softly, clasping her hands*)

And all these fourteen years,
He has been the old friend, who came to me
To be amusing.

CYRANO: Roxane!—

ROXANE: It was you.

CYRANO: No, no, Roxane, no!

ROXANE: And I might have known,
Every time that I heard you speak my name! . . .

CYRANO: No— It was not I—

ROXANE: It was . . . you!

CYRANO: I swear—

ROXANE: I understand everything now: The letters—
That was you . . .

CYRANO: No!

ROXANE: And the dear, foolish words—
That was you. . . .

CYRANO: No!

ROXANE: And the voice . . . in the dark. . . .
That was . . . you!

CYRANO: On my honor—

ROXANE: And . . . the Soul!—
That was all you.

CYRANO: I never loved you—

ROXANE: Yes,
You loved me.

CYRANO (*desperately*): No— He loved you—

ROXANE: Even now,
You love me!

CYRANO (*his voice weakens*): No!

ROXANE (*smiling*):   And why . . . so great a "No"?

CYRANO: No, no, my own dear love, I love you not! . . .
(*Pause.*)

ROXANE: How many things have died . . . and are new-
born! . . .
Why were you silent for so many years,
All the while, every night and every day,
He gave me nothing—you knew that— You knew
Here, in this letter lying on my breast,
Your tears— You knew they were your tears—

CYRANO (*holds the letter out to her*):   The blood
Was his.

ROXANE: Why do you break that silence now,
Today?

CYRANO: Why? Oh, because—

(LE BRET *and* RAGUENEAU *enter, running.*)

LE BRET: What recklessness—
I knew it! He is here!

CYRANO (*smiling, and trying to rise*): Well? Here I am!

RAGUENEAU: He has killed himself, Madame, coming here!

ROXANE: He— Oh God. . . . And that faintness . . . was
that—

CYRANO: No,
Nothing! I did not finish my Gazette—
Saturday, twenty-sixth: An hour or so
Before dinner, Monsieur de Bergerac
Died, foully murdered. (*He uncovers his head, and shows it
swathed in bandages.*)

ROXANE: Oh, what does he mean?—
Cyrano!— What have they done to you?—

CYRANO: "Struck down
By the sword of a hero, let me fall—
Steel in my heart, and laughter on my lips!"
Yes, I said that once. How Fate loves a jest!—
Behold me ambushed—taken in the rear—
My battlefield a gutter—my noble foe
A lackey, with a log of wood! . . . It seems
Too logical— I have missed everything,
Even my death!

RAGUENEAU (*breaks down*): Ah, monsieur!—

CYRANO: Ragueneau,
Stop blubbering! (*takes his hand*)
      What are you writing nowadays,
Old poet?

RAGUENEAU (*through his tears*): I am not a poet now;
I snuff the—light the candles—for Molière!

CYRANO: Oh—Molière!

RAGUENEAU: Yes, but I am leaving him
Tomorrow. Yesterday they played *Scapin*—
He has stolen your scene—

LE BRET: The whole scene—word for word!

RAGUENEAU: Yes: "What the devil was he doing there"—
That one!

LE BRET (*furious*): And Molière stole it all from you—
Bodily!—

CYRANO: Bah— He showed good taste. . . .
(*to* RAGUENEAU) The scene
Went well? . . .
RAGUENEAU: Ah, monsieur, they laughed—and laughed—
How they did laugh!
CYRANO: Yes—that has been my life. . . .
Do you remember that night Christian spoke
Under your window? It was always so!
While I stood in the darkness underneath,
Others climbed up to win the applause—the kiss!—
Well—that seems only justice— I still say,
Even now, on the threshold of my tomb—
"Molière has genius—Christian had good looks—"
(*The chapel bell is ringing. Along the avenue of trees above the stairway, the* NUNS *pass in procession to their prayers.*)
They are going to pray now; there is the bell.
ROXANE (*raises herself and calls to them*): Sister!
Sister!—
CYRANO (*holding on to her hand*): No,—do not go away—
I may not still be here when you return. . . .
(*The* NUNS *have gone into the chapel. The organ begins to play.*)
A little harmony is all I need—
Listen. . . .
ROXANE: You shall not die! I love you!—
CYRANO: No—
That is not in the story! You remember
When Beauty said "I love you" to the Beast
That was a fairy prince, his ugliness
Changed and dissolved, like magic. . . . But you see
I am still the same.
ROXANE: And I—I have done
This to you! All my fault—mine!
CYRANO: You? Why no,
On the contrary! I had never known
Womanhood and its sweetness but for you.
My mother did not love to look at me—
I never had a sister— Later on,
I feared the mistress with a mockery
Behind her smile. But you—because of you
I have had one friend not quite all a friend—
Across my life, one whispering silken gown! . . .
LE BRET (*points to the rising moon which begins to shine down between the trees*): Your other friend is looking at you.

CYRANO (*smiling at the moon*):   I see. . . .
ROXANE: I never loved but one man in my life,
And I have lost him—twice. . . .
CYRANO: Le Bret—I shall be up there presently
In the moon—without having to invent
Any flying machines!
ROXANE: What are you saying? . . .
CYRANO: The moon—yes, that would be the place for me—
My kind of paradise! I shall find there
Those other souls who should be friends of mine—
Socrates—Galileo—
LE BRET (*revolting*): No! No! No!
It is too idiotic—too unfair—
Such a friend—such a poet—such a man
To die so—to die so!
CYRANO (*affectionately*):   There goes Le Bret,
Growling!
LE BRET (*breaks down*): My friend!—
CYRANO (*half raises himself, his eye wanders*):
                    The Cadets of Gascoyne,
The Defenders. . . . The elementary mass—
Ah—there's the point! Now, then . . .
LE BRET: Delirious—
And all that learning—
CYRANO: On the other hand,
We have Copernicus—
ROXANE: Oh!
CYRANO (*more and more delirious*): "Very well,
But what the devil was he doing there?—
What the devil was he doing there, up there?" . . .
(*he declaims*)
    Philosopher and scientist,
        Poet, musician, duelist—
            He flew high, and fell back again!
    A pretty wit—whose like we lack—
    A lover . . . not like other men. . . .
        Here lies Hercule-Savinien
    De Cyrano de Bergerac
        Who was all things—and all in vain!
Well, I must go—pardon— I cannot stay!
My moonbeam comes to carry me away. . . .
(*He falls back into the chair, half fainting; the sobbing of*
ROXANE *recalls him to reality; gradually his mind comes back
to him; he looks at her, stroking the veil that hides her hair.*)
I would not have you mourn any the less

That good, brave, noble Christian; but perhaps—
I ask you only this—when the great cold
Gathers around my bones, that you may give
A double meaning to your widow's weeds
And the tears you let fall for him may be
For a little—my tears. . . .

    ROXANE (*sobbing*): Oh, my love! . . .

    CYRANO (*suddenly shaken as with a fever fit, he raises himself erect and pushes her away*):   —Not here!—
Not lying down! . . . (*They spring forward to help him; he motions them back.*)   Let no one help me—no one!—
Only the tree. . . . (*He sets his back against the trunk; pause.*) It is coming . . . I feel
Already shod with marble . . . gloved with lead . . .
(*joyously*) Let the old fellow come now! He shall find me
On my feet—sword in hand—(*draws his sword*).

    LE BRET: Cyrano!—

    ROXANE (*half fainting*): Oh,
Cyrano!

    CYRANO: I can see him there—he grins—
He is looking at my nose—that skeleton
—What's that you say? Hopeless?—Why, very well!—
But a man does not fight merely to win!
No—no—better to know one fights in vain! . . .
You there— Who are you? A hundred against one—
I know them now, my ancient enemies—
(*He lunges at the empty air.*) Falsehood! . . . There! There!
Prejudice— Compromise— Cowardice—(*thrusting*) What's
that? No! Surrender? No!
Never—never! . . .

               Ah, you too, Vanity!
I knew you would overthrow me in the end—
No! I fight on! I fight on! I fight on!
(*He swings the blade in great circles, then pauses, gasping; when he speaks again, it is in another tone.*)
Yes, all my laurels you have riven away
And all my roses; yet in spite of you,
There is one crown I bear away with me,
And tonight, when I enter before God,
My salute shall sweep all the stars away
From the blue threshold! One thing without stain,
Unspotted from the world, in spite of doom
Mine own!—(*He springs forward, his sword aloft.*)
And that is . . . (*The sword escapes from his hand; he totters and falls into the arms of* LE BRET *and* RAGUENEAU.)

ROXANE (*bends over him and kisses him on the forehead*):
—That is . . .

CYRANO (*opens his eyes and smiles up at her*):

                     My white plume. . . .

Thornton Wilder:

Our Town

Thornton Wilder (1897–   ) was born in Madison, Wisconsin, received his education in Madison and California. He attended Oberlin College and was later graduated from Yale in 1920, having interrupted his studies to serve in the Coast Artillery during World War I. He first achieved fame as a novelist, receiving his first Pulitzer Prize in 1928 for The Bridge of San Luis Rey. *Both* Our Town *(1938) and* The Skin of Our Teeth *(1942) won subsequent Pulitzer prizes, and his most recent novel,* The Eighth Day *(1967), received the National Book Award. Mr. Wilder served in the Air Force during World War II, taught at Lawrenceville Academy, the University of Chicago, and Harvard. He has lived the greater part of his life in and around New Haven, Connecticut.*

Although *Our Town* was written little more than thirty years ago, it is already an acknowledged classic and perhaps the most widely read play in America. The danger of a literary work's achieving the status of a classic lies in the possibility of its being read passively and uncritically. We lose sight of its limitations and, even worse, of its strengths.

For example does Wilder exert much effort to individualize his characters? Does he "flesh them out," so to speak? Or are they essentially stereotypes who fulfill their function in the playwright's overall design? Perhaps Wilder's comment, through the Stage Manager, provides some answers:

[The play is designed so that] people a thousand years from now'll know a few simple facts about us . . . the way we were in the provinces north of New York at the beginning of the twentieth century . . . in our growing up and in our marrying and in our living and in our dying.

But the difference between the artist and the technician

is that while each can deal in stereotypes, the artist—as though in spite of himself—transforms a type into a credible human being. One might see *Our Town* a dozen times and never fail, at least once in each act, to be so overpowered by emotion that tears come. Which is to say that while we may live remote from a rural New England town of the 1900s, *Our Town* somehow succeeds in evoking those central life experiences—the discovery of life's limitless possibilities, its joys and its excitements.

But the ultimate impact of the play derives from its mysterious essence that each of us must find for himself. For some, *Our Town* provides a glimpse into what Virgil described as *lacrimae rerum,* the tears of things. That is, as we grow older and gain intimations of the frailty and mortality of ourselves and of those we love, we discover—like Emily and George—the essential sadness inherent in human existence.

Aware of its underlying sadness, however, we should most of all take pleasure in *Our Town's* abounding humor, its briskness and common sense—qualities epitomized in Mrs. Webb's widely quoted response to Emily's tremulous question: "Mama . . am I pretty?" "Emily . . . now stop it. You're pretty enough for all normal purposes . . ."

Our Town

To Alexander Woollcott
of Castleton Township, Rutland County, Vermont

Characters

STAGE MANAGER.
DR. GIBBS.
JOE CROWELL.
HOWIE NEWSOME.
MRS. GIBBS.
MRS. WEBB.
GEORGE GIBBS.
REBECCA GIBBS.
WALLY WEBB.
EMILY WEBB.
PROFESSOR WILLARD.
MR. WEBB.
WOMAN IN THE BALCONY.
MAN IN THE AUDITORIUM.
LADY IN THE BOX.
SIMON STIMSON.
MRS. SOAMES.
CONSTABLE WARREN.
SI CROWELL.
THREE BASEBALL PLAYERS.
SAM CRAIG.
JOE STODDARD.

The entire play takes place in Grover's Corners, New Hampshire.

ACT I

STAGE MANAGER: This play is called *Our Town*. It was
written by Thornton Wilder; produced and directed by A.
. . . (or: produced by A. . . .; directed by B. . . .). In it
you will see Miss C. . . .; Miss D. . . .; Miss E. . . .; and
Mr. F. . . .; Mr. G. . . .; Mr. H. . . .; and many others. The
name of the town is Grover's Corners, New Hampshire—
just across the Massachusetts line: latitude 42 degrees 40
minutes; longitude 70 degrees 37 minutes. The First Act
shows a day in our town. The day is May 7, 1901. The time
is just before dawn. (*A rooster crows.*)

The sky is beginning to show some streaks of light over in
the East there, behind our mount'in.

The morning star always gets wonderful bright the minute
before it has to go—doesn't it? (*He stares at it for a moment,*
then goes upstage.)

Well, I'd better show you how our town lies. Up here
(*that is: parallel with the back wall*) is Main Street. Way
back there is the railway station: tracks go that way. Polish

Town's across the tracks, and some Canuck families (*toward the left*).

Over there is the Congregational Church; across the street's the Presbyterian.

Methodist and Unitarian are over there.

Baptist is down in the holla' by the river.

Catholic Church is over beyond the tracks.

Here's the Town Hall and Post Office combined; jail's in the basement.

Bryan once made a speech from these very steps here.

Along here's a row of stores. Hitching posts and horse blocks in front of them. First automobile's going to come along in about five years—belonged to Banker Cartwright, our richest citizen . . . lives in the big white house up on the hill.

Here's the grocery store and here's Mr. Morgan's drugstore. Most everybody in town manages to look into those two stores once a day.

Public School's over yonder. High School's still farther over. Quarter of nine mornings, noontimes, and three o'clock afternoons, the hull town can hear the yelling and screaming from those schoolyards. (*He approaches the table and chairs downstage right.*)

This is our doctor's house,—Doc Gibbs'. This is the back door. (*Two arched trellises, covered with vines and flowers, are pushed out, one by each proscenium pillar.*)

There's some scenery for those who think they have to have scenery.

This is Mrs. Gibbs' garden. Corn . . . peas . . . beans . . . hollyhocks . . . heliotrope . . . and a lot of burdock (*crosses the stage*).

In those days our newspaper come out twice a week—the Grover's Corners *Sentinel*—and this is Editor Webb's house.

And this is Mrs. Webb's garden.

Just like Mrs. Gibbs', only it's got a lot of sunflowers, too. (*He looks upward, center stage.*)

Right here . . . 's a big butternut tree. (*He returns to his place by the right proscenium pillar and looks at the audience for a minute.*)

Nice town, y'know what I mean?

Nobody very remarkable ever come out of it, s'far as we know.

The earliest tombstones in the cemetery up there on the mountain say 1670–1680—they're Grovers and Cartwrights and Gibbses and Herseys—same as are around here now.

Well, as I said: it's about dawn.

The only lights on in town are in a cottage over by the tracks where a Polish mother's just had twins. And in the Joe Crowell house, where Joe Junior's getting up so as to deliver the paper. And in the depot, where Shorty Hawkins is gettin' ready to flag the 5:45 for Boston. (*A train whistle is heard. The* STAGE MANAGER *takes out his watch and nods.*)

Naturally, out in the country—all around—there've been lights on for some time, what with milkin's and so on. But town people sleep late.

So—another day's begun.

There's Doc Gibbs comin' down Main Street now, comin' back from that baby case. And here's his wife comin' downstairs to get breakfast. (MRS. GIBBS, *a plump, pleasant woman in the middle thirties, comes "downstairs" right. She pulls up an imaginary window shade in her kitchen and starts to make a fire in her stove.*)

Doc Gibbs died in 1930. The new hospital's named after him.

Mrs. Gibbs died first—long time ago, in fact. She went out to visit her daughter, Rebecca, who married an insurance man in Canton, Ohio, and died there—pneumonia—but her body was brought back here. She's up in the cemetery there now—in with a whole mess of Gibbses and Herseys—she was Julia Hersey 'fore she married Doc Gibbs in the Congregational Church over there.

In our town we like to know the facts about everybody.

There's Mrs. Webb, coming downstairs to get her breakfast, too.—That's Doc Gibbs. Got that call at half past one this morning. And there comes Joe Crowell, Jr., delivering Mr. Webb's *Sentinel*.

(DR. GIBBS *has been coming along Main Street from the left. At the point where he would turn to approach his house, he stops, sets down his—imaginary—black bag, takes off his hat, and rubs his face with fatigue, using an enormous handkerchief.*

MRS. WEBB, *a thin, serious, crisp woman, has entered her kitchen, left, tying on an apron. She goes through the motions of putting wood into a stove, lighting it, and preparing breakfast.*

Suddenly, JOE CROWELL, JR., *eleven, starts down Main Street from the right, hurling imaginary newspapers into doorways.*)

JOE CROWELL, JR.: Morning, Doc Gibbs.

DR. GIBBS: Morning, Joe.

JOE CROWELL, JR.: Somebody been sick, Doc?

DR. GIBBS: No. Just some twins born over in Polish Town.

JOE CROWELL, JR.: Do you want your paper now?

DR. GIBBS: Yes, I'll take it.—Anything serious goin' on in the world since Wednesday?

JOE CROWELL, JR.: Yessir. My schoolteacher, Miss Foster, 's getting married to a fella over in Concord.

DR. GIBBS: I declare.—How do you boys feel about that?

JOE CROWELL, JR.: Well, of course, it's none of my business—but I think if a person starts out to be a teacher, she ought to stay one.

DR. GIBBS: How's your knee, Joe?

JOE CROWELL, JR.: Fine, Doc, I never think about it at all. Only like you said, it always tells me when it's going to rain.

DR. GIBBS: What's it telling you today? Goin' to rain?

JOE CROWELL, JR.: No, sir.

DR. GIBBS: Sure?

JOE CROWELL, JR.: Yessir.

DR. GIBBS: Knee ever make a mistake?

JOE CROWELL, JR.: No, sir.

(JOE *goes off.* DR. GIBBS *stands reading his paper.*)

STAGE MANAGER: Want to tell you something about that boy Joe Crowell there. Joe was awful bright—graduated from high school here, head of his class. So he got a scholarship to Massachusetts Tech. Graduated head of his class there, too. It was all wrote up in the Boston paper at the time. Goin' to be a great engineer, Joe was. But the war broke out and he died in France.—All that education for nothing.

HOWIE NEWSOME (*off left*): Giddap, Bessie! What's the matter with you today?

STAGE MANAGER: Here comes Howie Newsome, deliverin' the milk.

(HOWIE NEWSOME, *about thirty, in overalls, comes along Main Street from the left, walking beside an invisible horse and wagon and carrying an imaginary rack with milk bottles. The sound of clinking milk bottles is heard. He leaves some bottles at Mrs. Webb's trellis, then, crossing the stage to Mrs. Gibbs', he stops center to talk to Dr. Gibbs.*)

HOWIE NEWSOME: Morning, Doc.

DR. GIBBS: Morning, Howie.

HOWIE NEWSOME: Somebody sick?

DR. GIBBS: Pair of twins over to Mrs. Goruslawski's.

HOWIE NEWSOME: Twins, eh? This town's gettin' bigger every year.

DR. GIBBS: Going to rain, Howie?

HOWIE NEWSOME: No, no. Fine day—that'll burn through. Come on, Bessie.

DR. GIBBS: Hello, Bessie. (*He strokes the horse, which has remained up center.*) How old is she, Howie?

HOWIE NEWSOME: Going on seventeen. Bessie's all mixed up about the route ever since the Lockharts stopped takin' their quart of milk every day. She wants to leave 'em a quart just the same—keeps scolding me the hull trip. (*He reaches Mrs. Gibbs' back door. She is waiting for him.*)

MRS. GIBBS: Good morning, Howie.

HOWIE NEWSOME: Morning, Mrs. Gibbs. Doc's comin' down the street.

MRS. GIBBS: Is he? Seems like you're late today.

HOWIE NEWSOME: Yes, somep'n went wrong with the separator. Don't know what 'twas. (*He passes Dr. Gibbs up center.*) Doc!

DR. GIBBS: Howie!

MRS. GIBBS (*calling upstairs*): Children! Children! Time to get up.

HOWIE NEWSOME: Come on, Bessie! (*He goes off right.*)

MRS. GIBBS: George! Rebecca! (DR. GIBBS *arrives at his back door and passes through the trellis into his house.*)

MRS. GIBBS: Everything all right, Frank?

DR. GIBBS: Yes. I declare—easy as kittens.

MRS. GIBBS: Bacon'll be ready in a minute. Set down and drink your coffee. You can catch a couple hours' sleep this morning, can't you?

DR. GIBBS: Hm! . . . Mrs. Wentworth's coming at eleven. Guess I know what it's about, too. Her stummick ain't what it ought to be.

MRS. GIBBS: All told, you won't get more'n three hours' sleep. Frank Gibbs, I don't know what's goin' to become of you. I do wish I could get you to go away someplace and take a rest. I think it would do you good.

MRS. WEBB: Emileeee! Time to get up! Wally! Seven o'clock!

MRS. GIBBS: I declare, you got to speak to George. Seems like something's come over him lately. He's no help to me at all. I can't even get him to cut me some wood.

DR. GIBBS (*washing and drying his hands at the sink.* MRS. GIBBS *is busy at the stove.*): Is he sassy to you?

MRS. GIBBS: No. He just whines! All he thinks about is that baseball— George! Rebecca! You'll be late for school.

DR. GIBBS: M-m-m . . .

MRS. GIBBS: George!

DR. GIBBS: George, look sharp!

GEORGE'S VOICE: Yes, Pa!

DR. GIBBS (*as he goes off the stage*): Don't you hear your mother calling you? I guess I'll go upstairs and get forty winks.

MRS. WEBB: Walleee! Emileee! You'll be late for school! Walleee! You wash yourself good or I'll come up and do it myself.

REBECCA GIBBS' VOICE: Ma! What dress shall I wear?

MRS. GIBBS: Don't make a noise. Your father's been out all night and needs his sleep. I washed and ironed the blue gingham for you special.

REBECCA: Ma, I hate that dress.

MRS. GIBBS: Oh, hush-up-with-you.

REBECCA: Every day I go to school dressed like a sick turkey.

MRS. GIBBS: Now, Rebecca, you always look *very* nice.

REBECCA: Mama, George's throwing soap at me.

MRS. GIBBS: I'll come and slap the both of you,—that's what I'll do.

(*A factory whistle sounds. The* CHILDREN *dash in and take their places at the tables. Right,* GEORGE, *about sixteen, and* REBECCA, *eleven. Left,* EMILY *and* WALLY, *same ages. They carry strapped schoolbooks.*)

STAGE MANAGER: We've got a factory in our town too— hear it? Makes blankets. Cartwrights own it and it brung 'em a fortune.

MRS. WEBB: Children! Now I won't have it. Breakfast is just as good as any other meal and I won't have you gobbling like wolves. It'll stunt your growth,—that's a fact. Put away your book, Wally.

WALLY: Aw, Ma! By ten o'clock I got to know all about Canada.

MRS. WEBB: You know the rule's well as I do—no books at the table. As for me, I'd rather have my children healthy rather than bright.

EMILY: I'm both, Mama: you know I am. I'm the brightest girl in school for my age. I have a wonderful memory.

MRS. WEBB: Eat your breakfast.

WALLY: I'm bright, too, when I'm looking at my stamp collection.

MRS. GIBBS: I'll speak to your father about it when he's rested. Seems to me twenty-five cents a week's enough for a boy your age. I declare I don't know how you spend it all.

GEORGE: Aw, Ma,—I gotta lotta things to buy.

MRS. GIBBS: Strawberry phosphates—that's what you spend it on.

GEORGE: I don't see how Rebecca comes to have so much money. She has more'n a dollar.

REBECCA (*spoon in mouth, dreamily*): I've been saving it up gradual.

MRS. GIBBS: Well, dear, I think it's a good thing to spend some every now and then.

REBECCA: Mama, do you know what I love most in the world—do you?—Money.

MRS. GIBBS: Eat your breakfast.

THE CHILDREN: Mama, there's first bell.—I gotta hurry.— I don't want any more.—I gotta hurry.

(*The* CHILDREN *rise, seize their books and dash through the trellises. They meet, down center, and chattering, walk to Main Street, then turn left. The* STAGE MANAGER *goes off, unobtrusively, right.*)

MRS. WEBB: Walk fast, but you don't have to run. Wally, pull up your pants at the knee. Stand up straight, Emily.

MRS. GIBBS: Tell Miss Foster I send her my best congratulations—can you remember that?

REBECCA: Yes, Ma.

MRS. GIBBS: You look real nice, Rebecca. Pick up your feet.

ALL: Good-by.

MRS. GIBBS (*fills her apron with food for the chickens and comes down to the footlights*):

Here, chick, chick, chick.

No, go away, you. Go away.

What's the matter with *you?* Fight, fight, fight,—that's all you do.

Hm . . . *you* don't belong to me. Where'd you come from?

(*She shakes her apron.*) Oh, don't be so scared. Nobody's going to hurt you. (MRS. WEBB *is sitting on the bench by her trellis, stringing beans.*) Good morning, Myrtle. How's your cold?

MRS. WEBB: Well, I still get that tickling feeling in my throat. I told Charles I didn't know as I'd go to choir practice tonight. Wouldn't be any use.

MRS. GIBBS: Have you tried singing over your voice?

MRS. WEBB: Yes, but somehow I can't do that and stay

on the key. While I'm resting myself I thought I'd string some of these beans.

MRS. GIBBS (*rolling up her sleeves as she crosses the stage for a chat*): Let me help you. Beans have been good this year.

MRS. WEBB: I've decided to put up forty quarts if it kills me. The children say they hate 'em, but I notice they're able to get 'em down all winter.

(*Pause. Brief sound of chickens cackling.*)

MRS. GIBBS: Now, Myrtle. I've got to tell you something, because if I don't tell somebody I'll burst.

MRS. WEBB: Why, Julia Gibbs!

MRS. GIBBS: Here, give me some more of those beans. Myrtle, did one of those secondhand-furniture men from Boston come to see you last Friday?

MRS. WEBB: No-o.

MRS. GIBBS: Well, he called on me. First I thought he was a patient wantin' to see Dr. Gibbs. 'N he wormed his way into my parlor, and, Myrtle Webb, he offered me three hundred and fifty dollars for Grandmother Wentworth's highboy, as I'm sitting here!

MRS. WEBB: Why, Julia Gibbs!

MRS. GIBBS: He did! That old thing! Why, it was so big I didn't know where to put it and I almost gave it to Cousin Hester Wilcox.

MRS. WEBB: Well, you're going to take it, aren't you?

MRS. GIBBS: I don't know.

MRS. WEBB: You don't know—three hundred and fifty dollars! What's come over you?

MRS. GIBBS: Well, if I could get the Doctor to take the money and go away someplace on a real trip, I'd sell it like that.—Y'know, Myrtle, it's been the dream of my life to see Paris, France.—Oh, I don't know. It sounds crazy, I suppose, but for years I've been promising myself that if we ever had the chance—

MRS. WEBB: How does the Doctor feel about it?

MRS. GIBBS: Well, I did beat about the bush a little and said that if I got a legacy—that's the way I put it—I'd make him take me somewhere.

MRS. WEBB: M-m-m . . . What did he say?

MRS. GIBBS: You know how he is. I haven't heard a serious word out of him since I've known him. No, he said, it might make him discontented with Grover's Corners to go traipsin' about Europe; better let well enough alone, he says.

Every two years he makes a trip to the battlefields of the Civil War and that's enough treat for anybody, he says.

MRS. WEBB: Well, Mr. Webb just *admires* the way Dr. Gibbs knows everything about the Civil War. Mr. Webb's a good mind to give up Napoleon and move over to the Civil War, only Dr. Gibbs being one of the greatest experts in the country just makes him despair.

MRS. GIBBS: It's a fact! Dr. Gibbs is never so happy as when he's at Antietam or Gettysburg. The times I've walked over those hills, Myrtle, stopping at every bush and pacing it all out, like we were going to buy it.

MRS. WEBB: Well, if that secondhand man's really serious about buyin' it, Julia, you sell it. And then you'll get to see Paris, all right. Just keep droppin' hints from time to time—that's how I got to see the Atlantic Ocean, y'know.

MRS. GIBBS: Oh, I'm sorry I mentioned it. Only it seems to me that once in your life before you die you ought to see a country where they don't talk in English and don't even want to.

(*The* STAGE MANAGER *enters briskly from the right. He tips his hat to the ladies, who nod their heads.*)

STAGE MANAGER: Thank you, ladies. Thank you very much.

(MRS. GIBBS *and* MRS. WEBB *gather up their things, return into their homes and disappear.*)

Now we're going to skip a few hours.

But first we want a little more information about the town, kind of a scientific account, you might say.

So I've asked Professor Willard of our State University to sketch in a few details of our past history here.

Is Professor Willard here?

(PROFESSOR WILLARD, *a rural savant, pince-nez on a wide satin ribbon, enters from the right with some notes in his hand.*)

May I introduce Professor Willard of our State University.

A few brief notes, thank you, Professor,—unfortunately our time is limited.

PROFESSOR WILLARD: Grover's Corners . . . let me see . . . Grover's Corners lies on the old Pleistocene granite of the Appalachian range. I may say it's some of the oldest land in the world. We're very proud of that. A shelf of Devonian basalt crosses it with vestiges of Mesozoic shale, and some sandstone outcroppings; but that's all more recent: two hundred, three hundred million years old.

Some highly interesting fossils have been found . . . I may say: unique fossils . . . two miles out of town, in Silas Peckham's cow pasture. They can be seen at the museum in our University at any time—that is, at any reasonable time. Shall I read some of Professor Gruber's notes on the meteorological situation—mean precipitation, et cetera?

STAGE MANAGER: Afraid we won't have time for that, Professor. We might have a few words on the history of man here.

PROFESSOR WILLARD: Yes . . . anthropological data: Early Amerindian stock. Cotahatchee tribes . . . no evidence before the tenth century of this era . . . hm . . . now entirely disappeared . . . possible trace in three families. Migration toward the end of the seventeenth century of English brachiocephalic blue-eyed stock . . . for the most part. Since then some Slav and Mediterranean—

STAGE MANAGER: And the population, Professor Willard?

PROFESSOR WILLARD: Within the town limits: 2,640.

STAGE MANAGER: Just a moment, Professor. (*He whispers into the* PROFESSOR'S *ear.*)

PROFESSOR WILLARD: Oh, yes, indeed?—The population, *at the moment,* is 2,642. The Postal District brings in 507 more, making a total of 3,149.—Mortality and birth rates: constant. —By MacPherson's gauge: 6.032.

STAGE MANAGER: Thank you very much, Professor. We're all very much obliged to you, I'm sure.

PROFESSOR WILLARD: Not at all, sir; not at all.

STAGE MANAGER: This way, Professor, and thank you again.

(*Exit* PROFESSOR WILLARD.)

Now the political and social report: Editor Webb.—Oh, Mr. Webb?

MRS. WEBB (*appears at her back door*): He'll be here in a minute . . . He just cut his hand while he was eatin' an apple.

STAGE MANAGER: Thank you, Mrs. Webb.

MRS. WEBB: Charles! Everybody's waitin'.

(*Exit* MRS. WEBB.)

STAGE MANAGER: Mr. Webb is Publisher and Editor of the Grover's Corners *Sentinel.* That's our local paper, y'know.

(MR. WEBB *enters from his house, pulling on his coat. His finger is bound in a handkerchief.*)

MR. WEBB: Well . . . I don't have to tell you that we're run here by a Board of Selectmen.—All males vote at the age of twenty-one. Women vote indirect. We're lower middle class: sprinkling of professional men . . . ten per cent illiterate laborers. Politically, we're eighty-six per cent Republicans; six per cent Democrats; four per cent Socialists; rest, indifferent.

Religiously, we're eighty-five per cent Protestants; twelve per cent Catholics; rest, indifferent.

STAGE MANAGER: Have you any comments, Mr. Webb?

MR. WEBB: Very ordinary town, if you ask me. Little better behaved than most. Probably a lot duller.

But our young people here seem to like it well enough. Ninety per cent of 'em graduating from high school settle down right here to live—even when they've been away to college.

STAGE MANAGER: Now, is there anyone in the audience who would like to ask Editor Webb anything about the town?

WOMAN IN THE BALCONY: Is there much drinking in Grover's Corners?

MR. WEBB: Well, ma'am, I wouldn't know what you'd call *much.* Satiddy nights the farmhands meet down in Ellery Greenough's stable and holler some. We've got one or two town drunks, but they're always having remorses every time an evangelist comes to town. No, ma'am, I'd say likker ain't a regular thing in the homes here, except in the medicine chest. Right good for snake bite, y'know—always was.

BELLIGERENT MAN AT BACK OF AUDITORIUM: Is there no one in town aware of—

STAGE MANAGER: Come forward, will you, where we can all hear you.—What were you saying?

BELLIGERENT MAN: Is there no one in town aware of social injustice and industrial inequality?

MR. WEBB: Oh, yes, everybody is—somethin' terrible. Seems like they spend most of their time talking about who's rich and who's poor.

BELLIGERENT MAN: Then why don't they do something about it?

(*He withdraws without waiting for an answer.*)

MR. WEBB: Well, I dunno. . . . I guess we're all hunting like everybody else for a way the diligent and sensible can rise to the top and the lazy and quarrelsome can sink to the bottom. But it ain't easy to find. Meanwhile, we do all we can to help those that can't help themselves and those that can we leave alone.—Are there any other questions?

LADY IN A BOX: Oh, Mr. Webb, is there any culture or love of beauty in Grover's Corners?

MR. WEBB: Well, ma'am, there ain't much—not in the sense you mean. Come to think of it, there's some girls that play the piano at High School Commencement; but they ain't happy about it. No, ma'am, there isn't much culture; but maybe this is the place to tell you that we've got a lot of pleasures of a kind here: we like the sun comin' up over the mountain in the morning, and we all notice a good deal about the birds. We pay a lot of attention to them. And we watch the change of the seasons; yes, everybody knows about them. But those other things—you're right, ma'am,—there ain't much.—*Robinson Crusoe* and the Bible; and Handel's "Largo," we all know that; and Whistler's "Mother"—those are just about as far as we go.

LADY IN A BOX: So I thought. Thank you, Mr. Webb.

STAGE MANAGER: Thank you, Mr. Webb.

(MR. WEBB *retires.*)

Now, we'll go back to the town. It's early afternoon. All 2,642 have had their dinners and all the dishes have been washed.

(MR. WEBB, *having removed his coat, returns and starts pushing a lawn mower to and fro beside his house.*)

There's an early-afternoon calm in our town: a buzzin' and a hummin' from the school buildings; only a few buggies on Main Street—the horses dozing at the hitching posts; you all remember what it's like. Doc Gibbs in his office, tapping people and making them say "ah." Mr. Webb's cuttin' his lawn over there; one man in ten thinks it's a privilege to push his own lawn mower.

No, sir. It's later than I thought. There are the children coming home from school already.

(*Shrill girls' voices are heard, off left.* EMILY *comes along Main Street, carrying some books. There are some signs that she is imagining herself to be a lady of startling elegance.*)

EMILY: I *can't*, Lois. I've got to go home and help my mother. I *promised.*

MR. WEBB: Emily, walk simply. Who do you think you are today?

EMILY: Papa, you're terrible. One minute you tell me to stand up straight and the next minute you call me names. I just don't listen to you. (*She gives him an abrupt kiss.*)

MR. WEBB: Golly, I never got a kiss from such a great lady before.

(*He goes out of sight.* EMILY *leans over and picks some flowers by the gate of her house.*

GEORGE GIBBS *comes careening down Main Street. He is throwing a ball up to dizzying heights, and waiting to catch it again. This sometimes requires his taking six steps backward. He bumps into an* OLD LADY *invisible to us.*)

GEORGE: Excuse me, Mrs. Forrest.

STAGE MANAGER (*as* MRS. FORREST): Go out and play in the fields, young man. You got no business playing baseball on Main Street.

GEORGE: Awfully sorry, Mrs. Forrest.—Hello, Emily.

EMILY: H'lo.

GEORGE: You made a fine speech in class.

EMILY: Well . . . I was really ready to make a speech about the Monroe Doctrine, but at the last minute Miss Corcoran made me talk about the Louisiana Purchase instead. I worked an awful long time on both of them.

GEORGE: Gee, it's funny, Emily. From my window up there I can just see your head nights when you're doing your homework over in your room.

EMILY: Why, can you?

GEORGE: You certainly do stick to it, Emily. I don't see how you can sit still that long. I guess you like school.

EMILY: Well, I always feel it's something you have to go through.

GEORGE: Yeah.

EMILY: I don't mind it really. It passes the time.

GEORGE: Yeah.—Emily, what do you think? We might work out a kinda telegraph from your window to mine; and once in a while you could give me a kinda hint or two about one of those algebra problems. I don't mean the answers, Emily, of course not . . . just some little hint . . .

EMILY: Oh, I think *hints* are allowed.—So—ah—if you get stuck, George, you whistle to me; and I'll give you some hints.

GEORGE: Emily, you're just naturally bright, I guess.

EMILY: I figure that it's the way a person's born.

GEORGE: Yeah. But, you see, I want to be a farmer, and my Uncle Luke says whenever I'm ready I can come over and work on his farm and if I'm any good I can just gradually have it.

EMILY: You mean the house and everything?

(*Enter* MRS. WEBB *with a large bowl and sits on the bench by her trellis.*)

GEORGE: Yeah. Well, thanks . . . I better be getting out to the baseball field. Thanks for the talk, Emily.—Good afternoon, Mrs. Webb.

MRS. WEBB: Good afternoon, George.

GEORGE: So long, Emily.

EMILY: So long, George.

MRS. WEBB: Emily, come and help me string these beans for the winter. George Gibbs let himself have a real conversation, didn't he? Why, he's growing up. How old would George be?

EMILY: I don't know.

MRS. WEBB: Let's see. He must be almost sixteen.

EMILY: Mama, I made a speech in class today and I was very good.

MRS. WEBB: You must recite to your father at supper. What was it about?

EMILY: The Louisiana Purchase. It was like silk off a spool. I'm going to make speeches all my life.—Mama, are these big enough?

MRS. WEBB: Try and get them a little bigger if you can.

EMILY: Mama, will you answer me a question, serious?

MRS. WEBB: Seriously, dear—not serious.

EMILY: Seriously,—will you?

MRS. WEBB: Of course, I will.

EMILY: Mama, am I good-looking?

MRS. WEBB: Yes, of course you are. All my children have got good features; I'd be ashamed if they hadn't.

EMILY: Oh, Mama, that's not what I mean. What I mean is: am I *pretty*?

MRS. WEBB: I've already told you, yes. Now that's enough of that. You have a nice young pretty face. I never heard of such foolishness.

EMILY: Oh, Mama, you never tell us the truth about anything.

MRS. WEBB: I *am* telling you the truth.

EMILY: Mama, were *you* pretty?

MRS. WEBB: Yes, I was, if I do say it. I was the prettiest girl in town next to Mamie Cartwright.

EMILY: But, Mama, you've got to say something about me. Am I pretty enough . . . to get anybody . . . to get people interested in me?

MRS. WEBB: Emily, you make me tired. Now stop it. You're pretty enough for all normal purposes.—Come along now and bring that bowl with you.

EMILY: Oh, Mama, you're no help at all.

STAGE MANAGER: Thank you. Thank you! That'll do. We'll have to interrupt again here. Thank you, Mrs. Webb; thank you, Emily.

(MRS. WEBB *and* EMILY *withdraw*.)

There are some more things we want to explore about this town. (*He comes to the center of the stage. During the fol-*

*lowing speech the lights gradually dim to darkness, leaving
only a spot on him.*) I think this is a good time to tell you
that the Cartwright interests have just begun building a new
bank in Grover's Corners—had to go to Vermont for the
marble, sorry to say. And they've asked a friend of mine
what they should put in the cornerstone for people to dig
up . . . a thousand years from now. . . . Of course, they've
put in a copy of the *New York Times* and a copy of Mr.
Webb's *Sentinel*. . . . We're kind of interested in this because some scientific fellas have found a way of painting all
that reading matter with a glue—a silicate glue—that'll make
it keep a thousand—two thousand years.

We're putting in a Bible . . . and the Constitution of the
United States—and a copy of William Shakespeare's plays.
What do you say, folks? What do you think?

Y'know—Babylon once had two million people in it, and
all we know about 'em is the names of the kings and some
copies of wheat contracts . . . and contracts for the sale of
slaves. Yet every night all those families sat down to supper,
and the father came home from his work, and the smoke
went up the chimney,—same as here. And even in Greece
and Rome, all we know about the *real* life of the people
is what we can piece together out of the joking poems and
the comedies they wrote for the theater back then.

So I'm going to have a copy of this play put in the cornerstone and the people a thousand years from now'll know
a few simple facts about us—more than the Treaty of Ver-
sailles and the Lindbergh flight.

See what I mean?

So—people a thousand years from now—this is the way
we were in the provinces north of New York at the beginning of the twentieth century.—This is the way we were: in
our growing up and in our marrying and in our living and
in our dying.

(*A choir partially concealed in the orchestra pit has begun
singing "Blessed Be the Tie That Binds."*

SIMON STIMSON *stands directing them.*

*Two ladders have been pushed onto the stage; they serve
as indication of the second story in the Gibbs and Webb
houses.* GEORGE *and* EMILY *mount them, and apply themselves to their schoolwork.*

DR. GIBBS *has entered and is seated in his kitchen reading.*)

Well!—good deal of time's gone by. It's evening.

You can hear choir practice going on in the Congregational Church.

The children are at home doing their schoolwork.

The day's running down like a tired clock.

SIMON STIMSON: Now look here, everybody. Music come into the world to give pleasure.—Softer! Softer! Get it out of your heads that music's only good when it's loud. You leave loudness to the Methodists. You couldn't beat 'em, even if you wanted to. Now again. Tenors!

GEORGE: Hssst! Emily!

EMILY: Hello.

GEORGE: Hello!

EMILY: I can't work at all. The moonlight's so *terrible*.

GEORGE: Emily, did you get the third problem?

EMILY: Which?

GEORGE: The *third*?

EMILY: Why, yes, George—that's the easiest of them all.

GEORGE: I don't see it. Emily, can you give me a hint?

EMILY: I'll tell you one thing: the answer's in yards.

GEORGE: ! ! ! In yards? How do you mean?

EMILY: In *square* yards.

GEORGE: Oh . . . in square yards.

EMILY: Yes, George, don't you see?

GEORGE: Yeah.

EMILY: In square yards of *wallpaper*.

GEORGE: Wallpaper,—oh, I see. Thanks a lot, Emily.

EMILY: You're welcome. My, isn't the moonlight *terrible*? And choir practice going on.—I think if you hold your breath you can hear the train all the way to Contoocook. Hear it?

GEORGE: M-m-m—What do you know!

EMILY: Well, I guess I better go back and try to work.

GEORGE: Good night, Emily. And thanks.

EMILY: Good night, George.

SIMON STIMSON: Before I forget it: how many of you will be able to come in Tuesday afternoon and sing at Fred Hersey's wedding?—show your hands. That'll be fine; that'll be right nice. We'll do the same music we did for Jane Trowbridge's last month.

—Now we'll do: "Art Thou Weary; Art Thou Languid?" It's a question, ladies and gentlemen, make it talk. Ready.

DR. GIBBS: Oh, George, can you come down a minute?

GEORGE: Yes, Pa. (*He descends the ladder.*)

DR. GIBBS: Make yourself comfortable, George; I'll only keep you a minute. George, how old are you?

GEORGE: I? I'm sixteen, almost seventeen.

DR. GIBBS: What do you want to do after school's over?

GEORGE: Why, you know, Pa. I want to be a farmer on Uncle Luke's farm.

DR. GIBBS: You'll be willing, will you, to get up early and milk and feed the stock . . . and you'll be able to hoe and hay all day?

GEORGE: Sure, I will. What are you . . . what do you mean, Pa?

DR. GIBBS: Well, George, while I was in my office today I heard a funny sound . . . and what do you think it was? It was your mother chopping wood. There you see your mother—getting up early; cooking meals all day long; washing and ironing;—and still she has to go out in the back yard and chop wood. I suppose she just got tired of asking you. She just gave up and decided it was easier to do it herself. And you eat her meals, and put on the clothes she keeps nice for you, and you run off and play baseball,—like she's some hired girl we keep around the house but that we don't like very much. Well, I knew all I had to do was call your attention to it. Here's a handkerchief, son. George, I've decided to raise your spending money twenty-five cents a week. Not, of course, for chopping wood for your mother, because that's a present you give her, but because you're getting older—and I imagine there are lots of things you must find to do with it.

GEORGE: Thanks, Pa.

DR. GIBBS: Let's see—tomorrow's your payday. You can count on it—Hmm. Probably Rebecca'll feel she ought to have some more too. Wonder what could have happened to your mother. Choir practice never was as late as this before.

GEORGE: It's only half past eight, Pa.

DR. GIBBS: I don't know why she's in that old choir. She hasn't any more voice than an old crow. . . . Traipsin' around the streets at this hour of the night . . . Just about time you retired, don't you think?

GEORGE: Yes, Pa. (GEORGE *mounts to his place on the ladder.*

Laughter and good nights can be heard on stage left and presently MRS. GIBBS, MRS. SOAMES *and* MRS. WEBB *come down Main Street. When they arrive at the corner of the stage they stop.*)

MRS. SOAMES: Good night, Martha. Good night, Mr. Foster.

MRS. WEBB: I'll tell Mr. Webb; I *know* he'll want to put it in the paper.

MRS. GIBBS: My, it's late!

MRS. SOAMES: Good night, Irma.

MRS. GIBBS: Real nice choir practice, wa'n't it? Myrtle Webb! Look at that moon, will you! Tsk-tsk-tsk. Potato weather, for sure.

(*They are silent a moment, gazing up at the moon.*)

MRS. SOAMES: Naturally I didn't want to say a word about it in front of those others, but now we're alone—really, it's the worst scandal that ever was in this town!

MRS. GIBBS: What?

MRS. SOAMES: Simon Stimson!

MRS. GIBBS: Now, Louella!

MRS. SOAMES: But, Julia! To have the organist of a church *drink* and *drunk* year after year. You know he was drunk tonight.

MRS. GIBBS: Now, Louella! We all know about Mr. Stimson, and we all know about the troubles he's been through, and Dr. Ferguson knows too, and if Dr. Ferguson keeps him on there in his job the only thing the rest of us can do is just not to notice it.

MRS. SOAMES: *Not to notice it!* But it's getting worse.

MRS. WEBB: No, it isn't, Louella. It's getting better. I've been in that choir twice as long as you have. It doesn't happen anywhere near so often. . . . My, I hate to go to bed on a night like this.—I better hurry. Those children'll be sitting up till all hours. Good night, Louella.

(*They all exchange good nights. She hurries downstage, enters her house and disappears.*)

MRS. GIBBS: Can you get home safe, Louella?

MRS. SOAMES: It's as bright as day. I can see Mr. Soames scowling at the window now. You'd think we'd been to a dance the way the menfolk carry on.

(*More good nights.* MRS. GIBBS *arrives at her home and passes through the trellis into the kitchen.*)

MRS. GIBBS: Well, we had a real good time.

DR. GIBBS: You're late enough.

MRS. GIBBS: Why, Frank, it ain't any later 'n usual.

DR. GIBBS: And you stopping at the corner to gossip with a lot of hens.

MRS. GIBBS: Now, Frank, don't be grouchy. Come out and smell the heliotrope in the moonlight.

(*They stroll out arm in arm along the footlights.*)

Isn't that wonderful? What did you do all the time I was away?

DR. GIBBS: Oh, I read—as usual. What were the girls gossiping about tonight?

MRS. GIBBS: Well, believe me, Frank—there is something to gossip about.

DR. GIBBS: Hmm! Simon Stimson far gone, was he?

MRS. GIBBS: Worst I've ever seen him. How'll that end, Frank? Dr. Ferguson can't forgive him forever.

DR. GIBBS: I guess I know more about Simon Stimson's affairs than anybody in this town. Some people ain't made for small-town life. I don't know how that'll end; but there's nothing we can do but just leave it alone. Come, get in.

MRS. GIBBS: No, not yet . . . Frank, I'm worried about you.

DR. GIBBS: What are you worried about?

MRS. GIBBS: I think it's my duty to make plans for you to get a real rest and change. And if I get that legacy, well, I'm going to insist on it.

DR. GIBBS: Now, Julia, there's no sense in going over that again.

MRS. GIBBS: Frank, you're just *unreasonable!*

DR. GIBBS (*starting into the house*): Come on, Julia, it's getting late. First thing you know you'll catch cold. I gave George a piece of my mind tonight. I reckon you'll have your wood chopped for a while anyway. No, no, start getting upstairs.

MRS. GIBBS: Oh, dear. There's always so many things to pick up, seems like. You know, Frank, Mrs. Fairchild always locks her front door every night. All those people up that part of town do.

DR. GIBBS (*blowing out the lamp*): They're all getting citified, that's the trouble with them. They haven't got nothing fit to burgle and everybody knows it.

(*They disappear.* REBECCA *climbs up the ladder beside* GEORGE.)

GEORGE: Get out, Rebecca. There's only room for one at this window. You're always spoiling everything.

REBECCA: Well, let me look just a minute.

GEORGE: Use your own window.

REBECCA: I did, but there's no moon there. . . . George, do you know what I think, do you? I think maybe the moon's getting nearer and nearer and there'll be a big 'splosion.

GEORGE: Rebecca, you don't know anything. If the moon were getting nearer, the guys that sit up all night with telescopes would see it first and they'd tell about it, and it'd be in the newspapers.

REBECCA: George, is the moon shining on South America, Canada and half the whole world?

GEORGE: Well—prob'ly is.

(*The* STAGE MANAGER *strolls on. Pause. The sound of crickets is heard.*)

STAGE MANAGER: Nine thirty. Most of the lights are out. No, there's Constable Warren trying a few doors on Main Street. And here comes Editor Webb, after putting his newspaper to bed.

(MR. WARREN, *an elderly policeman, comes along Main Street from the right,* MR. WEBB *from the left.*)

MR. WEBB: Good evening, Bill.

CONSTABLE WARREN: Evenin', Mr. Webb.

MR. WEBB: Quite a moon!

CONSTABLE WARREN: Yepp.

MR. WEBB: All quiet tonight?

CONSTABLE WARREN: Simon Stimson is rollin' around a little. Just saw his wife movin' out to hunt for him so I looked the other way—there he is now.

(SIMON STIMSON *comes down Main Street from the left, only a trace of unsteadiness in his walk.*)

MR. WEBB: Good evening, Simon . . . Town seems to have settled down for the night pretty well. . . .

(SIMON STIMSON *comes up to him and pauses a moment and stares at him, swaying slightly.*)

Good evening . . . Yes, most of the town's settled down for the night, Simon. . . . I guess we better do the same. Can I walk along a ways with you?

(SIMON STIMSON *continues on his way without a word and disappears at the right.*)

Good night.

CONSTABLE WARREN: I don't know how that's goin' to end, Mr. Webb.

MR. WEBB: Well, he's seen a peck of trouble, one thing after another. . . . Oh, Bill . . . if you see my boy smoking cigarettes, just give him a word, will you? He thinks a lot of you, Bill.

CONSTABLE WARREN: I don't think he smokes no cigarettes, Mr. Webb. Leastways, not more'n two or three a year.

MR. WEBB: Hm . . . I hope not.—Well, good night, Bill.

CONSTABLE WARREN: Good night, Mr. Webb.

(*Exit.*)

MR. WEBB: Who's that up there? Is that you, Myrtle?

EMILY: No, it's me, Papa.

MR. WEBB: Why aren't you in bed?

EMILY: I don't know. I just can't sleep yet, Papa. The

moonlight's so *won*-derful. And the smell of Mrs. Gibbs'
heliotrope. Can you smell it?

MR. WEBB: Hm . . . Yes. Haven't any troubles on your
mind, have you, Emily?

EMILY: *Troubles*, Papa? *No.*

MR. WEBB: Well, enjoy yourself, but don't let your mother
catch you. Good night, Emily.

EMILY: Good night, Papa. (MR. WEBB *crosses into the
house, whistling "Blessed Be the Tie that Binds" and disappears.*)

REBECCA: I never told you about that letter Jane Crofut
got from her minister when she was sick. He wrote Jane a
letter and on the envelope the address was like this: It said:
Jane Crofut; The Crofut Farm; Grover's Corners; Sutton
County; New Hampshire; United States of America.

GEORGE: What's funny about that?

REBECCA: But listen, it's not finished: the United States of
America; Continent of North America; Western Hemisphere;
the Earth; the Solar System; the Universe; the Mind of
God—that's what it said on the envelope.

GEORGE: What do you know!

REBECCA: And the postman brought it just the same.

GEORGE: What do you know!

STAGE MANAGER: That's the end of the First Act, friends.
You can go and smoke now, those that smoke.

ACT II

(*The tables and chairs of the two kitchens are still on the
stage.*

The ladders and the small bench have been withdrawn.

The STAGE MANAGER *has been at his accustomed place
watching the audience return to its seats.*)

STAGE MANAGER: Three years have gone by.

Yes, the sun's come up over a thousand times.

Summers and winters have cracked the mountains a little
bit more and the rains have brought down some of the dirt.

Some babies that weren't even born before have begun
talking regular sentences already; and a number of people

who thought they were right young and spry have noticed that they can't bound up a flight of stairs like they used to, without their heart fluttering a little.

All that can happen in a thousand days.

Nature's been pushing and contriving in other ways, too: a number of young people fell in love and got married.

Yes, the mountain got bit away a few fractions of an inch; millions of gallons of water went by the mill; and here and there a new home was set up under a roof.

Almost everybody in the world gets married,—you know what I mean? In our town there aren't hardly any exceptions. Most everybody in the world climbs into their graves married.

The First Act was called the Daily Life. This act is called Love and Marriage. There's another act coming after this: I reckon you can guess what that's about.

So:

It's three years later. It's 1904.

It's July 7th, just after High School Commencement.

That's the time most of our young people jump up and get married.

Soon as they've passed their last examinations in solid geometry and Cicero's Orations, looks like they suddenly feel themselves fit to be married.

It's early morning. Only this time it's been raining. It's been pouring and thundering.

Mrs. Gibbs' garden, and Mrs. Webb's here: drenched.

All those bean poles and pea vines: drenched.

All yesterday over there on Main Street, the rain looked like curtains being blown along.

Hm . . . it may begin again any minute.

There! You can hear the 5:45 for Boston.

(MRS. GIBBS *and* MRS. WEBB *enter their kitchens and start the day as in the First Act.*)

And there's Mrs. Gibbs and Mrs. Webb come down to make breakfast, just as though it were an ordinary day. I don't have to point out to the women in my audience that those ladies they see before them, both of those ladies cooked three meals a day—one of 'em for twenty years, the other for forty—and no summer vacation. They brought up two children apiece, washed, cleaned the house,—and *never a nervous breakdown.*

It's like what one of those Middle West poets said: You've got to love life to have life, and you've got to have life to love life. . . .

It's what they call a vicious circle.

HOWIE NEWSOME (*off stage left*): Giddap, Bessie!

STAGE MANAGER: Here comes Howie Newsome delivering the milk. And there's Si Crowell delivering the papers like his brother before him.

(SI CROWELL *has entered hurling imaginary newspapers into doorways;* HOWIE NEWSOME *has come along Main Street with Bessie.*)

SI CROWELL: Morning, Howie.

HOWIE NEWSOME: Morning, Si.—Anything in the papers I ought to know?

SI CROWELL: Nothing much, except we're losing about the best baseball pitcher Grover's Corners ever had—George Gibbs.

HOWIE NEWSOME: Reckon he is.

SI CROWELL: He could hit and run bases, too.

HOWIE NEWSOME: Yep. Mighty fine ball player.—Whoa! Bessie! I guess I can stop and talk if I've a mind to!

SI CROWELL: I don't see how he could give up a thing like that just to get married. Would you, Howie?

HOWIE NEWSOME: Can't tell, Si. Never had no talent that way.

(CONSTABLE WARREN *enters. They exchange good mornings.*)

You're up early, Bill.

CONSTABLE WARREN: Seein' if there's anything I can do to prevent a flood. River's been risin' all night.

HOWIE NEWSOME: Si Crowell's all worked up here about George Gibbs' retiring from baseball.

CONSTABLE WARREN: Yes, sir; that's the way it goes. Back in '84 we had a player, Si—even George Gibbs couldn't touch him. Name of Hank Todd. Went down to Maine and become a parson. Wonderful ball player.—Howie, how does the weather look to you?

HOWIE NEWSOME: Oh, 'tain't bad. Think maybe it'll clear up for good.

(CONSTABLE WARREN *and* SI CROWELL *continue on their way.* HOWIE NEWSOME *brings the milk first to Mrs. Gibbs' house. She meets him by the trellis.*)

MRS. GIBBS: Good morning, Howie. Do you think it's going to rain again?

HOWIE NEWSOME: Morning, Mrs. Gibbs. It rained so heavy, I think maybe it'll clear up.

MRS. GIBBS: Certainly hope it will.

HOWIE NEWSOME: How much did you want today?

MRS. GIBBS: I'm going to have a houseful of relations,

Howie. Looks to me like I'll need three-a-milk and two-a-cream.

HOWIE NEWSOME: My wife says to tell you we both hope they'll be very happy, Mrs. Gibbs. Know they *will*.

MRS. GIBBS: Thanks a lot, Howie. Tell your wife I hope she gits there to the wedding.

HOWIE NEWSOME: Yes, she'll be there if she kin.

(HOWIE NEWSOME *crosses to Mrs. Webb's house.*)

Morning, Mrs. Webb.

MRS. WEBB: Oh, good morning, Mr. Newsome. I told you four quarts of milk, but I hope you can spare me another.

HOWIE NEWSOME: Yes'm . . . and the two of cream.

MRS. WEBB: Will it start raining again, Mr. Newsome?

HOWIE NEWSOME: Well. Just sayin' to Mrs. Gibbs as how it may lighten up. Mrs. Newsome told me to tell you as how we hope they'll both be very happy, Mrs. Webb. Know they *will*.

MRS. WEBB: Thank you, and thank Mrs. Newsome and we're counting on seeing you at the wedding.

HOWIE NEWSOME: Yes, Mrs. Webb. We hope to git there. Couldn't miss that. Come on, Bessie.

(*Exit* HOWIE NEWSOME.

DR. GIBBS *descends in shirt sleeves, and sits down at his breakfast table.*)

DR. GIBBS: Well, Ma, the day has come. You're losin' one of your chicks.

MRS. GIBBS: Frank Gibbs, don't you say another word. I feel like crying every minute. Sit down and drink your coffee.

DR. GIBBS: The groom's up shaving himself—only there ain't an awful lot to shave. Whistling and singing, like he's glad to leave us.—Every now and then he says "I do" to the mirror, but it don't sound convincing to me.

MRS. GIBBS: I declare, Frank, I don't know how he'll get along. I've arranged his clothes and seen to it he's put warm things on,—Frank! they're too *young*. Emily won't think of such things. He'll catch his death of cold within a week.

DR. GIBBS: I was remembering my wedding morning, Julia.

MRS. GIBBS: Now don't start that, Frank Gibbs.

DR. GIBBS: I was the scaredest young fella in the State of New Hampshire. I thought I'd make a mistake for sure. And when I saw you comin' down that aisle I thought you were the prettiest girl I'd ever seen, but the only trouble was that I'd never seen you before. There I was in the Congregational Church marryin' a total stranger.

MRS. GIBBS: And how do you think I felt!—Frank, weddings

are perfectly awful things. Farces,—that's what they are! (*She puts a plate before him.*) Here, I've made something for you.

DR. GIBBS: Why, Julia Hersey—French toast!

MRS. GIBBS: 'Tain't hard to make and I had to do *something.*

(*Pause.* DR. GIBBS *pours on the syrup.*)

DR. GIBBS: How'd you sleep last night, Julia?

MRS. GIBBS: Well, I heard a lot of the hours struck off.

DR. GIBBS: Ye-e-s! I get a shock every time I think of George setting out to be a family man—that great gangling thing!—I tell you Julia, there's nothing so terrifying in the world as a *son.* The relation of father and son is the darndest, awkwardest—

MRS. GIBBS: Well, mother and daughter's no picnic, let me tell you.

DR. GIBBS: They'll have a lot of troubles, I suppose, but that's none of our business. Everybody has a right to their own troubles.

MRS. GIBBS (*at the table, drinking her coffee, meditatively*): Yes . . . people are meant to go through life two by two. 'Tain't natural to be lonesome.

(*Pause.* DR. GIBBS *starts laughing.*)

DR. GIBBS: Julia, do you know one of the things I was scared of when I married you?

MRS. GIBBS: Oh, go along with you!

DR. GIBBS: I was afraid we wouldn't have material for conversation more'n'd last us a few weeks.

(*Both laugh.*)

I was afraid we'd run out and eat our meals in silence, that's a fact.—Well, you and I been conversing for twenty years now without any noticeable barren spells.

MRS. GIBBS: Well,—good weather, bad weather—'tain't very choice, but I always find something to say. (*She goes to the foot of the stairs.*) Did you hear Rebecca stirring around upstairs?

DR. GIBBS: No. Only day of the year Rebecca hasn't been managing everybody's business up there. She's hiding in her room.—I got the impression she's crying.

MRS. GIBBS: Lord's sakes!—This has got to stop.—Rebecca! Rebecca! Come and get your breakfast.

(GEORGE *comes rattling down the stairs, very brisk.*)

GEORGE: Good morning, everybody. Only five more hours to live (*makes the gesture of cutting his throat, and a loud "k-k-k," and starts through the trellis*).

MRS. GIBBS: George Gibbs, where are you going?

GEORGE: Just stepping across the grass to see my girl.

MRS. GIBBS: Now, George! You put on your overshoes. It's raining torrents. You don't go out of this house without you're prepared for it.

GEORGE: Aw, Ma. It's just a *step!*

MRS. GIBBS: George! You'll catch your death of cold and cough all through the service.

DR. GIBBS: George, do as your mother tells you!

(DR. GIBBS *goes upstairs.*)

GEORGE *returns reluctantly to the kitchen and pantomimes putting on overshoes.*)

MRS. GIBBS: From tomorrow on you can kill yourself in all weathers, but while you're in my house you'll live wisely, thank you.—Maybe Mrs. Webb isn't used to callers at seven in the morning.—Here, take a cup of coffee first.

GEORGE: Be back in a minute. (*He crosses the stage, leaping over the puddles.*) Good morning, Mother Webb.

MRS. WEBB: Goodness! You frightened me!—Now, George, you can come in a minute out of the wet, but you know I can't ask you in.

GEORGE: Why not—?

MRS. WEBB: George, you know's well as I do: the groom can't see his bride on his wedding day, not until he sees her in church.

GEORGE: Aw!—that's just a superstition.—Good morning, Mr. Webb.

(*Enter* MR. WEBB.)

MR. WEBB: Good morning, George.

GEORGE: Mr. Webb, you don't believe in that superstition, do you?

MR. WEBB: There's a lot of common sense in some superstitions, George. (*He sits at the table, facing right.*)

MRS. WEBB: Millions have folla'd it, George, and you don't want to be the first to fly in the face of custom.

GEORGE: How is Emily?

MRS. WEBB: She hasn't waked up yet. I haven't heard a sound out of her.

GEORGE: Emily's *asleep*!!!

MRS. WEBB: No wonder! We were up 'til all hours, sewing and packing. Now I'll tell you what I'll do; you set down here a minute with Mr. Webb and drink this cup of coffee; and I'll go upstairs and see she doesn't come down and surprise you. There's some bacon, too; but don't be long about it.

(*Exit* MRS. WEBB.

Embarrassed silence.

MR. WEBB *dunks doughnuts in his coffee.*

More silence.)

MR. WEBB (*suddenly and loudly*): Well, George, how are you?

GEORGE (*startled, choking over his coffee*): Oh, fine, I'm fine. (*pause*) Mr. Webb, what sense could there be in a superstition like that?

MR. WEBB: Well, you see,—on her wedding morning a girl's head's apt to be full of . . . clothes and one thing and another. Don't you think that's probably it?

GEORGE: Ye-e-es. I never thought of that.

MR. WEBB: A girl's apt to be a mite nervous on her wedding day.

(*Pause.*)

GEORGE: I wish a fellow could get married without all that marching up and down.

MR. WEBB: Every man that's ever lived has felt that way about it, George; but it hasn't been any use. It's the women-folk who've built up weddings, my boy. For a while now the women have it all their own. A man looks pretty small at a wedding, George. All those good women standing shoulder to shoulder making sure that the knot's tied in a mighty public way.

GEORGE: But . . . you *believe* in it, don't you, Mr. Webb?

MR. WEBB (*with alacrity*): Oh, yes; oh, yes. Don't you misunderstand me, my boy. Marriage is a wonderful thing,—wonderful thing. And don't you forget that, George.

GEORGE: No, sir.—Mr. Webb, how old were you when you got married?

MR. WEBB: Well, you see: I'd been to college and I'd taken a little time to get settled. But Mrs. Webb—she wasn't much older than what Emily is. Oh, age hasn't much to do with it, George,—not compared with . . . uh . . . other things.

GEORGE: What were you going to say, Mr. Webb?

MR. WEBB: Oh, I don't know.—Was I going to say something? (*pause*) George, I was thinking the other night of some advice my father gave me when I got married. Charles, he said, Charles, start out early showing who's boss, he said. Best thing to do is to give an order, even if it don't make sense; just so she'll learn to obey. And he said: if anything about your wife irritates you—her conversation, or any-thing—just get up and leave the house. That'll make it clear to her, he said. And, oh, yes! he said never, *never* let your wife know how much money you have, never.

GEORGE: Well, Mr. Webb . . . I don't think I could . . .

MR. WEBB: So I took the opposite of my father's advice and I've been happy ever since. And let that be a lesson to you, George, never to ask advice on personal matters.— George, are you going to raise chickens on your farm?

GEORGE: What?

MR. WEBB: Are you going to raise chickens on your farm?

GEORGE: Uncle Luke's never been much interested, but I thought—

MR. WEBB: A book came into my office the other day, George, on the Philo System of raising chickens. I want you to read it. I'm thinking of beginning in a small way in the back yard, and I'm going to put an incubator in the cellar—

(*Enter* MRS. WEBB.)

MRS. WEBB: Charles, are you talking about that old incubator again? I thought you two'd be talking about things worth while.

MR. WEBB (*bitingly*): Well, Myrtle, if you want to give the boy some good advice, I'll go upstairs and leave you alone with him.

MRS. WEBB (*pulling* GEORGE *up*): George, Emily's got to come downstairs and eat her breakfast. She sends you her love but she doesn't want to lay eyes on you. Good-by.

GEORGE: Good-by.

(GEORGE *crosses the stage to his own home, bewildered and crestfallen. He slowly dodges a puddle and disappears into his house.*)

MR. WEBB: Myrtle, I guess you don't know about that older superstition.

MRS. WEBB: What do you mean, Charles?

MR. WEBB: Since the cave men: no bridegroom should see his father-in-law on the day of the wedding, or near it. Now remember that.

(*Both leave the stage.*)

STAGE MANAGER: Thank you very much, Mr. and Mrs. Webb.—Now I have to interrupt again here. You see, we want to know how all this began—this wedding, this plan to spend a lifetime together. I'm awfully interested in how big things like that begin.

You know how it is: you're twenty-one or twenty-two and you make some decisions; then whisssh! you're seventy: you've been a lawyer for fifty years, and that white-haired lady at your side has eaten over fifty thousand meals with you.

How do such things begin?

George and Emily are going to show you now the conversation they had when they first knew that . . . that . . . as the saying goes . . . they were meant for one another.

But before they do it I want you to try and remember what it was like to have been very young.

And particularly the days when you were first in love; when you were like a person sleepwalking, and you didn't quite see the street you were in, and didn't quite hear everything that was said to you.

You're just a little bit crazy. Will you remember that, please?

Now they'll be coming out of high school at three o'clock. George has just been elected President of the Junior Class, and as it's June, that means he'll be President of the Senior Class all next year. And Emily's just been elected Secretary and Treasurer.

I don't have to tell you how important that is.

(*He places a board across the backs of two chairs, which he takes from those at the* GIBBS *family's table. He brings two high stools from the wings and places them behind the board. Persons sitting on the stools will be facing the audience. This is the counter of* MR. MORGAN'S *drugstore. The sounds of young people's voices are heard off left.*)

Yepp,—there they are coming down Main Street now.

(EMILY, *carrying an armful of—imaginary—schoolbooks, comes along Main Street from the left.*)

EMILY: I can't, Louise. I've got to go home. Good-by. Oh, Ernestine! Ernestine! Can you come over tonight and do Latin? Isn't that Cicero the worst thing—! Tell your mother you *have* to. G'by. G'by, Helen. G'by, Fred.

(GEORGE, *also carrying books, catches up with her.*)

GEORGE: Can I carry your books home for you, Emily?

EMILY (*coolly*): Why . . . uh . . . Thank you. It isn't far. (*She gives them to him.*)

GEORGE: Excuse me a minute, Emily.—Say, Bob, if I'm a little late, start practice anyway. And give Herb some long high ones.

EMILY: Good-by, Lizzy.

GEORGE: Good-by, Lizzy.—I'm awfully glad you were elected, too, Emily.

EMILY: Thank you.

(*They have been standing on Main Street, almost against the back wall. They take the first steps toward the audience when* GEORGE *stops and says:*)

GEORGE: Emily, why are you mad at me?

EMILY: I'm not mad at you.

GEORGE: You've been treating me so funny lately.

EMILY: Well, since you ask me, I might as well say it right out, George,—(*She catches sight of a teacher passing.*) Good-by, Miss Corcoran.

GEORGE: Good-by, Miss Corcoran.—Wha—what is it?

EMILY (*not scoldingly, finding it difficult to say*): I don't like the whole change that's come over you in the last year. I'm sorry if that hurts your feelings, but I've got to—tell the truth and shame the devil.

GEORGE: A *change?*—Wha—what do you mean?

EMILY: Well, up to a year ago I used to like you a lot. And I used to watch you as you did everything . . . because we'd been friends so long . . . and then you began spending all your time at *baseball* . . . and you never stopped to speak to anybody any more. Not even to your own family you didn't . . . and, George, it's a fact, you've got awful conceited and stuck-up, and all the girls say so. They may not say so to your face, but that's what they say about you behind your back, and it hurts me to hear them say it, but I've got to agree with them a little. I'm sorry if it hurts your feelings . . . but I can't be sorry I said it.

GEORGE: I . . . I'm glad you said it, Emily. I never thought that such a thing was happening to me. I guess it's hard for a fella not to have faults creep into his character.

(*They take a step or two in silence, then stand still in misery.*)

EMILY: I always expect a man to be perfect and I think he should be.

GEORGE: Oh . . . I don't think it's possible to be perfect, Emily.

EMILY: Well, my *father* is, and as far as I can see *your* father is. There's no reason on earth why you shouldn't be, too.

GEORGE: Well, I feel it's the other way round. That men aren't naturally good; but girls are.

EMILY: Well, you might as well know right now that I'm not perfect. It's not as easy for a girl to be perfect as a man, because we girls are more—more—nervous.—Now I'm sorry I said all that about you. I don't know what made me say it.

GEORGE: Emily,—

EMILY: Now I can see it's not the truth at all. And I suddenly feel that it isn't important, anyway.

GEORGE: Emily . . . would you like an ice-cream soda, or something, before you go home?

EMILY: Well, thank you. . . . I would.

(*They advance toward the audience and make an abrupt right turn, opening the door of Morgan's drugstore. Under strong emotion,* EMILY *keeps her face down.* GEORGE *speaks to some passers-by.*)

GEORGE: Hello, Stew,—how are you?—Good afternoon, Mrs. Slocum.

(*The* STAGE MANAGER, *wearing spectacles and assuming the role of* MR. MORGAN, *enters abruptly from the right and stands between the audience and the counter of his soda fountain.*)

STAGE MANAGER: Hello, George. Hello, Emily.—What'll you have?—Why, Emily Webb,—what you been crying about?

GEORGE (*He gropes for an explanation.*): She . . . she just got an awful scare, Mr. Morgan. She almost got run over by that hardware-store wagon. Everybody says that Tom Huckins drives like a crazy man.

STAGE MANAGER (*drawing a drink of water*): Well, now! You take a drink of water, Emily. You look all shook up. I tell you, you've got to look both ways before you cross Main Street these days. Gets worse every year.—What'll you have?

EMILY: I'll have a strawberry phosphate, thank you, Mr. Morgan.

GEORGE: No, no, Emily. Have an ice-cream soda with me. Two strawberry ice-cream sodas, Mr. Morgan.

STAGE MANAGER (*working the faucets*): Two strawberry ice-cream sodas, yes sir. Yes, sir. There are a hundred and twenty-five horses in Grover's Corners this minute I'm talking to you. State Inspector was in here yesterday. And now they're bringing in these auto-mo-biles, the best thing to do is to just stay home. Why, I can remember when a dog could go to sleep all day in the middle of Main Street and nothing come along to disturb him. (*He sets the imaginary glasses before them.*) There they are. Enjoy 'em. (*He sees a customer, right.*) Yes, Mrs. Ellis. What can I do for you? (*He goes out right.*)

EMILY: They're so expensive.

GEORGE: No, no,—don't you think of that. We're celebrating our election. And then do you know what else I'm celebrating?

EMILY: N-no.

GEORGE: I'm celebrating because I've got a friend who tells me all the things that ought to be told me.

EMILY: George, *please* don't think of that. I don't know why I said it. It's not true. You're—

GEORGE: No, Emily, you stick to it. I'm glad you spoke to me like you did. But you'll *see*: I'm going to change so quick—you bet I'm going to change. And, Emily, I want to ask you a favor.

EMILY: What?

GEORGE: Emily, if I go away to State Agriculture College next year, will you write me a letter once in a while?

EMILY: I certainly will. I certainly will, George . . .

(*Pause. They start sipping the sodas through the straws.*)

It certainly seems like being away three years you'd get out of touch with things. Maybe letters from Grover's Corners wouldn't be so interesting after a while. Grover's Corners isn't a very important place when you think of all—New Hampshire; but I think it's a very nice town.

GEORGE: The day wouldn't come when I wouldn't want to know everything that's happening here. I know *that's* true, Emily.

EMILY: Well, I'll try to make my letters interesting.

(*Pause.*)

GEORGE: Y'know, Emily, whenever I meet a farmer I ask him if he thinks it's important to go to Agriculture School to be a good farmer.

EMILY: Why, George—

GEORGE: Yeah, and some of them say that it's even a waste of time. You can get all those things, anyway, out of the pamphlets the government sends out. And Uncle Luke's getting old,—he's about ready for me to start in taking over his farm tomorrow, if I could.

EMILY: My!

GEORGE: And, like you say, being gone all that time . . . in other places and meeting other people . . . Gosh, if anything like that can happen I don't want to go away. I guess new people aren't any better than old ones. I'll bet they almost never are. Emily . . . I feel that you're as good a friend as I've got. I don't need to go and meet the people in other towns.

EMILY: But, George, maybe it's very important for you to go and learn all that about—cattle judging and soils and those things. . . . Of course, I don't know.

GEORGE (*after a pause, very seriously*): Emily, I'm going to make up my mind right now. I won't go. I'll tell Pa about it tonight.

EMILY: Why, George, I don't see why you have to decide right now. It's a whole year away.

GEORGE: Emily, I'm glad you spoke to me about that . . . that fault in my character. What you said was right; but there was *one* thing wrong in it, and that was when you said that for a year I wasn't noticing people, and . . . you, for instance. Why, you say you were watching me when I did everything . . . I was doing the same about you all the time. Why, sure,—I always thought about you as one of the chief people I thought about. I always made sure where you were sitting on the bleachers, and who you were with, and for three days now I've been trying to walk home with you; but something's always got in the way. Yesterday I was standing over against the wall waiting for you, and you walked home with *Miss Corcoran.*

EMILY: George! . . . Life's awful funny! How could I have known that? Why, I thought—

GEORGE: Listen, Emily, I'm going to tell you why I'm not going to Agriculture School. I think that once you've found a person that you're very fond of . . . I mean a person who's fond of you, too, and likes you enough to be interested in your character . . . Well, I think that's just as important as college is, and even more so. That's what I think.

EMILY: I think it's awfully important, too.

GEORGE: Emily.

EMILY: Y-yes, George.

GEORGE: Emily, if I *do* improve and make a big change . . . would you be . . . I mean: *could* you be . . .

EMILY: I . . . I am now; I always have been.

GEORGE (*pause*): So I guess this is an important talk we've been having.

EMILY: Yes . . . yes.

GEORGE (*takes a deep breath and straightens his back*): Wait just a minute and I'll walk you home.

(*With mounting alarm he digs into his pockets for the money.*

The STAGE MANAGER *enters, right.*

GEORGE, *deeply embarrassed, but direct, says to him*:)

Mr. Morgan, I'll have to go home and get the money to pay you for this. It'll only take me a minute.

STAGE MANAGER (*pretending to be affronted*): What's that? George Gibbs, do you mean to tell me—!

GEORGE: Yes, but I had reasons, Mr. Morgan.—Look, here's my gold watch to keep until I come back with the money.

STAGE MANAGER: That's all right. Keep your watch. I'll trust you.

GEORGE: I'll back in five minutes.

STAGE MANAGER: I'll trust you ten years, George,—not a day over.—Got all over your shock, Emily?

EMILY: Yes, thank you, Mr. Morgan. It was nothing.

GEORGE (*taking up the books from the counter*): I'm ready.

(*They walk in grave silence across the stage and pass through the trellis at the Webbs' back door and disappear.*

The STAGE MANAGER *watches them go out, then turns to the audience, removing his spectacles.*)

STAGE MANAGER: Well,— (*He claps his hands as a signal.*) Now we're ready to get on with the wedding.

(*He stands waiting while the set is prepared for the next scene.*

STAGEHANDS *remove the chairs, tables and trellises from the Gibbs and Webb houses.*

They arrange the pews for the church in the center of the stage. The congregation will sit facing the back wall.

The aisle of the church starts at the center of the back wall and comes toward the audience.

A small platform is placed against the back wall on which the STAGE MANAGER *will stand later, playing the minister.*

The image of a stained-glass window is cast from a lantern slide upon the back wall.

When all is ready the STAGE MANAGER *strolls to the center of the stage, down front, and, musingly, addresses the audience.*)

There are a lot of things to be said about a wedding; there are a lot of thoughts that go on during a wedding.

We can't get them all into one wedding, naturally, and especially not into a wedding at Grover's Corners, where they're awfully plain and short.

In this wedding I play the minister. That gives me the right to say a few more things about it.

For a while now, the play gets pretty serious.

Y'see, some churches say that marriage is a sacrament. I don't quite know what that means, but I can guess. Like Mrs. Gibbs said a few minutes ago: people were made to live two-by-two.

This is a good wedding, but people are so put together that even at a good wedding there's a lot of confusion way down deep in people's minds and we thought that that ought to be in our play, too.

The real hero of this scene isn't on the stage at all, and you know who that is. It's like what one of those European fellas said: every child born into the world is nature's attempt to make a perfect human being. Well, we've seen nature pushing and contriving for some time now. We all know that nature's interested in quantity; but I think she's interested in quality, too,—that's why I'm in the ministry.

And don't forget all the other witnesses at this wedding,— the ancestors. Millions of them. Most of them set out to live two-by-two, also. Millions of them.

Well, that's all my sermon. 'Twan't very long, anyway.

(*The organ starts playing Handel's "Largo."*)

The congregation streams into the church and sits in silence. Church bells are heard.

MRS. GIBBS *sits in the front row, the first seat on the aisle, the right section; next to her are* REBECCA *and* DR. GIBBS.

Across the aisle MRS. WEBB, WALLY *and* MR. WEBB. *A small choir takes its place, facing the audience under the stained-glass window.*

MRS. WEBB, *on the way to her place, turns back and speaks to the audience.*)

MRS. WEBB: I don't know why on earth I should be crying. I suppose there's nothing to cry about. It came over me at breakfast this morning; there was Emily eating her breakfast as she's done for seventeen years and now she's going off to eat it in someone else's house. I suppose that's it.

And Emily! She suddenly said: I can't eat another mouthful, and she put her head down on the table and *she* cried.

(*She starts toward her seat in the church, but turns back and adds:*) Oh, I've got to say it: you know, there's something downright cruel about sending our girls out into marriage this way.

I hope some of her girl friends have told her a thing or two. It's cruel, I know, but I couldn't bring myself to say anything. I went into it blind as a bat myself (*in half-amused exasperation*). The whole world's wrong, that's what's the matter.

There they come.

(*She hurries to her place in the pew.*

GEORGE *starts to come down the right aisle of the theater, through the audience.*

Suddenly THREE MEMBERS *of his baseball team appear by the right proscenium pillar and start whistling and catcalling to him. They are dressed for the ball field.*)

THE BASEBALL PLAYERS: Eh, George, George! Hast—

yaow! Look at him, fellas—he looks scared to death. Yaow!
George, don't look so innocent, you old geezer. We know
what you're thinking. Don't disgrace the team, big boy.
Whoo-oo-oo.

STAGE MANAGER: All right! All right! That'll do. That's
enough of that. (*Smiling, he pushes them off the stage. They
lean back to shout a few more catcalls.*) There used to be
an awful lot of that kind of thing at weddings in the old
days,—Rome, and later. We're more civilized now,—so they
say.

(*The choir starts singing "Love Divine, All Love Excell-
ing—"* GEORGE *has reached the stage. He stares at the congregation a moment, then takes a few steps of withdrawal,
toward the right proscenium pillar. His mother, from the
front row, seems to have felt his confusion. She leaves her
seat and comes down the aisle quickly to him.*)

MRS. GIBBS: George! George! What's the matter?

GEORGE: Ma, I don't want to grow old. Why's everybody
pushing me so?

MRS. GIBBS: Why, George . . . you wanted it.

GEORGE: No, Ma, listen to me—

MRS. GIBBS: No, no, George,—you're a man now.

GEORGE: Listen, Ma,—for the last time I ask you . . . All
I want to do is to be a fella—

MRS. GIBBS: George! If anyone should hear you! Now stop.
Why, I'm ashamed of you!

GEORGE (*He comes to himself and looks over the scene.*):
What? Where's Emily?

MRS. GIBBS (*relieved*): George! You gave me such a turn.

GEORGE: Cheer up, Ma. I'm getting married.

MRS. GIBBS: Let me catch my breath a minute.

GEORGE (*comforting her*): Now, Ma, you save Thursday
nights. Emily and I are coming over to dinner every Thursday
night . . . you'll see. Ma, what are you crying for? Come on;
we've got to get ready for this.

(MRS. GIBBS, *mastering her emotion, fixes his tie and whispers to him.*

In the meantime, EMILY, *in white and wearing her wedding veil, has come through the audience and mounted onto
the stage. She too draws back, frightened, when she sees the
congregation in the church. The choir begins: "Blessed Be the
Tie That Binds."*)

EMILY: I never felt so alone in my whole life. And George
over there, looking so . . . ! I *hate* him. I wish I were dead.
Papa! Papa!

MR. WEBB (*leaves his seat in the pews and comes toward her anxiously*): Emily! Emily! Now don't get upset . . . .

EMILY: But, Papa,—I don't want to get married. . . .

MR. WEBB: Sh—sh—Emily. Everything's all right.

EMILY: Why can't I stay for a while just as I am? Let's go away,—

MR. WEBB: No, no, Emily. Now stop and think a minute.

EMILY: Don't you remember that you used to say,—all the time you used to say—all the time: that I was *your* girl! There must be lots of places we can go to. I'll work for you. I could keep house.

MR. WEBB: Sh . . . You mustn't think of such things. You're just nervous, Emily. (*He turns and calls:*) George! George! Will you come here a minute? (*He leads her toward George.*) Why you're marrying the best young fellow in the world. George is a fine fellow.

EMILY: But Papa,—

(MRS. GIBBS *returns unobtrusively to her seat.*

MR. WEBB *has one arm around his daughter. He places his hand on* GEORGE's *shoulder.*)

MR. WEBB: I'm giving away my daughter, George. Do you think you can take care of her?

GEORGE: Mr. Webb, I want to . . . I want to try. Emily, I'm going to do my best. I love you, Emily. I need you.

EMILY: Well, if you love me, help me. All I want is someone to love me.

GEORGE: I will, Emily. Emily, I'll try.

EMILY: And I mean for *ever*. Do you hear? For ever and ever.

(*They fall into each other's arms.*

The March from Lohengrin *is heard.*

The STAGE MANAGER, *as* CLERGYMAN, *stands on the box, up center.*)

MR. WEBB: Come, they're waiting for us. Now you know it'll be all right. Come, quick.

(GEORGE *slips away and takes his place beside the* STAGE MANAGER-CLERGYMAN.

EMILY *proceeds up the aisle on her father's arm.*)

STAGE MANAGER: Do you, George, take this woman, Emily, to be your wedded wife, to have . . .

(MRS. SOAMES *has been sitting in the last row of the congregation.*

She now turns to her neighbors and speaks in a shrill voice. Her chatter drowns out the rest of the clergyman's words.)

MRS. SOAMES: Perfectly lovely wedding! Loveliest wedding I ever saw. Oh, I do love a good wedding, don't you? Doesn't she make a lovely bride?

GEORGE: I do.

STAGE MANAGER: Do you, Emily, take this man, George, to be your wedded husband,—

(*Again his further words are covered by those of* MRS. SOAMES.)

MRS. SOAMES: Don't know *when* I've seen such a lovely wedding. But I always cry. Don't know why it is but I always cry. I just like to see young people happy, don't you? Oh, I think it's lovely.

(*The ring.*
The kiss.
The stage is suddenly arrested into silent tableau.
The STAGE MANAGER, *his eyes on the distance, as though to himself:*)

STAGE MANAGER: I've married over two hundred couples in my day.

Do I believe in it?

I don't know.

M. . . . marries N. . . . millions of them.

The cottage, the go-cart, the Sunday-afternoon drives in the Ford, the first rheumatism, the grandchildren, the second rheumatism, the deathbed, the reading of the will,—(*He now looks at the audience for the first time, with a warm smile that removes any sense of cynicism from the next line.*) Once in a thousand times it's interesting.

—Well, let's have Mendelssohn's "Wedding March"!

(*The organ picks up the March.*
The BRIDE *and* GROOM *come down the aisle, radiant, but trying to be very dignified.*)

MRS. SOAMES: Aren't they a lovely couple? Oh, I've never been to such a nice wedding. I'm sure they'll be happy. I always say: *happiness*, that's the great thing! The important thing is to be happy.

(*The* BRIDE *and* GROOM *reach the steps leading into the audience. A bright light is thrown upon them. They descend into the auditorium and run up the aisle joyously.*)

STAGE MANAGER: That's all the Second Act, folks. Ten minutes' intermission.

ACT III

(*During the intermission the audience has seen the* STAGE-
HANDS *arranging the stage. On the right-hand side, a little
right of the center, ten or twelve ordinary chairs have been
placed in three openly spaced rows facing the audience.*

These are graves in the cemetery.

*Toward the end of the intermission the actors enter and
take their places. The front row contains: Toward the center of the stage, an empty chair; then* MRS. GIBBS; SIMON
STIMSON.

The second row contains, among others, MRS. SOAMES.

The third row has WALLY WEBB.

*The dead do not turn their heads or their eyes to right or
left, but they sit in a quiet without stiffness. When they
speak their tone is matter-of-fact, without sentimentality and,
above all, without lugubriousness.*

The STAGE MANAGER *takes his accustomed place and waits
for the house lights to go down.*)

STAGE MANAGER: This time nine years have gone by,
friends—summer, 1913.

Gradual changes in Grover's Corners. Horses are getting
rarer.

Farmers coming into town in Fords.

Everybody locks their house doors now at night. Ain't
been any burglars in town yet, but everybody's heard about
'em.

You'd be surprised, though—on the whole, things don't
change much around here.

This is certainly an important part of Grover's Corners.
It's on a hilltop—a windy hilltop—lots of sky, lots of
clouds,—often lots of sun and moon and stars.

You come up here on a fine afternoon and you can see
range on range of hills—awful blue they are—up there by
Lake Sunapee and Lake Winnipesaukee . . . and way up,
if you've got a glass, you can see the White Mountains and
Mt. Washington—where North Conway and Conway is.
And, of course, our favorite mountain, Mt. Monadnock, 's

right here—and all these towns that lie around it: Jaffrey, 'n East Jaffrey, 'n Peterborough, 'n Dublin; and (*then pointing down in the audience*) there, quite a ways down, is Grover's Corners.

Yes, beautiful spot up here. Mountain laurel and li-lacks. I often wonder why people like to be buried in Woodlawn and Brooklyn when they might pass the same time up here in New Hampshire.

Over there—(*pointing to stage left*) are the old stones.— 1670, 1680. Strong-minded people that come a long way to be independent. Summer people walk around there laughing at the funny words on the tombstones . . . it don't do any harm. And genealogists come up from Boston—get paid by city people for looking up their ancestors. They want to make sure they're Daughters of the American Revolution and of the *Mayflower*. . . . Well, I guess that don't do any harm, either. Wherever you come near the human race, there's layers and layers of nonsense. . . .

Over there are some Civil War veterans. Iron flags on their graves . . . New Hampshire boys . . . had a notion that the Union ought to be kept together, though they'd never seen more than fifty miles of it themselves. All they knew was the name, friends—the United States of America. The United States of America. And they went and died about it.

This here is the new part of the cemetery. Here's your friend Mrs. Gibbs. 'N let me see—Here's Mr. Stimson, organist at the Congregational Church. And Mrs. Soames who enjoyed the wedding so—you remember? Oh, and a lot of others. And Editor Webb's boy, Wallace, whose appendix burst while he was on a Boy Scout trip to Crawford Notch.

Yes, an awful lot of sorrow has sort of quieted down up here. People just wild with grief have brought their relatives up to this hill. We all know how it is . . . and then time . . . and sunny days . . . and rainy days . . . 'n snow . . . We're all glad they're in a beautiful place and we're coming up here ourselves when our fit's over.

Now there are some things we all know, but we don't take'm out and look at'm very often. We all know that *something* is eternal. And it ain't houses and it ain't names, and it ain't earth, and it ain't even the stars . . . everybody knows in their bones that *something* is eternal, and that something has to do with human beings. All the greatest people ever lived have been telling us that for five thousand years and yet you'd be surprised how people are always losing hold of it. There's something way down deep that's

eternal about every human being. (*pause*) You know as
well as I do that the dead don't stay interested in us living
people for very long. Gradually, gradually, they lose hold
of the earth . . . and the ambitions they had . . . and the
pleasures they had . . . and the things they suffered . . . and
the people they loved.

They get weaned away from the earth—that's the way I
put it,—weaned away.

And they stay here while the earth part of 'em burns
away, burns out; and all that time they slowly get indifferent
to what's goin' on in Grover's Corners.

They're waitin'. They're waitin' for something that they
feel is comin'. Something important, and great. Aren't they
waitin' for the eternal part in them to come out clear?

Some of the things they're going to say maybe'll hurt your
feelings—but that's the way it is: mother 'n daughter . . .
husband 'n wife . . . enemy 'n enemy . . . money 'n miser
. . . all those terribly important things kind of grow pale
around here. And what's left when memory's gone, and your
identity, Mrs. Smith? (*He looks at the audience a minute,
then turns to the stage.*) Well! There are some *living* people.
There's Joe Stoddard, our undertaker, supervising a new-
made grave. And here comes a Grover's Corners boy, that
left town to go out West.

(JOE STODDARD *has hovered about in the background.* SAM
CRAIG *enters left, wiping his forehead from the exertion. He
carries an umbrella and strolls front.*)

SAM CRAIG: Good afternoon, Joe Stoddard.

JOE STODDARD: Good afternoon, good afternoon. Let me
see now: do I know you?

SAM CRAIG: I'm Sam Craig.

JOE STODDARD: Gracious sakes' alive! Of all people! I
should'a knowed you'd be back for the funeral. You've been
away a long time, Sam.

SAM CRAIG: Yes, I've been away over twelve years. I'm in
business out in Buffalo now, Joe. But I was in the East when
I got news of my cousin's death, so I thought I'd combine
things a little and come and see the old home. You look well.

JOE STODDARD: Yes, yes, can't complain. Very sad, our
journey today, Samuel.

SAM CRAIG: Yes.

JOE STODDARD: Yes, yes. I always say I hate to supervise
when a young person is taken. They'll be here in a few
minutes now. I had to come here early today—my son's
supervisin' at the home.

SAM CRAIG (*reading stones*): Old Farmer McCarty, I used to do chores for him—after school. He had the lumbago.

JOE STODDARD: Yes, we brought Farmer McCarty here a number of years ago now.

SAM CRAIG (*staring at Mrs. Gibbs' knees*): Why, this is my Aunt Julia . . . I'd forgotten that she'd . . . of course, of course.

JOE STODDARD: Yes, Doc Gibbs lost his wife two-three years ago . . . about this time. And today's another pretty bad blow for him, too.

MRS. GIBBS (*to* SIMON STIMSON: *in an even voice*). That's my sister Carey's boy, Sam . . . Sam Craig.

SIMON STIMSON: I'm always uncomfortable when *they're* around.

MRS. GIBBS: Simon.

SAM CRAIG: Do they choose their own verses much, Joe?

JOE STODDARD: No . . . not usual. Mostly the bereaved pick a verse.

SAM CRAIG: Doesn't sound like Aunt Julia. There aren't many of those Hersey sisters left now. Let me see: where are . . . I wanted to look at my father's and mother's . . .

JOE STODDARD: Over there with the Craigs . . . Avenue F.

SAM CRAIG (*reading* SIMON STIMSON's *epitaph*): He was organist at church, wasn't he?—Hm, drank a lot, we used to say.

JOE STODDARD: Nobody was supposed to know about it. He'd seen a peck of trouble. (*behind his hand*) Took his own life, y'know?

SAM CRAIG: Oh, did he?

JOE STODDARD: Hung himself in the attic. They tried to hush it up, but of course it got around. He chose his own epy-taph. You can see it there. It ain't a verse exactly.

SAM CRAIG: Why, it's just some notes of music—what is it?

JOE STODDARD: Oh, I wouldn't know. It was wrote up in the Boston papers at the time.

SAM CRAIG: Joe, what did she die of?

JOE STODDARD: Who?

SAM CRAIG: My cousin.

JOE STODDARD: Oh, didn't you know? Had some trouble bringing a baby into the world. 'Twas her second, though. There's a little boy 'bout four years old.

SAM CRAIG (*opening his umbrella*): The grave's going to be over there?

JOE STODDARD: Yes, there ain't much more room over

here among the Gibbses, so they're opening up a whole new Gibbs section over by Avenue B. You'll excuse me now. I see they're comin'.

(*From left to center, at the back of the stage, comes a procession.* FOUR MEN *carry a casket, invisible to us. All the rest are under umbrellas. One can vaguely see:* DR. GIBBS, GEORGE, *the* WEBBS, *etc. They gather about a grave in the back center of the stage, a little to the left of center.*)

MRS. SOAMES: Who is it, Julia?

MRS. GIBBS (*without raising her eyes*): My daughter-in-law, Emily Webb.

MRS. SOAMES (*a little surprised, but no emotion*): Well, I declare! The road up here must have been awful muddy. What did she die of, Julia?

MRS. GIBBS: In childbirth.

MRS. SOAMES: Childbirth. (*almost with a laugh*) I'd forgotten all about that. My, wasn't life awful—(*with a sigh*) and wonderful.

SIMON STIMSON (*with a sideways glance*): Wonderful, was it?

MRS. GIBBS: Simon! Now remember!

MRS. SOAMES: I remember Emily's wedding. Wasn't it a lovely wedding! And I remember her reading the class poem at Graduation Exercises. Emily was one of the brightest girls ever graduated from High School. I've heard Principal Wilkins say so time after time. I called on them at their new farm, just before I died. Perfectly beautiful farm.

A WOMAN FROM AMONG THE DEAD: It's on the same road we lived on.

A MAN AMONG THE DEAD: Yepp, right smart farm. (*They subside. The group by the grave starts singing "Blessed Be the Tie That Binds."*)

A WOMAN AMONG THE DEAD: I always liked that hymn. I was hopin' they'd sing a hymn.

(*Pause. Suddenly* EMILY *appears from among the umbrellas. She is wearing a white dress. Her hair is down her back and tied by a white ribbon like a little girl. She comes slowly, gazing wonderingly at the dead, a little dazed.*

She stops halfway and smiles faintly. After looking at the mourners for a moment, she walks slowly to the vacant chair beside Mrs. Gibbs and sits down.)

EMILY (*to them all, quietly, smiling*): Hello.

MRS. SOAMES: Hello, Emily.

A MAN AMONG THE DEAD: Hello, M's Gibbs.

EMILY (*warmly*): Hello, Mother Gibbs.

MRS. GIBBS: Emily.

EMILY: Hello. (*with surprise*) It's raining. (*Her eyes drift back to the funeral company.*)

MRS. GIBBS: Yes . . . They'll be gone soon, dear. Just rest yourself.

EMILY: It seems like thousands and thousands of years since I . . . Papa remembered that that was my favorite hymn.

Oh, I wish I'd been here a long time. I don't like being new here.—How do you do, Mr. Stimson?

SIMON STIMSON: How do you do, Emily.

(*EMILY continues to look about her with a wondering smile; as though to shut out from her mind the thought of the funeral company she starts speaking to Mrs. Gibbs with a touch of nervousness.*)

EMILY: Mother Gibbs, George and I have made that farm into just the best place you ever saw. We thought of you all the time. We wanted to show you the new barn and a great long ce-ment drinking fountain for the stock. We bought that out of the money you left us.

MRS. GIBBS: I did?

EMILY: Don't you remember, Mother Gibbs—the legacy you left us? Why, it was over three hundred and fifty dollars.

MRS. GIBBS: Yes, yes, Emily.

EMILY: Well, there's a patent device on the drinking fountain so that it never overflows, Mother Gibbs, and it never sinks below a certain mark they have there. It's fine.

(*Her voice trails off and her eyes return to the funeral group.*) It won't be the same to George without me, but it's a lovely farm. (*Suddenly she looks directly at Mrs. Gibbs.*) Live people don't understand, do they?

MRS. GIBBS: No, dear—not very much.

EMILY: They're sort of shut up in little boxes, aren't they? I feel as though I knew them last a thousand years ago . . . My boy is spending the day at Mrs. Carter's. (*She sees* MR. CARTER *among the dead.*) Oh, Mr. Carter, my little boy is spending the day at your house.

MR. CARTER: Is he?

EMILY: Yes, he loves it there—Mother Gibbs, we have a Ford, too. Never gives any trouble. I don't drive, though. Mother Gibbs, when does this feeling go away?—Of being . . . one of *them?* How long does it . . . ?

MRS. GIBBS: Sh! dear. Just wait and be patient.

EMILY (*with a sigh*): I know.—Look, they're finished. They're going.

MRS. GIBBS: Sh——.

(*The umbrellas leave the stage.* DR. GIBBS *has come over to his wife's grave and stands before it a moment.* EMILY *looks up at his face.* MRS. GIBBS *does not raise her eyes.*)

EMILY: Look! Father Gibbs is bringing some of my flowers to you. He looks just like George, doesn't he? Oh, Mother Gibbs, I never realized before how troubled and how . . . how in the dark live persons are. Look at him. I loved him so. From morning till night, that's all they are—troubled.

(DR. GIBBS *goes off.*)

THE DEAD: Little cooler than it was.—Yes, that rain's cooled it off a little. Those northeast winds always do the same thing, don't they? If it isn't a rain, it's a three-day blow.—

(*A patient calm falls on the stage. The* STAGE MANAGER *appears at his proscenium pillar, smoking.* EMILY *sits up abruptly with an idea.*)

EMILY: But, Mother Gibbs, one can go back; one can go back there again . . . into living. I feel it. I know it. Why just then for a moment I was thinking about . . . about the farm . . . and for a minute I *was* there, and my baby was on my lap as plain as day.

MRS. GIBBS: Yes, of course you can.

EMILY: I can go back there and live all those days over again . . . why not?

MRS. GIBBS: All I can say is, Emily, don't.

EMILY (*She appeals urgently to the stage manager.*): But it's true, isn't it? I can go and live . . . back there . . . again.

STAGE MANAGER: Yes, some have tried—but they soon come back here.

MRS. GIBBS: Don't do it, Emily.

MRS. SOAMES: Emily, don't. It's not what you think it'd be.

EMILY: But I won't live over a sad day. I'll choose a happy one—I'll choose the day I first knew that I loved George. Why should that be painful?

(THEY *are silent. Her question turns to the* STAGE MANAGER.)

STAGE MANAGER: You not only live it; but you watch yourself living it.

EMILY: Yes?

STAGE MANAGER: And as you watch it, you see the thing that they—down there—never know. You see the future. You know what's going to happen afterwards.

EMILY: But is that—painful? Why?

MRS. GIBBS: That's not the only reason why you shouldn't

do it, Emily. When you've been here longer you'll see that our life here is to forget all that, and think only of what's ahead, and be ready for what's ahead. When you've been here longer you'll understand.

EMILY (*softly*): But, Mother Gibbs, how can I *ever* forget that life? It's all I know. It's all I had.

MRS. SOAMES: Oh, Emily. It isn't wise. Really, it isn't.

EMILY: But it's a thing I must know for myself. I'll choose a happy day, anyway.

MRS. GIBBS: *No!*—At least, choose an unimportant day. Choose the least important day in your life. It will be important enough.

EMILY (*to herself*): Then it can't be since I was married; or since the baby was born. (*to the* STAGE MANAGER, *eagerly*) I can choose a birthday at least, can't I?—I choose my twelfth birthday.

STAGE MANAGER: All right. February 11th, 1899. A Tuesday.—Do you want any special time of day?

EMILY: Oh, I want the whole day.

STAGE MANAGER: We'll begin at dawn. You remember it had been snowing for several days; but it had stopped the night before, and they had begun clearing the roads. The sun's coming up.

EMILY (*with a cry; rising*): There's Main Street . . . why, that's Mr. Morgan's drugstore before he changed it . . . And there's the livery stable.

(*The stage at no time in this act has been very dark; but now the left half of the stage gradually becomes very bright —the brightness of a crisp winter morning.* EMILY *walks toward Main Street.*)

STAGE MANAGER: Yes, it's 1899. This was fourteen years ago.

EMILY: Oh, that's the town I knew as a little girl. And, *look*, there's the old white fence that used to be around our house. Oh, I'd forgotten that! Oh, I love it so! Are they inside?

STAGE MANAGER: Yes, your mother'll be coming downstairs in a minute to make breakfast.

EMILY (*softly*): Will she?

STAGE MANAGER: And you remember: your father had been away for several days; he came back on the early-morning train.

EMILY: No . . . ?

STAGE MANAGER: He'd been back to his college to make a speech—in western New York, at Clinton.

EMILY: Look! There's Howie Newsome. There's our policeman. But he's *dead*; he *died*.

(*The voices of* HOWIE NEWSOME, CONSTABLE WARREN *and*
JOE CROWELL, JR., *are heard at the left of the stage.* EMILY
listens in delight.)

HOWIE NEWSOME: Whoa, Bessie!—Bessie! Morning, Bill.

CONSTABLE WARREN: Morning, Howie.

HOWIE NEWSOME: You're up early.

CONSTABLE WARREN: Been rescuin' a party; darn near
froze to death, down by Polish Town thar. Got drunk and
lay out in the snowdrifts. Thought he was in bed when I
shook'm.

EMILY: Why, there's Joe Crowell. . . .

JOE CROWELL: Good morning, Mr. Warren. Morning,
Howie.

(MRS. WEBB *has appeared in her kitchen, but* EMILY *does
not see her until she calls.*)

MRS. WEBB: Chil-*dren!* Wally! Emily! . . . Time to get up.

EMILY: Mama, I'm here! Oh; how young Mama looks! I
didn't know Mama was ever that young.

MRS. WEBB: You can come and dress by the kitchen fire,
if you like; but hurry.

(HOWIE NEWSOME *has entered along Main Street and brings
the milk to Mrs. Webb's door.*)

Good morning, Mr. Newsome. Whhhh—it's cold.

HOWIE NEWSOME: Ten below by my barn, Mrs. Webb.

MRS. WEBB: Think of it! Keep yourself wrapped up. (*She
takes her bottles in, shuddering.*)

EMILY (*with an effort*): Mama, I can't find my blue
hair ribbon anywhere.

MRS. WEBB: Just open your eyes, dear, that's all. I laid it
out for you special—on the dresser, there. If it were a snake
it would bite you.

EMILY: Yes, yes . . . (*She puts her hand on her heart.*
MR. WEBB *comes along Main Street, where he meets* CON-
STABLE WARREN. *Their movements and voices are increas-
ingly lively in the sharp air.*)

MR. WEBB: Good morning, Bill.

CONSTABLE WARREN: Good morning, Mr. Webb. You're
up early.

MR. WEBB: Yes, just been back to my old college in New
York State. Been any trouble here?

CONSTABLE WARREN: Well, I was called up this mornin'
to rescue a Polish fella—darn near froze to death he was.

MR. WEBB: We must get it in the paper.

CONSTABLE WARREN: 'Twan't much.

EMILY (*whispers*): Papa.

(MR. WEBB *shakes the snow off his feet and enters his house.* CONSTABLE WARREN *goes off, right.*)

MR. WEBB: Good morning, Mother.

MRS. WEBB: How did it go, Charles?

MR. WEBB: Oh, fine, I guess. I told'm a few things.— Everything all right here?

MRS. WEBB: Yes—can't think of anything that's happened, special. Been right cold. Howie Newsome says it's ten below over to his barn.

MR. WEBB: Yes, well, it's colder than that at Hamilton College. Students' ears are falling off. It ain't Christian.— Paper have any mistakes in it?

MRS. WEBB: None that I noticed. Coffee's ready when you want it. (*He starts upstairs.*) Charles! Don't forget; it's Emily's birthday. Did you remember to get her something?

MR. WEBB (*patting his pocket*): Yes, I've got something here. (*calling up the stairs*) Where's my girl? Where's my birthday girl?

(*He goes off left.*)

MRS. WEBB: Don't interrupt her now, Charles. You can see her at breakfast. She's slow enough as it is. Hurry up, children! It's seven o'clock. Now, I don't want to call you again.

EMILY (*softly, more in wonder than in grief*): I can't bear it. They're so young and beautiful. Why did they ever have to get old? Mama, I'm here. I'm grown up. I love you all, everything.—I can't look at everything hard enough.

(*She looks questioningly at the* STAGE MANAGER, *saying or suggesting: "Can I go in?" He nods briefly. She crosses to the inner door to the kitchen, left of her mother, and as though entering the room, says, suggesting the voice of a girl of twelve:*)

Good morning, Mama.

MRS. WEBB (*crossing to embrace and kiss her; in her characteristic matter-of-fact manner*): Well, now, dear, a very happy birthday to my girl and many happy returns. There are some surprises waiting for you on the kitchen table.

EMILY: Oh, Mama, you *shouldn't* have. (*She throws an anguished glance at the* STAGE MANAGER.)—I can't—I can't.

MRS. WEBB (*facing the audience, over her stove*): But birthday or no birthday, I want you to eat your breakfast good and slow. I want you to grow up and be a good strong girl.

That in the blue paper is from your Aunt Carrie; and I reckon you can guess who brought the post-card album. I found it on the doorstep when I brought in the milk—George Gibbs . . . must have come over in the cold pretty early . . . right nice of him.

EMILY (*to herself*): Oh, George! I'd forgotten that. . . .

MRS. WEBB: Chew that bacon good and slow. It'll help keep you warm on a cold day.

EMILY (*with mounting urgency*): Oh, Mama, just look at me one minute as though you really saw me. Mama, fourteen years have gone by. I'm dead. You're a grandmother, Mama. I married George Gibbs, Mama. Wally's dead, too. Mama, his appendix burst on a camping trip to North Conway. We felt just terrible about it—don't you remember? But, just for a moment now we're all together. Mama, just for a moment we're happy. *Let's look at one another.*

MRS. WEBB: That in the yellow paper is something I found in the attic among your grandmother's things. You're old enough to wear it now, and I thought you'd like it.

EMILY: And this is from you. Why, Mama, it's just lovely and it's just what I wanted. It's beautiful!

(*She flings her arms around her mother's neck. Her* MOTHER *goes on with her cooking, but is pleased.*)

MRS. WEBB: Well, I hoped you'd like it. Hunted all over. Your Aunt Norah couldn't find one in Concord, so I had to send all the way to Boston. (*laughing*) Wally's something for you, too. He made it at manual-training class and he's very proud of it. Be sure you make a big fuss about it.—Your father has a surprise for you, too; don't know what it is myself. Sh—here he comes.

MR. WEBB (*off stage*): Where's my girl? Where's my birthday girl?

EMILY (*in a loud voice to the* STAGE MANAGER): I can't. I can't go on. It goes so fast. We don't have time to look at one another.

(*She breaks down sobbing.*

The lights dim on the left half of the stage. MRS. WEBB *disappears.*)

I didn't realize. So all that was going on and we never noticed. Take me back—up the hill—to my grave. But first: Wait! One more look.

Good-by, Good-by, world. Good-by, Grover's Corners . . . Mama and Papa. Good-by to clocks ticking . . . and Mama's sunflowers. And food and coffee. And new-ironed dresses and hot baths . . . and sleeping and waking up. Oh, earth, you're too wonderful for anybody to realize you.

(*She looks toward the* STAGE MANAGER *and asks abruptly, through her tears:*)

Do any human beings ever realize life while they live it?— every, every minute?

STAGE MANAGER: No. (*pause*) The saints and poets, maybe—they do some.

EMILY: I'm ready to go back. (*She returns to her chair beside Mrs. Gibbs. Pause.*)

MRS. GIBBS: Were you happy?

EMILY: No . . . I should have listened to you. That's all human beings are! just blind people.

MRS. GIBBS: Look, it's clearing up. The stars are coming out.

EMILY: Oh, Mr. Stimson, I should have listened to them.

SIMON STIMSON (*with mounting violence; bitingly*): Yes, now you know. Now you know! That's what it was to be alive. To move about in a cloud of ignorance; to go up and down trampling on the feelings of those . . . of those about you. To spend and waste time as though you had a million years. To be always at the mercy of one self-centered passion, or another. Now you know—that's the happy existence you wanted to go back to. Ignorance and blindness.

MRS. GIBBS (*spiritedly*): Simon Stimson, that ain't the whole truth and you know it. Emily, look at that star. I forget its name.

A MAN AMONG THE DEAD: My boy Joel was a sailor,— knew 'em all. He'd set on the porch evenings and tell 'em all by name. Yes, sir, wonderful.

ANOTHER MAN AMONG THE DEAD: A star's mighty good company.

A WOMAN AMONG THE DEAD: Yes. Yes, 'tis.

SIMON STIMSON: Here's one of *them* coming.

THE DEAD: That's funny. 'Tain't no time for one of them to be here.—Goodness sakes.

EMILY: Mother Gibbs, it's George.

MRS. GIBBS: Sh, dear. Just rest yourself.

EMILY: It's George.

(GEORGE *enters from the left, and slowly comes toward them.*)

A MAN FROM AMONG THE DEAD: And my Joel, who knew the stars—he used to say it took millions of years for that speck o' light to git to the earth. Don't seem like a body could believe it, but that's what he used to say—millions of years.

(GEORGE *sinks to his knees then falls full length at Emily's feet.*)

A WOMAN AMONG THE DEAD: Goodness! That ain't no way to behave!

MRS. SOAMES: He ought to be home.

EMILY: Mother Gibbs?

MRS. GIBBS: Yes, Emily?

EMILY: They don't understand, do they?

MRS. GIBBS: No, dear. They don't understand.

(*The* STAGE MANAGER *appears at the right, one hand on a dark curtain which he slowly draws across the scene.*

In the distance a clock is heard striking the hour very faintly.)

STAGE MANAGER: Most everybody's asleep in Grover's Corners. There are a few lights on: Shorty Hawkins, down at the depot, has just watched the Albany train go by. And at the livery stable somebody's setting up late and talking.—Yes, it's clearing up. There are the stars—doing their old, old crisscross journeys in the sky. Scholars haven't settled the matter yet, but they seem to think there are no living beings up there. Just chalk . . . or fire. Only this one is straining away, straining away all the time to make something of itself. The strain's so bad that every sixteen hours everybody lies down and gets a rest. (*He winds his watch.*) Hm. . . . Eleven o'clock in Grover's Corners.—You get a good rest, too. Good night.

George Bernard Shaw:

Pygmalion

George Bernard Shaw (1856–1950) was born in Ireland and moved to England while he was still in his teens. In his twenties Shaw divided his time between writing unsuccessful novels and observing the wretched conditions of the London poor. In his thirties Shaw established himself as a critic of art, music, and drama. His career as a playwright coincided with the onset of middle age. His slow metamorphosis from an unknown, unsuccessful novelist to the best-known writer of his time has been the subject of a number of books, the best of which is St. John Ervine's Bernard Shaw. *His most representative plays are:* Mrs. Warren's Profession *(1893)*, Arms and the Man *(1894)*, Candida *(1894)*, The Devil's Disciple *(1896)*, Caesar and Cleopatra *(1899)*, Man and Superman *(1903)*, Major Barbara *(1905)*, The Doctor's Dilemma *(1906)*, Heartbreak House *(1920)*, Saint Joan *(1924)*, The Apple Cart *(1929)*, and Too True to be Good *(1932)*.

Bernard Shaw wrote in a 1942 preface to *Pygmalion* (1913) "that it is impossible for an Englishman to open his mouth without making some other Englishman despise him." In England (and even, to a certain extent, in the United States) speech is perhaps the most important clue in determining caste or class. *Pygmalion* has as its subject-theme the institutions man has constructed to help perpetuate both the privileges of the rich and the servility of the poor.

The passionate sincerity and the desperate earnestness that lie behind the surface play of Shaw's most successful comedy have as their origin the fact that Shaw spent the best part of his youth, the decade of his twenties, tramping the streets of London observing the extremes of wealth and poverty. Shocked by what he saw, he became a founding member of the Fabian Society, a political group committed to Socialism, the progenitor of Britain's Labour Party.

Shaw's earliest plays explicitly dealt with economic and social injustice. Sober, earnest, old-fashioned, they were failures. Not until Shaw found his own voice—in plays comically saturated with paradox and irreverence, a genre now known as Shavian comedy—did his impact on England and the world exceed that of any other playwright of our century.

What Shaw learned was that before he could persuade an audience to think, he must first provoke laughter—and then tears. At what point in the play do we become involved and indignant about the plight of Eliza Doolittle? Like her benefactors, we continue to regard her as something not unlike a trained dog—until the moment we realize that because of the accident of birth a young woman of character and intelligence has been condemned to a lifetime of squalor and hopelessness. Then, and only then, do we realize that Shaw has used his Cockney Cinderella as a symbol of the world's dispossessed whose hope lies in the availability of education and the good will of those more fortunate among us.

Pygmalion

[*Passages following the asterisked sections of the text were added by Bernard Shaw for inclusion in the motion picture adaptation of the play*] *ed.*

ACT I

(*London at 11:15 p.m. Torrents of heavy summer rain. Cab whistles blowing frantically in all directions. Pedestrians running for shelter into the portico of St. Paul's church (not Wren's cathedral but Inigo Jones's church in Covent Garden vegetable market), among them a lady and her daughter in evening dress. All are peering out gloomily at the rain, except one man with his back turned to the rest, wholly preoccupied with a notebook in which he is writing.*
The church clock strikes the first quarter.)

THE DAUGHTER (*in the space between the central pillars, close to the one on her left*): I'm getting chilled to the bone. What can Freddy be doing all this time? He's been gone twenty minutes.

THE MOTHER (*on her daughter's right*): Not so long. But he ought to have got us a cab by this.

A BYSTANDER (*on the lady's right*): He wont get no cab not until half-past eleven, missus, when they come back after dropping their theatre fares.

THE MOTHER: But we must have a cab. We cant stand here until half-past eleven. It's too bad.

THE BYSTANDER: Well, it aint my fault, missus.

THE DAUGHTER: If Freddy had a bit of gumption, he would have got one at the theatre door.

THE MOTHER: What could he have done, poor boy?

THE DAUGHTER: Other people got cabs. Why couldnt he?

(FREDDY *rushes in out of the rain from the Southampton Street side, and comes between them closing a dripping umbrella. He is a young man of twenty, in evening dress, very wet round the ankles.*)

THE DAUGHTER: Well havnt you got a cab?

FREDDY: Theres not one to be had for love or money.

THE MOTHER: Oh, Freddy, there must be one. You cant have tried.

THE DAUGHTER: It's too tiresome. Do you expect us to go and get one ourselves?

FREDDY: I tell you theyre all engaged. The rain was so sudden: nobody was prepared; and everybody had to take a cab. Ive been to Charing Cross one way and nearly to Ludgate Circus the other; and they were all engaged.

THE MOTHER: Did you try Trafalgar Square?

FREDDY: There wasn't one at Trafalgar Square.

THE DAUGHTER: Did you try?

FREDDY: I tried as far as Charing Cross Station. Did you expect me to walk to Hammersmith?

THE DAUGHTER: You havnt tried at all.

THE MOTHER: You really are very helpless, Freddy. Go again; and dont come back until you have found a cab.

FREDDY: I shall simply get soaked for nothing.

THE DAUGHTER: And what about us? Are we to stay here all night in this draught, with next to nothing on? You selfish pig—

FREDDY: Oh, very well: I'll go, I'll go. (*He opens his umbrella and dashes off Strandwards, but comes into collision with a* FLOWER GIRL *who is hurrying for shelter, knocking her basket out of her hands. A blinding flash of lightning, followed instantly by a rattling peal of thunder, orchestrates the incident.*)

THE FLOWER GIRL: Nah then, Freddy: look wh' y' gowin, deah.

FREDDY: Sorry.

(*He rushes off.*)

THE FLOWER GIRL (*picking up her scattered flowers and replacing them in the basket*): Theres menners f' yer! Te-oo banches o voylets trod into the mad. (*She sits down on the plinth of the column, sorting her flowers, on the lady's right. She is not at all a romantic figure. She is perhaps eighteen, perhaps twenty, hardly older. She wears a little sailor hat of black straw that has long been exposed to the dust and soot of London and has seldom if ever been brushed. Her hair needs washing rather badly: its mousy color can hardly be natural. She wears a shoddy black coat that reaches nearly to her knees and is shaped to her waist. She has a brown skirt with a coarse apron. Her boots are much the worse for wear.*)

She is no doubt as clean as she can afford to be; but com-pared to the ladies she is very dirty. Her features are no worse than theirs; but their condition leaves something to be desired; and she needs the services of a dentist.)

THE MOTHER: How do you know that my son's name is Freddy, pray?

THE FLOWER GIRL: Ow, eez ye-ooa san, is e? Wal, fewd dan y' de-ooty bawmz a mather should, eed now bettern to spawl a pore gel's flahrzn than ran awy athaht pyin. Will ye-oo py me f'them? (*Here, with apologies, this desperate attempt to represent her dialect without a phonetic alphabet must be abandoned as unintelligible outside London.*)

THE DAUGHTER: Do nothing of the sort, mother. The idea!

THE MOTHER: Please allow me, Clara. Have you any pen-nies?

THE DAUGHTER: No. Ive nothing smaller than sixpence.

THE FLOWER GIRL (*hopefully*): I can give you change for a tanner, kind lady.

THE MOTHER (*to* CLARA): Give it to me. (CLARA *parts re-luctantly.*) Now. (*to the* GIRL) This is for your flowers.

THE FLOWER GIRL: Thank you kindly, lady.

THE DAUGHTER: Make her give you the change. These things are only a penny a bunch.

THE MOTHER: Do hold your tongue, Clara. (*to the* GIRL) You can keep the change.

THE FLOWER GIRL: Oh, thank you, lady.

THE MOTHER: Now tell me how you know that young gentleman's name.

THE FLOWER GIRL: I didnt.

THE MOTHER: I heard you call him by it. Dont try to deceive me.

THE FLOWER GIRL (*protesting*): Who's trying to deceive you? I called him Freddy or Charlie same as you might your-self if you was talking to a stranger and wished to be pleasant.

THE DAUGHTER: Sixpence thrown away! Really, mamma, you might have spared Freddy that. (*She retreats in disgust behind the pillar.*)

(*An elderly* GENTLEMAN *of the amiable military type rushes into the shelter, and closes a dripping umbrella. He is in the same plight as* FREDDY, *very wet about the ankles. He is in evening dress, with a light overcoat. He takes the place left vacant by the daughter.*)

THE GENTLEMAN: Phew!

THE MOTHER (*to the* GENTLEMAN): Oh, sir, is there any sign of its stopping?

THE GENTLEMAN: I'm afraid not. It started worse than ever about two minutes ago. (*He goes to the plinth beside the* FLOWER GIRL; *puts up his foot on it; and stoops to turn down his trouser ends.*)

THE MOTHER: Oh dear! (*She retires sadly and joins her* DAUGHTER.)

THE FLOWER GIRL (*taking advantage of the military* GENTLEMAN's *proximity to establish friendly relations with him*): If it's worse, it's a sign it's nearly over. So cheer up, Captain; and buy a flower off a poor girl.

THE GENTLEMAN: I'm sorry. I havnt any change.

THE FLOWER GIRL: I can give you change, Captain.

THE GENTLEMAN: For a sovereign? Ive nothing less.

THE FLOWER GIRL: Garn! Oh do buy a flower off me, Captain. I can change half-a-crown. Take this for tuppence.

THE GENTLEMAN: Now dont be troublesome: theres a good girl (*trying his pockets*). I really havnt any change—Stop: heres three hapence, if thats any use to you. (*He retreats to the other pillar.*)

THE FLOWER GIRL (*disappointed, but thinking three halfpence better than nothing*): Thank you, sir.

THE BYSTANDER (*to the* GIRL): You be careful: give him a flower for it. Theres a bloke here behind taking down every blessed word youre saying. (*All turn to the man who is taking notes.*)

THE FLOWER GIRL (*springing up terrified*): I aint done nothing wrong by speaking to the gentleman. Ive a right to sell flowers if I keep off the kerb. (*hysterically*) I'm a respectable girl: so help me, I never spoke to him except to ask him to buy a flower off me.

(*General hubbub, mostly sympathetic to the* FLOWER GIRL, *but deprecating her excessive sensibility. Cries of* Dont start hollerin. Who's hurting you? Nobody's going to touch you. Whats the good of fussing? Steady on. Easy easy, etc., *come from the elderly staid spectators, who pat her comfortingly. Less patient ones bid her shut her head, or ask her roughly what is wrong with her. A remoter group, not knowing what the matter is, crowd in and increase the noise with question and answer:* Whats the row? What-she do? Where is he? A tec taking her down. What! him? Yes: him over there: Took money off the gentleman, etc.)

THE FLOWER GIRL (*breaking through them to the* GENTLEMAN, *crying wildly*): Oh, sir, dont let him charge me. You dunno what it means to me. Theyll take away my character and drive me on the streets for speaking to gentlemen. They—

THE NOTE TAKER (*coming forward on her right, the rest crowding after him*): There! there! there! there! who's hurting you, you silly girl? What do you take me for?

THE BYSTANDER: It's aw rawt: e's a genleman: look at his be-oots. (*explaining to the* NOTE TAKER) She thought you was a copper's nark, sir.

THE NOTE TAKER (*with quick interest*): Whats a copper's nark?

THE BYSTANDER (*inapt at definition*): It's a—well, it's a copper's nark, as you might say. What else would you call it? A sort of informer.

THE FLOWER GIRL (*still hysterical*): I take my Bible oath I never said a word—

THE NOTE TAKER (*overbearing but good-humored*): Oh, shut up, shut up. Do I look like a policeman?

THE FLOWER GIRL (*far from reassured*): Then what did you take down my words for? How do I know whether you took me down right? You just shew me what youve wrote about me. (*The* NOTE TAKER *opens his book and holds it steadily under her nose, though the pressure of the mob trying to read it over his shoulders would upset a weaker man.*) Whats that? That aint proper writing. I cant read that.

THE NOTE TAKER: I can. (*reads, reproducing her pronunciation exactly*) "Cheer ap, Keptin; n' baw ya flahr orf a pore gel."

THE FLOWER GIRL (*much distressed*): It's because I called him Captain. I meant no harm. (*to the* GENTLEMAN) Oh, sir, dont let him lay a charge agen me for a word like that. You—

THE GENTLEMAN: Charge! I make no charge. (*to the* NOTE TAKER) Really, sir, if you are a detective, you need not begin protecting me against molestation by young women until I ask you. Anybody could see that the girl meant no harm.

THE BYSTANDERS GENERALLY (*demonstrating against police espionage*): Course they could. What business is it of yours? You mind your own affairs. He wants promotion, he does. Taking down people's words! Girl never said a word to him. What harm if she did? Nice thing a girl cant shelter from the rain without being insulted, etc., etc., etc. (*She is conducted by the more sympathetic demonstrators back to her plinth, where she resumes her seat and struggles with her emotion.*)

THE BYSTANDER: He aint a tec. He's a bloming busybody: thats what he is. I tell you, look at his be-oots.

THE NOTE TAKER (*turning on him genially*): And how are all your people down at Selsey?

THE BYSTANDER (*suspiciously*): Who told you my people come from Selsey?

THE NOTE TAKER: Never you mind. They did. (*to the* GIRL) How do you come to be up so far east? You were born in Lisson Grove.

THE FLOWER GIRL (*appalled*): Oh, what harm is there in my leaving Lisson Grove? It wasnt fit for a pig to live in; and I had to pay four-and-six a week. (*in tears*) Oh, boo—hoo—oo—

THE NOTE TAKER: Live where you like; but stop that noise.

THE GENTLEMAN (*to the* GIRL): Come, come! he cant touch you: you have a right to live where you please.

A SARCASTIC BYSTANDER (*thrusting himself between the* NOTE TAKER *and the* GENTLEMAN): Park Lane, for instance. I'd like to go into the Housing Question with you, I would.

THE FLOWER GIRL (*subsiding into a brooding melancholy over her basket, and talking very low-spiritedly to herself*): I'm a good girl, I am.

THE SARCASTIC BYSTANDER (*not attending to her*): Do you know where *I* come from?

THE NOTE TAKER (*promptly*): Hoxton.

(*Titterings. Popular interest in the* NOTE TAKER'S *performance increases.*)

THE SARCASTIC ONE (*amazed*): Well, who said I didnt? Bly me! you know everything, you do.

THE FLOWER GIRL (*still nursing her sense of injury*): Aint no call to meddle with me, he aint.

THE BYSTANDER (*to her*): Of course he aint. Dont you stand it from him. (*to the* NOTE TAKER) See here: what call have you to know about people what never offered to meddle with you?

THE FLOWER GIRL: Let him say what he likes. I dont want to have no truck with him.

THE BYSTANDER: You take us for dirt under your feet, dont you? Catch you taking liberties with a gentleman!

THE SARCASTIC BYSTANDER: Yes: tell him where he come from if you want to go fortune-telling.

THE NOTE TAKER: Cheltenham, Harrow, Cambridge, and India.

THE GENTLEMAN: Quite right.

(*Great laughter. Reaction in the* NOTE TAKER'S *favor. Exclamations of* He knows all about it. Told him proper. Hear him tell the toff where he come from? *etc.*)

...MAN: May I ask, sir, do you do this for your
...sic hall?

... TAKER: I've thought of that. Perhaps I shall some

... rain has stopped; and the persons on the outside of the crowd begin to drop off.)

THE FLOWER GIRL (*resenting the reaction*): He's no gentleman, he aint, to interfere with a poor girl.

THE DAUGHTER (*out of patience, pushing her way rudely to the front and displacing the* GENTLEMAN, *who politely retires to the other side of the pillar*): What on earth is Freddy doing? I shall get pneumownia if I stay in this draught any longer.

THE NOTE TAKER (*to himself, hastily making a note of her pronunciation of "monia"*): Earlscourt.

THE DAUGHTER (*violently*): Will you please keep your impertinent remarks to yourself.

THE NOTE TAKER: Did I say that out loud? I didnt mean to. I beg your pardon. Your mother's Epsom, unmistakeably.

THE MOTHER (*advancing between the* DAUGHTER *and the* NOTE TAKER): How very curious! I was brought up in Largelady Park, near Epsom.

THE NOTE TAKER (*uproariously amused*): Ha! ha! What a devil of a name! Excuse me. (*to the* DAUGHTER) You want a cab, do you?

THE DAUGHTER: Dont dare speak to me.

THE MOTHER: Oh please, please, Clara. (*Her* DAUGHTER *repudiates her with an angry shrug and retires haughtily.*) We should be so grateful to you, sir, if you found us a cab. (*The* NOTE TAKER *produces a whistle.*) Oh, thank you. (*She joins her* DAUGHTER.)

(*The* NOTE TAKER *blows a piercing blast.*)

THE SARCASTIC BYSTANDER: There! I knowed he was a plain-clothes copper.

THE BYSTANDER: That aint a police whistle; thats a sporting whistle.

THE FLOWER GIRL (*still preoccupied with her wounded feelings*): He's no right to take away my character. My character is the same to me as any lady's.

THE NOTE TAKER: I dont know whether youve noticed it; but the rain stopped about two minutes ago.

THE BYSTANDER: So it has. Why didn't you say so before? and us losing our time listening to your silliness! (*He walks off towards the Strand.*)

THE SARCASTIC BYSTANDER: I can tell where you come from. You come from Anwell. Go back there.

THE NOTE TAKER (*helpfully*): *H*anwell.

THE SARCASTIC BYSTANDER (*affecting great distinction of speech*): Thenk you, teacher. Haw haw! So long. (*He touches his hat with mock respect and strolls off.*)

THE FLOWER GIRL: Frightening people like that! How would he like it himself?

THE MOTHER: It's quite fine now, Clara. We can walk to a motor bus. Come. (*She gathers her skirts above her ankles and hurries off towards the Strand.*)

THE DAUGHTER: But the cab—(*Her mother is out of hearing.*) Oh, how tiresome! (*She follows angrily.*)

(*All the rest have gone except the* NOTE TAKER, *the* GENTLEMAN, *and the* FLOWER GIRL, *who sits arranging her basket, and still pitying herself in murmurs.*)

THE FLOWER GIRL: Poor girl! Hard enough for her to live without being worrited and chivied.

THE GENTLEMAN (*returning to his former place on the* NOTE TAKER'S *left*): How do you do it, if I may ask?

THE NOTE TAKER: Simply phonetics. The science of speech. Thats my profession: also my hobby. Happy is the man who can make a living by his hobby! You can spot an Irishman or a Yorkshireman by his brogue. *I* can place any man within six miles. I can place him within two miles in London. Sometimes within two streets.

THE FLOWER GIRL: Ought to be ashamed of himself, unmanly coward!

THE GENTLEMAN: But is there a living in that?

THE NOTE TAKER: Oh yes. Quite a fat one. This is an age of upstarts. Men begin in Kentish Town with £80 a year, and end in Park Lane with a hundred thousand. They want to drop Kentish Town; but they give themselves away every time they open their mouths. Now I can teach them—

THE FLOWER GIRL: Let him mind his own business and leave a poor girl—

THE NOTE TAKER (*explosively*): Woman: cease this detestable boohooing instantly; or else seek the shelter of some other place of worship.

THE FLOWER GIRL (*with feeble defiance*): Ive a right to be here if I like, same as you.

THE NOTE TAKER: A woman who utters such depressing and disgusting sounds has no right to be anywhere—no right to live. Remember that you are a human being with a soul and the divine gift of articulate speech; that your native language is the language of Shakespear and Milton and The Bible; and dont sit there crooning like a bilious pigeon.

THE FLOWER GIRL (*quite overwhelmed, looking up at him in mingled wonder and deprecation without daring to raise her head*): Ah-ah-ah-ow-ow-ow-oo!

THE NOTE TAKER (*whipping out his book*): Heavens! what a sound! (*He writes; then holds out the book and reads, reproducing her vowels exactly.*) Ah-ah-ah-ow-ow-ow-oo!

THE FLOWER GIRL (*tickled by the performance, and laughing in spite of herself*): Garn!

THE NOTE TAKER: You see this creature with her kerbstone English: the English that will keep her in the gutter to the end of her days. Well, sir, in three months I could pass that girl off as a duchess at an ambassador's garden party. I could even get her a place as lady's maid or shop assistant, which requires better English.

THE FLOWER GIRL: Whats that you say?

THE NOTE TAKER: Yes, you squashed cabbage leaf, you disgrace to the noble architecture of these columns, you incarnate insult to the English language: I could pass you off as the Queen of Sheba. (*to the* GENTLEMAN) Can you believe that?

THE GENTLEMAN: Of course I can. I am myself a student of Indian dialects; and—

THE NOTE TAKER (*eagerly*): Are you? Do you know Colonel Pickering, the author of Spoken Sanscrit?

THE GENTLEMAN: I am Colonel Pickering. Who are you?

THE NOTE TAKER: Henry Higgins, author of Higgins's Universal Alphabet.

PICKERING (*with enthusiasm*): I came from India to meet you.

HIGGINS: I was going to India to meet you.

PICKERING: Where do you live?

HIGGINS: 27A Wimpole Street. Come and see me tomorrow.

PICKERING: I'm at the Carlton. Come with me now and lets have a jaw over some supper.

HIGGINS: Right you are.

THE FLOWER GIRL (*to* PICKERING, *as he passes her*): Buy a flower, kind gentleman. I'm short for my lodging.

PICKERING: I really havnt any change. I'm sorry. (*He goes away.*)

HIGGINS (*shocked at the* GIRL's *mendacity*): Liar. You said you could change half-a-crown.

THE FLOWER GIRL (*rising in desperation*): You ought to be

stuffed with nails, you ought. (*flinging the basket at his feet*) Take the whole blooming basket for sixpence.

(*The church clock strikes the second quarter.*)

HIGGINS (*hearing in it the voice of God, rebuking him for his Pharisaic want of charity to the poor girl*): A reminder. (*He raises his hat solemnly; then throws a handful of money into the basket and follows* PICKERING.)

THE FLOWER GIRL (*picking up a half-crown*): Ah-ow-ooh! (*picking up a couple of florins*) Aaah-ow-ooh! (*picking up several coins*) Aaaah-ow-ooh! (*picking up a half-sovereign*) Aaaaaaaaaaaah-ow-ooh!!!

FREDDY (*springing out of a taxicab*): Got one at last. Hallo! (*to the* GIRL) Where are the two ladies that were here?

THE FLOWER GIRL: They walked to the bus when the rain stopped.

FREDDY: And left me with a cab on my hands! Damnation!

THE FLOWER GIRL (*with grandeur*): Never mind, young man. I'm going home in a taxi. (*She sails off to the cab. The driver puts his hand behind him and holds the door firmly shut against her. Quite understanding his mistrust, she shews him her handful of money.*) A taxi fare aint no object to me, Charlie. (*He grins and opens the door.*) Here. What about the basket?

THE TAXIMAN: Give it here. Tuppence extra.

LIZA: No: I dont want nobody to see it. (*She crushes it into the cab and gets in continuing the conversation through the window.*) Goodbye, Freddy.

FREDDY (*dazedly raising his hat*): Goodbye.

TAXIMAN: Where to?

LIZA: Bucknam Pellis (Buckingham Palace).

TAXIMAN: What d'ye mean—Bucknam Pellis?

LIZA: Dont you know where it is? In the Green Park, where the King lives. Goodbye, Freddy. Dont let me keep you standing there. Goodbye.

FREDDY: Goodbye.

(*He goes.*)

TAXIMAN: Here? Whats this about Bucknam Pellis? What business have you at Bucknam Pellis?

LIZA: Of course I havnt none. But I wasnt going to let him know that. You drive me home.

TAXIMAN: And wheres home?

LIZA: Angel Court, Drury Lane, next Meiklejohn's oil shop.

TAXIMAN: That sounds more like it, Judy. (*He drives off.*)

*   *   *   *   *   *   *   *   *   *   *

(*Let us follow the taxi to the entrance to Angel Court, a narrow little archway between two shops, one of them Meiklejohn's oil shop. When it stops there,* ELIZA *gets out, dragging her basket with her.*)

LIZA: How much?

TAXIMAN (*indicating the taximeter*): Cant you read? A shilling.

LIZA: A shilling for two minutes!!

TAXIMAN: Two minutes or ten: it's all the same.

LIZA: Well, I dont call it right.

TAXIMAN: Ever been in a taxi before?

LIZA (*with dignity*): Hundreds and thousands of times, young man.

TAXIMAN (*laughing at her*): Good for you, Judy. Keep the shilling, darling, with best love from all at home. Good luck! (*He drives off.*)

LIZA (*humiliated*): Impidence!

(*She picks up the basket and trudges up the alley with it to her lodging: a small room with very old wall paper hanging loose in the damp places. A broken pane in the window is mended with paper. A portrait of a popular actor and a fashion plate of ladies' dresses, all wildly beyond poor* ELIZA'S *means, both torn from newspapers, are pinned up on the wall. A birdcage hangs in the window; but its tenant died long ago: it remains as a memorial only.*

These are the only visible luxuries: the rest is the irreducible minimum of poverty's needs: a wretched bed heaped with all sorts of coverings that have any warmth in them, a draped packing case with a basin and jug on it and a little looking glass over it, a chair and table, the refuse of some suburban kitchen, and an American alarum clock on the shelf above the unused fireplace: the whole lighted with a gas lamp with a penny in the slot meter. Rent: four shillings a week.

Here ELIZA, *chronically weary, but too excited to go to bed, sits, counting her new riches and dreaming and planning what to do with them, until the gas goes out, when she enjoys for the first time the sensation of being able to put in another penny without grudging it. This prodigal mood does not extinguish her gnawing sense of the need for economy sufficiently to prevent her from calculating that she can dream and plan in bed more cheaply and warmly than sitting up without a fire. So she takes off her shawl and skirt and adds them to the miscellaneous bedclothes. Then she kicks off her shoes and gets into bed without any further change.*

ACT II

(*Next day at 11 a.m.* HIGGINS's *laboratory in Wimpole Street. It is a room on the first floor, looking on the street, and was meant for the drawing room. The double doors are in the middle of the back wall; and persons entering find in the corner to their right two tall file cabinets at right angles to one another against the walls. In this corner stands a flat writing-table, on which are a phonograph, a laryngoscope, a row of tiny organ pipes with a bellows, a set of lamp chimneys for singing flames with burners attached to a gas plug in the wall by an indiarubber tube, several tuning-forks of different sizes, a life-size image of half a human head, shewing in section the vocal organs, and a box containing a supply of wax cylinders for the phonograph.*

Further down the room, on the same side, is a fireplace, with a comfortable leather-covered easy-chair at the side of the hearth nearest the door, and a coal-scuttle. There is a clock on the mantelpiece. Between the fireplace and the phonograph table is a stand for newspapers.

On the other side of the central door, to the left of the visitor, is a cabinet of shallow drawers. On it is a telephone and the telephone directory. The corner beyond, and most of the side wall, is occupied by a grand piano, with the keyboard at the end furthest from the door, and a bench for the players extending the full length of the keyboard. On the piano is a dessert dish heaped with fruit and sweets, mostly chocolates.

The middle of the room is clear. Besides the easy-chair, the piano bench, and two chairs at the phonograph table, there is one stray chair. It stands near the fireplace. On the walls, engravings: mostly Piranesis and mezzotint portraits. No paintings.

PICKERING *is seated at the table, putting down some cards and a tuning-fork which he has been using.* HIGGINS *is standing up near him, closing two or three file drawers which are hanging out. He appears in the morning light as a robust, vital, appetizing sort of man of forty or thereabouts, dressed in a professional-looking black frock-coat with a white linen collar and black silk tie. He is of energetic, scientific type, heartily, even violently interested in everything that can be studied as a scientific subject, and careless about himself and other people, including their feelings. He is, in fact, but for his years and size, rather like a very impetuous baby "taking notice" eagerly and loudly, and requiring almost as much watching to keep him out of unintended mischief. His manner varies from genial bullying when he is in a good humor to stormy petulance when anything goes wrong; but he is so entirely frank and void of malice that he remains likeable even in his least reasonable moments.*

HIGGINS (*as he shuts the last drawer*): Well, I think thats the whole show.

PICKERING: It's really amazing. I havnt taken half of it in, you know.

HIGGINS: Would you like to go over any of it again?

PICKERING (*rising and coming to the fireplace, where he plants himself with his back to the fire*): No, thank you: not now. I'm quite done up for this morning.

HIGGINS (*following him, and standing beside him on his left*): Tired of listening to sounds?

PICKERING: Yes. It's a fearful strain. I rather fancied myself because I can pronounce twenty-four distinct vowel sounds; but your hundred and thirty beat me. I cant hear a bit of difference between most of them.

HIGGINS (*chuckling, and going over to the piano to eat sweets*): Oh, that comes with practice. You hear no difference at first; but you keep on listening, and presently you find theyre all as different as A from B. (MRS PEARCE *looks in: She is* HIGGINS's *housekeeper.*) Whats the matter?

MRS PEARCE (*hesitating, evidently perplexed*): A young woman asks to see you, sir.

HIGGINS: A young woman! What does she want?

MRS PEARCE: Well, sir, she says youll be glad to see her when you know what she's come about. She's quite a common girl, sir. Very common indeed. I should have sent her away, only I thought perhaps you wanted her to talk into your machines. I hope Ive not done wrong; but really you see such queer people sometimes—youll excuse me, I'm sure, sir—

HIGGINS: Oh, thats all right, Mrs Pearce. Has she an interesting accent?

MRS PEARCE: Oh, something dreadful, sir, really. I dont know how you can take an interest in it.

HIGGINS (*to* PICKERING): Lets have her up. Shew her up, Mrs Pearce. (*He rushes across to his working table and picks out a cylinder to use on the phonograph.*)

MRS PEARCE (*only half resigned to it*): Very well, sir. It's for you to say. (*She goes downstairs.*)

HIGGINS: This is rather a bit of luck. I'll shew you how I make records. We'll set her talking; and I'll take it down first in Bell's Visible Speech; then in broad Romic; and then we'll get her on the phonograph so that you can turn her on as often as you like with the written transcript before you.

MRS PEARCE (*returning*): This is the young woman, sir.

(*The* FLOWER GIRL *enters in state. She has a hat with three ostrich feathers, orange, sky-blue, and red. She has a nearly clean apron, and the shoddy coat has been tidied a little. The pathos of this deplorable figure, with its innocent vanity and consequential air, touches* PICKERING, *who has already straightened himself in the presence of* MRS PEARCE. *But as to* HIGGINS, *the only distinction he makes between men and women is that when he is neither bullying nor exclaiming to the heavens against some feather-weight cross, he coaxes women as a child coaxes its nurse when it wants to get anything out of her.*)

HIGGINS (*brusquely, recognizing her with unconcealed disappointment, and at once, babylike, making an intolerable grievance of it*): Why, this is the girl I jotted down last night. She's no use: Ive got all the records I want of the Lisson Grove lingo; and I'm not going to waste another cylinder on it. (*to the* GIRL) Be off with you: I dont want you.

THE FLOWER GIRL: Dont you be so saucy. You aint heard what I come for yet. (*to* MRS PEARCE, *who is waiting at the door for further instructions*) Did you tell him I come in a taxi?

MRS PEARCE: Nonsense, girl! what do you think a gentleman like Mr. Higgins cares what you came in?

THE FLOWER GIRL: Oh, we are proud! He aint above giving lessons, not him: I heard him say so. Well, I aint come here to ask for any compliment; and if my money's not good enough I can go elsewhere.

HIGGINS: Good enough for what?

THE FLOWER GIRL: Good enough for ye-oo. Now you know, dont you? I've come to have lessons, I am. And to pay for em te-oo: make no mistake.

HIGGINS (*stupent*): Well!!! (*recovering his breath with a gasp*) What do you expect me to say to you?

THE FLOWER GIRL: Well, if you was a gentleman, you might ask me to sit down, I think. Dont I tell you I'm bringing you business?

HIGGINS: Pickering: shall we ask this baggage to sit down, or shall we throw her out of the window?

THE FLOWER GIRL (*running away in terror to the piano, where she turns at bay*): Ah-ah-oh-ow-ow-ow-oo! (*wounded and whimpering*) I wont be called a baggage when Ive offered to pay like any lady.

(*Motionless, the two men stare at her from the other side of the room, amazed.*)

PICKERING (*gently*): But what is it you want?

THE FLOWER GIRL: I want to be a lady in a flower shop stead of sellin at the corner of Tottenham Court Road. But they wont take me unless I can talk more genteel. He said he could teach me. Well, here I am ready to pay him—not asking any favor—and he treats me zif I was dirt.

MRS PEARCE: How can you be such a foolish ignorant girl as to think you could afford to pay Mr Higgins?

THE FLOWER GIRL: Why shouldnt I? I know what lessons cost as well as you do; and I'm ready to pay.

HIGGINS: How much?

THE FLOWER GIRL (*coming back to him, triumphant*): Now youre talking! I thought youd come off it when you saw a chance of getting back a bit of what you chucked at me last night. (*confidentially*) Youd had a drop in, hadnt you?

HIGGINS (*peremptorily*): Sit down.

THE FLOWER GIRL: Oh, if youre going to make a compliment of it—

HIGGINS (*thundering at her*): Sit down.

MRS PEARCE (*severely*): Sit down, girl. Do as youre told.

THE FLOWER GIRL: Ah-ah-ah-ow-ow-oo! (*She stands, half rebellious, half bewildered.*)

PICKERING (*very courteous*): Wont you sit down? (*He places the stray chair near the hearthrug between himself and HIGGINS.*)

LIZA (*coyly*): Dont mind if I do. (*She sits down.* PICKERING *returns to the hearthrug.*)

HIGGINS: Whats your name?

THE FLOWER GIRL: Liza Doolittle.

HIGGINS (*declaiming gravely*):

Eliza, Elizabeth, Betsy and Bess,
They went to the woods to get a bird's nes':
PICKERING: They found a nest with four eggs in it:
HIGGINS: They took one apiece, and left three in it.
(*They laugh heartily at their own fun.*)
LIZA: Oh, dont be silly.

MRS PEARCE (*placing herself behind* ELIZA's *chair*): You mustnt speak to the gentlemen like that.

LIZA: Well, why wont he speak sensible to me?

HIGGINS: Come back to business. How much do you propose to pay me for the lessons?

LIZA: Oh, I know whats right. A lady friend of mine gets French lessons for eighteenpence an hour from a real French gentleman. Well, you wouldnt have the face to ask me the same for teaching me my own language as you would for French; so I wont give more than a shilling. Take it or leave it.

HIGGINS (*walking up and down the room, rattling his keys and his cash in his pockets*): You know, Pickering, if you consider a shilling, not as a simple shilling, but as a percentage of this girl's income, it works out as fully equivalent to sixty or seventy guineas from a millionaire.

PICKERING: How so?

HIGGINS: Figure it out. A millionaire has about £150 a day. She earns about half-a-crown.

LIZA (*haughtily*): Who told you I only—

HIGGINS (*continuing*): She offers me two-fifths of her day's income for a lesson. Two-fifths of a millionaire's income for a day would be somewhere about £60. It's handsome. By George, it's enormous! it's the biggest offer I ever had.

LIZA (*rising, terrified*): Sixty pounds! What are you talking about? I never offered you sixty pounds. Where would I get—

HIGGINS: Hold your tongue.

LIZA (*weeping*): But I aint got sixty pounds. Oh—

MRS PEARCE: Dont cry, you silly girl. Sit down. Nobody is going to touch your money.

HIGGINS: Somebody is going to touch you, with a broomstick, if you dont stop snivelling. Sit down.

LIZA (*obeying slowly*): Ah-ah-ah-ow-oo-o! One would think you was my father.

HIGGINS: If I decide to teach you, I'll be worse than two fathers to you. Here! (*He offers her his silk handkerchief.*)

LIZA: Whats this for?

HIGGINS: To wipe your eyes. To wipe any part of your

face that feels moist. Remember: thats your handkerchief; and thats your sleeve. Dont mistake the one for the other if you wish to become a lady in a shop.

(LIZA, *utterly bewildered, stares helplessly at him.*)

MRS PEARCE: It's no use talking to her like that, Mr. Higgins: she doesnt understand you. Besides, youre quite wrong: she doesnt do it that way at all. (*She takes the handkerchief.*)

LIZA (*snatching it*): Here! You give me that handkerchief. He gev it to me, not to you.

PICKERING (*laughing*): He did. I think it must be regarded as her property, Mrs Pearce.

MRS PEARCE (*resigning herself*): Serve you right, Mr Higgins.

PICKERING: Higgins: I'm interested. What about the ambassador's garden party? I'll say youre the greatest teacher alive if you make that good. I'll bet you all the expenses of the experiment you cant do it. And I'll pay for the lessons.

LIZA: Oh, you are real good. Thank you, Captain.

HIGGINS (*tempted, looking at her*): It's almost irresistible. She's so deliciously low—so horribly dirty—

LIZA (*protesting extremely*): Ah-ah-ah-ah-ow-ow-oo-oo!!! I aint dirty: I washed my face and hands afore I come, I did.

PICKERING: Youre certainly not going to turn her head with flattery, Higgins.

MRS PEARCE (*uneasy*): Oh, dont say that, sir: theres more ways than one of turning a girl's head; and nobody can do it better than Mr Higgins, though he may not always mean it. I do hope, sir, you wont encourage him to do anything foolish.

HIGGINS (*becoming excited as the idea grows on him*): What is life but a series of inspired follies? The difficulty is to find them to do. Never lose a chance: it doesnt come every day. I shall make a duchess of this draggletailed guttersnipe.

LIZA (*strongly deprecating this view of her*): Ah-ah-ah-ow-ow-oo!

HIGGINS (*carried away*): Yes: in six months—in three if she has a good ear and a quick tongue—I'll take her anywhere and pass her off as anything. We'll start today: now! this moment! Take her away and clean her, Mrs Pearce. Monkey Brand, if it wont come off any other way. Is there a good fire in the kitchen?

MRS PEARCE (*protesting*): Yes; but—

HIGGINS (*storming on*): Take all her clothes off and burn

them. Ring up Whitely or somebody for new ones. Wrap her up in brown paper til they come.

LIZA: Youre no gentleman, youre not, to talk of such things. I'm a good girl, I am; and I know what the like of you are, I do.

HIGGINS: We want none of your Lisson Grove prudery here, young woman. Youve got to learn to behave like a duchess. Take her away, Mrs Pearce. If she gives you any trouble, wallop her.

LIZA (*springing up and running between* PICKERING *and* MRS PEARCE *for protection*): No! I'll call the police, I will.

MRS PEARCE: But Ive no place to put her.

HIGGINS: Put her in the dustbin.

LIZA: Ah-ah-ah-ow-ow-oo!

PICKERING: Oh come, Higgins! be reasonable.

MRS PEARCE (*resolutely*): You must be reasonable, Mr Higgins: really you must. You cant walk over everybody like this.

(HIGGINS, *thus scolded, subsides. The hurricane is succeeded by a zephyr of amiable surprise.*)

HIGGINS (*with professional exquisiteness of modulation*): *I* walk over everybody! My dear Mrs Pearce, my dear Pickering, I never had the slightest intention of walking over anyone. All I propose is that we should be kind to this poor girl. We must help her to prepare and fit herself for her new station in life. If I did not express myself clearly it was because I did not wish to hurt her delicacy, or yours.

(LIZA, *reassured, steals back to her chair.*)

MRS PEARCE (*to* PICKERING): Well, did you ever hear anything like that, sir?

PICKERING (*laughing heartily*): Never, Mrs Pearce: never.

HIGGINS (*patiently*): Whats the matter?

MRS PEARCE: Well, the matter is, sir, that you cant take a girl up like that as if you were picking up a pebble on the beach.

HIGGINS: Why not?

MRS PEARCE: Why not! But you dont know anything about her. What about her parents? She may be married.

LIZA: Garn!

HIGGINS: There! As the girl very properly says, Garn! Married indeed! Dont you know that a woman of that class looks a worn out drudge of fifty a year after she's married?

LIZA: Whood marry me?

HIGGINS (*suddenly resorting to the most thrillingly beautiful low tones in his best elocutionary style*): By George,

Eliza, the streets will be strewn with the bodies of men shooting themselves for your sake before Ive done with you.

MRS PEARCE: Nonsense, sir. You mustnt talk like that to her.

LIZA (*rising and squaring herself determinedly*): I'm going away. He's off his chump, he is. I dont want no balmies teaching me.

HIGGINS (*wounded in his tenderest point by her insensibility to his elocution*): Oh, indeed! I'm mad, am I? Very well, Mrs Pearce: you neednt order the new clothes for her. Throw her out.

LIZA (*whimpering*): Nah-ow. You got no right to touch me.

MRS PEARCE: You see now what comes of being saucy. (*indicating the door*) This way, please.

LIZA (*almost in tears*): I didnt want no clothes. I wouldnt have taken them. (*She throws away the handkerchief.*) I can buy my own clothes.

HIGGINS (*deftly retrieving the handkerchief and intercepting her on her reluctant way to the door*): Youre an ungrateful wicked girl. This is my return for offering to take you out of the gutter and dress you beautifully and make a lady of you.

MRS PEARCE: Stop, Mr Higgins. I won't allow it. It's you that are wicked. Go home to your parents, girl; and tell them to take better care of you.

LIZA: I aint got no parents. They told me I was big enough to earn my own living and turned me out.

MRS PEARCE: Wheres your mother?

LIZA: I aint got no mother. Her that turned me out was my sixth stepmother. But I done without them. And I'm a good girl, I am.

HIGGINS: Very well, then, what on earth is all this fuss about? The girl doesnt belong to anybody—is no use to anybody but me. (*He goes to* MRS PEARCE *and begins coaxing.*) You can adopt her, Mrs Pearce: I'm sure a daughter would be a great amusement to you. Now dont make any more fuss. Take her downstairs; and—

MRS PEARCE: But whats to become of her? Is she to be paid anything? Do be sensible, sir.

HIGGINS: Oh, pay her whatever is necessary: put it down in the housekeeping book. (*impatiently*) What on earth will she want with money? She'll have her food and her clothes. She'll only drink if you give her money.

LIZA (*turning on him*): Oh you are a brute. It's a lie; nobody ever saw the sign of liquor on me. (*to* PICKERING) Oh, sir: youre a gentleman: dont let him speak to me like that.

PICKERING (*in good-humored remonstrance*): Does it occur to you, Higgins, that the girl has some feelings?

HIGGINS (*looking critically at her*): Oh no, I dont think so. Not any feelings that we need bother about. (*cheerily*) Have you, Eliza?

LIZA: I got my feelings same as anyone else.

HIGGINS (*to* PICKERING, *reflectively*): You see the difficulty?

PICKERING: Eh? What difficulty?

HIGGINS: To get her to talk grammar. The mere pronunciation is easy enough.

LIZA: I dont want to talk grammar. I want to talk like a lady in a flower-shop.

MRS PEARCE: Will you please keep to the point, Mr Higgins. I want to know on what terms the girl is to be here. Is she to have any wages? And what is to become of her when youve finished your teaching? You must look ahead a little.

HIGGINS (*impatiently*): Whats to become of her if I leave her in the gutter? Tell me that, Mrs Pearce.

MRS PEARCE: Thats her own business, not yours, Mr Higgins.

HIGGINS: Well, when Ive done with her, we can throw her back into the gutter; and then it will be her own business again; so thats all right.

LIZA: Oh, youve no feeling heart in you: you dont care for nothing but yourself. (*She rises and takes the floor resolutely.*) Here! Ive had enough of this. I'm going (*making for the door*). You ought to be ashamed of yourself, you ought.

HIGGINS (*snatching a chocolate cream from the piano, his eyes suddenly beginning to twinkle with mischief*): Have some chocolates, Eliza.

LIZA (*halting, tempted*): How do I know what might be in them? Ive heard of girls being drugged by the like of you.

(HIGGINS *whips out his penknife; cuts a chocolate in two; puts one half into his mouth and bolts it; and offers her the other half.*)

HIGGINS: Pledge of good faith, Eliza. I eat one half: you eat the other. (LIZA *opens her mouth to retort: he pops the half chocolate into it.*) You shall have boxes of them, barrels of them, every day. You shall live on them. Eh?

LIZA (*who has disposed of the chocolate after being nearly choked by it*): I wouldnt have ate it, only I'm too ladylike to take it out of my mouth.

HIGGINS: Listen, Eliza. I think you said you came in a taxi.

LIZA: Well, what if I did? Ive as good a right to take a taxi as anyone else.

HIGGINS: You have, Eliza; and in future you shall have as many taxis as you want. You shall go up and down and round the town in a taxi every day. Think of that, Eliza.

MRS PEARCE: Mr Higgins: youre tempting the girl. It's not right. She should think of the future.

HIGGINS: At her age! Nonsense! Time enough to think of the future when you havnt any future to think of. No, Eliza: do as this lady does: think of other people's futures; but never think of your own. Think of chocolates, and taxis, and gold, and diamonds.

LIZA: No: I dont want no gold and no diamonds. I'm a good girl, I am. (*She sits down again, with an attempt at dignity.*)

HIGGINS: You shall remain so, Eliza, under the care of Mrs Pearce. And you shall marry an officer in the Guards, with a beautiful moustache: the son of a marquis, who will disinherit him for marrying you, but will relent when he sees your beauty and goodness—

PICKERING: Excuse me, Higgins; but I really must interfere. Mrs Pearce is quite right. If this girl is to put herself in your hands for six months for an experiment in teaching, she must understand thoroughly what she's doing.

HIGGINS: How can she? She's incapable of understanding anything. Besides, do any of us understand what we are doing? If we did, would we ever do it?

PICKERING: Very clever, Higgins; but not to the present point. (*to* ELIZA) Miss Doolittle—

LIZA (*overwhelmed*): Ah-ah-ow-oo!

HIGGINS: There! Thats all youll get out of Eliza. Ah-ah-ow-oo! No use explaining. As a military man you ought to know that. Give her her orders: thats enough for her. Eliza: you are to live here for the next six months, learning how to speak beautifully, like a lady in a florist's shop. If youre good and do whatever youre told, you shall sleep in a proper bed-room, and have lots to eat, and money to buy chocolates and take rides in taxis. If youre naughty and idle you will sleep in the back kitchen among the black beetles, and be walloped by Mrs Pearce with a broomstick. At the end of six months you shall go to Buckingham Palace in a carriage, beautifully

HIGGINS (*sternly*): Of course. I'm always particular about what I say. Why do you say this to me?

MRS PEARCE (*unmoved*): No, sir: youre not at all particular when youve mislaid anything or when you get a little impatient. Now it doesnt matter before me: I'm used to it. But you really must not swear before the girl.

HIGGINS (*indignantly*): *I* swear! (*most emphatically*) I never swear. I detest the habit. What the devil do you mean?

MRS PEARCE (*stolidly*): Thats what I mean, sir. You swear a great deal too much. I dont mind your damning and blasting, and what the devil and where the devil and who the devil—

HIGGINS: Mrs Pearce: this language from your lips! Really!

MRS PEARCE (*not to be put off*): —but there is a certain word I must ask you not to use. The girl used it herself when she began to enjoy the bath. It begins with the same letter as bath. She knows no better: she learnt it at her mother's knee. But she must not hear it from your lips.

HIGGINS (*loftily*): I cannot charge myself with having ever uttered it, Mrs Pearce. (*She looks at him steadfastly. He adds, hiding an uneasy conscience with a judicial air.*) Except perhaps in a moment of extreme and justifiable excitement.

MRS PEARCE: Only this morning, sir, you applied it to your boots, to the butter, and to the brown bread.

HIGGINS: Oh, that! Mere alliteration, Mrs Pearce, natural to a poet.

MRS PEARCE: Well, sir, whatever you choose to call it, I beg you not to let the girl hear you repeat it.

HIGGINS: Oh, very well, very well. Is that all?

MRS PEARCE: No, sir. We shall have to be very particular with this girl as to personal cleanliness.

HIGGINS: Certainly. Quite right. Most important.

MRS PEARCE: I mean not to be slovenly about her dress or untidy in leaving things about.

HIGGINS (*going to her solemnly*): Just so. I intended to call your attention to that. (*He passes on to* PICKERING, *who is enjoying the conversation immensely.*) It is these little things that matter, Pickering. Take care of the pence and the pounds will take care of themselves is as true of personal habits as of money. (*He comes to anchor on the hearthrug, with the air of a man in an unassailable position.*)

MRS PEARCE: Yes, sir. Then might I ask you not to come down to breakfast in your dressing-gown, or at any rate not to use it as a napkin to the extent you do, sir. And if you would be so good as not to eat everything off the same plate, and to remember not to put the porridge saucepan out of your hand on the clean tablecloth, it would be a better example to the girl. You know you nearly choked yourself with a fishbone in a jam only last week.

HIGGINS (*routed from the hearthrug and drifting back to the piano*): I may do these things sometimes in absence of mind; but surely I dont do them habitually. (*angrily*) By the way: my dressing-gown smells most damnably of benzine.

MRS PEARCE: No doubt it does, Mr Higgins. But if you will wipe your fingers—

HIGGINS (*yelling*): Oh very well, very well: I'll wipe them in my hair in future.

MRS PEARCE: I hope youre not offended, Mr Higgins.

HIGGINS (*shocked at finding himself thought capable of an unamiable sentiment*): Not at all, not at all. Youre quite right, Mrs Pearce: I shall be particularly careful before the girl. Is that all?

MRS PEARCE: No, sir. Might she use some of those Japanese dresses you brought from abroad? I really cant put her back into her old things.

HIGGINS: Certainly. Anything you like. Is that all?

MRS PEARCE: Thank you, sir. Thats all. (*She goes out.*)

HIGGINS: You know, Pickering, that woman has the most extraordinary ideas about me. Here I am, a shy, diffident sort of man. Ive never been able to feel really grown-up and tremendous, like other chaps. And yet she's firmly persuaded that I'm an arbitrary overbearing bossing kind of person. I cant account for it.

(MRS PEARCE *returns*.)

MRS PEARCE: If you please, sir, the trouble's beginning already. Theres a dustman downstairs, Alfred Doolittle, wants to see you. He says you have his daughter here.

PICKERING (*rising*): Phew! I say!

HIGGINS (*promptly*): Send the blackguard up.

MRS PEARCE: Oh, very well, sir. (*She goes out.*)

PICKERING: He may not be a blackguard, Higgins.

HIGGINS: Nonsense. Of course he's a blackguard.

PICKERING: Whether he is or not, I'm afraid we shall have some trouble with him.

HIGGINS (*confidently*): Oh no: I think not. If theres any trouble he shall have it with me, not I with him. And we are sure to get something interesting out of him.

PICKERING: About the girl?

HIGGINS: No. I mean his dialect.

PICKERING: Oh!

MRS PEARCE (*at the door*): Doolittle, sir.

(*She admits* DOOLITTLE *and retires.*

ALFRED *is an elderly but vigorous dustman, clad in the costume of his profession, including a hat with a back brim covering his neck and shoulders. He has well marked and rather interesting features, and seems equally free from fear and conscience. He has a remarkably expressive voice, the result of a habit of giving vent to his feelings without reserve. His present pose is that of wounded honor and stern resolution.*)

DOOLITTLE (*at the door, uncertain which of the two gentlemen is his man*): Professor Iggins?

HIGGINS: Here. Good morning. Sit down.

DOOLITTLE: Morning, Governor. (*He sits down magisterially.*) I come about a very serious matter, Governor.

HIGGINS (*to* PICKERING): Brought up in Hounslow. Mother Welsh, I should think. (DOOLITTLE *opens his mouth, amazed.* HIGGINS *continues.*) What do you want, Doolittle?

DOOLITTLE (*menacingly*): I want my daughter: thats what I want. See?

HIGGINS: Of course you do. Youre her father, arnt you? You dont suppose anyone else wants her, do you? I'm glad to see you have some spark of family feeling left. She's upstairs. Take her away at once.

DOOLITTLE (*rising, fearfully taken aback*): What!

HIGGINS: Take her away. Do you suppose I'm going to keep your daughter for you?

DOOLITTLE (*remonstrating*): Now, now, look here, Governor. Is this reasonable? Is it fair to take advantage of a man like this? The girl belongs to me. You got her. Where do I come in? (*He sits down again.*)

HIGGINS: Your daughter had the audacity to come to my house and ask me to teach her how to speak properly so that she could get a place in a flower-shop. This gentleman and my housekeeper have been here all the time. (*bullying him*) How dare you come here and attempt to blackmail me? You sent her here on purpose.

DOOLITTLE (*protesting*): No, Governor.

HIGGINS: You must have. How else could you possibly know that she is here?

DOOLITTLE: Don't take a man up like that, Governor.

HIGGINS: The police shall take you up. This is a plant—a plot to extort money by threats. I shall telephone for the police. (*He goes resolutely to the telephone and opens the directory.*)

DOOLITTLE: Have I asked you for a brass farthing? I leave it to the gentleman here: have I said a word about money?

HIGGINS (*throwing the book aside and marching down on* DOOLITTLE *with a poser*): What else did you come for?

DOOLITTLE (*sweetly*): Well, what would a man come for? Be human, Governor.

HIGGINS (*disarmed*): Alfred: did you put her up to it?

DOOLITTLE: So help me, Governor, I never did. I take my Bible oath I aint seen the girl these two months past.

HIGGINS: Then how did you know she was here?

DOOLITTLE (*"most musical, most melancholy"*): I'll tell you, Governor, if youll only let me get a word in. I'm willing to tell you. I'm wanting to tell you. I'm waiting to tell you.

HIGGINS: Pickering: this chap has a certain natural gift of rhetoric. Observe the rhythm of his native woodnotes wild. "I'm willing to tell you: I'm wanting to tell you: I'm waiting to tell you." Sentimental rhetoric! thats the Welsh strain in him. It also accounts for his mendacity and dishonesty.

PICKERING: Oh, please, Higgins: I'm west country myself. (*to* DOOLITTLE) How did you know the girl was here if you didnt send her?

DOOLITTLE: It was like this, Governor. The girl took a boy in the taxi to give him a jaunt. Son of her landlady, he is. He hung about on the chance of her giving him another ride home. Well, she sent him back for her luggage when she heard you was willing for her to stop here. I met the boy at the corner of Long Acre and Endell Street.

HIGGINS: Public house. Yes?

DOOLITTLE: The poor man's club, Governor: why shouldnt I?

PICKERING: Do let him tell his story, Higgins.

DOOLITTLE: He told me what was up. And I ask you, what was my feelings and my duty as a father? I says to the boy, "You bring me the luggage," I says—

PICKERING: Why didnt you go for it yourself?

DOOLITTLE: Landlady wouldnt have trusted me with it, Governor. She's that kind of woman: you know. I had to give the boy a penny afore he trusted me with it, the little swine. I brought it to her just to oblige you like, and make myself agreeable. Thats all.

HIGGINS: How much luggage?

DOOLITTLE: Musical instrument, Governor. A few pictures, a trifle of jewelry, and a bird-cage. She said she didnt want no clothes. What was I to think from that, Governor? I ask you as a parent what was I to think?

HIGGINS: So you came to rescue her from worse than death, eh?

DOOLITTLE (*appreciatively: relieved at being so well understood*): Just so, Governor. Thats right.

PICKERING: But why did you bring her luggage if you intended to take her away?

DOOLITTLE: Have I said a word about taking her away? Have I now?

HIGGINS (*determinedly*): Youre going to take her away, double quick. (*He crosses to the hearth and rings the bell.*)

DOOLITTLE (*rising*): No, Governor. Dont say that. I'm not the man to stand in my girl's light. Heres a career opening for her, as you might say; and—

(MRS PEARCE *opens the door and awaits orders.*)

HIGGINS: Mrs Pearce: this is Eliza's father. He has come to take her away. Give her to him. (*He goes back to the piano, with an air of washing his hands of the whole affair.*)

DOOLITTLE: No. This is a misunderstanding. Listen here—

MRS PEARCE: He cant take her away, Mr Higgins: how can he? You told me to burn her clothes.

DOOLITTLE: Thats right. I cant carry the girl through the streets like a blooming monkey, can I? I put it to you.

HIGGINS: You have put it to me that you want your daughter. Take your daughter. If she has no clothes go out and buy her some.

DOOLITTLE (*desperate*): Wheres the clothes she come in? Did I burn them or did your missus here?

MRS PEARCE: I am the housekeeper, if you please. I have sent for some clothes for your girl. When they come you can take her away. You can wait in the kitchen. This way, please.

(DOOLITTLE, *much troubled, accompanies her to the door; then hesitates; finally turns confidentially to* HIGGINS.)

DOOLITTLE: Listen here, Governor. You and me is men of the world, aint we?

HIGGINS: Oh! Men of the world, are we? Youd better go, Mrs Pearce.

MRS PEARCE: I think so, indeed, sir. (*She goes, with dignity.*)

PICKERING: The floor is yours, Mr Doolittle.

DOOLITTLE (*to* PICKERING): I thank you, Governor. (*to* HIGGINS, *who takes refuge on the piano bench, a little overwhelmed by the proximity of his visitor; for* DOOLITTLE *has a professional flavor of dust about him*) Well, the truth is,

I've taken a sort of fancy to you, Governor; and if you want the girl, I'm not so set on having her back home again but what I might be open to an arrangement. Regarded in the light of a young woman, she's a fine handsome girl. As a daughter she's not worth her keep; and so I tell you straight. All I ask is my rights as a father; and youre the last man alive to expect me to let her go for nothing; for I can see youre one of the straight sort, Governor. Well, whats a five-pound note to you? and whats Eliza to me? (*He turns to his chair and sits down judicially.*)

PICKERING: I think you ought to know, Doolittle, that Mr Higgins's intentions are entirely honorable.

DOOLITTLE: Course they are, Governor. If I thought they wasnt, I'd ask fifty.

HIGGINS (*revolted*): Do you mean to say that you would sell your daughter for £50?

DOOLITTLE: Not in a general way I would; but to oblige a gentleman like you I'd do a good deal, I do assure you.

PICKERING: Have you no morals, man?

DOOLITTLE (*unabashed*): Cant afford them, Governor. Neither could you if you was as poor as me. Not that I mean any harm, you know. But if Liza is going to have a bit out of this, why not me too?

HIGGINS (*troubled*): I dont know what to do, Pickering. There can be no question that as a matter of morals it's a positive crime to give this chap a farthing. And yet I feel a sort of rough justice in his claim.

DOOLITTLE: Thats it, Governor. Thats all I say. A father's heart, as it were.

PICKERING: Well, I know the feeling; but really it seems hardly right—

DOOLITTLE: Dont say that, Governor. Dont look at it that way. What am I, Governors both? I ask you, what am I? I'm one of the undeserving poor: thats what I am. Think of what that means to a man. It means that he's up agen middle class morality all the time. If theres anything going, and I put in for a bit of it, it's always the same story: "Youre undeserving; so you cant have it." But my needs is as great as the most deserving widow's that ever got money out of six different charities in one week for the death of the same husband. I dont need less than a deserving man: I need more. I dont eat less hearty than him; and I drink a lot more. I want a bit of amusement, cause I'm a thinking man. I want cheerfulness and a song and a band when I feel low. Well, they charge me just the same for everything as they charge

the deserving. What is middle class morality? Just an excuse
for never giving me anything. Therefore, I ask you, as two
gentlemen, not to play that game on me. I'm playing straight
with you. I aint pretending to be deserving. I'm undeserving;
and I mean to go on being undeserving. I like it; and thats
the truth. Will you take advantage of a man's nature to do
him out of the price of his own daughter what he's brought
up and fed and clothed by the sweat of his brow until she's
growed big enough to be interesting to you two gentlemen?
Is five pounds unreasonable? I put it to you; and I leave it
to you.

HIGGINS (*rising, and going over to* PICKERING): Pickering:
if we were to take this man in hand for three months, he
could choose between a seat in the Cabinet and a popular
pulpit in Wales.

PICKERING: What do you say to that, Doolittle?

DOOLITTLE: Not me, Governor, thank you kindly. Ive
heard all the preachers and all the prime ministers—for I'm a
thinking man and game for politics or religion or social reform same as all the other amusements—and I tell you it's a
dog's life any way you look at it. Undeserving poverty is my
line. Taking one station in society with another, it's—it's—
well, it's the only one that has any ginger in it, to my taste.

HIGGINS: I suppose we must give him a fiver.

PICKERING: He'll make a bad use of it, I'm afraid.

DOOLITTLE: Not me, Governor, so help me I wont. Dont
you be afraid that I'll save it and spare it and live idle on it.
There wont be a penny of it left by Monday: I'll have to go
to work same as if I'd never had it. It wont pauperize me,
you bet. Just one good spree for myself and the missus,
giving pleasure to ourselves and employment to others, and
satisfaction to you to think it's not been throwed away. You
couldnt spend it better.

HIGGINS (*taking out his pocket book and coming between*
DOOLITTLE *and the piano*): This is irresistible. Lets give him
ten. (*He offers two notes to the dustman.*)

DOOLITTLE: No, Governor. She wouldnt have the heart to
spend ten; and perhaps I shouldnt neither. Ten pounds is a
lot of money: it makes a man feel prudent like; and then
goodbye to happiness. You give me what I ask you, Governor: not a penny more, and not a penny less.

PICKERING: Why dont you marry that missus of yours?
I rather draw the line at encouraging that sort of immorality.

DOOLITTLE: Tell her so, Governor: tell her so. *I'*m willing.
It's me that suffers by it. Ive no hold on her. I got to be

agreeable to her. I got to give her presents. I got to buy her clothes something sinful. I'm a slave to that woman, Governor, just because I'm not her lawful husband. And she knows it too. Catch her marrying me! Take my advice, Governor: marry Eliza while she's young and dont know no better. If you dont youll be sorry for it after. If you do, she'll be sorry for it after; but better her than you, because youre a man, and she's only a woman and dont know how to be happy anyhow.

HIGGINS: Pickering: if we listen to this man another minute, we shall have no convictions left. (*to* DOOLITTLE) Five pounds I think you said.

DOOLITTLE: Thank you kindly, Governor.

HIGGINS: Youre sure you wont take ten?

DOOLITTLE: Not now. Another time, Governor.

HIGGINS (*handing him a five-pound note*): Here you are.

DOOLITTLE: Thank you, Governor. Good morning. (*He hurries to the door, anxious to get away with his booty. When he opens it he is confronted with a dainty and exquisitely clean young Japanese lady in a simple blue cotton kimono printed cunningly with small white jasmine blossoms.* MRS PEARCE *is with her. He gets out of her way deferentially and apologizes.*) Beg pardon, miss.

THE JAPANESE LADY: Garn! Dont you know your own daughter?

DOOLITTLE	*exclaiming*	Bly me! it's Eliza!
HIGGINS	*simul-*	Whats that? This!
PICKERING	*taneously*	By Jove!

LIZA: Dont I look silly?

HIGGINS: Silly?

MRS PEARCE (*at the door*): Now, Mr Higgins, please dont say anything to make the girl conceited about herself.

HIGGINS (*conscientiously*): Oh! Quite right, Mrs Pearce. (*to* ELIZA) Yes: damned silly.

MRS PEARCE: Please, sir.

HIGGINS (*correcting himself*): I mean extremely silly.

LIZA: I should look all right with my hat on. (*She takes up her hat; puts it on; and walks across the room to the fireplace with a fashionable air.*)

HIGGINS: A new fashion, by George! And it ought to look horrible!

DOOLITTLE (*with fatherly pride*): Well, I never thought she'd clean up as good looking as that, Governor. She's a credit to me, aint she?

LIZA: I tell you, it's easy to clean up here. Hot and cold

water on tap, just as much as you like, there is. Woolly
towels, there is; and a towel horse so hot, it burns your fingers. Soft brushes to scrub yourself, and a wooden bowl of
soap smelling like primroses. Now I know why ladies is so
clean. Washing's a treat for them. Wish they could see what
it is for the like of me!

HIGGINS: I'm glad the bathroom met with your approval.

LIZA: It didnt: not all of it; and I dont care who hears me
say it. Mrs Pearce knows.

HIGGINS: What was wrong, Mrs Pearce?

MRS PEARCE (*blandly*): Oh, nothing, sir. It doesnt matter.

LIZA: I had a good mind to break it. I didnt know which
way to look. But I hung a towel over it, I did.

HIGGINS: Over what?

MRS PEARCE: Over the looking-glass, sir.

HIGGINS: Doolittle: you have brought your daughter up too
strictly.

DOOLITTLE: Me! I never brought her up at all, except to
give her a lick of a strap now and again. Dont put it on me,
Governor. She aint accustomed to it, you see: thats all. But
she'll soon pick up your free-and-easy ways.

LIZA: I'm a good girl, I am; and I wont pick up no free-
and-easy ways.

HIGGINS: Eliza: if you say again that youre a good girl,
your father shall take you home.

LIZA: Not him. You dont know my father. All he come
here for was to touch you for some money to get drunk on.

DOOLITTLE: Well, what else would I want money for? To
put into the plate in church, I suppose. (*She puts out her
tongue at him. He is so incensed by this that* PICKERING
presently finds it necessary to step between them.) Dont you
give me none of your lip; and dont let me hear you giving
this gentleman any of it neither, or youll hear from me about
it. See?

HIGGINS: Have you any further advice to give her before
you go, Doolittle? Your blessing, for instance.

DOOLITTLE: No, Governor: I aint such a mug as to put up
my children to all I know myself. Hard enough to hold them
in without that. If you want Eliza's mind improved, Governor, you do it yourself with a strap. So long, gentlemen. (*He
turns to go.*)

HIGGINS (*impressively*): Stop. Youll come regularly to see
your daughter. It's your duty, you know. My brother is a
clergyman; and he could help you in your talks with her.

DOOLITTLE (*evasively*): Certainly, I'll come, Governor.

Not just this week, because I have a job at a distance. But later on you may depend on me. Afternoon, gentlemen. Afternoon, maam.

(*He touches his hat to* MRS PEARCE, *who disdains the salutation and goes out. He winks at* HIGGINS, *thinking him probably a fellower-sufferer from* MRS PEARCE'S *difficult disposition, and follows her.*)

LIZA: Dont you believe the old liar. He'd as soon you set a bulldog on him as a clergyman. You wont see him again in a hurry.

HIGGINS: I dont want to, Eliza. Do you?

LIZA: Not me. I dont never want to see him again, I dont. He's a disgrace to me, he is, collecting dust, instead of working at his trade.

PICKERING: What is his trade, Eliza?

LIZA: Talking money out of other people's pockets into his own. His proper trade's a navvy; and he works at it sometimes too—for exercise—and earns good money at it. Aint you going to call me Miss Doolittle any more?

PICKERING: I beg your pardon, Miss Doolittle. It was a slip of the tongue.

LIZA: Oh, I dont mind; only it sounded so genteel. I should just like to take a taxi to the corner of Tottenham Court Road and get out there and tell it to wait for me, just to put the girls in their place a bit. I wouldnt speak to them, you know.

PICKERING: Better wait til we get you something really fashionable.

HIGGINS: Besides, you shouldnt cut your old friends now that you have risen in the world. Thats what we call snobbery.

LIZA: You dont call the like of them my friends now, I should hope. Theyve took it out of me often enough with their ridicule when they had the chance; and now I mean to get a bit of my own back. But if I'm to have fashionable clothes, I'll wait. I should like to have some. Mrs Pearce says youre going to give me some to wear in bed at night different to what I wear in the daytime; but it do seem a waste of money when you could get something to shew. Besides, I never could fancy changing into cold things on a winter night.

MRS PEARCE (*coming back*): Now, Eliza. The new things have come for you to try on.

LIZA: Ah-ow-oo-ooh! (*She rushes out.*)

MRS PEARCE (*following her*): Oh, dont rush about like that, girl. (*She shuts the door behind her.*)

HIGGINS: Pickering: we have taken on a stiff job.

PICKERING (*with conviction*): Higgins: we have.

*   *   *   *   *   *

(*There seems to be some curiosity as to what* HIGGINS'S *lessons to* ELIZA *were like. Well, here is a sample: the first one.*

Picture ELIZA, *in her new clothes, and feeling her inside put out of step by a lunch, dinner, and breakfast of a kind to which it is unaccustomed, seated with* HIGGINS *and the* COLONEL *in the study, feeling like a hospital out-patient at a first encounter with the doctors.*

HIGGINS, *constitutionally unable to sit still, discomposes her still more by striding restlessly about. But for the reassuring presence and quietude of her friend the* COLONEL *she would run for her life, even back to Drury Lane.*)

HIGGINS: Say your alphabet.

LIZA: I know my alphabet. Do you think I know nothing? I dont need to be taught like a child.

HIGGINS (*thundering*): Say your alphabet.

PICKERING: Say it, Miss Doolittle. You will understand presently. Do what he tells you; and let him teach you in his own way.

LIZA: Oh well, if you put it like that—Ahyee, beyee, ceyee, deyee—

HIGGINS (*with the roar of a wounded lion*): Stop. Listen to this, Pickering. This is what we pay for as elementary education. This unfortunate animal has been locked up for nine years in school at our expense to teach her to speak and read the language of Shakespear and Milton. And the result is Ahyee, Be-yee, Ce-yee, Deyee. (*to Eliza*) Say A, B, C, D.

LIZA (*almost in tears*): But I'm sayin it. Ahyee, Beyee, Ce-yee—

HIGGINS: Stop. Say a cup of tea.

LIZA: A cappee-ee.

HIGGINS: Put your tongue forward until it squeezes against the top of your lower teeth. Now say cup.

LIZA: C-c-c—I cant. C-Cup.

PICKERING: Good. Splendid, Miss Doolittle.

HIGGINS: By Jupiter, she's done it the first shot. Pickering: we shall make a duchess of her. (*to* ELIZA) Now do you think you could possibly say tea? Not te-yee, mind: if you ever say be-yee ce-yee de-yee again you shall be dragged round the room three times by the hair of your head. (*fortissimo*) T, T, T, T.

LIZA (*weeping*): I cant hear no difference cep that it sounds more genteel-like when you say it.

HIGGINS: Well, if you can hear that difference, what the devil are you crying for? Pickering: give her a chocolate.

PICKERING: No, no. Never mind crying a little, Miss Doolittle: you are doing very well; and the lessons wont hurt. I promise you I wont let him drag you round the room by your hair.

HIGGINS: Be off with you to Mrs Pearce and tell her about it. Think about it. Try to do it by yourself: and keep your tongue well forward in your mouth instead of trying to roll it up and swallow it. Another lesson at half-past four this afternoon. Away with you.

(ELIZA, *still sobbing, rushes from the room.*

And that is the sort of ordeal poor ELIZA *has to go through for months before we meet her again on her first appearance in London society of the professional class.*)

ACT III

(*It is* MRS HIGGINS'S *at-home day. Nobody has yet arrived. Her drawing room, in a flat on Chelsea Embankment, has three windows looking on the river; and the ceiling is not so lofty as it would be in an older house of the same pretension. The windows are open, giving access to a balcony with flowers in pots. If you stand with your face to the windows, you have the fireplace on your left and the door in the right-hand wall close to the corner nearest the windows.*

MRS HIGGINS *was brought up on Morris and Burne Jones; and her room, which is very unlike her son's room in Wimpole Street, is not crowded with furniture and little tables and nicknacks. In the middle of the room there is a big ottoman; and this, with the carpets, the Morris wall-papers, and the Morris chintz window curtains and brocade covers of the ottoman and its cushions, supply all the ornament, and are much too handsome to be hidden by odds and ends of useless things. A few good oil-paintings from the exhibitions in the Grosvenor Gallery thirty years ago (the Burne Jones, not the*

Whistler side of them) are on the walls. The only landscape is a Cecil Lawson on the scale of a Rubens. There is a portrait of Mrs Higgins as she was when she defied the fashion in her youth in one of the beautiful Rossettian costumes which, when caricatured by people who did not understand, led to the absurdities of popular estheticism in the eighteen-seventies.

In the corner diagonally opposite the door MRS HIGGINS, *now over sixty and long past taking the trouble to dress out of the fashion, sits writing at an elegantly simple writing-table with a bell button within reach of her hand. There is a Chippendale chair further back in the room between her and the window nearest her side. At the other side of the room, further forward, is an Elizabethan chair roughly carved in the taste of Inigo Jones. On the same side a piano in a decorated case. The corner between the fireplace and the window is occupied by a divan cushioned in Morris chintz.*

It is between four and five in the afternoon.

The door is opened violently; and HIGGINS *enters with his hat on.)*

MRS HIGGINS (*dismayed*): Henry! (*scolding him*) What are you doing here today? It is my at-home day: you promised not to come. (*As he bends to kiss her, she takes his hat off, and presents it to him.*)

HIGGINS: Oh bother! (*He throws the hat down on the table.*)

MRS HIGGINS: Go home at once.

HIGGINS (*kissing her*): I know, mother. I came on purpose.

MRS HIGGINS: But you mustnt. I'm serious, Henry. You offend all my friends: they stop coming whenever they meet you.

HIGGINS: Nonsense! I know I have no small talk; but people dont mind. (*He sits on the settee.*)

MRS HIGGINS: Oh! dont they? Small talk indeed! What about your large talk? Really, dear, you mustnt stay.

HIGGINS: I must. Ive a job for you. A phonetic job.

MRS HIGGINS: No use, dear. I'm sorry; but I cant get round your vowels; and though I like to get pretty postcards in your patent shorthand, I always have to read the copies in ordinary writing you so thoughtfully send me.

HIGGINS: Well, this isnt a phonetic job.

MRS HIGGINS: You said it was.

HIGGINS: Not your part of it. Ive picked up a girl.

MRS HIGGINS: Does that mean that some girl has picked you up?

HIGGINS: Not at all. I dont mean a love affair.

MRS HIGGINS: What a pity!

HIGGINS: Why?

MRS HIGGINS: Well, you never fall in love with anyone under forty-five. When will you discover that there are some rather nice-looking young women about?

HIGGINS: Oh, I cant be bothered with young women. My idea of a lovable woman is somebody as like you as possible. I shall never get into the way of seriously liking young women: some habits lie too deep to be changed. (*rising abruptly and walking about, jingling his money and his keys in his trouser pockets*) Besides, theyre all idiots.

MRS HIGGINS: Do you know what you would do if you really loved me, Henry?

HIGGINS: Oh bother! What? Marry, I suppose.

MRS HIGGINS: No. Stop fidgeting and take your hands out of your pockets. (*With a gesture of despair, he obeys and sits down again.*) Thats a good boy. Now tell me about the girl.

HIGGINS: She's coming to see you.

MRS HIGGINS: I dont remember asking her.

HIGGINS: You didnt. *I* asked her. If youd known her you wouldnt have asked her.

MRS HIGGINS: Indeed! Why?

HIGGINS: Well, it's like this. She's a common flower girl. I picked her off the kerbstone.

MRS HIGGINS: And invited her to my at-home!

HIGGINS (*rising and coming to her to coax her*): Oh, thatll be all right. Ive taught her to speak properly; and she has strict orders as to her behavior. She's to keep to two subjects: the weather and everybody's health—Fine day and How do you do, you know—and not to let herself go on things in general. That will be safe.

MRS HIGGINS: Safe! To talk about our health! about our insides! perhaps about our outsides! How could you be so silly, Henry?

HIGGINS (*impatiently*): Well, she must talk about something. (*He controls himself and sits down again.*) Oh, she'll be all right: dont you fuss. Pickering is in it with me. Ive a sort of bet on that I'll pass her off as a duchess in six months. I started on her some months ago; and she's getting on like a house on fire. I shall win my bet. She has a quick ear; and she's easier to teach than my middle-class pupils because she's had to learn a complete new language. She talks English almost as you talk French.

MRS HIGGINS: Thats satisfactory, at all events.

HIGGINS: Well, it is and it isnt.

MRS HIGGINS: What does that mean?

HIGGINS: You see, Ive got her pronunciation all right; but you have to consider not only how a girl pronounces, but what she pronounces; and thats where—

(*They are interrupted by the* PARLOR-MAID, *announcing guests.*)

THE PARLOR-MAID: Mrs and Miss Eynsford Hill. (*She withdraws.*)

HIGGINS: Oh Lord! (*He rises; snatches his hat from the table; and makes for the door; but before he reaches it his mother introduces him.*)

(MRS *and* MISS EYNSFORD HILL *are the mother and daughter who sheltered from the rain in Covent Garden. The mother is well bred, quiet, and has the habitual anxiety of straitened means. The daughter has acquired a gay air of being very much at home in society: the bravado of genteel poverty.*)

MRS EYNSFORD HILL (*to* MRS HIGGINS): How do you do? (*They shake hands.*)

MISS EYNSFORD HILL: How d'you do? (*She shakes.*)

MRS HIGGINS (*introducing*): My son Henry.

MRS EYNSFORD HILL: Your celebrated son! I have so longed to meet you, Professor Higgins.

HIGGINS (*glumly, making no movement in her direction*): Delighted. (*He backs against the piano and bows brusquely.*)

MISS EYNSFORD HILL (*going to him with confident familiarity*): How do you do?

HIGGINS (*staring at her*): Ive seen you before somewhere. I havnt the ghost of a notion where; but Ive heard your voice. (*drearily*) It doesnt matter. Youd better sit down.

MRS HIGGINS: I'm sorry to say that my celebrated son has no manners. You mustnt mind him.

MISS EYNSFORD HILL (*gaily*): I don't. (*She sits in the Elizabethan chair.*)

MRS EYNSFORD HILL (*a little bewildered*): Not at all. (*She sits on the ottoman between her daughter and* MRS HIGGINS, *who has turned her chair away from the writing-table.*)

HIGGINS: Oh, have I been rude? I didnt mean to be.

(*He goes to the central window, through which, with his back to the company, he contemplates the river and the flowers in Battersea Park on the opposite bank as if they were a frozen desert.*

The PARLOR-MAID *returns, ushering in* PICKERING.)

THE PARLOR-MAID: Colonel Pickering. (*She withdraws.*)

PICKERING: How do you do, Mrs Higgins?

MRS HIGGINS: So glad youve come. Do you know Mrs Eynsford Hill—Miss Eynsford Hill? (*Exchange of bows. The* COLONEL *brings the Chippendale chair a little forward between* MRS HILL *and* MRS HIGGINS, *and sits down.*)

PICKERING: Has Henry told you what weve come for?

HIGGINS (*over his shoulder*): We were interrupted: damn it!

MRS HIGGINS: Oh Henry, Henry, really!

MRS EYNSFORD HILL (*half rising*): Are we in the way?

MRS HIGGINS (*rising and making her sit down again*): No, no. You couldnt have come more fortunately: we want you to meet a friend of ours.

HIGGINS (*turning hopefully*): Yes, by George! We want two or three people. Youll do as well as anybody else.

(*The* PARLOR-MAID *returns, ushering* FREDDY.)

THE PARLOR-MAID: Mr Eynsford Hill.

HIGGINS (*almost audibly, past endurance*): God of Heaven! another of them.

FREDDY (*shaking hands with* MRS HIGGINS): Ahdedo?

MRS HIGGINS: Very good of you to come. (*introducing*) Colonel Pickering.

FREDDY (*bowing*): Ahdedo?

MRS HIGGINS: I dont think you know my son, Professor Higgins.

FREDDY (*going to* HIGGINS): Ahdedo?

HIGGINS (*looking at him much as if he were a pickpocket*): I'll take my oath Ive met you before somewhere. Where was it?

FREDDY: I dont think so.

HIGGINS (*resignedly*): It doesnt matter, anyhow. Sit down. (*He shakes* FREDDY'S *hand, and almost slings him on to the ottoman with his face to the window; then comes round to the other side of it.*)

HIGGINS: Well, here we are, anyhow! (*He sits down on the ottoman next to* MRS EYNSFORD HILL, *on her left.*) And now, what the devil are we going to talk about until Eliza comes?

MRS HIGGINS: Henry: you are the life and soul of the Royal Society's soirées; but really youre rather trying on more commonplace occasions.

HIGGINS: Am I? Very sorry. (*beaming suddenly*) I suppose I am, you know. (*uproariously*) Ha, ha!

MISS EYNSFORD HILL (*who considers* HIGGINS *quite eligible matrimonially*): I sympathize. *I* havnt any small talk. If people would only be frank and say what they really think!

HIGGINS (*relapsing into gloom*): Lord forbid!

MRS EYNSFORD HILL (*taking up her daughter's cue*): But why?

HIGGINS: What they think they ought to think is bad enough, Lord knows; but what they really think would break up the whole show. Do you suppose it would be really agreeable if I were to come out now with what *I* really think?

MISS EYNSFORD HILL (*gaily*): Is it so very cynical?

HIGGINS: Cynical! Who the dickens said it was cynical? I mean it wouldnt be decent.

MRS EYNSFORD HILL (*seriously*): Oh! I'm sure you dont mean that, Mr Higgins.

HIGGINS: You see, we're all savages, more or less. We're supposed to be civilized and cultured—to know all about poetry and philosophy and art and science, and so on; but how many of us know even the meanings of these names? (*to* MISS HILL) What do you know of poetry? (*to* MRS HILL) What do you know of science? (*indicating* FREDDY) What does he know of art or science or anything else? What the devil do you imagine I know of philosophy?

MRS HIGGINS (*warningly*): Or of manners, Henry?

THE PARLOR-MAID (*opening the door*): Miss Doolittle. (*She withdraws.*)

HIGGINS (*rising hastily and running to* MRS HIGGINS): Here she is, mother. (*He stands on tiptoe and makes signs over his mother's head to* ELIZA *to indicate to her which lady is her hostess.*

ELIZA (*who is exquisitely dressed, produces an impression of such remarkable distinction and beauty as she enters that they all rise, quite fluttered. Guided by* HIGGINS'S *signals, she comes to* MRS HIGGINS *with studied grace.*)

LIZA (*speaking with pedantic correctness of pronunciation and great beauty of tone*): How do you do, Mrs Higgins? (*She gasps slightly in making sure of the H in Higgins, but is quite successful.*) Mr Higgins told me I might come.

MRS HIGGINS (*cordially*): Quite right: I'm very glad indeed to see you.

PICKERING: How do you do, Miss Doolittle?

LIZA (*shaking hands with him*): Colonel Pickering, is it not?

MRS EYNSFORD HILL: I feel sure we have met before, Miss Doolittle. I remember your eyes.

LIZA: How do you do? (*She sits down on the ottoman gracefully in the place just left vacant by* HIGGINS.)

MRS EYNSFORD HILL (*introducing*): My daughter Clara.

LIZA: How do you do?

CLARA (*impulsively*): How do you do? (*She sits down on the ottoman beside* ELIZA, *devouring her with her eyes.*)

FREDDY (*coming to their side of the ottoman*): Ive certainly had the pleasure.

MRS EYNSFORD HILL (*introducing*): My son Freddy.

LIZA: How do you do?

(FREDDY *bows and sits down in the Elizabethan chair, infatuated.*)

HIGGINS (*suddenly*): By George, yes: it all comes back to me! (*They stare at him.*) Covent Garden! (*lamentably*) What a damned thing!

MRS HIGGINS: Henry, please! (*He is about to sit on the edge of the table.*) Dont sit on my writing-table: youll break it.

HIGGINS (*sulkily*): Sorry.

(*He goes to the divan, stumbling into the fender and over the fire-irons on his way; extricating himself with muttered imprecations; and finishing his disastrous journey by throwing himself so impatiently on the divan that he almost breaks it.* MRS. HIGGINS *looks at him, but controls herself and says nothing.*

A long and painful pause ensues.)

MRS HIGGINS (*at last, conversationally*): Will it rain, do you think?

LIZA: The shallow depression in the west of these islands is likely to move slowly in an easterly direction. There are no indications of any great change in the barometrical situation.

FREDDY: Ha! ha! how awfully funny!

LIZA: What is wrong with that, young man? I bet I got it right.

FREDDY: Killing!

MRS EYNSFORD HILL: I'm sure I hope it wont turn cold. Theres so much influenza about. It runs right through our whole family regularly every spring.

LIZA (*darkly*): My aunt died of influenza: so they said.

MRS EYNSFORD HILL (*clicks her tongue sympathetically*): !!!

LIZA (*in the same tragic tone*): But it's my belief they done the old woman in.

MRS HIGGINS (*puzzled*): Done her in?

LIZA: Y-e-e-e-es, Lord love you! Why should she die of influenza? She come through diphtheria right enough the year before. I saw her with my own eyes. Fairly blue with it, she was. They all thought she was dead; but my father he kept ladling gin down her throat til she came to so sudden that she bit the bowl off the spoon.

MRS EYNSFORD HILL (*startled*): Dear me!

LIZA (*piling up the indictment*): What call would a woman with that strength in her have to die of influenza? What become of her new straw hat that should have come to me? Somebody pinched it; and what I say is, them as pinched it done her in.

MRS EYNSFORD HILL: What does doing her in mean?

HIGGINS (*hastily*): Oh, thats the new small talk. To do a person in means to kill them.

MRS EYNSFORD HILL (*to* ELIZA, *horrified*): You surely dont believe that your aunt was killed?

LIZA: Do I not! Them she lived with would have killed her for a hat-pin, let alone a hat.

MRS EYNSFORD HILL: But it cant have been right for your father to pour spirits down her throat like that. It might have killed her.

LIZA: Not her. Gin was mother's milk to her. Besides, he'd poured so much down his own throat that he knew the good of it.

MRS EYNSFORD HILL: Do you mean that he drank?

LIZA: Drank! My word! Something chronic.

MRS EYNSFORD HILL: How dreadful for you!

LIZA: Not a bit. It never did him no harm what I could see. But then he did not keep it up regular. (*cheerfully*) On the burst, as you might say, from time to time. And always more agreeable when he had a drop in. When he was out of work, my mother used to give him fourpence and tell him to go out and not come back until he'd drunk himself cheerful and loving-like. Theres lots of women has to make their husbands drunk to make them fit to live with. (*now quite at her ease*) You see, it's like this. If a man has a bit of conscience, it always takes him when he's sober; and then it makes him low-spirited. A drop of booze just takes that off and makes him happy. (*to* FREDDY, *who is in convulsions of suppressed laughter*) Here! what are you sniggering at?

FREDDY: The new small talk. You do it so awfully well.

LIZA: If I was doing it proper, what was you laughing at? (*to* HIGGINS) Have I said anything I oughtnt?

MRS HIGGINS (*interposing*): Not at all, Miss Doolittle.

LIZA: Well, thats a mercy, anyhow. (*expansively*) What I always say is—

HIGGINS (*rising and looking at his watch*): Ahem!

LIZA (*looking round at him; taking the hint; and rising*): Well: I must go. (*They all rise.* FREDDY *goes to the door.*) So pleased to have met you. Goodbye. (*She shakes hands with* MRS HIGGINS.)

MRS HIGGINS: Goodbye.

LIZA: Goodbye, Colonel Pickering.

PICKERING: Goodbye, Miss Doolittle. (*They shake hands.*)

LIZA (*nodding to the others*): Goodbye, all.

FREDDY (*opening the door for her*): Are you walking across the Park, Miss Doolittle? If so—

LIZA (*with perfectly elegant diction*): Walk! Not bloody likely. (*sensation*) I am going in a taxi. (*She goes out.*)

(PICKERING *gasps and sits down.* FREDDY *goes out on the balcony to catch another glimpse of* ELIZA.)

MRS EYNSFORD HILL (*suffering from shock*): Well, I really cant get used to the new ways.

CLARA (*throwing herself discontentedly into the Elizabethan chair*): Oh, it's all right, mamma, quite right. People will think we never go anywhere or see anybody if you are so old-fashioned.

MRS EYNSFORD HILL: I daresay I am very old-fashioned; but I do hope you wont begin using that expression, Clara. I have got accustomed to hear you talking about men as rotters, and calling everything filthy and beastly; though I do think it horrible and unladylike. But this last is really too much. Dont you think so, Colonel Pickering?

PICKERING: Dont ask me. Ive been away in India for several years; and manners have changed so much that I sometimes dont know whether I'm at a respectable dinnertable or in a ship's forecastle.

CLARA: It's all a matter of habit. Theres no right or wrong in it. Nobody means anything by it. And it's so quaint, and gives such a smart emphasis to things that are not in themselves very witty. I find the new small talk delightful and quite innocent.

MRS EYNSFORD HILL (*rising*): Well, after that, I think it's time for us to go.

(PICKERING *and* HIGGINS *rise.*)

CLARA (*rising*): Oh yes: we have three at-homes to go to

still. Goodbye, Mrs Higgins. Goodbye, Colonel Pickering. Goodbye, Professor Higgins.

HIGGINS (*coming grimly at her from the divan, and accompanying her to the door*): Goodbye. Be sure you try on that small talk at the three at-homes. Dont be nervous about it. Pitch it in strong.

CLARA (*all smiles*): I will. Goodbye. Such nonsense, all this early Victorian prudery!

HIGGINS (*tempting her*): Such damned nonsense!

CLARA: Such bloody nonsense!

MRS EYNSFORD HILL (*convulsively*): Clara!

CLARA: Ha! ha!

(*She goes out radiant, conscious of being thoroughly up to date, and is heard descending the stairs in a stream of silvery laughter.*)

FREDDY (*to the heavens at large*): Well, I ask you— (*He gives it up, and comes to* MRS HIGGINS.) Goodbye.

MRS HIGGINS (*shaking hands*): Goodbye. Would you like to meet Miss Doolittle again?

FREDDY (*eagerly*): Yes, I should, most awfully.

MRS HIGGINS: Well, you know my days.

FREDDY: Yes. Thanks awfully. Goodbye.

(*He goes out.*)

MRS EYNSFORD HILL: Goodbye, Mr Higgins.

HIGGINS: Goodbye. Goodbye.

MRS EYNSFORD HILL (*to* PICKERING): It's no use. I shall never be able to bring myself to use that word.

PICKERING: Dont. It's not compulsory, you know. Youll get on quite well without it.

MRS EYNSFORD HILL: Only, Clara is so down on me if I am not positively reeking with the latest slang. Goodbye.

PICKERING: Goodbye. (*They shake hands.*)

MRS EYNSFORD HILL (*to* MRS HIGGINS): You mustnt mind Clara. (PICKERING, *catching from her lowered tone that this is not meant for him to hear, discreetly joins* HIGGINS *at the window.*) We're so poor! and she gets so few parties, poor child! She doesnt quite know. (MRS HIGGINS, *seeing that her eyes are moist, takes her hand sympathetically and goes with her to the door.*) But the boy is nice. Don't you think so?

MRS HIGGINS: Oh, quite nice. I shall always be delighted to see him.

MRS EYNSFORD HILL: Thank you, dear. Goodbye.

(*She goes out.*)

HIGGINS (*eagerly*): Well? Is Eliza presentable? (*He swoops on his mother and drags her to the ottoman, where she sits down in* ELIZA'S *place with her son on her left.*

PICKERING *returns to his chair on her right.*)

MRS HIGGINS: You silly boy, of course she's not presentable. She's a triumph of your art and of her dressmaker's; but if you suppose for a moment that she doesn't give herself away in every sentence she utters, you must be perfectly cracked about her.

PICKERING: But dont you think something might be done? I mean something to eliminate the sanguinary element from her conversation.

MRS HIGGINS: Not as long as she is in Henry's hands.

HIGGINS (*aggrieved*): Do you mean that my language is improper?

MRS HIGGINS: No, dearest: it would be quite proper—say on a canal barge; but it would not be proper for her at a garden party.

HIGGINS (*deeply injured*): Well I must say—

PICKERING (*interrupting him*): Come, Higgins: you must learn to know yourself. I havent heard such language as yours since we used to review the volunteers in Hyde Park twenty years ago.

HIGGINS (*sulkily*): Oh, well, if you say so, I suppose I dont always talk like a bishop.

MRS HIGGINS (*quieting* HENRY *with a touch*): Colonel Pickering: will you tell me what is the exact state of things in Wimpole Street?

PICKERING (*cheerfully: as if this completely changed the subject*): Well, I have come to live there with Henry. We work together at my Indian Dialects; and we think it more convenient—

MRS HIGGINS: Quite so. I know all about that: it's an excellent arrangement. But where does this girl live?

HIGGINS: With us, of course. Where should she live?

MRS HIGGINS: But on what terms? Is she a servant? If not, what is she?

PICKERING (*slowly*): I think I know what you mean, Mrs Higgins.

HIGGINS: Well, dash me if *I* do! Ive had to work at the girl every day for months to get her to her present pitch. Besides, she's useful. She knows where my things are, and remembers my appointments and so forth.

MRS HIGGINS: How does your housekeeper get on with her?

HIGGINS: Mrs Pearce? Oh, she's jolly glad to get so much taken off her hands; for before Eliza came, she used to have to find things and remind me of my appointments. But she's got some silly bee in her bonnet about Eliza. She keeps saying "You dont think, sir": doesnt she, Pick?

PICKERING: Yes: thats the formula. "You dont think, sir." Thats the end of every conversation about Eliza.

HIGGINS: As if I ever stop thinking about the girl and her confounded vowels and consonants. I'm worn out, thinking about her, and watching her lips and her teeth and her tongue, not to mention her soul, which is the quaintest of the lot.

MRS HIGGINS: You certainly are a pretty pair of babies, playing with your live doll.

HIGGINS: Playing! The hardest job I ever tackled: make no mistake about that, mother. But you have no idea how frightfully interesting it is to take a human being and change her into a quite different human being by creating a new speech for her. It's filling up the deepest gulf that separates class from class and soul from soul.

PICKERING (*drawing his chair closer to* MRS HIGGINS *and bending over to her eagerly*): Yes: it's enormously interesting. I assure you, Mrs Higgins, we take Eliza very seriously. Every week—every day almost—there is some new change. (*closer again*) We keep records of every stage—dozens of gramophone disks and photographs—

HIGGINS (*assailing her at the other ear*): Yes, by George: it's the most absorbing experiment I ever tackled. She regularly fills our lives up: doesnt she, Pick?

PICKERING: We're always talking Eliza.

HIGGINS: Teaching Eliza.

PICKERING: Dressing Eliza.

MRS HIGGINS: What!

HIGGINS: Inventing new Elizas.

HIGGINS:	(*speaking together*)	You know, she has the most extraordinary quickness of ear:
PICKERING:		I assure you, my dear Mrs Higgins, that girl
HIGGINS:		just like a parrot. Ive tried her with every
PICKERING:		is a genius. She can play the piano quite beautifully.
HIGGINS:		possible sort of sound that a human being can make—
PICKERING:		We have taken her to classical concerts and to music

HIGGINS:	(*speaking together*)	Continental dialects, African dialects, Hottentot
PICKERING:		halls; and it's all the same to her: she plays everything
HIGGINS:		clicks, things it took me years to get hold of; and
PICKERING:		she hears right off when she comes home, whether it's
HIGGINS:		she picks them up like a shot, right away, as if she had
PICKERING:		Beethoven and Brahms or Lehar and Lionel Monckton;
HIGGINS:		been at it all her life.
PICKERING:		though six months ago, she'd never as much as touched a piano—

MRS HIGGINS (*putting her fingers in her ears, as they are by this time shouting one another down with an intolerable noise*): Sh-sh-sh——sh! (*They stop.*)

PICKERING: I beg your pardon. (*He draws his chair back apologetically.*)

HIGGINS: Sorry. When Pickering starts shouting nobody can get a word in edgeways.

MRS HIGGINS: Be quiet, Henry. Colonel Pickering: dont you realize that when Eliza walked in Wimpole Street, something walked in with her?

PICKERING: Her father did. But Henry soon got rid of him.

MRS HIGGINS: It would have been more to the point if her mother had. But as her mother didnt something else did.

PICKERING: But what?

MRS HIGGINS (*unconsciously dating herself by the word*): A problem.

PICKERING: Oh, I see. The problem of how to pass her off as a lady.

HIGGINS: I'll solve that problem. Ive half solved it already.

MRS HIGGINS: No, you two infinitely stupid male creatures: the problem of what is to be done with her afterwards.

HIGGINS: I dont see anything in that. She can go her own way, with all the advantages I have given her.

MRS HIGGINS: The advantages of that poor woman who was here just now! The manners and habits that disqualify a fine lady from earning her own living without giving her a fine lady's income! Is that what you mean?

PICKERING (*indulgently, being rather bored*): Oh, that will be all right, Mrs Higgins. (*He rises to go.*)

HIGGINS (*rising also*): We'll find her some light employment.

PICKERING: She's happy enough. Dont you worry about her. Goodbye. (*He shakes hands as if he were consoling a frightened child, and makes for the door.*)

HIGGINS: Anyhow, theres no good bothering now. The thing's done. Goodbye, mother. (*He kisses her, and follows* PICKERING.)

PICKERING (*turning for a final consolation*): There are plenty of openings. We'll do whats right. Goodbye.

HIGGINS (*to* PICKERING *as they go out together*): Lets take her to the Shakespear exhibition at Earls Court.

PICKERING: Yes: lets. Her remarks will be delicious.

HIGGINS: She'll mimic all the people for us when we get home.

PICKERING: Ripping. (*Both are heard laughing as they go downstairs.*)

MRS HIGGINS (*rises with an impatient bounce, and returns to her work at the writing-table. She sweeps a litter of disarranged papers out of the way; snatches a sheet of paper from her stationery case; and tries resolutely to write. At the third time she gives it up; flings down her pen; grips the table angrily and exclaims*): Oh, men! men!! men!!!

*   *   *   *   *   *

(*Clearly* ELIZA *will not pass as a duchess yet; and* HIGGINS's *bet remains unwon. But the six months are not yet exhausted and just in time* ELIZA *does actually pass as a princess. For a glimpse of how she did it imagine an Embassy in London one summer evening after dark. The hall door has an awning and a carpet across the sidewalk to the kerb, because a grand reception is in progress. A small crowd is lined up to see the guests arrive.*

A Rolls-Royce car drives up. PICKERING *in evening dress, with medals and orders, alights, and hands out* ELIZA, *in opera cloak, evening dress, diamonds, fan, flowers and all accessories.* HIGGINS *follows. The car drives off; and the three go up the steps and into the house, the door opening for them as they approach.*

Inside the house they find themselves in a spacious hall from which the grand staircase rises. On the left are the ar-

rangements for the gentlemen's cloaks. The male guests are depositing their hats and wraps there.

On the right is a door leading to the ladies' cloakroom. Ladies are going in cloaked and coming out in splendor. PICKERING *whispers to* ELIZA *and points out the ladies' room. She goes into it.* HIGGINS *and* PICKERING *take off their overcoats and take tickets for them from the attendant.*

One of the guests, occupied in the same way, has his back turned. Having taken his ticket, he turns round and reveals himself as an important looking young man with an astonishingly hairy face. He has an enormous moustache, flowing out into luxuriant whiskers. Waves of hair cluster on his brow. His hair is cropped closely at the back, and glows with oil. Otherwise he is very smart. He wears several worthless orders. He is evidently a foreigner, guessable as a whiskered Pandour from Hungary; but in spite of the ferocity of his moustache he is amiable and genially voluble.

Recognizing HIGGINS, *he flings his arms wide apart and approaches him enthusiastically.*)

WHISKERS: Maestro, maestro. (*He embraces* HIGGINS *and kisses him on both cheeks.*) You remember me?

HIGGINS: No I dont. Who the devil are you?

WHISKERS: I am your pupil: your first pupil, your best and greatest pupil. I am little Nepommuck, the marvelous boy. I have made your name famous throughout Europe. You teach me phonetic. You cannot forget ME.

HIGGINS: Why don't you shave?

NEPOMMUCK: I have not your imposing appearance, your chin, your brow. Nobody notice me when I shave. Now I am famous: they call me Hairy Faced Dick.

HIGGINS: And what are you doing here among all these swells?

NEPOMMUCK: I am interpreter. I speak 32 languages. I am indispensable at these international parties. You are great cockney specialist: you place a man anywhere in London the moment he open his mouth. I place any man in Europe.

(*A footman hurries down the grand staircase and comes to* NEPOMMUCK.)

FOOTMAN: You are wanted upstairs. Her Excellency cannot understand the Greek gentleman.

NEPOMMUCK: Thank you, yes, immediately.

(*The* FOOTMAN *goes and is lost in the crowd.*)

NEPOMMUCK (*to* HIGGINS): This Greek diplomatist pretends he cannot speak nor understand English. He cannot deceive me. He is the son of a Clerkenwell watchmaker. He speaks English so villainously that he dare not utter a word of it without betraying his origin. I help him to pretend; but I make him pay through the nose. I make them all pay. Ha ha! (*He hurries upstairs.*)

PICKERING: Is this fellow really an expert? Can he find out Eliza and blackmail her?

HIGGINS: We shall see. If he finds her out I lose my bet.

(ELIZA *comes from the cloakroom and joins them.*)

PICKERING: Well, Eliza, now for it. Are you ready?

LIZA: Are you nervous, Colonel?

PICKERING: Frightfully. I feel exactly as I felt before my first battle. It's the first time that frightens.

LIZA: It is not the first time for me, Colonel. I have done this fifty times—hundreds of times—in my little piggery in Angel Court in my day-dreams. I am in a dream now. Promise me not to let Professor Higgins wake me; for if he does I shall forget everything and talk as I used to in Drury Lane.

PICKERING: Not a word, Higgins. (*to* ELIZA) Now, ready?

LIZA: Ready.

PICKERING: Go.

(*They mount the stairs,* HIGGINS *last.* PICKERING *whispers to the* FOOTMAN *on the first landing.*)

FIRST LANDING FOOTMAN: Miss Doolittle, Colonel Pickering, Professor Higgins.

SECOND LANDING FOOTMAN: Miss Doolittle, Colonel Pickering, Professor Higgins.

(*At the top of the staircase the* AMBASSADOR *and his wife, with* NEPOMMUCK *at her elbow, are receiving.*)

HOSTESS (*taking* ELIZA'S *hand*): How d'ye do?

HOST (*same play*): How d'ye do? How d'ye do, Pickering?

LIZA (*with a beautiful gravity that awes her hostess*): How do you do? (*She passes on to the drawing room.*)

HOSTESS: Is that your adopted daughter, Colonel Pickering? She will make a sensation.

PICKERING: Most kind of you to invite her for me. (*He passes on.*)

HOSTESS (*to* NEPOMMUCK): Find out all about her.

NEPOMMUCK (*bowing*): Excellency—(*He goes into the crowd.*)

HOST: How d'ye do, Higgins? You have a rival here tonight. He introduced himself as your pupil. Is he any good?

HIGGINS: He can learn a language in a fortnight—knows dozens of them. A sure mark of a fool. As a phonetician, no good whatever.

HOSTESS: How d'ye do, Professor?

HIGGINS: How do you do? Fearful bore for you this sort of thing. Forgive my part in it. (*He passes on.*)

(*In the drawing room and its suite of salons the reception is in full swing.* ELIZA *passes through. She is so intent on her ordeal that she walks like a somnambulist in a desert instead of a débutante in a fashionable crowd. They stop talking to look at her, admiring her dress, her jewels, and her strangely attractive style. Some of the younger ones at the back stand on their chairs to see.*

The HOST *and* HOSTESS *come in from the staircase and mingle with their guests.* HIGGINS, *gloomy and contemptuous of the whole business, comes into the group where they are chatting.*)

HOSTESS: Ah, here is Professor Higgins: he will tell us. Tell us all about the wonderful young lady, Professor.

HIGGINS (*almost morosely*): What wonderful young lady?

HOSTESS: You know very well. They tell me there has been nothing like her in London since people stood on their chairs to look at Mrs Langtry.

(NEPOMMUCK *joins the group, full of news.*)

HOSTESS: Ah, here you are at last, Nepommuck. Have you found out all about the Doolittle lady?

NEPOMMUCK: I have found out all about her. She is a fraud.

HOSTESS: A fraud! Oh no.

NEPOMMUCK: YES, yes. She cannot deceive me. Her name cannot be Doolittle.

HIGGINS: Why?

NEPOMMUCK: Because Doolittle is an English name. And she is not English.

HOSTESS: Oh, nonsense! She speaks English perfectly.

NEPOMMUCK: Too perfectly. Can you shew me any English woman who speaks English as it should be spoken? Only foreigners who have been taught to speak it speak it well.

HOSTESS: Certainly she terrified me by the way she said How d'ye do. I had a schoolmistress who talked like that; and I was mortally afraid of her. But if she is not English what is she?

NEPOMMUCK: Hungarian.

ALL THE REST: Hungarian!

NEPOMMUCK: Hungarian. And of royal blood. I am Hungarian. My blood is royal.

HIGGINS: Did you speak to her in Hungarian?

NEPOMMUCK: I did. She was very clever. She said "Please speak to me in English: I do not understand French." French!

She pretend not to know the difference between Hungarian and French. Impossible: she knows both.

HIGGINS: And the blood royal? How did you find that out?

NEPOMMUCK: Instinct, maestro, instinct. Only the Magyar races can produce that air of the divine right, those resolute eyes. She is a princess.

HOST: What do you say, Professor?

HIGGINS: I say an ordinary London girl out of the gutter and taught to speak by an expert. I place her in Drury Lane.

NEPOMMUCK: Ha ha ha! Oh, maestro, maestro, you are mad on the subject of cockney dialects. The London gutter is the whole world for you.

HIGGINS (*to the* HOSTESS): What does your Excellency say?

HOSTESS: Oh, of course I agree with Nepommuck. She must be a princess at least.

HOST: Not necessarily legitimate, of course. Morganatic perhaps. But that is undoubtedly her class.

HIGGINS: I stick to my opinion.

HOSTESS: Oh, you are incorrigible.

(*The group breaks up, leaving* HIGGINS *isolated.* PICKERING *joins him.*)

PICKERING: Where is Eliza? We must keep an eye on her.

(ELIZA *joins them.*)

LIZA: I don't think I can bear much more. The people all stare so at me. An old lady has just told me that I speak exactly like Queen Victoria. I am sorry if I have lost your bet. I have done my best; but nothing can make me the same as these people.

PICKERING: You have not lost it, my dear. You have won it ten times over.

HIGGINS: Let us get out of this. I have had enough of chattering to these fools.

PICKERING: Eliza is tired; and I am hungry. Let us clear out and have supper somewhere.

ACT IV

(*The Wimpole Street laboratory. Midnight. Nobody in the room. The clock on the mantelpiece strikes twelve. The fire is not alight: it is a summer night.*

Presently HIGGINS *and* PICKERING *are heard on the stairs.*)

HIGGINS (*calling down to* PICKERING): I say, Pick: lock up, will you? I shant be going out again.

PICKERING: Right. Can Mrs Pearce go to bed? We dont want anything more, do we?

HIGGINS: Lord, no!

(ELIZA *opens the door and is seen on the lighted landing in all the finery in which she has just won* HIGGINS'S *bet for him. She comes to the hearth, and switches on the electric lights there. She is tired: her pallor contrasts strongly with her dark eyes and hair; and her expression is almost tragic. She takes off her cloak; puts her fan and gloves on the piano; and sits down on the bench, brooding and silent.* HIGGINS, *in evening dress, with overcoat and hat, comes in, carrying a smoking jacket which he has picked up downstairs. He takes off the hat and overcoat; throws them carelessly on the newspaper stand; disposes of his coat in the same way; puts on the smoking jacket; and throws himself wearily into the easy-chair at the hearth.* PICKERING, *similarly attired, comes in. He also takes off his hat and overcoat, and is about to throw them on* HIGGINS'S *when he hesitates.*)

PICKERING: I say: Mrs Pearce will row if we leave these things lying about in the drawing room.

HIGGINS: Oh, chuck them over the bannisters into the hall. She'll find them there in the morning and put them away all right. She'll think we were drunk.

PICKERING: We are, slightly. Are there any letters?

HIGGINS: I didnt look. (PICKERING *takes the overcoats and hats and goes downstairs.* HIGGINS *begins half singing half yawning an air from* "La Fanciulla del Golden West." *Suddenly he stops and exclaims.*) I wonder where the devil my slippers are!

(ELIZA *looks at him darkly; then rises suddenly and leaves the room.*

HIGGINS *yawns again, and resumes his song.*

PICKERING *returns, with the contents of the letter-box in his hand.*)

PICKERING: Only circulars, and this coroneted billet-doux for you. (*He throws the circulars into the fender, and posts himself on the hearthrug, with his back to the grate.*)

HIGGINS (*glancing at the billet-doux*): Money-lender. (*He throws the letter after the circulars.*

ELIZA *returns with a pair of large down-at-heel slippers.*

She places them on the carpet before HIGGINS, *and sits as before without a word.*)

HIGGINS (*yawning again*): Oh Lord! What an evening! What a crew! What a silly tomfoolery! (*He raises his shoe to unlace it, and catches sight of the slippers. He stops unlacing and looks at them as if they had appeared there of their own accord.*) Oh! theyre there, are they?

PICKERING (*stretching himself*): Well, I feel a bit tired. It's been a long day. The garden party, a dinner party, and the reception! Rather too much of a good thing. But youve won your bet, Higgins. Eliza did the trick, and something to spare, eh?

HIGGINS (*fervently*): Thank God it's over!

(ELIZA *flinches violently; but they take no notice of her, and she recovers herself and sits stonily as before.*)

PICKERING: Were you nervous at the garden party? *I* was. Eliza didnt seem a bit nervous.

HIGGINS: Oh, she wasnt nervous. I knew she'd be all right. No: it's the strain of putting the job through all these months that has told on me. It was interesting enough at first, while we were at the phonetics; but after that I got deadly sick of it. If I hadnt backed myself to do it I should have chucked the whole thing up two months ago. It was a silly notion: the whole thing has been a bore.

PICKERING: Oh come! the garden party was frightfully exciting. My heart began beating like anything.

HIGGINS: Yes, for the first three minutes. But when I saw we were going to win hands down, I felt like a bear in a cage, hanging about doing nothing. The dinner was worse: sitting gorging there for over an hour, with nobody but a damned fool of a fashionable woman to talk to! I tell you, Pickering, never again for me. No more artificial duchesses. The whole thing has been simple purgatory.

PICKERING: Youve never been broken in properly to the social routine. (*strolling over to the piano*) I rather enjoy dipping into it occasionally myself: it makes me feel young again. Anyhow, it was a great success: an immense success. I was quite frightened once or twice because Eliza was doing it so well. You see, lots of the real people cant do it at all: theyre such fools that they think style comes by nature to people in their position; and so they never learn. Theres always something professional about doing a thing superlatively well.

HIGGINS: Yes: thats what drives me mad: the silly people dont know their own silly business. (*rising*) However, it's over and done with; and now I can go to bed at last without dreading tomorrow.

(ELIZA's *beauty becomes murderous.*)

PICKERING: I think I shall turn in too. Still, it's been a great occasion: a triumph for you. Goodnight. (*He goes.*)

HIGGINS (*following him*): Goodnight. (*over his shoulder, at the door*) Put out the lights, Eliza; and tell Mrs Pearce not to make coffee for me in the morning: I'll take tea. (*He goes out.*)

ELIZA *tries to control herself and feel indifferent as she rises and walks across to the hearth to switch off the lights. By the time she gets there she is on the point of screaming. She sits down in* HIGGINS's *chair and holds on hard to the arms. Finally she gives way and flings herself furiously on the floor, raging.*)

HIGGINS (*in despairing wrath outside*): What the devil have I done with my slippers? (*He appears at the door.*)

LIZA (*snatching up the slippers, and hurling them at him one after the other with all her force*): There are your slippers. And there. Take your slippers; and may you never have a day's luck with them!

HIGGINS (*astounded*): What on earth—! (*He comes to her.*) Whats the matter? Get up. (*He pulls her up.*) Anything wrong?

LIZA (*breathless*): Nothing wrong—with you. Ive won your bet for you, havent I? Thats enough for you. *I* don't matter, I suppose.

HIGGINS: You won my bet! You! Presumptuous insect! *I* won it. What did you throw those slippers at me for?

LIZA: Because I wanted to smash your face. I'd like to kill you, you selfish brute. Why didn't you leave me where you picked me out of—in the gutter? You thank God it's all over, and that now you can throw me back again there, do you? (*She crisps her fingers frantically.*)

HIGGINS (*looking at her in cool wonder*): The creature is nervous after all.

LIZA (*gives a suffocated scream of fury, and instinctively darts her nails at his face*): !!

HIGGINS (*catching her wrists*): Ah! would you? Claws in, you cat. How dare you shew your temper to me? Sit down and be quiet. (*He throws her roughly into the easy-chair.*)

LIZA (*crushed by superior strength and weight*): Whats to become of me? Whats to become of me?

HIGGINS: How the devil do I know whats to become of you? What does it matter what becomes of you?

LIZA: You dont care. I know you dont care. You wouldnt care if I was dead. I'm nothing to you—not so much as them slippers.

HIGGINS (*thundering*): Those slippers.

LIZA (*with bitter submission*): Those slippers. I didnt think it made any difference now.

(*A pause.* ELIZA *hopeless and crushed.* HIGGINS *a little uneasy.*)

HIGGINS (*in his loftiest manner*): Why have you begun going on like this? May I ask whether you complain of your treatment here?

LIZA: No.

HIGGINS: Has anybody behaved badly to you? Colonel Pickering? Mrs Pearce? Any of the servants?

LIZA: No.

HIGGINS: I presume you dont pretend that *I* have treated you badly?

LIZA: No.

HIGGINS: I am glad to hear it. (*He moderates his tone.*) Perhaps youre tired after the strain of the day. Will you have a glass of champagne? (*He moves towards the door.*)

LIZA: No. (*recollecting her manners*) Thank you.

HIGGINS (*good-humored again*): This has been coming on you for some days. I suppose it was natural for you to be anxious about the garden party. But thats all over now. (*He pats her kindly on the shoulder. She writhes.*) Theres nothing more to worry about.

LIZA: No. Nothing more for you to worry about. (*She suddenly rises and gets away from him by going to the piano bench, where she sits and hides her face.*) Oh God! I wish I was dead.

HIGGINS (*staring after her in sincere surprise*): Why? In heaven's name, why? (*reasonably, going to her*) Listen to me, Eliza. All this irritation is purely subjective.

LIZA: I dont understand. I'm too ignorant.

HIGGINS: It's only imagination. Low spirits and nothing else. Nobody's hurting you. Nothing's wrong. You go to bed like a good girl and sleep it off. Have a little cry and say your prayers: that will make you comfortable.

LIZA: I heard your prayers. "Thank God it's all over!"

HIGGINS (*impatiently*): Well, dont you thank God it's all over? Now you are free and can do what you like.

LIZA (*pulling herself together in desperation*): What am I fit for? What have you left me fit for? Where am I to go? What am I to do? Whats to become of me?

HIGGINS (*enlightened, but not at all impressed*): Oh, thats whats worrying you, is it? (*He thrusts his hands into his pockets, and walks about in his usual manner, rattling the contents of his pockets, as if condescending to a trivial subject out of pure kindness.*) I shouldnt bother about it if I were you. I should imagine you wont have much difficulty in settling yourself somewhere or other, though I hadnt quite realized that you were going away. (*She looks quickly at him; he does not look at her, but examines the dessert stand on the piano and decides that he will eat an apple.*) You might marry, you know. (*He bites a large piece out of the apple and munches it noisily.*) You see, Eliza, all men are not confirmed old bachelors like me and the Colonel. Most men are the marrying sort (poor devils!); and youre not bad-looking: it's quite a pleasure to look at you sometimes—not now, of course, because youre crying and looking as ugly as the very devil; but when youre all right and quite yourself, youre what I should call attractive. That is, to the people in the marrying line, you understand. You go to bed and have a good nice rest; and then get up and look at yourself in the glass; and you wont feel so cheap.

(ELIZA *again looks at him, speechless, and does not stir.*

The look is quite lost on him: he eats his apple with a dreamy expression of happiness, as it is quite a good one.)

HIGGINS (*a genial afterthought occurring to him*): I daresay my mother could find some chap or other who would do very well.

LIZA: We were above that at the corner of Tottenham Court Road.

HIGGINS (*waking up*): What do you mean?

LIZA: I sold flowers. I didnt sell myself. Now youve made a lady of me I'm not fit to sell anything else. I wish youd left me where you found me.

HIGGINS (*slinging the core of the apple decisively into the grate*): Tosh, Eliza. Dont you insult human relations by dragging all this cant about buying and selling into it. You neednt marry the fellow if you dont like him.

LIZA: What else am I to do?

HIGGINS: Oh, lots of things. What about your old idea of a florist's shop? Pickering could set you up in one: he has lots of money. (*chuckling*) He'll have to pay for all those togs you have been wearing today; and that, with the hire of the jewelry, will make a big hole in two hundred pounds. Why, six months ago you would have thought it the millennium to have a flower-shop of your own. Come! youll be all right. I must clear off to bed: I'm devilish sleepy. By the way, I came down for something: I forget what it was.

LIZA: Your slippers.

HIGGINS: Oh yes, of course. You shied them at me. (*He picks them up, and is going out when she rises and speaks to him.*)

LIZA: Before you go, sir—

HIGGINS (*dropping the slippers in his surprise at her calling him Sir*): Eh?

LIZA: Do my clothes belong to me or to Colonel Pickering?

HIGGINS (*coming back into the room as if her question were the very climax of unreason*): What the devil use would they be to Pickering?

LIZA: He might want them for the next girl you pick up to experiment on.

HIGGINS (*shocked and hurt*): Is that the way you feel towards us?

LIZA: I dont want to hear anything more about that. All I want to know is whether anything belongs to me. My own clothes were burnt.

HIGGINS: But what does it matter? Why need you start bothering about that in the middle of the night?

LIZA: I want to know what I may take away with me. I dont want to be accused of stealing.

HIGGINS (*now deeply wounded*): Stealing! You shouldnt have said that, Eliza. That shews a want of feeling.

LIZA: I'm sorry. I'm only a common ignorant girl; and in my station I have to be careful. There cant be any feelings between the like of you and the like of me. Please will you tell me what belongs to me and what doesnt?

HIGGINS (*very sulky*): You may take the whole damned houseful if you like. Except the jewels. Theyre hired. Will that satisfy you? (*He turns on his heel and is about to go in extreme dudgeon.*)

LIZA (*drinking in his emotion like nectar, and nagging him to provoke a further supply*): Stop, please. (*She takes off her jewels.*) Will you take these to your room and keep them safe? I dont want to run the risk of their being missing.

HIGGINS (*furious*): Hand them over. (*She puts them into his hands.*) If these belonged to me instead of the jeweller, I'd ram them down your ungrateful throat. (*He perfunctorily thrusts them into his pockets, unconsciously decorating himself with the protruding ends of the chains.*)

LIZA (*taking a ring off*): This ring isnt the jeweller's: it's the one you bought me in Brighton. I dont want it now.

(HIGGINS *dashes the ring violently into the fireplace, and turns on her so threateningly that she crouches over the piano with her hands over her face, and exclaims*) Dont you hit me.

HIGGINS: Hit you! You infamous creature, how dare you accuse me of such a thing? It is you who have hit me. You have wounded me to the heart.

LIZA (*thrilling with hidden joy*): I'm glad. I've got a little of my own back, anyhow.

HIGGINS (*with dignity, in his finest professional style*): You have caused me to lose my temper: a thing that has hardly ever happened to me before. I prefer to say nothing more tonight. I am going to bed.

LIZA (*pertly*): Youd better leave a note for Mrs Pearce about the coffee; for she wont be told by me.

HIGGINS (*formally*): Damn Mrs Pearce; and damn the coffee; and damn you; and (*wildly*) damn my own folly in having lavished my hard-earned knowledge and the treasure of my regard and intimacy on a heartless guttersnipe. (*He goes out with impressive decorum, and spoils it by slamming the door savagely.*)

(ELIZA *goes down on her knees on the hearthrug to look for the ring. When she finds it she considers for a moment what to do with it. Finally she flings it down on the dessert stand and goes upstairs in a tearing rage.*

*   *   *   *   *   *

The furniture of ELIZA's *room has been increased by a big wardrobe and a sumptuous dressing-table. She comes in and switches on the electric light. She goes to the wardrobe; opens it; and pulls out a walking dress, a hat, and a pair of shoes, which she throws on the bed. She takes off her evening dress and shoes; then takes a padded hanger from the wardrobe; adjusts it carefully in the evening dress; and hangs it in the wardrobe, which she shuts with a slam. She puts on her walking shoes, her walking dress, and hat. She takes her wrist watch from the dressing-table and fastens it on. She pulls on her gloves; takes her vanity bag; and looks into it to see that her purse is there before hanging it on her wrist. She makes for the door. Every movement expresses her furious resolution.*

She takes a last look at herself in the glass.

She suddenly puts out her tongue at herself; then leaves the room, switching off the electric light at the door.

Meanwhile, in the street outside, FREDDY EYNSFORD HILL, *lovelorn, is gazing up at the second floor, in which one of the windows is still lighted.*

The light goes out.)

FREDDY: Goodnight, darling, darling, darling.

(ELIZA *comes out, giving the door a considerable bang behind her.)*

LIZA: Whatever are you doing here?

FREDDY: Nothing. I spend most of my nights here. It's the only place where I'm happy. Dont laugh at me, Miss Doolittle.

LIZA: Dont you call me Miss Doolittle, do you hear? Liza's good enough for me. (*She breaks down and grabs him by the shoulders.*) Freddy: you dont think I'm a heartless guttersnipe, do you?

FREDDY: Oh no, no, darling: how can you imagine such a thing? You are the loveliest, dearest—

(*He loses all self-control and smothers her with kisses. She, hungry for comfort, responds. They stand there in one another's arms.*

An elderly police constable arrives.)

CONSTABLE (*scandalized*): Now then! Now then!! Now then!!!

(*They release one another hastily.)*

FREDDY: Sorry, constable. Weve only just become engaged.

(*They run away.*

The CONSTABLE *shakes his head, reflecting on his own courtship and on the vanity of human hopes. He moves off in the opposite direction with slow professional steps.*

The flight of the lovers takes them to Cavendish Square. There they halt to consider their next move.)

LIZA (*out of breath*): He didnt half give me a fright, that copper. But you answered him proper.

FREDDY: I hope I havent taken you out of your way. Where were you going?

LIZA: To the river.

FREDDY: What for?

LIZA: To make a hole in it.

FREDDY (*horrified*): Eliza, darling. What do you mean? What's the matter?

LIZA: Never mind. It doesnt matter now. There's nobody in the world now but you and me, is there?

FREDDY: Not a soul.

(*They indulge in another embrace, and are again surprised by a much younger constable.)*

SECOND CONSTABLE: Now then, you two! What's this? Where do you think you are? Move along here, double quick.

FREDDY: As you say, sir, double quick.

(*They run away again, and are in Hanover Square before they stop for another conference.*)

FREDDY: I had no idea the police were so devilishly prudish.

LIZA: It's their business to hunt girls off the streets.

FREDDY: We must go somewhere. We cant wander about the streets all night.

LIZA: Cant we? I think it'd be lovely to wander about forever.

FREDDY: Oh, darling.

(*They embrace again, oblivious of the arrival of a crawling taxi. It stops.*)

TAXIMAN: Can I drive you and the lady anywhere, sir?

(*They start asunder.*)

LIZA: Oh, Freddy, a taxi. The very thing.

FREDDY: But, damn it, Ive no money.

LIZA: I have plenty. The Colonel thinks you should never go out without ten pounds in your pocket. Listen. We'll drive about all night; and in the morning I'll call on old Mrs Higgins and ask her what I ought to do. I'll tell you all about it in the cab. And the police wont touch us there.

FREDDY: Righto! Ripping. (*to the* TAXIMAN) Wimbledon Common. (*They drive off.*)

ACT V

(MRS HIGGINS'S *drawing room. She is at her writing-table as before. The* PARLOR-MAID *comes in.*)

THE PARLOR-MAID (*at the door*): Mr Henry, maam, is downstairs with Colonel Pickering.

MRS HIGGINS: Well, shew them up.

THE PARLOR-MAID: Theyre using the telephone, maam. Telephoning to the police, I think.

MRS HIGGINS: What!

THE PARLOR-MAID (*coming further in and lowering her voice*): Mr Henry is in a state, maam. I thought I'd better tell you.

MRS HIGGINS: If you had told me that Mr Henry was not in a state it would have been more surprising. Tell them to come up when theyve finished with the police. I suppose he's lost something.

THE PARLOR-MAID: Yes, maam (*going*).

MRS HIGGINS: Go upstairs and tell Miss Doolittle that Mr Henry and the Colonel are here. Ask her not to come down til I send for her.

THE PARLOR-MAID: Yes, maam.

(HIGGINS *bursts in. He is, as the* PARLOR-MAID *has said, in a state.*)

HIGGINS: Look here, mother: heres a confounded thing!

MRS HIGGINS: Yes, dear. Good morning. (*He checks his impatience and kisses her, whilst the* PARLOR-MAID *goes out.*) What is it?

HIGGINS: Eliza's bolted.

MRS HIGGINS (*calmly continuing her writing*): You must have frightened her.

HIGGINS: Frightened her! nonsense! She was left last night, as usual, to turn out the lights and all that; and instead of going to bed she changed her clothes and went right off: her bed wasnt slept in. She came in a cab for her things before seven this morning; and that fool Mrs Pearce let her have them without telling me a word about it. What am I to do?

MRS HIGGINS: Do without, I'm afraid, Henry. The girl has a perfect right to leave if she chooses.

HIGGINS (*wandering distractedly across the room*): But I cant find anything. I dont know what appointments Ive got. I'm—(PICKERING *comes in.* MRS HIGGINS *puts down her pen and turns away from the writing-table.*)

PICKERING (*shaking hands*): Good morning, Mrs Higgins. Has Henry told you? (*He sits down on the ottoman.*)

HIGGINS: What does that ass of an inspector say? Have you offered a reward?

MRS HIGGINS (*rising in indignant amazement*): You dont mean to say you have set the police after Eliza.

HIGGINS: Of course. What are the police for? What else could we do? (*He sits in the Elizabethan chair.*)

PICKERING: The inspector made a lot of difficulties. I really think he suspected us of some improper purpose.

MRS HIGGINS: Well, of course he did. What right have you to go to the police and give the girl's name as if she were a thief, or a lost umbrella, or something? Really! (*She sits down again, deeply vexed.*)

HIGGINS: But we want to find her.

PICKERING: We cant let her go like this, you know, Mrs Higgins. What were we to do?

MRS HIGGINS: You have no more sense, either of you, than two children. Why—

(*The* PARLOR-MAID *comes in and breaks off the conversation.*)

THE PARLOR-MAID: Mr Henry: a gentleman wants to see you very particular. He's been sent on from Wimpole Street.

HIGGINS: Oh, bother! I cant see anyone now. Who is it?

THE PARLOR-MAID: A Mr Doolittle, sir.

PICKERING: Doolittle! Do you mean the dustman?

THE PARLOR-MAID: Dustman! Oh no, sir: a gentleman.

HIGGINS (*springing up excitedly*): By George, Pick, it's some relative of hers that she's gone to. Somebody we know nothing about. (*to the* PARLOR-MAID) Send him up, quick.

THE PARLOR-MAID: Yes, sir. (*She goes.*)

HIGGINS (*eagerly, going to his mother*): Genteel relatives! now we shall hear something. (*He sits down in the Chippendale chair.*)

MRS HIGGINS: Do you know any of her people?

PICKERING: Only her father: the fellow we told you about.

THE PARLOR-MAID (*announcing*): Mr Doolittle. (*She withdraws.*)

(DOOLITTLE *enters. He is resplendently dressed as for a fashionable wedding, and might, in fact, be the bridegroom. A flower in his buttonhole, a dazzling silk hat, and patent leather shoes complete the effect. He is too concerned with the business he has come on to notice* MRS HIGGINS. *He walks straight to* HIGGINS, *and accosts him with vehement reproach.*)

DOOLITTLE (*indicating his own person*): See here! Do you see this? You done this.

HIGGINS: Done what, man?

DOOLITTLE: This, I tell you. Look at it. Look at this hat. Look at this coat.

PICKERING: Has Eliza been buying you clothes?

DOOLITTLE: Eliza! not she. Why would she buy me clothes?

MRS HIGGINS: Good morning, Mr Doolittle. Wont you sit down?

DOOLITTLE (*taken aback as he becomes conscious that he has forgotten his hostess*): Asking your pardon, maam. (*He approaches her and shakes her proffered hand.*) Thank you. (*He sits down on the ottoman, on* PICKERING'S *right.*) I am that full of what has happened to me that I cant think of anything else.

HIGGINS: What the dickens has happened to you?

DOOLITTLE: I shouldnt mind if it had only happened to me: anything might happen to anybody and nobody to blame but Providence, as you might say. But this is something that you done to me: yes, you, Enry Iggins.

HIGGINS: Have you found Eliza?

DOOLITTLE: Have you lost her?

HIGGINS: Yes.

DOOLITTLE: You have all the luck, you have. I aint found her; but she'll find me quick enough now after what you done to me.

MRS HIGGINS: But what has my son done to you, Mr Doolittle?

DOOLITTLE: Done to me! Ruined me. Destroyed my happiness. Tied me up and delivered me into the hands of middle class morality.

HIGGINS (*rising intolerantly and standing over* DOOLITTLE): Youre raving. Youre drunk. Youre mad. I gave you five pounds. After that I had two conversations with you, at half-a-crown an hour. Ive never seen you since.

DOOLITTLE: Oh! Drunk am I? Mad am I? Tell me this. Did you or did you not write a letter to an old blighter in America that was giving five millions to found Moral Reform Societies all over the world, and that wanted you to invent a universal language for him?

HIGGINS: What! Ezra D. Wannafeller! He's dead. (*He sits down again carelessly.*)

DOOLITTLE: Yes: he's dead; and I'm done for. Now did you or did you not write a letter to him to say that the most original moralist at present in England, to the best of your knowledge, was Alfred Doolittle, a common dustman?

HIGGINS: Oh, after your first visit I remember making some silly joke of the kind.

DOOLITTLE: Ah! you may well call it a silly joke. It put the lid on me right enough. Just give him the chance he wanted to shew that Americans is not like us: that they reckonize and respect merit in every class of life, however humble. Them words is in his blooming will, in which, Henry Higgins, thanks to your silly joking, he leaves me a share in his Pre-digested Cheese Trust worth four thousand a year on condition that I lecture for his Wannafeller Moral Reform World League as often as they ask me up to six times a year.

HIGGINS: The devil he does! Whew! (*brightening suddenly*) What a lark!

PICKERING: A safe thing for you, Doolittle. They wont ask you twice.

DOOLITTLE: It aint the lecturing I mind. I'll lecture them blue in the face, I will, and not turn a hair. It's making a gentleman of me that I object to. Who asked him to make a gentleman of me? I was happy. I was free. I touched pretty nigh everybody for money when I wanted it, same as I touched you, Enry Iggins. Now I am worrited; tied neck and heels; and everybody touches me for money. It's a fine thing for you, says my solicitor. Is it? says I. You mean it's a good thing for you, I says. When I was a poor man and had a solicitor once when they found a pram in the dust cart, he got me off, and got shut of me and got me shut of him as quick as he could. Same with the doctors; used to shove me out of the hospital before I could hardly stand on my legs, and nothing to pay. Now they finds out that I'm not a healthy man and cant live unless they looks after me twice a day. In the house I'm not let do a hand's turn for myself: somebody else must do it and touch me for it. A year ago I hadnt a relative in the world except two or three that wouldnt speak to me. Now Ive fifty, and not a decent week's wages among the lot of them. I have to live for others and not for myself: that middle class morality. You talk of losing Eliza. Dont you be anxious: I bet she's on my doorstep by this: she that could support herself easy by selling flowers if I wasnt respectable. And the next one to touch me will be you, Enry Iggins. I'll have to learn to speak middle class language from you, instead of speaking proper English. Thats where youll come in; and I daresay thats what you done it for.

MRS HIGGINS: But, my dear Mr Doolittle, you need not suffer all this if you are really in earnest. Nobody can force you to accept this bequest. You can repudiate it. Isnt that so, Colonel Pickering?

PICKERING: I believe so.

DOOLITTLE (*softening his manner in deference to her sex*): Thats the tragedy of it, maam. It's easy to say chuck it; but I havnt the nerve. Which of us has? We're all intimidated. Intimidated, maam: thats what we are. What is there for me if I chuck it but the workhouse in my old age? I have to dye my hair already to keep my job as a dustman. If I was one of the deserving poor, and had put by a bit, I could chuck it; but then why should I, acause the deserving poor might as well be millionaires for all the happiness they ever has. They dont know what happiness is. But I, as one of the undeserving poor, have nothing between me and the pauper's uniform but this here blasted four thousand a year that shoves me into the middle class. (*Excuse the expression, maam; youd use it yourself if you had my provocation.*) Theyve got you every way you turn: it's a choice between the Skilly of the workhouse and the Char Bydis of the middle class; and I havnt the nerve for the workhouse. Intimidated: thats what I am. Broke. Bought up. Happier men than me will call for my dust, and touch me for their tip; and I'll look on helpless, and envy them. And thats what your son has brought me to. (*He is overcome by emotion.*)

MRS HIGGINS: Well, I'm very glad youre not going to do anything foolish, Mr Doolittle. For this solves the problem of Eliza's future. You can provide for her now.

DOOLITTLE (*with melancholy resignation*): Yes, maam: I'm expected to provide for everyone now, out of four thousand a year.

HIGGINS (*jumping up*): Nonsense! he cant provide for her. He shant provide for her. She doesnt belong to him. I paid him five pounds for her. Doolittle: either youre an honest man or a rogue.

DOOLITTLE (*tolerantly*): A little of both, Henry, like the rest of us: a little of both.

HIGGINS: Well, you took that money for the girl; and you have no right to take her as well.

MRS HIGGINS: Henry: dont be absurd. If you want to know where Eliza is, she is upstairs.

HIGGINS (*amazed*): Upstairs!!! Then I shall jolly soon fetch her downstairs. (*He makes resolutely for the door.*)

MRS HIGGINS (*rising and following him*): Be quiet, Henry. Sit down.

HIGGINS: I—

MRS HIGGINS: Sit down, dear; and listen to me.

HIGGINS: Oh very well, very well, very well. (*He throws himself ungraciously on the ottoman, with his face towards the windows.*) But I think you might have told us this half an hour ago.

MRS HIGGINS: Eliza came to me this morning. She told me of the brutal way you two treated her.

HIGGINS (*bounding up again*): What!

PICKERING (*rising also*): My dear Mrs Higgins, she's been telling you stories. We didnt treat her brutally. We hardly said a word to her; and we parted on particularly good terms. (*turning on* HIGGINS) Higgins: did you bully her after I went to bed?

HIGGINS: Just the other way about. She threw my slippers in my face. She behaved in the most outrageous way. I never gave her the slightest provocation. The slippers came bang into my face the moment I entered the room—before I had uttered a word. And used perfectly awful language.

PICKERING (*astonished*): But why? What did we do to her?

MRS HIGGINS: I think I know pretty well what you did. The girl is naturally rather affectionate, I think. Isnt she, Mr Doolittle?

DOOLITTLE: Very tender-hearted, maam. Takes after me.

MRS HIGGINS: Just so. She had become attached to you both. She worked very hard for you, Henry. I dont think you quite realize what anything in the nature of brain work means to a girl of her class. Well, it seems that when the great day of trial came, and she did this wonderful thing for you without making a single mistake, you two sat there and never said a word to her, but talked together of how glad you were that it was all over and how you had been bored with the whole thing. And then you were surprised because she threw your slippers at you! *I* should have thrown the fire-irons at you.

HIGGINS: We said nothing except that we were tired and wanted to go to bed. Did we, Pick?

PICKERING (*shrugging his shoulders*): That was all.

MRS HIGGINS (*ironically*): Quite sure?

PICKERING: Absolutely. Really, that was all.

MRS HIGGINS: You didnt thank her, or pet her, or admire her, or tell her how splendid she'd been.

HIGGINS (*impatiently*): But she knew all about that. We didnt make speeches to her, if thats what you mean.

PICKERING (*conscience-stricken*): Perhaps we were a little inconsiderate. Is she very angry?

MRS HIGGINS (*returning to her place at the writing-table*): Well, I'm afraid she wont go back to Wimpole Street, especially now that Mr Doolittle is able to keep up the position you have thrust on her; but she says she is quite willing to meet you on friendly terms and to let bygones be bygones.

HIGGINS (*furious*): Is she, by George? Ho!

MRS HIGGINS: If you promise to behave yourself, Henry, I'll ask her to come down. If not, go home; for you have taken up quite enough of my time.

HIGGINS: Oh, all right. Very well. Pick: you behave yourself. Let us put on our best Sunday manners for this creature that we picked out of the mud. (*He flings himself sulkily into the Elizabethan chair.*)

DOOLITTLE (*remonstrating*): Now, now, Enry Iggins! Have some consideration for my feelings as a middle class man.

MRS HIGGINS: Remember your promise, Henry. (*She presses the bell-button on the writing-table.*) Mr Doolittle: will you be so good as to step out on the balcony for a moment. I dont want Eliza to have the shock of your news until she has made it up with these two gentlemen. Would you mind?

DOOLITTLE: As you wish, lady. Anything to help Henry to keep her off my hands. (*He disappears through the window. The* PARLOR-MAID *answers the bell.* PICKERING *sits down in* DOOLITTLE'S *place.*)

MRS HIGGINS: Ask Miss Doolittle to come down, please.

THE PARLOR-MAID: Yes, maam. (*She goes out.*)

MRS HIGGINS: Now, Henry: be good.

HIGGINS: I am behaving myself perfectly.

PICKERING: He is doing his best, Mrs Higgins.

(*A pause.* HIGGINS *throws back his head; stretches out his legs; and begins to whistle.*)

MRS HIGGINS: Henry, dearest, you dont look at all nice in that attitude.

HIGGINS (*pulling himself together*): I was not trying to look nice, mother.

MRS HIGGINS: It doesnt matter, dear. I only wanted to make you speak.

HIGGINS: Why?

MRS HIGGINS: Because you cant speak and whistle at the same time.

(HIGGINS *groans. Another very trying pause.*)

HIGGINS (*springing up, out of patience*): Where the devil is that girl? Are we to wait here all day?

(ELIZA *enters, sunny, self-possessed, and giving a staggeringly convincing exhibition of ease of manner. She carries a little workbasket, and is very much at home.* PICKERING *is too much taken aback to rise.*)

LIZA: How do you do, Professor Higgins? Are you quite well?

HIGGINS (*choking*): Am I— (*He can say no more.*)

LIZA: But of course you are: you are never ill. So glad to see you again, Colonel Pickering. (*He rises hastily; and they shake hands.*) Quite chilly this morning, isn't it? (*She sits down on his left. He sits beside her.*)

HIGGINS: Dont you dare try this game on me. I taught it

to you; and it doesnt take me in. Get up and come home; and dont be a fool.

(ELIZA *takes a piece of needlework from her basket, and begins to stitch at it, without taking the least notice of this outburst.*)

MRS HIGGINS: Very nicely put, indeed, Henry. No woman could resist such an invitation.

HIGGINS: You let her alone, mother. Let her speak for herself. You will jolly soon see whether she has an idea that I havnt put into her head or a word that I havnt put into her mouth. I tell you I have created this thing out of the squashed cabbage leaves of Covent Garden; and now she pretends to play the fine lady with me.

MRS HIGGINS (*placidly*): Yes, dear; but youll sit down, wont you?

(HIGGINS *sits down again, savagely.*)

LIZA (*to* PICKERING, *taking no apparent notice of* HIGGINS, *and working away deftly*): Will you drop me altogether now that the experiment is over, Colonel Pickering?

PICKERING: Oh dont. You mustnt think of it as an experiment. It shocks me, somehow.

LIZA: Oh, I'm only a squashed cabbage leaf—

PICKERING (*impulsively*): No.

LIZA (*continuing quietly*):—but I owe so much to you that I should be very unhappy if you forgot me.

PICKERING: It's very kind of you to say so, Miss Doolittle.

LIZA: It's not because you paid for my dresses. I know you are generous to everybody with money. But it was from you that I learnt really nice manners; and that is what makes one a lady, isnt it? You see it was so very difficult for me with the example of Professor Higgins always before me. I was brought up to be just like him, unable to control myself, and using bad language on the slightest provocation. And I should never have known that ladies and gentlemen didnt behave like that if you hadnt been there.

HIGGINS: Well!!

PICKERING: Oh, thats only his way, you know. He doesnt mean it.

LIZA: Oh, *I* didnt mean it either, when I was a flower girl. It was only my way. But you see I did it; and thats what makes the difference after all.

PICKERING: No doubt. Still, he taught you to speak; and I couldnt have done that, you know.

LIZA (*trivially*): Of course: that is his profession.

HIGGINS: Damnation!

LIZA (*continuing*): It was just like learning to dance in the fashionable way: there was nothing more than that in it. But do you know what began my real education?

PICKERING: What?

LIZA (*stopping her work for a moment*): Your calling me Miss Doolittle that day when I first came to Wimpole Street. That was the beginning of self-respect for me. (*She resumes her stitching.*) And there were a hundred little things you never noticed, because they came naturally to you. Things about standing up and taking off your hat and opening doors—

PICKERING: Oh, that was nothing.

LIZA: Yes: things that shewed you thought and felt about me as if I were something better than a scullery-maid; though of course I know you would have been just the same to a scullery-maid if she had been let into the drawing room. You never took off your boots in the dining room when I was there.

PICKERING: You mustnt mind that. Higgins takes off his boots all over the place.

LIZA: I know. I am not blaming him. It is his way, isnt it? But it made such a difference to me that you didnt do it. You see, really and truly, apart from the things anyone can pick up (the dressing and the proper way of speaking, and so on), the difference between a lady and a flower girl is not how she behaves, but how she's treated. I shall always be a flower girl to Professor Higgins, because he always treats me as a flower girl, and always will; but I know I can be a lady to you, because you always treat me as a lady, and always will.

MRS HIGGINS: Please dont grind your teeth, Henry.

PICKERING: Well, this is really very nice of you, Miss Doolittle.

LIZA: I should like you to call me Eliza, now, if you would.

PICKERING: Thank you. Eliza, of course.

LIZA: And I should like Professor Higgins to call me Miss Doolittle.

HIGGINS: I'll see you damned first.

MRS HIGGINS: Henry, Henry!

PICKERING (*laughing*): Why dont you slang back at him? Dont stand it. It would do him a lot of good.

LIZA: I cant. I could have done it once; but now I cant go back to it. You told me, you know, that when a child is brought to a foreign country, it picks up the language in a few weeks, and forgets its own. Well, I am a child in your country. I have forgotten my own language, and can speak nothing but yours. Thats the real break-off with the corner of Tottenham Court Road. Leaving Wimpole Street finishes it.

PICKERING (*much alarmed*): Oh! but youre coming back to Wimpole Street, arnt you? Youll forgive Higgins?

HIGGINS (*rising*): Forgive! Will she, by George! Let her go. Let her find out how she can get on without us. She will relapse into the gutter in three weeks without me at her elbow.

(DOOLITTLE *appears at the center window. With a look of dignified reproach at* HIGGINS, *he comes slowly and silently to his daughter, who, with her back to the window, is unconscious of his approach.*)

PICKERING: He's incorrigible, Eliza. You wont relapse, will you?

LIZA: No: not now. Never again. I have learnt my lesson. I dont believe I could utter one of the old sounds if I tried.

(*Doolittle touches her on the left shoulder. She drops her work, losing her self-possession utterly at the spectacle of her father's splendor.*) A-a-a-a-ah-ow-ooh!

HIGGINS (*with a crow of triumph*): Aha! Just so. A-a-a-a-ahowooh! A-a-a-a-ahowooh! A-a-a-a-ahowooh! Victory! Victory! (*He throws himself on the divan, folding his arms, and spraddling arrogantly.*)

DOOLITTLE: Can you blame the girl? Dont look at me like that, Eliza. It aint my fault. Ive come into some money.

LIZA: You must have touched a millionaire this time, dad.

DOOLITTLE: I have. But I'm dressed something special today. I'm going to St. George's, Hanover Square. Your stepmother is going to marry me.

LIZA (*angrily*): Youre going to let yourself down to marry that low common woman!

PICKERING (*quietly*): He ought to, Eliza. (*to* DOOLITTLE) Why has she changed her mind?

DOOLITTLE (*sadly*): Intimidated, Governor. Intimidated. Middle class morality claims its victim. Wont you put on your hat, Liza, and come and see me turned off?

LIZA: If the Colonel says I must, I—I'll (*almost sobbing*) I'll demean myself. And get insulted for my pains, like enough.

DOOLITTLE: Dont be afraid: she never comes to words with anyone now, poor woman! respectability has broke all the spirit out of her.

PICKERING (*squeezing* ELIZA'S *elbow gently*): Be kind to them, Eliza. Make the best of it.

LIZA (*forcing a little smile for him through her vexation*): Oh well, just to shew theres no ill feeling. I'll be back in a moment. (*She goes out.*)

DOOLITTLE (*sitting down beside* PICKERING): I feel uncommon nervous about the ceremony, Colonel. I wish youd come and see me through it.

PICKERING: But youve been through it before, man. You were married to Eliza's mother.

DOOLITTLE: Who told you that, Colonel?

PICKERING: Well, nobody told me. But I concluded—naturally—

DOOLITTLE: No: that aint the natural way, Colonel: it's only the middle class way. My way was always the undeserving way. But dont say nothing to Eliza. She dont know: I always had a delicacy about telling her.

PICKERING: Quite right. We'll leave it so, if you dont mind.

DOOLITTLE: And youll come to the church, Colonel, and put me through straight?

PICKERING: With pleasure. As far as a bachelor can.

MRS HIGGINS: May I come, Mr Doolittle? I should be very sorry to miss your wedding.

DOOLITTLE: I should indeed be honored by your condescension, maam; and my poor old woman would take it as a tremenjous compliment. She's been very low, thinking of the happy days that are no more.

MRS HIGGINS (*rising*): I'll order the carriage and get ready. (*The men rise, except* HIGGINS.) I shant be more than fifteen minutes. (*As she goes to the door* ELIZA *comes in, hatted and buttoning her gloves.*) I'm going to the church to see your father married, Eliza. You had better come in the brougham with me. Colonel Pickering can go on with the bridegroom.

(MRS HIGGINS *goes out.* ELIZA *comes to the middle of the room between the center window and the ottoman.* PICKERING *joins her.*)

DOOLITTLE: Bridegroom. What a word! It makes a man realize his position, somehow. (*He takes up his hat and goes towards the door.*)

PICKERING: Before I go, Eliza, do forgive Higgins and come back to us.

LIZA: I dont think dad would allow me. Would you, dad?

DOOLITTLE (*sad but magnanimous*): They played you off very cunning, Eliza, them two sportsmen. If it had been only one of them, you could have nailed him. But you see, there was two; and one of them chaperoned the other, as you might say. (*to* PICKERING) It was artful of you, Colonel; but I bear no malice: I should have done the same myself. I been the victim of one woman after another all my life, and I dont grudge you two getting the better of Liza. I shant interfere. It's time for us to go, Colonel. So long, Henry. See you in St George's, Eliza. (*He goes out.*)

PICKERING (*coaxing*): Do stay with us, Eliza. (*He follows* DOOLITTLE.

ELIZA *goes out on the balcony to avoid being alone with* HIGGINS. *He rises and joins her there. She immediately comes back into the room and makes for the door; but he goes along the balcony and gets his back to the door before she reaches it.*)

HIGGINS: Well, Eliza, youve had a bit of your own back, as you call it. Have you had enough? and are you going to be reasonable? Or do you want any more?

LIZA: You want me back only to pick up your slippers and put up with your tempers and fetch and carry for you.

HIGGINS: I havnt said I wanted you back at all.

LIZA: Oh, indeed. Then what are we talking about?

HIGGINS: About you, not about me. If you come back I shall treat you just as I have always treated you. I cant change my nature; and I dont intend to change my manners. My manners are exactly the same as Colonel Pickering's.

LIZA: Thats not true. He treats a flower girl as if she was a duchess.

HIGGINS: And I treat a duchess as if she was a flower girl.

LIZA: I see. (*She turns away composedly, and sits on the ottoman, facing the window.*) The same to everybody.

HIGGINS: Just so.

LIZA: Like father.

HIGGINS (*grinning, a little taken down*): Without accepting the comparison at all points, Eliza, it's quite true that your father is not a snob, and that he will be quite at home in any station of life to which his eccentric destiny may call him. (*seriously*) The great secret, Eliza, is not having bad manners or good manners or any other particular sort of manners, but having the same manner for all human souls: in short, behaving as if you were in Heaven, where there are no third-class carriages, and one soul is as good as another.

LIZA: Amen. You are a born preacher.

HIGGINS (*irritated*): The question is not whether I treat you rudely, but whether you ever heard me treat anyone else better.

LIZA (*with sudden sincerity*): I dont care how you treat me. I dont mind your swearing at me. I shouldnt mind a black eye: Ive had one before this. But (*standing up and facing him*) I wont be passed over.

HIGGINS: Then get out of my way; for I wont stop for you. You talk about me as if I were a motor bus.

LIZA: So you are a motor bus: all bounce and go, and no consideration for anyone. But I can do without you: dont think I cant.

HIGGINS: I know you can. I told you you could.

LIZA (*wounded, getting away from him to the other side of the ottoman with her face to the hearth*): I know you did, you brute. You wanted to get rid of me.

HIGGINS: Liar.

LIZA: Thank you. (*She sits down with dignity.*)

HIGGINS: You never asked yourself, I suppose, whether *I* could do without you.

LIZA (*earnestly*): Dont you try to get round me. Youll have to do without me.

HIGGINS (*arrogant*): I can do without anybody. I have my own soul: my own spark of divine fire. But (*with sudden humility*) I shall miss you, Eliza. (*He sits down near her on the ottoman.*) I have learnt something from your idiotic notions: I confess that humbly and gratefully. And I have grown accustomed to your voice and appearance. I like them, rather.

LIZA: Well, you have both of them on your gramophone and in your book of photographs. When you feel lonely without me, you can turn the machine on. It's got no feelings to hurt.

HIGGINS: I cant turn your soul on. Leave me those feelings; and you can take away the voice and the face. They are not you.

LIZA: Oh, you are a devil. You can twist the heart in a girl as easy as some could twist her arms to hurt her. Mrs Pearce warned me. Time and again she has wanted to leave you; and you always got round her at the last minute. And you dont care a bit for her. And you dont care a bit for me.

HIGGINS: I care for life, for humanity; and you are a part of it that has come my way and been built into my house. What more can you or anyone ask?

LIZA: I wont care for anybody that doesnt care for me.

HIGGINS: Commercial principles, Eliza. Like (*reproducing her Covent Garden pronunciation with professional exactness*): s'yollin voylets [selling violets], isnt it?

LIZA: Dont sneer at me. It's mean to sneer at me.

HIGGINS: I have never sneered in my life. Sneering doesnt become either the human face or the human soul. I am expressing my righteous contempt for Commercialism. I dont and wont trade in affection. You call me a brute because you couldnt buy a claim on me by fetching my slippers and finding my spectacles. You were a fool: I think a woman fetching a man's slippers is a disgusting sight: did I ever fetch your slippers? I think a good deal more of you for throwing them in my face. No use slaving for me and then saying you want to be cared for: who cares for a slave? If you come back, come back for the sake of good fellowship; for youll get nothing else. Youve had a thousand times as much out of me as I have out of you; and if you dare to set up your little dog's tricks of fetching and carrying slippers against my creation of a Duchess Eliza, I'll slam the door in your silly face.

LIZA: What did you do it for if you didnt care for me?

HIGGINS (*heartily*): Why, because it was my job.

LIZA: You never thought of the trouble it would make for me.

HIGGINS: Would the world ever have been made if its maker had been afraid of making trouble? Making life means making trouble. Theres only one way of escaping trouble; and thats killing things. Cowards, you notice, are always shrieking to have troublesome people killed.

LIZA: I'm no preacher: I dont notice things like that. I notice that you dont notice me.

HIGGINS (*jumping up and walking about intolerantly*): Eliza: youre an idiot. I waste the treasures of my Miltonic mind by spreading them before you. Once for all, understand that I go my way and do my work without caring twopence what happens to either of us. I am not intimidated, like your father and your stepmother. So you can come back or go to the devil: which you please.

LIZA: What am I to come back for?

HIGGINS (*bouncing up on his knees on the ottoman and leaning over it to her*): For the fun of it. Thats why I took you on.

LIZA (*with averted face*): And you may throw me out tomorrow if I dont do everything you want me to?

HIGGINS: Yes; and you may walk out tomorrow if I dont do everything you want me to.

LIZA: And live with my stepmother?

HIGGINS: Yes, or sell flowers.

LIZA: Oh! if I only could go back to my flower basket! I should be independent of both you and father and all the world! Why did you take my independence from me? Why did I give it up? I'm a slave now, for all my fine clothes.

HIGGINS: Not a bit. I'll adopt you as my daughter and settle money on you if you like. Or would you rather marry Pickering?

LIZA (*looking fiercely round at him*): I wouldnt marry you if you asked me; and youre nearer my age than what he is.

HIGGINS (*gently*): Than he is: not "than what he is."

LIZA (*losing her temper and rising*): I'll talk as I like. Youre not my teacher now.

HIGGINS (*reflectively*): I dont suppose Pickering would, though. He's as confirmed an old bachelor as I am.

LIZA: Thats not what I want; and dont you think it. I've always had chaps enough wanting me that way. Freddy Hill writes to me twice and three times a day, sheets and sheets.

HIGGINS (*disagreeably surprised*): Damn his impudence! (*He recoils and finds himself sitting on his heels.*)

LIZA: He has a right to if he likes, poor lad. And he does love me.

HIGGINS (*getting off the ottoman*): You have no right to encourage him.

LIZA: Every girl has a right to be loved.

HIGGINS: What! By fools like that?

LIZA: Freddy's not a fool. And if he's weak and poor and wants me, may be he'd make me happier than my betters that bully me and dont want me.

HIGGINS: Can he make anything of you? Thats the point.

LIZA: Perhaps I could make something of him. But I never thought of us making anything of one another; and you never think of anything else. I only want to be natural.

HIGGINS: In short, you want me to be as infatuated about you as Freddy? Is that it?

LIZA: No I dont. Thats not the sort of feeling I want from you. And dont you be too sure of yourself or of me. I could have been a bad girl if I'd liked. Ive seen more of some things than you, for all your learning. Girls like me can drag gentlemen down to make love to them easy enough. And they wish each other dead the next minute.

HIGGINS: Of course they do. Then what in thunder are we quarrelling about?

LIZA (*much troubled*): I want a little kindness. I know I'm a common ignorant girl, and you a book-learned gentleman; but I'm not dirt under your feet. What I done (*correcting herself*) what I did was not for the dresses and the taxis: I did it because we were pleasant together and I come—came—to care for you; not to want you to make love to me, and not forgetting the difference between us, but more friendly like.

HIGGINS: Well, of course. Thats just how I feel. And how Pickering feels. Eliza; youre a fool.

LIZA: Thats not a proper answer to give me. (*She sinks on the chair at the writing-table in tears.*)

HIGGINS: It's all youll get until you stop being a common idiot. If youre going to be a lady, youll have to give up feeling neglected if the men you know dont spend half their time snivelling over you and the other half giving you black eyes. If you cant stand the coldness of my sort of life, and the strain of it, go back to the gutter. Work til youre more a brute than a human being; and then cuddle and squabble and drink til you fall asleep. Oh, it's a fine life, the life of the gutter. It's real: it's warm: it's violent: you can feel it through the thickest skin: you can taste it and smell it without any training or any work. Not like Science and Literature and Classical Music and Philosophy and Art. You find me cold, unfeeling, selfish, dont you? Very well: be off with you to the sort of people you like. Marry some sentimental hog or other with lots of money, and a thick pair of lips to kiss you with and a thick pair of boots to kick you with. If you cant appreciate what youve got, youd better get what you can appreciate.

LIZA (*desperate*): Oh, you are a cruel tyrant. I cant talk to you: you turn everything against me: I'm always in the wrong. But you know very well all the time that youre nothing but a bully. You know I cant go back to the gutter, as you call it, and that I have no real friends in the world but you and the Colonel. You know well I couldnt bear to live with a low common man after you two; and it's wicked and cruel of you to insult me by pretending I could. You think I must go back to Wimpole Street because I have nowhere else to go but father's. But dont you be too sure that you have me under your feet to be trampled on and talked down. I'll marry Freddy, I will, as soon as I'm able to support him.

HIGGINS (*thunderstruck*): Freddy!!! that young fool! That poor devil who couldnt get a job as an errand boy even if he had the guts to try for it! Woman: do you not understand that I have made you a consort for a king?

LIZA: Freddy loves me: that makes him king enough for me. I dont want him to work: he wasnt brought up to it as I was. I'll go and be a teacher.

HIGGINS: Whatll you teach, in heaven's name?

LIZA: What you taught me. I'll teach phonetics.

HIGGINS: Ha! ha! ha!

LIZA: I'll offer myself as an assistant to that hairyfaced Hungarian.

HIGGINS (*rising in a fury*): What! That impostor! that humbug! that toadying ignoramus! Teach him my methods! my discoveries! You take one step in his direction and I'll wring your neck. (*He lays hands on her.*) Do you hear?

LIZA (*defiantly non-resistant*): Wring away. What do I care? I knew youd strike me some day. (*He lets her go, stamping with rage at having forgotten himself, and recoils so hastily that he stumbles back into his seat on the ottoman.*) Aha! Now I know how to deal with you. What a fool I was not to think of it before! You cant take away the knowledge you gave me. You said I had a finer ear than you. And I can be civil and kind to people, which is more than you can. Aha! (*purposely dropping her aitches to annoy him*) Thats done you, Enry Iggins, it az. Now I dont care that (*snapping her finger*) for your bullying and your big talk. I'll advertise it in the papers that your duchess is only a flower girl that you taught, and that she'll teach anybody to be a duchess just the same in six months for a thousand guineas. Oh, when I think of myself crawling under your feet and being trampled on and called names, when all the time I had only to lift up my finger to be as good as you, I could just kick myself.

HIGGINS (*wondering at her*): You damned impudent slut, you! But it's better than snivelling; better than fetching slippers and finding spectacles, isnt it? (*rising*) By George, Eliza, I said I'd make a woman of you; and I have. I like you like this.

LIZA: Yes: you turn round and make up to me now that I'm not afraid of you, and can do without you.

HIGGINS: Of course I do, you little fool. Five minutes ago you were like a millstone round my neck. Now youre a tower of strength: a consort battleship. You and I and Pickering will be three old bachelors instead of only two men and a silly girl.

(MRS HIGGINS *returns, dressed for the wedding.* ELIZA *instantly becomes cool and elegant.*)

MRS HIGGINS: The carriage is waiting, Eliza. Are you ready?

LIZA: Quite. Is the Professor coming?

MRS HIGGINS: Certainly not. He cant behave himself in

church. He makes remarks out loud all the time on the clergyman's pronunciation.

LIZA: Then I shall not see you again, Professor. Goodbye. (*She goes to the door.*)

MRS HIGGINS (*coming to* HIGGINS): Goodbye, dear.

HIGGINS: Goodbye, mother. (*He is about to kiss her, when he recollects something.*) Oh, by the way, Eliza, order a ham and a Stilton cheese, will you? And buy me a pair of reindeer gloves, number eights, and a tie to match that new suit of mine. You can choose the color. (*His cheerful, careless, vigorous voice shews that he is incorrigible.*)

LIZA (*disdainfully*): Number eights are too small for you if you want them lined with lamb's wool. You have three new ties that you have forgotten in the drawer of your washstand. Colonel Pickering prefers double Gloucester to Stilton; and you dont notice the difference. I telephoned Mrs Pearce this morning not to forget the ham. What you are to do without me I cannot imagine. (*She sweeps out.*)

MRS HIGGINS: I'm afraid youve spoilt that girl, Henry. I should be uneasy about you and her if she were less fond of Colonel Pickering.

HIGGINS: Pickering! Nonsense: she's going to marry Freddy. Ha ha! Freddy! Freddy!! Ha ha ha ha ha!!!!! (*He roars with laughter as the play ends.*)

Arthur Miller:

The Crucible

Arthur Miller (1915–   ), a native of New York City and a graduate of the University of Michigan where he wrote his first plays, achieved success in 1947 with All My Sons, *a play clearly in the tradition of Ibsen. Miller consolidated his position in his second Broadway play,* Death of a Salesman, *which won for him the 1949 Pulitzer Prize. After his second Pulitzer prizewinning play,* A View from the Bridge, *Miller became less productive, more estranged from the new directions taken by the theater in the late fifties and sixties. But his most recent play,* The Price, *though it is composed in a conventional mode, reestablished Miller as a still vital force in the American theater.* The Crucible *was written in 1952 during the Communist investigations by the late Senator Joseph McCarthy.*

The reader of *The Crucible* is subjected to an initial difficulty. Before the play begins the dramatist offers us a sermon. And when the sermon ends, the reader is subjected to a long first act which is almost entirely expository and which, except for the brief scene between Proctor and Abigail, contains little dramatic conflict.

Ultimately, once we are caught up in the tension of the play, the necessity for the protracted exposition of Act I becomes clear. All of which is in character with the earnest, uncompromising, almost dour Arthur Miller who regards the theater—like the Greeks, like Ibsen—as a temple where we undergo spiritual purification. Miller sees *The Crucible,* like most of his other plays, as a modern tragedy; and there is reason for us to accept them on that basis.

In tragedy, we recall, there must be a sacrificial victim, a man (or woman) of nobility and consequence who must die before the evil force that threatens a state can be dispelled. Tragedy, also, usually requires that there be a peripety (the

289

sudden reversal of circumstance) followed by a recognition, wherein the source of evil becomes known. In *The Crucible* John Proctor is the sacrificial victim. But Miller deliberately omits the peripety and recognition, a reversal that could only be undergone by the leaders of the community itself, since it is the community that is the true protagonist of the play.

A crucible is a symbol of a severe testing. The Salem witch trials, while they were a test for the accused, were even more a test of the principles on which the New England community was founded. Miller's inescapable implication is that America continues to be tested and it is ultimately the people of America who are the protagonist of *The Crucible,* a modern tragedy.

The Crucible

Characters

REVEREND PARRIS.
BETTY PARRIS.
TITUBA.
ABIGAIL WILLIAMS.
SUSANNA WALCOTT.
MRS. ANN PUTNAM.
THOMAS PUTNAM.
MERCY LEWIS.
MARY WARREN.
JOHN PROCTOR.
REBECCA NURSE.
GILES COREY.
REVEREND JOHN HALE.
ELIZABETH PROCTOR.
FRANCIS NURSE.
EZEKIEL CHEEVER.
MARSHAL HERRICK.
JUDGE HATHORNE.
DEPUTY GOVERNOR DANFORTH.
SARAH GOOD.
HOPKINS.

A NOTE ON THE HISTORICAL ACCURACY
OF THIS PLAY

This play is not history in the sense in which the word is used by the academic historian. Dramatic purposes have sometimes required many characters to be fused into one; the number of girls involved in the "crying-out" has been reduced; Abigail's age has been raised; while there were several judges of almost equal authority, I have symbolized them all in Hathorne and Danforth. However, I believe that the reader will discover here the essential nature of one of the strangest and most awful chapters in human history. The fate of each character is exactly that of his historical model, and there is no one in the drama who did not play a similar—and in some cases exactly the same—role in history.

As for the characters of the persons, little is known about most of them excepting what may be surmised from a few letters, the trial record, certain broadsides written at the time, and references to their conduct in sources of varying reliability. They may therefore be taken as creations of my own, drawn to the best of my ability in conformity with their known behavior, except as indicated in the commentary I have written for this text.

ACT I

(AN OVERTURE)

(*A small upper bedroom in the home of* REVEREND SAMUEL
PARRIS, *Salem, Massachusetts, in the spring of the year 1692.*

*There is a narrow window at the left. Through its leaded
panes the morning sunlight streams. A candle still burns near
the bed, which is at the right. A chest, a chair, and a small
table are the other furnishings. At the back a door opens on
the landing of the stairway to the ground floor. The room
gives off an air of clean spareness. The roof rafters are exposed, and the wood colors are raw and unmellowed.*

As the curtain rises, REVEREND PARRIS *is discovered kneel-
ing beside the bed, evidently in prayer. His daughter,* BETTY
PARRIS, *aged ten, is lying on the bed, inert.*

At the time of these events PARRIS was in his middle forties.
In history he cut a villainous path, and there is very little
good to be said for him. He believed he was being persecuted
wherever he went, despite his best efforts to win people and
God to his side. In meeting, he felt insulted if someone rose
to shut the door without first asking his permission. He was
a widower with no interest in children, or talent with them.
He regarded them as young adults, and until this strange
crisis he, like the rest of Salem, never conceived that the children were anything but thankful for being permitted to walk
straight, eyes slightly lowered, arms at the sides, and mouths
shut until bidden to speak.

His house stood in the "town"—but we today would hardly
call it a village. The meeting house was nearby, and from
this point outward—toward the bay or inland—there were
a few small-windowed, dark houses snuggling against the raw
Massachusetts winter. Salem had been established hardly forty
years before. To the European world the whole province was
a barbaric frontier inhabited by a sect of fanatics who, never-

293

theless, were shipping out products of slowly increasing quantity and value.

No one can really know what their lives were like. They had no novelists—and would not have permitted anyone to read a novel if one were handy. Their creed forbade anything resembling a theater or "vain enjoyment." They did not celebrate Christmas, and a holiday from work meant only that they must concentrate even more upon prayer.

Which is not to say that nothing broke into this strict and somber way of life. When a new farmhouse was built, friends assembled to "raise the roof," and there would be special foods cooked and probably some potent cider passed around. There was a good supply of ne'er-do-wells in Salem, who dallied at the shovelboard in Bridget Bishop's tavern. Probably more than the creed, hard work kept the morals of the place from spoiling, for the people were forced to fight the land like heroes for every grain of corn, and no man had very much time for fooling around.

That there were some jokers, however, is indicated by the practice of appointing a two-man patrol whose duty was to "walk forth in the time of God's worship to take notice of such as either lye about the meeting house, without attending to the word and ordinances, or that lye at home or in the fields without giving good account thereof, and to take the names of such persons, and to present them to the magistrates, whereby they may be accordingly proceeded against." This predilection for minding other people's business was time-honored among the people of Salem, and it undoubtedly created many of the suspicions which were to feed the coming madness. It was also, in my opinion, one of the things that a JOHN PROCTOR would rebel against, for the time of the armed camp had almost passed, and since the country was reasonably—although not wholly—safe, the old disciplines were beginning to rankle. But, as in all such matters, the issue was not clear-cut, for danger was still a possibility, and in unity still lay the best promise of safety.

The edge of the wilderness was close by. The American continent stretched endlessly west, and it was full of mystery for them. It stood, dark and threatening, over their shoulders night and day, for out of it Indian tribes marauded from time to time, and Reverend Parris had parishioners who had lost relatives to these heathen.

The parochial snobbery of these people was partly responsible for their failure to convert the Indians. Probably they also preferred to take land from heathens rather than from fellow

Christians. At any rate, very few Indians were converted, and the Salem folk believed that the virgin forest was the Devil's last preserve, his home base and the citadel of his final stand. To the best of their knowledge the American forest was the last place on earth that was not paying homage to God.

For these reasons, among others, they carried about an air of innate resistance, even of persecution. Their fathers had, of course, been persecuted in England. So now they and their church found it necessary to deny any other sect its freedom, lest their New Jerusalem be defiled and corrupted by wrong ways and deceitful ideas.

They believed, in short, that they held in their steady hands the candle that would light the world. We have inherited this belief, and it has helped and hurt us. It helped them with the discipline it gave them. They were a dedicated folk, by and large, and they had to be to survive the life they had chosen or been born into in this country.

The proof of their belief's value to them may be taken from the opposite character of the first Jamestown settlement, farther south, in Virginia. The Englishmen who landed there were motivated mainly by a hunt for profit. They had thought to pick off the wealth of the new country and then return rich to England. They were a band of individualists, and a much more ingratiating group than the Massachusetts men. But Virginia destroyed them. Massachusetts tried to kill off the Puritans, but they combined; they set up a communal society which, in the beginning, was little more than an armed camp with an autocratic and very devoted leadership. It was, however, an autocracy by consent, for they were united from top to bottom by a commonly held idealogy whose perpetuation was the reason and justification for all their sufferings. So their self-denial, their purposefulness, their suspicion of all vain pursuits, their hard-handed justice, were altogether perfect instruments for the conquest of this space so antagonistic to man.

But the people of Salem in 1692 were not quite the dedicated folk that arrived on the *Mayflower*. A vast differentiation had taken place, and in their own time a revolution had unseated the royal government and substituted a junta which was at this moment in power. The times, to their eyes, must have been out of joint, and to the common folk must have seemed as insoluble and complicated as do ours today. It is not hard to see how easily many could have been led to believe that the time of confusion had been brought upon them by deep and darkling forces. No hint of such speculation appears on the court record, but social disorder in any age breeds such mystical suspicions, and when, as in Salem, wonders are brought forth from below the social surface, it is too much to expect people to hold back very long from laying on the victims with all the force of their frustrations.

The Salem tragedy, which is about to begin in these pages, developed from a paradox. It is a paradox in whose grip we still live, and there is no prospect yet that we will discover its resolution. Simply, it was this: for good purposes, even high purposes, the people of Salem developed a theocracy, a combine of state and religious power whose function was to keep the community together, and to prevent any kind of disunity that might open it to destruction by material or ideological enemies. It was forged for a necessary purpose and accomplished that purpose. But all organization is and must be grounded on the idea of exclusion and prohibition, just as two objects cannot occupy the same space. Evidently the time came in New England when the repressions of order were heavier than seemed warranted by the dangers against which the order was organized. The witch-hunt was a perverse manifestation of the panic which set in among all classes when the balance began to turn toward greater individual freedom.

When one rises above the individual villainy displayed, one can only pity them all, just as we shall be pitied someday. It is still impossible for man to organize his social life without repressions, and the balance has yet to be struck between order and freedom.

The witch-hunt was not, however, a mere repression. It was also, and as importantly, a long overdue opportunity for everyone so inclined to express publicly his guilt and sins, under the cover of accusations against the victims. It suddenly became possible—and patriotic and holy—for a man to say that MARTHA COREY had come into his bedroom at night, and that, while his wife was sleeping at his side, MARTHA laid herself down on his chest and "nearly suffocated him." Of course it was her spirit only, but his satisfaction at confessing himself was no lighter than if it had been MARTHA herself. One could not ordinarily speak such things in public.

Long-held hatreds of neighbors could now be openly expressed, and vengeance taken, despite the Bible's charitable injunctions. Land-lust which had been expressed before by constant bickering over boundaries and deeds, could now be elevated to the arena of morality; one could cry witch against one's neighbor and feel perfectly justified in the bargain. Old scores could be settled on a plane of heavenly combat between Lucifer and the Lord; suspicions and the envy of the miserable toward the happy could and did burst out in the general revenge.

REVEREND PARRIS *is praying now, and, though we cannot hear his words, a sense of his confusion hangs about him. He mumbles, then seems about to weep; then he weeps, then prays again; but his daughter does not stir on the bed.*

The door opens, and his Negro slave enters. TITUBA *is in her forties.* PARRIS *brought her with him from Barbados, where he spent some years as a merchant before entering the ministry. She enters as one does who can no longer bear to be barred from the sight of her beloved, but she is also very frightened because her slave sense has warned her that, as always, trouble in this house eventually lands on her back.)*

TITUBA (*already taking a step backward*): My Betty be hearty soon?

PARRIS: Out of here!

TITUBA (*backing to the door*): My Betty not goin' die . . .

PARRIS (*scrambling to his feet in a fury*): Out of my sight! (*She is gone.*) Out of my—(*He is overcome with sobs. He clamps his teeth against them and closes the door and leans against it, exhausted.*) Oh, my God! God help me! (*Quaking with fear, mumbling to himself through his sobs, he goes to the bed and gently takes* BETTY'S *hand.*) Betty. Child. Dear child. Will you wake, will you open up your eyes! Betty, little one . . .

(*He is bending to kneel again when his niece,* ABIGAIL WILLIAMS, *seventeen, enters—a strikingly beautiful girl, an orphan, with an endless capacity for dissembling. Now she is all worry and apprehension and propriety.*)

ABIGAIL: Uncle? (*He looks to her.*) Susanna Walcott's here from Doctor Griggs.

PARRIS: Oh? Let her come, let her come.

ABIGAIL (*leaning out the door to call to* SUSANNA, *who is down the hall a few steps*): Come in, Susanna.

(SUSANNA WALCOTT, *a little younger than* ABIGAIL, *a nervous, hurried girl, enters.*)

PARRIS (*eagerly*): What does the doctor say, child?

SUSANNA (*craning around* PARRIS *to get a look at* BETTY): He bid me come and tell you, reverend sir, that he cannot discover no medicine for it in his books.

PARRIS: Then he must search on.

SUSANNA: Aye, sir, he have been searchin' his books since he left you, sir. But he bid me tell you, that you might look to unnatural things for the cause of it.

PARRIS (*his eyes going wide*): No—no. There be no un-natural cause here. Tell him I have sent for Reverend Hale of Beverly, and Mr. Hale will surely confirm that. Let him look to medicine and put out all thought of unnatural causes here. There be none.

SUSANNA: Aye, sir. He bid me tell you. (*She turns to go.*)

ABIGAIL: Speak nothin' of it in the village, Susanna.

PARRIS: Go directly home and speak nothing of unnatural causes.

SUSANNA: Aye, sir. I pray for her.

(*She goes out.*)

ABIGAIL: Uncle, the rumor of witchcraft is all about; I think you'd best go down and deny it yourself. The parlor's packed with people, sir. I'll sit with her.

PARRIS (*pressed, turns on her*): And what shall I say to them? That my daughter and my niece I discovered dancing like heathen in the forest?

ABIGAIL: Uncle, we did dance; let you tell them I confessed it—and I'll be whipped if I must be. But they're speakin' of witchcraft. Betty's not witched.

PARRIS: Abigail, I cannot go before the congregation when I know you have not opened with me. What did you do with her in the forest?

ABIGAIL: We did dance, uncle, and when you leaped out of the bush so suddenly, Betty was frightened and then she fainted. And there's the whole of it.

PARRIS: Child. Sit you down.

ABIGAIL (*quavering, as she sits*): I would never hurt Betty. I love her dearly.

PARRIS: Now look you, child, your punishment will come in its time. But if you trafficked with spirits in the forest I must know it now, for surely my enemies will, and they will ruin me with it.

ABIGAIL: But we never conjured spirits.

PARRIS: Then why can she not move herself since mid-night? This child is desperate! (ABIGAIL *lowers her eyes.*) It must come out—my enemies will bring it out. Let me know what you done there. Abigail, do you understand that I have many enemies?

ABIGAIL: I have heard of it, uncle.

PARRIS: There is a faction that is sworn to drive me from my pulpit. Do you understand that?

ABIGAIL: I think so, sir.

PARRIS: Now then, in the midst of such disruption, my own household is discovered to be the very center of some obscene practice. Abominations are done in the forest—

ABIGAIL: It were sport, uncle!

PARRIS (*pointing at* BETTY): You call this sport? (*She lowers her eyes. He pleads.*) Abigail, if you know something that may help the doctor, for God's sake tell it to me. (*She is silent.*) I saw Tituba waving her arms over the fire when I came on you. Why was she doing that? And I heard a screeching and gibberish coming from her mouth. She were swaying like a dumb beast over that fire!

ABIGAIL: She always sings her Barbados songs, and we dance.

PARRIS: I cannot blink what I saw, Abigail, for my enemies will not blink it. I saw a dress lying on the grass.

ABIGAIL (*innocently*): A dress?

PARRIS (*It is very hard to say.*): Aye, a dress. And I thought I saw—someone naked running through the trees!

ABIGAIL (*in terror*): No one was naked! You mistake your self, uncle!

PARRIS (*with anger*): I saw it! (*He moves from her. Then, resolved*) Now tell me true, Abigail. And I pray you feel the weight of truth upon you, for now my ministry's at stake, my ministry and perhaps your cousin's life. Whatever abomination you have done, give me all of it now, for I dare not be taken unaware when I go before them down there.

ABIGAIL: There is nothin' more. I swear it, uncle.

PARRIS (*studies her, then nods, half convinced*): Abigail, I have fought here three long years to bend these stiff-necked people to me, and now, just now when some good respect is rising for me in the parish, you compromise my very charac- ter. I have given you a home, child, I have put clothes upon your back—now give me upright answer. Your name in the town—it is entirely white, is it not?

ABIGAIL (*with an edge of resentment*): Why, I am sure it is, sir. There be no blush about my name.

PARRIS (*to the point*): Abigail, is there any other cause than you have told me, for your being discharged from Goody Proctor's service? I have heard it said, and I tell you as I heard it, that she comes so rarely to the church this year for she will not sit so close to something soiled. What signified that remark?

ABIGAIL: She hates me, uncle, she must, for I would not be her slave. It's a bitter woman, a lying, cold, sniveling woman, and I will not work for such a woman!

PARRIS: She may be. And yet it has troubled me that you are now seven month out of their house, and in all this time no other family has ever called for your service.

ABIGAIL: They want slaves, not such as I. Let them send to

Barbados for that. I will not black my face for any of them! (*with ill-concealed resentment at him*) Do you begrudge my bed, uncle?

PARRIS: No—no.

ABIGAIL (*in a temper*): My name is good in the village! I will not have it said my name is soiled! Goody Proctor is a gossiping liar!

(*Enter* MRS. ANN PUTNAM. *She is a twisted soul of forty-five, a death-ridden woman, haunted by dreams.*)

PARRIS (*as soon as the door begins to open*): No—no, I cannot have anyone. (*He sees her, and a certain deference springs into him, although his worry remains.*) Why, Goody Putnam, come in.

MRS. PUTNAM (*full of breath, shiny-eyed*): It is a marvel. It is surely a stroke of hell upon you.

PARRIS: No, Goody Putnam, it is—

MRS. PUTNAM (*glancing at* BETTY): How high did she fly, how high?

PARRIS: No, no, she never flew—

MRS. PUTNAM (*very pleased with it*): Why, it's sure she did. Mr. Collins saw her goin' over Ingersoll's barn, and come down light as bird, he says!

PARRIS: Now, look you, Goody Putnam, she never—(*Enter* THOMAS PUTNAM, *a well-to-do, hard-handed land-owner, near fifty.*) Oh, good morning, Mr. Putnam.

PUTNAM: It is a providence the thing is out now! It is a providence. (*He goes directly to the bed.*)

PARRIS: What's out, sir, what's—?

(MRS. PUTNAM *goes to the bed.*)

PUTNAM (*looking down at* BETTY): Why, *her* eyes is closed! Look you, Ann.

MRS. PUTNAM: Why, that's strange. (*to* PARRIS) Ours is open.

PARRIS (*shocked*): Your Ruth is sick?

MRS. PUTNAM (*with vicious certainty*): I'd not call it sick; the Devil's touch is heavier than sick. It's death, y'know, it's death drivin' into them, forked and hoofed.

PARRIS: Oh, pray not! Why, how does Ruth ail?

MRS. PUTNAM: She ails as she must—she never waked this morning, but her eyes open and she walks, and hears naught, sees naught, and cannot eat. Her soul is taken, surely.

(PARRIS *is struck.*)

PUTNAM (*as though for further details*): They say you've sent for Reverend Hale of Beverly?

PARRIS (*with dwindling conviction now*): A precaution only. He has much experience in all demonic arts, and I—

MRS. PUTNAM: He has indeed; and found a witch in Beverly last year, and let you remember that.

PARRIS: Now, Goody Ann, they only thought that were a witch, and I am certain there be no element of witchcraft here.

PUTNAM: No witchcraft! Now look you, Mr. Parris—

PARRIS: Thomas, Thomas, I pray you, leap not to witchcraft. I know that you—you least of all, Thomas, would ever wish so disastrous a charge laid upon me. We cannot leap to witchcraft. They will howl me out of Salem for such corruption in my house.

(A word about THOMAS PUTNAM. He was a man with many grievances, at least one of which appears justified. Some time before, his wife's brother-in-law, James Bayley, had been turned down as minister at Salem. Bayley had all the qualifications, and a two-thirds vote into the bargain, but a faction stopped his acceptance, for reasons that are not clear.

THOMAS PUTNAM was the eldest son of the richest man in the village. He had fought the Indians at Narragansett, and was deeply interested in parish affairs. He undoubtedly felt it poor payment that the village should so blatantly disregard his candidate for one of its more important offices, especially since he regarded himself as the intellectual superior of most of the people around him.

His vindictive nature was demonstrated long before the witchcraft began. Another former Salem minister, George Burroughs, had had to borrow money to pay for his wife's funeral, and, since the parish was remiss in his salary, he was soon bankrupt. Thomas and his brother John had Burroughs jailed for debts the man did not owe. The incident is important only in that Burroughs succeeded in becoming minister where Bayley, Thomas Putnam's brother-in-law, had been rejected; the motif of resentment is clear here. Thomas Putnam felt that his own name and the honor of his family had been smirched by the village, and he meant to right matters however he could.

Another reason to believe him a deeply embittered man was his attempt to break his father's will, which left a disproportionate amount to a stepbrother. As with every other public cause in which he tried to force his way, he failed in this.

So it is not surprising to find that so many accusations against people are in the handwriting of THOMAS PUTNAM, or that his name is so often found as a witness corroborating the supernatural testimony, or that his daughter led the crying-out at the most opportune junctures of the trials, especially when——But we'll speak of that when we come to it.)

PUTNAM (*At the moment he is intent upon getting* PARRIS, *for whom he has only contempt, to move toward the abyss.*): Mr. Parris, I have taken your part in all contention here, and I would continue; but I cannot if you hold back in this. There are hurtful, vengeful spirits layin' hands on these children.

PARRIS: But, Thomas, you cannot——

PUTNAM: Ann! Tell Mr. Parris what you have done.

MRS. PUTNAM: Reverend Parris, I have laid seven babies unbaptized in the earth. Believe me, sir, you never saw more hearty babies born. And yet, each would wither in my arms the very night of their birth. I have spoke nothin', but my heart has clamored intimations. And now, this year, my Ruth, my only—— I see her turning strange. A secret child she has become this year, and shrivels like a sucking mouth were pullin' on her life too. And so I thought to send her to your Tituba——

PARRIS: To Tituba! What may Tituba——?

MRS. PUTNAM: Tituba knows how to speak to the dead, Mr. Parris.

PARRIS: Goody Ann, it is a formidable sin to conjure up the dead!

MRS. PUTNAM: I take it on my soul, but who else may surely tell us what person murdered my babies?

PARRIS (*horrified*): Woman!

MRS. PUTNAM: They were murdered, Mr. Parris! And mark this proof! Mark it! Last night my Ruth were ever so close to their little spirits; I know it, sir. For how else is she struck dumb now except some power of darkness would stop her mouth? It is a marvelous sign, Mr. Parris!

PUTNAM: Don't you understand it, sir? There is a murdering witch among us, bound to keep herself in the dark. (PARRIS *turns to* BETTY, *a frantic terror rising in him.*) Let your names make of it what they will, you cannot blink it more.

PARRIS (*to* ABIGAIL): Then you were conjuring spirits last night.

ABIGAIL (*whispering*): Not I, sir——Tituba and Ruth.

PARRIS (*turns now, with new fear, and goes to* BETTY, *looks down at her, and then, gazing off*): Oh, Abigail, what proper payment for my charity! Now I am undone.

PUTNAM: You are not undone! Let you take hold here. Wait for no one to charge you——declare it yourself. You have discovered witchcraft——

PARRIS: In my house? In my house, Thomas? They will topple me with this! They will make of it a—

(*Enter* MERCY LEWIS, *the Putnams' servant, a fat, sly, merciless girl of eighteen.*)

MERCY: Your pardons. I only thought to see how Betty is.

PUTNAM: Why aren't you home? Who's with Ruth?

MERCY: Her grandma come. She's improved a little, I think—she give a powerful sneeze before.

MRS. PUTNAM: Ah, there's a sign of life!

MERCY: I'd fear no more, Goody Putnam. It were a grand sneeze; another like it will shake her wits together, I'm sure. (*She goes to the bed to look.*)

PARRIS: Will you leave me now, Thomas? I would pray a while alone.

ABIGAIL: Uncle, you've prayed since midnight. Why do you not go down and—

PARRIS: No—no. (*to* PUTNAM) I have no answer for that crowd. I'll wait till Mr. Hale arrives. (*to get* MRS. PUTNAM *to leave*) If you will, Goody Ann . . .

PUTNAM: Now look you, sir. Let you strike out against the Devil, and the village will bless you for it! Come down, speak to them—pray with them. They're thirsting for your word, Mister! Surely you'll pray with them.

PARRIS (*swayed*): I'll lead them in a psalm, but let you say nothing of witchcraft yet. I will not discuss it. The cause is yet unknown. I have had enough contention since I came; I want no more.

MRS. PUTNAM: Mercy, you go home to Ruth, d'y'hear?

MERCY: Aye, mum.

(MRS. PUTNAM *goes out.*)

PARRIS (*to* ABIGAIL): If she starts for the window, cry for me at once.

ABIGAIL: I will, uncle.

PARRIS (*to Putnam*): There is a terrible power in her arms today. (*He goes out with* PUTNAM.)

ABIGAIL (*with hushed trepidation*): How is Ruth sick?

MERCY: It's weirdish, I know not—she seems to walk like a dead one since last night.

ABIGAIL (*turns at once and goes to* BETTY, *and now, with fear in her voice*): Betty? (BETTY *doesn't move. She shakes her.*) Now stop this! Betty! Sit up now!

(BETTY *doesn't stir.* MERCY *comes over.*)

MERCY: Have you tried beatin' her? I gave Ruth a good one and it waked her for a minute. Here, let me have her.

ABIGAIL (*holding* MERCY *back*): No, he'll be comin' up.

Listen, now; if they be questioning us, tell them we danced—
I told him as much already.

MERCY: Aye. And what more?

ABIGAIL: He knows Tituba conjured Ruth's sisters to come
out of the grave.

MERCY: And what more?

ABIGAIL: He saw you naked.

MERCY (*clapping her hands together with a frightened
laugh*): Oh, Jesus!

(*Enter* MARY WARREN, *breathless. She is seventeen, a sub-
servient, naive, lonely girl.*)

MARY WARREN: What'll we do? The village is out! I just
come from the farm; the whole country's talkin' witchcraft!
They'll be callin' us witches, Abby!

MERCY (*pointing and looking at* MARY WARREN): She
means to tell, I know it.

MARY WARREN: Abby, we've got to tell. Witchery's a
hangin' error, a hangin' like they done in Boston two year ago!
We must tell the truth, Abby! You'll only be whipped for
dancin', and the other things!

ABIGAIL: Oh, *we'll* be whipped!

MARY WARREN: I never done none of it, Abby. I only
looked!

MERCY (*moving menacingly toward* MARY): Oh, you're a
great one for lookin', aren't you, Mary Warren? What a
grand peeping courage you have!

(BETTY, *on the bed, whimpers.* ABIGAIL *turns to her at once.*)

ABIGAIL: Betty? (*She goes to* BETTY.) Now, Betty, dear,
wake up now. It's Abigail. (*She sits* BETTY *up and furiously
shakes her.*) I'll beat you, Betty! (BETTY *whimpers.*) My, you
seem improving. I talked to your papa and I told him everything. So there's nothing to—

BETTY (*darts off the bed, frightened of* ABIGAIL, *and flattens
herself against the wall*): I want my mama!

ABIGAIL (*with alarm, as she cautiously approaches* BETTY):
What ails you, Betty? Your mama's dead and buried.

BETTY: I'll fly to Mama. Let me fly! (*She raises her arms as
though to fly, and streaks for the window, gets one leg out.*)

ABIGAIL (*pulling her away from the window*): I told him
everything; he knows now, he knows everything we—

BETTY: You drank blood, Abby! You didn't tell him that!

ABIGAIL: Betty, you never say that again! You will never—

BETTY: You did, you did! You drank a charm to kill John
Proctor's wife! You drank a charm to kill Goody Proctor!

ABIGAIL (*smashes her across the face*): Shut it! Now shut it!

BETTY (*collapsing on the bed*): Mama, Mama! (*She dissolves into sobs.*)

ABIGAIL: Now look you. All of you. We danced. And Tituba conjured Ruth Putnam's dead sisters. And that is all. And mark this. Let either of you breathe a word, or the edge of a word, about the other things, and I will come to you in the black of some terrible night and I will bring a pointy reckoning that will shudder you. And you know I can do it; I saw Indians smash my dear parents' heads on the pillow next to mine, and I have seen some reddish work done at night, and I can make you wish you had never seen the sun go down! (*She goes to* BETTY *and roughly sits her up.*) Now, you— sit up and stop this!

(*But* BETTY *collapses in her hands and lies inert on the bed.*)

MARY WARREN (*with hysterical fright*): What's got her? (*Abigail stares in fright at* BETTY.) Abby, she's going to die! It's a sin to conjure, and we—

ABIGAIL (*starting for* MARY): I say shut it, Mary Warren!

(*Enter* JOHN PROCTOR. *On seeing him,* MARY WARREN *leaps in fright.*

PROCTOR was a farmer in his middle thirties. He need not have been a partisan of any faction in the town, but there is evidence to suggest that he had a sharp and biting way with hypocrites. He was the kind of man—powerful of body, even-tempered, and not easily led—who cannot refuse support to partisans without drawing their deepest resentment. In PROCTOR'S presence a fool felt his foolishness instantly—and a PROCTOR is always marked for calumny therefore.

But as we shall see, the steady manner he displays does not spring from an untroubled soul. He is a sinner, a sinner not only against the moral fashion of the time, but against his own vision of decent conduct. These people had no ritual for the washing away of sins. It is another trait we inherited from them, and it has helped to discipline us as well as to breed hypocrisy among us. PROCTOR, respected and even feared in Salem, has come to regard himself as a kind of fraud. But no hint of this has yet appeared on the surface, and as he enters from the crowded parlor below it is a man in his prime we see, with a quiet confidence and an unexpressed, hidden force. MARY WARREN, his servant, can barely speak for embarrassment and fear.)

MARY WARREN: Oh! I'm just going home, Mr. Proctor.

PROCTOR: Be you foolish, Mary Warren? Be you deaf? I

forbid you leave the house, did I not? Why shall I pay you? I am looking for you more often than my cows!

MARY WARREN: I only come to see the great doings in the world.

PROCTOR: I'll show you a great doin' on your arse one of these days. Now get you home; my wife is waitin' with your work! (*Trying to retain a shred of dignity, she goes slowly out.*)

MERCY LEWIS (*both afraid of him and strangely titillated*): I'd best be off. I have my Ruth to watch. Good morning, Mr. Proctor.

(MERCY *sidles out. Since* PROCTOR'S *entrance,* ABIGAIL *has stood as though on tiptoe, absorbing his presence, wide-eyed. He glances at her then goes to* BETTY *on the bed.*)

ABIGAIL: Gad. I'd almost forgot how strong you are, John Proctor!

PROCTOR (*looking at* ABIGAIL *now, the faintest suggestion of a knowing smile on his face*): What's this mischief here?

ABIGAIL (*with a nervous laugh*): Oh, she's only gone silly somehow.

PROCTOR: The road past my house is a pilgrimage to Salem all morning. The town's mumbling witchcraft.

ABIGAIL: Oh, posh! (*Winningly she comes a little closer, with a confidential, wicked air.*) We were dancin' in the woods last night, and my uncle leaped in on us. She took fright, is all.

PROCTOR (*his smile widening*): Ah, you're wicked yet, aren't y'! (*A trill of expectant laughter escapes her, and she dares come closer, feverishly looking into his eyes.*) You'll be clapped in the stocks before you're twenty.

(*He takes a step to go, and she springs into his path.*)

ABIGAIL: Give me a word, John. A soft word. (*Her concentrated desire destroys his smile.*)

PROCTOR: No, no, Abby. That's done with.

ABIGAIL (*tauntingly*): You come five mile to see a silly girl fly? I know you better.

PROCTOR (*setting her firmly out of his path*): I come to see what mischief your uncle's brewin' now. (*with final emphasis*) Put it out of mind, Abby.

ABIGAIL (*grasping his hand before he can release her*): John —I am waitin' for you every night.

PROCTOR: Abby, I never give you hope to wait for me.

ABIGAIL (*now beginning to anger—she can't believe it*): I have something better than hope, I think!

PROCTOR: Abby, you'll put it out of mind. I'll not be comin' for you more.

ABIGAIL: You're surely sportin' with me.

PROCTOR: You know me better.

ABIGAIL: I know how you clutched my back behind your house and sweated like a stallion whenever I come near! Or did I dream that? It's she put me out, you cannot pretend it were you. I saw your face when she put me out, and you loved me then and you do now!

PROCTOR: Abby, that's a wild thing to say—

ABIGAIL: A wild thing may say wild things. But not so wild, I think. I have seen you since she put me out; I have seen you nights.

PROCTOR: I have hardly stepped off my farm this seven-month.

ABIGAIL: I have a sense for heat, John, and yours has drawn me to my window, and I have seen you looking up, burning in your loneliness. Do you tell me you've never looked up at my window?

PROCTOR: I may have looked up.

ABIGAIL (*now softening*): And you must. You are no wintry man. I know you, John. I *know* you. (*She is weeping.*) I cannot sleep for dreamin'; I cannot dream but I wake and walk about the house as though I'd find you comin' through some door. (*She clutches him desperately.*)

PROCTOR (*gently pressing her from him, with great sympathy but firmly*): Child—

ABIGAIL (*with a flash of anger*): How do you call me child!

PROCTOR: Abby, I may think of you softly from time to time. But I will cut off my hand before I'll ever reach for you again. Wipe it out of mind. We never touched, Abby.

ABIGAIL: Aye, but we did.

PROCTOR: Aye, but we did not.

ABIGAIL (*with a bitter anger*): Oh, I marvel how such a strong man may let such a sickly wife be—

PROCTOR (*angered—at himself as well*): You'll speak nothin' of Elizabeth!

ABIGAIL: She is blackening my name in the village! She is telling lies about me! She is a cold, sniveling woman, and you bend to her! Let her turn you like a—

PROCTOR (*shaking her*): Do you look for whippin'?

(*A psalm is heard being sung below.*)

ABIGAIL (*in tears*): I look for John Proctor that took me from my sleep and put knowledge in my heart! I never knew what pretense Salem was, I never knew the lying lessons I was taught by all these Christian women and their covenanted men! And now you bid me tear the light out of my eyes? I will not, I cannot! You loved me, John Proctor, and whatever sin it is, you love me yet! (*He turns abruptly to go out. She rushes to him.*) John, pity me, pity me!

(*The words "going up to Jesus" are heard in the psalm, and* BETTY *claps her ears suddenly and whines loudly.*)

ABIGAIL: Betty? (*She hurries to* BETTY, *who is now sitting up and screaming.* PROCTOR *goes to* BETTY *as* ABIGAIL *is trying to pull her hands down, calling "Betty!"*)

PROCTOR (*growing unnerved*): What's she doing? Girl, what ails you? Stop that wailing!

(*The singing has stopped in the midst of this, and now* PARRIS *rushes in.*)

PARRIS: What happened? What are you doing to her? Betty!

(*He rushes to the bed, crying, "Betty, Betty!"* MRS. PUTNAM *enters, feverish with curiosity, and with her* THOMAS PUTNAM *and* MERCY LEWIS. PARRIS, *at the bed, keeps lightly slapping* BETTY'S *face, while she moans and tries to get up.*)

ABIGAIL: She heard you singin' and suddenly she's up and screamin'.

MRS. PUTNAM: The psalm! The psalm! She cannot bear to hear the Lord's name!

PARRIS: No, God forbid. Mercy, run to the doctor! Tell him what's happened here! (MERCY LEWIS *rushes out.*)

MRS. PUTNAM: Mark it for a sign, mark it!

(REBECCA NURSE, *seventy-two, enters. She is white-haired, leaning upon her walking-stick.*)

PUTNAM (*pointing at the whimpering* BETTY): That is a notorious sign of witchcraft afoot, Goody Nurse, a prodigious sign!

MRS. PUTNAM: My mother told me that! When they cannot bear to hear the name of—

PARRIS (*trembling*): Rebecca, Rebecca, go to her, we're lost. She suddenly cannot bear to hear the Lord's—

(GILES COREY, *eighty-three, enters. He is knotted with muscle, canny, inquisitive, and still powerful.*)

REBECCA: There is hard sickness here, Giles Corey, so please to keep the quiet.

GILES: I've not said a word. No one here can testify I've said a word. Is she going to fly again? I hear she flies.

PUTNAM: Man, be quiet now!

(*Everything is quiet.* REBECCA *walks across the room to the bed. Gentleness exudes from her.* BETTY *is quietly whimpering, eyes shut.* REBECCA *simply stands over the child, who gradually quiets.*

And while they are so absorbed, we may put a word in for REBECCA. REBECCA was the wife of FRANCIS NURSE, who, from all accounts, was one of those men for whom both sides of the argument had to have respect. He was called upon to arbitrate disputes as though he were an unofficial judge, and REBECCA also enjoyed the high opinion most people had for him. By the time of the delusion, they had three hundred acres, and their children were settled in separate homesteads within the same estate. However FRANCIS had originally rented the land, and one theory has it that, as he gradually paid for it and raised his social status, there were those who resented his rise.

Another suggestion to explain the systematic campaign against REBECCA, and inferentially against FRANCIS, is the land war he fought with his neighbors, one of whom was a Putnam. This squabble grew to the proportions of a battle in the woods between partisans of both sides, and it is said to have lasted for two days. As for REBECCA herself, the general opinion of her character was so high that to explain how anyone dared cry her out for a witch—and more, how adults could bring themselves to lay hands on her—we must look to the fields and boundaries of that time.

As we have seen, THOMAS PUTNAM'S man for the Salem ministry was Bayley. The Nurse clan had been in the faction that prevented Bayley's taking office. In addition, certain families allied to the NURSES by blood or friendship, and whose farms were contiguous with the Nurse farm or close to it, combined to break away from the Salem town authority and set up Topsfield, a new and independent entity whose existence was resented by old Salemites.

That the guiding hand behind the outcry was PUTNAM'S is indicated by the fact that, as soon as it began, this Topsfield-Nurse faction absented themselves from church in protest and disbelief. It was Edward and Jonathan Putnam who signed the first complaint against REBECCA; and THOMAS PUTNAM'S little daughter was the one who fell into a fit at the hearing and pointed to REBECCA as her attacker. To top it all, MRS. PUTNAM—who is now staring at the bewitched child on the bed—soon accused REBECCA'S spirit of "tempting her to iniquity," a charge that had more truth in it than MRS. PUTNAM could know.)

MRS. PUTNAM (*astonished*): What have you done?

(REBECCA, *in thought, now leaves the bedside and sits.*)

PARRIS (*wondrous and relieved*): What do you make of it, Rebecca?

PUTNAM (*eagerly*): Goody Nurse, will you go to my Ruth and see if you can wake her?

REBECCA (*sitting*): I think she'll wake in time. Pray calm yourselves. I have eleven children, and I am twenty-six times a grandma, and I have seen them all through their silly seasons, and when it come on them they will run the Devil bowlegged keeping up with their mischief. I think she'll wake when she tires of it. A child's spirit is like a child, you can never catch it by running after it; you must stand still, and, for love, it will soon itself come back.

PROCTOR: Aye, that's the truth of it, Rebecca.

MRS. PUTNAM: This is no silly season, Rebecca. My Ruth is bewildered, Rebecca; she cannot eat.

REBECCA: Perhaps she is not hungered yet. (*to* PARRIS) I hope you are not decided to go in search of loose spirits, Mr. Parris. I've heard promise of that outside.

PARRIS: A wide opinion's running in the parish that the Devil may be among us, and I would satisfy them that they are wrong.

PROCTOR: Then let you come out and call them wrong. Did you consult the wardens before you called this minister to look for devils?

PARRIS: He is not coming to look for devils!

PROCTOR: Then what's he coming for?

PUTNAM: There be children dyin' in the village, Mister!

PROCTOR: I seen none dyin'. This society will not be a bag to swing around your head, Mr. Putnam. (*to* PARRIS) Did you call a meeting before you—?

PUTNAM: I am sick of meetings; cannot the man turn his head without he have a meeting?

PROCTOR: He may turn his head, but not to Hell!

REBECCA: Pray, John, be calm. (*Pause. He defers to her.*) Mr. Parris, I think you'd best send Reverend Hale back as soon as he come. This will set us all to arguin' again in the society, and we thought to have peace this year. I think we ought rely on the doctor now, and good prayer.

MRS. PUTNAM: Rebecca, the doctor's baffled!

REBECCA: If so he is, then let us go to God for the cause of it. There is prodigious danger in the seeking of loose spirits. I fear it, I fear it. Let us rather blame ourselves and—

PUTNAM: How may we blame ourselves? I am one of nine

sons; the Putnam seed have peopled this province. And yet I
have but one child left of eight—and now she shrivels!

REBECCA: I cannot fathom that.

MRS. PUTNAM (*with a growing edge of sarcasm*): But I
must! You think it God's work you should never lose a child,
nor grandchild either, and I bury all but one? There are
wheels within wheels in this village, and fires within fires!

PUTNAM (*to Parris*): When Reverend Hale comes, you will
proceed to look for signs of witchcraft here.

PROCTOR (*to* PUTNAM): You cannot command Mr. Parris.
We vote by name in this society, not by acreage.

PUTNAM: I never heard you worried so on this society,
Mr. Proctor. I do not think I saw you at Sabbath meeting
since snow flew.

PROCTOR: I have trouble enough without I come five mile
to hear him preach only hellfire and bloody damnation. Take
it to heart, Mr. Parris. There are many others who stay away
from church these days because you hardly ever mention
God any more.

PARRIS (*now aroused*): Why, that's a drastic charge!

REBECCA: It's somewhat true; there are many that quail to
bring their children—

PARRIS: I do not preach for children, Rebecca. It is not the
children who are unmindful of their obligations toward this
ministry.

REBECCA: Are there really those unmindful?

PARRIS: I should say the better half of Salem village—

PUTNAM: And more than that!

PARRIS: Where is my wood? My contract provides I be
supplied with all my firewood. I am waiting since November
for a stick, and even in November I had to show my frost-
bitten hands like some London beggar!

GILES: You are allowed six pound a year to buy your wood,
Mr. Parris.

PARRIS: I regard that six pound as part of my salary. I am
paid little enough without I spend six pound on firewood.

PROCTOR: Sixty, plus six for firewood—

PARRIS: The salary is sixty-six pound, Mr. Proctor! I am
not some preaching farmer with a book under my arm; I
am a graduate of Harvard College.

GILES: Aye, and well instructed in arithmetic!

PARRIS: Mr. Corey, you will look far for a man of my
kind at sixty pound a year! I am not used to this poverty; I
left a thrifty business in the Barbados to serve the Lord. I
do not fathom it, why am I persecuted here? I cannot offer

one proposition but there be a howling riot of argument. I have often wondered if the Devil be in it somewhere; I cannot understand you people otherwise.

PROCTOR: Mr. Parris, you are the first minister ever did demand the deed to this house—

PARRIS: Man! Don't a minister deserve a house to live in?

PROCTOR: To live in, yes. But to ask ownership is like you shall own the meeting house itself; the last meeting I were at you spoke so long on deeds and mortgages I thought it were an auction.

PARRIS: I want a mark of confidence, is all! I am your third preacher in seven years. I do not wish to be put out like the cat whenever some majority feels the whim. You people seem not to comprehend that a minister is the Lord's man in the parish; a minister is not to be so lightly crossed and contradicted—

PUTNAM: Aye!

PARRIS: There is either obedience or the church will burn like Hell is burning!

PROCTOR: Can you speak one minute without we land in Hell again? I am sick of Hell!

PARRIS: It is not for you to say what is good for you to hear!

PROCTOR: I may speak my heart, I think!

PARRIS (*in a fury*): What, are we Quakers? We are not Quakers here yet, Mr. Proctor. And you may tell that to your followers!

PROCTOR: My followers!

PARRIS (*Now he's out with it.*): There is a party in this church. I am not blind; there is a faction and a party.

PROCTOR: Against you?

PUTNAM: Against him and all authority!

PROCTOR: Why, then I must find it and join it.

(*There is shock among the others.*)

REBECCA: He does not mean that.

PUTNAM: He confessed it now!

PROCTOR: I mean it solemnly, Rebecca; I like not the smell of this "authority."

REBECCA: No, you cannot break charity with your minister. You are another kind, John. Clasp his hand, make your peace.

PROCTOR: I have a crop to sow and lumber to drag home. (*He goes angrily to the door and turns to* COREY *with a smile.*) What say you, Giles, let's find the party. He says there's a party.

GILES: I've changed my opinion of this man, John. Mr. Parris, I beg your pardon. I never thought you had so much iron in you.

PARRIS (*surprised*): Why, thank you, Giles!

GILES: It suggests to the mind what the trouble be among us all these years. (*to all*) Think on it. Wherefore is everybody suing everybody else? Think on it now, it's a deep thing, and dark as a pit. I have been six time in court this year—

PROCTOR (*familiarly, with warmth, although he knows he is approaching the edge of* GILES' *tolerance with this*): Is it the Devil's fault that a man cannot say you good morning without you clap him for defamation? You're old, Giles, and you're not hearin' so well as you did.

GILES (*He cannot be crossed.*): John Proctor, I have only last month collected four pound damages for you publicly sayin' I burned the roof off your house, and I—

PROCTOR (*laughing*): I never said no such thing, but I've paid you for it, so I hope I can call you deaf without charge. Now come along, Giles, and help me drag my lumber home.

PUTNAM: A moment, Mr. Proctor. What lumber is that you're draggin', if I may ask you?

PROCTOR: My lumber. From out my forest by the riverside.

PUTNAM: Why, we are surely gone wild this year. What anarchy is this? That tract is in my bounds, it's in my bounds, Mr. Proctor.

PROCTOR: In your bounds! (*indicating* REBECCA) I bought that tract from Goody Nurse's husband five months ago.

PUTNAM: He had no right to sell it. It stands clear in my grandfather's will that all the land between the river and—

PROCTOR: Your grandfather had a habit of willing land that never belonged to him, if I may say it plain.

GILES: That's God's truth; he nearly willed away my north pasture but he knew I'd break his fingers before he'd set his name to it. Let's get your lumber home, John. I feel a sudden will to work coming on.

PUTNAM: You load one oak of mine and you'll fight to drag it home!

GILES: Aye, and we'll win too, Putnam—this fool and I. Come on! (*He turns to* PROCTOR *and starts out.*)

PUTNAM: I'll have my men on you, Corey! I'll clap a writ on you!

(*Enter* REVEREND JOHN HALE *of Beverly*.

MR. HALE is nearing forty, a tight-skinned, eager-eyed intellectual. This is a beloved errand for him; on being called here to ascertain witchcraft he felt the pride of the specialist whose unique knowledge has at last been publicly called for. Like almost all men of learning, he spent a good deal of his time pondering the invisible world, especially since he had himself encountered a witch in his parish not long before. That woman, however, turned into a mere pest under his searching scrutiny, and the child she had allegedly been afflicting recovered her normal behavior after HALE had given her his kindness and a few days of rest in his own house. However, that experience never raised a doubt in his mind as to the reality of the underworld or the existence of Lucifer's many-faced lieutenants. And his belief is not to his discredit. Better minds than Hale's were—and still are—convinced that there is a society of spirits beyond our ken. One cannot help noting that one of his lines has never yet raised a laugh in any audience that has seen this play; it is his assurance that "We cannot look to superstition in this. The Devil is precise." Evidently we are not quite certain even now whether diabolism is holy and not to be scoffed at. And it is no accident that we should be so bemused.

Like REVEREND HALE and the others on this stage, we conceive the Devil as a necessary part of a respectable view of cosmology. Ours is a divided empire in which certain ideas and emotions and actions are of God, and their opposites are of Lucifer. It is as impossible for most men to conceive of a morality without sin as of an earth without "sky." Since 1692 a great but superficial change has wiped out God's beard and the Devil's horns, but the world is still gripped between two diametrically opposed absolutes. The concept of unity, in which positive and negative are attributes of the same force, in which good and evil are relative, ever-changing, and always joined to the same phenomenon—such a concept is still reserved to the physical sciences and to the few who have grasped the history of ideas. When it is recalled that until the Christian era the underworld was never regarded as a hostile area, that all gods were useful and essentially friendly to man despite occasional lapses; when we see the steady and methodical inculcation into humanity of the idea of man's worthlessness—until redeemed—the necessity of the Devil may become evident as a weapon, a weapon designed and used time and time again in every age to whip men into a surrender to a particular church or church-state.

Our difficulty in believing the—for want of a better word—political inspiration of the Devil is due in great part to the fact that he is called up and damned not only by our social antagonists but by our own side, whatever it may be. The Catholic Church, through its Inquisition, is famous for cultivating Lucifer as the arch-fiend, but the Church's enemies relied no less upon the Old Boy to keep the human mind enthralled. Luther was himself accused of alliance with Hell, and he in turn accused his enemies. To complicate matters further, he believed that he had had contact with the Devil and had argued theology with him. I am not surprised at this, for at my own university a professor of history—a Lutheran, by the way—used to assemble his graduate students, draw the shades, and commune in the classroom with Erasmus. He was never, to my knowledge, officially scoffed at for this, the reason being that the university officials, like most of us, are the children of a history which still sucks at the Devil's teats. At this writing, only England has held back before the temptations of contemporary diabolism. In the countries of the Communist ideology, all resistance of any import is linked to the totally malign capitalist succubi, and in America any man who is not reactionary in his views is open to the charge of alliance with the Red hell. Political opposition, thereby, is given an inhumane overlay which then justifies the abrogation of all normally applied customs of civilized intercourse. A political policy is equated with moral right, and opposition to it with diabolical malevolence. Once such an equation is effectively made, society becomes a congeries of plots and counterplots, and the main role of government changes from that of the arbiter to that of the scourge of God.

The results of this process are no different now from what they ever were, except sometimes in the degree of cruelty inflicted, and not always even in that department. Normally the actions and deeds of a man were all that society felt comfortable in judging. The secret intent of an action was left to the ministers, priests, and rabbis to deal with. When diabolism rises, however, actions are the least important manifests of the true nature of a man. The Devil, as REVEREND HALE said, is a wily one, and until an hour before he fell, even God thought him beautiful in Heaven.

The analogy, however, seems to falter when one considers that, while there were no witches then, there are Communists and capitalists now, and in each camp there is certain proof that spies of each side are at work undermining the other. But this is a snobbish objection and not

at all warranted by the facts. I have no doubt that people
were communing with, and even worshiping, the Devil in
Salem, and if the whole truth could be known in this case,
as it is in others, we should discover a regular and con-
ventionalized propitiation of the dark spirit. One certain
evidence of this is the confession of TITUBA, the slave of
REVEREND PARRIS, and another is the behavior of the children who were known to have indulged in sorceries with
her.

There are accounts of similar *klatches* in Europe, where
the daughters of the towns would assemble at night and,
sometimes with fetishes, sometimes with a selected young
man, give themselves to love, with some bastardly results.
The Church, sharp-eyed as it must be when gods long
dead are brought to life, condemned these orgies as witchcraft and interpreted them, rightly, as a resurgence of the
Dionysiac forces it had crushed long before. Sex, sin, and
the Devil were early linked, and so they continued to be
in Salem, and are today. From all accounts there are no
more puritanical mores in the world than those enforced
by the Communists in Russia, where women's fashions,
for instance, are as prudent and all-covering as any American Baptist would desire. The divorce laws lay a tremendous responsibility on the father for the care of his children. Even the laxity of divorce regulations in the early
years of the revolution was undoubtedly a revulsion from
the nineteenth-century Victorian immobility of marriage
and the consequent hypocrisy that developed from it. If
for no other reasons, a state so powerful, so jealous of the
uniformity of its citizens, cannot long tolerate the atomiza-
tion of the family. And yet, in American eyes at least,
there remains the conviction that the Russian attitude toward women is lascivious. It is the Devil working again,
just as he is working within the Slav who is shocked at the
very idea of a woman's disrobing herself in a burlesque
show. Our opposites are always robed in sexual sin, and
it is from this unconscious conviction that demonology
gains both its attractive sensuality and its capacity to in-
furiate and frighten.

Coming into Salem now, REVEREND HALE conceives of
himself much as a young doctor on his first call. His painfully acquired armory of symptoms, catchwords, and diag-
nostic procedures are now to be put to use at last. The
road from Beverly is unusually busy this morning, and he
has passed a hundred rumors that make him smile at the

ignorance of the yeomanry in this most precise science. He feels himself allied with the best minds of Europe—kings, philosophers, scientists, and ecclesiasts of all churches. His goal is light, goodness and its preservation, and he knows the exaltation of the blessed whose intelligence, sharpened by minute examinations of enormous tracts, is finally called upon to face what may be a bloody fight with the Fiend himself.

(*He appears loaded down with half a dozen heavy books.*)

HALE: Pray you, someone take these!

PARRIS (*delighted*): Mr. Hale! Oh! it's good to see you again! (*taking some books*) My, they're heavy!

HALE (*setting down his books*): They must be; they are weighted with authority.

PARRIS (*a little scared*): Well, you do come prepared!

HALE: We shall need hard study if it comes to tracking down the Old Boy. (*noticing* REBECCA) You cannot be Rebecca Nurse?

REBECCA: I am, sir. Do you know me?

HALE: It's strange how I knew you, but I suppose you look as such a good soul should. We have all heard of your great charities in Beverly.

PARRIS: Do you know this gentleman? Mr. Thomas Putnam. And his good wife Ann.

HALE: Putnam! I had not expected such distinguished company, sir.

PUTNAM (*pleased*): It does not seem to help us today, Mr. Hale. We look to you to come to our house and save our child.

HALE: Your child ails too?

MRS. PUTNAM: Her soul, her soul seems flown away. She sleeps and yet she walks . . .

PUTNAM: She cannot eat.

HALE: Cannot eat! (*thinks on it; then, to* PROCTOR *and* GILES COREY) Do you men have afflicted children?

PARRIS: No, no, these are farmers. John Proctor—

GILES COREY: He don't believe in witches.

PROCTOR (*to* HALE): I never spoke on witches one way or the other. Will you come, Giles?

GILES: No—no, John, I think not. I have some few queer questions of my own to ask this fellow.

PROCTOR: I've heard you to be a sensible man, Mr. Hale. I hope you'll leave some of it in Salem.

(PROCTOR *goes.* HALE *stands embarrassed for an instant.*)

PARRIS (*quickly*): Will you look at my daughter, sir? (*leads* HALE *to the bed*) She has tried to leap out the window; we discovered her this morning on the highroad, waving her arms as though she'd fly.

HALE (*narrowing his eyes*): Tries to fly.

PUTNAM: She cannot bear to hear the Lord's name, Mr. Hale; that's a sure sign of witchcraft afloat.

HALE (*holding up his hands*): No, no. Now let me instruct you. We cannot look to superstition in this. The Devil is precise; the marks of his presence are definite as stone, and I must tell you all that I shall not proceed unless you are prepared to believe me if I should find no bruise of hell upon her.

PARRIS: It is agreed, sir—it is agreed—we will abide by your judgment.

HALE: Good then. (*He goes to the bed, looks down at* BETTY. *To* PARRIS) Now, sir, what were your first warnings of this strangeness?

PARRIS: Why, sir—I discovered her (*indicating* ABIGAIL) and my niece and ten or twelve of the other girls, dancing in the forest last night.

HALE (*surprised*): You permit dancing?

PARRIS: No, no, it were secret—

MRS. PUTNAM (*unable to wait*): Mr. Parris's slave has knowledge of conjurin', sir.

PARRIS (*to* MRS. PUTNAM): We cannot be sure of that, Goody Ann—

MRS. PUTNAM (*frightened, very softly*): I know it, sir. I sent my child—she should learn from Tituba who murdered her sisters.

REBECCA (*horrified*): Goody Ann! You sent a child to conjure up the dead?

MRS. PUTNAM: Let God blame me, not you, not you, Rebecca! I'll not have you judging me any more! (*to* HALE) Is it natural work to lose seven children before they live a day?

PARRIS: Sssh!

(REBECCA, *with great pain, turns her face away. There is a pause.*)

HALE: Seven dead in childbirth.

MRS. PUTNAM (*softly*): Aye. (*Her voice breaks; she looks up at him. Silence.* HALE *is impressed.* PARRIS *looks to him. He goes to his books, opens one, turns pages, then reads. All wait, avidly.*)

PARRIS (*hushed*): What book is that?

MRS. PUTNAM: What's there, sir?

HALE (*with a tasty love of intellectual pursuit*): Here is all the invisible world, caught, defined, and calculated. In these books the Devil stands stripped of all his brute disguises. Here are all your familiar spirits—your incubi and succubi; your witches that go by land, by air, and by sea; your wizards of the night and of the day. Have no fear now—we shall find him out if he has come among us, and I mean to crush him utterly if he has shown his face! (*He starts for the bed.*)

REBECCA: Will it hurt the child, sir?

HALE: I cannot tell. If she is truly in the Devil's grip we may have to rip and tear to get her free.

REBECCA: I think I'll go, then. I am too old for this. (*She rises.*)

PARRIS (*striving for conviction*): Why, Rebecca, we may open up the boil of all our troubles today!

REBECCA: Let us hope for that. I go to God for you, sir.

PARRIS (*with trepidation—and resentment*): I hope you do not mean to go to Satan here! (*Slight pause.*)

REBECCA: I wish I knew.

(*She goes out; they feel resentful of her note of moral superiority.*)

PUTNAM (*abruptly*): Come, Mr. Hale, let's get on. Sit you here.

GILES: Mr. Hale, I have always wanted to ask a learned man—what signifies the readin' of strange books?

HALE: What books?

GILES: I cannot tell; she hides them.

HALE: Who does this?

GILES: Martha, my wife. I have waked at night many a time and found her in a corner, readin' of a book. Now what do you make of that?

HALE: Why, that's not necessarily—

GILES: It discomfits me! Last night—mark this—I tried and tried and could not say my prayers. And then she closes her book and walks out of the house, and suddenly —mark this—I could pray again!

(Old GILES must be spoken for, if only because his fate was to be so remarkable and so different from that of all the others. He was in his early eighties at this time, and was the most comical hero in the history. No man has ever been blamed for so much. If a cow was missed, the first thought was to look for her around COREY'S house; a fire blazing up at night brought suspicion of arson to his door. He didn't give a hoot for public opinion, and only in his last years—after he had married MARTHA—did he bother much with the church. That she stopped his prayer is very probable, but he forgot to say that he'd only recently learned any prayers and it didn't take much to make him stumble over them. He was a crank and a nuisance, but withal a deeply innocent and brave man. In court, once, he was asked if it were true that he had been frightened by the strange behavior of a hog and had then said he knew it to be the Devil in an animal's shape. "What frighted you?" he was asked. He forgot everything but the word "frighted," and instantly replied, "I do not know that I ever spoke that word in my life.")

HALE: Ah! The stoppage of prayer—that is strange. I'll speak further on that with you.

GILES: I'm not sayin' she's touched the Devil, now, but I'd admire to know what books she reads and why she hides them. She'll not answer me, y'see.

HALE: Aye, we'll discuss it. (*to all*) Now mark me, if the Devil is in her you will witness some frightful wonders in this room, so please to keep your wits about you. Mr. Putnam, stand close in case she flies. Now, Betty, dear, will you sit up? (PUTNAM *comes in closer, ready-handed.* HALE *sits* BETTY *up, but she hangs limp in his hands.*) Hmmm. (*He observes her carefully. The others watch breathlessly.*) Can you hear me? I am John Hale, minister of Beverly. I have come to help you, dear. Do you remember my two little girls in Beverly? (*She does not stir in his hands.*)

PARRIS (*in fright*): How can it be the Devil? Why would he choose my house to strike? We have all manner of licentious people in the village!

HALE: What victory would the Devil have to win a soul already bad? It is the best the Devil wants, and who is better than the minister?

GILES: That's deep, Mr. Parris, deep, deep!

PARRIS (*with resolution now*): Betty! Answer Mr. Hale! Betty!

HALE: Does someone afflict you, child? It need not be a woman, mind you, or a man. Perhaps some bird invisible to others comes to you—perhaps a pig, a mouse, or any beast at all. Is there some figure bids you fly? (*The child remains limp in his hands. In silence he lays her back on the pillow. Now, holding out his hands toward her, he intones.*) In nomine Domini Sabaoth sui filique ite ad infernos. (*She does not stir. He turns to Abigail, his eyes narrowing.*) Abigail, what sort of dancing were you doing with her in the forest?

ABIGAIL: Why—common dancing is all.

PARRIS: I think I ought to say that I—I saw a kettle in the grass where they were dancing.

ABIGAIL: That were only soup.

HALE: What sort of soup were in this kettle, Abigail?

ABIGAIL: Why, it were beans—and lentils, I think, and—

HALE: Mr. Parris, you did not notice, did you, any living thing in the kettle? A mouse, perhaps, a spider, a frog—?

PARRIS (*fearfully*): I—do believe there were some movement—in the soup.

ABIGAIL: That jumped in, we never put it in!

HALE (*quickly*): What jumped in?

ABIGAIL: Why, a very little frog jumped—

PARRIS: A frog, Abby!

HALE (*grasping Abigail*): Abigail, it may be your cousin is dying. Did you call the Devil last night?

ABIGAIL: I never called him! Tituba, Tituba . . .

PARRIS (*blanched*): She called the Devil?

HALE: I should like to speak with Tituba.

PARRIS: Goody Ann, will you bring her up? (MRS. PUTNAM *exits.*)

HALE: How did she call him?

ABIGAIL: I know not—she spoke Barbados.

HALE: Did you feel any strangeness when she called him? A sudden cold wind, perhaps? A trembling below the ground?

ABIGAIL: I didn't see no Devil! (*shaking* BETTY) Betty, wake up. Betty! Betty!

HALE: You cannot evade me, Abigail. Did your cousin drink any of the brew in that kettle?

ABIGAIL: She never drank it!

HALE: Did you drink it?

ABIGAIL: No, sir!

HALE: Did Tituba ask you to drink it?

ABIGAIL: She tried, but I refused.

HALE: Why are you concealing? Have you sold yourself to Lucifer?

ABIGAIL: I never sold myself! I'm a good girl! I'm a proper girl!

(MRS. PUTNAM *enters with* TITUBA, *and instantly* ABIGAIL *points at* TITUBA.)

ABIGAIL: She made me do it! She made Betty do it!

TITUBA (*shocked and angry*): Abby!

ABIGAIL: She makes me drink blood!

PARRIS: Blood!!

MRS. PUTNAM: My baby's blood?

TITUBA: No, no, chicken blood. I give she chicken blood!

HALE: Woman, have you enlisted these children for the Devil?

TITUBA: No, no, sir, I don't truck with no Devil!

HALE: Why can she not wake? Are you silencing this child?

TITUBA: I love me Betty!

HALE: You have sent your spirit out upon this child, have you not? Are you gathering souls for the Devil?

ABIGAIL: She sends her spirit on me in church; she makes me laugh at prayer!

PARRIS: She have often laughed at prayer!

ABIGAIL: She comes to me every night to go and drink blood!

TITUBA: You beg *me* to conjure! She beg *me* make charm—

ABIGAIL: Don't lie! (*to* HALE) She comes to me while I sleep; she's always making me dream corruptions!

TITUBA: Why you say that, Abby?

ABIGAIL: Sometimes I wake and find myself standing in the open doorway and not a stitch on my body! I always hear her laughing in my sleep. I hear her singing her Barbados songs and tempting me with—

TITUBA: Mister Reverend, I never—

HALE (*resolved now*): Tituba, I want you to wake this child.

TITUBA: I have no power on this child, sir.

HALE: You most certainly do, and you will free her from it now! When did you compact with the Devil?

TITUBA: I don't compact with no Devil!

PARRIS: You will confess yourself or I will take you out and whip you to your death, Tituba!

PUTNAM: This woman must be hanged! She must be taken and hanged!

TITUBA (*terrified, falls to her knees*): No, no, don't hang Tituba! I tell him I don't desire to work for him, sir.

PARRIS: The Devil?

HALE: Then you saw him! (TITUBA *weeps.*) Now Tituba, I

know that when we bind ourselves to Hell it is very hard to break with it. We are going to help you tear yourself free—

TITUBA (*frightened by the coming process*): Mister Reverend, I do believe somebody else be witchin' these children.

HALE: Who?

TITUBA: I don't know, sir, but the Devil got him numerous witches.

HALE: Does he! *It is a clue.* Tituba, look into my eyes. Come, look into me. (*She raises her eyes to his fearfully.*) You would be a good Christian woman, would you not, Tituba?

TITUBA: Aye, sir, a good Christian woman.

HALE: And you love these little children?

TITUBA: Oh, yes, sir, I don't desire to hurt little children.

HALE: And you love God, Tituba?

TITUBA: I love God with all my bein'.

HALE: Now, in God's holy name—

TITUBA: Bless Him. Bless Him. (*She is rocking on her knees, sobbing in terror.*)

HALE: And to His glory—

TITUBA: Eternal glory. Bless Him—bless God . . .

HALE: Open yourself, Tituba—open yourself and let God's holy light shine on you.

TITUBA: Oh, bless the Lord.

HALE: When the Devil comes to you does he ever come —with another person? (*She stares up into his face.*) Perhaps another person in the village? Someone you know.

PARRIS: Who came with him?

PUTNAM: Sarah Good? Did you ever see Sarah Good with him? Or Osburn?

PARRIS: Was it man or woman came with him?

TITUBA: Man or woman. Was—was woman.

PARRIS: What woman? A woman, you said. What woman?

TITUBA: It was black dark, and I—

PARRIS: You could see him, why could you not see her?

TITUBA: Well, they was always talking; they was always runnin' round and carryin' on—

PARRIS: You mean out of Salem? Salem witches?

TITUBA: I believe so, yes, sir.

(*Now* HALE *takes her hand. She is surprised.*)

HALE: Tituba. You must have no fear to tell us who they are, do you understand? We will protect you. The Devil can never overcome a minister. You know that, do you not?

TITUBA (*kisses* HALE's *hand*): Aye, sir, oh, I do.

HALE: You have confessed yourself to witchcraft, and that speaks a wish to come to Heaven's side. And we will bless you, Tituba.

TITUBA (*deeply relieved*): Oh, God bless you, Mr. Hale!

HALE (*with rising exaltation*): You are God's instrument put in our hands to discover the Devil's agent among us. You are selected, Tituba, you are chosen to help us cleanse our village. So speak utterly, Tituba, turn your back on him and face God—face God, Tituba, and God will protect you.

TITUBA (*joining with him*): Oh, God, protect Tituba!

HALE (*kindly*): Who came to you with the Devil? Two? Three? Four? How many?

(TITUBA *pants, and begins rocking back and forth again, staring ahead.*)

TITUBA: There was four. There was four.

PARRIS (*pressing in on her*): Who? Who? Their names, their names!

TITUBA (*suddenly bursting out*): Oh, how many times he bid me kill you, Mr. Parris!

PARRIS: Kill me!

TITUBA (*in a fury*): He say Mr. Parris must be kill! Mr. Parris no goodly man, Mr. Parris mean man and no gentle man, and he bid me rise out of my bed and cut your throat! (*They gasp.*) But I tell him "No! I don't hate that man. I don't want kill that man." But he say, "You work for me, Tituba, and I make you free! I give you pretty dress to wear, and put you way high up in the air, and you gone fly back to Barbados!" And I say, "You lie, Devil, you lie!" And then he come one stormy night to me, and he say, "Look! I have *white* people belong to me." And I look—and there was Goody Good.

PARRIS: Sarah Good!

TITUBA (*rocking and weeping*): Aye, sir, and Goody Osburn.

MRS. PUTNAM: I knew it! Goody Osburn were midwife to me three times. I begged you, Thomas, did I not? I begged him not to call Osburn because I feared her. My babies always shriveled in her hands!

HALE: Take courage, you must give us all their names. How can you bear to see this child suffering? Look at her, Tituba. (*He is indicating* BETTY *on the bed.*) Look at her God-given innocence; her soul is so tender; we must protect her, Tituba; the Devil is out and preying on her like a beast upon the flesh of the pure lamb. God will bless you for your help.

(*Abigail rises, staring as though inspired, and cries out.*)

ABIGAIL: I want to open myself! (*They turn to her, startled. She is enraptured, as though in a pearly light.*) I want the light of God, I want the sweet love of Jesus! I danced for the Devil; I saw him; I wrote in his book; I go back to Jesus; I kiss His hand. I saw Sarah Good with the Devil! I saw Goody Osburn with the Devil! I saw Bridget Bishop with the Devil!

(*As she is speaking,* BETTY *is rising from the bed, a fever in her eyes, and picks up the chant.*)

BETTY (*staring too*): I saw George Jacobs with the Devil! I saw Goody Howe with the Devil!

PARRIS: She speaks! (*He rushes to embrace* BETTY.) She speaks!

HALE: Glory to God! It is broken, they are free!

BETTY (*calling out hysterically and with great relief*): I saw Martha Bellows with the Devil!

ABIGAIL: I saw Goody Sibber with the Devil! (*It is rising to a great glee.*)

PUTNAM: The marshal, I'll call the marshal!

(PARRIS *is shouting a prayer of thanksgiving.*)

BETTY: I saw Alice Barrow with the Devil!

(*The curtain begins to fall.*)

HALE (*as* PUTNAM *goes out*): Let the marshal bring irons!

ABIGAIL: I saw Goody Hawkins with the Devil!

BETTY: I saw Goody Bibber with the Devil!

ABIGAIL: I saw Goody Booth with the Devil!

(*On their ecstatic cries the curtain falls.*)

ACT II

(*The common room of* PROCTOR'S *house, eight days later.*

At the right is a door opening on the fields outside. A fireplace is at the left, and behind it a stairway leading upstairs. It is the low, dark, and rather long living room of the time. As the curtain rises, the room is empty. From above, ELIZABETH *is heard softly singing to the children.*

Presently the door opens and JOHN PROCTOR *enters, carrying his gun. He glances about the room as he comes toward the fireplace, then halts for an instant as he hears her singing. He continues on to the fireplace, leans the gun against the wall as he swings a pot out of the fire and smells it. Then he lifts out the ladle and tastes. He is not quite pleased. He reaches to a cupboard, takes a pinch of salt, and drops it into the pot. As he is tasting again, her footsteps are heard on the stair. He swings the pot into the fireplace and goes to a basin and washes his hands and face.* ELIZABETH *enters.*)

ELIZABETH: What keeps you so late? It's almost dark.

PROCTOR: I were planting far out to the forest edge.

ELIZABETH: Oh, you're done then.

PROCTOR: Aye, the farm is seeded. The boys asleep?

ELIZABETH: They will be soon. (*And she goes to the fireplace, proceeds to ladle up stew in a dish.*)

PROCTOR: Pray now for a fair summer.

ELIZABETH: Aye.

PROCTOR: Are you well today?

ELIZABETH: I am. (*She brings the plate to the table, and, indicating the food.*) It is a rabbit.

PROCTOR (*going to the table*): Oh, is it! In Jonathan's trap?

ELIZABETH: No, she walked into the house this afternoon; I found her sittin' in the corner like she come to visit.

PROCTOR: Oh, that's a good sign walkin' in.

ELIZABETH: Pray God. It hurt my heart to strip her, poor rabbit. (*She sits and watches him taste it.*)

PROCTOR: It's well seasoned.

ELIZABETH (*blushing with pleasure*): I took great care. She's tender?

PROCTOR: Aye. (*He eats. She watches him.*) I think we'll see green fields soon. It's warm as blood beneath the clods.

ELIZABETH: That's well.

(PROCTOR *eats, then looks up.*)

PROCTOR: If the crop is good I'll buy George Jacobs' heifer. How would that please you?

ELIZABETH: Aye, it would.

PROCTOR (*with a grin*): I mean to please you, Elizabeth.

ELIZABETH (*It is hard to say.*): I know it, John.

(*He gets up, goes to her, kisses her. She receives it. With a certain disappointment, he returns to the table.*)

PROCTOR (*as gently as he can*): Cider?

ELIZABETH (*with a sense of reprimanding herself for having forgot*): Aye! (*She gets up and goes and pours a glass for him. He now arches his back.*)

PROCTOR: This farm's a continent when you go foot by foot droppin' seeds in it.

ELIZABETH (*coming with the cider*): It must be.

PROCTOR (*drinks a long draught, then, putting the glass down*): You ought to bring some flowers in the house.

ELIZABETH: Oh! I forgot! I will tomorrow.

PROCTOR: It's winter in here yet. On Sunday let you come with me, and we'll walk the farm together; I never see such a load of flowers on the earth. (*With good feeling he goes and looks up at the sky through the open doorway.*) Lilacs have a purple smell. Lilac is the smell of nightfall, I think. Massachusetts is a beauty in the spring!

ELIZABETH: Aye, it is.

(*There is a pause. She is watching him from the table as he stands there absorbing the night. It is as though she would speak but cannot. Instead, now, she takes up his plate and glass and fork and goes with them to the basin. Her back is turned to him. He turns to her and watches her. A sense of their separation rises.*)

PROCTOR: I think you're sad again. Are you?

ELIZABETH (*She doesn't want friction, and yet she must.*): You come so late I thought you'd gone to Salem this afternoon.

PROCTOR: Why? I have no business in Salem.

ELIZABETH: You did speak of going, earlier this week.

PROCTOR (*He knows what she means.*): I thought better of it since.

ELIZABETH: Mary Warren's there today.

PROCTOR: Why'd you let her? You heard me forbid her go to Salem any more!

ELIZABETH: I couldn't stop her.

PROCTOR (*holding back a full condemnation of her*): It is a fault, it is a fault, Elizabeth—you're the mistress here, not Mary Warren.

ELIZABETH: She frightened all my strength away.

PROCTOR: How may that mouse frighten you, Elizabeth? You—

ELIZABETH: It is a mouse no more. I forbid her go, and she raises up her chin like the daughter of a prince and says to me, "I must go to Salem, Goody Proctor; I am an official of the court!"

PROCTOR: Court! What court?

ELIZABETH: Aye, it is a proper court they have now. They've sent four judges out of Boston, she says, weighty magistrates of the General Court, and at the head sits the Deputy Governor of the Province.

PROCTOR (*astonished*): Why, she's mad.

ELIZABETH: I would to God she were. There be fourteen people in the jail now, she says. (PROCTOR *simply looks at her, unable to grasp it.*) And they'll be tried, and the court have power to hang them too, she says.

PROCTOR (*scoffing, but without conviction*): Ah, they'd never hang—

ELIZABETH: The Deputy Governor promise hangin' if they'll not confess, John. The town's gone wild, I think. She speak of Abigail, and I thought she were a saint, to hear her. Abigail brings the other girls into the court, and where she walks the crowd will part like the sea for Israel, and folks are brought before them, and if they scream and howl and fall to the floor—the person's clapped in the jail for bewitchin' them.

PROCTOR (*wide-eyed*): Oh, it is a black mischief.

ELIZABETH: I think you must go to Salem, John. (*He turns to her.*) I think so. You must tell them it is a fraud.

PROCTOR (*thinking beyond this*): Aye, it is, it is surely.

ELIZABETH: Let you go to Ezekiel Cheever—he knows you well. And tell him what she said to you last week in her uncle's house. She said it had naught to do with witchcraft, did she not?

PROCTOR (*in thought*): Aye, she did, she did. (*now, a pause*)

ELIZABETH (*quietly, fearing to anger him by prodding*): God forbid you keep that from the court, John. I think they must be told.

PROCTOR (*quietly, struggling with his thought*): Aye, they must, they must. It is a wonder they do believe her.

ELIZABETH: I would go to Salem now, John—let you go tonight.

PROCTOR: I'll think on it.

ELIZABETH (*with her courage now*): You cannot keep it, John.

PROCTOR (*angering*): I know I cannot keep it. I say I will think on it!

ELIZABETH (*hurt, and very coldly*): Good, then, let you think on it. (*She stands and starts to walk out of the room.*)

PROCTOR: I am only wondering how I may prove what she told me, Elizabeth. If the girl's a saint now, I think it is not easy to prove she's fraud, and the town gone so silly. She told it to me in a room alone—I have no proof for it.

ELIZABETH: You were alone with her?

PROCTOR (*stubbornly*): For a moment alone, aye.

ELIZABETH: Why, then, it is not as you told me.

PROCTOR (*his anger rising*): For a moment, I say. The others come in soon after.

ELIZABETH (*quietly—she has suddenly lost all faith in him*): Do as you wish, then. (*She starts to turn.*)

PROCTOR: Woman. (*She turns to him.*) I'll not have your suspicion any more.

ELIZABETH (*a little loftily*): I have no—

PROCTOR: I'll not have it!

ELIZABETH: Then let you not earn it.

PROCTOR (*with a violent undertone*): You doubt me yet?

ELIZABETH (*with a smile, to keep her dignity*): John, if it were not Abigail that you must go to hurt, would you falter now? I think not.

PROCTOR: Now look you—

ELIZABETH: I see what I see, John.

PROCTOR (*with solemn warning*): You will not judge me more, Elizabeth. I have good reason to think before I charge fraud on Abigail, and I will think on it. Let you look to your own improvement before you go to judge your husband any more. I have forgot Abigail, and—

ELIZABETH: And I.

PROCTOR: Spare me! You forget nothin' and forgive nothin'. Learn charity, woman. I have gone tiptoe in this house all seven month since she is gone. I have not moved from there to there without I think to please you, and still an everlasting funeral marches round your heart. I cannot speak but I am doubted, every moment judged for lies, as though I come into a court when I come into this house!

ELIZABETH: John, you are not open with me. You saw her with a crowd, you said. Now you—

PROCTOR: I'll plead my honesty no more, Elizabeth.

ELIZABETH (*Now she would justify herself.*): John, I am only—

PROCTOR: No more! I should have roared you down when first you told me your suspicion. But I wilted, and, like a Christian, I confessed. Confessed! Some dream I had must have mistaken you for God that day. But you're not,

you're not, and let you remember it! Let you look sometimes for the goodness in me, and judge me not.

ELIZABETH: I do not judge you. The magistrate sits in
your heart that judges you. I never thought you but a good
man, John (*with a smile*) only somewhat bewildered.

PROCTOR (*laughing bitterly*): Oh, Elizabeth, your justice
would freeze beer! (*He turns suddenly toward a sound
outside. He starts for the door as* MARY WARREN *enters.
As soon as he sees her, he goes directly to her and grabs
her by the cloak, furious.*) How do you go to Salem when
I forbid it? Do you mock me? (*shaking her*) I'll whip you
if you dare leave this house again!

(*Strangely, she doesn't resist him, but hangs limply by
his grip.*)

MARY WARREN: I am sick, I am sick, Mr. Proctor. Pray,
pray, hurt me not. (*Her strangeness throws him off, and her
evident pallor and weakness. He frees her.*) My insides are
all shuddery; I am in the proceedings all day, sir.

PROCTOR (*with draining anger—his curiosity is draining
it*): And what of these proceedings here? When will you
proceed to keep this house, as you are paid nine pound a
year to do—and my wife not wholly well?

(*As though to compensate,* MARY WARREN *goes to* ELIZA-
BETH *with a small rag doll.*)

MARY WARREN: I made a gift for you today, Goody Proctor. I had to sit long hours in a chair, and passed the time
with sewing.

ELIZABETH (*perplexed, looking at the doll*): Why, thank
you, it's a fair poppet.

MARY WARREN (*with a trembling, decayed voice*): We
must all love each other now, Goody Proctor.

ELIZABETH (*amazed at her strangeness*): Aye, indeed we
must.

MARY WARREN (*glancing at the room*): I'll get up early
in the morning and clean the house. I must sleep now.
(*She turns and starts off.*)

PROCTOR: Mary. (*She halts.*) Is it true? There be fourteen
women arrested?

MARY WARREN: No, sir. There be thirty-nine now—(*She
suddenly breaks off and sobs and sits down, exhausted.*)

ELIZABETH: Why, she's weepin'! What ails you, child?

MARY WARREN: Goody Osburn—will hang!

(*There is a shocked pause, while she sobs.*)

PROCTOR: Hang! (*He calls into her face.*) Hang, y'say?

MARY WARREN (*through her weeping*): Aye.

PROCTOR: The Deputy Governor will permit it?

MARY WARREN: He sentenced her. He must. (*to ameliorate it*) But not Sarah Good. For Sarah Good confessed, y'see.

PROCTOR: Confessed! To what?

MARY WARREN: That she (*in horror at the memory*) she sometimes made a compact with Lucifer, and wrote her name in his black book—with her blood—and bound herself to torment Christians till God's thrown down—and we all must worship Hell forevermore.

(*Pause.*)

PROCTOR: But—surely you know what a jabberer she is. Did you tell them that?

MARY WARREN: Mr. Proctor, in open court she near to choked us all to death.

PROCTOR: How, choked you?

MARY WARREN: She sent her spirit out.

ELIZABETH: Oh, Mary, Mary, surely you—

MARY WARREN (*with an indignant edge*): She tried to kill me many times, Goody Proctor!

ELIZABETH: Why, I never heard you mention that before.

MARY WARREN: I never knew it before. I never knew anything before. When she come into the court I say to myself, I must not accuse this woman, for she sleep in ditches, and so very old and poor. But then—then she sit there, denying and denying, and I feel a misty coldness climbin' up my back, and the skin on my skull begin to creep, and I feel a clamp around my neck and I cannot breathe air; and then (*entranced*) I hear a voice, a screamin' voice, and it were my voice—and all at once I remembered everything she done to me!

PROCTOR: Why? What did she do to you?

MARY WARREN (*like one awakened to a marvelous secret insight*): So many time, Mr. Proctor, she come to this very door, beggin' bread and a cup of cider—and mark this: whenever I turned her away empty, she *mumbled*.

ELIZABETH: Mumbled! She may mumble if she's hungry.

MARY WARREN: But *what* does she mumble? You must remember, Goody Proctor. Last month—a Monday, I think—she walked away, and I thought my guts would burst for two days after. Do you remember it?

ELIZABETH: Why—I do, I think, but—

MARY WARREN: And so I told that to Judge Hathorne, and he asks her so. "Goody Osburn," says he, "what curse do you mumble that this girl must fall sick after turning you away?" And then she replies (*mimicking an old crone*), "Why, your excellence, no curse at all. I only say my commandments; I hope I may say my commandments," says she!

ELIZABETH: And that's an upright answer.

MARY WARREN: Aye, but then Judge Hathorne say, "Recite for us your commandments!" (*leaning avidly toward them*) and of all the ten she could not say a single one. She never knew no commandments, and they had her in a flat lie!

PROCTOR: And so condemned her?

MARY WARREN (*now a little strained, seeing his stubborn doubt*): Why, they must when she condemned herself.

PROCTOR: But the proof, the proof!

MARY WARREN (*with greater impatience with him*): I told you the proof. It's hard proof, hard as rock, the judges said.

PROCTOR (*pauses an instant, then*): You will not go to court again, Mary Warren.

MARY WARREN: I must tell you, sir, I will be gone every day now. I am amazed you do not see what weighty work we do.

PROCTOR: What work you do! It's strange work for a Christian girl to hang old women!

MARY WARREN: But, Mr. Proctor, they will not hang them if they confess. Sarah Good will only sit in jail some time (*recalling*) and here's a wonder for you; think on this. Goody Good is pregnant!

ELIZABETH: Pregnant! Are they mad? The woman's near to sixty!

MARY WARREN: They had Doctor Griggs examine her, and she's full to the brim. And smokin' a pipe all these years, and no husband either! But she's safe, thank God, for they'll not hurt the innocent child. But be that not a marvel? You must see it, sir, it's God's work we do. So I'll be gone every day for some time. I'm—I am an official of the court, they say, and I— (*She has been edging toward offstage.*)

PROCTOR: I'll official you! (*He strides to the mantel, takes down the whip hanging there.*)

MARY WARREN (*terrified, but coming erect, striving for her authority*): I'll not stand whipping any more!

ELIZABETH (*hurriedly, as PROCTOR approaches*): Mary, promise you'll stay at home—

MARY WARREN (*backing from him, but keeping her erect posture, striving, striving for her way*): The Devil's loose in Salem, Mr. Proctor; we must discover where he's hiding!

PROCTOR: I'll whip the Devil out of you! (*With whip raised he reaches out for her, and she streaks away and yells.*)

MARY WARREN (*pointing at* ELIZABETH): I saved her life today!

(*Silence. His whip comes down.*)

ELIZABETH (*softly*): I am accused?

MARY WARREN (*quaking*): Somewhat mentioned. But I said I never see no sign you ever sent your spirit out to hurt no one, and seeing I do live so closely with you, they dismissed it.

ELIZABETH: Who accused me?

MARY WARREN: I am bound by law, I cannot tell it. (*to* PROCTOR) I only hope you'll not be so sarcastical no more. Four judges and the King's deputy sat to dinner with us but an hour ago. I—I would have you speak civilly to me, from this out.

PROCTOR (*in horror, muttering in disgust at her*): Go to bed.

MARY WARREN (*with a stamp of her foot*): I'll not be ordered to bed no more, Mr. Proctor! I am eighteen and a woman, however single!

PROCTOR: Do you wish to sit up? Then sit up.

MARY WARREN: I wish to go to bed!

PROCTOR (*in anger*): Good night, then!

MARY WARREN: Good night.

(*Dissatisfied, uncertain of herself, she goes out. Wide-eyed, both,* PROCTOR *and* ELIZABETH *stand staring.*)

ELIZABETH (*quietly*): Oh, the noose, the noose is up!

PROCTOR: There'll be no noose.

ELIZABETH: She wants me dead. I knew all week it would come to this!

PROCTOR (*without conviction*): They dismissed it. You heard her say—

ELIZABETH: And what of tomorrow? She will cry me out until they take me!

PROCTOR: Sit you down.

ELIZABETH: She wants me dead, John, you know it!

PROCTOR: I say sit down! (*She sits, trembling. He speaks quickly, trying to keep his wits.*) Now we must be wise, Elizabeth.

ELIZABETH (*with sarcasm, and a sense of being lost*): Oh, indeed, indeed!

PROCTOR: Fear nothing. I'll find Ezekiel Cheever. I'll tell him she said it were all sport.

ELIZABETH: John, with so many in the jail, more than

Cheever's help is needed now, I think. Would you favor me with this? Go to Abigail.

PROCTOR (*his soul hardening as he senses . . .*): What have I to say to Abigail?

ELIZABETH (*delicately*): John—grant me this. You have a faulty understanding of young girls. There is a promise made in any bed—

PROCTOR (*striving against his anger*): What promise!

ELIZABETH: Spoke or silent, a promise is surely made, And she may dote on it now—I am sure she does—and thinks to kill me, then to take my place.

(PROCTOR'S *anger is rising; he cannot speak.*)

ELIZABETH: It is her dearest hope, John, I know it. There be a thousand names; why does she call mine? There be a certain danger in calling such a name—I am no Goody Good that sleeps in ditches, nor Osburn, drunk and half-witted. She'd dare not call out such a farmer's wife but there be monstrous profit in it. She thinks to take my place, John.

PROCTOR: She cannot think it! (*He knows it is true.*)

ELIZABETH ("*reasonably*"): John, have you ever shown her somewhat of contempt? She cannot pass you in the church but you will blush—

PROCTOR: I may blush for my sin.

ELIZABETH: I think she sees another meaning in that blush.

PROCTOR: And what see you? What see you, Elizabeth?

ELIZABETH ("*conceding*"): I think you be somewhat ashamed, for I am there, and she so close.

PROCTOR: When will you know me, woman? Were I stone I would have cracked for shame this seven month!

ELIZABETH: Then go and tell her she's a whore. Whatever promise she may sense—break it, John, break it.

PROCTOR (*between his teeth*): Good, then. I'll go. (*He starts for his rifle.*)

ELIZABETH (*trembling, fearfully*): Oh, how unwillingly!

PROCTOR (*turning on her, rifle in hand*): I will curse her hotter than the oldest cinder in hell. But pray, begrudge me not my anger!

ELIZABETH: Your anger! I only ask you—

PROCTOR: Woman, am I so base? Do you truly think me base?

ELIZABETH: I never called you base.

PROCTOR: Then how do you charge me with such a promise? The promise that a stallion gives a mare I gave that girl!

ELIZABETH: Then why do you anger with me when I bid you break it?

PROCTOR: Because it speaks deceit, and I am honest! But I'll plead no more! I see now your spirit twists around the single error of my life, and I will never tear it free!

ELIZABETH (*crying out*): You'll tear it free—when you come to know that I will be your only wife, or no wife at all! She has an arrow in you yet, John Proctor, and you know it well!

(*Quite suddenly, as though from the air, a figure appears in the doorway. They start slightly. It is* MR. HALE. *He is different now—drawn a little, and there is a quality of deference, even of guilt, about his manner now.*)

HALE: Good evening.

PROCTOR (*still in his shock*): Why, Mr. Hale! Good evening to you, sir. Come in, come in.

HALE (*to* ELIZABETH): I hope I do not startle you.

ELIZABETH: No, no, it's only that I heard no horse—

HALE: You are Goodwife Proctor.

PROCTOR: Aye; Elizabeth.

HALE (*nods, then*): I hope you're not off to bed yet.

PROCTOR (*setting down his gun*): No, no. (HALE *comes further into the room. And* PROCTOR, *to explain his nervousness*) We are not used to visitors after dark, but you're welcome here. Will you sit you down, sir?

HALE: I will. (*He sits.*) Let you sit, Goodwife Proctor.

(*She does, never letting him out of her sight. There is a pause as* HALE *looks about the room.*)

PROCTOR (*to break the silence*): Will you drink cider, Mr. Hale?

HALE: No, it rebels my stomach; I have some further traveling yet tonight. Sit you down, sir. (PROCTOR *sits.*) I will not keep you long, but I have some business with you.

PROCTOR: Business of the court?

HALE: No—no, I come of my own, without the court's authority. Hear me. (*He wets his lips.*) I know not if you are aware, but your wife's name is—mentioned in the court.

PROCTOR: We know it, sir. Our Mary Warren told us. We are entirely amazed.

HALE: I am a stranger here, as you know. And in my ignorance I find it hard to draw a clear opinion of them that come accused before the court. And so this afternoon, and now tonight, I go from house to house—I come now from Rebecca Nurse's house and—

ELIZABETH (*shocked*): Rebecca's charged!

HALE: God forbid such a one be charged. She is, however —mentioned somewhat.

ELIZABETH (*with an attempt at a laugh*): You will never believe, I hope, that Rebecca trafficked with the Devil.

HALE: Woman, it is possible.

PROCTOR (*taken aback*): Surely you cannot think so.

HALE: This is a strange time, Mister. No man may longer doubt the powers of the dark are gathered in monstrous attack upon this village. There is too much evidence now to deny it. You will agree, sir?

PROCTOR (*evading*): I—have no knowledge in that line. But it's hard to think so pious a woman be secretly a Devil's bitch after seventy year of such good prayer.

HALE: Aye. But the Devil is a wily one, you cannot deny it. However, she is far from accused, and I know she will not be. (*pause*) I thought, sir, to put some questions as to the Christian character of this house, if you'll permit me.

PROCTOR (*coldly, resentful*): Why, we—have no fear of questions, sir.

HALE: Good, then. (*He makes himself more comfortable.*) In the book of record that Mr. Parris keeps, I note that you are rarely in the church on Sabbath Day.

PROCTOR: No, sir, you are mistaken.

HALE: Twenty-six time in seventeen month, sir. I must call that rare. Will you tell me why you are so absent?

PROCTOR: Mr. Hale, I never knew I must account to that man for I come to church or stay at home. My wife were sick this winter.

HALE: So I am told. But you, Mister, why could you not come alone?

PROCTOR: I surely did come when I could, and when I could not I prayed in this house.

HALE: Mr. Proctor, your house is not a church; your theology must tell you that.

PROCTOR: It does, sir, it does; and it tells me that a minister may pray to God without he have golden candlesticks upon the altar.

HALE: What golden candlesticks?

PROCTOR: Since we built the church there were pewter candlesticks upon the altar; Francis Nurse made them, y'know, and a sweeter hand never touched the metal. But Parris came, and for twenty week he preach nothin' but golden candlesticks until he had them. I labor the earth from dawn of day to blink of night, and I tell you true, when I look to heaven and see my money glaring at his elbows—it hurt my prayer, sir, it hurt my prayer. I think, sometimes, the man dreams cathedrals, not clapboard meetin' houses.

HALE (*thinks, then*): And yet, Mister, a Christian on Sabbath Day must be in church. (*pause*) Tell me—you have three children?

PROCTOR: Aye. Boys.

HALE: How comes it that only two are baptized?

PROCTOR (*starts to speak, then stops, then, as though unable to restrain this*): I like it not that Mr. Parris should lay his hand upon my baby. I see no light of God in that man. I'll not conceal it.

HALE: I must say it, Mr. Proctor; that is not for you to decide. The man's ordained, therefore the light of God is in him.

PROCTOR (*flushed with resentment but trying to smile*): What's your suspicion, Mr. Hale?

HALE: No, no, I have no—

PROCTOR: I nailed the roof upon the church, I hung the door—

HALE: Oh, did you! That's a good sign, then.

PROCTOR: It may be I have been too quick to bring the man to book, but you cannot think we ever desired the destruction of religion. I think that's in your mind, is it not?

HALE (*not altogether giving way*): I—have—there is a softness in your record, sir, a softness.

ELIZABETH: I think, maybe, we have been too hard with Mr. Parris. I think so. But sure we never loved the Devil here.

HALE (*nods, deliberating this; then, with the voice of one administering a secret test*): Do you know your Commandments, Elizabeth?

ELIZABETH (*without hesitation, even eagerly*): I surely do. There be no mark of blame upon my life, Mr. Hale. I am a covenanted Christian woman.

HALE: And you, Mister?

PROCTOR (*a trifle unsteadily*): I—am sure I do, sir.

HALE (*glances at her open face, then at* JOHN, *then*): Let you repeat them, if you will.

PROCTOR: The Commandments.

HALE: Aye.

PROCTOR (*looking off, beginning to sweat*): Thou shalt not kill.

HALE: Aye.

PROCTOR (*counting on his fingers*): Thou shalt not steal.

Thou shalt not covet thy neighbor's goods, nor make unto thee any graven image. Thou shalt not take the name of the Lord in vain; thou shalt have no other gods before me. (*with some hesitation*) Thou shalt remember the Sabbath Day and keep it holy. (*pause; then*) Thou shalt honor thy father and mother. Thou shalt not bear false witness. (*He is stuck. He counts back on his fingers, knowing one is missing.*) Thou shalt not make unto thee any graven image.

HALE: You have said that twice, sir.

PROCTOR (*lost*): Aye. (*He is flailing for it.*)

ELIZABETH (*delicately*): Adultery, John.

PROCTOR (*as though a secret arrow had pained his heart*): Aye. (*trying to grin it away—to* HALE) You see, sir, between the two of us we do know them all. (HALE *only looks at* PROCTOR, *deep in his attempt to define this man.* PROCTOR *grows more uneasy.*) I think it be a small fault.

HALE: Theology, sir, is a fortress; no crack in a fortress may be accounted small. (*He rises; he seems worried now. He paces a little, in deep thought.*)

PROCTOR: There be no love for Satan in this house, Mister.

HALE: I pray it, I pray it dearly. (*He looks to both of them, an attempt at a smile on his face, but his misgivings are clear.*) Well, then—I'll bid you good night.

ELIZABETH (*unable to restrain herself*): Mr. Hale. (*He turns.*) I do think you are suspecting me somewhat? Are you not?

HALE (*obviously disturbed—and evasive*): Goody Proctor, I do not judge you. My duty is to add what I may to the godly wisdom of the court. I pray you both good health and good fortune. (*to* JOHN) Good night, sir. (*He starts out.*)

ELIZABETH (*with a note of desperation*): I think you must tell him, John.

HALE: What's that?

ELIZABETH (*restraining a call*): Will you tell him?

(*Slight pause.* HALE *looks questioningly at* JOHN.)

PROCTOR (*with difficulty*): I—I have no witness and cannot prove it, except my word be taken. But I know the children's sickness had naught to do with witchcraft.

HALE (*stopped, struck*): Naught to do—?

PROCTOR: Mr. Parris discovered them sportin' in the woods. They were startled and took sick.

(*Pause.*)

HALE: Who told you this?

PROCTOR (*hesitates, then*): Abigail Williams.

HALE: Abigail!

PROCTOR: Aye.

HALE (*his eyes wide*): Abigail Williams told you it had naught to do with witchcraft!

PROCTOR: She told me the day you came, sir.

HALE (*suspiciously*): Why—why did you keep this?

PROCTOR: I never knew until tonight that the world is gone daft with this nonsense.

HALE: Nonsense! Mister, I have myself examined Tituba, Sarah Good, and numerous others that have confessed to dealing with the Devil. They have *confessed* it.

PROCTOR: And why not, if they must hang for denyin' it? There are them that will swear to anything before they'll hang; have you never thought of that?

HALE: I have. I—I have indeed. (*It is his own suspicion, but he resists it. He glances at* ELIZABETH, *then at* JOHN.) And you—would you testify to this in court?

PROCTOR: I—had not reckoned with goin' into court. But if I must I will.

HALE: Do you falter here?

PROCTOR: I falter nothing, but I may wonder if my story will be credited in such a court. I do wonder on it, when such a steady-minded minister as you will suspicion such a woman that never lied, and cannot, and the world knows she cannot! I may falter somewhat, Mister; I am no fool.

HALE (*quietly—it has impressed him*): Proctor, let you open with me now, for I have a rumor that troubles me. It's said you hold no belief that there may even be witches in the world. Is that true, sir?

PROCTOR (*He knows this is critical, and is striving against his disgust with* HALE *and with himself for even answering.*): I know not what I have said, I may have said it. I have wondered if there be witches in the world—although I cannot believe they come among us now.

HALE: Then you do not believe—

PROCTOR: I have no knowledge of it; the Bible speaks of witches, and I will not deny them.

HALE: And you, woman?

ELIZABETH: I—I cannot believe it.

HALE (*shocked*): You cannot!

PROCTOR: Elizabeth, you bewilder him!

ELIZABETH (*to* HALE): I cannot think the Devil may own a woman's soul, Mr. Hale, when she keeps an upright way, as I have. I am a good woman, I know it; and if you believe I may do only good work in the world, and yet be secretly bound to Satan, then I must tell you, sir, I do not believe it.

HALE: But, woman, you do believe there are witches in—

ELIZABETH: If you think that I am one, then I say there are none.

HALE: You surely do not fly against the Gospel, the Gospel—

PROCTOR: She believe in the Gospel, every word!

ELIZABETH: Question Abigail Williams about the Gospel, not myself!

(HALE *stares at her.*)

PROCTOR: She do not mean to doubt the Gospel, sir, you cannot think it. This be a Christian house, sir, a Christian house.

HALE: God keep you both; let the third child be quickly baptized, and go you without fail each Sunday in to Sabbath prayer; and keep a solemn, quiet way among you. I think—

(GILES COREY *appears in doorway.*)

GILES: John!

PROCTOR: Giles! What's the matter?

GILES: They take my wife.

(FRANCIS NURSE *enters.*)

GILES: And his Rebecca!

PROCTOR (*to* FRANCIS): Rebecca's in the *jail!*

FRANCIS: Aye, Cheever come and take her in his wagon. We've only now come from the jail, and they'll not even let us in to see them.

ELIZABETH: They've surely gone wild now, Mr. Hale!

FRANCIS (*going to* HALE): Reverend Hale! Can you not speak to the Deputy Governor? I'm sure he mistakes these people—

HALE: Pray calm yourself, Mr. Nurse.

FRANCIS: My wife is the very brick and mortar of the church, Mr. Hale (*indicating* GILES) and Martha Corey, there cannot be a woman closer yet to God than Martha.

HALE: How is Rebecca charged, Mr. Nurse?

FRANCIS (*with a mocking, half-hearted laugh*): For murder, she's charged! (*mockingly quoting the warrant*) "For the marvelous and supernatural murder of Goody Putnam's babies." What am I to do, Mr. Hale?

HALE (*turns from* FRANCIS, *deeply troubled, then*): Believe me, Mr. Nurse, if Rebecca Nurse be tainted, then nothing's left to stop the whole green world from burning. Let you rest upon the justice of the court; the court will send her home, I know it.

FRANCIS: You cannot mean she will be tried in court!

HALE (*pleading*): Nurse, though our hearts break, we cannot flinch; these are new times, sir. There is a misty plot afoot so subtle we should be criminal to cling to old respects and ancient friendships. I have seen too many frightful proofs in court—the Devil is alive in Salem, and we dare not quail to follow wherever the accusing finger points!

PROCTOR (*angered*): How may such a woman murder children?

HALE (*in great pain*): Man, remember, until an hour before the Devil fell, God thought him beautiful in Heaven.

GILES: I never said my wife were a witch, Mr. Hale; I only said she were reading books!

HALE: Mr. Corey, exactly what complaint were made on your wife?

GILES: That bloody mongrel Walcott charge her. Y'see he buy a pig of my wife four or five year ago, and the pig died soon after. So he come dancin' in for his money back. So my Martha, she says to him, "Walcott, if you haven't the wit to feed a pig properly, you'll not live to own many," she says. Now he goes to court and claims that from that day to this he cannot keep a pig alive for more than four weeks because my Martha bewitch them with her books!

(*Enter* EZEKIEL CHEEVER. *A shocked silence.*)

CHEEVER: Good evening to you, Proctor.

PROCTOR: Why, Mr. Cheever. Good evening.

CHEEVER: Good evening, all. Good evening, Mr. Hale.

PROCTOR: I hope you come not on business of the court.

CHEEVER: I do, Proctor, aye. I am clerk of the court now, y'know.

(*Enter* MARSHAL HERRICK, *a man in his early thirties, who is somewhat shamefaced at the moment.*)

GILES: It's a pity, Ezekiel, that an honest tailor might have gone to Heaven must burn in Hell. You'll burn for this, do you know it?

CHEEVER: You know yourself I must do as I'm told. You surely know that, Giles. And I'd as lief you'd not be sending me to Hell. I like not the sound of it, I tell you; I like not the sound of it. (*He fears* PROCTOR, *but starts to reach inside his coat.*) Now believe me, Proctor, how heavy be the law, all its tonnage I do carry on my back tonight. (*He takes out a warrant.*) I have a warrant for your wife.

PROCTOR (*to* HALE): You said she were not charged!

HALE: I know nothin' of it. (*to* CHEEVER) When were she charged?

CHEEVER: I am given sixteen warrant tonight, sir, and she is one.

PROCTOR: Who charged her?

CHEEVER: Why, Abigail Williams charge her.

PROCTOR: On what proof, what proof?

CHEEVER (*looking about the room*): Mr. Proctor, I have little time. The court bid me search your house, but I like not to search a house. So will you hand me any poppets that your wife may keep here?

PROCTOR: Poppets?

ELIZABETH: I never kept no poppets, not since I were a girl.

CHEEVER (*embarrassed, glancing toward the mantel where sits* MARY WARREN'S *poppet*): I spy a poppet, Goody Proctor.

ELIZABETH: Oh! (*going for it*) Why, this is Mary's.

CHEEVER (*shyly*): Would you please to give it to me?

ELIZABETH (*handing it to him, asks* HALE): Has the court discovered a text in poppets now?

CHEEVER (*carefully holding the poppet*): Do you keep any others in this house?

PROCTOR: No, nor this one either till tonight. What signifies a poppet?

CHEEVER: Why, a poppet— (*He gingerly turns the poppet over.*) a poppet may signify— Now, woman, will you please to come with me?

PROCTOR: She will not! (*to* ELIZABETH) Fetch Mary here.

CHEEVER (*ineptly reaching toward* ELIZABETH): No, no, I am forbid to leave her from my sight.

PROCTOR (*pushing his arm away*): You'll leave her out of sight and out of mind, Mister. Fetch Mary, Elizabeth.

(ELIZABETH *goes upstairs.*)

HALE: What signifies a poppet, Mr. Cheever?

CHEEVER (*turning the poppet over in his hands*): Why, they say it may signify that she— (*He has lifted the poppet's skirt, and his eyes widen in astonished fear.*) Why, this, this—

PROCTOR (*reaching for the poppet*): What's there?

CHEEVER: Why— (*He draws out a long needle from the poppet.*) it is a needle! Herrick, Herrick, it is a needle!

(HERRICK *comes toward him.*)

PROCTOR (*angrily, bewildered*): And what signifies a needle!

CHEEVER (*his hands shaking*): Why, this go hard with her, Proctor, this—I had my doubts, Proctor, I had my

doubts, but here's calamity. (*to* HALE, *showing the needle*)
You see it, sir, it is a needle!

HALE: Why? What meanin' has it?

CHEEVER (*wide-eyed, trembling*): The girl, the Williams
girl, Abigail Williams, sir. She sat to dinner in Reverend Parris's house tonight, and without word nor warnin' she falls to
the floor. Like a struck beast, he says, and screamed a scream
that a bull would weep to hear. And he goes to save her, and,
stuck two inches in the flesh of her belly, he draw a needle
out. And demandin' of her how she come to be so stabbed,
she (*to* PROCTOR *now*) testify it were your wife's familiar
spirit pushed it in.

PROCTOR: Why, she done it herself! (*to* HALE) I hope
you're not takin' this for proof, Mister!

(HALE, *struck by the proof, is silent.*)

CHEEVER: 'Tis hard proof! (*to* HALE) I find here a poppet
Goody Proctor keeps. I have found it, sir. And in the belly
of the poppet a needle's stuck. I tell you true, Proctor, I never
warranted to see such proof of Hell, and I bid you obstruct
me not, for I——

(*Enter* ELIZABETH *with* MARY WARREN. PROCTOR, *seeing*
MARY WARREN, *draws her by the arm to* HALE.)

PROCTOR: Here now! Mary, how did this poppet come
into my house?

MARY WARREN (*frightened for herself, her voice very
small*): What poppet's that, sir?

PROCTOR (*impatiently, points at the doll in* CHEEVER'S
hand): This poppet, this poppet.

MARY WARREN (*evasively, looking at it*): Why, I——I think
it is mine.

PROCTOR: It is your poppet, is it not?

MARY WARREN (*not understanding the direction of this*):
It——is, sir.

PROCTOR: And how did it come into this house?

MARY WARREN (*glancing about at the avid faces*): Why——I
made it in the court, sir, and——give it to Goody Proctor
tonight.

PROCTOR (*to* HALE): Now, sir——do you have it?

HALE: Mary Warren, a needle have been found inside this
poppet.

MARY WARREN (*bewildered*): Why, I meant no harm by it,
sir.

PROCTOR (*quickly*): You stuck that needle in yourself?

MARY WARREN: I——I believe I did, sir, I——

PROCTOR (*to* HALE): What say you now?

HALE (*watching* MARY WARREN *closely*): Child, you are certain this be your natural memory? May it be, perhaps, that someone conjures you even now to say this?

MARY WARREN: Conjures me? Why, no, sir, I am entirely myself, I think. Let you ask Susanna Walcott—she saw me sewin' it in court. (*or better still*) Ask Abby, Abby sat beside me when I made it.

PROCTOR (*to* HALE, *of* CHEEVER): Bid him begone. Your mind is surely settled now. Bid him out, Mr. Hale.

ELIZABETH: What signifies a needle?

HALE: Mary—you charge a cold and cruel murder on Abigail.

MARY WARREN: Murder! I charge no—

HALE: Abigail were stabbed tonight; a needle were found stuck into her belly—

ELIZABETH: And she charges me?

HALE: Aye.

ELIZABETH (*her breath knocked out*): Why—! The girl is murder! She must be ripped out of the world!

CHEEVER (*pointing at* ELIZABETH): You've heard that, sir! Ripped out of the world! Herrick, you heard it!

PROCTOR (*suddenly snatching the warrant out of* CHEEVER'S *hands*): Out with you.

CHEEVER: Proctor, you dare not touch the warrant.

PROCTOR (*ripping the warrant*): Out with you!

CHEEVER: You've ripped the Deputy Governor's warrant, man!

PROCTOR: Damn the Deputy Governor! Out of my house!

HALE: Now, Proctor, Proctor!

PROCTOR: Get y'gone with them! You are a broken minister.

HALE: Proctor, if she is innocent, the court—

PROCTOR: If *she* is innocent! Why do you never wonder if Parris be innocent, or Abigail? Is the accuser always holy now? Were they born this morning as clean as God's fingers? I'll tell you what's walking Salem—vengeance is walking Salem. We are what we always were in Salem, but now the little crazy children are jangling the keys of the kingdom, and common vengeance writes the law! This warrant's vengeance! I'll not give my wife to vengeance!

ELIZABETH: I'll go, John—

PROCTOR: You will not go!

HERRICK: I have nine men outside. You cannot keep her. The law binds me, John, I cannot budge.

PROCTOR (*to* HALE, *ready to break him*): Will you see her taken?

HALE: Proctor, the court is just—

PROCTOR: Pontius Pilate! God will not let you wash your hands of this!

ELIZABETH: John—I think I must go with them. (*He cannot bear to look at her.*) Mary, there is bread enough for the morning; you will bake, in the afternoon. Help Mr. Proctor as you were his daughter—you owe me that, and much more. (*She is fighting her weeping; to* PROCTOR) When the children wake, speak nothing of witchcraft—it will frighten them. (*She cannot go on.*)

PROCTOR: I will bring you home. I will bring you soon.

ELIZABETH: Oh, John, bring me soon!

PROCTOR: I will fall like an ocean on that court! Fear nothing, Elizabeth.

ELIZABETH (*with great fear*): I will fear nothing. (*She looks about the room, as though to fix it in her mind.*) Tell the children I have gone to visit someone sick.

(*She walks out the door,* HERRICK *and* CHEEVER *behind her. For a moment,* PROCTOR *watches from the doorway. The clank of chain is heard.*)

PROCTOR: Herrick! Herrick, don't chain her! (*He rushes out the door. From outside*) Damn you, man, you will not chain her! Off with them! I'll not have it! I will not have her chained!

(*There are other men's voices against his.* HALE, *in a fever of guilt and uncertainty, turns from the door to avoid the sight;* MARY WARREN *bursts into tears and sits weeping.* GILES COREY *calls to* HALE.)

GILES: And yet silent, minister? It is fraud, you know it is fraud! What keeps you, man?

(PROCTOR *is half braced, half pushed into the room by two deputies and* HERRICK.)

PROCTOR: I'll pay you, Herrick, I will surely pay you!

HERRICK (*panting*): In God's name, John, I cannot help myself. I must chain them all. Now let you keep inside this house till I am gone!

(*He goes out with his deputies.*

PROCTOR *stands there, gulping air. Horses and a wagon creaking are heard.*)

HALE (*in great uncertainty*): Mr. Proctor—

PROCTOR: Out of my sight!

HALE: Charity, Proctor, charity. What I have heard in her favor, I will not fear to testify in court. God help me, I cannot judge her guilty or innocent—I know not. Only this consider: the world goes mad, and it profit nothing you should lay the cause to the vengeance of a little girl.

PROCTOR: You are a coward! Though you be ordained in God's own tears, you are a coward now!

HALE: Proctor, I cannot think God be provoked so grandly by such a petty cause. The jails are packed—our greatest judges sit in Salem now—and hangin's promised. Man, we must look to cause proportionate. Were there murder done, perhaps, and never brought to light? Abomination? Some secret blasphemy that stinks to Heaven? Think on cause, man, and let you help me to discover it. For there's your way, believe it, there is your only way, when such confusion strikes upon the world. (*He goes to* GILES *and* FRANCIS.) Let you counsel among yourselves; think on your village and what may have drawn from heaven such thundering wrath upon you all. I shall pray God open up our eyes.

(HALE *goes out.*)

FRANCIS (*struck by* HALE'S *mood*): I never heard no murder done in Salem.

PROCTOR (*He has been reached by* HALE'S *words.*): Leave me, Francis, leave me.

GILES (*shaken*): John—tell me, are we lost?

PROCTOR: Go home now, Giles. We'll speak on it tomorrow.

GILES: Let you think on it. We'll come early, eh?

PROCTOR: Aye. Go now, Giles.

GILES: Good night, then.

(GILES COREY *goes out. After a moment*)

MARY WARREN (*in a fearful squeak of a voice*): Mr. Proctor, very likely they'll let her come home once they're given proper evidence.

PROCTOR: You're coming to the court with me, Mary. You will tell it in the court.

MARY WARREN: I cannot charge murder on Abigail.

PROCTOR (*moving menacingly toward her*): You will tell the court how that poppet come here and who stuck the needle in.

MARY WARREN: She'll kill me for sayin' that! (PROCTOR *continues toward her.*) Abby'll charge lechery on you, Mr. Proctor!

PROCTOR (*halting*): She's told you!

MARY WARREN: I have known it, sir. She'll ruin you with it, I know she will.

PROCTOR (*hesitating, and with deep hatred of himself*):

Good. Then her saintliness is done with. (MARY *backs from him.*) We will slide together into our pit; you will tell the court what you know.

MARY WARREN (*in terror*): I cannot, they'll turn on me—

(PROCTOR *strides and catches her, and she is repeating, "I cannot, I cannot!"*)

PROCTOR: My wife will never die for me! I will bring your guts into your mouth but that goodness will not die for me!

MARY WARREN (*struggling to escape him*): I cannot do it, I cannot!

PROCTOR (*grasping her by the throat as though he would strangle her*): Make your peace with it! Now Hell and Heaven grapple on our backs, and all our old pretense is ripped away—make your peace! (*He throws her to the floor, where she sobs, "I cannot, I cannot . . ."; and now, half to himself, staring, and turning to the open door*) Peace. It is a providence, and no great change; we are only what we always were, but naked now. (*He walks as though toward a great horror, facing the open sky.*) Aye, naked! And the wind, God's icy wind, will blow!

(*And she is over and over again sobbing, "I cannot, I cannot, I cannot," as the curtain falls.*)

ACT III

(*The vestry room of the Salem meeting house, now serving as the anteroom of the General Court.*

As the curtain rises, the room is empty, but for sunlight pouring through two high windows in the back wall. The room is solemn, even forbidding. Heavy beams jut out, boards of random widths make up the walls. At the right are two doors leading into the meeting house proper, where the court is being held. At the left another door leads outside.

There is a plain bench at the left, and another at the right. In the center a rather long meeting table, with stools and a considerable armchair snugged up to it.

Through the partitioning wall at the right we hear a prosecutor's voice, JUDGE HATHORNE'S, asking a question; then a woman's voice, MARTHA COREY'S, replying.)

HATHORNE'S VOICE: Now, Martha Corey, there is abundant evidence in our hands to show that you have given yourself to the reading of fortunes. Do you deny it?

MARTHA COREY'S VOICE: I am innocent to a witch. I know not what a witch is.

HATHORNE'S VOICE: How do you know, then, that you are not a witch?

MARTHA COREY'S VOICE: If I were, I would know it.

HATHORNE'S VOICE: Why do you hurt these children?

MARTHA COREY'S VOICE: I do not hurt them. I scorn it!

GILES' VOICE (*roaring*): I have evidence for the court!

(*Voices of townspeople rise in excitement.*)

DANFORTH'S VOICE: You will keep your seat!

GILES' VOICE: Thomas Putnam is reaching out for land!

DANFORTH'S VOICE: Remove that man, Marshal!

GILES' VOICE: You're hearing lies, lies!

(*A roaring goes up from the people.*)

HATHORNE'S VOICE: Arrest him, excellency!

GILES' VOICE: I have evidence. Why will you not hear my evidence?

(*The door opens and* GILES *is half carried into the vestry room by* HERRICK.)

GILES: Hands off, damn you, let me go!

HERRICK: Giles, Giles!

GILES: Out of my way, Herrick! I bring evidence—

HERRICK: You cannot go in there, Giles; it's a court!

(*Enter* HALE *from the court.*)

HALE: Pray be calm a moment.

GILES: You, Mr. Hale, go in there and demand I speak.

HALE: A moment, sir, a moment.

GILES: They'll be hangin' my wife!

(JUDGE HATHORNE *enters. He is in his sixties, a bitter, remorseless Salem judge.*)

HATHORNE: How do you dare come roarin' into this court! Are you gone daft, Corey?

GILES: You're not a Boston judge, Hathorne. You'll not call me daft!

(*Enter* DEPUTY GOVERNOR DANFORTH *and, behind him,* EZEKIEL CHEEVER *and* PARRIS. *On his appearance, silence falls.* DANFORTH *is a grave man in his sixties, of some humor and sophistication that does not, however, interfere with an exact loyalty to his position and his cause. He comes down to* GILES, *who awaits his wrath.*)

DANFORTH (*looking directly at* GILES): Who is this man?

PARRIS: Giles Corey, sir, and a more contentious—

GILES (*to* PARRIS): I am asked the question, and I am old enough to answer it! (*to* DANFORTH, *who impresses him and to whom he smiles through his strain*) My name is Corey, sir, Giles Corey. I have six hundred acres, and timber in addition. It is my wife you be condemning now. (*He indicates the courtroom.*)

DANFORTH: And how do you imagine to help her cause with such contemptuous riot? Now be gone. Your old age alone keeps you out of jail for this.

GILES (*beginning to plead*): They be tellin' lies about my wife, sir, I—

DANFORTH: Do you take it upon yourself to determine what this court shall believe and what it shall set aside?

GILES: Your Excellency, we mean no disrespect for—

DANFORTH: Disrespect indeed! It is disruption, Mister. This is the highest court of the supreme government of this province, do you know it?

GILES (*beginning to weep*): Your Excellency, I only said she were readin' books, sir, and they come and take her out of my house for—

DANFORTH (*mystified*): Books! What books?

GILES (*through helpless sobs*): It is my third wife, sir; I never had no wife that be so taken with books, and I thought to find the cause of it, d'y'see, but it were no witch I blamed her for. (*He is openly weeping.*) I have broke charity with the woman, I have broke charity with her. (*He covers his face, ashamed.* DANFORTH *is respectfully silent.*)

HALE: Excellency, he claims hard evidence for his wife's defense. I think that in all justice you must—

DANFORTH: Then let him submit his evidence in proper affidavit. You are certainly aware of our procedure here, Mr. Hale. (*to* HERRICK) Clear this room.

HERRICK: Come now, Giles. (*He gently pushes* COREY *out.*)

FRANCIS: We are desperate, sir; we come here three days now and cannot be heard.

DANFORTH: Who is this man?

FRANCIS: Francis Nurse, Your Excellency.

HALE: His wife's Rebecca that were condemned this morning.

DANFORTH: Indeed! I am amazed to find you in such uproar. I have only good report of your character, Mr. Nurse.

HATHORNE: I think they must both be arrested in contempt, sir.

DANFORTH (*to* FRANCIS): Let you write your plea, and in due time I will—

FRANCIS: Excellency, we have proof for your eyes; God forbid you shut them to it. The girls, sir, the girls are frauds.

DANFORTH: What's that?

FRANCIS: We have proof of it, sir. They are all deceiving you.

(DANFORTH *is shocked, but studying* FRANCIS.)

HATHORNE: This is contempt, sir, contempt!

DANFORTH: Peace, Judge Hathorne. Do you know who I am, Mr. Nurse?

FRANCIS: I surely do, sir, and I think you must be a wise judge to be what you are.

DANFORTH: And do you know that near to four hundred are in the jails from Marblehead to Lynn, and upon my signature?

FRANCIS: I—

DANFORTH: And seventy-two condemned to hang by that signature?

FRANCIS: Excellency, I never thought to say it to such a weighty judge, but you are deceived.

(*Enter* GILES COREY *from left. All turn to see as he beckons in* MARY WARREN *with* PROCTOR. MARY *is keeping her eyes to the ground;* PROCTOR *has her elbow as though she were near collapse.*)

PARRIS (*on seeing her, in shock*): Mary Warren! (*He goes directly to bend close to her face.*) What you about here?

PROCTOR (*pressing* PARRIS *away from her with a gentle but firm motion of protectiveness*): She would speak with the Deputy Governor.

DANFORTH (*shocked by this, turns to* HERRICK): Did you not tell me Mary Warren were sick in bed?

HERRICK: She were, Your Honor. When I go to fetch her to the court last week, she said she were sick.

GILES: She has been strivin' with her soul all week, Your Honor; she comes now to tell the truth of this to you.

DANFORTH: Who is this?

PROCTOR: John Proctor, sir. Elizabeth Proctor is my wife.

PARRIS: Beware this man, Your Excellency, this man is mischief.

HALE (*excitedly*): I think you must hear the girl, sir, she—

DANFORTH (*who has become very interested in* MARY WAR-REN *and only raises a hand toward* HALE): Peace. What would you tell us, Mary Warren?

(PROCTOR *looks at her, but she cannot speak.*)

PROCTOR: She never saw no spirits, sir.

DANFORTH (*with great alarm and surprise, to* MARY): Never saw no spirits!

GILES (*eagerly*): Never.

PROCTOR (*reaching into his jacket*): She has signed a deposition, sir—

DANFORTH (*instantly*): No, no, I accept no depositions. (*He is rapidly calculating this; he turns from her to* PROCTOR.) Tell me, Mr. Proctor, have you given out this story in the village?

PROCTOR: We have not.

PARRIS: They've come to overthrow the court, sir! This man is—

DANFORTH: I pray you, Mr. Parris. Do you know, Mr. Proctor, that the entire contention of the state in these trials is that the voice of Heaven is speaking through the children?

PROCTOR: I know that, sir.

DANFORTH (*thinks, staring at* PROCTOR, *then turns to* MARY WARREN): And you, Mary Warren, how came you to cry out people for sending their spirits against you?

MARY WARREN: It were pretense, sir.

DANFORTH: I cannot hear you.

PROCTOR: It were pretense, she says.

DANFORTH: Ah? And the other girls? Susanna Walcott, and—the others? They are also pretending?

MARY WARREN: Aye, sir.

DANFORTH (*wide-eyed*): Indeed. (*Pause. He is baffled by this. He turns to study* PROCTOR'S *face.*)

PARRIS (*in a sweat*): Excellency, you surely cannot think to let so vile a lie be spread in open court.

DANFORTH: Indeed not, but it strike hard upon me that she will dare come here with such a tale. Now, Mr. Proctor, before I decide whether I shall hear you or not, it is my duty to tell you this. We burn a hot fire here; it melts down all concealment.

PROCTOR: I know that, sir.

DANFORTH: Let me continue. I understand well, a husband's tenderness may drive him to extravagance in defense of a wife. Are you certain in your conscience, Mister, that your evidence is the truth?

PROCTOR: It is. And you will surely know it.

DANFORTH: And you thought to declare this revelation in the open court before the public?

PROCTOR: I thought I would, aye—with your permission.

DANFORTH (*his eyes narrowing*): Now, sir, what is your purpose in so doing?

PROCTOR: Why, I—I would free my wife, sir.

DANFORTH: There lurks nowhere in your heart, nor hidden in your spirit, any desire to undermine this court?

PROCTOR (*with the faintest faltering*): Why, no, sir.

CHEEVER (*clears his throat, awakening*): I— Your Excellency.

DANFORTH: Mr. Cheever.

CHEEVER: I think it be my duty, sir— (*kindly, to* PROCTOR) You'll not deny it, John. (*to* DANFORTH) When we come to take his wife, he damned the court and ripped your warrant.

PARRIS: Now you have it!

DANFORTH: He did that, Mr. Hale?

HALE (*takes a breath*): Aye, he did.

PROCTOR: It were a temper, sir. I knew not what I did.

DANFORTH (*studying him*): Mr. Proctor.

PROCTOR: Aye, sir.

DANFORTH (*straight into his eyes*): Have you ever seen the Devil?

PROCTOR: No, sir.

DANFORTH: You are in all respects a Gospel Christian?

PROCTOR: I am, sir.

PARRIS: Such a Christian that will not come to church but once in a month!

DANFORTH (*restrained—he is curious*): Not come to church?

PROCTOR: I—I have no love for Mr. Parris. It is no secret. But God I surely love.

CHEEVER: He plow on Sunday, sir.

DANFORTH: Plow on Sunday!

CHEEVER (*apologetically*): I think it be evidence, John. I am an official of the court, I cannot keep it.

PROCTOR: I—I have once or twice plowed on Sunday. I have three children, sir, and until last year my land give little.

GILES: You'll find other Christians that do plow on Sunday if the truth be known.

HALE: Your Honor, I cannot think you may judge the man on such evidence.

DANFORTH: I judge nothing. (*Pause. He keeps watching* PROCTOR, *who tries to meet his gaze.*) I tell you straight, Mister—I have seen marvels in this court. I have seen people choked before my eyes by spirits; I have seen them stuck by pins and slashed by daggers. I have until this moment not the slightest reason to suspect that the children may be deceiving me. Do you understand my meaning?

PROCTOR: Excellency, does it not strike upon you that so

many of these women have lived so long with such upright reputation, and—

PARRIS: Do you read the Gospel, Mr. Proctor?

PROCTOR: I read the Gospel.

PARRIS: I think not, or you should surely know that Cain were an upright man, and yet he did kill Abel.

PROCTOR: Aye, God tells us that. (*to* DANFORTH) But who tells us Rebecca Nurse murdered seven babies by sending out her spirit on them? It is the children only, and this one will swear she lied to you.

(DANFORTH *considers, then beckons* HATHORNE *to him.* HATHORNE *leans in, and he speaks in his ear.* HATHORNE *nods.*)

HATHORNE: Aye, she's the one.

DANFORTH: Mr. Proctor, this morning, your wife send me a claim in which she states that she is pregnant now.

PROCTOR: My wife pregnant!

DANFORTH: There be no sign of it—we have examined her body.

PROCTOR: But if she say she is pregnant, then she must be! That woman will never lie, Mr. Danforth.

DANFORTH: She will not?

PROCTOR: Never, sir, never.

DANFORTH: We have thought it too convenient to be credited. However, if I should tell you now that I will let her be kept another month; and if she begin to show her natural signs, you shall have her living yet another year until she is delivered—what say you to that? (JOHN PROCTOR *is struck silent.*) Come now. You say your only purpose is to save your wife. Good, then, she is saved at least this year, and a year is long. What say you, sir? It is done now. (*In conflict,* PROCTOR *glances at* FRANCIS *and* GILES.) Will you drop this charge?

PROCTOR: I—I think I cannot.

DANFORTH (*now an almost imperceptible hardness in his voice*): Then your purpose is somewhat larger.

PARRIS: He's come to overthrow this court, Your Honor!

PROCTOR: These are my friends. Their wives are also accused—

DANFORTH (*with a sudden briskness of manner*): I judge you not, sir. I am ready to hear your evidence.

PROCTOR: I come not to hurt the court; I only—

DANFORTH (*cutting him off*): Marshal, go into the court and bid Judge Stoughton and Judge Sewall declare recess for one hour. And let them go to the tavern, if they will. All witnesses and prisoners are to be kept in the building.

HERRICK: Aye, sir. (*very deferentially*) If I may say it, sir, I know this man all my life. It is a good man, sir.

DANFORTH (*It is the reflection on himself he resents.*): I am sure of it, Marshal. (HERRICK *nods, then goes out.*) Now, what deposition do you have for us, Mr. Proctor? And I beg you be clear, open as the sky, and honest.

PROCTOR (*as he takes out several papers*): I am no lawyer, so I'll—

DANFORTH: The pure in heart need no lawyers. Proceed as you will.

PROCTOR (*handing* DANFORTH *a paper*): Will you read this first, sir? It's a sort of testament. The people signing it declare their good opinion of Rebecca, and my wife, and Martha Corey. (DANFORTH *looks down at the paper.*)

PARRIS (*to enlist* DANFORTH'S *sarcasm*): Their good opinion! (*But* DANFORTH *goes on reading, and* PROCTOR *is heartened.*)

PROCTOR: These are all landholding farmers, members of the church. (*delicately, trying to point out a paragraph*) If you'll notice, sir—they've known the women many years and never saw no sign they had dealings with the Devil.

(PARRIS *nervously moves over and reads over* DANFORTH'S *shoulder.*)

DANFORTH (*glancing down a long list*): How many names are here?

FRANCIS: Ninety-one, Your Excellency.

PARRIS (*sweating*): These people should be summoned. (DANFORTH *looks up at him questioningly.*) For questioning.

FRANCIS (*trembling with anger*): Mr. Danforth, I gave them all my word no harm would come to them for signing this.

PARRIS: This is a clear attack upon the court!

HALE (*to* PARRIS, *trying to contain himself*): Is every defense an attack upon the court? Can no one—?

PARRIS: All innocent and Christian people are happy for the courts in Salem! These people are gloomy for it. (*to* DANFORTH *directly*) And I think you will want to know, from each and every one of them, what discontents them with you!

HATHORNE: I think they ought to be examined, sir.

DANFORTH: It is not necessarily an attack, I think. Yet—

FRANCIS: These are all covenanted Christians, sir.

DANFORTH: Then I am sure they may have nothing to fear. (*hands* CHEEVER *the paper*) Mr. Cheever, have warrants drawn for all of these—arrest for examination. (*to* PROCTOR)

Now, Mister, what other information do you have for us? (FRANCIS *is still standing, horrified.*) You may sit, Mr. Nurse.

FRANCIS: I have brought trouble on these people; I have—

DANFORTH: No, old man, you have not hurt these people if they are of good conscience. But you must understand, sir, that a person is either with this court or he must be counted against it, there be no road between. This is a sharp time, now, a precise time—we live no longer in the dusky afternoon when evil mixed itself with good and befuddled the world. Now, by God's grace, the shining sun is up, and them that fear not light will surely praise it. I hope you will be one of those. (MARY WARREN *suddenly sobs.*) She's not hearty, I see.

PROCTOR: No, she's not, sir. (*to* MARY, *bending to her, holding her hand, quietly*) Now remember what the angel Raphael said to the boy Tobias. Remember it.

MARY WARREN (*hardly audible*): Aye.

PROCTOR: "Do that which is good, and no harm shall come to thee."

MARY WARREN: Aye.

DANFORTH: Come, man, we wait you.

(MARSHAL HERRICK *returns, and takes his post at the door.*)

GILES: John, my deposition, give him mine.

PROCTOR: Aye. (*He hands* DANFORTH *another paper.*) This is Mr. Corey's deposition.

DANFORTH: Oh? (*He looks down at it. Now* HATHORNE *comes behind him and reads with him.*)

HATHORNE (*suspiciously*): What lawyer drew this, Corey?

GILES: You know I never hired a lawyer in my life, Hathorne.

DANFORTH (*finishing the reading*): It is very well phrased. My compliments. Mr. Parris, if Mr. Putnam is in the court, will you bring him in? (HATHORNE *takes the deposition, and walks to the window with it.* PARRIS *goes into the court.*) You have no legal training, Mr. Corey?

GILES (*very pleased*): I have the best, sir—I am thirty-three time in court in my life. And always plaintiff, too.

DANFORTH: Oh, then you're much put-upon.

GILES: I am never put-upon; I know my rights, sir, and I will have them. You know, your father tried a case of mine—might be thirty-five year ago, I think.

DANFORTH: Indeed.

GILES: He never spoke to you of it?

DANFORTH: No, I cannot recall it.

GILES: That's strange, he give me nine pound damages.

He were a fair judge, your father. Y'see, I had a white mare that time, and the fellow come to borrow the mare— (*Enter* PARRIS *with* THOMAS PUTNAM. *When he sees* PUTNAM, GILES' *ease goes; he is hard.*) Aye, there he is.

DANFORTH: Mr. Putnam, I have here an accusation by Mr. Corey against you. He states that you coldly prompted your daughter to cry witchery upon George Jacobs that is now in jail.

PUTNAM: It is a lie.

DANFORTH (*turning to* GILES): Mr. Putnam states your charge is a lie. What say you to that?

GILES (*furious, his fists clenched*): A fart on Thomas Putnam, that is what I say to that!

DANFORTH: What proof do you submit for your charge, sir?

GILES: My proof is there! (*pointing to the paper*) If Jacobs hangs for a witch he forfeit up his property—that's law! And there is none but Putnam with the coin to buy so great a piece. This man is killing his neighbors for their land!

DANFORTH: But proof, sir, proof.

GILES (*pointing at his deposition*): The proof is there! I have it from an honest man who heard Putnam say it! The day his daughter cried out on Jacobs, he said he'd given him a fair gift of land.

HATHORNE: And the name of this man?

GILES (*taken aback*): What name?

HATHORNE: The man that give you this information.

GILES (*hesitates, then*): Why, I—I cannot give you his name.

HATHORNE: And why not?

GILES (*hesitates, then bursts out*): You know well why not! He'll lay in jail if I give his name!

HATHORNE: This is contempt of the court, Mr. Danforth!

DANFORTH (*to avoid that*): You will surely tell us the name.

GILES: I will not give you no name. I mentioned my wife's name once and I'll burn in hell long enough for that. I stand mute.

DANFORTH: In that case, I have no choice but to arrest you for contempt of this court, do you know that?

GILES: This is a hearing; you cannot clap me for contempt of a hearing.

DANFORTH: Oh, it is a proper lawyer! Do you wish me to declare the court in full session here? Or will you give me good reply?

GILES (*faltering*): I cannot give you no name, sir, I cannot.

DANFORTH: You are a foolish old man. Mr. Cheever, begin the record. The court is now in session. I ask you, Mr. Corey—

PROCTOR (*breaking in*): Your Honor—he has the story in confidence, sir, and he—

PARRIS: The Devil lives on such confidences! (*to* DANFORTH) Without confidences there could be no conspiracy, Your Honor!

HATHORNE: I think it must be broken, sir.

DANFORTH (*to* GILES): Old man, if your informant tells the truth let him come here openly like a decent man. But if he hide in anonymity I must know why. Now sir, the government and central church demand of you the name of him who reported Mr. Thomas Putnam a common murderer.

HALE: Excellency—

DANFORTH: Mr. Hale.

HALE: We cannot blink it more. There is a prodigious fear of this court in the country—

DANFORTH: Then there is a prodigious guilt in the country. Are *you* afraid to be questioned here?

HALE: I may only fear the Lord, sir, but there is fear in the country nevertheless.

DANFORTH (*angered now*): Reproach me not with the fear in the country; there is fear in the country because there is a moving plot to topple Christ in the country!

HALE: But it does not follow that everyone accused is part of it.

DANFORTH: No uncorrupt man may fear this court, Mr. Hale! None! (*to* GILES) You are under arrest in contempt of this court. Now sit you down and take counsel with yourself, or you will be set in the jail until you decide to answer all questions.

(GILES COREY *makes a rush for* PUTNAM. PROCTOR *lunges and holds him.*)

PROCTOR: No, Giles!

GILES (*over* PROCTOR's *shoulder at* PUTNAM): I'll cut your throat, Putnam, I'll kill you yet!

PROCTOR (*forcing him into a chair*): Peace, Giles, peace. (*releasing him*) We'll prove ourselves. Now we will. (*He starts to turn to* DANFORTH.)

GILES: Say nothin' more, John. (*pointing at* DANFORTH) He's only playin' you! He means to hang us all!

(MARY WARREN *bursts into sobs.*)

DANFORTH: This is a court of law, Mister. I'll have no effrontery here!

PROCTOR: Forgive him, sir, for his old age. Peace, Giles, we'll prove it all now. (*He lifts up* MARY'S *chin.*) You cannot weep, Mary. Remember the angel, what he say to the boy. Hold to it, now; there is your rock. (MARY *quiets. He takes out a paper, and turns to* DANFORTH.) This is Mary Warren's deposition. I—I would ask you remember, sir, while you read it, that until two week ago she were no different than the other children are today. (*He is speaking reasonably, restraining all his fears, his anger, his anxiety.*) You saw her scream, she howled, she swore familiar spirits choked her; she even testified that Satan, in the form of women now in jail, tried to win her soul away, and then when she refused—

DANFORTH: We know all this.

PROCTOR: Aye, sir. She swears now that she never saw Satan; nor any spirit, vague or clear, that Satan may have sent to hurt her. And she declares her friends are lying now.

(PROCTOR *starts to hand* DANFORTH *the deposition, and* HALE *comes up to* DANFORTH *in a trembling state.*)

HALE: Excellency, a moment. I think this goes to the heart of the matter.

DANFORTH (*with deep misgiving*): It surely does.

HALE: I cannot say he is an honest man; I know him little. But in all justice, sir, a claim so weighty cannot be argued by a farmer. In God's name, sir, stop here; send him home and let him come again with a lawyer—

DANFORTH (*patiently*): Now look you, Mr. Hale—

HALE: Excellency, I have signed seventy-two death warrants; I am a minister of the Lord, and I dare not take a life without there be a proof so immaculate no slightest qualm of conscience may doubt it.

DANFORTH: Mr. Hale, you surely do not doubt my justice.

HALE: I have this morning signed away the soul of Rebecca Nurse, Your Honor. I'll not conceal it, my hand shakes yet as with a wound! I pray you, sir, *this* argument let lawyers present to you.

DANFORTH: Mr. Hale, believe me; for a man of such terrible learning you are most bewildered—I hope you will forgive me. I have been thirty-two year at the bar, sir, and I should be confounded were I called upon to defend these people. Let you consider, now— (*to* PROCTOR *and the others*) And I bid you all do likewise. In all ordinary crime, how does one defend the accused? One calls up witnesses to prove his innocence. But witchcraft is *ipso facto*, on its face and by its nature, an invisible crime, is it not? Therefore, who may possibly be witness to it? The witch and the victim. None other. Now we cannot hope the witch will accuse herself; granted? Therefore, we must rely upon her victims—and they do testify, the children certainly do testify. As for the witches, none will deny that we are most eager for all their confessions. Therefore, what is left for a lawyer to bring out? I think I have made my point. Have I not?

HALE: But this child claims the girls are not truthful, and if they are not—

DANFORTH: That is precisely what I am about to consider, sir. What more may you ask of me? Unless you doubt my probity?

HALE (*defeated*): I surely do not, sir. Let you consider it, then.

DANFORTH: And let you put your heart to rest. Her deposition, Mr. Proctor.

(PROCTOR *hands it to him.* HATHORNE *rises, goes beside* DANFORTH, *and starts reading.* PARRIS *comes to his other side.* DANFORTH *looks at* JOHN PROCTOR, *then proceeds to read.* HALE *gets up, finds position near the judge, reads too.* PROCTOR *glances at* GILES. FRANCIS *prays silently, hands pressed together.* CHEEVER *waits placidly, the sublime official, dutiful.* MARY WARREN *sobs once.* JOHN PROCTOR *touches her head reassuringly. Presently* DANFORTH *lifts his eyes, stands up, takes out a kerchief and blows his nose. The others stand aside as he moves in thought toward the window.*)

PARRIS (*hardly able to contain his anger and fear*): I should like to question—

DANFORTH (*his first real outburst, in which his contempt for* PARRIS *is clear*): Mr. Parris, I bid you be silent! (*He stands in silence, looking out the window; now, having established that he will set the gait*) Mr. Cheever, will you go into the court and bring the children here? (CHEEVER *gets up and goes out upstage.* DANFORTH *now turns to* MARY.) Mary Warren, how came you to this turnabout? Has Mr. Proctor threatened you for this deposition?

MARY WARREN: No, sir.

DANFORTH: Has he ever threatened you?

MARY WARREN (*weaker*): No, sir.

DANFORTH (*sensing a weakening*): Has he threatened you?

MARY WARREN: No, sir.

DANFORTH: Then you tell me that you sat in my court, callously lying, when you knew that people would hang by your evidence? (*She does not answer.*) Answer me!

MARY WARREN (*almost inaudibly*): I did, sir.

DANFORTH: How were you instructed in your life? Do

you not know that God damns all liars? (*She cannot speak.*) Or is it now that you lie?

MARY WARREN: No, sir—I am with God now.

DANFORTH: You are with God now.

MARY WARREN: Aye, sir.

DANFORTH (*containing himself*): I will tell you this—you are either lying now, or you were lying in the court, and in either case you have committed perjury and you will go to jail for it. You cannot lightly say you lied, Mary. Do you know that?

MARY WARREN: I cannot lie no more. I am with God, I am with God.

(*But she breaks into sobs at the thought of it, and the right door opens, and enter* SUSANNA WALCOTT, MERCY LEWIS, BETTY PARRIS, *and finally* ABIGAIL. CHEEVER *comes to* DANFORTH.)

CHEEVER: Ruth Putnam's not in the court, sir, nor the other children.

DANFORTH: These will be sufficient. Sit you down, children. (*Silently they sit.*) Your friend, Mary Warren, has given us a deposition. In which she swears that she never saw familiar spirits, apparitions, nor any manifest of the Devil. She claims as well that none of you have seen these things either. (*slight pause*) Now, children, this is a court of law. The law, based upon the Bible, and the Bible, writ by Almighty God, forbid the practice of witchcraft, and describe death as the penalty thereof. But likewise, children, the law and Bible damn all bearers of false witness. (*slight pause*) Now then. It does not escape me that this deposition may be devised to blind us; it may well be that Mary Warren has been conquered by Satan, who sends her here to distract our sacred purpose. If so, her neck will break for it. But if she speak true, I bid you now drop your guile and confess your pretense, for a quick confession will go easier with you. (*pause*) Abigail Williams, rise. (ABIGAIL *slowly rises.*) Is there any truth in this?

ABIGAIL: No, sir.

DANFORTH (*thinks, glances at* MARY, *then back to* ABIGAIL): Children, a very augur bit will now be turned into your souls until your honesty is proved. Will either of you change your positions now, or do you force me to hard questioning?

ABIGAIL: I have naught to change, sir. She lies.

DANFORTH (*to* MARY): You would still go on with this?

MARY WARREN (*faintly*): Aye, sir.

DANFORTH (*turning to* ABIGAIL): A poppet were discovered in Mr. Proctor's house, stabbed by a needle. Mary Warren claims that you sat beside her in the court when she made it, and that you saw her make it and witnessed how she herself stuck the needle into it for safe-keeping. What say you to that?

ABIGAIL (*with a slight note of indignation*): It is a lie, sir.

DANFORTH (*after a slight pause*): While you worked for Mr. Proctor, did you see poppets in that house?

ABIGAIL: Goody Proctor always kept poppets.

PROCTOR: Your Honor, my wife never kept no poppets. Mary Warren confesses it was her poppet.

CHEEVER: Your Excellency.

DANFORTH: Mr. Cheever.

CHEEVER: When I spoke with Goody Proctor in that house, she said she never kept no poppets. But she said she did keep poppets when she were a girl.

PROCTOR: She has not been a girl these fifteen years, Your Honor.

HATHORNE: But a poppet will keep fifteen years, will it not?

PROCTOR: It will keep if it is kept, but Mary Warren swears she never saw no poppets in my house, nor anyone else.

PARRIS: Why could there not have been poppets hid where no one ever saw them?

PROCTOR (*furious*): There might also be a dragon with five legs in my house, but no one has ever seen it.

PARRIS: We are here, Your Honor, precisely to discover what no one has ever seen.

PROCTOR: Mr. Danforth, what profit this girl to turn herself about? What may Mary Warren gain but hard questioning and worse?

DANFORTH: You are charging Abigail Williams with a marvelous cool plot to murder, do you understand that?

PROCTOR: I do, sir. I believe she means to murder.

DANFORTH (*pointing at* ABIGAIL, *incredulously*): This child would murder your wife?

PROCTOR: It is not a child. Now hear me, sir. In the sight of the congregation she were twice this year put out of this meetin' house for laughter during prayer.

DANFORTH (*shocked, turning to* ABIGAIL): What's this? Laughter during—!

PARRIS: Excellency, she were under Tituba's power at that time, but she is solemn now.

GILES: Aye, now she is solemn and goes to hang people!

DANFORTH: Quiet, man.

HATHORNE: Surely it have no bearing on the question, sir. He charges contemplation of murder.

DANFORTH: Aye. (*he studies* ABIGAIL *for a moment, then*) Continue, Mr. Proctor.

PROCTOR: Mary. Now tell the Governor how you danced in the woods.

PARRIS (*instantly*): Excellency, since I come to Salem this man is blackening my name. He—

DANFORTH: In a moment, sir. (*to* MARY WARREN, *sternly, and surprised*) What is this dancing?

MARY WARREN: I— (*She glances at* ABIGAIL, *who is staring down at her remorselessly. Then, appealing to* PROCTOR) Mr. Proctor—

PROCTOR (*taking it right up*): Abigail leads the girls to the woods, Your Honor, and they have danced there naked—

PARRIS: Your Honor, this—

PROCTOR (*at once*): Mr. Parris discovered them himself in the dead of night! There's the "child" she is!

DANFORTH (*It is growing into a nightmare, and he turns, astonished, to* PARRIS.): Mr. Parris—

PARRIS: I can only say, sir, that I never found any of them naked, and this man is—

DANFORTH: But you discovered them dancing in the woods? (*Eyes on* PARRIS, *he points at* ABIGAIL.) Abigail?

HALE: Excellency, when I first arrived from Beverly, Mr. Parris told me that.

DANFORTH: Do you deny it, Mr. Parris?

PARRIS: I do not, sir, but I never saw any of them naked.

DANFORTH: But she have *danced*?

PARRIS (*unwillingly*): Aye, sir.

(DANFORTH, *as though with new eyes, looks at* ABIGAIL.)

HATHORNE: Excellency, will you permit me? (*He points at* MARY WARREN.)

DANFORTH (*with great worry*): Pray, proceed.

HATHORNE: You say you never saw no spirits, Mary, were never threatened or afflicted by any manifest of the Devil or the Devil's agents.

MARY WARREN (*very faintly*): No, sir.

HATHORNE (*with a gleam of victory*): And yet, when people accused of witchery confronted you in court, you would faint, saying their spirits came out of their bodies and choked you—

MARY WARREN: That were pretense, sir.

DANFORTH: I cannot hear you.

MARY WARREN: Pretense, sir.

PARRIS: But you did turn cold, did you not? I myself picked you up many times, and your skin were icy. Mr. Danforth, you—

DANFORTH: I saw that many times.

PROCTOR: She only pretended to faint, Your Excellency. They're all marvelous pretenders.

HATHORNE: Then can she pretend to faint now?

PROCTOR: Now?

PARRIS: Why not? Now there are no spirits attacking her, for none in this room is accused of witchcraft. So let her turn herself cold now, let her pretend she is attacked now, let her faint. (*He turns to* MARY WARREN.) Faint!

MARY WARREN: Faint?

PARRIS: Aye, faint. Prove to us how you pretended in the court so many times.

MARY WARREN (*looking to* PROCTOR): I—cannot faint now, sir.

PROCTOR (*alarmed, quietly*): Can you not pretend it?

MARY WARREN: I— (*She looks about as though searching for the passion to faint.*) I—have no *sense* of it now, I—

DANFORTH: Why? What is lacking now?

MARY WARREN: I—cannot tell, sir, I—

DANFORTH: Might it be that here we have no afflicting spirit loose, but in the court there were some?

MARY WARREN: I never saw no spirits.

PARRIS: Then see no spirits now, and prove to us that you can faint by your own will, as you claim.

MARY WARREN (*stares, searching for the emotion of it, and then shakes her head*): I—cannot do it.

PARRIS: Then you will confess, will you not? It were attacking spirits made you faint!

MARY WARREN: No, sir, I—

PARRIS: Your Excellency, this is a trick to blind the court!

MARY WARREN: It's not a trick! (*She stands.*) I—I used to faint because I—I thought I saw spirits.

DANFORTH: *Thought* you saw them!

MARY WARREN: But I did not, Your Honor.

HATHORNE: How could you think you saw them unless you saw them?

MARY WARREN: I—I cannot tell how, but I did. I—I heard the other girls screaming, and you, Your Honor, you seemed to believe them, and I— It were only sport in the beginning, sir, but then the whole world cried spirits, spirits, and I—I promise you, Mr. Danforth, I only thought I saw them but I did not.

(DANFORTH *peers at her.*)

PARRIS (*smiling, but nervous because* DANFORTH *seems to be struck by* MARY WARREN'S *story*): Surely Your Excellency is not taken by this simple lie.

DANFORTH (*turning worriedly to* ABIGAIL): Abigail. I bid you now search your heart and tell me this—and beware of it, child, to God every soul is precious and His vengeance is terrible on them that take life without cause. Is it possible, child, that the spirits you have seen are illusion only, some deception that may cross your mind when—

ABIGAIL: Why, this—this—is a base question, sir.

DANFORTH: Child, I would have you consider it—

ABIGAIL: I have been hurt, Mr. Danforth; I have seen my blood runnin' out! I have been near to murdered every day because I done my duty pointing out the Devil's people— and this is my reward? To be mistrusted, denied, questioned like a—

DANFORTH (*weakening*): Child, I do not mistrust you—

ABIGAIL (*in an open threat*): Let *you* beware, Mr. Danforth. Think you to be so mighty that the power of Hell may not turn *your* wits? Beware of it! There is— (*Suddenly, from an accusatory attitude, her face turns, looking into the air above—it is truly frightened.*)

DANFORTH (*apprehensively*): What is it, child?

ABIGAIL (*looking about in the air, clasping her arms about her as though cold*): I—I know not. A wind, a cold wind, has come. (*Her eyes fall on* MARY WARREN.)

MARY WARREN (*terrified, pleading*): Abby!

MERCY LEWIS (*shivering*): Your Honor, I freeze!

PROCTOR: They're pretending!

HATHORNE (*touching* ABIGAIL'S *hand*): She is cold, Your Honor, touch her!

MERCY LEWIS (*through chattering teeth*): Mary, do you send this shadow on me?

MARY WARREN: Lord, save me!

SUSANNA WALCOTT: I freeze, I freeze!

ABIGAIL (*shivering visibly*): It is a wind, a wind!

MARY WARREN: Abby, don't do that!

DANFORTH (*himself engaged and entranced by* ABIGAIL): Mary Warren, do you witch her? I say to you, do you send your spirit out?

(*With a hysterical cry* MARY WARREN *starts to run.* PROCTOR *catches her.*)

MARY WARREN (*almost collapsing*): Let me go, Mr. Proctor, I cannot, I cannot—

ABIGAIL (*crying to Heaven*): Oh, Heavenly Father, take away this shadow!

(*Without warning or hesitation,* PROCTOR *leaps at* ABIGAIL *and, grabbing her by the hair, pulls her to her feet. She screams in pain.* DANFORTH, *astonished, cries, "What are you about?" and* HATHORNE *and* PARRIS *call, "Take your hands off her!" and out of it all comes* PROCTOR'S *roaring voice.*)

PROCTOR: How do you call Heaven! Whore! Whore!

(HERRICK *breaks* PROCTOR *from her.*)

HERRICK: John!

DANFORTH: Man! Man, what do you—

PROCTOR (*breathless and in agony*): It is a whore!

DANFORTH (*dumfounded*): You charge—?

ABIGAIL: Mr. Danforth, he is lying!

PROCTOR: Mark her! Now she'll suck a scream to stab me with, but—

DANFORTH: You will prove this! This will not pass!

PROCTOR (*trembling, his life collapsing about him*): I have known her, sir. I have known her.

DANFORTH: You—you are a lecher?

FRANCIS (*horrified*): John, you cannot say such a—

PROCTOR: Oh, Francis, I wish you had some evil in you that you might know me! (*to* DANFORTH) A man will not cast away his good name. You surely know that.

DANFORTH (*dumfounded*): In—in what time? In what place?

PROCTOR (*his voice about to break, and his shame great*): In the proper place—where my beasts are bedded. On the last night of my joy, some eight months past. She used to serve me in my house, sir. (*He has to clamp his jaw to keep from weeping.*) A man may think God sleeps, but God sees everything. I know it now. I beg you, sir, I beg you—see her what she is. My wife, my dear good wife, took this girl soon after, sir, and put her out on the highroad. And being what she is, a lump of vanity, sir— (*He is being overcome.*) Excellency, forgive me, forgive me. (*Angrily against himself, he turns away from the* GOVERNOR *for a moment; then, as though to cry out is his only means of speech left*) She thinks to dance with me on my wife's grave! And well she might, for I thought of her softly. God help me, I lusted, and there *is* a promise in such sweat. But it is a whore's vengeance, and you must see it; I set myself entirely in your hands. I know you must see it now.

DANFORTH (*blanched, in horror, turning to* ABIGAIL): You deny every scrap and tittle of this?

ABIGAIL: If I must answer that, I will leave and I will not come back again!

(DANFORTH *seems unsteady*.)

PROCTOR: I have made a bell of my honor! I have rung the doom of my good name—you will believe me, Mr. Danforth! My wife is innocent, except she knew a whore when she saw one!

ABIGAIL (*stepping up to* DANFORTH): What look do you give me? (DANFORTH *cannot speak*.) I'll not have such looks! (*She turns and starts for the door*.)

DANFORTH: You will remain where you are! (HERRICK *steps into her path. She comes up short, fire in her eyes*.) Mr. Parris, go into the court and bring Goodwife Proctor out.

PARRIS (*objecting*): Your Honor, this is all a—

DANFORTH (*sharply to* PARRIS): Bring her out! And tell her not one word of what's been spoken here. And let you knock before you enter. (PARRIS *goes out*.) Now we shall touch the bottom of this swamp. (*to* PROCTOR) Your wife, you say, is an honest woman.

PROCTOR: In her life, sir, she have never lied. There are them that cannot sing, and them that cannot weep—my wife cannot lie. I have paid much to learn it, sir.

DANFORTH: And when she put this girl out of your house, she put her out for a harlot?

PROCTOR: Aye, sir.

DANFORTH: And knew her for a harlot?

PROCTOR: Aye, sir, she knew her for a harlot.

DANFORTH: Good then. (*to* ABIGAIL) And if she tell me, child, it were for harlotry, may God spread His mercy on you! (*There is a knock. He calls to the door*.) Hold! (*to* ABIGAIL) Turn your back. Turn your back. (*to* PROCTOR) Do likewise. (*Both turn their backs*—ABIGAIL *with indignant slowness*.) Now let neither of you turn to face Goody Proctor. No one in this room is to speak one word, or raise a gesture aye or nay. (*He turns toward the door, calls*) Enter! (*The door opens.* ELIZABETH *enters with* PARRIS. PARRIS *leaves her. She stands alone, her eyes looking for* PROCTOR.) Mr. Cheever, report this testimony in all exactness. Are you ready?

CHEEVER: Ready, sir.

DANFORTH: Come here, woman. (ELIZABETH *comes to him, glancing at* PROCTOR'S *back*.) Look at me only, not at your husband. In my eyes only.

ELIZABETH (*faintly*): Good, sir.

DANFORTH: We are given to understand that at one time you dismissed your servant, Abigail Williams.

ELIZABETH: That is true, sir.

DANFORTH: For what cause did you dismiss her? (*Slight pause. Then* ELIZABETH *tries to glance at* PROCTOR.) You will look in my eyes only and not at your husband. The answer is in your memory and you need no help to give it to me. Why did you dismiss Abigail Williams?

ELIZABETH (*not knowing what to say, sensing a situation, wetting her lips to stall for time*): She—dissatisfied me. (*pause*) And my husband.

DANFORTH: In what way dissatisfied you?

ELIZABETH: She were— (*She glances at* PROCTOR *for a cue.*)

DANFORTH: Woman, look at me! (ELIZABETH *does.*) Were she slovenly? Lazy? What disturbance did she cause?

ELIZABETH: Your Honor, I—in that time I were sick. And I— My husband is a good and righteous man. He is never drunk as some are, nor wastin' his time at the shovelboard, but always at his work. But in my sickness—you see, sir, I were a long time sick after my last baby, and I thought I saw my husband somewhat turning from me. And this girl— (*She turns to* ABIGAIL.)

DANFORTH: Look at me.

ELIZABETH: Aye, sir. Abigail Williams— (*She breaks off.*)

DANFORTH: What of Abigail Williams?

ELIZABETH: I came to think he fancied her. And so one night I lost my wits, I think, and put her out on the highroad.

DANFORTH: Your husband—did he indeed turn from you?

ELIZABETH (*in agony*): My husband—is a goodly man, sir.

DANFORTH: Then he did not turn from you.

ELIZABETH (*starting to glance at* PROCTOR): He—

DANFORTH (*reaches out and holds her face, then*): Look at me! To your own knowledge, has John Proctor ever committed the crime of lechery? (*In a crisis of indecision she cannot speak.*) Answer my question! Is your husband a lecher!

ELIZABETH (*faintly*): No, sir.

DANFORTH: Remove her, Marshal.

PROCTOR: Elizabeth, tell the truth!

DANFORTH: She has spoken. Remove her!

PROCTOR (*crying out*): Elizabeth, I have confessed it!

ELIZABETH: Oh, God! (*The door closes behind her.*)

PROCTOR: She only thought to save my name!

HALE: Excellency, it is a natural lie to tell; I beg you, stop now before another is condemned! I may shut my conscience to it no more—private vengeance is working through this testimony! From the beginning this man has struck me true. By my oath to Heaven, I believe him now, and I pray you call back his wife before we—

DANFORTH: She spoke nothing of lechery, and this man has lied!

HALE: I believe him! (*pointing at* ABIGAIL) This girl has always struck me false! She has—

(ABIGAIL, *with a weird, wild, chilling cry, screams up to the ceiling.*)

ABIGAIL: You will not! Begone! Begone, I say!

DANFORTH: What is it, child? (*But* ABIGAIL, *pointing with fear, is now raising up her frightened eyes, her awed face, toward the ceiling—the girls are doing the same—and now* HATHORNE, HALE, PUTNAM, CHEEVER, HERRICK, *and* DANFORTH *do the same.*) What's there? (*He lowers his eyes from the ceiling, and now he is frightened; there is real tension in his voice.*) Child! (*She is transfixed—with all the girls, she is whimpering open-mouthed, agape at the ceiling.*) Girls! Why do you—?

MERCY LEWIS (*pointing*): It's on the beam! Behind the rafter!

DANFORTH (*looking up*): Where!

ABIGAIL: Why—? (*She gulps.*) Why do you come, yellow bird?

PROCTOR: Where's a bird? I see no bird!

ABIGAIL (*to the ceiling*): My face? My face?

PROCTOR: Mr. Hale—

DANFORTH: Be quiet!

PROCTOR (*to* HALE): Do you see a bird?

DANFORTH: Be quiet!

ABIGAIL (*to the ceiling, in a genuine conversation with the "bird," as though trying to talk it out of attacking her*): But God made my face; you cannot want to tear my face. Envy is a deadly sin, Mary.

MARY WARREN (*on her feet with a spring, and horrified, pleading*): Abby!

ABIGAIL (*unperturbed, continuing to the "bird"*): Oh, Mary, this is a black art to change your shape. No, I cannot, I cannot stop my mouth; it's God's work I do.

MARY WARREN: Abby, I'm *here*!

PROCTOR (*frantically*): They're pretending, Mr. Danforth!

ABIGAIL (*now takes a backward step, as though in fear the*

bird will swoop down momentarily): Oh, please, Mary! Don't come down.

SUSANNA WALCOTT: Her claws, she's stretching her claws!

PROCTOR: Lies, lies.

ABIGAIL (*backing further, eyes still fixed above*): Mary, please don't hurt me!

MARY WARREN (*to* DANFORTH): I'm not hurting her!

DANFORTH (*to* MARY WARREN): Why does she see this vision?

MARY WARREN: She sees nothin'!

ABIGAIL (*now staring full front as though hypnotized, and mimicking the exact tone of* MARY WARREN'S *cry*): She sees nothin'!

MARY WARREN (*pleading*): Abby, you mustn't!

ABIGAIL AND ALL THE GIRLS (*all transfixed*): Abby, you mustn't!

MARY WARREN (*to all the girls*): I'm here, I'm here!

GIRLS: I'm here, I'm here!

DANFORTH (*horrified*): Mary Warren! Draw back your spirit out of them!

MARY WARREN: Mr. Danforth!

GIRLS (*cutting her off*): Mr. Danforth!

DANFORTH: Have you compacted with the Devil? Have you?

MARY WARREN: Never, never!

GIRLS: Never, never!

DANFORTH (*growing hysterical*): Why can they only repeat you?

PROCTOR: Give me a whip—I'll stop it!

MARY WARREN: They're sporting. They—!

GIRLS: They're sporting!

MARY WARREN (*turning on them all hysterically and stamping her feet*): Abby, stop it!

GIRLS (*stamping their feet*): Abby, stop it!

MARY WARREN: Stop it!

GIRLS: Stop it!

MARY WARREN (*screaming it out at the top of her lungs, and raising her fists*): Stop it!!

GIRLS (*raising their fists*): Stop it!!

(MARY WARREN, *utterly confounded, and becoming overwhelmed by* ABIGAIL'S—*and the girls'—utter conviction, starts to whimper, hands half raised, powerless, and all the girls begin whimpering exactly as she does.*)

DANFORTH: A little while ago you were afflicted. Now it seems you afflict others; where did you find this power?

MARY WARREN (*staring at* ABIGAIL): I—have no power.

GIRLS: I have no power.

PROCTOR: They're gulling you, Mister!

DANFORTH: Why did you turn about this past two weeks? You have seen the Devil, have you not?

HALE (*indicating* ABIGAIL *and the girls*): You cannot believe them!

MARY WARREN: I—

PROCTOR (*sensing her weakening*): Mary, God damns all liars!

DANFORTH (*pounding it into her*): You have seen the Devil, you have made compact with Lucifer, have you not?

PROCTOR: God damns liars, Mary!

(MARY *utters something unintelligible, staring at* ABIGAIL, *who keeps watching the "bird" above.*)

DANFORTH: I cannot hear you. What do you say? (MARY *utters again unintelligibly.*) You will confess yourself or you will hang! (*He turns her roughly to face him.*) Do you know who I am? I say you will hang if you do not open with me!

PROCTOR: Mary, remember the angel Raphael—do that which is good and—

ABIGAIL (*pointing upward*): The wings! Her wings are spreading! Mary, please, don't, don't—!

HALE: I see nothing, Your Honor!

DANFORTH: Do you confess this power! (*He is an inch from her face.*) Speak!

ABIGAIL: She's going to come down! She's walking the beam!

DANFORTH: Will you speak!

MARY WARREN (*staring in horror*): I cannot!

GIRLS: I cannot!

PARRIS: Cast the Devil out! Look him in the face! Trample him! We'll save you, Mary, only stand fast against him and—

ABIGAIL (*looking up*): Look out! She's coming down!

(*She and all the girls run to one wall, shielding their eyes. And now, as though cornered, they let out a gigantic scream, and* MARY, *as though infected, opens her mouth and screams with them. Gradually* ABIGAIL *and the girls leave off, until only* MARY *is left there, staring up at the "bird," screaming madly. All watch her, horrified by this evident fit.* PROCTOR *strides to her.*)

PROCTOR: Mary, tell the Governor what they— (*He has hardly got a word out, when, seeing him coming for her, she rushes out of his reach, screaming in horror.*)

MARY WARREN: Don't touch me—don't touch me! (*At which the girls halt at the door.*)

PROCTOR (*astonished*): Mary!

MARY WARREN (*pointing at* PROCTOR): You're the Devil's man!

(*He is stopped in his tracks.*)

PARRIS: Praise God!

GIRLS: Praise God!

PROCTOR (*numbed*): Mary, how——?

MARY WARREN: I'll not hang with you! I love God, I love God.

DANFORTH (*to* MARY): He bid you do the Devil's work?

MARY WARREN (*hysterically, indicating* PROCTOR): He come at me by night and every day to sign, to sign, to——

DANFORTH: Sign what?

PARRIS: The Devil's book? He come with a book?

MARY WARREN (*hysterically, pointing at* PROCTOR, *fearful of him*): My name, he want my name. "I'll murder you," he says, "if my wife hangs! We must go and overthrow the court," he says!

(DANFORTH'S *head jerks toward* PROCTOR, *shock and horror in his face.*)

PROCTOR (*turning, appealing to* HALE): Mr. Hale!

MARY WARREN (*her sobs beginning*): He wake me every night, his eyes were like coals and his fingers claw my neck, and I sign, I sign . . .

HALE: Excellency, this child's gone wild!

PROCTOR (*as* DANFORTH'S *wide eyes pour on him*): Mary, Mary!

MARY WARREN (*screaming at him*): No, I love God; I go your way no more. I love God, I bless God. (*Sobbing, she rushes to* ABIGAIL.) Abby, Abby, I'll never hurt you more! (*They all watch, as* ABIGAIL, *out of her infinite charity, reaches out and draws the sobbing* MARY *to her, and then looks up to* DANFORTH.)

DANFORTH (*to* PROCTOR): What are you? (PROCTOR *is beyond speech in his anger.*) You are combined with anti-Christ, are you not? I have seen your power; you will not deny it! What say you, Mister?

HALE: Excellency—

DANFORTH: I will have nothing from you, Mr. Hale! (*to* PROCTOR) Will you confess yourself befouled with Hell, or do you keep that black allegiance yet? What say you?

PROCTOR (*his mind wild, breathless*): I say—I say—God is dead!

PARRIS: Hear it, hear it!

PROCTOR (*laughs insanely, then*): A fire, a fire is burning! I hear the boot of Lucifer, I see his filthy face! And it is my face, and yours, Danforth! For them that quail to bring men out of ignorance, as I have quailed, and as you quail now when you know in all your black hearts that this be fraud— God damns our kind especially, and we will burn, we will burn together.

DANFORTH: Marshal! Take him and Corey with him to the jail!

HALE (*starting across to the door*): I denounce these proceedings!

PROCTOR: You are pulling Heaven down and raising up a whore!

HALE: I denounce these proceedings, I quit this court! (*He slams the door to the outside behind him.*)

DANFORTH (*calling to him in a fury*): Mr. Hale! Mr. Hale!

ACT IV

(*A cell in Salem jail, that fall.*

At the back is a high barred window; near it, a great, heavy door. Along the walls are two benches.

The place is in darkness but for the moonlight seeping through the bars. It appears empty. Presently footsteps are heard coming down a corridor beyond the walls, keys rattle and the door swings open. MARSHAL HERRICK *enters with a lantern.*

He is nearly drunk, and heavy-footed. He goes to a bench and nudges a bundle of rags lying on it.)

HERRICK: Sarah, wake up! Sarah Good! (*He then crosses to the other bench.*)

SARAH GOOD (*rising in her rags*): Oh, Majesty! Comin', comin'! Tituba, he's here, His Majesty's come!

HERRICK: Go to the north cell; this place is wanted now. (*He hangs his lantern on the wall.* TITUBA *sits up.*)

TITUBA: That don't look to me like His Majesty: look to ~e like the marshal.

HERRICK (*taking out a flask*): Get along with you now, clear this place. (*He drinks, and* SARAH GOOD *comes and peers up into his face.*)

SARAH GOOD: Oh, it is you, Marshal! I thought sure you be the Devil comin' for us. Could I have a sip of cider for me goin'-away?

HERRICK (*handing her the flask*): And where are you off to, Sarah?

TITUBA (*as* SARAH *drinks*): We goin' to Barbados, soon the Devil gits here with the feathers and the wings.

HERRICK: Oh? A happy voyage to you.

SARAH GOOD: A pair of bluebirds wingin' southerly, the two of us! Oh, it be a grand transformation, Marshal! (*She raises the flask to drink again.*)

HERRICK (*taking the flask from her lips*): You'd best give me that or you'll never rise off the ground. Come along now.

TITUBA: I'll speak to him for you, if you desires to come along, Marshal.

HERRICK: I'd not refuse it, Tituba; it's the proper morning to fly into Hell.

TITUBA: Oh, it be no Hell in Barbados. Devil, him be pleasureman in Barbados, him be singin' and dancin' in Barbados. It's you folks—you riles him up 'round here; it be too cold 'round here for that Old Boy. He freeze his soul in Massachusetts, but in Barbados he just as sweet and—(*A bellowing cow is heard, and* TITUBA *leaps up and calls to the window*): Aye, sir! That's him, Sarah!

SARAH GOOD: I'm here, Majesty! (*They hurriedly pick up their rags as* HOPKINS, *a guard, enters.*)

HOPKINS: The Deputy Governor's arrived.

HERRICK (*grabbing* TITUBA): Come along, come along.

TITUBA (*resisting him*): No, he comin' for me. I goin' home!

HERRICK (*pulling her to the door*): That's not Satan, just a poor old cow with a hatful of milk. Come along now, out with you!

TITUBA (*calling to the window*): Take me home, Devil! Take me home!

SARAH GOOD (*following the shouting* TITUBA *out*): Tell him I'm goin', Tituba! Now you tell him Sarah Good is goin' too!

(*In the corridor outside* TITUBA *calls on*—"*Take me home, Devil; Devil take me home!*" *and* HOPKINS' *voice orders her to move on.* HERRICK *returns and begins to push old rags and straw into a corner. Hearing footsteps, he turns, and enter* DANFORTH *and* JUDGE HATHORNE. *They are in great-coats and wear hats against the bitter cold. They àre followed by* CHEEVER, *who carries a dispatch case and a flat wooden box containing his writing materials.*)

HERRICK: Good morning, Excellency.

DANFORTH: Where is Mr. Parris?

HERRICK: I'll fetch him. (*He starts for the door.*)

DANFORTH: Marshal. (HERRICK *stops.*) When did Reverend Hale arrive?

HERRICK: It were toward midnight, I think.

DANFORTH (*suspiciously*): What is he about here?

HERRICK: He goes among them that will hang, sir. And he prays with them. He sits with Goody Nurse now. And Mr. Parris with him.

DANFORTH: Indeed. That man have no authority to enter here, Marshal. Why have you let him in?

HERRICK: Why, Mr. Parris command me, sir. I cannot deny him.

DANFORTH: Are you drunk, Marshal?

HERRICK: No, sir; it is a bitter night, and I have no fire here.

DANFORTH (*containing his anger*): Fetch Mr. Parris.

HERRICK: Aye, sir.

DANFORTH: There is a prodigious stench in this place.

HERRICK: I have only now cleared the people out for you.

DANFORTH: Beware hard drink, Marshal.

HERRICK: Aye, sir.

(*He waits an instant for further orders. But* DANFORTH, *in dissatisfaction, turns his back on him, and* HERRICK *goes out. There is a pause.* DANFORTH *stands in thought.*)

HATHORNE: Let you question Hale, Excellency; I should not be surprised he have been preaching in Andover lately.

DANFORTH: We'll come to that; speak nothing of Andover. Parris prays with him. That's strange. (*He blows on his hand, moves toward the window, and looks out.*)

HATHORNE: Excellency, I wonder if it be wise to let Mr. Parris so continuously with the prisoners. (DANFORTH *turns to him, interested.*) I think, sometimes, the man has a mad look these days.

DANFORTH: Mad?

HATHORNE: I met him yesterday coming out of his house, and I bid him good morning—and he wept and went his way. I think it is not well the village sees him so unsteady.

DANFORTH: Perhaps he have some sorrow.

CHEEVER (*stamping his feet against the cold*): I think it be the cows, sir.

DANFORTH: Cows?

CHEEVER: There be so many cows wanderin' the high-roads, now their masters are in the jails, and much disagreement who they will belong to now. I know Mr. Parris be arguin' with farmers all yesterday—there is great contention, sir, about the cows. Contention make him weep, sir; it were always a man that weep for contention. (*He turns, as do* HATHORNE *and* DANFORTH, *hearing someone coming up the corridor.* DANFORTH *raises his head as* PARRIS *enters. He is gaunt, frightened, and sweating in his great-coat.*)

PARRIS (*to* DANFORTH, *instantly*): Oh, good morning, sir, thank you for coming. I beg your pardon wakin' you so early. Good morning, Judge Hathorne.

DANFORTH: Reverend Hale have no right to enter this—

PARRIS: Excellency, a moment. (*He hurries back and shuts the door.*)

HATHORNE: Do you leave him alone with the prisoners?

DANFORTH: What's his business here?

PARRIS (*prayerfully holding up his hands*): Excellency, hear me. It is a providence. Reverend Hale has returned to bring Rebecca Nurse to God.

DANFORTH (*surprised*): He bids her confess?

PARRIS (*sitting*): Hear me. Rebecca have not given me a word this three month since she came. Now she sits with him, and her sister and Martha Corey and two or three others, and he pleads with them, confess their crimes and save their lives.

DANFORTH: Why—this is indeed a providence. And they soften, they soften?

PARRIS: Not yet, not yet. But I thought to summon you, sir, that we might think on whether it be not wise, to— (*He dares not say it.*) I had thought to put a question, sir, and I hope you will not—

DANFORTH: Mr. Parris, be plain, what troubles you?

PARRIS: There is news, sir, that the court—the court must reckon with. My niece, sir, my niece—I believe she has vanished.

DANFORTH: Vanished!

PARRIS: I had thought to advise you of it earlier in the week, but—

DANFORTH: Why? How long is she gone?

PARRIS: This be the third night. You see, sir, she told me

she would stay a night with Mercy Lewis. And next day, when she does not return, I send to Mr. Lewis to inquire. Mercy told him she would sleep in *my* house for a night.

DANFORTH: They are both gone?

PARRIS (*in fear of him*): They are, sir.

DANFORTH (*alarmed*): I will send a party for them. Where may they be?

PARRIS: Excellency, I think they be aboard a ship. (DANFORTH *stands agape.*) My daughter tells me how she heard them speaking of ships last week, and tonight I discover my—my strongbox is broke into. (*He presses his fingers against his eyes to keep back tears.*)

HATHORNE (*astonished*): She have robbed you?

PARRIS: Thirty-one pound is gone. I am penniless. (*He covers his face and sobs.*)

DANFORTH: Mr. Parris, you are a brainless man! (*He walks in thought, deeply worried.*)

PARRIS: Excellency, it profit nothing you should blame me. I cannot think they would run off except they fear to keep in Salem any more. (*He is pleading.*) Mark it, sir, Abigail had close knowledge of the town, and since the news of Andover has broken here—

DANFORTH: Andover is remedied. The court returns there on Friday, and will resume examinations.

PARRIS: I am sure of it, sir. But the rumor here speaks rebellion in Andover, and it—

DANFORTH: There is no rebellion in Andover!

PARRIS: I tell you what is said here, sir. Andover have thrown out the court, they say, and will have no part of witchcraft. There be a faction here, feeding on that news, and I tell you true, sir, I fear there will be riot here.

HATHORNE: Riot! Why at every execution I have seen naught but high satisfaction in town.

PARRIS: Judge Hathorne—it were another sort that hanged till now. Rebecca Nurse is no Bridget that lived three year with Bishop before she married him. John Proctor is not Isaac Ward that drank his family to ruin. (*to* DANFORTH) I would to God it were not so, Excellency, but these people have great weight yet in the town. Let Rebecca stand upon the gibbet and send up some righteous prayer, and I fear she'll wake a vengeance on you.

HATHORNE: Excellency, she is condemned a witch. The court have—

DANFORTH (*in deep concern, raising a hand to* HATHORNE): Pray you. (*to* PARRIS) How do you propose, then?

PARRIS: Excellency, I would postpone these hangin's for a time.

DANFORTH: There will be no postponement.

PARRIS: Now Mr. Hale's returned, there is hope, I think —for if he bring even one of these to God, that confession surely damns the others in the public eye, and none may doubt more that they are all linked to Hell. This way, unconfessed and claiming innocence, doubts are multiplied, many honest people will weep for them, and our good purpose is lost in their tears.

DANFORTH (*after thinking a moment, then going to* CHEEVER): Give me the list.

(CHEEVER *opens the dispatch case, searches.*)

PARRIS: It cannot be forgot, sir, that when I summoned the congregation for John Proctor's excommunication there were hardly thirty people come to hear it. That speak a discontent, I think, and—

DANFORTH (*studying the list*): There will be no postponement.

PARRIS: Excellency—

DANFORTH: Now, sir—which of these in your opinion may be brought to God? I will myself strive with him till dawn. (*He hands the list to* PARRIS, *who merely glances at it.*)

PARRIS: There is not sufficient time till dawn.

DANFORTH: I shall do my utmost. Which of them do you have hope for?

PARRIS (*not even glancing at the list now, and in a quavering voice, quietly*): Excellency—a dagger—(*He chokes up.*)

DANFORTH: What do you say?

PARRIS: Tonight, when I open my door to leave my house —a dagger clattered to the ground. (*Silence.* DANFORTH *absorbs this; now* PARRIS *cries out*) You cannot hang this sort. There is danger for me. I dare not step outside at night!

(REVEREND HALE *enters. They look at him for an instant in silence. He is steeped in sorrow, exhausted, and more direct than he ever was.*)

DANFORTH: Accept my congratulations, Reverend Hale; we are gladdened to see you returned to your good work.

HALE (*coming to* DANFORTH *now*): You must pardon them. They will not budge.

(HERRICK *enters, waits.*)

DANFORTH (*conciliatory*): You misunderstand, sir; I cannot pardon these when twelve are already hanged for the same crime. It is not just.

PARRIS (*with failing heart*): Rebecca will not confess?

HALE: The sun will rise in a few minutes. Excellency, I must have more time.

DANFORTH: Now hear me, and beguile yourselves no more. I will not receive a single plea for pardon or postponement. Them that will not confess will hang. Twelve are already executed; the names of these seven are given out, and the village expects to see them die this morning. Postponement now speaks of floundering on my part; reprieve or pardon must cast doubt upon the guilt of them that died till now. While I speak God's law, I will not crack its voice with whimpering. If retaliation is your fear, know this—I should hang ten thousand that dared to rise against the law, and an ocean of salt tears could not melt the resolution of the statutes. Now draw yourselves up like men and help me, as you are bound by Heaven to do. Have you spoken with them all, Mr. Hale?

HALE: All but Proctor. He is in the dungeon.

DANFORTH (*to* HERRICK): What's Proctor's way now?

HERRICK: He sits like some great bird; you'd not know he lived except he will take food from time to time.

DANFORTH (*after thinking a moment*): His wife—his wife must be well on with child now.

HERRICK: She is, sir.

DANFORTH: What think you, Mr. Parris? You have closer knowledge of this man; might her presence soften him?

PARRIS: It is possible, sir. He have not laid eyes on her these three months. I should summon her.

DANFORTH (*to* HERRICK): Is he yet adamant? Has he struck at you again?

HERRICK: He cannot, sir, he is chained to the wall now.

DANFORTH (*after thinking on it*): Fetch Goody Proctor to me. Then let you bring him up.

HERRICK: Aye, sir.

(HERRICK *goes. There is silence.*)

HALE: Excellency, if you postpone a week and publish to the town that you are striving for their confessions, that speak mercy on your part, not faltering.

DANFORTH: Mr. Hale, as God have not empowered me like Joshua to stop this sun from rising, so I cannot withhold from them the perfection of their punishment.

HALE (*harder now*): If you think God wills you to raise rebellion, Mr. Danforth, you are mistaken!

DANFORTH (*instantly*): You have heard rebellion spoken in the town?

HALE: Excellency, there are orphans wandering from house to house; abandoned cattle bellow on the highroads, the stink of rotting crops hangs everywhere, and no man knows when the harlots' cry will end his life—and you wonder yet if rebellion's spoke? Better you should marvel how they do not burn your province!

DANFORTH: Mr. Hale, have you preached in Andover this month?

HALE: Thank God they have no need of me in Andover.

DANFORTH: You baffle me, sir. Why have you returned here?

HALE: Why, it is all simple. I come to do the Devil's work. I come to counsel Christians they should belie themselves. (*His sarcasm collapses.*) There is blood on my head! Can you not see the blood on my head!!

PARRIS: Hush! (*For he has heard footsteps. They all face the door.* HERRICK *enters with* ELIZABETH. *Her wrists are linked by heavy chain, which* HERRICK *now removes. Her clothes are dirty; her face is pale and gaunt.*

HERRICK *goes out.*)

DANFORTH (*very politely*): Goody Proctor. (*She is silent.*) I hope you are hearty?

ELIZABETH (*as a warning reminder*): I am yet six months before my time.

DANFORTH: Pray be at your ease, we come not for your life. We (*uncertain how to plead, for he is not accustomed to it*) Mr. Hale, will you speak with the woman?

HALE: Goody Proctor, your husband is marked to hang this morning.

(*Pause.*)

ELIZABETH (*quietly*): I have heard it.

HALE: You know, do you not, that I have no connection with the court? (*She seems to doubt it.*) I come of my own, Goody Proctor. I would save your husband's life, for if he is taken I count myself his murderer. Do you understand me?

ELIZABETH: What do you want of me?

HALE: Goody Proctor, I have gone this three month like our Lord into the wilderness. I have sought a Christian way, for damnation's doubled on a minister who counsels men to lie.

HATHORNE: It is no lie, you cannot speak of lies.

HALE: It is a lie! They are innocent!

DANFORTH: I'll hear no more of that!

HALE (*continuing to* ELIZABETH): Let you not mistake

your duty as I mistook my own. I came into this village like a bridegroom to his beloved, bearing gifts of high religion; the very crowns of holy law I brought, and what I touched with my bright confidence, it died; and where I turned the eye of my great faith, blood flowed up. Beware, Goody Proctor—cleave to no faith when faith brings blood. It is mistaken law that leads you to sacrifice. Life, woman, life is God's most precious gift; no principle, however glorious, may justify the taking of it. I beg you, woman, prevail upon your husband to confess. Let him give his lie. Quail not before God's judgment in this, for it may well be God damns a liar less than he that throws his life away for pride. Will you plead with him? I cannot think he will listen to another.

ELIZABETH (*quietly*): I think that be the Devil's argument.

HALE (*with climactic desperation*): Woman, before the laws of God we are as swine! We cannot read His will!

ELIZABETH: I cannot dispute with you, sir; I lack learning for it.

DANFORTH (*going to her*): Goody Proctor, you are not summoned here for disputation. Be there no wifely tenderness within you? He will die with the sunrise. Your husband. Do you understand it? (*She only looks at him.*) What say you? Will you contend with him? (*She is silent.*) Are you stone? I tell you true, woman, had I no other proof of your unnatural life, your dry eyes now would be sufficient evidence that you delivered up your soul to Hell! A very ape would weep at such calamity! Have the devil dried up any tear of pity in you? (*She is silent.*) Take her out. It profit nothing she should speak to him!

ELIZABETH (*quietly*): Let me speak with him, Excellency.

PARRIS (*with hope*): You'll strive with him? (*She hesitates.*)

DANFORTH: Will you plead for his confession or will you not?

ELIZABETH: I promise nothing. Let me speak with him.

(*A sound—the sibilance of dragging feet on stone. They turn. A pause.* HERRICK *enters with* JOHN PROCTOR. *His wrists are chained. He is another man, bearded, filthy, his eyes misty as though webs had overgrown them. He halts inside the doorway, his eye caught by the sight of* ELIZABETH. *The emotion flowing between them prevents anyone from speaking for an instant. Now* HALE, *visibly affected, goes to* DANFORTH *and speaks quietly.*)

HALE: Pray, leave them, Excellency.

DANFORTH (*pressing* HALE *impatiently aside*): Mr. Proctor, you have been notified, have you not? (PROCTOR *is silent, staring at* ELIZABETH.) I see light in the sky, Mister; let you counsel with your wife, and may God help you turn your back on Hell. (PROCTOR *is silent, staring at* ELIZABETH.)

HALE (*quietly*): Excellency, let—

(DANFORTH *brushes past* HALE *and walks out.* HALE *follows.* CHEEVER *stands and follows,* HATHORNE *behind.* HERRICK *goes.* PARRIS, *from a safe distance, offers*)

PARRIS: If you desire a cup of cider, Mr. Proctor, I am sure I— (PROCTOR *turns an icy stare at him, and he breaks off.* PARRIS *raises his palms toward* PROCTOR.) God lead you now.

(PARRIS *goes out.*)

(*Alone.* PROCTOR *walks to her, halts. It is as though they stood in a spinning world. It is beyond sorrow, above it. He reaches out his hand as though toward an embodiment not quite real, and as he touches her, a strange soft sound, half laughter, half amazement, comes from his throat. He pats her hand. She covers his hand with hers. And then, weak, he sits. Then she sits, facing him.*)

PROCTOR: The child?

ELIZABETH: It grows.

PROCTOR: There is no word of the boys?

ELIZABETH: They're well. Rebecca's Samuel keeps them.

PROCTOR: You have not seen them?

ELIZABETH: I have not. (*She catches a weakening in herself and downs it.*)

PROCTOR: You are a—marvel, Elizabeth.

ELIZABETH: You—have been tortured?

PROCTOR: Aye. (*Pause. She will not let herself be drowned in the sea that threatens her.*) They come for my life now.

ELIZABETH: I know it.

(*Pause.*)

PROCTOR: None—have yet confessed?

ELIZABETH: There be many confessed.

PROCTOR: Who are they?

ELIZABETH: There be a hundred or more, they say. Goody Ballard is one; Isaiah Goodkind is one. There be many.

PROCTOR: Rebecca?

ELIZABETH: Not Rebecca. She is one foot in Heaven now; naught may hurt her more.

PROCTOR: And Giles?

ELIZABETH: You have not heard of it?

PROCTOR: I hear nothin', where I am kept.

ELIZABETH: Giles is dead.

(*He looks at her incredulously.*)

PROCTOR: When were he hanged?

ELIZABETH (*quietly, factually*): He were not hanged. He would not answer aye or nay to his indictment; for if he denied the charge they'd hang him surely, and auction out his property. So he stand mute, and died Christian under the law. And so his sons will have his farm. It is the law, for he could not be condemned a wizard without he answer the indictment, aye or nay.

PROCTOR: Then how does he die?

ELIZABETH (*gently*): They press him, John.

PROCTOR: Press?

ELIZABETH: Great stones they lay upon his chest until he plead aye or nay. (*with a tender smile for the old man*) They say he give them but two words. "More weight," he says. And died.

PROCTOR (*numbed—a thread to weave into his agony*): "More weight."

ELIZABETH: Aye. It were a fearsome man, Giles Corey.
(*Pause.*)

PROCTOR (*with great force of will, but not quite looking at her*): I have been thinking I would confess to them, Elizabeth. (*She shows nothing.*) What say you? If I give them that?

ELIZABETH: I cannot judge you, John.
(*Pause.*)

PROCTOR (*simply—a pure question*): What would you have me do?

ELIZABETH: As you will, I would have it. (*slight pause*) I want you living, John. That's sure.

PROCTOR (*pauses, then with a flailing of hope*): Giles' wife? Have she confessed?

ELIZABETH: She will not.
(*Pause.*)

PROCTOR: It is a pretense, Elizabeth.

ELIZABETH: What is?

PROCTOR: I cannot mount the gibbet like a saint. It is a fraud. I am not that man. (*She is silent.*) My honesty is broke, Elizabeth; I am no good man. Nothing's spoiled by giving them this lie that were not rotten long before.

ELIZABETH: And yet you've not confessed till now. That speak goodness in you.

PROCTOR: Spite only keeps me silent. It is hard to give a lie to dogs. (*Pause. For the first time he turns directly to her.*) I would have your forgiveness, Elizabeth.

ELIZABETH: It is not for me to give, John, I am—

PROCTOR: I'd have you see some honesty in it. Let them that never lied die now to keep their souls. It is pretense for me, a vanity that will not blind God nor keep my children out of the wind. (*pause*) What say you?

ELIZABETH (*upon a heaving sob that always threatens*): John, it come to naught that I should forgive you, if you'll not forgive yourself. (*Now he turns away a little, in great agony.*) It is not my soul, John, it is yours. (*He stands, as though in physical pain, slowly rising to his feet with a great immortal longing to find his answer. It is difficult to say, and she is on the verge of tears.*) Only be sure of this, for I know it now: Whatever you will do, it is a good man does it. (*He turns his doubting, searching gaze upon her.*) I have read my heart this three month, John. (*pause*) I have sins of my own to count. It needs a cold wife to prompt lechery.

PROCTOR (*in great pain*): Enough, enough—

ELIZABETH (*now pouring out her heart*): Better you should know me!

PROCTOR: I will not hear it! I know you!

ELIZABETH: You take my sins upon you, John—

PROCTOR (*in agony*): No, I take my own, my own!

ELIZABETH: John, I counted myself so plain, so poorly made, no honest love could come to me! Suspicion kissed you when I did; I never knew how I should say my love. It were a cold house I kept! (*In fright, she swerves, as* HATHORNE *enters.*)

HATHORNE: What say you, Proctor? The sun is soon up.

(PROCTOR, *his chest heaving, stares, turns to* ELIZABETH. *She comes to him as though to plead, her voice quaking.*)

ELIZABETH: Do what you will. But let none be your judge. There be no higher judge under Heaven than Proctor is! Forgive me, forgive me, John—I never knew such goodness in the world! (*She covers her face, weeping.*)

(PROCTOR *turns from her to* HATHORNE; *he is off the earth, his voice hollow.*)

PROCTOR: I want my life.

HATHORNE (*electrified, surprised*): You'll confess yourself?

PROCTOR: I will have my life.

HATHORNE (*with a mystical tone*): God be praised! It is a providence! (*He rushes out the door, and his voice is heard calling down the corridor.*) He will confess! Proctor will confess!

PROCTOR (*with a cry, as he strides to the door*): Why do you cry it? (*In great pain he turns back to her.*) It is evil, is it not? It is evil.

ELIZABETH (*in terror, weeping*): I cannot judge you, John, I cannot!

PROCTOR: Then who will judge me? (*suddenly clasping his hands*) God in Heaven, what is John Proctor, what is John Proctor? (*He moves as an animal, and a fury is riding in him, a tantalized search.*) I think it is honest, I think so; I am no saint. (*As though she had denied this he calls angrily at her*) Let Rebecca go like a saint; for me it is fraud!

(*Voices are heard in the hall, speaking together in suppressed excitement.*)

ELIZABETH: I am not your judge, I cannot be. (*as though giving him release*) Do as you will, do as you will!

PROCTOR: Would you give them such a lie? Say it. Would you ever give them this? (*She cannot answer.*) You would not; if tongs of fire were singeing you you would not! It is evil. Good, then—it is evil, and I do it!

(HATHORNE *enters with* DANFORTH *and, with them,* CHEEVER, PARRIS, *and* HALE. *It is a businesslike, rapid entrance, as though the ice had been broken.*)

DANFORTH (*with great relief and gratitude*): Praise to God, man, praise to God; you shall be blessed in Heaven for this. (CHEEVER *has hurried to the bench with pen, ink, and paper.* PROCTOR *watches him.*) Now then, let us have it. Are you ready, Mr. Cheever?

PROCTOR (*with a cold, cold horror at their efficiency*): Why must it be written?

DANFORTH: Why, for the good instruction of the village, Mister; this we shall post upon the church door! (*to* PARRIS, *urgently*) Where is the marshal?

PARRIS (*runs to the door and calls down the corridor*): Marshal! Hurry!

DANFORTH: Now, then, Mister, will you speak slowly, and directly to the point, for Mr. Cheever's sake. (*He is on record now, and is really dictating to* CHEEVER, *who writes.*) Mr. Proctor, have you seen the Devil in your life? (PROCTOR'S *jaws lock.*) Come, man, there is light in the sky; the town waits at the scaffold; I would give out this news. Did you see the Devil?

PROCTOR: I did.

PARRIS: Praise God!

DANFORTH: And when he come to you, what were his demand? (PROCTOR *is silent.* DANFORTH *helps.*) Did he bid you to do his work upon the earth?

PROCTOR: He did.

DANFORTH: And you bound yourself to his service? (DAN-

FORTH *turns, as* REBECCA NURSE *enters, with* HERRICK *helping to support her. She is barely able to walk.*) Come in, come in, woman!

REBECCA (*brightening as she sees* PROCTOR): Ah, John! You are well, then, eh?

(PROCTOR *turns his face to the wall.*)

DANFORTH: Courage, man, courage—let her witness your good example that she may come to God herself. Now hear it, Goody Nurse! Say on, Mr. Proctor. Did you bind yourself to the Devil's service?

REBECCA (*astonished*): Why, John!

PROCTOR (*through his teeth, his face turned from* REBECCA): I did.

DANFORTH: Now, woman, you surely see it profit nothin' to keep this conspiracy any further. Will you confess yourself with him?

REBECCA: Oh, John—God send his mercy on you!

DANFORTH: I say, will you confess yourself, Goody Nurse?

REBECCA: Why, it is a lie, it is a lie; how may I damn myself? I cannot, I cannot.

DANFORTH: Mr. Proctor. When the Devil came to you did you see Rebecca Nurse in his company? (PROCTOR *is silent.*) Come, man, take courage—did you ever see her with the Devil?

PROCTOR (*almost inaudibly*): No.

(DANFORTH, *now sensing trouble, glances at* JOHN *and goes to the table, and picks up a sheet—the list of condemned.*)

DANFORTH: Did you ever see her sister, Mary Easty, with the Devil?

PROCTOR: No, I did not.

DANFORTH (*His eyes narrow on* PROCTOR.): Did you ever see Martha Corey with the Devil?

PROCTOR: I did not.

DANFORTH (*realizing, slowly putting the sheet down*): Did you ever see anyone with the Devil?

PROCTOR: I did not.

DANFORTH: Proctor, you mistake me. I am not empowered to trade your life for a lie. You have most certainly seen some person with the Devil. (PROCTOR *is silent.*) Mr. Proctor, a score of people have already testified they saw this woman with the Devil.

PROCTOR: Then it is proved. Why must I say it?

DANFORTH: Why "must" you say it! Why, you should rejoice to say it if your soul is truly purged of any love for Hell!

PROCTOR: They think to go like saints. I like not to spoil their names.

DANFORTH (*inquiring, incredulous*): Mr. Proctor, do you think they go like saints?

PROCTOR (*evading*): This woman never thought she done the Devil's work.

DANFORTH: Look you, sir. I think you mistake your duty here. It matters nothing what she thought—she is convicted of the unnatural murder of children, and you for sending your spirit out upon Mary Warren. Your soul alone is the issue here, Mister, and you will prove its whiteness or you cannot live in a Christian country. Will you tell me now what persons conspired with you in the Devil's company? (PROCTOR *is silent*.) To your knowledge was Rebecca Nurse ever—

PROCTOR: I speak my own sins; I cannot judge another. (*crying out, with hatred*) I have no tongue for it.

HALE (*quickly to* DANFORTH): Excellency, it is enough he confess himself. Let him sign it, let him sign it.

PARRIS (*feverishly*): It is a great service, sir. It is a weighty name; it will strike the village that Proctor confess. I beg you, let him sign it. The sun is up, Excellency!

DANFORTH (*considers; then with dissatisfaction*): Come, then, sign your testimony. (*to* CHEEVER) Give it to him. (CHEEVER *goes to* PROCTOR, *the confession and a pen in hand*. PROCTOR *does not look at it*.) Come, man, sign it.

PROCTOR (*after glancing at the confession*): You have all witnessed it—it is enough.

DANFORTH: You will not sign it?

PROCTOR: You have all witnessed it; what more is needed?

DANFORTH: Do you sport with me? You will sign your name or it is no confession, Mister! (*His breast heaving with agonizing breathing*, PROCTOR *now lays the paper down and signs his name*.)

PARRIS: Praise be to the Lord!

(PROCTOR *has just finished signing when* DANFORTH *reaches for the paper. But* PROCTOR *snatches it up, and now a wild terror is rising in him, and a boundless anger*.)

DANFORTH (*perplexed, but politely extending his hand*): If you please, sir.

PROCTOR: No.

DANFORTH (*as though* PROCTOR *did not understand*): Mr. Proctor, I must have—

PROCTOR: No, no. I have signed it. You have seen me. It is done! You have no need for this.

PARRIS: Proctor, the village must have proof that—

PROCTOR: Damn the village! I confess to God, and God has seen my name on this! It is enough!

DANFORTH: No, sir, it is—

PROCTOR: You came to save my soul, did you not? Here! I have confessed myself; it is enough!

DANFORTH: You have not con—

PROCTOR: I have confessed myself! Is there no good penitence but it be public? God does not need my name nailed upon the church! God sees my name; God knows how black my sins are! It is enough!

DANFORTH: Mr. Proctor—

PROCTOR: You will not use me! I am no Sarah Good or Tituba, I am John Proctor! You will not use me! It is no part of salvation that you should use me!

DANFORTH: I do not wish to—

PROCTOR: I have three children—how may I teach them to walk like men in the world, and I sold my friends?

DANFORTH: You have not sold your friends—

PROCTOR: Beguile me not! I blacken all of them when this is nailed to the church the very day they hang for silence!

DANFORTH: Mr. Proctor, I must have good and legal proof that you—

PROCTOR: You are the high court, your word is good enough! Tell them I confessed myself; say Proctor broke his knees and wept like a woman; say what you will, but my name cannot—

DANFORTH (*with suspicion*): It is the same, is it not? If I report it or you sign to it?

PROCTOR (*He knows it is insane.*): No, it is not the same! What others say and what I sign to is not the same!

DANFORTH: Why? Do you mean to deny this confession when you are free?

PROCTOR: I mean to deny nothing!

DANFORTH: Then explain to me, Mr. Proctor, why you will not let—

PROCTOR (*with a cry of his whole soul*): Because it is my name! Because I cannot have another in my life! Because I lie and sign myself to lies! Because I am not worth the dust on the feet of them that hang! How may I live without my name? I have given you my soul; leave me my name!

DANFORTH (*pointing at the confession in* PROCTOR'S *hand*): Is that document a lie? If it is a lie I will not accept it! What say you? I will not deal in lies, Mister! (PROCTOR *is motion-*

less.) You will give me your honest confession in my hand, or I cannot keep you from the rope. (PROCTOR *does not reply.*) Which way do you go, Mister?

(*His breast heaving, his eyes staring,* PROCTOR *tears the paper and crumples it, and he is weeping in fury, but erect.*)

DANFORTH: Marshal!

PARRIS (*hysterically, as though the tearing paper were his life*): Proctor, Proctor!

HALE: Man, you will hang! You cannot!

PROCTOR (*his eyes full of tears*): I can. And there's your first marvel, that I can. You have made your magic now, for now I do think I see some shred of goodness in John Proctor. Not enough to weave a banner with, but white enough to keep it from such dogs. (ELIZABETH, *in a burst of terror, rushes to him and weeps against his hand.*) Give them no tear! Tears pleasure them! Show honor now, show a stony heart and sink them with it! (*He has lifted her, and kisses her now with great passion.*)

REBECCA: Let you fear nothing! Another judgment waits us all!

DANFORTH: Hang them high over the town! Who weeps for these, weeps for corruption! (*He sweeps out past them.* HERRICK *starts to lead* REBECCA, *who almost collapses, but* PROCTOR *catches her, and she glances up at him apologetically.*)

REBECCA: I've had no breakfast.

HERRICK: Come, man.

(HERRICK *escorts them out,* HATHORNE *and* CHEEVER *behind them.* ELIZABETH *stands staring at the empty doorway.*)

PARRIS (*in deadly fear, to* ELIZABETH): Go to him, Goody Proctor! There is yet time!

(*From outside a drumroll strikes the air.* PARRIS *is startled.* ELIZABETH *jerks about toward the window.*)

PARRIS: Go to him! (*He rushes out the door, as though to hold back his fate.*) Proctor! Proctor!

(*Again, a short burst of drums.*)

HALE: Woman, plead with him! (*He starts to rush out the door, and then goes back to her.*) Woman! It is pride, it is vanity. (*She avoids his eyes, and moves to the window. He drops to his knees.*) Be his helper!—What profit him to bleed? Shall the dust praise him? Shall the worms declare his truth? Go to him, take his shame away!

ELIZABETH (*supporting herself against collapse, grips the*

bars of the window, and with a cry): He have his goodness now. God forbid I take it from him!

(The final drumroll crashes, then heightens violently. HALE *weeps in frantic prayer, and the new sun is pouring in upon her face, and the drums rattle like bones in the morning air.)*

Henrik Ibsen:

An Enemy of the People

Henrik Ibsen (1828–1906), Norwegian poet-playwright, in-augurated the realistic tradition in modern theater and im-posed his powerful ideas upon contemporary thought. He began his career in the theater at twenty-three as a director and resident playwright but was nearly forty when he com-pleted his first masterpiece, Peer Gynt, *a verse drama in the romantic tradition. The publication of* Peer Gynt, *in Ibsen's fortieth year, marked a significant change in his life. Two years before, he had been granted a government pension; for the better part of a quarter-century Ibsen exiled himself from Norway, preferring to live and work in Italy, Austria, and Germany. The period of his exile coincided with the com-position of most of the major plays that followed* Peer Gynt: Emperor and Galilean *(1873);* The Pillars of Society *(1877);* A Doll's House *(1879);* Ghosts *(1881);* An Enemy of the People *(1882);* The Wild Duck *(1884);* Rosmersholm *(1886);* The Lady from the Sea *(1888);* Hedda Gabbler *(1890);* The Master Builder *(1892);* John Gabriel Borkman *(1896);* When We Dead Awaken *(1899). Ibsen did not re-turn to live in Norway until 1891, when he settled in Oslo, where he remained until his death.*

An Enemy of the People is an indignant play, and it is a means by which Ibsen could express a number of his social ideas, some of which were a reaction to the suppression and the obloquy which attended his publication of *Ghosts*. In this play we view the ruin of a man (and his family) whose position on a vital community issue is clearly and ineluct-ably right. Ibsen polarizes Stockmann's opposition so that it is wholly in the wrong. But this is no melodrama. As we read the play we discover that Stockmann is not intended to symbolize pure idealism, nor are his opponents unmiti-gated blackguards. Stockmann is tactless and arrogant. His position is sound, but the complexities, the tensions, the delicate dependencies of modern urban life make absurd the self-important individualism that Stockmann assumes for himself.

But what is the alternative to Stockmann's position? Compromise? Delay? Surrender? When a man finds his community threatened by profound corruption what else can he do but speak out loud and clear? The evil that threatened Ibsen's Norwegian coastal town has its counterpart in the conditions infesting our cities today. But it is one thing to identify and diagnose a cancer; it is another thing to expunge it. The cure cannot be effected by one man nor even by a small group of men.

In his play, Ibsen has dramatized a central issue of our own time. If we could grasp the relevance of Ibsen's implications, we might better provide more rational answers than those society has come up with in the past.

An Enemy of the People

THE R. FARQUHARSON SHARP TRANSLATION
NEWLY REVISED AND MODERNIZED
FOR THIS EDITION

Characters

DR. THOMAS STOCKMANN, Medical Officer of the Municipal Baths.

MRS. STOCKMANN, his wife.

PETRA, their daughter, a teacher.

EJLIF
MORTEN } their sons (aged 13 and 10 respectively).

PETER STOCKMANN, the Doctor's elder brother; Mayor of the Town and Chief Constable, Chairman of the Baths' Committee, etc., etc.

MORTEN KIIL, a tanner (Mrs. Stockmann's adoptive father).

HOVSTAD, editor of the *People's Messenger*.

BILLING, sub-editor.

CAPTAIN HORSTER.

ASLAKSEN, a printer.

Men of various conditions and occupations, some few women, and a troop of schoolboys—the audience at a public meeting.

(The action takes place in a coast town in southern Norway.)

ACT I

(DR. STOCKMANN'S *sitting room. It is evening. The room is plainly but neatly appointed and furnished. In the right-hand wall are two doors; the farther leads out to the hall, the nearer to the doctor's study. In the left-hand wall, opposite the door leading to the hall, is a door leading to the other rooms occupied by the family. In the middle of the same wall stands the stove, and, further forward, a couch with a looking glass hanging over it and an oval table in front of it. On the table, a lighted lamp, with a lampshade. At the back of the room, an open door leads to the dining room.* BILLING *is seen sitting at the dining table, on which a lamp is burning. He has a napkin tucked under his chin, and* MRS. STOCKMANN *is standing by the table handing him a large plateful of roast beef. The other places at the table are empty, and the table somewhat in disorder, a meal having evidently recently been finished.*)

MRS. STOCKMANN: Coming an hour late, Mr. Billing, you have to put up with a cold supper.

BILLING (*eating*): It's very good, thank you, it's really very good.

MRS. STOCKMANN: My husband insists on having his meals on time . . .

BILLING: That doesn't bother me a bit. I think I prefer eating by myself.

MRS. STOCKMANN: So long as you're enjoying it. (*turns to the hall door, listening*) I expect that is Mr. Hovstad coming too.

BILLING: Very likely.

(PETER STOCKMANN *enters wearing an overcoat, carrying a top hat and walking stick.*)

PETER STOCKMANN: Good evening, Katherine.

MRS. STOCKMANN (*coming forward into the sitting room*):

394

Ah, good evening—is it you? How good of you to come up and see us!

PETER STOCKMANN: I happened to be passing, and so— (*looks into the dining room*) But you have company with you, I see.

MRS. STOCKMANN (*a little embarrassed*): Oh, no—it was quite by chance he came in. (*hurriedly*) Won't you come in and have something, too?

PETER STOCKMANN: I! No, thank you. Good gracious— meat at night! Not with my digestion.

MRS. STOCKMANN: Oh, but just once in a while—

PETER STOCKMANN: No, no, my dear lady; I stick to my tea and bread and butter. It is much more wholesome in the long run—and a little more economical, too.

MRS. STOCKMANN (*smiling*): Now you mustn't think that Thomas and I are spendthrifts.

PETER STOCKMANN: Not you, my dear; I would never think that of you. (*points to the* DOCTOR'S *study*) Is he not at home?

MRS. STOCKMANN: No, he went for a little turn after supper—he and the boys.

PETER STOCKMANN: I doubt if that is a wise thing to do. (*listens*) I fancy I hear him coming now.

MRS. STOCKMANN: No, I don't think it is he. (*A knock is heard at the door.*) Come in! (HOVSTAD *comes in from the hall.*) Oh, it is you, Mr. Hovstad!

HOVSTAD: Yes, I hope you will forgive me, but I was delayed at the printers. Good evening, Mr. Mayor.

PETER STOCKMANN (*bowing a little distantly*): Good evening. You have come on business, no doubt.

HOVSTAD: Partly. It's about an article for the paper.

PETER STOCKMANN: So I imagined. I hear my brother has become a prolific contributor to the *People's Messenger*.

HOVSTAD: Yes, he is good enough to write in the *People's Messenger* when he has any home truths to tell.

MRS. STOCKMANN (*to* HOVSTAD): But won't you—? (*points to the dining room*)

PETER STOCKMANN: Quite so, quite so. I don't blame him in the least, as a writer, for addressing himself to the quarters where he will find the readiest sympathy. And, besides that, I personally have no reason to bear any ill will to your paper, Mr. Hovstad.

HOVSTAD: I quite agree with you.

PETER STOCKMANN: Taking one thing with another, there is an excellent spirit of toleration in the town—an admirable municipal spirit. And it all springs from the fact of our having a great common interest to unite us—an interest that is in an equally high degree the concern of every right-minded citizen—

HOVSTAD: The Baths, yes.

PETER STOCKMANN: Exactly—our fine, new, handsome Baths. Mark my words, Mr. Hovstad—the Baths will become the focus of our municipal life! No doubt about it!

MRS. STOCKMANN: That is just what Thomas says.

PETER STOCKMANN: Think how extraordinarily the place has developed within the last year or two! Money has been flowing in, and there is some life and some business doing in the town. Houses and landed property are rising in value every day.

HOVSTAD: And unemployment is going down.

PETER STOCKMANN: Yes, that is another thing. The burden of the poor rates has been lightened, to the great relief of the propertied classes; and that relief will be even greater if only we get a really good summer this year, and lots of visitors—plenty of invalids, who will make the Baths talked about.

HOVSTAD: And there is a good prospect of that, I hear.

PETER STOCKMANN: It looks very promising. Inquiries about apartments and that sort of thing are reaching us every day.

HOVSTAD: Well, the doctor's article will come in very suitably.

PETER STOCKMANN: Has he been writing something just lately?

HOVSTAD: This is something he wrote in the winter; a recommendation of the Baths—an account of the excellent sanitary conditions here. But I held the article over, temporarily.

PETER STOCKMANN: Ah,—some little difficulty about it, I suppose?

HOVSTAD: No, not at all; I thought it would be better to wait till the spring, because it is just at this time that people begin to think seriously about their summer quarters.

PETER STOCKMANN: Quite right; you were perfectly right, Mr. Hovstad.

HOVSTAD: Yes, Thomas is really indefatigable when it is a question of the Baths.

PETER STOCKMANN: Well—remember, he is the Medical Officer to the Baths.

HOVSTAD: Yes, and what is more, they owe their existence to him.

PETER STOCKMANN: To him? Indeed! It is true I have heard from time to time that some people are of that opinion. At the same time I must say I imagined that I took a modest part in the enterprise.

MRS. STOCKMANN: Yes, that is what Thomas is always saying.

HOVSTAD: But who denies it, Mr. Stockmann? You set the thing going and made a practical concern of it; we all know that. I only meant that the idea of it came first from the doctor.

PETER STOCKMANN: Oh, ideas—yes! My brother has had plenty of them in his time—unfortunately. But when it is a question of putting an idea into practical shape, you have to apply to a man of different mettle, Mr. Hovstad. And I certainly should have thought that in this house at least—

MRS. STOCKMANN: My dear Peter—

HOVSTAD: How can you think that—?

MRS. STOCKMANN: Won't you go in and have something, Mr. Hovstad? My husband is sure to be back directly.

HOVSTAD: Thank you, perhaps just a morsel (*goes into the dining room*).

PETER STOCKMANN (*lowering his voice a little*): It is a curious thing that these farmers' sons never seem to lose their lack of tact.

MRS. STOCKMANN: Surely it is not worth bothering about! Cannot you and Thomas share the credit as brothers?

PETER STOCKMANN: I should have thought so; but apparently some people are not satisfied with a share.

MRS. STOCKMANN: What nonsense! You and Thomas get on so well together. (*listens*) There he is at last, I think (*goes out and opens the door leading to the hall*).

DR. STOCKMANN (*laughing and talking outside*): Look here—here is another guest for you, Katherine. Isn't that jolly! Come in, Captain Horster; hang your coat upon this peg. Ah, you don't wear an overcoat. Just think, Katherine; I met him in the street and could hardly persuade him to come up! (CAPTAIN HORSTER *comes into the room and greets* MRS. STOCKMANN. *He is followed by* DR. STOCKMANN.) Come along in, boys. They are ravenously hungry again, you know. Come along, Captain Horster; you must have a slice of beef (*pushes* HORSTER *into the dining room*; EJLIF *and* MORTEN *go in after them*).

MRS. STOCKMANN: But, Thomas, don't you see—?

DR. STOCKMANN (*turning in the doorway*): Oh, is it you, Peter? (*shakes hands with him*) Now that is very delightful.

PETER STOCKMANN: Unfortunately I must go in a moment—

DR. STOCKMANN: Nonsense! There is some toddy just coming in. You haven't forgotten the toddy, Katherine?

MRS. STOCKMANN: Of course not; the water is boiling now (*goes into the dining room*).

PETER STOCKMANN: Toddy too!

DR. STOCKMANN: Yes, sit down and we will have it comfortably.

PETER STOCKMANN: Thanks, I never care about an evening's drinking.

DR. STOCKMANN: But this isn't an evening's drinking.

PETER STOCKMANN: It seems to me—. (*looks towards the dining room*) It is extraordinary how they can put away all that food.

DR. STOCKMANN (*rubbing his hands*): Yes, isn't it splendid to see young people eat? They have always got an appetite, you know! That's as it should be. Lots of food—to build up their strength! They are the people who are going to stir up the fermenting forces of the future, Peter.

PETER STOCKMANN: May I ask what they will find here to "stir up," as you put it?

DR. STOCKMANN: Ah, you must ask the young people that—when the time comes. We shan't be able to see it, of course. That stands to reason—two old fogies, like us—

PETER STOCKMANN: Really, really! I must say that is an extremely odd expression to—

DR. STOCKMANN: Oh, you mustn't take me too literally, Peter. I am so heartily happy and contented, you know. I think it is such an extraordinary piece of good fortune to be in the middle of all this growing, germinating life. It is a splendid time to live in! It is as if a whole new world were being created around one.

PETER STOCKMANN: Do you really think so?

DR. STOCKMANN: Ah, naturally you can't appreciate it as keenly as I. You have lived all your life in these surroundings, and your impressions have got blunted. But I, who have been buried all these years in my little corner up north, almost without ever seeing a stranger who might bring new ideas with him—well, in my case it has just the same effect as if I had been transported into the middle of a crowded city.

PETER STOCKMANN: Oh, a city—!

DR. STOCKMANN: I know, I know; it is all cramped enough here, compared with many other places. But there is life here—there is promise—there are innumerable things to work for and fight for; and that is the main thing. (*calls*) Katherine, hasn't the postman been here?

MRS. STOCKMANN (*from the dining room*): No.

DR. STOCKMANN: And then to be comfortably off, Peter! That is something one learns to value, when one has been on the brink of starvation, as we have.

PETER STOCKMANN: Oh, surely—

DR. STOCKMANN: Indeed I can assure you we have often been very hard up, up there. And now to be able to live like a lord! Today, for instance, we had roast beef for dinner—and, what is more, for supper too. Won't you come and have a little bit? Or let me show it to you, at any rate? Come here—

PETER STOCKMANN: No, no—not for worlds!

DR. STOCKMANN: Well, but just come here then. Do you see, we have got a table cover?

PETER STOCKMANN: Yes, I noticed it.

DR. STOCKMANN: And we have got a lampshade too. Do you see? All out of Katherine's savings! It makes the room so cosy. Don't you think so? Just stand here for a moment—no, no, not there—right here, that's it! Look now, when you get the light on it altogether—I really think it looks very nice, doesn't it?

PETER STOCKMANN: Oh, if you can afford luxuries of this kind—

DR. STOCKMANN: Yes, I can afford it now. Katherine tells me I earn almost as much as we spend.

PETER STOCKMANN: Almost—yes!

DR. STOCKMANN: But a scientific man must live in a little bit of style. I am quite sure an ordinary civil servant spends more in a year than I do.

PETER STOCKMANN: I daresay. A civil servant—a man in a well-paid position—

DR. STOCKMANN: Well, any ordinary merchant, then! A man in that position spends two or three times as much as—

PETER STOCKMANN: It just depends on circumstances.

DR. STOCKMANN: At all events I assure you I don't waste money unprofitably. But I can't find it in my heart to deny myself the pleasure of entertaining my friends. I need that sort of thing, you know. I have lived for so long shut out of it all, that it is a necessity of life to me to mix with young, eager, ambitious men, men of liberal and active minds; and that describes every one of those fellows who are enjoying their supper in there. I wish you knew more of Hovstad—

PETER STOCKMANN: By the way, Hovstad was telling me he was going to print another article of yours.

DR. STOCKMANN: An article of mine?

PETER STOCKMANN: Yes, about the Baths. An article you wrote in the winter.

DR. STOCKMANN: Oh, that one! No, I don't intend that to appear just for the present.

PETER STOCKMANN: Why not? It seems to me that this would be the most opportune moment.

DR. STOCKMANN: Yes, very likely—under normal conditions (*crosses the room*).

PETER STOCKMANN (*following him with his eyes*): Is there anything abnormal about the present conditions?

DR. STOCKMANN (*standing still*): To tell you the truth, Peter, I can't say just at this moment—at all events not to-night. There may be much that is very abnormal about the present conditions—and it is possible there may be nothing abnormal about them at all. It is quite possible it may be merely my imagination.

PETER STOCKMANN: I must say it all sounds most mysterious. Is there something going on that I am to be kept in ignorance of? I should have imagined that I, as Chairman of the governing body of the Baths—

DR. STOCKMANN: And I should have imagined that I—. Oh, come, don't let us fly out at one another, Peter.

PETER STOCKMANN: Heaven forbid! I am not in the habit of flying out at people, as you call it. But I am entitled to request most emphatically that all arrangements shall be made in a business-like manner, through the proper channels, and shall be dealt with by the legally constituted authorities. I can allow no going behind our backs by any roundabout means.

DR. STOCKMANN: Have I ever at any time tried to go behind your backs!

PETER STOCKMANN: You have an ingrained tendency to take your own way, at all events; and that is almost equally inadmissible in a well ordered community. The individual ought undoubtedly to acquiesce in subordinating himself to the community—or, to speak more accurately, to the authorities who have the care of the community's welfare.

DR. STOCKMANN: Very likely. But what the blazes has all this got to do with me?

PETER STOCKMANN: That is exactly what you never appear

to be willing to learn, my dear Thomas. But, mark my words, some day you will have to suffer for it—sooner or later. Now I have told you. Good-bye.

DR. STOCKMANN: Have you taken leave of your senses? You are on the wrong track altogether.

PETER STOCKMANN: I am not usually that. You must excuse me now if I—(*calls into the dining room*). Good night, Katherine. Good night, gentlemen (*goes out*).

MRS. STOCKMANN (*coming from the dining room*): Has he gone?

DR. STOCKMANN: Yes, and in such bad temper.

MRS. STOCKMANN: But, dear Thomas, what have you been doing to him again?

DR. STOCKMANN: Nothing at all. And, anyhow, he can't oblige me to make my report before the proper time.

MRS. STOCKMANN: What have you got to make a report to him about?

DR. STOCKMANN: Hm! Leave that to me, Katherine.—It is an extraordinary thing that the postman doesn't come.

(HOVSTAD, BILLING *and* HORSTER *have got up from the table and come into the sitting room.* EJLIF *and* MORTEN *come in after them.*)

BILLING (*stretching himself*): Ah!—one feels a new man after a meal like that.

HOVSTAD: The Mayor wasn't in a very sweet temper to-night, then.

DR. STOCKMANN: It is his stomach; he has a wretched digestion.

HOVSTAD: I rather think it was us two of the *People's Messenger* that he couldn't digest.

MRS. STOCKMANN: I thought you came out of it pretty well with him.

HOVSTAD: Oh yes; but it is only a sort of truce.

BILLING: That is just what it is! That word sums up the situation.

DR. STOCKMANN: We must remember that Peter is a lonely man, poor chap. He has no home comforts of any kind; nothing but everlasting business. And all that infernal weak tea wash that he pours into himself! Now then, my boys, bring chairs up to the table. Aren't we going to have that toddy, Katherine?

MRS. STOCKMANN (*going into the dining room*): I am just getting it.

DR. STOCKMANN: Sit down here on the couch beside me, Captain Horster. We so seldom see you—. Please sit down, my friends. (*They sit down at the table.* MRS. STOCKMANN *brings a tray, with a spirit lamp, glasses, bottles, etc., upon it.*)

MRS. STOCKMANN: There you are! This is arrack, and this is rum, and this one is the brandy. Now every one must help himself.

DR. STOCKMANN (*taking a glass*): We will. (*They all mix themselves some toddy.*) And let us have the cigars. Ejlif, you know where the box is. And you, Morten, can fetch my pipe. (*The two boys go into the room on the right.*) I have a suspicion that Ejlif pockets a cigar now and then!—but I take no notice of it. (*calls out*) And my smoking cap too, Morten. Katherine, you can tell him where I left it. Ah, he has got it. (*The boys bring the various things.*) Now, my friends. I stick to my pipe, you know. This one has seen plenty of bad weather with me up north. (*touches glasses with them*) Your good health! Ah, it is good to be sitting snug and warm here.

MRS. STOCKMANN (*who sits knitting*): Do you sail soon, Captain Horster?

HORSTER: I expect to be ready to sail next week.

MRS. STOCKMANN: I suppose you are going to America?

HORSTER: Yes, that is the plan.

MRS. STOCKMANN: Then you won't be able to take part in the coming election.

HORSTER: Is there going to be an election?

BILLING: Didn't you know?

HORSTER: No, I don't mix myself up with those things.

BILLING: But do you not take an interest in public affairs?

HORSTER: No, I don't know anything about politics.

BILLING: All the same, one ought to vote, at any rate.

HORSTER: Even if one doesn't know anything about what is going on?

BILLING: Doesn't know? What do you mean by that? A community is like a ship; every one ought to be prepared to take the helm.

HORSTER: May be that is all very well on shore; but on board ship it wouldn't work.

HOVSTAD: It is astonishing how little most sailors care about what goes on on shore.

BILLING: Very extraordinary.

DR. STOCKMANN: Sailors are like birds of passage; they feel equally at home in any latitude. And that is another reason for our being all the more keen, Hovstad. Is there to be anything of public interest in tomorrow's *Messenger*?

HOVSTAD: Nothing about municipal affairs. But the day after tomorrow I was thinking of printing your article—

DR. STOCKMANN: Ah, blazes—my article! Look, that has to wait a bit.

HOVSTAD: Really? We have just the right space for it, and I thought it was the opportune moment—

DR. STOCKMANN: Yes, yes, very likely you are right; but it must wait all the same. I will explain to you later.

(PETRA *comes in from the hall, in hat and cloak and with a bundle of exercise books under her arm.*)

PETRA: Good evening.

DR. STOCKMANN: Good evening, Petra; come along.

(*Mutual greetings;* PETRA *takes off her things and puts them down on a chair by the door.*)

PETRA: And you have all been sitting here enjoying your-selves, while I have been out slaving!

DR. STOCKMANN: Well, come and enjoy yourself too!

BILLING: May I mix a glass for you?

PETRA (*coming to the table*): Thanks, I would rather do it; you always mix it too strong. But I forgot, father—I have a letter for you (*goes to the chair where she has laid her things*).

DR. STOCKMANN: A letter? From whom?

PETRA (*looking in her coat pocket*): The postman gave it to me just as I was going out—

DR. STOCKMANN (*getting up and going to her*): And you only give to me now!

PETRA: I really didn't have time to run up again. There it is!

DR. STOCKMANN (*seizing the letter*): Let's see, let's see, child! (*looks at the address*) Yes, that's all right!

MRS. STOCKMANN: Is it the one you have been expecting so anxiously, Thomas?

DR. STOCKMANN: Yes, it is. I must go to my room now and—. Where shall I get a light, Katherine? Is there no lamp in my room again?

MRS. STOCKMANN: Yes, your lamp is all ready lit on your desk.

DR. STOCKMANN: Good, good. Excuse me for a moment— (*goes into his study*).

PETRA: What do you suppose it is, mother?

MRS. STOCKMANN: I don't know; for the last day or two he has always been asking if the postman has come.

BILLING: Probably some country patient.

PETRA: Poor old dad!—he will overwork himself soon. (*mixes a glass for herself*) There, that will taste good!

HOVSTAD: Have you been teaching in the evening school again today?

PETRA (*sipping from her glass*): Two hours.

BILLING: And four hours of school in the morning—

PETRA: Five hours.

MRS. STOCKMANN: And you have still got exercises to correct, I see.

PETRA: A whole heap, yes.

HORSTER: You are pretty full up with work too, it seems to me.

PETRA: Yes—but that is good. One is so delightfully tired after it.

BILLING: Do you like that?

PETRA: Yes, because one sleeps so well then.

MORTEN: You must be dreadfully wicked, Petra.

PETRA: Wicked?

MORTEN: Yes, because you work so much. Mr. Rörlund says work is a punishment for our sins.

EJLIF: Pooh, what a dummy you are, to believe a thing like that!

MRS. STOCKMANN: Come, come, Ejlif!

BILLING (*laughing*): That's great!

HOVSTAD: Don't you want to work as hard as that, Morten?

MORTEN: No, indeed. I sure don't.

HOVSTAD: What do you want to be, then?

MORTEN: I'd like to be a Viking.

EJLIF: You would have to be a pagan then.

MORTEN: Well, I could become a pagan, couldn't I?

BILLING: I agree with you, Morten! My sentiments, exactly.

MRS. STOCKMANN (*signaling to him*): I am sure that is not true, Mr. Billing.

BILLING: Yes, I swear it is! I am a pagan, and I am proud of it. Believe me, before long we shall all be pagans.

MORTEN: And then we can do anything we like?

BILLING: Well, you see, Morten—.

MRS. STOCKMANN: You must go to your room now, boys; I am sure you have some lessons to learn for tomorrow.

EJLIF: I want to stay a little longer—

MRS. STOCKMANN: No, no; away you go, both of you.

(*The boys say good night and go into the room on the left.*)

HOVSTAD: Do you really think it can do the boys any harm to hear such things?

MRS. STOCKMANN: I don't know; but I don't like it.

PETRA: But you know, mother, I think you really are wrong about it.

MRS. STOCKMANN: Maybe, but I don't like it—not in our own home.

PETRA: There is so much falsehood both at home and at school. At home one must not speak, and at school we have to stand and tell lies to the children.

HORSTER: Tell lies?

PETRA: Yes, don't you suppose we have to teach them all sorts of things that we don't believe?

BILLING: That is perfectly true.

PETRA: If only I had the means I would start a school of my own, and it would be run very differently.

BILLING: Oh, forget the means—!

HORSTER: Well, if you are thinking of that, Miss Stockmann, I shall be delighted to provide you with a schoolroom. The great big old house my father left me is standing almost empty; there is an immense dining room downstairs—

PETRA (*laughing*): Thank you very much; but I am afraid nothing will come of it.

HOVSTAD: No, Miss Petra is much more likely to take to journalism, I expect. By the way, have you had time to do anything with that English story you promised to translate for us?

PETRA: No, not yet; but you shall have it.

(DR. STOCKMANN *comes in from his room with an open letter in his hand.*)

DR. STOCKMANN (*waving the letter*): Well, now the town will have something new to talk about, I can tell you!

BILLING: Something new?

MRS. STOCKMANN: What is this?

DR. STOCKMANN: A great discovery, Katherine.

HOVSTAD: Really?

MRS. STOCKMANN: A discovery of yours?

DR. STOCKMANN: A discovery of mine. (*walks up and down*) Just let them come saying, as usual, that it is all fancy and a crazy man's imagination! But they will be careful what they say this time, I can tell you!

PETRA: But, father, tell us what it is.

DR. STOCKMANN: Yes, yes—only give me time, and you shall know all about it. If only I had Peter here now! It just shows how we men can go about forming our judgments, when in reality we are as blind as any moles—

HOVSTAD: What are you driving at, Doctor?

DR. STOCKMANN (*standing still by the table*): Isn't it the universal opinion that our town is a healthy spot?

HOVSTAD: Certainly.

DR. STOCKMANN: Quite an unusually healthy spot, in fact —a place that deserves to be recommended in the warmest possible manner either for invalids or for people who are well—

MRS. STOCKMANN: Yes, but my dear Thomas—

DR. STOCKMANN: And we have been recommending it and praising it—I have written and written, both in the *Messenger* and in pamphlets—

HOVSTAD: Well, what then?

DR. STOCKMANN: And the Baths—we have called them the "main artery of the town's life-blood," the "nerve-center of our town," and the devil knows what else—

BILLING: "The town's pulsating heart" was the expression I once used on an important occasion—

DR. STOCKMANN: Quite so. Well, do you know what they really are, these great, splendid, much praised Baths, that have cost so much money—do you know what they are?

HOVSTAD: No, what are they?

MRS. STOCKMANN: Yes, what are they?

DR. STOCKMANN: The whole place is a pesthouse!

PETRA: The Baths, father?

MRS. STOCKMANN (*at the same time*): Our Baths!

HOVSTAD: But, Doctor—

BILLING: Absolutely incredible!

DR. STOCKMANN: The whole Bath establishment is a whited, poisoned sepulcher, I tell you—the gravest possible danger to the public health! All the nastiness up at Mölledal, all that stinking filth, is infecting the water in the conduit-pipes leading to the reservoir; and the same cursed, filthy poison oozes out on the shore too—

HORSTER: Where the bathing place is?

DR. STOCKMANN: Just there.

HOVSTAD: How do you come to be so certain of all this, Doctor?

DR. STOCKMANN: I have investigated the matter most conscientiously. For a long time past I have suspected something of the kind. Last year we had some very strange cases of illness among the visitors—typhoid cases, and cases of gastric fever—

MRS. STOCKMANN: Yes, that is quite true.

DR. STOCKMANN: At the time, we supposed the visitors had been infected before they came; but later on, in the winter, I began to have a different opinion; and so I set myself to examine the water, as well as I could.

MRS. STOCKMANN: Then that is what you have been so busy with?

DR. STOCKMANN: Indeed I have been busy, Katherine. But here I had none of the necessary scientific apparatus; so I sent samples, both of the drinking water and of the sea water, up to the University, to have an accurate analysis made by a chemist.

HOVSTAD: And have you got that?

DR. STOCKMANN (showing him the letter): Here it is! It proves the presence of decomposing organic matter in the water—it is full of infusoria. The water is absolutely dangerous to use, either internally or externally.

MRS. STOCKMANN: What a mercy you discovered it in time.

DR. STOCKMANN: You may well say so.

HOVSTAD: And what do you propose to do now, Doctor?

DR. STOCKMANN: To see the matter put right—naturally.

HOVSTAD: Can that be done?

DR. STOCKMANN: It must be done. Otherwise the Baths will be absolutely useless and wasted. But we need not anticipate that; I have a very clear idea what we shall have to do.

MRS. STOCKMANN: But why have you kept this all so secret, dear?

DR. STOCKMANN: Do you suppose I was going to run about the town gossiping about it, before I had absolute proof? No, thank you. I am not such a fool.

PETRA: Still, you might have told us—

DR. STOCKMANN: Not a living soul. But tomorrow you may run around to the old Badger—

MRS. STOCKMANN: Oh, Thomas! Thomas!

DR. STOCKMANN: Well, to your grandfather, then. The old boy will have something to be astonished at! I know he thinks I am cracked—and there are lots of other people think so too, I have noticed. But now these good folks shall see—they shall just see—! (walks about, rubbing his hands) There will be a nice upset in the town, Katherine; you can't imagine what it will be. All the conduit pipes will have to be relaid.

HOVSTAD (getting up): All the conduit pipes—?

DR. STOCKMANN: Yes, of course. The intake is too low down; it will have to be lifted to a position much higher up.

PETRA: Then you were right after all.

DR. STOCKMANN: Ah, you remember, Petra—I wrote opposing the plans before the work was begun. But at that time no one would listen to me. Well, I am going to let them have it, now! Of course I have prepared a report for the Baths Committee; I have had it ready for a week, and was only waiting for this to come. (*shows the letter*) Now it shall go off at once. (*goes into his room and comes back with some papers*) Look at that! Four closely written sheets! —and the letter shall go with them. Give me a bit of paper, Katherine—something to wrap them up in. That will do! Now give it to—to—(*stamps his foot*)—what the blazes is her name?—give it to the maid, and tell her to take it at once to the Mayor.

(MRS. STOCKMANN *takes the packet and goes out through the dining room.*)

PETRA: What do you think uncle Peter will say, father?

DR. STOCKMANN: What is there for him to say? I should think he would be very glad that such an important truth has been brought to light.

HOVSTAD: Will you let me print a short note about your discovery in the *Messenger*?

DR. STOCKMANN: I shall be very much obliged if you will.

HOVSTAD: It is very desirable that the public should be informed of it without delay.

DR. STOCKMANN: Certainly.

MRS. STOCKMANN (*coming back*): She has just gone with it.

BILLING: Upon my soul, Doctor, you are going to be the foremost man in the town!

DR. STOCKMANN (*walking about happily*): Nonsense! As a matter of fact I have done nothing more than my duty. I have only made a lucky find—that's all. Still, all the same—

BILLING: Hovstad, don't you think the town ought to give Dr. Stockmann some sort of testimonial?

HOVSTAD: I will suggest it, anyway.

BILLING: And I will speak to Aslaksen about it.

DR. STOCKMANN: No, my good friends, don't let us have any of that nonsense. I won't hear of anything of the kind. And if the Baths Committee should think of voting me an increase of salary, I will not accept it. Do you hear, Katherine?—I won't accept it.

MRS. STOCKMANN: You are quite right, Thomas.

PETRA (*lifting her glass*): Your health, father!

HOVSTAD and BILLING: Your health, Doctor! Good health!

HORSTER (*touches glasses with* DR. STOCKMANN): I hope it will bring you nothing but good luck.

DR. STOCKMANN: Thank you, thank you, my dear fellows! I feel tremendously happy! It is a splendid thing for a man to be able to feel that he has done a service to his native town and to his fellow-citizens! Hurrah, Katherine! (*He puts his arms round her and whirls her round and round, while she protests with laughing cries. They all laugh, clap their hands, and cheer the* DOCTOR. *The boys put their heads in at the door to see what is going on.*)

ACT II

(*The same setting. The door into the dining room is shut. It is morning.* MRS. STOCKMANN, *with a sealed letter in her hand, comes in from the dining room, goes to the door of the* DOCTOR'S *study, and peeps in.*)

MRS. STOCKMANN: Are you in, Thomas?

DR. STOCKMANN (*from within his room*): Yes, I have just come in. (*comes into the room*) What is it?

MRS. STOCKMANN: A letter from your brother.

DR. STOCKMANN: Aha, let us see! (*opens the letter and reads*) "I return herewith the manuscript you sent me"— (*reads on in a low murmur*) Hm!—

MRS. STOCKMANN: What does he say?

DR. STOCKMANN (*putting the papers in his pocket*): Oh, he only writes that he will come up here himself about midday.

MRS. STOCKMANN: Well, try and remember to be at home this time.

DR. STOCKMANN: That will be no trouble; I have got through all my morning visits.

MRS. STOCKMANN: I am extremely curious to know how he takes it.

DR. STOCKMANN: You will see he won't like its having been I, and not he, that made the discovery.

MRS. STOCKMANN: Aren't you a little nervous about that?

DR. STOCKMANN: Oh, he really will be pleased enough, you know. But, at the same time, Peter is so confoundedly afraid of anyone's doing any service to the town except himself.

MRS. STOCKMANN: I will tell you what, Thomas—you should be good-natured, and share the credit of this with him. Couldn't you make out that it was he who set you on the scent of this discovery?

DR. STOCKMANN: I am quite willing. If only I can get the thing set right. I—

(MORTEN KIIL *puts his head in through the door leading from the hall, looks round in an inquiring manner, and chuckles.*)

MORTEN KIIL (*slyly*): Is it—is it true?

MRS. STOCKMANN (*going to the door*): Father!—is it you?

DR. STOCKMANN: Ah, Mr. Kiil—good morning, good morning!

MRS. STOCKMANN: But come along in.

MORTEN KIIL: If it is true, I will; if not, I am off.

DR. STOCKMANN: If what is true?

MORTEN KIIL: This tale about the water supply. Is it true?

DR. STOCKMANN: Certainly it is true. But how did you come to hear it?

MORTEN KIIL (*coming in*): Petra ran in on her way to the school—

DR. STOCKMANN: Did she?

MORTEN KIIL: Yes; and she declares that—. I thought she was only making a fool of me, but it isn't like Petra to do that.

DR. STOCKMANN: Of course not. How could you imagine such a thing!

MORTEN KIIL: Oh well, it is better never to trust anybody; you may find you have been made a fool of before you know where you are. But it is really true, all the same?

DR. STOCKMANN: You can depend upon it that it is true. Won't you sit down? (*settles him on the couch*) Isn't it a real bit of luck for the town—

MORTEN KIIL (*suppressing his laughter*): A bit of luck for the town?

DR. STOCKMANN: Yes, that I made the discovery in good time.

MORTEN KIIL (*as before*): Yes, yes, yes!—But I should never have thought you the sort of man to pull your own brother's leg like this!

DR. STOCKMANN: Pull his leg!

MRS. STOCKMANN: Really, father dear—

MORTEN KIIL (*resting his hands and his chin on the handle of his stick and winking slyly at the* DOCTOR): Let me see, what was the story? Some kind of beast that had got into the water pipes, wasn't it?

DR. STOCKMANN: Infusoria—yes.

MORTEN KIIL: And a lot of these beasts had got in, according to Petra—a tremendous lot.

DR. STOCKMANN: Certainly; hundreds of thousands of them, probably.

MORTEN KIIL: But no one can see them—isn't that so?

DR. STOCKMANN: Yes; you can't see them.

MORTEN KIIL (*with a quiet chuckle*): Damme—it's the finest story I have ever heard!

DR. STOCKMANN: What do you mean?

MORTEN KIIL: But you will never get the Mayor to believe a thing like that.

DR. STOCKMANN: We shall see.

MORTEN KIIL: Do you think he will be fool enough to—?

DR. STOCKMANN: I hope the whole town will be fools enough.

MORTEN KIIL: The whole town! Well, it wouldn't be a bad thing. It would just serve them right, and teach them a lesson. They think themselves so much cleverer than we old fellows. They hounded me out of the council; they did, I tell you—they hounded me out. Now they shall pay for it. You pull their legs too, Thomas!

DR. STOCKMANN: Really, I—

MORTEN KIIL: You pull their legs! (*gets up*) If you can work it so that the Mayor and his friends all swallow the same bait, I will give ten pounds to a charity—like a shot!

DR. STOCKMANN: That is very kind of you.

MORTEN KIIL: Yes, I haven't got much money to throw away, I can tell you; but if you can work this, I will give five pounds to a charity at Christmas.

(HOVSTAD *comes in by the hall door.*)

HOVSTAD: Good morning! (*stops*) Oh, I beg your pardon—

DR. STOCKMANN: Not at all; come in.

MORTEN KIIL (*with another chuckle*): Oho!—is he in this too?

HOVSTAD: What do you mean?

DR. STOCKMANN: Certainly he is.

MORTEN KIIL: I might have known it! It must get into the papers. You know how to do it, Thomas! Set your wits to work. Now I must go.

DR. STOCKMANN: Won't you stay a little while?

MORTEN KIIL: No, I must be off now. You keep up this game for all it is worth; you won't repent it, I'm damned if you will!

(*He goes out;* MRS. STOCKMANN *follows him into the hall.*)

DR. STOCKMANN (*laughing*): Just imagine—the old chap doesn't believe a word of all this about the water supply.

HOVSTAD: Oh that was it, then?

DR. STOCKMANN: Yes, that was what we were talking about. Perhaps it is the same thing that brings you here?

HOVSTAD: Yes, it is. Can you spare me a few minutes, Doctor?

DR. STOCKMANN: As long as you like, my dear fellow.

HOVSTAD: Have you heard from the Mayor yet?

DR. STOCKMANN: Not yet. He is coming here later.

HOVSTAD: I have given the matter a great deal of thought since last night.

DR. STOCKMANN: Well?

HOVSTAD: From your point of view, as a doctor and a man of science, this affair of the water supply is an isolated matter. I mean, you do not realize that it involves a great many other things.

DR. STOCKMANN: How do you mean?—Let us sit down, my dear fellow. No, sit here on the couch. (HOVSTAD *sits down on the couch,* DR. STOCKMANN *on a chair on the other side of the table.*) Now then. You mean that—?

HOVSTAD: You said yesterday that the pollution of the water was due to impurities in the soil.

DR. STOCKMANN: Yes, unquestionably it is due to that poisonous morass up at Mölledal.

HOVSTAD: Begging your pardon, Doctor, I fancy it is due to quite another morass altogether.

DR. STOCKMANN: What morass?

HOVSTAD: The morass that the whole life of our town is built on and is rotting in.

DR. STOCKMANN: What the deuce are you driving at, Hovstad?

HOVSTAD: The whole of the town's interests have, little by little, got into the hands of a pack of officials.

DR. STOCKMANN: Oh, come!—they are not all officials.

HOVSTAD: No, but those that are not officials are at any rate the officials' friends and adherents; it is the wealthy folk, the old families in the town, that have got us entirely in their hands.

DR. STOCKMANN: Yes, but after all they are men of ability and knowledge.

HOVSTAD: Did they show any ability or knowledge when they laid the conduit pipes where they are now?

DR. STOCKMANN: No, of course that was a great piece of stupidity on their part. But that is going to be set right now.

HOVSTAD: Do you think that will be all such plain sailing?

DR. STOCKMANN: Plain sailing or no, it has got to be done, anyway.

HOVSTAD: Yes, provided the press takes up the question.

DR. STOCKMANN: I don't think that will be necessary, my dear fellow, I am certain my brother—

HOVSTAD: Excuse me, Doctor; I feel bound to tell you I am inclined to take the matter up.

DR. STOCKMANN: In the paper?

HOVSTAD: Yes. When I took over the *People's Messenger* my idea was to break up this ring of self-opinionated old fossils who had got hold of all the influence.

DR. STOCKMANN: But you know you told me yourself what the result had been; you nearly ruined your paper.

HOVSTAD: Yes, at the time we were obliged to climb down a peg or two, it is quite true; because there was a danger of the whole project of the Baths coming to nothing if they failed us. But now the scheme has been carried through, and we can dispense with these grand gentlemen.

DR. STOCKMANN: Dispense with them, yes; but we owe them a great debt of gratitude.

HOVSTAD: That shall be recognized ungrudgingly. But a journalist of my democratic tendencies cannot let such an opportunity as this slip. The bubble of official infallibility must be pricked. This superstition must be destroyed, like any other.

DR. STOCKMANN: I am wholeheartedly with you in that, Mr. Hovstad; if it is a superstition, away with it!

HOVSTAD: I should be very reluctant to bring the Mayor into it, because he is your brother. But I am sure you will agree with me that truth should be the first consideration.

DR. STOCKMANN: That goes without saying. (*with sudden emphasis*) Yes, but—but—

HOVSTAD: You must not misjudge me. I am neither more self-interested nor more ambitious than most men.

DR. STOCKMANN: My dear fellow—who suggests anything of that kind?

HOVSTAD: I am of humble origin, as you know; and that has given me opportunities of knowing what is the most crying need in the humbler ranks of life. It is that they should be allowed some part in the direction of public affairs, Doctor. That is what will develop their faculties and intelligence and self-respect—

DR. STOCKMANN: I quite appreciate that.

HOVSTAD: Yes—and in my opinion a journalist incurs a heavy responsibility if he neglects a favorable opportunity of emancipating the masses—the humble and oppressed. I know well enough that in exalted circles I shall be called an agitator, and all that sort of thing; but they may call me what they like. If only my conscience doesn't reproach me, then—

DR. STOCKMANN: Quite right! Quite right, Mr. Hovstad. But all the same—oh, blazes! (*A knock is heard at the door.*) Come in!

(ASLAKSEN *appears at the door. He is poorly but decently dressed, in black, with a slightly crumpled white neckcloth; he wears gloves and has a felt hat in his hand.*)

ASLAKSEN (*bowing*): Excuse my taking the liberty, Doctor—

DR. STOCKMANN (*getting up*): Ah, it is you, Aslaksen!

ASLAKSEN: Yes, Doctor.

HOVSTAD (*standing up*): Is it me you want, Aslaksen?

ASLAKSEN: No; I didn't know I should find you here. No, it was the Doctor I—

DR. STOCKMANN: I am quite at your service. What is it?

ASLAKSEN: Is what I heard from Mr. Billing true, sir—that you mean to improve our water supply?

DR. STOCKMANN: Yes, for the Baths.

ASLAKSEN: Quite so, I understand. Well, I have come to say that I will back that up by every means in my power.

HOVSTAD (*to the* DOCTOR): You see!

DR. STOCKMANN: I shall be very grateful to you, but—

ASLAKSEN: Because it may be no bad thing to have us small tradesmen at your back. We form, as it were, a compact majority in the town—if we choose. And it is always a good thing to have the majority with you, Doctor.

DR. STOCKMANN: This is undeniably true; but I confess I don't see why such unusual precautions should be necessary in this case. It seems to me that such a plain, straightforward thing—

ASLAKSEN: Oh, it may be very desirable, all the same. I know our local authorities so well; officials are not generally very ready to act on proposals that come from other people. That is why I think it would not be at all amiss if we made a little demonstration.

HOVSTAD: That's right.

DR. STOCKMANN: Demonstration, did you say? What on earth are you going to make a demonstration about?

ASLAKSEN: We shall proceed with the greatest moderation, Doctor. Moderation is always my aim; it is the greatest virtue in a citizen—at least, I think so.

DR. STOCKMANN: It is well known to be a characteristic of yours, Mr. Aslaksen.

ASLAKSEN: Yes, I think I may pride myself on that. And this matter of the water supply is of the greatest importance to us small tradesmen. The Baths promise to be a regular gold mine for the town. We shall all make our living out of them, especially those of us who are householders. That is why we will back up the project as strongly as possible. And as I am at present Chairman of the Householders' Association—

DR. STOCKMANN: Yes—?

ASLAKSEN: And, what is more, local secretary of the Temperance Society—you know, sir, I suppose, that I am a worker in the temperance cause?

DR. STOCKMANN: Of course, of course.

ASLAKSEN: Well, you can understand that I come into contact with a great many people. And as I have the reputation of a temperate and law-abiding citizen—like yourself, Doctor—I have a certain influence in the town, a little bit of power, if I may be allowed to say so.

DR. STOCKMANN: I know that quite well, Mr. Aslaksen.

ASLAKSEN: So you see it would be an easy matter for me to set on foot some testimonial, if necessary.

DR. STOCKMANN: A testimonial?

ASLAKSEN: Yes, some kind of an address of thanks from the townsmen for your share in a matter of such importance to the community. I need scarcely say that it would have to be drawn up with the greatest regard to moderation, so as not to offend the authorities—who, after all, have the reins in their hands. If we pay strict attention to that, no one can take it amiss, I should think!

HOVSTAD: Well, and even supposing they didn't like it—

ASLAKSEN: No, no, no; there must be no discourtesy to the authorities, Mr. Hovstad. It is no use falling foul of those upon whom our welfare so closely depends. I have done that in my time, and no good ever comes of it. But no one can take exception to a reasonable and frank expression of a citizen's views.

DR. STOCKMANN (*shaking him by the hand*): I can't tell

you, dear Mr. Aslaksen, how extremely pleased I am to find such hearty support among my fellow-citizens. I am delighted —delighted! Now, you will take a small glass of sherry, eh?

ASLAKSEN: No, thank you; I never drink alcohol of that kind.

DR. STOCKMANN: Well, what do you say to a glass of beer, then?

ASLAKSEN: Nor that either, thank you, Doctor. I never drink anything as early as this. I am going into town now to talk this over with one or two householders, and prepare the ground.

DR. STOCKMANN: It is tremendously kind of you, Mr. Aslaksen; but I really cannot understand the necessity for all these precautions. It seems to me that the thing should go of itself.

ASLAKSEN: The authorities are somewhat slow to move, Doctor. Far be it from me to seem to blame them—

HOVSTAD: We are going to stir them up in the paper tomorrow, Aslaksen.

ASLAKSEN: But not violently, I trust, Mr. Hovstad. Proceed with moderation, or you will do nothing with them. You may take my advice; I have gathered my experience in the school of life. Well, I must say good-bye, Doctor. You may know now that we small tradesmen are at your back at all events, like a solid wall. You have the compact majority on your side, Doctor.

DR. STOCKMANN: I am very much obliged, dear Mr. Aslaksen. (*shakes hands with him*) Good-bye, good-bye.

ASLAKSEN: Are you going my way, towards the printing office, Mr. Hovstad?

HOVSTAD: I will come later; I have something to settle up first.

ASLAKSEN: Very well.

(*Bows and goes out;* STOCKMANN *follows him into the hall.*)

HOVSTAD (*as* STOCKMANN *comes in again*): Well, what do you think of that, Doctor? Don't you think it is high time we stirred a little life into all this slackness and vacillation and cowardice?

DR. STOCKMANN: Are you referring to Aslaksen?

HOVSTAD: Yes, I am. He is one of those who are floundering in a bog—decent enough fellow though he may be, otherwise. And most of the people here are in just the same case—see-sawing and edging first to one side and then to the other, so overcome with caution and scruple that they never dare to take any decided step.

DR. STOCKMANN: Yes, but Aslaksen seemed to me so thoroughly well-intentioned.

HOVSTAD: There is one thing I esteem higher than that; and that is for a man to be self-reliant and sure of himself.

DR. STOCKMANN: I think you are perfectly right there.

HOVSTAD: That is why I want to seize this opportunity, and try if I cannot manage to put a little virility into these well-intentioned people for once. The idol of Authority must be shattered in this town. This gross and inexcusable blunder about the water supply must be brought home to the mind of every municipal voter.

DR. STOCKMANN: Very well; if you are of the opinion that it is for the good of the community, so be it. But not until I have had a talk with my brother.

HOVSTAD: Anyway, I will get a leading article ready; and if the Mayor refuses to take the matter up—

DR. STOCKMANN: How can you suppose such a thing possible?

HOVSTAD: It is conceivable. And in that case—

DR. STOCKMANN: In that case I promise you—. Look here, in that case you may print my report—every word of it.

HOVSTAD: May I? Have I your word for it?

DR. STOCKMANN (*giving him the MS*): Here it is; take it with you. It can do no harm for you to read it through, and you can give it back to me later on.

HOVSTAD: Good, good! That is what I will do. And now good-bye, Doctor.

DR. STOCKMANN: Good-bye, good-bye. You will see everything will run quite smoothly, Mr. Hovstad—quite smoothly.

HOVSTAD: Hm!—we shall see.

(*Bows and goes out.*)

DR. STOCKMANN (*opens the dining room door and looks in*): Katherine! Oh, you are back, Petra?

PETRA (*coming in*): Yes, I have just come from the school.

MRS. STOCKMANN (*coming in*): Has he not been here yet?

DR. STOCKMANN: Peter? No. But I have had a long talk with Hovstad. He is quite excited about my discovery. I find it has a much wider bearing than I at first imagined. And he has put his paper at my disposal if necessity should arise.

MRS. STOCKMANN: Do you think it will?

DR. STOCKMANN: Not for a moment. But at all events it makes me feel proud to know that I have the liberal-minded independent press on my side. Yes, and—just imagine—I have had a visit from the Chairman of the Householders' Association!

MRS. STOCKMANN: Oh! What did he want?

DR. STOCKMANN: To offer me his support too. They will support me in a body if it should be necessary. Katherine— do you know what I have got behind me?

MRS. STOCKMANN: Behind you? No, what have you got behind you?

DR. STOCKMANN: The compact majority.

MRS. STOCKMANN: Really? Is that a good thing for you, Thomas?

DR. STOCKMANN: I should think it was a good thing. (*walks up and down rubbing his hands*) By heaven, it's a fine thing to feel this bond of brotherhood between oneself and one's fellow citizens!

PETRA: And to be able to do so much that is good and useful, father!

DR. STOCKMANN: And for one's own native town into the bargain, my child!

MRS. STOCKMANN: That was a ring at the bell.

DR. STOCKMANN: It must be he, then. (*A knock is heard at the door.*) Come in!

PETER STOCKMANN (*comes in from the hall*): Good morning.

DR. STOCKMANN: Glad to see you, Peter!

MRS. STOCKMANN: Good morning, Peter. How are you?

PETER STOCKMANN: So so, thank you. (*to* DR. STOCKMANN) I received from you yesterday, after office hours, a report dealing with the condition of the water at the Baths.

DR. STOCKMANN: Yes. Have you read it?

PETER STOCKMANN: Yes, I have.

DR. STOCKMANN: And what have you to say to it?

PETER STOCKMANN (*with a sidelong glance*): Hm!—

MRS. STOCKMANN: Come along, Petra. (*She and* PETRA *go into the room on the left.*)

PETER STOCKMANN (*after a pause*): Was it necessary to make all these investigations behind my back?

DR. STOCKMANN: Yes, because until I was absolutely certain about it—

PETER STOCKMANN: Then you mean that you are absolutely certain now?

DR. STOCKMANN: Surely you are convinced of that.

PETER STOCKMANN: Is it your intention to bring this document before the Baths Committee as a sort of official communication?

DR. STOCKMANN: Certainly. Something must be done in the matter—and that quickly.

PETER STOCKMANN: As usual, you employ violent expressions in your report. You say, amongst other things, that what we offer visitors in our Baths is a permanent supply of poison.

DR. STOCKMANN: Well, can you describe it any other way, Peter? Just think—water that is poisonous, whether you drink it or bathe in it! And this we offer to the poor sick folk who come to us trustfully and pay us at an exorbitant rate to be made well again!

PETER STOCKMANN: And your reasoning leads you to this conclusion, that we must build a sewer to draw off the alleged impurities from Mölledal and must relay the water conduits.

DR. STOCKMANN: Yes. Do you see any other way out of it? I don't.

PETER STOCKMANN: I made a pretext this morning to go and see the town engineer, and, as if only half seriously, broached the subject of these proposals as a thing we might perhaps have to take under consideration some time later on.

DR. STOCKMANN: Some time later on!

PETER STOCKMANN: He smiled at what he considered to be my extravagance, naturally. Have you taken the trouble to consider what your proposed alterations would cost? According to the information I obtained, the expenses would probably mount up to fifteen or twenty thousand pounds.

DR. STOCKMANN: Would it cost so much?

PETER STOCKMANN: Yes; and the worst part of it would be that the work would take at least two years.

DR. STOCKMANN: Two years? Two whole years?

PETER STOCKMANN: At least. And what are we to do with the Baths in the meantime? Close them? Indeed we should be obliged to. And do you suppose any one would come near the place after it had got about that the water was dangerous?

DR. STOCKMANN: Yes, but, Peter, that is what it is.

PETER STOCKMANN: And all this at this juncture—just as the Baths are beginning to be known. There are other towns in the neighborhood with qualifications to attract visitors for bathing purposes. Don't you suppose they would immediately strain every nerve to divert the entire stream of strangers to themselves? Unquestionably they would; and then where should we be? We should probably have to abandon the whole thing, which has cost us so much money—and then you would have ruined your native town.

DR. STOCKMANN: I—should have ruined—!

PETER STOCKMANN: It is simply and solely through the Baths that the town has before it any future worth mentioning. You know that just as well as I.

DR. STOCKMANN: But what do you think ought to be done, then?

PETER STOCKMANN: Your report has not convinced me that the condition of the water at the Baths is as bad as you represent it to be.

DR. STOCKMANN: I tell you it is even worse!—or at all events it will be in summer, when the warm weather comes.

PETER STOCKMANN: As I said, I believe you exaggerate the matter considerably. A capable physician ought to know what measures to take—he ought to be capable of preventing injurious influences or of remedying them if they become obviously persistent.

DR. STOCKMANN: Well? What more?

PETER STOCKMANN: The water supply for the Baths is now an established fact, and in consequence must be treated as such. But probably the Committee, at its discretion, will not be disinclined to consider the question of how far it might be possible to introduce certain improvements consistently with a reasonable expenditure.

DR. STOCKMANN: And do you suppose that I will have anything to do with such a piece of trickery as that?

PETER STOCKMANN: Trickery!!

DR. STOCKMANN: Yes, it would be a trick—a fraud, a lie, a downright crime towards the public, towards the whole community!

PETER STOCKMANN: I have not, as I remarked before, been able to convince myself that there is actually any imminent danger.

DR. STOCKMANN: You have! It is impossible that you should not be convinced. I know I have represented the facts absolutely truthfully and fairly. And you know it very well, Peter, only you won't acknowledge it. It was owing to your action that both the Baths and the water conduits were built where they are; and that is what you won't acknowledge— that damn blunder of yours. Pooh!—do you suppose I don't see through you?

PETER STOCKMANN: And even if that were true? If I perhaps guard my reputation somewhat anxiously, it is in the best interests of the town. Without moral authority I am powerless to direct public affairs as seems, to my judgment, to be best for the common good. And on that account—and for various other reasons too—it appears to me to be a matter of importance that your report should not be delivered to the Committee. In the interests of the public, you must withhold it. Then, later on, I will raise the question and we will do our best, privately; but nothing of this unfortunate affair—not a single word of it—must come to the ears of the public.

DR. STOCKMANN: I am afraid you will not be able to prevent that now, my dear Peter.

PETER STOCKMANN: It must and shall be prevented.

DR. STOCKMANN: It is no use, I tell you. There are too many people that know about it.

PETER STOCKMANN: That know about it? Who? Surely you don't mean those fellows on the *People's Messenger?*

DR. STOCKMANN: Yes, they know. The liberal-minded independent press is going to see that you do your duty.

PETER STOCKMANN (*after a short pause*): You are an extraordinarily independent man, Thomas. Have you given no thought to the consequences this may have for yourself?

DR. STOCKMANN: Consequences?—for me?

PETER STOCKMANN: For you and yours, yes.

DR. STOCKMANN: What the blazes do you mean?

PETER STOCKMANN: I believe I have always behaved in a brotherly way to you—have always been ready to oblige or to help you?

DR. STOCKMANN: Yes, you have, and I am grateful to you for it.

PETER STOCKMANN: There is no need. Indeed, to some extent I was forced to do so—for my own sake. I always hoped that, if I helped to improve your financial position, I should be able to keep some check on you.

DR. STOCKMANN: What!! Then it was only for your own sake—!

PETER STOCKMANN: Up to a certain point, yes. It is painful for a man in an official position to have his nearest relative compromise himself time after time.

DR. STOCKMANN: And do you consider that I do that?

PETER STOCKMANN: Yes, unfortunately, you do, without even being aware of it. You have a restless, pugnacious, rebellious disposition. And then there is that disastrous propensity of yours to want to write about every sort of possible and impossible thing. The moment an idea comes into your head, you must needs go and write a newspaper article or a whole pamphlet about it.

DR. STOCKMANN: Well, but is it not the duty of a citizen to let the public share in any new ideas he may have?

PETER STOCKMANN: Oh, the public doesn't require any new

ideas. The public is best served by the good, old-fashioned ideas it already has.

DR. STOCKMANN: And that is your honest opinion?

PETER STOCKMANN: Yes, and for once I must talk frankly to you. Hitherto I have tried to avoid doing so, because I know how irritable you are; but now I must tell you the truth, Thomas. You have no conception what an amount of harm you do yourself by your impetuosity. You complain of the authorities, you even complain of the government—you are always pulling them to pieces; you insist that you have been neglected and persecuted. But what else can such a cantankerous man as you expect?

DR. STOCKMANN: What next! Cantankerous, am I?

PETER STOCKMANN: Yes, Thomas, you are an extremely cantankerous man to work with—I know that to my cost. You disregard everything that you ought to have consideration for. You seem completely to forget that it is me you have to thank for your appointment here as medical officer to the Baths—

DR. STOCKMANN: I was entitled to it as a matter of course! —I and nobody else! I was the first person to see that the town could be made into a flourishing watering-place, and I was the only one who saw it at that time. I had to fight single-handed in support of the idea for many years; and I wrote and wrote—

PETER STOCKMANN: Undoubtedly. But things were not ripe for the scheme then—though, of course, you could not judge of that in your out-of-the-way corner up north. But as soon as the opportune moment came, I—and the others—took the matter into our hands—

DR. STOCKMANN: Yes, and made this mess of all my beautiful plan. It is pretty obvious now what clever fellows you were!

PETER STOCKMANN: To my mind the whole thing only seems to mean that you are seeking another outlet for your combativeness. You want to pick a quarrel with your superiors—an old habit of yours. You cannot put up with any authority over you. You look askance at anyone who occupies a superior official position; you regard him as a personal enemy, and then any stick is good enough to beat him with. But now I have called your attention to the fact that the town's interests are at stake—and, incidentally, my own too. And therefore I must tell you, Thomas, that you will find me inexorable with regard to what I am about to require you to do.

DR. STOCKMANN: And what is that?

PETER STOCKMANN: As you have been so indiscreet as to speak of this delicate matter to outsiders, despite the fact that you ought to have treated it as entirely official and confidential, it is obviously impossible to hush it up now. All sorts of rumors will get about directly, and everybody who has a grudge against us will take care to embellish these rumors. So it will be necessary for you to refute them publicly.

DR. STOCKMANN: I! How? I don't understand.

PETER STOCKMANN: What we shall expect is that, after making further investigations, you will come to the conclusion that the matter is not by any means as dangerous or as critical as you imagined in the first instance.

DR. STOCKMANN: Oho!—so that is what you expect!

PETER STOCKMANN: And, what is more, we shall expect you to make public profession of your confidence in the Committee and in their readiness to consider fully and conscientiously what steps may be necessary to remedy any possible defects.

DR. STOCKMANN: But you will never be able to do that by patching and tinkering at it—never! Take my word for it, Peter; I mean what I say, as deliberately and emphatically as possible.

PETER STOCKMANN: As an officer under the Committee, you have no right to any individual opinion.

DR. STOCKMANN (*amazed*): No right?

PETER STOCKMANN: In your official capacity, no. As a private person, it is quite another matter. But as a subordinate member of the staff of the Baths, you have no right to express any opinion which runs contrary to that of your superiors.

DR. STOCKMANN: This is too much! I, a doctor, a man of science, have no right to—!

PETER STOCKMANN: The matter in hand is not simply a scientific one. It is a complicated matter, and has its economic as well as its technical side.

DR. STOCKMANN: I don't care what it is! I intend to be free to express my opinion on any subject under the sun.

PETER STOCKMANN: As you please—but not on any subject concerning the Baths. That we forbid.

DR. STOCKMANN (*shouting*): You forbid—! You! A pack of—

PETER STOCKMANN: *I* forbid it—I, your chief; and if I forbid it, you have to obey.

DR. STOCKMANN (*controlling himself*): Peter—if you were not my brother—

PETRA (*throwing open the door*): Father, you shan't stand this!

MRS. STOCKMANN (*coming in after her*): Petra, Petra!

PETER STOCKMANN: Oh, so you have been eavesdropping.

MRS. STOCKMANN: You were talking so loud, we couldn't help—

PETRA: Yes, I was listening.

PETER STOCKMANN: Well, after all, I am very glad—

DR. STOCKMANN (*going up to him*): You were saying something about forbidding and obeying?

PETER STOCKMANN: You obliged me to take that tone with you.

DR. STOCKMANN: And so I am to give myself the lie, publicly?

PETER STOCKMANN: We consider it absolutely necessary that you should make some such public statement as I have asked for.

DR. STOCKMANN: And if I do not—obey?

PETER STOCKMANN: Then we shall publish a statement ourselves to reassure the public.

DR. STOCKMANN: Very well; but in that case I shall use my pen against you. I stick to what I have said; I will show that I am right and that you are wrong. And what will you do then?

PETER STOCKMANN: Then I shall not be able to prevent your being dismissed.

DR. STOCKMANN: What—?

PETRA: Father—dismissed!

MRS. STOCKMANN: Dismissed!

PETER STOCKMANN: Dismissed from the staff of the Baths. I shall be obliged to propose that you shall immediately be given notice, and shall not be allowed any further participation in the Baths' affairs.

DR. STOCKMANN: You would dare to do that!

PETER STOCKMANN: It is you that are playing the daring game.

PETRA: Uncle, that is a shameful way to treat a man like father!

MRS. STOCKMANN: Do hold your tongue, Petra!

PETER STOCKMANN (*looking at* PETRA): Oh, so we volunteer our opinions already, do we? Of course. (*to* MRS. STOCKMANN) Katherine, I imagine you are the most sensible person in this house. Use any influence you may have over your husband, and make him see what this will entail for his family as well as—

DR. STOCKMANN: My family is my own concern and nobody else's!

PETER STOCKMANN: —for his own family, as I was saying, as well as for the town he lives in.

DR. STOCKMANN: It is I who have the real good of the town at heart! I want to lay bare the defects that sooner or later must come to the light of day. I will show whether I love my native town.

PETER STOCKMANN: You, who in your blind obstinacy want to cut off the most important source of the town's welfare?

DR. STOCKMANN: The source is poisoned, man! Are you mad? We are making our living by retailing filth and corruption! The whole of our flourishing municipal life derives its sustenance from a lie!

PETER STOCKMANN: All imagination—or something even worse. The man who can throw out such offensive insinuations about his native town must be an enemy to our community.

DR. STOCKMANN (*going up to him*): Do you dare to—!

MRS. STOCKMANN (*throwing herself between them*): Thomas!

PETRA (*catching her father by the arm*): Don't lose your temper, father!

PETER STOCKMANN: I will not expose myself to violence. Now you have had a warning; so reflect on what you owe to yourself and your family. Good-bye (*goes out*).

DR. STOCKMANN (*walking up and down*): Am I to put up with such treatment as this? In my own house, Katherine! What do you think of that!

MRS. STOCKMANN: Indeed it is both shameful and absurd, Thomas—

PETRA: If only I could give uncle a piece of my mind—

DR. STOCKMANN: It is my own fault. I ought to have flown out at him long ago!—shown my teeth!—bitten! To hear him call me an enemy to our community! Me! I shall not take that lying down, upon my soul!

MRS. STOCKMANN: But, dear Thomas, your brother has power on his side—

DR. STOCKMANN: Yes, but I have right on mine, I tell you.

MRS. STOCKMANN: Oh yes, right—right. What is the use of having right on your side if you have not got might?

PETRA: Oh, mother!—how can you say such a thing!

DR. STOCKMANN: Do you imagine that in a free country it is no use having right on your side? You are absurd, Katherine. Besides, haven't I got the liberal-minded independent press to lead the way, and the compact majority behind me? That is might enough, I should think!

MRS. STOCKMANN: But, good heavens, Thomas, you don't mean to—?

DR. STOCKMANN: Don't mean to what?

MRS. STOCKMANN: To set yourself up in opposition to your brother.

DR. STOCKMANN: In God's name, what else do you suppose I should do but take my stand on right and truth?

PETRA: Yes, I was just going to say that.

MRS. STOCKMANN: But it won't do you any earthly good. If they won't do it, they won't.

DR. STOCKMANN: Oho, Katherine! Just give me time, and you will see how I will carry the war into their camp.

MRS. STOCKMANN: Yes, you carry the war into their camp, and you get your dismissal—that is what you will do.

DR. STOCKMANN: In any case I shall have done my duty towards the public—towards the community. I, who am called its enemy!

MRS. STOCKMANN: But towards your family, Thomas? Towards your own home! Do you think that is doing your duty towards those you have to provide for?

PETRA: Ah, don't think always first of us, mother.

MRS. STOCKMANN: Oh, it is easy for you to talk; you are able to shift for yourself, if need be. But remember the boys, Thomas; and think a little too of yourself, and of me—

DR. STOCKMANN: I think you are out of your senses, Katherine! If I were to be such a miserable coward as to go on my knees to Peter and his damned crew, do you suppose I should ever know an hour's peace of mind all my life afterwards?

MRS. STOCKMANN: I don't know anything about that; but God preserve us from the peace of mind we shall have, all the same, if you go on defying him! You will find yourself again without the means of subsistence, with no income to count upon. I should think we had had enough of that in the old days. Remember that, Thomas; think what that means.

DR. STOCKMANN (collecting himself with a struggle and clenching his fists): And this is what this slavery can bring upon a free, honorable man! Isn't it horrible, Katherine?

MRS. STOCKMANN: Yes, it is sinful to treat you so, it is perfectly true. But, good heavens, one has to put up with so much injustice in this world.—There are the boys, Thomas! Look at them! What is to become of them? Oh, no, you can never have the heart—. (EJLIF *and* MORTEN *have come in while she was speaking, with their school books in their hands.*)

DR. STOCKMANN: The boys—! (*recovers himself suddenly*) No, even if the whole world goes to pieces, I will never bow my neck to this yoke! (*goes towards his room*)

MRS. STOCKMANN (*following him*): Thomas—what are you going to do!

DR. STOCKMANN (*at his door*): I mean to have the right to look my sons in the face when they are grown men (*goes into his room*).

MRS. STOCKMANN (*bursting into tears*): God help us all!

PETRA: Father is splendid! He will not give in.

(*The boys look on in amazement;* PETRA *signs to them not to speak.*)

ACT III

(*The editorial office of the* People's Messenger. *The entrance door is on the left-hand side of the back wall; on the right-hand side is another door with glass panels through which the printing room can be seen. Another door in the right-hand wall. In the middle of the room is a large table covered with papers, newspapers and books. In the foreground on the left a window, before which stands a desk and a high stool. There are a couple of easy chairs by the table, and other chairs standing along the wall. The room is dingy and uncomfortable; the furniture is old, the chairs stained and torn. In the printing room the compositors are seen at work, and a printer is working a handpress.* HOVSTAD *is sitting at the desk, writing.* BILLING *comes in from the right with* DR. STOCKMANN'S *manuscript in his hand.*)

BILLING: Well, I must say!

HOVSTAD (*still writing*): Have you read it through?

BILLING (*laying the MS on the desk*): Yes, indeed I have.

HOVSTAD: Don't you think the Doctor hits them pretty hard?

BILLING: Hard? Bless my soul, he's crushing! Every word falls like—how shall I put it?—like the blow of a sledge-hammer.

HOVSTAD: Yes, but they are not the people to throw in the sponge at the first blow.

BILLING: That is true; and for that reason we must strike blow upon blow until the whole of this aristocracy tumbles to pieces. As I sat there reading this, I almost seemed to see a revolution in being.

HOVSTAD (*turning round*): Hush!—speak so that Aslaksen cannot hear you.

BILLING (*lowering his voice*): Aslaksen is a chicken-hearted chap, a coward; there is nothing of the man in him. But this time you will insist on your own way, won't you? You will put the Doctor's article in?

HOVSTAD: Yes, and if the Mayor doesn't like it—

BILLING: That will be a problem.

HOVSTAD: Well, fortunately we can turn the situation to good account, whatever happens. If the Mayor will not fall in with the Doctor's project, he will have all the small trades-men down on him—the whole of the Householders' Associa-tion and the rest of them. And if he does fall in with it, he will fall out with the whole crowd of large shareholders in the Baths, who up to now have been his most valuable sup-porters—

BILLING: Yes, because they will certainly have to fork out a pretty penny—

HOVSTAD: Yes, you may be sure they will. And in this way the ring will be broken up, you see, and then in every issue of the paper we will enlighten the public on the Mayor's incapability on one point and another, and make it clear that all the positions of trust in the town, the whole control of municipal affairs, ought to be put in the hand of the Liberals.

BILLING: That is perfectly true! I see it coming—I see it coming; we are on the threshold of a revolution!

(*A knock is heard at the door.*)

HOVSTAD: Hush! (*calls out*) Come in! (DR. STOCKMANN *comes in by the street door.* HOVSTAD *goes to meet him.*) Ah, it is you, Doctor! Well?

DR. STOCKMANN: You may set to work and print it, Mr. Hovstad!

HOVSTAD: Has it come to that, then?

BILLING: Hurrah!

DR. STOCKMANN: Yes, print away. Undoubtedly it has come

to that. Now they must take what they get. There is going to be a fight in the town, Mr. Billing!

BILLING: War to the knife, I hope! We will have our knives at their throats, Doctor!

DR. STOCKMANN: This article is only a beginning. I have already got four or five more sketched out in my head. Where is Aslaksen?

BILLING (*calls into the printing room*): Aslaksen, just come here for a minute!

HOVSTAD: Four or five more articles, did you say? On the same subject?

DR. STOCKMANN: No—far from it, my dear fellow. No, they are about quite another matter. But they all spring from the question of the water supply and the drainage. One thing leads to another, you know. It is like beginning to pull down an old house, exactly.

BILLING: Upon my soul, it's true; you find you are not done till you have pulled all the old rubbish down.

ASLAKSEN (*coming in*): Pulled down? You are not thinking of pulling down the Baths surely, Doctor?

HOVSTAD: Far from it, don't be afraid.

DR. STOCKMANN: No, we meant something quite different. Well, what do you think of my article, Mr. Hovstad?

HOVSTAD: I think it is simply a masterpiece—

DR. STOCKMANN: Do you really think so? Well, I am very pleased, very pleased.

HOVSTAD: It is so clear and intelligible. One need have no special knowledge to understand the bearing of it. You will have every enlightened man on your side.

ASLAKSEN: And every prudent man too, I hope?

BILLING: The prudent and the imprudent—almost the whole town.

ASLAKSEN: In that case we may venture to print it.

DR. STOCKMANN: I should think so!

HOVSTAD: We will put it in tomorrow morning.

DR. STOCKMANN: Of course—you must not lose a single day. What I wanted to ask you, Mr. Aslaksen, was if you would supervise the printing of it yourself.

ASLAKSEN: With pleasure.

DR. STOCKMANN: Take care of it as if it were a treasure! No misprints—every word is important. I will look in again a little later; perhaps you will be able to let me see a proof. I can't tell you how eager I am to see it in print, and see it burst upon the public—

BILLING: Burst upon them—yes, like a flash of lightning!

DR. STOCKMANN: —and to have it submitted to the judgment of my intelligent fellow-townsmen. You cannot imagine what I have gone through today. I have been threatened first with one thing and then with another; they have tried to rob me of my most elementary rights as a man—

BILLING: What! Your rights as a man!

DR. STOCKMANN: —they have tried to degrade me, to make a coward of me, to force me to put personal interests before my most sacred convictions—

BILLING: That is too much—I'm damned if it isn't.

HOVSTAD: Oh, you mustn't be surprised at anything from that quarter.

DR. STOCKMANN: Well, they will get the worst of it with me; they may assure themselves of that. I shall consider the *People's Messenger* my sheet-anchor now, and every single day I will bombard them with one article after another, like bomb shells—

ASLAKSEN: Yes, but—

BILLING: Hurrah!—it is war, it is war!

DR. STOCKMANN: I shall smite them to the ground—I shall crush them—I shall break down all their defenses, before the eyes of the honest public! That is what I shall do!

ASLAKSEN: Yes, but in moderation, Doctor—proceed with moderation—

BILLING: Not a bit of it, not a bit of it! Don't spare the dynamite!

DR. STOCKMANN: Because it is not merely a question of water supply and drains now, you know. No—it is the whole of our social life that we have got to purify and disinfect—

BILLING: Spoken like a deliverer!

DR. STOCKMANN: All the defectives must be turned out, you understand—in every walk of life! Endless vistas have opened themselves to my mind's eye today. I cannot see it all quite clearly yet, but I shall in time. Young and vigorous standard-bearers—those are what we need and must seek, my friends; we must have new men in command at all our outposts.

BILLING: Hear, hear!

DR. STOCKMANN: We only need to stand by one another, and it will all be perfectly easy. The revolution will be launched like a ship that runs smoothly off the stocks. Don't you think so?

HOVSTAD: For my part I think we have now a prospect of getting the municipal authority into the hands where it should lie.

ASLAKSEN: And if only we proceed with moderation, I cannot imagine that there will be any risk.

DR. STOCKMANN: Who the devil cares whether there is any risk or not! What I am doing, I am doing in the name of truth and for the sake of my conscience.

HOVSTAD: You are a man who deserves to be supported, Doctor.

ASLAKSEN: Yes, there is no denying that the Doctor is a true friend to the town—a real friend to the community, that he is.

BILLING: Take my word for it, Aslaksen, Dr. Stockmann is a friend of the people.

ASLAKSEN: I fancy the Householders' Association will make use of that expression before long.

DR. STOCKMANN (*affected, grasps their hands*): Thank you, thank you, my dear staunch friends. It is very refreshing to me to hear you say that; my brother called me something quite different. By Jove, he shall have it back, with interest! But now I must be off to see a poor devil—. I will come back, as I said. Keep a very careful eye on the manuscript, Aslaksen, and don't leave out any of my exclamation marks! Instead put one or two more in! Great! Great! Well, good-bye for the present—good-bye, good-bye!

(*They show him to the door, and bow him out.*)

HOVSTAD: He may prove an invaluably useful man to us.

ASLAKSEN: Yes, so long as he confines himself to this matter of the Baths. But if he goes farther afield, I don't think it would be advisable to follow him.

HOVSTAD: Hm!—that all depends—

BILLING: You are so infernally timid, Aslaksen!

ASLAKSEN: Timid? Yes, when it is a question of the local authorities, I am timid, Mr. Billing; it is a lesson I have learned in the school of experience, let me tell you. But try me in higher politics, in matters that concern the government itself, and then see if I am timid.

BILLING: No, you aren't, I admit. But this is simply contradicting yourself.

ASLAKSEN: I am a man with a conscience, and that is the whole matter. If you attack the government, you don't do the community any harm, anyway; those fellows pay no attention to attacks, you see—they go on just as they are, in spite of them. But *local* authorities are different; they *can* be turned out, and then perhaps you may get an ignorant lot into office who may do irreparable harm to the householders and everybody else.

HOVSTAD: But what of the education of citizens by self-government—don't you attach any importance to that?

ASLAKSEN: When a man has interests of his own to protect, he cannot think of everything, Mr. Hovstad.

HOVSTAD: Then I hope I shall never have interests of my own to protect!

BILLING: Hear, hear!

ASLAKSEN (with a smile): Hm! (points to the desk) Mr. Sheriff Stensgaard was your predecessor at that editorial desk.

BILLING (spitting): Bah! That turncoat.

HOVSTAD: I am not a weathervane—and never will be.

ASLAKSEN: A politician should never be too certain of anything, Mr. Hovstad. And as for you, Mr. Billing, I should think it is time for you to be taking in a reef or two in your sails, seeing that you are applying for the post of secretary to the Bench.

BILLING: I—!

HOVSTAD: Are you, Billing?

BILLING: Well, yes—but you must clearly understand I am only doing it to annoy the bigwigs.

ASLAKSEN: Anyhow, it is no business of mine. But if I am to be accused of timidity and of inconsistency in my principles, this is what I want to point out: my political past is an open book. I have never changed, except perhaps to become a little more moderate, you see. My heart is still with the people; but I don't deny that my reason has a certain bias towards the authorities—the local ones, I mean (goes into the printing room).

BILLING: Shouldn't we try to get rid of him, Hovstad?

HOVSTAD: Do you know anyone else who will advance the money for our paper and printing bill?

BILLING: It is an infernal nuisance that we don't have some capital to trade on.

HOVSTAD (sitting down at his desk): Yes, if we only had that, then—

BILLING: Suppose you were to apply to Dr. Stockmann?

HOVSTAD (turning over some papers): What is the use? He has got nothing.

BILLING: No, but he has got a warm man in the background, old Morten Kiil—"the Badger," as they call him.

HOVSTAD (writing): Are you so sure he has got anything?

BILLING: Good Lord, of course he has! And some of it must come to the Stockmanns. Most probably he will do something for the children, at all events.

HOVSTAD (turning half round): Are you counting on that?

BILLING: Counting on it? Of course I am not counting on anything.

HOVSTAD: That is right. And I should not count on the secretaryship to the Bench either, if I were you; for I can assure you—you won't get it.

BILLING: Do you think I am not quite aware of that? My object is precisely *not* to get it. A slight of that kind stimulates a man's fighting power—it is like getting a supply of fresh bile—and I am sure one needs that badly enough in a hole-and-corner place like this, where it is so seldom anything happens to stir one up.

HOVSTAD (*writing*): Right, right.

BILLING: Ah, I shall be heard of yet!—Now I shall go and write the appeal to the Householders' Association (*goes into the room on the right*).

HOVSTAD (*sitting at his desk, biting his penholder, says slowly*): Hm!—that's it, that is it. (*A knock is heard.*) Come in! (PETRA *comes in by the other door*. HOVSTAD *gets up.*) What, you!—here?

PETRA: Yes, you must forgive me—

HOVSTAD (*pulling a chair forward*): Won't you sit down?

PETRA: No, thank you; I must go again in a moment.

HOVSTAD: Have you come with a message from your father, by any chance?

PETRA: No, I have come on my own account. (*takes a book out of her coat pocket*) Here is the English story.

HOVSTAD: Why have you brought it back?

PETRA: Because I am not going to translate it.

HOVSTAD: But you promised me faithfully—

PETRA: Yes, but then I had not read it. I don't suppose you have read it either?

HOVSTAD: No, you know quite well I don't understand English; but—

PETRA: Quite so. That is why I wanted to tell you that you must find something else. (*lays the book on the table*) You can't use this for the *People's Messenger*.

HOVSTAD: Why not?

PETRA: Because it conflicts with all your opinions.

HOVSTAD: Oh, for that matter—

PETRA: You don't understand me. The burden of this story is that there is a supernatural power that looks after the so-called good people in this world and makes everything happen for the best in their case—while all the so-called bad people are punished.

HOVSTAD: Well, but that is all right. That is just what our readers want.

PETRA: And are you going to be the one to give it to them? For myself, I do not believe a word of it. You know quite well that things do not happen so in reality.

HOVSTAD: You are perfectly right; but an editor cannot always act as he would prefer. He is often obliged to bow to the wishes of the public in unimportant matters. Politics are the most important thing in life—for a newspaper, anyway; and if I want to carry my public with me on the path that leads to liberty and progress, I must not frighten them away. If they find a moral tale of this sort in the serial at the bottom of the page, they will be all the more ready to read what is printed above it; they feel more secure, as it were.

PETRA: For shame! You would never go and set a snare like that for your readers; you are not a spider!

HOVSTAD (smiling): Thank you for having such a good opinion of me. No; as a matter of fact that is Billing's idea and not mine.

PETRA: Billing's!

HOVSTAD: Yes; anyway he propounded that theory here one day. And it is Billing who is so anxious to have that story in the paper; I don't know anything about the book.

PETRA: But how can Billing, with his emancipated views—

HOVSTAD: Oh, Billing is a many-sided man. He is applying for the post of secretary to the Bench, too, I hear.

PETRA: I don't believe it, Mr. Hovstad. How could he possibly bring himself to do such a thing?

HOVSTAD: Ah, you must ask him that.

PETRA: I should never have thought it of him.

HOVSTAD (looking more closely at her): No? Does it really surprise you so much?

PETRA: Yes. Or perhaps not altogether. Really, I don't quite know—

HOVSTAD: We journalists are not much worth, Miss Stockmann.

PETRA: Do you really mean that?

HOVSTAD: I think so sometimes.

PETRA: Yes, in the ordinary affairs of everyday life, perhaps; I can understand that. But now, when you have taken a weighty matter in hand—

HOVSTAD: This matter of your father's, you mean?

PETRA: Exactly. It seems to me that now you must feel you are a man worth more than most.

HOVSTAD: Yes, today I do feel something of that sort.

PETRA: Of course you do, don't you? It is a splendid voca-
tion you have chosen—to smooth the way for the march of
unappreciated truths, and new and courageous lines of
thought. If it were nothing more than because you stand
fearlessly in the open and take up the cause of an injured
man—

HOVSTAD: Especially when that injured man is—ahem!—I
don't rightly know how to—

PETRA: When that man is so upright and so honest, you
mean?

HOVSTAD (*more gently*): Especially when he is your father,
I meant.

PETRA (*suddenly checked*): *That?*

HOVSTAD: Yes, Petra—Miss Petra.

PETRA: Is it *that*, that is first and foremost with you? Not
the matter itself? Not the truth?—not my father's big generous heart?

HOVSTAD: Certainly—of course—that too.

PETRA: No, thank you; you have betrayed yourself, Mr.
Hovstad, and now I shall never trust you again in anything.

HOVSTAD: Can you really take it so amiss in me that it is
mostly for your sake—?

PETRA: What I am angry with you for, is for not having
been honest with my father. You talked to him as if the
truth and the good of the community were what lay nearest
to your heart. You have made fools of both my father and
me. You are not the man you made yourself out to be. And
that I shall never forgive you—never!

HOVSTAD: You ought not to speak so bitterly, Miss Petra
—least of all now.

PETRA: Why not now, especially?

HOVSTAD: Because your father cannot do without my help.

PETRA (*looking him up and down*): Are you that sort of
man too? For shame!

HOVSTAD: No, no, I am not. This came upon me so un-
expectedly—you must believe that.

PETRA: I know what to believe. Good-bye.

ASLAKSEN (*coming from the printing room, hurriedly and
with an air of mystery*): Damnation, Hovstad!—(*sees* PETRA)
Oh, this is awkward—

PETRA: There is the book; you must give it to some one
else (*goes towards the door*).

HOVSTAD (*following her*): But, Miss Stockmann—

PETRA: Good-bye (*goes out*).

ASLAKSEN: Listen, Mr. Hovstad—

HOVSTAD: Well, well!—what is it?

ASLAKSEN: The Mayor is outside in the printing room.

HOVSTAD: The Mayor, did you say?

ASLAKSEN: Yes, he wants to speak to you. He came in by the back door—didn't want to be seen, you understand.

HOVSTAD: What can he want? Wait a bit—I will go myself. (*goes to the door of the printing room, opens it, bows and invites* PETER STOCKMANN *in*) Just see, Aslaksen, that no one—

ASLAKSEN: Quite so (*goes into the printing room*).

PETER STOCKMANN: You did not expect to see me here, Mr. Hovstad?

HOVSTAD: No, I confess I did not.

PETER STOCKMANN (*looking round*): You are very snug in here—very nice indeed.

HOVSTAD: Oh—

PETER STOCKMANN: And here I come, without any notice, to take up your time!

HOVSTAD: By all means, Mr. Mayor. I am at your service. But let me relieve you of your— (*takes* STOCKMANN'S *hat and stick and puts them on a chair*) Won't you sit down?

PETER STOCKMANN (*sitting down by the table*): Thank you. (HOVSTAD *sits down*.) I have had an extremely annoying experience today, Mr. Hovstad.

HOVSTAD: Really? Ah well, I expect with all the various business you have to attend to—

PETER STOCKMANN: The Medical Officer of the Baths is responsible for what happened today.

HOVSTAD: Indeed? The Doctor?

PETER STOCKMANN: He has addressed a kind of report to the Baths Committee on the subject of certain supposed defects in the Baths.

HOVSTAD: Has he indeed?

PETER STOCKMANN: Yes—has he not told you? I thought he said—

HOVSTAD: Ah, yes—it is true he did mention something about—

ASLAKSEN (*coming from the printing room*): I ought to have that copy—

HOVSTAD (*angrily*): Ahem!—there it is on the desk.

ASLAKSEN (*taking it*): Right.

PETER STOCKMANN: But look there—that is the thing I was speaking of!

ASLAKSEN: Yes, that is the Doctor's article, Mr. Mayor.

HOVSTAD: Oh, is *that* what you were speaking about?

PETER STOCKMANN: Yes, that is it. What do you think of it?

HOVSTAD: Oh, I am only a layman—and I have only taken a very cursory glance at it.

PETER STOCKMANN: But you are going to print it?

HOVSTAD: I cannot very well refuse a distinguished man—

ASLAKSEN: I have nothing to do with editing the paper, Mr. Mayor—

PETER STOCKMANN: I understand.

ASLAKSEN: I merely print what is put into my hands.

PETER STOCKMANN: Quite so.

ASLAKSEN: And so I must— (*moves off towards the printing room*).

PETER STOCKMANN: No, wait a moment, Mr. Aslaksen. You will allow me, Mr. Hovstad?

HOVSTAD: If you please, Mr. Mayor.

PETER STOCKMANN: You are a discreet and thoughtful man, Mr. Aslaksen.

ASLAKSEN: I am delighted to hear you think so, sir.

PETER STOCKMANN: And a man of very considerable influence.

ASLAKSEN: Chiefly among the small tradesmen, sir.

PETER STOCKMANN: The small taxpayers are the majority —here as everywhere else.

ASLAKSEN: That is true.

PETER STOCKMANN: And I have no doubt you know the general trend of opinion among them, don't you?

ASLAKSEN: Yes I think I may say I do, Mr. Mayor.

PETER STOCKMANN: Yes. Well, since there is such a praiseworthy spirit of self-sacrifice among the less wealthy citizens of our town—

ASLAKSEN: What?

HOVSTAD: Self-sacrifice?

PETER STOCKMANN: It is pleasing evidence of a public-spirited feeling, extremely pleasing evidence. I might almost say I hardly expected it. But you have a closer knowledge of public opinion than I.

ASLAKSEN: But, Mr. Mayor—

PETER STOCKMANN: And indeed it is no small sacrifice that the town is going to make.

HOVSTAD: The town?

ASLAKSEN: But I don't understand. Is it the Baths—?

PETER STOCKMANN: At a provisional estimate, the alterations that the Medical Officer asserts to be desirable will cost somewhere about twenty thousand pounds.

ASLAKSEN: That is a lot of money, but—

PETER STOCKMANN: Of course it will be necessary to raise a municipal loan.

HOVSTAD (*getting up*): Surely you never mean that the town must pay—?

ASLAKSEN: Do you mean that it must come out of the municipal funds?—out of the ill-filled pockets of the small tradesmen?

PETER STOCKMANN: Well, my dear Mr. Aslaksen, where else is the money to come from?

ASLAKSEN: The gentlemen who own the Baths ought to provide that.

PETER STOCKMANN: The proprietors of the Baths are not in a position to incur any further expense.

ASLAKSEN: Is that absolutely certain, Mr. Mayor?

PETER STOCKMANN: I have satisfied myself that it is so. If the town wants these very extensive alterations, it will have to pay for them.

ASLAKSEN: But, damn it all—I beg your pardon—this is quite another matter, Mr. Hovstad!

HOVSTAD: It is, indeed.

PETER STOCKMANN: The most fatal part of it is that we shall be obliged to shut the Baths for a couple of years.

HOVSTAD: Shut them? Shut them altogether?

ASLAKSEN: For two years?

PETER STOCKMANN: Yes, the work will take as long as that —at least.

ASLAKSEN: I'm damned if we will stand for that, Mr. Mayor! What are we householders to live upon in the meantime?

PETER STOCKMANN: Unfortunately that is an extremely difficult question to answer, Mr. Aslaksen. But what would you have us do? Do you suppose we shall have a single visitor in the town, if we go about proclaiming that our water is polluted, that we are living over a plague spot, that the entire town—

ASLAKSEN: And the whole thing is merely imagination?

PETER STOCKMANN: With the best will in the world, I have not been able to come to any other conclusion.

ASLAKSEN: Well then I must say it is absolutely unjustifiable of Dr. Stockmann—I beg your pardon, Mr. Mayor—

PETER STOCKMANN: What you say is lamentably true, Mr. Aslaksen. My brother has unfortunately always been a headstrong man.

ASLAKSEN: After this, do you mean to give him your support, Mr. Hovstad?

HOVSTAD: Can you suppose for a moment that I—?

PETER STOCKMANN: I have drawn up a short *résumé* of the situation as it appears from a reasonable man's point of view. In it I have indicated how certain possible defects might suitably be remedied without out-running the resources of the Baths Committee.

HOVSTAD: Have you got it with you, Mr. Mayor?

PETER STOCKMANN (*fumbling in his pocket*): Yes, I brought it with me in case you should—

ASLAKSEN: Good Lord, there he is!

PETER STOCKMANN: Who? My brother?

HOVSTAD: Where? Where?

ASLAKSEN: He has just gone through the printing room.

PETER STOCKMANN: How unlucky! I don't want to meet him here, and I had still several things to speak to you about.

HOVSTAD (*pointing to the door on the right*): Go in there for the present.

PETER STOCKMANN: But—?

HOVSTAD: You will only find Billing in there.

ASLAKSEN: Quick, quick, Mr. Mayor—he is just coming.

PETER STOCKMANN: Yes, very well; but see that you get rid of him quickly (*goes out through the door on the right, which* ASLAKSEN *opens for him and shuts after him*).

HOVSTAD: Pretend to be doing something, Aslaksen. (*Sits down and writes;* ASLAKSEN *begins foraging among a heap of newspapers that are lying on a chair.*)

DR. STOCKMANN (*coming in from the printing room*): Here I am again (*puts down his hat and stick*).

HOVSTAD (*writing*): Already, Doctor? Hurry up with what we were speaking about, Aslaksen. We are very pressed for time today.

DR. STOCKMANN (*to* ASLAKSEN): No proof for me to see yet, I hear.

ASLAKSEN (*without turning round*): You couldn't expect it yet, Doctor.

DR. STOCKMANN: No, no; but I am impatient, as you can understand. I shall not know a moment's peace of mind till I see it in print.

HOVSTAD: Hm!—It will take a good while yet, won't it, Aslaksen?

ASLAKSEN: Yes, I am almost afraid it will.

DR. STOCKMANN: All right, my dear friends; I will come back. I do not mind coming back twice if necessary. A matter of such great importance—the welfare of the town at stake—it is no time to shirk trouble. (*is just going, but stops and comes back*) Look here—there is one thing more I want to speak to you about.

HOVSTAD: Excuse me, but could it not wait till some other time?

DR. STOCKMANN: I can tell you in half a dozen words. It is only this. When my article is read tomorrow and it is realized that I have been quietly working the whole winter for the welfare of the town—

HOVSTAD: Yes but, Doctor—

DR. STOCKMANN: I know what you are going to say. You don't see how on earth it was any more than my duty—my obvious duty as a citizen. Of course it wasn't; I know that as well as you. But my fellow-citizens, you know—! Good Lord, think of all the good souls who think so highly of me—!

ASLAKSEN: Yes, our townsfolk have had a very high opinion of you so far, Doctor.

DR. STOCKMANN: Yes, and that is just why I am afraid they—. Well, this is the point; when this reaches them, especially the poorer classes, and sounds in their ears like a summons to take the town's affairs into their own hands for the future—

HOVSTAD (*getting up*): Ahem! Doctor, I won't conceal from you the fact—

DR. STOCKMANN: Ah—I knew there was something in the wind! But I won't hear a word of it. If anything of that sort is being set on foot—

HOVSTAD: Of what sort?

DR. STOCKMANN: Well, whatever it is—whether it is a demonstration in my honor, or a banquet, or a subscription list for some presentation to me—whatever it is, you must promise me solemnly and faithfully to put a stop to it. You too, Mr. Aslaksen; do you understand?

HOVSTAD: You must forgive me, Doctor, but sooner or later we must tell you the plain truth—

(*He is interrupted by the entrance of* MRS. STOCKMANN, *who comes in from the street door.*)

MRS. STOCKMANN (*seeing her husband*): Just as I thought!

HOVSTAD (*going towards her*): You too, Mrs. Stockmann?

DR. STOCKMANN: What on earth do *you* want here, Katherine?

MRS. STOCKMANN: I should think you know very well what I want.

HOVSTAD: Won't you sit down? Or perhaps—

MRS. STOCKMANN: No, thank you; don't trouble. And you

must not be offended at my coming to fetch my husband; I am the mother of three children, you know.

DR. STOCKMANN: Nonsense!—we know all about that.

MRS. STOCKMANN: Well, one would not give you credit for much thought for your wife and children today; if you had had that, you would not have gone and dragged us all into misfortune.

DR. STOCKMANN: Are you out of your senses, Katherine! Because a man has a wife and children, is he not to be allowed to proclaim the truth—is he not to be allowed to be an actively useful citizen—is he not to be allowed to do a service to his native town!

MRS. STOCKMANN: Yes, Thomas—in reason.

ASLAKSEN: Just what I say. Moderation in everything.

MRS. STOCKMANN: And that is why you wrong us, Mr. Hovstad, in enticing my husband away from his home and making a dupe of him in all this.

HOVSTAD: I certainly am making a dupe of no one—

DR. STOCKMANN: Making a dupe of me! Do you suppose *I* should allow myself to be duped!

MRS. STOCKMANN: It is just what you do. I know quite well you have more brains than anyone in the town, but you are extremely easily duped, Thomas. (*to* HOVSTAD) Please realize that he loses his post at the Baths if you print what he has written—

ASLAKSEN: What!

HOVSTAD: Look here, Doctor—

DR. STOCKMANN (*laughing*): Ha—ha!—just let them try! No, no—they will take good care not to. I have got the compact majority behind me, let me tell you!

MRS. STOCKMANN: Yes, that is just the worst of it—your having any such horrid thing behind you.

DR. STOCKMANN: Rubbish, Katherine!—Go home and look after your house and leave me to look after the community. How can you be so afraid, when I am so confident and happy? (*walks up and down, rubbing his hands*) Truth and the People will win the fight, you may be certain! I see the whole of the broad-minded middle class marching like a victorious army—! (*stops beside a chair*) What is that lying there?

ASLAKSEN: Good Lord!

HOVSTAD: Ahem!

DR. STOCKMANN: Here we have the topmost pinnacle of authority! (*takes the* MAYOR'S *official hat carefully between his finger-tips and holds it up in the air*)

MRS. STOCKMANN: The Mayor's hat!

DR. STOCKMANN: And here is the staff of office too. How in the name of all that's wonderful—?

HOVSTAD: Well, you see—

DR. STOCKMANN: Oh, I understand. He has been here trying to talk you over. Ha—ha!—he made rather a mistake there! And as soon as he caught sight of me in the printing room—. (*bursts out laughing*) Did he run away, Mr. Aslaksen?

ASLAKSEN (*hurriedly*): Yes, he ran away, Doctor.

DR. STOCKMANN: Ran away without his stick or his—. Fiddlesticks! Peter doesn't run away and leave his belongings behind him. But what the blazes have you done with him? Ah!—in there, of course. Now you shall see, Katherine!

MRS. STOCKMANN: Thomas—please don't—!

ASLAKSEN: Don't be rash, Doctor.

(DR. STOCKMANN *has put on the* MAYOR'S *hat and taken his stick in his hand. He goes up to the door, opens it, and stands with his hand to his hat at the salute.* PETER STOCKMANN *comes in, red with anger.* BILLING *follows him.*)

PETER STOCKMANN: What does this tomfoolery mean?

DR. STOCKMANN: Be respectful, my good Peter. I am the chief authority in the town now (*walks up and down*).

MRS. STOCKMANN (*almost in tears*): Really, Thomas!

PETER STOCKMANN (*following him about*): Give me my hat and stick.

DR. STOCKMANN (*in the same tone as before*): If you are chief constable, let me tell you that I am the Mayor—I am the master of the whole town, please understand!

PETER STOCKMANN: Take off my hat, I tell you. Remember it is part of an official uniform.

DR. STOCKMANN: Pooh! Do you think the newly awakened lion-hearted people are going to be frightened by an official hat? There is going to be a revolution in the town tomorrow, let me tell you. You thought you could turn me out; but now I shall turn you out—turn you out of all your various offices. Do you think I cannot? Listen to me. I have triumphant social forces behind me. Hovstad and Billing will thunder in the *People's Messenger*, and Aslaksen will take the field at the head of the whole Householders' Association—

ASLAKSEN: That I won't, Doctor.

DR. STOCKMANN: Of course you will—

PETER STOCKMANN: Ah!—may I ask then if Mr. Hovstad intends to join this agitation.

HOVSTAD: No, Mr. Mayor.

ASLAKSEN: No, Mr. Hovstad is not such a fool as to go and

ruin his paper and himself for the sake of an imaginary grievance.

DR. STOCKMANN (*looking round him*): What does this mean?

HOVSTAD: You have represented your case in a false light, Doctor, and therefore I am unable to give you my support.

BILLING: And after what the Mayor was so kind as to tell me just now, I—

DR. STOCKMANN: A false light! Leave that part of it to me. Only print my article; I am quite capable of defending it.

HOVSTAD: I am not going to print it. I cannot and will not and dare not print it.

DR. STOCKMANN: You dare not? What nonsense!—you are the editor; and an editor controls his paper, I suppose!

ASLAKSEN: No, it is the subscribers, Doctor.

PETER STOCKMANN: Fortunately, yes.

ASLAKSEN: It is public opinion—the enlightened public—householders and people of that kind; they control the newspapers.

DR. STOCKMANN (*composedly*): And I have all these influences against me?

ASLAKSEN: Yes, you have. It would mean the absolute ruin of the community if your article were to appear.

DR. STOCKMANN: Indeed.

PETER STOCKMANN: My hat and stick, if you please. (DR. STOCKMANN *takes off the hat and lays it on the table with the stick.* PETER STOCKMANN *takes them up.*) Your authority as mayor has come to an untimely end.

DR. STOCKMANN: We have not got to the end yet. (*to* HOVSTAD) Then it is quite impossible for you to print my article in the *People's Messenger*?

HOVSTAD: Quite impossible—out of regard for your family as well.

MRS. STOCKMANN: You need not concern yourself about his family, thank you, Mr. Hovstad.

PETER STOCKMANN (*taking a paper from his pocket*): It will be sufficient, for the guidance of the public, if this appears. It is an official statement. May I trouble you?

HOVSTAD (*taking the paper*): Certainly; I will see that it is printed.

DR. STOCKMANN: But not mine. Do you imagine that you can silence me and stifle the truth! You will not find it so easy as you suppose. Mr. Aslaksen, kindly take my manuscript at once and print it as a pamphlet—at my expense. I will have four hundred copies—no, five—six hundred.

ASLAKSEN: If you offered me its weight in gold, I could not lend my press for any such purpose, Doctor. It would be flying in the face of public opinion. You will not get it printed anywhere in the town.

DR. STOCKMANN: Then give it back to me.

HOVSTAD (*giving him the MS*): Here it is.

DR. STOCKMANN (*taking his hat and stick*): It shall be made public all the same. I will read it out at a mass meeting of the townspeople. All my fellow-citizens shall hear the voice of truth!

PETER STOCKMANN: You will not find any public body in the town that will give you the use of their hall for such a purpose.

ASLAKSEN: Not a single one, I am certain.

BILLING: No, I'm damned if you will find one.

MRS. STOCKMANN: But this is too shameful! Why should every one turn against you like that?

DR. STOCKMANN (*angrily*): I will tell you why. It is because all the men in this town are old women—like you; they all think of nothing but their families, and never of the community.

MRS. STOCKMANN (*putting her arm into his*): Then I will show them that an—an old woman can be a man for once. I am going to stand by you, Thomas!

DR. STOCKMANN: Bravely said, Katherine! It shall be made public—as I am a living soul! If I can't hire a hall, I shall hire a drum, and parade the town with it and read it at every street corner.

PETER STOCKMANN: You are surely not such an arrant fool as that!

DR. STOCKMANN: Yes, I am.

ASLAKSEN: You won't find a single man in the whole town to go with you.

BILLING: No, I'm damned if you will.

MRS. STOCKMANN: Don't give in, Thomas. I will tell the boys to go with you.

DR. STOCKMANN: That is a splendid idea!

MRS. STOCKMANN: Morten will be delighted; and Ejlif will do whatever he can.

DR. STOCKMANN: Yes, and Petra!—and you too, Katherine!

MRS. STOCKMANN: No, I won't do that; but I will stand at the window and watch you, that's what I will do.

DR. STOCKMANN (*puts his arms round her and kisses her*): Thank you, my dear! Now you and I are going to try a fall, my fine gentlemen! I am going to see whether a pack of cowards can succeed in gagging a patriot who wants to purify society!

(*He and his wife go out by the street door.*)

PETER STOCKMANN (*shaking his head seriously*): Now he has sent *her* out of her senses, too.

ACT IV

(*A big old-fashioned room in* CAPTAIN HORSTER'S *house. At the back folding doors, which are standing open, lead to an anteroom. Three windows in the left-hand wall. In the middle of the opposite wall a platform has been erected. On this is a small table with two candles, a water bottle and glass, and a bell. The room is lit by lamps placed between the windows. In the foreground on the left there is a table with candles and a chair. To the right is a door and some chairs standing near it. The room is nearly filled with a crowd of townspeople of all sorts, a few women and schoolboys being amongst them. People are still streaming in from the back, and the room is soon filled.*)

FIRST CITIZEN (*meeting another*): Hullo, Lamstad! You here too?

SECOND CITIZEN: I go to every public meeting, I do.

THIRD CITIZEN: Brought your whistle too, I expect!

SECOND CITIZEN: I should think so. Haven't you?

THIRD CITIZEN: Rather! And old Evensen said he was going to bring a cow-horn, he did.

SECOND CITIZEN: Good old Evensen! (*laughter among the crowd*)

FOURTH CITIZEN (*coming up to them*): I say, tell me what is going on here tonight.

SECOND CITIZEN: Dr. Stockmann is going to deliver an address attacking the Mayor.

FOURTH CITIZEN: But the Mayor is his brother.

FIRST CITIZEN: That doesn't matter; Dr. Stockmann's not the chap to be afraid.

THIRD CITIZEN: But he is in the wrong; it said so in the *People's Messenger*.

SECOND CITIZEN: Yes, I expect he must be in the wrong

this time, because neither the Householders' Association nor the Citizens' Club would lend him their hall for his meeting.

FIRST CITIZEN: He couldn't even get the loan of the hall at the Baths.

SECOND CITIZEN: No, I should think not.

A MAN IN ANOTHER PART OF THE CROWD: Listen—who do we support in this?

ANOTHER MAN (*beside him*): Watch Aslaksen, and do as he does.

BILLING (*pushing his way through the crowd with a writing case under his arm*): Excuse me, gentlemen—do you mind letting me through? I am reporting for the *People's Messenger*. Thank you very much! (*He sits down at the table on the left.*)

A WORKMAN: Who was that?

SECOND WORKMAN: Don't you know him? It's Billing, who writes for Aslaksen's paper.

(CAPTAIN HORSTER *brings in* MRS. STOCKMANN *and* PETRA *through the door on the right.* EJLIF *and* MORTEN *follow them in.*)

HORSTER: I thought you might all sit here; you can slip out easily from here, if things get too lively.

MRS. STOCKMANN: Do you think there will be a disturbance?

HORSTER: One can never tell—with such a crowd. But sit down, and don't be uneasy.

MRS. STOCKMANN (*sitting down*): It was extremely kind of you to offer my husband the room.

HORSTER: Well, if nobody else would—

PETRA (*who has sat down beside her mother*): And it was a plucky thing to do, Captain Horster.

HORSTER: Oh, it is not such a great matter as all that.

(HOVSTAD *and* ASLAKSEN *make their way through the crowd.*)

ASLAKSEN (*going up to* HORSTER): Has the Doctor not come yet?

HORSTER: He is waiting in the next room (*movement in the crowd by the door at the back*).

HOVSTAD: Look—here comes the Mayor!

BILLING: Yes, I'm damned if he hasn't come after all!

(PETER STOCKMANN *makes his way gradually through the crowd, bows courteously, and takes up a position by the wall on the left. Shortly afterwards* DR. STOCKMANN *comes in by the right-hand door. He is dressed in a black frock-coat, with a white tie. There is a little feeble applause, which is hushed down. Silence is obtained.*)

DR. STOCKMANN (*in an undertone*): How do you feel, Katherine?

MRS. STOCKMANN: All right, thank you. (*lowering her voice*) Be sure not to lose your temper, Thomas.

DR. STOCKMANN: Oh, I know how to control myself. (*looks at his watch, steps on to the platform, and bows*) It is a quarter past—so I will begin (*takes his MS out of his pocket*).

ASLAKSEN: I think we ought to elect a chairman first.

DR. STOCKMANN: No, it is quite unnecessary.

SOME OF THE CROWD: Yes—yes!

PETER STOCKMANN: I certainly think too that we ought to have a chairman.

DR. STOCKMANN: But I have called this meeting to deliver a lecture, Peter.

PETER STOCKMANN: Dr. Stockmann's lecture may possibly lead to a considerable conflict of opinion.

VOICES IN THE CROWD: A chairman! A chairman!

HOVSTAD: The general wish of the meeting seems to be that a chairman should be elected.

DR. STOCKMANN (*restraining himself*): Very well—let the meeting have its way.

ASLAKSEN: Will the Mayor be good enough to undertake the task?

THREE MEN (*clapping their hands*): Bravo! Bravo!

PETER STOCKMANN: For various reasons, which you will easily understand, I must beg to be excused. But fortunately we have amongst us a man who I think will be acceptable to you all. I refer to the President of the Householders' Association, Mr. Aslaksen!

SEVERAL VOICES: Yes—Aslaksen! Bravo Aslaksen!

(DR. STOCKMANN *takes up his MS and walks up and down the platform.*)

ASLAKSEN: Since my fellow-citizens choose to entrust me with this duty, I cannot refuse.

(*Loud applause.* ASLAKSEN *mounts the platform.*)

BILLING (*writing*): "Mr. Aslaksen was elected with enthusiasm."

ASLAKSEN: And now, as I am in this position, I should like to say a few brief words. I am a quiet and peaceable man, who believes in discreet moderation, and—and—in moderate discretion. All my friends can bear witness to that.

SEVERAL VOICES: That's right! That's right, Aslaksen!

ASLAKSEN: I have learned in the school of life and experience that moderation is the most valuable virtue a citizen can possess—

PETER STOCKMANN: Hear, hear!

ASLAKSEN: —And moreover that discretion and moderation are what enable a man to be of most service to the community. I would therefore suggest to our esteemed fellow-citizen, who has called this meeting, that he should strive to keep strictly within the bounds of moderation.

A MAN BY THE DOOR: Three cheers for the Moderation Society!

A VOICE: Shame!

SEVERAL VOICES: Sh!—Sh!

ASLAKSEN: No interruptions, gentlemen, please! Does anyone wish to make any remarks?

PETER STOCKMANN: Mr. Chairman.

ASLAKSEN: The Mayor will address the meeting.

PETER STOCKMANN: In consideration of the close relationship in which, as you all know, I stand to the present Medical Officer of the Baths, I should have preferred not to speak this evening. But my official position with regard to the Baths and my solicitude for the vital interests of the town compel me to bring forward a motion. I venture to presume that there is not a single one of our citizens present who considers it desirable that unreliable and exaggerated accounts of the sanitary condition of the Baths and the town should be spread abroad.

SEVERAL VOICES: No, no! Certainly not! We protest against it!

PETER STOCKMANN: Therefore I should like to propose that the meeting should not permit the Medical Officer either to read or to comment on his proposed lecture.

DR. STOCKMANN (*impatiently*): Not permit—! What the devil—!

MRS. STOCKMANN (*coughing*): Ahem!—ahem!

DR. STOCKMANN (*collecting himself*): Very well. Go ahead!

PETER STOCKMANN: In my communication to the *People's Messenger*, I have put the essential facts before the public in such a way that every fair-minded citizen can easily form his own opinion. From it you will see that the main result of the Medical Officer's proposals—apart from their constituting a vote of censure on the leading men of the town—would be to saddle the ratepayers with an unnecessary expenditure of at least some thousands of pounds.

(*Sounds of disapproval among the audience, and some catcalls.*)

ASLAKSEN (*ringing his bell*): Silence, please, gentlemen! I beg to support the Mayor's motion. I quite agree with him that there is something behind this agitation started by the Doctor. He talks about the Baths; but it is a revolution he is aiming at—he wants to get the administration of the town put into new hands. No one doubts the honesty of the Doctor's intentions—no one will suggest that there can be any two opinions as to that. I myself am a believer in self-government for the people, provided it does not fall too heavily on the ratepayers. But that would be the case here; and that is why I will see Dr. Stockmann damned—I beg your pardon—before I go with him in the matter. You can pay too dearly for a thing sometimes; that is my opinion.

(*Loud applause on all sides.*)

HOVSTAD: I, too, feel called upon to explain my position. Dr. Stockmann's agitation appeared to be gaining a certain amount of sympathy at first, so I supported it as impartially as I could. But presently we had reason to suspect that we had allowed ourselves to be misled by misrepresentation of the state of affairs—

DR. STOCKMANN: Misrepresentation—!

HOVSTAD: Well, let us say a not entirely trustworthy representation. The Mayor's statement has proved that. I hope no one here has any doubt as to my liberal principles; the attitude of the *People's Messenger* towards important political questions is well known to every one. But the advice of experienced and thoughtful men has convinced me that in purely local matters a newspaper ought to proceed with a certain caution.

ASLAKSEN: I entirely agree with the speaker.

HOVSTAD: And, in the matter before us, it is now an undoubted fact that Dr. Stockmann has public opinion against him. Now, what is an editor's first and most obvious duty, gentlemen? Is it not to work in harmony with his readers? Has he not received a sort of tacit mandate to work persistently and assiduously for the welfare of those whose opinions he represents? Or is it possible I am mistaken in that?

VOICES FROM THE CROWD: No, no! You are absolutely right!

HOVSTAD: It has cost me a severe struggle to break with a man in whose house I have been lately a frequent guest—a man who till today has been able to pride himself on the undivided goodwill of his fellow-citizens—a man whose only, or at all events whose essential failing, is that he is swayed by his heart rather than his head.

A FEW SCATTERED VOICES: That is true! Bravo, Stockmann!

HOVSTAD: But my duty to the community obliged me to break with him. And there is another consideration that impels me to oppose him, and, as far as possible, to arrest him on the perilous course he has adopted; that is, consideration for his family—

DR. STOCKMANN: Please stick to the water supply and drainage!

HOVSTAD: —consideration, I repeat, for his wife and his children for whom he has made no provision.

MORTEN: Is that us, mother?

MRS. STOCKMANN: Hush!

ASLAKSEN: I will now put the Mayor's proposition to the vote.

DR. STOCKMANN: There is no necessity! Tonight I have no intention of dealing with all that filth down at the Baths. No; I have something quite different to say to you.

PETER STOCKMANN (aside): What is coming now?

A DRUNKEN MAN (by the entrance door): I am a ratepayer! And therefore I have a right to speak too! And my entire—firm—inconceivable opinion is—

A NUMBER OF VOICES: Be quiet, at the back there!

OTHERS: He is drunk! Turn him out! (They turn him out.)

DR. STOCKMANN: Am I allowed to speak?

ASLAKSEN (ringing his bell): Dr. Stockmann will address the meeting.

DR. STOCKMANN: I should like to have seen any one, a few days ago, dare to attempt to silence me as has been done tonight! I would have defended my sacred rights as a man, like a lion! But now it is all one to me; I have something of even weightier importance to say to you. (The crowd presses nearer to him, MORTEN KIIL conspicuous among them.)

DR. STOCKMANN (continuing): I have thought and pondered a great deal, these last few days—pondered over such a variety of things that in the end my head seemed too full to hold them—

PETER STOCKMANN (with a cough): Ahem!

DR. STOCKMANN: —but I got them clear in my mind at last, and then I saw the whole situation lucidly. And that is why I am standing here tonight. I have a great revelation to make to you, my fellow-citizens! I will impart to you a discovery of a far wider scope than the trifling matter that our water supply is poisoned and our medicinal Baths are standing on pestiferous soil.

A NUMBER OF VOICES (*shouting*): Don't talk about the Baths! We won't hear you! None of that!

DR. STOCKMANN: I have already told you that what I want to speak about is the great discovery I have made lately—the discovery that all the sources of our *moral* life are poisoned and that the whole fabric of our civic community is founded on the pestiferous soil of falsehood.

VOICES OF DISCONCERTED CITIZENS: What is that he says?

PETER STOCKMANN: Such an insinuation—!

ASLAKSEN (*with his hand on his bell*): I call upon the speaker to moderate his language.

DR. STOCKMANN: I have always loved my native town as a man only can love the home of his youthful days. I was not old when I went away from here; and exile, longing and memories cast as it were an additional halo over both the town and its inhabitants. (*some clapping and applause*) And there I stayed, for many years, in a horrible hole far away up north. When I came into contact with some of the people that lived scattered about among the rocks, I often thought it would of been more service to the poor half-starved creatures if a veterinary doctor had been sent up there, instead of a man like me (*murmurs among the crowd*).

BILLING (*laying down his pen*): I'm damned if I have ever heard—!

HOVSTAD: It is an insult to a respectable population!

DR. STOCKMANN: Wait a bit! I do not think any one will charge me with having forgotten my native town up there. I was like one of the eider-ducks brooding on its nest, and what I hatched was—the plans for these Baths. (*applause and protests*) And then when fate at last decreed for me the great happiness of coming home again—I assure you, gentlemen, I thought I had nothing more in the world to wish for. Or rather, there was one thing I wished for—eagerly, untiringly, ardently—and that was to be able to be of service to my native town and the good of the community.

PETER STOCKMANN (*looking at the ceiling*): You chose a strange way of doing it—ahem!

DR. STOCKMANN: And so, with my eyes blinded to the real facts, I reveled in happiness. But yesterday morning—no, to be precise, it was yesterday afternoon—the eyes of my mind were opened wide, and the first thing I realized was the colossal stupidity of the authorities— (*Uproar, shouts and laughter.* MRS. STOCKMANN *coughs persistently.*)

PETER STOCKMANN: Mr. Chairman!

ASLAKSEN (*ringing his bell*): By virtue of my authority—!

DR. STOCKMANN: It is a pretty thing to catch me up on a word, Mr. Aslaksen. What I mean is only that I got scent of the unbelievable piggishness our leading men had been responsible for down at the Baths. I can't stand leading men at any price!—I have had enough of such people in my time. They are like billy-goats in a young plantation; they do mischief everywhere. They stand in a free man's way, whichever way he turns, and what I should like best would be to see them exterminated like any other vermin—(*uproar*).

PETER STOCKMANN: Mr. Chairman, can we allow such expressions to pass?

ASLAKSEN (*with his hand on his bell*): Doctor—!

DR. STOCKMANN: I cannot understand how it is that I have only now acquired a clear conception of what these gentry are, when I had almost daily before my eyes in this town such an excellent specimen of them—my brother Peter—slow-witted and hidebound in prejudice—. (*Laughter, uproar and hisses.* MRS. STOCKMANN *sits coughing assiduously.* ASLAKSEN *rings his bell violently.*)

THE DRUNKEN MAN (*who has got in again*): Is it me he is talking about? My name's Petersen, all right—but devil take me if I—

ANGRY VOICES: Turn out that drunken man! Turn him out. (*He is turned out again.*)

PETER STOCKMANN: Who was that person?

FIRST CITIZEN: I don't know who he is, Mr. Mayor.

SECOND CITIZEN: He doesn't belong here.

THIRD CITIZEN: I expect he is a dock worker from over at —(*The rest is inaudible.*)

ASLAKSEN: He has obviously had too much beer.—Proceed, Doctor; but please strive to be moderate in your language.

DR. STOCKMANN: Very well, gentlemen, I will say no more about our leading men. And if anyone imagines, from what I have just said, that my object is to attack these people this evening, he is wrong—absolutely wide of the mark. For I cherish the comforting conviction that these parasites—all these venerable relics of a dying school of thought—are most admirably paving the way for their own extinction; they need no doctor's help to hasten their end. Nor is it folk of that kind who constitute the most pressing danger to the community. It is not they who are most instrumental in poisoning the sources of our moral life and infecting the ground on which

we stand. It is not they who are the most dangerous enemies
of truth and freedom amongst us.

SHOUTS FROM ALL SIDES: Who then? Who is it? Name!
Name!

DR. STOCKMANN: You may depend upon it I shall name
them! That is precisely the great discovery I made yesterday.
(*raises his voice*) The most dangerous enemy of truth and
freedom amongst us is the compact majority—yes, the
damned compact Liberal majority—that is it! Now you know!
(*Tremendous uproar. Most of the crowd are shouting, stamping and hissing. Some of the older men among them exchange
stolen glances and seem to be enjoying themselves.* MRS.
STOCKMANN *gets up, looking anxious.* EJLIF *and* MORTEN
*advance threateningly upon some schoolboys who are playing
pranks.* ASLAKSEN *rings his bell and begs for silence.* HOVSTAD
and BILLING *both talk at once, but are inaudible. At last quiet
is restored.*)

ASLAKSEN: As chairman, I call upon the speaker to withdraw the ill-considered expression he has just used.

DR. STOCKMANN: Never, Mr. Aslaksen! It is the majority
in our community that denies me my freedom and seeks to
prevent my speaking the truth.

HOVSTAD: The majority always has right on its side.

BILLING: And truth too, by God!

DR. STOCKMANN: The majority *never* has right on its side.
Never, I say! That is one of these social lies against which
an independent, intelligent man must wage war. Who is it that
constitute the majority of the population in a country? Is it
the clever folk or the stupid? I don't imagine you will dispute
the fact that at present the stupid people are in an absolutely
overwhelming majority all the world over. But, good Lord!—
you can never pretend that it is right that the stupid folk
should govern the clever ones! (*uproar and cries*) Oh, yes—
you can shout me down, I know! but you cannot answer
me. The majority has *might* on its side—unfortunately; but
right it has *not*. I am in the right—I and a few other scattered
individuals. The minority is always in the right (*renewed
uproar*).

HOVSTAD: Aha!—so Dr. Stockmann has become an aristo-
crat since the day before yesterday!

DR. STOCKMANN: I have already said that I don't intend
to waste a word on the puny, narrow-chested, short-winded
crew whom we are leaving astern. Pulsating life no longer
concerns itself with them. I am thinking of the few, the scattered few amongst us, who have absorbed new and vigorous

truths. Such men stand, as it were, at the outposts, so far ahead that the compact majority has not yet been able to come up with them; and there they are fighting for truths that are too newly-born into the world of consciousness to have any considerable number of people on their side as yet.

HOVSTAD: So the Doctor is a revolutionary now!

DR. STOCKMANN: Good heavens—of course I am, Mr. Hovstad! I propose to raise a revolution against the lie that the majority has the monopoly on the truth. What sort of truths are they that the majority usually supports? They are truths that are of such advanced age that they are beginning to break up. And if a truth is as old as that, it is also in a fair way of becoming a lie, gentlemen. (*laughter and mocking cries*) Yes, believe me or not, as you like; but truths are by no means as long-lived as Methuselah—as some folks imagine. A normally constituted truth lives, let us say, as a rule seventeen or eighteen, or at most twenty years; seldom longer. But truths as aged as that are always worn frightfully thin, and nevertheless it is only then that the majority recognizes them and recommends them to the community as wholesome moral nourishment. There is no great nutritive value in that sort of fare, I can assure you; and, as a doctor, I ought to know. These "majority truths" are like last year's cured meat —like rancid, tainted ham; and they are the origin of the moral scurvy that is rampant in our communities.

ASLAKSEN: It appears to me that the speaker is wandering a long way from his subject.

PETER STOCKMANN: I quite agree with the Chairman.

DR. STOCKMANN: Have you gone clean out of your senses, Peter? I am sticking as closely to my subject as I can; for my subject is precisely this, that it is the masses, the majority —this infernal compact majority—that poisons the sources of our moral life and infects the ground we stand on.

HOVSTAD: And all this because the great, broad-minded majority of the people is prudent enough to show deference only to well-ascertained and well-approved truths?

DR. STOCKMANN: Ah, my good Mr. Hovstad, don't talk nonsense about well-ascertained truths! The truths of which the masses now approve are the very truths that the fighters at the outposts held to in the days of our grandfathers. We fighters at the outposts nowadays no longer approve of them; and I do not believe there is any other well-ascertained truth except this, that no community can live a healthy life if it is nourished only on such old marrowless truths.

HOVSTAD: But instead of standing there using vague generalities, it would be interesting if you would tell us what these old marrowless truths are, that we are nourished on.

(*Applause from many quarters.*)

DR. STOCKMANN: Oh, I could give you a whole string of such abominations; but to begin with I will confine myself to one well-approved truth, which at bottom is a foul lie, but upon which nevertheless Mr. Hovstad and the *People's Messenger* and all the *Messenger's* supporters are nourished.

HOVSTAD: And that is——?

DR. STOCKMANN: That is, the doctrine you have inherited from your forefathers and proclaim thoughtlessly far and wide —the doctrine that the public, the crowd, the masses, are the essential part of the population—that they constitute the People—that the common folk, the ignorant and incomplete element in the community, have the same right to pronounce judgment and to approve, to direct and to govern, as the isolated, intellectually superior personalities in it.

BILLING: Well, damn me if ever I——

HOVSTAD (*at the same time, shouting out*): Fellow-citizens, take good note of that!

A NUMBER OF VOICES (*angrily*): Oho!—we are not the People! Only the superior folk are to govern, are they!

A WORKMAN: Turn the fellow out, for talking such rubbish!

ANOTHER: Out with him!

ANOTHER (*calling out*): Blow your horn, Evensen!

(*A horn is blown loudly, amidst hisses and an angry uproar.*)

DR. STOCKMANN (*when the noise has somewhat abated*): Be reasonable! Can't you stand hearing the voice of truth for once? I don't in the least expect you to agree with me all at once; but I must say I did expect Mr. Hovstad to admit I was right, when he had recovered his composure a little. He claims to be a freethinker—

VOICES (*in murmurs of astonishment*): Freethinker, did he say? Is Hovstad a freethinker?

HOVSTAD (*shouting*): Prove it, Dr. Stockmann! When have I said so in print?

DR. STOCKMANN (*reflecting*): No, confound it, you are right!—you have never had the courage to. Well, I won't put you in a hole, Mr. Hovstad. Let us say it is I that am the freethinker, then. I am going to prove to you, scientifically, that the *People's Messenger* leads you by the nose in a shameful manner when it tells you that you—that the common people, the crowd, the masses, are the real essence of the People. That is only a newspaper lie, I tell you! The common

people are nothing more than the raw material of which a
People is made. (*groans, laughter and uproar*) Well, isn't that
the case? Isn't there an enormous difference between a well-
bred and an ill-bred strain of animals? Take, for instance, a
common barn-door hen. What sort of eating do you get from
a shriveled-up old scrag of a fowl like that? Not much, do
you! And what sort of eggs does it lay? A fairly good crow
or a raven can lay pretty nearly as good an egg. But take a
well-bred Spanish or Japanese hen, or a good pheasant or a
turkey—then you will see the difference. Or take the case of
dogs, with whom we humans are on such intimate terms.
Think first of an ordinary common cur—I mean one of the
horrible, coarse-haired, low-bred curs that do nothing but
run about the streets and befoul the walls of the houses.
Compare one of these curs with a poodle whose sires for
many generations have been bred in a gentleman's house,
where they have had the best of food and had the opportunity
of hearing soft voices and music. Do you not think that the
poodle's brain is developed to quite a different degree from
that of the cur? Of course it is. It is puppies of well-bred
poodles like that, that showmen train to do incredibly clever
tricks—things that a common cur could never learn to do
even if it stood on its head (*uproar and mocking cries*).

A CITIZEN (*calls out*): Are you going to make out we are
dogs, now?

ANOTHER CITIZEN: We are not animals, Doctor!

DR. STOCKMANN: Yes but, bless my soul, we *are*, my friend!
It is true we are the finest animals anyone could wish for;
but, even amongst us, exceptionally fine animals are rare.
There is a tremendous difference between poodle-men and
cur-men. And the amusing part of it is, that Mr. Hovstad
quite agrees with me as long as it is a question of four-
footed animals—

HOVSTAD: Yes, it is true enough as far as they are concerned.

DR. STOCKMANN: Very well. But as soon as I extend the
principle and apply it to two-legged animals, Mr. Hovstad
stops short. He no longer dares to think independently, or to
pursue his ideas to their logical conclusion; so he turns the
whole theory upside down and proclaims in the *People's
Messenger* that it is the barn-door hens and street curs that
are the finest specimens in the menagerie. But that is always
the way, as long as a man retains the traces of common origin
and has not worked his way up to intellectual distinction.

HOVSTAD: I lay no claim to any sort of distinction. I am the son of humble countryfolk, and I am proud that the stock I come from is rooted deep among the common people he insults.

VOICES: Bravo, Hovstad! Bravo! Bravo!

DR. STOCKMANN: The kind of common people I mean are not only to be found low down in the social scale; they crawl and swarm all around us—even in the highest social positions. You have only to look at your own fine, distinguished Mayor! My brother Peter is every bit as plebeian as anyone that walks in two shoes—(*laughter and hisses*).

PETER STOCKMANN: I protest against personal allusions of this kind.

DR. STOCKMANN (*imperturbably*): —and that, not because he is, like myself, descended from some old rascal of a pirate from Pomerania or thereabouts—because that is who we are descended from—

PETER STOCKMANN: An absurd legend. I deny it!

DR. STOCKMANN: —but because he thinks what his superiors think and holds the same opinions as they. People who do that are, intellectually speaking, common people; and that is why my magnificent brother Peter is in reality so very far from any distinction—and consequently also so far from being liberal-minded.

PETER STOCKMANN: Mr. Chairman—!

HOVSTAD: So it is only the distinguished men that are liberal-minded in this country? We are learning something quite new! (*laughter*)

DR. STOCKMANN: Yes, that is part of my new discovery too. And another part of it is that broad-mindedness is almost precisely the same thing as morality. That is why I maintain that it is absolutely inexcusable in the *People's Messenger* to proclaim, day in and day out, the false doctrine that it is the masses, the crowd, the compact majority, that have the monopoly of broad-mindedness and morality—and that vice and corruption and every kind of intellectual depravity are the result of culture, just as all the filth that is draining into our Baths is the result of the tanneries up at Mölledal! (*Uproar and interruptions.* DR. STOCKMANN *is undisturbed, and goes on, carried away by his ardor, with a smile.*) And yet this same *People's Messenger* can go on preaching that the masses ought to be elevated to higher conditions of life! But, bless my soul, if the *Messenger's* teaching is to be depended upon, this very raising up the masses would mean nothing more or less than setting them straightway upon the paths of depravity! Happily the theory that culture demoralizes is only an old falsehood that our forefathers believed in and we have inherited. No, it is ignorance, poverty, ugly conditions of life, that do the devil's work! In a house which does not get aired and swept every day—my wife Katherine maintains that the floor ought to be scrubbed as well, but that is a debatable question—in such a house, let me tell you, people will lose within two or three years the power of thinking or acting in a moral manner. Lack of oxygen weakens the conscience. And there must be a plentiful lack of oxygen in very many houses in this town, I should think, judging from the fact that the whole compact majority can be unconscientious enough to wish to build the town's prosperity on a quagmire of falsehood and deceit.

ASLAKSEN: We cannot allow such a grave accusation to be flung at a citizen community.

A CITIZEN: I move that the Chairman direct the speaker to sit down.

VOICES (*angrily*): Hear, hear! Right! Make him sit down!

DR. STOCKMANN (*losing his self-control*): Then I will go and shout the truth at every street corner! I will write it in other towns' newspapers! The whole country shall know what is going on here!

HOVSTAD: It almost seems as if Dr. Stockmann's intention were to ruin the town.

DR. STOCKMANN: Yes, my native town is so dear to me that I would rather ruin it than see it flourishing upon a lie.

ASLAKSEN: This is really serious. (*Uproar and catcalls.* MRS. STOCKMANN *coughs, but to no purpose; her husband does not listen to her any longer.*)

HOVSTAD (*shouting above the din*): A man must be a public enemy to wish to ruin a whole community!

DR. STOCKMANN (*with growing fervor*): What does the destruction of a community matter, if it lives on lies! It ought to be razed to the ground, I tell you! All who live by lies ought to be exterminated like vermin! You will end by infecting the whole country; you will bring about such a state of things that the whole country will deserve to be ruined. And if things come to that pass, I shall say from the bottom of my heart: Let the whole country perish, let all these people be exterminated!

VOICES FROM THE CROWD: That is talking like an out-and-out enemy of the people!

BILLING: There sounded the voice of the people, by all that's holy!

THE WHOLE CROWD (*shouting*): Yes, yes! He is an enemy

of the people! He hates his country! He hates his own people!

ASLAKSEN: Both as a citizen and as an individual, I am profoundly disturbed by what we have had to listen to. Dr. Stockmann has shown himself in a light I should never have dreamed of. I am unhappily obliged to subscribe to the opinion which I have just heard my estimable fellow-citizens utter; and I propose that we should give expression to that opinion in a resolution. I propose a resolution as follows: "This meeting declares that it considers Dr. Thomas Stockmann, Medical Officer of the Baths, to be an enemy of the people." (*A storm of cheers and applause. A number of men surround the* DOCTOR *and hiss him.* MRS. STOCKMANN *and* PETRA *have got up from their seats.* MORTEN *and* EJLIF *are fighting the other schoolboys for hissing; some of their elders separate them.*)

DR. STOCKMANN (*to the men who are hissing him*): Oh, you fools! I tell you that—

ASLAKSEN (*ringing his bell*): We cannot hear you now, Doctor. A formal vote is about to be taken; but, out of regard for personal feelings, it shall be by ballot and not verbal. Have you any clean paper, Mr. Billing?

BILLING: I have both blue and white here.

ASLAKSEN (*going to him*): That will do nicely; we shall get on more quickly that way. Cut it up into small strips— yes, that's it. (*to the meeting*) Blue means no; white means yes. I will come round myself and collect votes. (PETER STOCKMANN *leaves the hall.* ASLAKSEN *and one or two others go round the room with the slips of paper in their hats.*)

FIRST CITIZEN (*to* HOVSTAD): I say, what has come over the Doctor? What are we to think of it?

HOVSTAD: Oh, you know how headstrong he is.

SECOND CITIZEN (*to* BILLING): Billing, you go to their house—have you ever noticed if the fellow drinks?

BILLING: Well I'm hanged if I know what to say. There are always spirits on the table when you go.

THIRD CITIZEN: I rather think he goes quite off his head sometimes.

FIRST CITIZEN: I wonder if there is any madness in his family?

BILLING: I shouldn't wonder if there were.

FOURTH CITIZEN: No, it is nothing more than sheer malice; he wants to get even with somebody for something or other.

BILLING: Well certainly he suggested a rise in his salary on one occasion lately, and did not get it.

THE CITIZENS (*together*): Ah!—then it is easy to understand how it is!

THE DRUNKEN MAN (*who has got amongst the audience again*): I want a blue one, I do! And I want a white one too!

VOICES: It's that drunken chap again! Turn him out!

MORTEN KIIL (*going up to* DR. STOCKMANN): Well, Stockmann, do you see what these monkey tricks of yours lead to?

DR. STOCKMANN: I have done my duty.

MORTEN KIIL: What was that you said about the tanneries at Mölledal?

DR. STOCKMANN: You heard well enough. I said they were the source of all the filth.

MORTEN KIIL: My tannery too?

DR. STOCKMANN: Unfortunately your tannery is by far the worst.

MORTEN KIIL: Are you going to put that in the papers?

DR. STOCKMANN: I shall conceal nothing.

MORTEN KIIL: That may cost you dear, Stockmann (*goes out*).

A STOUT MAN (*going up to* CAPTAIN HORSTER, *without taking any notice of the ladies*): Well, Captain, so you lend your house to enemies of the people?

HORSTER: I imagine I can do what I like with my own possessions, Mr. Vik.

THE STOUT MAN: Then you can have no objection to my doing the same with mine.

HORSTER: What do you mean, sir?

THE STOUT MAN: You shall hear from me in the morning (*turns his back on him and moves off*).

PETRA: Was that not your owner, Captain Horster?

HORSTER: Yes, that was Mr. Vik, the shipowner.

ASLAKSEN (*with the voting-papers in his hands, gets up on to the platform and rings his bell*): Gentlemen, allow me to announce the result. By the votes of every one here except one person—

A YOUNG MAN: That is the drunk chap!

ASLAKSEN: By the votes of every one here except a tipsy man, this meeting of citizens declares Dr. Thomas Stockmann to be an enemy of the people. (*shouts and applause*) Three cheers for our ancient and honorable citizen community! (*renewed applause*) Three cheers for our able and energetic Mayor, who has so loyally suppressed the promptings of family feeling! (*cheers*) The meeting is dissolved (*gets down*).

BILLING: Three cheers for the Chairman!

THE WHOLE CROWD: Three cheers for Aslaksen! Hurrah!

DR. STOCKMANN: My hat and coat, Petra! Captain, have
you room on your ship for passengers to the New World?

HORSTER: For you and yours we will make room, Doctor.

DR. STOCKMANN (*as* PETRA *helps him into his coat*): Good.
Come, Katherine! Come, boys!

MRS. STOCKMANN (*in an undertone*): Thomas, dear, let
us go out by the back way.

DR. STOCKMANN: No back ways for me, Katherine. (*raising his voice*) You will hear more of this enemy of the
people, before he shakes the dust off his shoes upon you! I
am not so forgiving as a certain Person; I do not say: "I
forgive you, for ye know not what ye do."

ASLAKSEN (*shouting*): That is a blasphemous comparison,
Dr. Stockmann!

BILLING: It is, by God! It's dreadful for an earnest man to
listen to.

A COARSE VOICE: Threatens us now, does he!

OTHER VOICES (*excitedly*): Let's go and break his windows!
Duck him in the fjord!

ANOTHER VOICE: Blow your horn, Evensen! Pip, pip!

(*Horn-blowing, hisses, and wild cries.* DR. STOCKMANN *goes
out through the hall with his family,* HORSTER *elbowing a way
for them.*)

THE WHOLE CROWD (*howling after them as they go*): Enemy of the People! Enemy of the People!

BILLING (*as he puts his papers together*): Well, I'm damned
if I go and drink toddy with the Stockmanns tonight!

(*The crowd press towards the exit. The uproar continues
outside; shouts of* "Enemy of the People!" *are heard from
without.*)

ACT V

(DR. STOCKMANN'S *study. Bookcases, and cabinets containing specimens, line the walls. At the back is a door leading
to the hall; in the foreground on the left, a door leading to
the sitting room. In the right-hand wall are two windows, of
which all the panes are broken. The* DOCTOR'S *desk, littered
with books and papers, stands in the middle of the room,
which is in disorder. It is morning.* DR. STOCKMANN *in dress-*

ing gown, slippers and a smoking cap, is bending down and raking with an umbrella under one of the cabinets. After a little while he rakes out a stone.)

DR. STOCKMANN (*calling through the open sitting room door*): Katherine, I have found another one.

MRS. STOCKMANN (*from the sitting room*): Oh, you will find a lot more yet, I expect.

DR. STOCKMANN (*adding the stone to a heap of others on the table*): I shall treasure these stones as relics. Ejlif and Morten shall look at them every day, and when they are grown up they shall inherit them as heirlooms. (*rakes about under a bookcase*) Hasn't—what *is* her name?—the girl, you know—hasn't she been to fetch the glazier yet?

MRS. STOCKMANN (*coming in*): Yes, but she said he didn't know if he would be able to come today.

DR. STOCKMANN: You will see he won't dare to come.

MRS. STOCKMANN: Well, that is just what Randine thought —that he didn't dare to, on account of the neighbors. (*calls into the sitting room*) What is it you want, Randine? Give it to me. (*goes in, and comes out again directly*) Here is a letter for you, Thomas.

DR. STOCKMANN: Let me see it. (*opens and reads it*) Ah!— of course.

MRS. STOCKMANN: Who is it from?

DR. STOCKMANN: From the landlord. Notice to get out.

MRS. STOCKMANN: Is it possible? Such a nice man—

DR. STOCKMANN (*looking at the letter*): Does not dare do otherwise, he says. Doesn't like doing it, but dare not do otherwise—on account of his fellow-citizens—out of regard for public opinion. Is in a dependent position—dare not offend certain influential men—

MRS. STOCKMANN: There, you see, Thomas!

DR. STOCKMANN: Yes, yes, I see well enough; the whole lot of them in the town are cowards; not a man among them dares do anything for fear of the others. (*throws the letter on to the table*) But it doesn't matter to us, Katherine. We are going to sail away to the New World, and—

MRS. STOCKMANN: But, Thomas, are you sure we are well advised to take this step?

DR. STOCKMANN: Are you suggesting that I should stay here, where they have pilloried me as an enemy of the people—branded me—broken my windows! And just look here, Katherine—they have torn a great rent in my black trousers too!

MRS. STOCKMANN: Oh, dear!—and they are the best pair you have got!

DR. STOCKMANN: You should never wear your best trousers when you go out to fight for freedom and truth. It is not that I care so much about the trousers, you know; you can always sew them up again for me. But that the common herd should dare to make this attack on me, as if they were my equals— that is what I cannot, for the life of me, swallow!

MRS. STOCKMANN: There is no doubt they have behaved very badly to you, Thomas; but is that sufficient reason for our leaving our native country for good and all?

DR. STOCKMANN: If we went to another town, do you suppose we should not find the common people just as insolent as they are here? Depend upon it, there is not much to choose between them. Oh, well, let the curs snap—that is not the worst part of it. The worst is that, from one end of this country to the other, every man is the slave of his Party. Although, as far as that goes, I daresay it is not much better in the free West either; the compact majority, and liberal public opinion, and all that infernal old bag of tricks are probably rampant there too. But there things are done on a larger scale, you see. They may kill you, but they won't put you to death by slow torture. They don't squeeze a free man's soul in a vise, as they do here. And, if need be, one can live in solitude. (*walks up and down*) If I only knew where there was a virgin forest or a small South Sea island for sale, cheap—

MRS. STOCKMANN: But think of the boys, Thomas!

DR. STOCKMANN (*standing still*): What a strange woman you are, Katherine! Would you prefer to have the boys grow up in a society like this? You saw for yourself last night that half the population are out of their minds; and if the other half have not lost their senses, it is because they are mere brutes, with no sense to lose.

MRS. STOCKMANN: But, Thomas dear, the imprudent things you said had something to do with it, you know.

DR. STOCKMANN: Well, isn't what I said perfectly true? Don't they turn every idea topsy-turvy? Don't they make a regular hotch-potch of right and wrong? Don't they say that the things I know are true, are lies? The craziest part of it all is the fact of these "liberals," men of full age, going about in crowds imagining that they are the broad-minded party! Did you ever hear anything like it, Katherine!

MRS. STOCKMANN: Yes, yes, it's mad enough of them,

certainly; but—(PETRA *comes in from the sitting room.*) Back from school already?

PETRA: Yes. I have been given notice of dismissal.

MRS. STOCKMANN: Dismissal?

DR. STOCKMANN: You too?

PETRA: Mrs. Busk gave me my notice; so I thought it was best to go at once.

DR. STOCKMANN: You were perfectly right, too!

MRS. STOCKMANN: Who would have thought Mrs. Busk was a woman like that!

PETRA: Mrs. Busk isn't a bit like that, mother; I saw quite plainly how it hurt her to do it. But she didn't dare do otherwise, she said; and so I got my notice.

DR. STOCKMANN (*laughing and rubbing his hands*): She didn't dare do otherwise, either! It's delicious!

MRS. STOCKMANN: Well, after the dreadful scenes last night—

PETRA: It was not only that. Just listen to this, father!

DR. STOCKMANN: Well?

PETRA: Mrs. Busk showed me no less than three letters she received this morning—

DR. STOCKMANN: Anonymous, I suppose?

PETRA: Yes.

DR. STOCKMANN: Yes, because they didn't dare to risk signing their names, Katherine!

PETRA: And two of them were to the effect that a man, who has been our guest here, was declaring last night at the Club that my views on various subjects are extremely emancipated—

DR. STOCKMANN: You did not deny that, I hope?

PETRA: No, you know I wouldn't. Mrs. Busk's own views are tolerably emancipated, when we are alone together; but now that this report about me is being spread, she dare not keep me on any longer.

MRS. STOCKMANN: And some one who had been a guest of ours! That shows you the return you get for your hospitality, Thomas!

DR. STOCKMANN: We won't live in such a disgusting hole any longer. Pack up as quickly as you can, Katherine; the sooner we can get away, the better.

MRS. STOCKMANN: Be quiet—I think I hear some one in the hall. See who it is, Petra.

PETRA (*opening the door*): Oh, it's you, Captain Horster! Do come in.

HORSTER (*coming in*): Good morning. I thought I would just come in and see how you were.

DR. STOCKMANN (*shaking his hand*): Thanks—that is really kind of you.

MRS. STOCKMANN: And thank you, too, for helping us through the crowd, Captain Horster.

PETRA: How did you manage to get home again?

HORSTER: Oh, somehow or other. I am fairly strong, and there is more sound than fury about these folk.

DR. STOCKMANN: Yes, isn't their swinish cowardice astonishing? Look here, I will show you something! There are all the stones they have thrown through my windows. Just look at them! I'm hanged if there are more than two decently large bits of hardstone in the whole heap; the rest are nothing but gravel—wretched little things. And yet they stood out there bawling and swearing that they would do me some violence; but as for *doing* anything—you don't see much of that in this town.

HORSTER: Just as well for you this time, Doctor!

DR. STOCKMANN: True enough. But it makes one angry all the same; because if some day it should be a question of a national fight in real earnest, you will see that public opinion will be in favor of taking to one's heels, and the compact majority will turn tail like a flock of sheep, Captain Horster. That is what is so mournful to think of; it gives me so much concern, that—. No, forget that, it is ridiculous to care about it! They have called me an enemy of the people, so an enemy of the people let me be!

MRS. STOCKMANN: You will never be that, Thomas.

DR. STOCKMANN: Don't swear to that, Katherine. To be called an ugly name may have the same effect as a pin-scratch in the lung. And that hateful name—I can't get rid of it. It is sticking here in the pit of my stomach, eating into me like a corrosive acid. And no magnesia will remove it.

PETRA: Bah!—you should only laugh at them, father.

HORSTER: They will change their minds some day, Doctor.

MRS. STOCKMANN: Yes, Thomas, as sure as you are standing here.

DR. STOCKMANN: Perhaps, when it is too late. Much good may it do them! They may wallow in their filth then and rue the day when they drove a patriot into exile. When do you sail, Captain Horster?

HORSTER: Hm!—that was just what I had come to speak about—

DR. STOCKMANN: Why, has anything gone wrong with the ship?

HORSTER: No; but what has happened is that I am not to sail in it.

PETRA: Do you mean that you have been dismissed from your command?

HORSTER (*smiling*): Yes, that's just it.

PETRA: You too.

MRS. STOCKMANN: There, you see, Thomas!

DR. STOCKMANN: And that for the truth's sake! Oh, if I had thought such a thing possible—

HORSTER: You mustn't take it to heart! I shall be sure to find a job with some shipowner or other, elsewhere.

DR. STOCKMANN: And that is this man Vik—a wealthy man, independent of every one and everything—! Shame on him!

HORSTER: He is quite an excellent fellow otherwise; he told me himself he would willingly have kept me on, if only he had dared—

DR. STOCKMANN: But he didn't dare? No, of course not.

HORSTER: It is not such an easy matter, he said, for a party man—

DR. STOCKMANN: The worthy man spoke the truth. A party is like a sausage machine; it mashes up all sorts of heads together into the same mincemeat—fatheads and blockheads, all in one mash!

MRS. STOCKMANN: Come, come, Thomas dear!

PETRA (*to* HORSTER): If only you had not come home with us, things might not have come to this pass.

HORSTER: I do not regret it.

PETRA (*holding out her hand to him*): Thank you for that!

HORSTER (*to* DR. STOCKMANN): And so what I came to say was that if you are determined to go away, I have thought of another plan—

DR. STOCKMANN: That's splendid—if only we can get away at once.

MRS. STOCKMANN: Hush!—wasn't that some one knocking?

PETRA: That is uncle, surely.

DR. STOCKMANN: Aha! (*calls out*) Come in!

MRS. STOCKMANN: Dear Thomas, promise me, definitely—.

(PETER STOCKMANN *comes in from the hall.*)

PETER STOCKMANN: Oh, you are engaged. In that case, I will—

DR. STOCKMANN: No, no, come in.

PETER STOCKMANN: But I wanted to speak to you alone.

MRS. STOCKMANN: We will go into the sitting room in the meanwhile.

HORSTER: And I will look in again later.

DR. STOCKMANN: No, go in there with them, Captain Horster; I want to hear more about—.

HORSTER: Very well, I will wait, then. (*He follows* MRS. STOCKMANN *and* PETRA *into the sitting room.*)

DR. STOCKMANN: I daresay you find it rather draughty here today. Put your hat on.

PETER STOCKMANN: Thank you, if I may. (*does so*) I think I caught cold last night; I stood and shivered—

DR. STOCKMANN: Really? I found it warm enough.

PETER STOCKMANN: I regret it was not in my power to prevent those excesses last night.

DR. STOCKMANN: Have you anything particular to say to me besides that?

PETER STOCKMANN (*taking a big letter from his pocket*): I have this document for you, from the Baths Committee.

DR. STOCKMANN: My dismissal?

PETER STOCKMANN: Yes, dating from today. (*lays the letter on the table*) It gives us pain to do it; but, to speak frankly, we dared not do otherwise on account of public opinion.

DR. STOCKMANN (*smiling*): Dared not? I seem to have heard that word before, today.

PETER STOCKMANN: I must beg you to understand your position clearly. For the future you must not count on any practice whatever in the town.

DR. STOCKMANN: Hang the practice! But why are you so sure of that?

PETER STOCKMANN: The Householders' Association is circulating a list from house to house. All right-minded citizens are being called upon to give up employing you; and I can assure you that not a single head of a family will risk refusing his signature. They simply dare not.

DR. STOCKMANN: No, no; I don't doubt it. But what then?

PETER STOCKMANN: If I might advise you, it would be best to leave the place for a little while—

DR. STOCKMANN: Yes, the propriety of leaving the place *has* occurred to me.

PETER STOCKMANN: Good. And then, when you have had six months to think things over, if, after mature consideration, you can persuade yourself to write a few words of regret, acknowledging your error—

DR. STOCKMANN: I might have my appointment restored to me, do you mean?

PETER STOCKMANN: Perhaps. It is not at all impossible.

DR. STOCKMANN: But what about public opinion, then? Surely you would not dare to do it on account of public feeling.

PETER STOCKMANN: Public opinion is an extremely mutable thing. And, to be quite candid with you, it is a matter of great importance to us to have some admission of that sort from you in writing.

DR. STOCKMANN: Oh, that's what you are after, is it! I will trouble you to remember what I said to you lately about foxy tricks of that sort!

PETER STOCKMANN: Your position was quite different then. At that time you had reason to suppose you had the whole town at your back—

DR. STOCKMANN: Yes, and now I feel I have the whole town *on* my back—(*flaring up*) I would not do it if I had the devil and his wife on my back—! Never—never, I tell you!

PETER STOCKMANN: A man with a family has no right to behave as you do. You have no right to do it, Thomas.

DR. STOCKMANN: I have no right! There is only one single thing in the world a free man has no right to do. Do you know what that is?

PETER STOCKMANN: No.

DR. STOCKMANN: Of course you don't, but I will tell you. A free man has no right to soil himself with filth; he has no right to behave in a way that would justify his spitting in his own face.

PETER STOCKMANN: This sort of thing sounds extremely plausible, of course; and if there were no other explanation for your obstinacy—. But as it happens, there is.

DR. STOCKMANN: What do you mean?

PETER STOCKMANN: You understand very well what I mean. But, as your brother and as a man of discretion, I advise you not to build too much upon expectations and prospects that may so very easily fail you.

DR. STOCKMANN: What in the world is all this about?

PETER STOCKMANN: Do you really ask me to believe that you are ignorant of the terms of Mr. Kiil's will?

DR. STOCKMANN: I know that the small amount he possesses is to go to an institution for indigent old workpeople. How does that concern me?

PETER STOCKMANN: In the first place, it is by no means a small amount that is in question. Mr. Kiil is a fairly wealthy man.

DR. STOCKMANN: I had no notion of that!

PETER STOCKMANN: Hm!—hadn't you really? Then I suppose you had no notion, either, that a considerable portion of his wealth will come to your children, you and your wife having a life-rent of the capital. Has he never told you so?

DR. STOCKMANN: Never, on my honor! Quite the reverse; he has consistently done nothing but fume at being so unconscionably heavily taxed. But are you perfectly certain of this, Peter?

PETER STOCKMANN: I have it from an absolutely reliable source.

DR. STOCKMANN: Then, thank God, Katherine is provided for—and the children too! I must tell her this at once—(*calls out*) Katherine, Katherine!

PETER STOCKMANN (*restraining him*): Hush, don't say a word yet!

MRS. STOCKMANN (*opening the door*): What is the matter?

DR. STOCKMANN: Oh, nothing, nothing; you can go back. (*She shuts the door.* DR. STOCKMANN *walks up and down in his excitement.*) Provided for!—Just think of it, we are all provided for! And for life! What a blessed feeling it is to know one is provided for!

PETER STOCKMANN: Yes, but that is just exactly what you are not. Mr. Kiil can alter his will any day he likes.

DR. STOCKMANN: But he won't do that, my dear Peter. The "Badger" is much too delighted at my attack on you and your wise friends.

PETER STOCKMANN (*starts and looks intently at him*): Ah, that throws a light on various things.

DR. STOCKMANN: What things?

PETER STOCKMANN: I see that the whole thing was a combined maneuver on your part and his. These violent, reckless attacks that you have made against the leading men of the town, under the pretense that it was in the name of truth—

DR. STOCKMANN: What about them?

PETER STOCKMANN: I see that they were nothing else than the stipulated price for that vindictive old man's will.

DR. STOCKMANN (*almost speechless*): Peter—you are the most disgusting plebeian I have ever met in all my life.

PETER STOCKMANN: All is over between us. Your dismissal is irrevocable—we have a weapon against you now (*goes out*).

DR. STOCKMANN: For shame! For shame! (*calls out*) Katherine, you must have the floor scrubbed after him! Let—

what's her name—hang it, the girl who has always got soot
on her nose—

MRS. STOCKMANN (*in the sitting room*): Hush, Thomas,
be quiet!

PETRA (*coming to the door*): Father, grandfather is here,
asking if he may speak to you alone.

DR. STOCKMANN: Certainly he may. (*going to the door*)
Come in, Mr. Kiil. (MORTEN KIIL *comes in.* DR. STOCKMANN
shuts the door after him.) What can I do for you? Won't
you sit down?

MORTEN KIIL: I won't sit. (*looks around*) You look very
comfortable here today, Thomas.

DR. STOCKMANN: Yes, don't we!

MORTEN KIIL: Very comfortable—plenty of fresh air. I
should think you have got enough today of that oxygen you
were talking about yesterday. Your conscience must be in
splendid order today, I should think.

DR. STOCKMANN: It is.

MORTEN KIIL: So I should think. (*taps his chest*) Do you
know what I have got here?

DR. STOCKMANN: A good conscience, too, I hope.

MORTEN KIIL: Bah!—No, it is something better than that.
(*He takes a thick pocketbook from his breast pocket, opens
it, and displays a packet of papers.*)

DR. STOCKMANN (*looking at him in astonishment*): Shares
in the Baths?

MORTEN KIIL: They were not difficult to get today.

DR. STOCKMANN: And you have been buying—?

MORTEN KIIL: As many as I could pay for.

DR. STOCKMANN: But, my dear Mr. Kiil—consider the state
of the Baths' affairs!

MORTEN KIIL: If you behave like a reasonable man, you
can soon set the Baths on their feet again.

DR. STOCKMANN: Well, you can see for yourself that I have
done all I can, but—. They are all mad in this town!

MORTEN KIIL: You said yesterday that the worst of this
pollution came from my tannery. If that is true, then my
grandfather and my father before me, and I myself, for many
years past, have been poisoning the town like three destroying
angels. Do you think I am going to sit quiet under that reproach?

DR. STOCKMANN: Unfortunately I am afraid you will have
to.

MORTEN KIIL: No, thank you. I am jealous of my name
and reputation. They call me "the Badger," I am told. A

badger is a kind of pig, I believe; but I am not going to give them the right to call me that. I mean to live and die a clean man.

DR. STOCKMANN: And how are you going to set about it?

MORTEN KIIL: You shall cleanse me, Thomas.

DR. STOCKMANN: I!

MORTEN KIIL: Do you know what money I have bought these shares with? No, of course you can't know—but I will tell you. It is the money that Katherine and Petra and the boys have when I am gone. Because I have been able to save a little bit after all, you know.

DR. STOCKMANN (*flaring up*): And you have gone and taken Katherine's money for *this!*

MORTEN KIIL: Yes, the whole of the money is invested in the Baths now. And now I just want to see whether you are quite stark, staring mad, Thomas! If you still make out that these animals and other nasty things of that sort come from my tannery, it will be exactly as if you were to flay broad strips of skin from Katherine's body, and Petra's and the boys; and no decent man would do that—unless he were mad.

DR. STOCKMANN (*walking up and down*): Yes, but I *am* mad; I *am* mad!

MORTEN KIIL: You cannot be so absurdly mad as all that, when it is a question of your wife and children.

DR. STOCKMANN (*standing still in front of him*): Why couldn't you consult me about it, before you went and bought all that trash?

MORTEN KIIL: What is done cannot be undone.

DR. STOCKMANN (*walks about uneasily*). If only I were not so certain about it—! But I am absolutely convinced that I am right.

MORTEN KIIL (*weighing the pocketbook in his hand*): If you stick to your mad idea, this won't be worth much, you know (*puts the pocketbook in his pocket*).

DR. STOCKMANN: But, hang it all! it might be possible for science to discover some prophylactic, I should think—or some antidote of some kind—

MORTEN KIIL: To kill these animals, do you mean?

DR. STOCKMANN: Yes, or to make them innocuous.

MORTEN KIIL: Couldn't you try some rat's-bane?

DR. STOCKMANN: Don't talk nonsense! They all say it is only imagination, you know. Well, let it go at that! Let them have their own way about it! Haven't the ignorant, narrow-minded curs reviled me as an enemy of the people?—and haven't they been ready to tear the clothes off my back too?

MORTEN KIIL: And broken all your windows to pieces!

DR. STOCKMANN: And then there is my duty to my family. I must talk it over with Katherine; she is great on those things.

MORTEN KIIL: That is right; be guided by a reasonable woman's advice.

DR. STOCKMANN (*advancing towards him*): To think you could do such a preposterous thing! Risking Katherine's money in this way, and putting me in such a horribly painful dilemma! When I look at you, I think I see the devil himself—.

MORTEN KIIL: Then I had better go. But I must have an answer from you before two o'clock—yes or no. If it is no, the shares go to a charity, and that this very day.

DR. STOCKMANN: And what does Katherine get?

MORTEN KIIL: Not a halfpenny. (*The door leading to the hall opens, and* HOVSTAD *and* ASLAKSEN *make their appearance.*) Look at those two!

DR. STOCKMANN (*staring at them*): What the devil!—have *you* actually the face to come into my house?

HOVSTAD: Certainly.

ASLAKSEN: We have something to say to you, you see.

MORTEN KIIL (*in a whisper*): Yes or no—before two o'clock.

ASLAKSEN (*glancing at* HOVSTAD): Aha!

(MORTEN KIIL *goes out.*)

DR. STOCKMANN: Well, what do you want with me? Be brief.

HOVSTAD: I can quite understand that you are annoyed with us for our attitude at the meeting yesterday—

DR. STOCKMANN: Attitude, do you call it? Yes, it was a charming attitude! I call it weak, womanish—damnably shameful!

HOVSTAD: Call it what you like, we could not do otherwise.

DR. STOCKMANN: You *dared* not do otherwise—isn't that it?

HOVSTAD: Well, if you like to put it that way.

ASLAKSEN: But why did you not let us have word of it beforehand?—just a hint to Mr. Hovstad or to me?

DR. STOCKMANN: A hint? Of what?

ASLAKSEN: Of what was behind it all.

DR. STOCKMANN: I don't understand you in the least.

ASLAKSEN (*with a confidential nod*): Oh yes, you do, Dr. Stockmann.

HOVSTAD: It is no good making a mystery of it any longer.

DR. STOCKMANN (*looking first at one of them and then at the other*): What the devil do you both mean?

ASLAKSEN: May I ask if your father-in-law is not going round the town buying up all the shares in the Baths?

DR. STOCKMANN: Yes, he has been buying Baths shares today; but—

ASLAKSEN: It would have been more prudent to get some one else to do it—some one less nearly related to you.

HOVSTAD: And you should not have let your name appear in the affair. There was no need for anyone to know that the attack on the Baths came from you. You ought to have consulted me, Dr. Stockmann.

DR. STOCKMANN (*looks in front of him; then a light seems to dawn on him and he says in amazement*): Are such things conceivable? Are such things possible?

ASLAKSEN (*with a smile*): Evidently they are. But it is better to use a little *finesse*, you know.

HOVSTAD: And it is much better to have several persons in a thing of that sort; because the responsibility of each individual is lessened, when there are others with him.

DR. STOCKMANN (*composedly*): Come to the point, gentlemen. What do you want?

ASLAKSEN: Perhaps Mr. Hovstad had better—

HOVSTAD: No, you tell him, Aslaksen.

ASLAKSEN: Well, the fact is that, now we know the bearings of the whole affair, we think we might venture to put the *People's Messenger* at your disposal.

DR. STOCKMANN: Do you dare do that now? What about public opinion? Are you not afraid of a storm breaking upon our heads?

HOVSTAD: We will try to weather it.

ASLAKSEN: And you must be ready to go off quickly on a new tack, Doctor. As soon as your invective has done its work—

DR. STOCKMANN: Do you mean, as soon as my father-in-law and I have got hold of the shares at a low figure?

HOVSTAD: Your reasons for wishing to get the control of the Baths are mainly scientific, I take it.

DR. STOCKMANN: Of course; it was for scientific reasons that I persuaded old "Badger" to stand in with me in the matter. So we will tinker at the conduit pipes a little, and dig up a little bit of the shore, and it shan't cost the town a sixpence. That will be all right—eh?

HOVSTAD: I think so—if you have the *People's Messenger* behind you.

ASLAKSEN: The Press is a power in a free community, Doctor.

DR. STOCKMANN: Quite so. And so is public opinion. And you, Mr. Aslaksen—I suppose you will be answerable for the Householders' Association?

ASLAKSEN: Yes, and for the Temperance Society. You may rely on that.

DR. STOCKMANN: But, gentlemen—I really am ashamed to ask the question—but, what return do you—?

HOVSTAD: We should prefer to help you without any return whatever, believe me. But the *People's Messenger* is in rather a shaky condition; it doesn't go really well; and I should be very unwilling to suspend the paper now, when there is so much work to do here in the political way.

DR. STOCKMANN: Quite so; that would be a great trial to such a friend of the people as you are. (*flares up*) But I am an enemy of the people, remember! (*walks about the room*) Where have I put my stick? Where the devil is my stick?

HOVSTAD: What's that?

ASLAKSEN: Surely you never mean—?

DR. STOCKMANN (*standing still*): And suppose I don't give you a single penny of all I get out of it? Money is not very easy to get out of us rich folk, please to remember!

HOVSTAD: And you please to remember that this affair of the shares can be represented in two ways!

DR. STOCKMANN: Yes, and you are just the man to do it. If I don't come to the rescue of the *People's Messenger,* you will certainly take an evil view of the affair; you will hunt me down, I can well imagine—pursue me—try to throttle me as a dog does a hare.

HOVSTAD: It is a natural law; every animal must fight for its own livelihood.

ASLAKSEN: And get its food where it can, you know.

DR. STOCKMANN (*walking about the room*): Then you go and look for yours in the gutter; because I am going to show you which is the strongest animal of us three! (*finds an umbrella and brandishes it above his head*) Ah, now—!

HOVSTAD: You are surely not going to use violence!

ASLAKSEN: Take care what you are doing with that umbrella.

DR. STOCKMANN: Out of the window with you, Mr. Hovstad!

HOVSTAD (*edging to the door*): Are you quite mad!

DR. STOCKMANN: Out of the window, Mr. Aslaksen! Jump, I tell you! You will have to do it, sooner or later.

ASLAKSEN (*running round the writing table*): Moderation, Doctor—I am a delicate man—I can stand so little—(*calls out*) help, help!

(MRS. STOCKMANN, PETRA *and* HORSTER *come in from the sitting room.*)

MRS. STOCKMANN: Good gracious, Thomas! What is happening?

DR. STOCKMANN (*brandishing the umbrella*): Jump out, I tell you! Out into the gutter!

HOVSTAD: An assault on an unoffending man! I call you to witness, Captain Horster (*hurries out through the hall*).

ASLAKSEN (*irresolutely*): If only I knew the way about here— (*steals out through the sitting room*).

MRS. STOCKMANN (*holding her husband back*): Control yourself, Thomas!

DR. STOCKMANN (*throwing down the umbrella*): Upon my soul, they have escaped after all.

MRS. STOCKMANN: What did they want you to do?

DR. STOCKMANN: I will tell you later on; I have something else to think about now. (*goes to the table and writes something on a calling card*) Look there, Katherine; what is written there?

MRS. STOCKMANN: Three big *Noes;* what does that mean?

DR. STOCKMANN: I will tell you that too, later on. (*holds out the card to* PETRA) There, Petra; tell sooty-face to run over to the Badger's with that, as quick as she can. Hurry up! (PETRA *takes the card and goes out to the hall.*)

DR. STOCKMANN: Well, I think I have had a visit from every one of the devil's messengers today! But now I am going to sharpen my pen till they can feel its point; I shall dip it in venom and gall; I shall hurl my inkpot at their heads!

MRS. STOCKMANN: Yes, but we are going away, you know, Thomas.

(PETRA *comes back.*)

DR. STOCKMANN: Well?

PETRA: She has gone with it.

DR. STOCKMANN: Good.—Going away, did you say? No, I'll be hanged if we are going away! We are going to stay where we are, Katherine!

PETRA: Stay here?

MRS. STOCKMANN: Here, in the town?

DR. STOCKMANN: Yes, here. This is the field of battle—this is where the fight will be. This is where I shall triumph! As soon as I have had my trousers sewn up I shall go out and

look for another house. We must have a roof over our heads
for the winter.

HORSTER: That you shall have in my house.

DR. STOCKMANN: Can I?

HORSTER: Yes, quite well. I have plenty of room, and I am
almost never at home.

MRS. STOCKMANN: How good of you, Captain Horster!

PETRA: Thank you!

DR. STOCKMANN (*grasping his hand*): Thank you, thank
you! That is one trouble over! Now I can set to work in
earnest at once. There is an endless amount of things to look
through here, Katherine! Luckily I shall have all my time at
my disposal; because I have been dismissed from the Baths,
you know.

MRS. STOCKMANN (*with a sigh*): Oh yes, I expected that.

DR. STOCKMANN: And they want to take my practice away
from me too. Let them! I have got the poor people to fall back
upon, anyway—those that don't pay anything! and, after all,
they need me most, too. But, by heaven, they will have to
listen to me; I shall preach to them in season and out of season, as it says somewhere.

MRS. STOCKMANN: But, dear Thomas, I should have thought
events had showed you what use it is to preach.

DR. STOCKMANN: You are really ridiculous, Katherine. Do
you want me to let myself be beaten off the field by public
opinion and the compact majority and all that deviltry? No,
thank you! And what I want to do is so simple and clear and
straightforward. I only want to drum into the heads of these
curs the fact that the liberals are the most insidious enemies
of freedom—that party programs strangle every young and
vigorous truth—that considerations of expediency turn morality and justice upside down—and that they will end by
making life here unbearable. Don't you think, Captain Horster, that I ought to be able to make people understand that?

HORSTER: Very likely; I don't know much about such
things myself.

DR. STOCKMANN: Well, look here—I will explain! It is the
party leaders that must be exterminated. A party leader is
like a wolf, you see—like a voracious wolf. He requires a
certain number of smaller victims to prey upon every year,
if he is to live. Just look at Hovstad and Aslaksen! How
many smaller victims have they not put an end to—or at any
rate maimed and mangled until they are fit for nothing except
to be householders or subscribers to the *People's Messenger!*
(*sits down on the edge of the table*) Come here, Katherine—

look how beautifully the sun shines today! And this lovely spring air I am drinking in!

MRS. STOCKMANN: Yes, if only we could live on sunshine and spring air, Thomas.

DR. STOCKMANN: Oh, you will have to pinch and save a bit —then we shall get along. That gives me very little concern. What is much worse is, that I know of no one who is liberal-minded and high-minded enough to venture to take up my work after me.

PETRA: Don't think about that, father; you have plenty of time before you.—Hullo, here are the boys already!

(EJLIF *and* MORTEN *come in from the sitting room.*)

MRS. STOCKMANN: Have you got a holiday?

MORTEN: No; but we were fighting with the other boys between lessons—

EJLIF: That isn't true; it was the other boys were fighting with us.

MORTEN: Well, and then Mr. Rörlund said we had better stay at home for a day or two.

DR. STOCKMANN (*snapping his fingers and getting up from the table*): I have it! I have it, by heaven! You shall never set foot in the school again!

THE BOYS: No more school!

MRS. STOCKMANN: But Thomas—

DR. STOCKMANN: Never, I say. I will educate you myself; that is to say, you shan't learn a blessed thing—

MORTEN: Hooray!

DR. STOCKMANN: —but I will make liberal-minded and high-minded men of you. You must help me with that, Petra.

PETRA: Yes, father, you may be sure I will.

DR. STOCKMANN: And my school shall be in the room where they insulted me and called me an enemy of the people. But we are too few as we are; I must have at least twelve boys to begin with.

MRS. STOCKMANN: You will certainly never get them in this town.

DR. STOCKMANN: We shall. (*to the boys*) Don't you know any street urchins—regular ragamuffins—?

MORTEN: Yes, father, I know lots!

DR. STOCKMANN: That's great! Bring me some specimens of them. I am going to experiment with curs, just for once; there may be some exceptional heads amongst them.

MORTEN: And what are we going to do, when you have made liberal-minded and high-minded men of us?

DR. STOCKMANN: Then you shall drive all the wolves out of the country, my boys!

(EJLIF *looks rather doubtful about it;* MORTEN *jumps about crying* "Hurrah!")

MRS. STOCKMANN: Let us hope it won't be the wolves that will drive you out of the country, Thomas.

DR. STOCKMANN: Are you out of your mind, Katherine? Drive me out! Now—when I am the strongest man in the town!

MRS. STOCKMANN: The strongest—now?

DR. STOCKMANN: Yes, and I will go so far as to say that now I am the strongest man in the whole world.

MORTEN: I say!

DR. STOCKMANN (*lowering his voice*): Hush! You mustn't say anything about it yet; but I have made a great discovery.

MRS. STOCKMANN: Another one?

DR. STOCKMANN: Yes. (*gathers them round him, and says confidentially*) It is this, let me tell you—that the strongest man in the world is he who stands most alone.

MRS. STOCKMANN (*smiling and shaking her head*): Oh, Thomas, Thomas!

PETRA (*encouragingly, as she grasps her father's hands*): Father!

havnt. I find that the moment I let a woman make friends with me, she becomes jealous, exacting, suspicious, and a damned nuisance. I find that the moment I let myself make friends with a woman, I become selfish and tyrannical. Women upset everything. When you let them into your life, you find that the woman is driving at one thing and youre driving at another.

PICKERING: At what, for example?

HIGGINS (*coming off the piano restlessly*): Oh, Lord knows! I suppose the woman wants to live her own life; and the man wants to live his; and each tries to drag the other on to the wrong track. One wants to go north and the other south; and the result is that both have to go east, though they both hate the east wind. (*He sits down on the bench at the keyboard.*) So here I am, a confirmed old bachelor, and likely to remain so.

PICKERING (*rising and standing over him gravely*): Come, Higgins! You know what I mean. If I'm to be in this business I shall feel responsible for that girl. I hope it's understood that no advantage is to be taken of her position.

HIGGINS: What! That thing! Sacred, I assure you. (*rising to explain*) You see, she'll be a pupil; and teaching would be impossible unless pupils were sacred. Ive taught scores of American millionairesses how to speak English: the best looking women in the world. I'm seasoned. They might as well be blocks of wood. *I* might as well be a block of wood. It's——

(MRS. PEARCE *opens the door. She has* ELIZA'S *hat in her hand.* PICKERING *retires to the easy-chair at the hearth and sits down.*)

HIGGINS (*eagerly*): Well, Mrs Pearce: is it all right?

MRS PEARCE (*at the door*): I just wish to trouble you with a word, if I may, Mr Higgins.

HIGGINS: Yes, certainly. Come in. (*She comes forward.*) Dont burn that, Mrs Pearce. I'll keep it as a curiosity. (*He takes the hat.*)

MRS PEARCE: Handle it carefully, sir, please. I had to promise her not to burn it; but I had better put it in the oven for a while.

HIGGINS (*putting it down hastily on the piano*): Oh! thank you. Well, what have you to say to me?

PICKERING: Am I in the way?

MRS PEARCE: Not in the least, sir. Mr Higgins: Will you please be very particular what you say before the girl?

MRS PEARCE: I want to change you from a frowzy slut to a clean respectable girl fit to sit with the gentlemen in the study. Are you going to trust me and do what I tell you or be thrown out and sent back to your flower basket?

LIZA: But you dont know what the cold is to me. You dont know how I dread it.

MRS PEARCE: Your bed won't be be cold here: I will put a hot water bottle in it. (*pushing her into the bedroom*) Off with you and undress.

LIZA: Oh, if only I'd known what a dreadful thing it is to be clean I'd never have come. I didnt know when I was well off. I—(MRS PEARCE *pushes her through the door, but leaves it partly open lest her prisoner should take to flight.*

MRS PEARCE *puts on a pair of white rubber sleeves, and fills the bath, mixing hot and cold, and testing the result with the bath thermometer. She perfumes it with a handful of bath salts and adds a palmful of mustard. She then takes a formidable-looking long-handled scrubbing brush and soaps it profusely with a ball of scented soap.*

ELIZA *comes back with nothing on but the bath gown huddled tightly around her, a piteous spectacle of abject terror.*)

MRS PEARCE: Now come along. Take that thing off.

LIZA: Oh I couldnt, Mrs Pearce: I reely couldnt. I never done such a thing.

MRS PEARCE: Nonsense. Here: step in and tell me whether it's hot enough for you.

LIZA: Ah-oo! Ah-oo! It's too hot.

MRS PEARCE (*deftly snatching the gown away and throwing ELIZA down on her back*): It wont hurt you. (*She sets to work with the scrubbing brush.*

ELIZA'S *screams are heartrending.*

*   *   *   *   *   *

Meanwhile the COLONEL *has been having it out with* HIGGINS *about* ELIZA. PICKERING *has come from the hearth to the chair and seated himself astride of it with his arms on the back to cross-examine him.*)

PICKERING: Excuse the straight question, Higgins. Are you a man of good character where women are concerned?

HIGGINS (*moodily*): Have you ever met a man of good character where women are concerned?

PICKERING: Yes: very frequently.

HIGGINS (*dogmatically, lifting himself on his hands to the level of the piano, and sitting on it with a bounce*): Well, I

the likes of me. I should be afraid to touch anything. I aint
a duchess yet, you know.

MRS PEARCE: You have got to make yourself as clean as
the room: then you wont be afraid of it. And you must call
me Mrs Pearce, not missus. (*She throws open the door of
the dressing room, now modernized as a bathroom.*)

LIZA: Gawd! whats this? Is this where you wash clothes?
Funny sort of copper I call it.

MRS PEARCE: It is not a copper. This is where we wash
ourselves, Eliza, and where I am going to wash you.

LIZA: You expect me to get into that and wet myself all
over! Not me. I should catch my death. I knew a woman did
it every Saturday night; and she died of it.

MRS PEARCE: Mr Higgins has the gentlemen's bathroom
downstairs; and he has a bath every morning, in cold water.

LIZA: Ugh! He's made of iron, that man.

MRS PEARCE: If you are to sit with him and the Colonel
and be taught you will have to do the same. They wont like
the smell of you if you dont. But you can have the water as
hot as you like. There are two taps: hot and cold.

LIZA (*weeping*): I couldnt. I dursnt. It's not natural: it
would kill me. Ive never had a bath in my life: not what
youd call a proper one.

MRS PEARCE: Well, dont you want to be clean and sweet
and decent, like a lady? You know you cant be a nice girl
inside if youre a dirty slut outside.

LIZA: Boohoo!!!!

MRS PEARCE: Now stop crying and go back into your room
and take off all your clothes. Then wrap yourself in this
(*taking down a gown from its peg and handing it to her*)
and come back to me. I will get the bath ready.

LIZA (*all tears*): I cant. I wont. I'm not used to it. Ive
never took off all my clothes before. It's not right: it's not
decent.

MRS PEARCE: Nonsense, child. Dont you take off all your
clothes every night when you go to bed?

LIZA (*amazed*): No. Why should I? I should catch my
death. Of course I take off my skirt.

MRS PEARCE: Do you mean that you sleep in the under-
clothes you wear in the daytime?

LIZA: What else have I to sleep in?

MRS PEARCE: You will never do that again as long as you
live here. I will get you a proper nightdress.

LIZA: Do you mean change into cold things and lie awake
shivering half the night? You want to kill me, you do.

dressed. If the King finds out youre not a lady, you will be taken by the police to the Tower of London, where your head will be cut off as a warning to other presumptuous flower girls. If you are not found out, you shall have a present of seven-and-sixpence to start life with as a lady in a shop. If you refuse this offer you will be a most ungrateful wicked girl; and the angels will weep for you. (*to* PICKERING) Now are you satisfied, Pickering? (*to* MRS PEARCE) Can I put it more plainly and fairly, Mrs Pearce?

MRS PEARCE (*patiently*): I think youd better let me speak to the girl properly in private. I dont know that I can take charge of her or consent to the arrangement at all. Of course I know you dont mean her any harm; but when you get what you call interested in people's accents, you never think or care what may happen to them or you. Come with me, Eliza.

HIGGINS: Thats all right. Thank you, Mrs Pearce. Bundle her off to the bathroom.

LIZA (*rising reluctantly and suspiciously*): Youre a great bully, you are. I wont stay here if I dont like. I wont let nobody wallop me. I never asked to go to Bucknam Palace, I didnt. I was never in trouble with the police, not me. I'm a good girl—

MRS PEARCE: Dont answer back, girl. You dont understand the gentleman. Come with me. (*She leads the way to the door, and holds it open for* ELIZA.)

LIZA (*as she goes out*): Well, what I say is right. I wont go near the King, not if I'm going to have my head cut off. If I'd known what I was letting myself in for, I wouldnt have come here. I always been a good girl; and I never offered to say a word to him; and I dont owe him nothing; and I dont care; and I wont be put upon; and I have my feelings the same as anyone else—

(MRS PEARCE *shuts the door; and* ELIZA'S *plaints are no longer audible.*

* * * * * *

ELIZA *is taken upstairs to the third floor greatly to her surprise; for she expected to be taken down to the scullery. There* MRS PEARCE *opens a door and takes her into a spare bedroom.*)

MRS PEARCE: I will have to put you here. This will be your bedroom.

LIZA: O-h, I couldnt sleep here, missus. It's too good for